BERMUDA

ROSEMARY JONES

SEP - - 2018

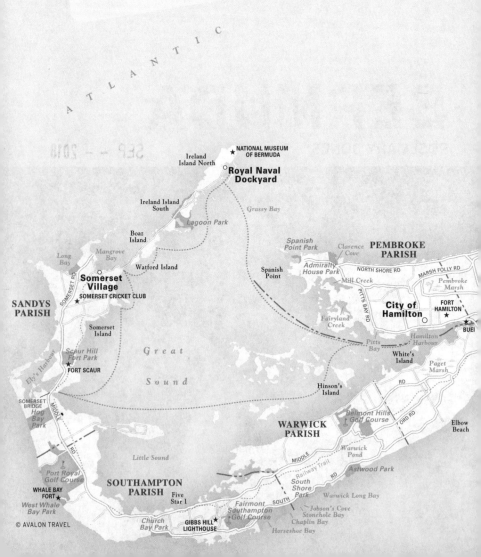

BERMUDA

ATLANTIC OCEAN

★ NATIONAL MUSEUM OF BERMUDA

Ireland Island North

○ **Royal Naval Dockyard**

Ireland Island South

Grassy Bay

Boaz Island

Lagoon Park

Spanish Point Park

Watford Island

Clarence Cove

PEMBROKE PARISH

Spanish Point

Admiralty House Park

NORTH SHORE RD

MARSH FOLLY RD

Mill Creek

Pembroke Marsh

Long Bay

Mangrove Bay

★ **Somerset Village**

SOMERSET RD

SOMERSET CRICKET CLUB ★

SANDYS PARISH

Somerset Island

City of Hamilton ○

★ **FORT HAMILTON**

★ BUEI

Fairyland Creek

PITTS BAY RD

Hamilton Harbour

Scaur Hill Fort Park

★ **FORT SCAUR**

Great Sound

Pitts Bay

White's Island

Paget Marsh

SOMERSET BRIDGE

Hog Bay Park

Ely's Harbour

MIDDLE RD

Hinson's Island

RD

Belmont Hills Golf Course

ORD RD

Elbow Beach

Port Royal Golf Course

Little Sound

WARWICK PARISH

MIDDLE

Warwick Pond

Astwood Park

★ **WHALE BAY FORT**

West Whale Bay Park

SOUTHAMPTON PARISH

Five Star 1

Railway Trail

South Shore Park

SOUTH SHORE RD

SOUTH

Johson's Cove

Stonehole Bay

Chaplin Bay

Warwick Long Bay

Church Bay Park

★ **GIBBS HILL LIGHTHOUSE**

Fairmont Southampton Golf Course

Horseshoe Bay

Achilles Bay ★ FORT ST. CATHERINE
Tobacco Bay St. Catherine's Beach

Town of
St. George

ST. GEORGE'S ○ DELIVERANCE ALEXANDRA BATTERY
CRICKET CLUB ★ GATES FORT
Mullet Bay WORLD HERITAGE Ordnance Town Cut
CENTRE Island Paget
ST. GEORGE'S Island
PARISH St. George's
Harbour Smith's
BERMUDA INSTITUTE Island ST. DAVID'S
OF OCEAN SCIENCES BATTERY ★
St. George's
Island Great
Head Park
Ferry Point ✈ L.F. WADE
National Park INTERNATIONA
Ferry Beach L AIRPORT ST. DAVID'S
MARTELLO TOWER ★ LIGHTHOUSE
St. David's
Island Clearwater
Coney Beach
Island Park Coney
Island Cooper's
Castle Island Cooper's Island
Harbour Nature Reserve
Blue Hole Park Nonsuch
Walsingham Island
HAMILTON Nature
PARISH Reserve

Shelly Bay Harrington Tucker's Point
Beach Park Golf Course
Shark
Shelly Hole TUCKER'S
Bay Sound Mid Ocean TOWN
Golf Course
BERMUDA AQUARIUM, Mangrove Trott's Pond
MUSEUM & ZOO Lake
Gibbet
Island ○ Flatts Village
Flatts
Inlet John Smith's Bay
Penhurst Spittal Pond Watch
Park Nature Reserve Hill Park
Robinson's SMITH'S PARISH
Bay Park
Devonshire
Marsh ★ VERDMONT
Ocean View MUSEUM
Golf Course
The Devonshire
Arboretum Bay Park
Devonshire Bay
Botanical DEVONSHIRE
Gardens PARISH

PAGET PARISH

0   1 mi

0   1 km

UNITED   ATLANTIC
STATES

Bermuda

OCEAN

CUBA DOMINICAN
REPUBLIC

HAITI PUERTO
RICO
Caribbean Sea

Contents

Discover Bermuda 6
  8 Top Experiences 10
  Planning Your Trip 16
  The Best of Bermuda 19
  A Romantic Retreat 20
  • Best Beaches 21
  • Scuba Diving Shipwrecks 22
  Family Vacation 23
  • Extreme Water Sports 24
  Exploring the Railway Trail 25
  • On the Wild Side 26

City of Hamilton and Pembroke
  Parish 28
  City of Hamilton 32
  Pembroke Parish 64

Devonshire and Paget
  Parishes 79
  Devonshire Parish 82
  Paget Parish 92

Warwick and Southampton
  Parishes 109
  Warwick Parish 112
  Southampton Parish 123

Sandys Parish 140
  Royal Naval Dockyard 145
  Somerset Village 157
  Around Sandys 161

Smith's and Hamilton
  Parishes 169
  Smith's Parish 172
  Hamilton Parish 182

St. George's Parish **196**
  The Old Town of St. George 201
  Around the Old Town 213
  St. David's Island and Southside 222

Background **229**
  The Landscape 230
  Plants and Animals 237
  History........................ 250
  Government 257
  Economy....................... 260
  People and Culture 268

Essentials **271**
  Transportation.................. 272

Visas and Officialdom 283
Recreation...................... 285
Food 291
Accommodations 293
Conduct and Customs 296
Health and Safety 297
Travel Tips 304
Information and Services 309

Resources **317**
  Suggested Reading and Films....... 317
  Internet Resources 323

Index **328**

List of Maps **334**

DISCOVER

Bermuda

Bermudians often refer to the "Real World" as if theirs isn't. Perhaps it's truer to say the island is "Another World," as local crooner Hubert Smith and his 1960s band the Coral Islanders sang in Bermuda's unofficial national anthem. He was right, of course—there is an ephemeral, otherworldly feel to the 21-square-mile island with its hallmark hue of confectionery pink that brands buses, hibiscus, cottages, and those legendary linen shorts.

That element of pure fantasy has drawn visitors here for centuries, and this British Overseas Territory's charms cast just as strong a spell today. Arriving over impossibly turquoise bays, so translucent you can almost spot the parrotfish beneath the silky surface, is to experience a suspension of disbelief. The trilling tree frogs, wobbly scooter rides, perfumed breezes, and laid-back lifestyle probably won't do much to shatter the illusion.

For Bermuda's residents, this piece of paradise is home—a quirky combo of British, North American, West Indian, and Portuguese influences that feels alternately sophisticated and small-town. With their heritage of pioneers and pirates, islanders embody a pragmatic stoicism, jaunty pride, and wicked humor wrapped in an easy friendliness that relaxes you faster than your first rum

Clockwise from top left: frangipani flowers; snorkeling; typical island architecture; Port Royal Golf Course; dark 'n' stormy; Bermuda landscape.

swizzle. Bermudians go with the flow, literally: The Gulf Stream—the warm current, not the private jet, though there are plenty of those here too—has shaped their destiny.

Bermuda's allure is truly unforgettable. Mark Twain likened it to heaven. John Lennon discovered *Double Fantasy* here. And when you head back to that Real World, you might just wonder if it's all been a brilliant figment of your own imagination.

Clockwise from top left: humpback whales breach off Southampton; ripe peaches; Bermuda home; Admiralty House Park.

8 TOP EXPERIENCES

1 **Beaches:** Bermuda's beaches are among the world's most stunning, offering sun, serenity, swimming, and snorkeling (page 21).

v
v
v

2 **Summer Festivals and Events:**
Dance at **Bermuda Heroes Weekend** (page 46), watch the **Bermuda Fitted Dinghy Races** (page 159), and party with locals at **Cup Match** (pages 165 and 219).

>>>

3 **Railway Trail:**
Walk, bike, or ride a horse along this historic rail trail that runs throughout the island (page 25).

<<<

4 **Water Sports:**
Bermuda's irresistible turquoise waters invite every brand of active encounter (pages 149 and 190).

>>>

5 **Romantic Escapes:** Enjoy quality couple time in the form of dreamy resorts, spa treatments, and alfresco dinners (page 20).

^
^
^

6 **Historic Forts:** Explore 400 years of history through Bermuda's chain of forts at dramatic examples such as **Fort Hamilton** (page 68), **Fort Scaur and Park** (page 162), and **Fort St. Catherine** (page 214).

7 **Green Spaces:** From the **Arboretum** (page 84) to the **Bermuda Botanical Gardens** (page 94) to the **Spittal Pond Nature Reserve** (page 175), this island offers options aplenty for verdant exploration.

>>>

8 **Golfing:** With the most courses per square mile in the world—including world-class championship varieties—Bermuda is the ultimate golf getaway (pages 88, 117, 129, and 218).

Planning Your Trip

Where to Go

City of Hamilton and Pembroke Parish

Whether you foray into "Town" for **shopping, restaurants,** or **nightclubs,** or use the capital as a base from which to explore the rest of the island, the city and its environs are a logical place to start a tour of the parishes. Hamilton currently has no hotels, but nearby neighborhoods in Pembroke have several excellent options offering access to the city and bus and ferry terminals. Attractions include **art galleries, parks, cathedrals,** and an **1870s fort. Harbor cruises** and **ferries** for Paget, Warwick, Dockyard, Royal Naval Dockyard, and St. George's leave from the waterfront, where a tour center can help you book adventures island-wide and year-round.

Devonshire and Paget Parishes

Deep country is found in Devonshire, with **old estates, farmland,** and **seaside communities.** Paget offers suburban attractions such as **golf, tennis,** and **top-notch restaurants.** Resorts and guesthouses abound in Paget, while colorful local eateries, **churches,** and **nature reserves** enhance Devonshire's allure. Key attractions include the **Arboretum, Bermuda Botanical Gardens, Masterworks Museum of Bermuda Art,** and **Elbow Beach.**

Warwick and Southampton Parishes

Beach bums beware: You might never leave the pink-sand confines of these western parishes.

church in Hamilton

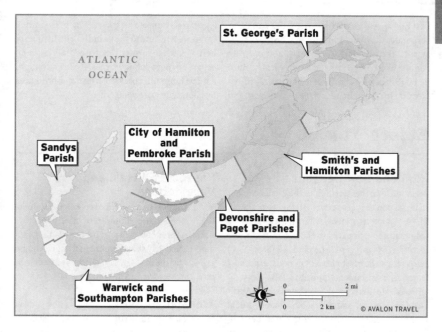

This is the realm of **scuba, water sports, horseback riding,** and **snorkeling,** not to mention **tennis, golf,** and pampering **spas** at several major resorts. Jocks and sun-worshippers will find nirvana here. There are a few historic sites, including **Gibbs Hill Lighthouse**—which provides the island's best view. Both parishes offer a plethora of gourmet and comfort food, and accommodations to suit various budgets.

Sandys Parish

The historic military gems of the fortified **Royal Naval Dockyard,** including the **National Museum of Bermuda,** are the biggest collective magnet drawing visitors to the West End. This outer parish has a quaint, countrified character that invites gentle exploration. **Somerset Village** and its surroundings provide rural lanes to meander, plus shops, restaurants, and water sports. **Deep-sea fishing** boats are also based in this parish. One major resort and several guesthouses provide accommodations, but fast ferries

from Hamilton can get you (and your scooter) here in 20 minutes.

Smith's and Hamilton Parishes

Packed with attractions, Smith's Parish and Hamilton Parish—the latter not to be confused with the capital city—offer plenty to see, plus pretty pathways to the East End. Explore history and nature at **Verdmont Museum,** a historic home, before taking a hike at the 34-acre oceanfront bird sanctuary **Spittal Pond Nature Reserve,** both in Smith's. **Bermuda Aquarium, Museum & Zoo** in Hamilton Parish is a favorite island attraction. The cave-honeycombed Harrington Sound provides a scenic route east, and several beautiful beaches—**Shelly Bay Beach, John Smith's Bay**—are inviting distractions.

St. George's Parish

A UNESCO World Heritage Site, the 400-year-old Town of St. George and its related forts in the

East End appeal to history lovers. The parish incorporates the island's first capital, along with the airport, the island of St. David's, and outlying regions like Ferry Point National Park. Built by English settlers, St. George's boasts winding streets, many landmarks, a public square, and a yacht-laden waterfront. The surrounding forts are a tribute to the island's British military heritage, while former U.S. base lands boast an expanse of now-public beaches. Parish accommodations range from backstreet bed-and-breakfasts to a boutique Rosewood hotel.

Before You Go

High and Low Seasons

Bermuda is farther north than the Caribbean hot spots, so don't expect perfect weather year-round. The winter season (Nov.-Mar.) has average 68°F temperatures, compared to the high 80s of midsummer. Spring (Apr.-May) and fall (Sept.-Nov.) are perhaps the most pleasant periods, especially October, as summer's humidity falls away. In terms of rates and crowds, high season is April-October and low season is November-March. Bermuda makes a pleasant year-round destination, however, as it has no defined rainy season, nor a period when shops and restaurants are closed seasonally, as elsewhere in the Caribbean.

You may want to time your visit around cultural and sports events. Local favorites include Bermuda Heroes Weekend (a multiple-day, round-the-clock soca carnival in mid-June), Cup Match (a four-day extravaganza combining cricket, concerts, boating, and beaching in late July or early August) and Bermuda Day (a public holiday the last Friday in May, with a festive parade and half-marathon). Easter brings kites and Christmas boasts a boat parade and festival of lights. International events include the Bermuda Festival of the Performing Arts (dance, opera, theater) in January and February, and November's World Rugby Classic.

Passports, Visas, and Vaccinations

Valid passports are required to enter Bermuda. Visitors must also show a return or departure ticket, or proof of transport off the island, and it saves time to have handy your hotel or guesthouse address for the immigration officer. No vaccinations are needed for travel to Bermuda.

Transportation

Major airlines and cruise ships serve Bermuda daily from U.S. and Canadian cities, as well as from the United Kingdom. On the island, you can rent scooters or two-person electric cars, tour the parishes by bus, or hop on reliable ferries. Taxis are relatively expensive but provide service to all nine parishes.

Reservations

Hotels' best rooms can become fully booked in the high season, particularly at popular small resorts, where repeat visitors book up to a year in advance. If you're planning scuba outings, fishing trips, or golf and spa packages, you should arrange tee times, treatments, and reservations in advance. Tickets to premier events also need to be purchased early. Check for details on www.gotobermuda.com.

The Best of Bermuda

With its short distances and efficient public transportation, Bermuda reveals much of itself to energetic travelers during a weeklong stay. Look below the surface of this reef-fringed paradox and you'll discover a melting pot of culture, history, and outdoor adventure encompassing all nine parishes.

Day 1

Touch down at L. F. Wade International Airport and grab a cab to your hotel. Ask the driver where to find the island's best fish sandwich, a Bermudian staple. Shake off your mainland cobwebs with an afternoon at Elbow Beach, strolling the soft sand and testing the turquoise waters. Later, choose a waterfront terrace, such as the trendy Seabreeze Lounge on Paget's South Shore, The Dock in Southampton, or sunset-soaked 1609 Bar & Restaurant on Hamilton Harbour for an alfresco dinner.

Day 2

Head into Hamilton for home-grown breakfast with Bermudians at the Cottage Café & Bistro. Spend the morning exploring Front, Reid, and Church Streets' boutiques, art galleries, and churches. Climb Holy Trinity Cathedral's landmark tower to overlook the city. Try lunch at sushi hot spot Beluga Seafood Bar or farm-to-table Devil's Isle Kitchen and Bar. In the afternoon, rent a scooter or hop on a bus and cruise the North Shore to visit Crystal Cave and Fantasy Cave. Watch the daylight dwindle aboard a Hamilton Harbour sunset cruise, then head to Marcus', celebrity chef Marcus Samuelsson's restaurant that puts his award-winning spin on island cuisine.

Day 3

Cool out on the beach today. Go to pristine Warwick Long Bay for bodysurfing,

bodysurfing on the South Shore

sandcastles, and snorkeling. Follow the trail west through protected, dune-cradled South Shore National Park to sample Jobson's Cove, followed by Chaplin, Stonehole, and Horseshoe Bays. Take a dip at each. Have lunch at the foot of Gibbs Hill Lighthouse inside The Dining Room. In the late afternoon, escape the sun and indulge in a spa treatment at a resort (book your treatment days in advance if possible).

Day 4

Take the ferry from Hamilton across the Great Sound to the Royal Naval Dockyard, scooter optional. Book a half-day scuba outing, rent a kayak, or take a snorkeling or paragliding tour of the West End. Celebrate the neighborhood's British heritage with a pub lunch, then learn stories of soldiers, slaves, immigrants, and war vets at the National Museum of Bermuda. Grab a rum cake, a piece of blown glass, or a painting from the Bermuda Arts Centre to take home.

Day 5

Take the ferry along the North Shore to St. George's. Explore the museums and backstreets of the old town, a UNESCO World Heritage Site.

Visit area forts (also UNESCO gems), including Gates Fort, Alexandra Battery, the Martello Tower at Ferry Reach, and Fort St. Catherine, with its commanding views of the bay where the first settlers landed. Have lunch at one of the wharfside eateries, then do some souvenir scouting.

Day 6

Walk in John Lennon's footsteps at the Bermuda Botanical Gardens in Paget, where *Double Fantasy* was born, and pay a visit to the Masterworks Museum of Bermuda Art. Head to North Hamilton for a Caribbean-style lunch at one of the many cafés, such as Jamaican Grill, Juice 'n' Beans or Fish & Tings. Climb up to nearby Fort Hamilton for moat gardens and panoramic views, and stroll the backstreets to glimpse gingerbread architecture. If it's a Wednesday, return to the city for a stroll around Harbour Nights, or go for an evening pool dip or a chilled dark 'n' stormy.

Day 7

Grab an early-morning beach run or walk along the South Shore and cool off with a dip in the balmy water before your flight out.

A Romantic Retreat

TOP EXPERIENCE

Moon gates, hidden beaches, star-speckled skies, and blossom-scented breezes—Bermuda's charms, like the setting of an over-the-top pulp romance, soon put lovebirds in the mood. The island is a popular destination for couples planning a romantic long weekend, a honeymoon, wedding anniversary, or trendy "babymoon," not least because of the easy flight from North American East Coast cities (flight times range from 1.5-2.5 hours). Bermuda's natural beauty and languorous pace are seductive to anyone hoping to celebrate a new romance, toast coupledom, or fall in love all over again.

Day 1

Most flights from North America arrive in Bermuda at midday or early afternoon, leaving lots of time to begin unwinding. Check into the gorgeously renovated "Pink Palace," the historic Hamilton Princess & Beach Club, where you can sip swizzles or mango lemonade beside the infinity pool overlooking the superyachts and passing spinnakers. Stretch your legs along Front Street, where you and your honey can compare perfumes at Lili Bermuda, or buy a pair of bona fide Bermuda shorts. In the evening, stroll through the lush gardens at Ascot's before dinner-for-two in the charming former mansion.

Best Beaches

Bermuda's beaches are world-renowned, and there are hundreds of them around the island. Whether you're staying at a dedicated beach resort or an inland guesthouse, you're never far from shore. Although some are officially private, belonging to resorts or restricted neighborhoods, most of Bermuda's beaches are open to the public sunrise-sunset, from the water's edge to the high-tide mark.

MOST BEAUTIFUL BEACHES

- **Elbow Beach:** This beach offers pillow-soft sand and frolicking parrotfish, along with volleyball and kitesurfing (page 100).

- **Warwick Long Bay:** Presenting a serene antidote to neighboring beach crowds, this bay has deep white sands and crashing surf (page 116).

- **Horseshoe Bay:** Find a sweeping pink stretch hemmed by emerald foliage and sparkling turquoise—plus showers, restrooms, a café and bar, lifeguards, and beach gear rentals. Local teens and twentysomethings lend a beach-party atmosphere to summer weekend afternoons here (page 127).

- **John Smith's Bay:** Framed by coconut palms, this picturesque bay has shady caves, lifeguards, and nearby reefs for snorkeling (page 178).

MOST SECLUDED BEACHES

- **Astwood Cove:** This is hard to access, except by a steep cliffside path, but the privacy and crystal-clear water are worth the trouble (page 115).

- **Chaplin Bay:** Between Horseshoe and Warwick Long Bay, Chaplin is connected to both via South Shore Park and a string of idyllic coves that invite beach-hopping. It's also good for watching longtails soaring to and from limestone cliff nests (page 116).

- **West Whale Bay:** Hidden below Whale Bay Fort far from the main road, a string of coves and soft, sandy stretches offer wading, swimming, and turtle-spotting at low-tide (page 128).

- **Turtle Bay, Long Bay,** and **Soldier Bay:** This 44-acre peninsula offers a plethora of gorgeous, off-the-beaten-track beaches, facing both Castle Harbour and South Shore and bordered by bird and turtle sanctuaries (page 226).

Horseshoe Bay

BEST SNORKELING BEACHES

- **Clarence Cove:** A sheltered, reef-fringed bay inside a national park, this cove is popular with scuba divers, snorkelers, and children (page 69).

- **Church Bay:** Easy-to-reach boiler reefs make this a perennial top pick among devoted snorkelers (page 128).

- **Tobacco Bay:** This is a snorkeler's heaven (when not crowded with cruise ship passengers), thanks to its natural underwater columns and reef life (page 217).

WHERE LOCALS GO

- **Somerset Long Bay:** Turtles can be seen grazing in the shallows, alongside a public park and nature reserve (page 164).

- **St. Catherine's Beach:** Here's a sandy arc on the island's easternmost tip where shipwrecked English colonists struggled ashore (page 217).

- **Clearwater Beach:** With its accessible water and nearby playground, parkland, and fast-food restaurants, this aptly named swimming venue is a summer hot spot with locals (page 226).

Scuba Diving Shipwrecks

Bermuda is known as the shipwreck capital of the Atlantic, with 500 years of human history snared on its 280-square-mile reef platform. Most of these unfortunate vessels, from treasure-laden galleons to U.S. Civil War-era steamers, lie less than 60 feet deep, making accessibility a breeze. Bermuda water temperatures vary from an average 65°F in the winter months (though water clarity is better then) to average highs of 85°F in the summer. Here are a few of the best dive sites:

• *Sea Venture:* The most recent artificial dive site, this decommissioned 75-foot ferry is named for the shipwreck that accidentally brought the first English settlers in 1609. It was sunk off Bermuda's northwest corner in 2007. The wreck sits in about 50 feet of water at Eastern Blue Cut, one of several "cuts," or "breaks," in the necklace of reefs around the island, attracting plenty of sealife (page 149).

• *Constellation:* A 192-foot, four-masted, wooden American schooner that served as a cargo ship in World War II before it sank off the West End in 1943, this ship inspired Peter Benchley's novel *The Deep.* The wreck lies scattered on a coral and sand bottom in about 30 feet of water, exposing sacks of petrified cement, cups, glass bottles, and other small items (page 149).

• *L'Herminie:* An impressive warship wreck, this three-masted French wooden frigate crashed in 1838, scattering dozens of cannons over the ocean floor on the island's western side. Today, it lies in 25-30 feet of water, and ship timbers, hull sheathing, and copper nails can be seen (page 149).

• *Cristóbal Colón:* The biggest of Bermuda's shipwrecks, a 499-foot Spanish luxury liner that went down off the island's northeast corner in 1936 lies 55 feet below the surface. It has become a haven for large groupers and other reef fish. The

scuba diver exploring *Cristóbol Colón*

ship's wreckage is spread over thousands of square feet of seafloor, providing hours of exploration opportunities (page 190).

Check out the website of the **Bermuda Tourism Authority** (www.gotobermuda.com) for more details on wrecks, dive operators, rates, and seasonal schedules, plus photo galleries of the most intriguing caverns, swim-throughs, and reef life, as well as **Bermuda100** (http://bermuda100.ucsd.edu), a collaboration between UC San Diego and Bermuda's Department of Environment and Natural Resources, whose website offers an archive of available data and multimedia on Bermuda's shipwrecks.

Day 2

Share a scooter or a tiny **Twizy** (an electric car perfect for two) and enjoy exploring the postcard-pretty West End. Explore **Somerset**'s pastel lanes on foot, then pick up a takeout lunch from the **Village Café, Woody's Drive-in Two Bar and Restaurant,** or **Gloria's Kitchen** for a private picnic and swim at **Black Bay.** Enjoy an early dinner at alfresco restaurant **Breezes** before heading back to stargaze amid the tree frogs.

Day 3

Head east for a magical underground couple's

massage inside **Prospero's Cave Spa** at Grotto Bay Beach Resort. Continue on to **Cooper's Island Nature Reserve,** a 44-acre peninsula bordered by secluded azure beaches. Then drop into historic **St. George's** for afternoon tea at **The Bermuda Perfumery.** Don't miss a visit to gather a turquoise treasure from **Davidrose Jewelry** on the cobblestoned waterfront.

Day 4
Make sure you book an afternoon flight out, if possible, to make the most of the morning. Have another swim, or tour the harbor and Great Sound by ferry before you leave.

Family Vacation

Being a kid in Bermuda is like stepping into *Fantasia* or *Alice in Wonderland*. There are plenty of weird animals—lizards, trilling tree frogs, and manta rays gliding like UFOs under Flatts Bridge. Roadsides are dotted with trails of Technicolor blossoms, perfect for pretend princesses. Sunshine-packed days spill over with sandcastles, real-life forts, and bubblegum-colored buses. For a calendar of kid-friendly activities, check www.nothingtodoinbermuda.com. Tickets for a wide range of music, cultural, and sporting events can be purchased online at www.ptix.bm.

Sights and Recreation
ROYAL NAVAL DOCKYARD
The ferry ride to the West End alone is entertainment enough, but little ones will adore up-close encounters with dolphins inside the National Museum grounds, plus the adjacent playground with its mini-lighthouse entwined by a 70-foot moray eel. Outside in the Dockyard, don't miss the games room in the Frog and Onion Pub, or the popsicle, fudge, and ice cream vendors at Dockyard Terrace and the Clocktower Mall.

Bermuda Aquarium, Museum & Zoo

a replica of *Deliverance*

While many Bermuda residents spend weekends and downtime testing their limits against the island's physical challenges, visitor activities were often somewhat, well, sedate. That's all changed in recent years with the arrival of numerous vendors offering outsiders a feel of the "real"—read extreme—Bermuda, typically involving its beckoning waters. Book in advance with the vendors directly or through the Island Tour Centre (www.islandtourcentre.bm):

- Get airborne with **Coconut Rockets/ Bermuda Flyboard.** Attached via boots and bindings to a pressurized flyboard, the "pilot" is propelled by the water jet pack up to 35 feet above the ocean surface. Experience stuntman-style antics in and over the water (page 150).

- Hawaii Ironman and multisport athlete Kent Richardson is the real deal when it comes to conquering the outdoors. At **Bermuda Waterski & Wakeboard Centre** (tel. 441/234-3354 or 441/335-1012, www.island-windsbermuda.com), he'll test your mettle with thrills like jumping off Diving Board Island or full-throttle waterskiing along the North Shore. If you're up for tamer stuff, he's happy to show off Bermuda with snorkeling or sightseeing too (page 165).

- If you balk at riding the killer wakes of his awesome speedboat, John Martin will simply tell you he taught his five-year-old twins to do it. His company, **AXIS Adrenaline Projects,** picks up island-wide and will zoom you past eye-popping scenery to Castle Harbour or other turquoise expanses where you can get your

wakeboarding in Bermuda

balance and learn mastery of such extreme arts from a true maestro (page 190).

- The wow factor of **North Rock**'s barrier reef has even bona fide Bermudians catching their breath. If you have a spare afternoon, book a truly unforgettable trip to the landmark beacon nine miles off the North Shore. The **Bermuda Zoological Society** run four-hour snorkel trips to the spectacular underwater world that's like diving into a scene from *Finding Nemo* (190).

WORLD HERITAGE CENTRE

Make a beeline for the East End, where kids can be immersed in history they will actually enjoy. The World Heritage Centre in St. George's lets youngsters dress up and experience the sights and sounds of times gone by. Children can also imagine long-gone life at sea by clambering aboard *Deliverance,* the replica 17th-century vessel on the old town's waterfront. Head up to Fort St. Catherine to hide out in tunnels or climb atop

cannons with panoramic views. Who can't be a pirate with those kinds of props?

BERMUDA AQUARIUM, MUSEUM & ZOO

Ring-tailed lemurs, harbor seals, sharks, and seahorses keep youngsters, and their adult companions, entertained for hours at the island's favorite attraction. There's also a playground on-site with a conveniently situated café for lunch—or a glass of grownup vino while the kids try out the slides.

Beaches

JOBSON'S COVE AND BABY BEACH

Bodysurfers may love the sweeping, wave-crashed strands of Warwick Long Bay or Southampton's Horseshoe, but less experienced beach bums may feel more confident in the adjoining coves, protected and shaded by tall limestone cliffs. Kids can entertain themselves for hours here playing in rock pools, collecting shells, or spying on reef life with a mask and snorkel. Make sure to bring hats, shades, and plenty of sunblock.

CLARENCE COVE

This gentle, picture-perfect bay within Pembroke's Admiralty House Park is on bus routes and accessible from all central parishes. A soft sandy beach, a dock, and coastal reefs provide all the ingredients for hours of fun whether you're traveling with toddlers or teens. They'll likely meet some local counterparts to play with too.

Entertainment and Events

HARBOUR NIGHTS

Kids can sip fresh-made lemonade, try the bouncy castles, or dance to the rhythms of gombeys at the high season's stay-up-late Wednesday night street festival, where loads of local food and craft vendors shut down Front and Queen Streets to allow pedestrian-only traffic.

BERMUDA KITEFEST

Easter weekend is a riot of colorful attractions as traditional local kites take to the skies, many with long homemade tails that buzz loudly over every parish neighborhood. At Horseshoe Bay, kites miniscule and gargantuan compete for attention—and prizes. Armed with the day's mandatory fish cake sandwich, who wouldn't be captivated?

CHRISTMAS BOAT PARADE

The sight of motor yachts, sailboats, and even pint-size dinghies decked out in themed lights provides no-holds-barred magic for kids. Watch contestants encircle Hamilton Harbour, choose your favorite, and then top off the night with the shower of fireworks that wraps up the festivities.

Exploring the Railway Trail

TOP EXPERIENCE

Stretching the length of the island, the Railway Trail provides a serene 20-mile artery through Bermuda's parishes, safely away from trafficked thoroughfares. Abandoned as a train route when the island's railway fell into disrepair after a brief run in the 1930s and 1940s, the trail today belongs to the National Parks System. Well maintained and signposted with interpretive historical information as well as historic limestone parish markers, the trail is popular with runners, walkers, horseback riders, and nature-lovers. Try two of the best sections on foot or bicycle:

Paget-Southampton

The trail provides a green getaway in these busy central commuter parishes, making a perfect nature-filled expedition through residential neighborhoods. Enter at Rural Hill, Paget, on South Road just west of the Trimingham Hill roundabout. You can park a scooter here at the entrance gates or rent a mountain bike from nearby Oleander Cycles for an out-and-back of your desired distance (the huge limestone quarry at Khyber Pass, near St. Mary's Church, and back is about five miles; out and back to Gibbs Hill Lighthouse is closer to nine miles). Proceed west, through a limestone-walled tunnel, past Paget Marsh and Elbow Beach—accessible via tribe roads—and onward past scenic Belmont Hills Golf Club and through thick spice tree woodlands populated with cardinals, lizards, and wild fruits like loquats and cherries. Various main roads intersect the journey; be extremely careful when crossing, as there are no speed bumps, stoplights, or crosswalks. You'll also have to lift

Bermuda may seem like a manicured garden, but its somewhat limited open spaces nevertheless give an intriguing glimpse of the island's wildlife. Well-managed government national parks in many parishes, as well as nature reserves owned by the Bermuda National Trust and Bermuda Audubon Society, account for 850 acres of green space and boast spectacular scenery.

PEMBROKE PARISH

Bermuda Underwater Exploration Institute (BUEI)

Part museum (with exhibits on Bermuda shells, geology, wildlife, and shipwrecks), part conference center, and hub for ocean-based activities around the island, BUEI attracts the ecologically inclined. Sign up for monthly lectures, spring whale-watching tours, or moonlit cruises to watch phosphorescent glowworms.

DEVONSHIRE PARISH

Arboretum

Devonshire's largest open space is a beautifully unkempt 19-acre spread of rolling meadows, upland forest, and bluebird and cardinal sanctuaries. Cedars, avocado trees, giant rubber trees, and fiddlewood groves abound.

SANDYS PARISH

Hog Bay Park

This is a rugged, 38-acre reserve in Sandys Parish where hikers can walk undulating trails through farmland, forest, and coastline, stopping to spot turtles and take a dip.

SMITH'S PARISH

Spittal Pond Nature Reserve

A magnet for migratory birds, this 34-acre park hugs the South Shore in Smith's Parish. Trails, brackish ponds, and phenomenal ocean outlooks draw birders, cross-country runners, and local families, but like all the parks, it is quiet and underused.

bird-of-paradise flower

HAMILTON PARISH

Bermuda Aquarium, Museum & Zoo

Tour this historic Flatts facility, home to more than 200 local fish and invertebrate species, a 140,000-gallon reef tank, and a Natural History Museum that tells the story of Bermuda's origins. Zoo exhibits reflect links with island environments around the globe. Its support charity runs snorkeling and turtle-spotting marine excursions.

ST. GEORGE'S PARISH

Bermuda Institute of Ocean Sciences

Visitors are welcome at this world-renowned institution at Ferry Reach in the East End. Take a free morning tour of the station, where scientists come to study global warming, natural disasters, genomes, marine science technology, and potential medicines from the sea.

Mangrove Bay

your bike over the metal trail gates meant to prevent motorized traffic. At Tribe Road 2, scoot up to **Gibbs Hill** for lunch at the **The Dining Room** restaurant, or just ogle the stunning 360-degree views, before retracing your steps.

Sandys

The beauty of the Railway Trail is that it offers a fairly flat, as-the-crow-flies route for taking in most of Bermuda. The Sandys section is a perfect example, including tarmacadam sections that make it the smoothest stretch for riding a pedal bike. If you're on a scooter, park at **Somerset Bridge,** the world's smallest drawbridge, and watch occasional boats making their way between the Great Sound and Ely's Harbour. Walk

west through fascinating deep limestone cuts in the cliffsides, now covered in rubber tree roots and other exotic foliage. The trail hugs the coastline for long stretches, giving marvelous views of the **Great Sound.** You can venture down to the shore, where several spots offer good **swimming** points to cool off. Continuing on, it's worth climbing up to historic **Fort Scaur** to check out the cannons and views. At **Mangrove Bay,** where the final Somerset Station stood, you can explore **Somerset Village** before heading back (about 3.5 miles round-trip).

If you start at Dockyard instead, you can do the route in reverse, bringing a **scooter or pedal bike** on the ferry from Hamilton, or renting them at Dockyard's Oleander Cycles outlet.

City of Hamilton and Pembroke Parish

City of Hamilton 32   Pembroke Parish. 64

At the center of Bermuda, the City of Hamilton—and Pembroke, the parish in which it lies—form the crux of island life on multiple levels.

Home to the seat of government, including the House of Assembly and the Senate, the city is also the island's main port and its major headquarters for business, the civil service, the courts, restaurants, and nightclubs. The island's central ferry and bus terminals are located here. And because it is where most Bermudians work, shop, and eat, Hamilton and Pembroke are also the barometers of national mood: Here is where you'll find the political issues of the day hotly discussed, the latest gossip relayed, the merriment of an imminent public holiday bursting forth, or the staid pomp and ceremony of events such as Budget Day or the Throne Speech celebrated. It is where you may rub shoulders with both Bermuda's richest—the old-money merchants or insurance CEOs—and its least privileged, as it is probably the only place on the island where you'll see a few homeless panhandlers.

The city, named for its first mayor, Henry Hamilton, has morphed over two centuries from a sleepy port for sailing ships into a global insurance powerhouse second only to London. Hamilton's exponential growth in international business ("IB" in local speak) since the 1980s has changed the city and its social dynamics. Today, while quaint china and linen stores do business as ever behind pastel waterfront facades, multibillion-dollar deals are struck down the block. While it may sometimes look like Toytown, given its tropical hues and diminutive size, Hamilton is a hub for business with a global impact; the best example is its reinsurance industry, which protects nations around the world from financial disasters caused by tornadoes, tsunamis, or terrorism. Those directly employed in insurance and other financial services are the ones with the high-end clothing and restaurant charge accounts, and the sector powers the island's whole economy. Hamilton's thoroughfares are busy with brokers, accountants, lawyers, actuaries, and underwriters year-round. Corporate visitors stick out among the residents as they shuttle between the airport and city boardrooms, pulling their luggage to meetings.

Previous: kayaks in tranquil Admiralty House Park; Front Street. **Above:** Chancery Lane.

Look for ★ to find recommended
sights, activities, dining, and lodging.

Highlights

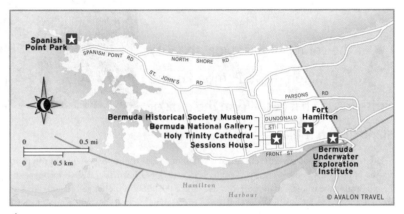

★ **Bermuda Historical Society Museum:** Rooms full of antiquities tell the territory's history at this museum inside the Bermuda National Library (page 34).

★ **Bermuda National Gallery:** Explore high-profile shows, a respected biennial exhibition, and an internationally renowned collection (page 36).

★ **Holy Trinity Cathedral:** Climb up the 155 winding stairs to the top platform of this church tower for dramatic views of Hamilton (page 37).

★ **Sessions House:** Bermuda's Italianate Parliament building holds the boisterous Friday afternoon House of Assembly meetings upstairs

and bewigged Supreme Court sessions below—all open to the public (page 39).

★ **Spanish Point Park:** A grassy promontory stretching into the main sea channel into Hamilton, this oft-forgotten park is a neighborhood favorite (page 66).

★ **Fort Hamilton:** In addition to a stunning panorama, this well-preserved 1870s fort boasts historic ramparts, a cannon, an exotic moat garden, and, in winter, bagpipers (page 68).

★ **Bermuda Underwater Exploration Institute:** Make like explorers William Beebe and Jacques Cousteau at this showcase for the surrounding deep ocean (page 69).

Pembroke, once the countrified outskirts of the city, is now—with a few neighborhood exceptions—a heavily trafficked suburban parish, catching Hamilton's commercial overflow, providing housing and schools, and playing noisy hub for public and private transport to other points on the island. Pembroke's accommodations cater to a variety of budgets, though most are geared to higher-end business travelers not seeking beaches or water sports. Theatrical events, art show openings, the annual film festival, and big sporting events are also rooted in Hamilton and Pembroke.

PLANNING YOUR TIME

Unless you're staying in the Town of St. George or the West End, each with its own culinary and retail offerings, Hamilton will likely be your first point of reference as you explore Bermuda. If you are a business visitor, you would be wise to stay in outlying Pembroke, in the cluster of Pitts Bay hotels and guesthouses, which offer quick access to city meetings and also cater to corporate needs and schedules.

Both the East End (St. George's) and the West End (Sandys, including the Royal Naval Dockyard) are a 30- to 40-minute drive from the city; quicker if you hop on the westbound fast ferry, longer if you board a leisurely pink bus. Hamilton makes a perfect starting place to visit either by public transport or rental scooter, as its main routes run through Pembroke and launch you on your way to other parishes.

Sightseeing in Hamilton could take a few hours or several days. Make sure to spend time poking around its boutiques and art galleries, walking its busy streets. Drifting amid the daily hustle and bustle is a great way to get a feel for Bermudians and the way they live. You could break up your day by, for example, spending a morning shopping and sightseeing, then going to the beach or another parish before returning for happy hour and dinner in one of the city's clubs or restaurants.

Hop on a ferry—around Paget and Warwick, or to Dockyard and back—and see the juxtaposition of insurance-industry towers and age-old landmarks; nowhere is the city's skyline as dramatic as from the waterfront. Ferry rides are also a good place to mix with locals and see the smaller islands of Hamilton Harbour and the Pembroke shore.

The city's size means it is entirely walkable if you are able, and, though there are a few steep hills, Hamilton is easy to cover in a day. If you have a scooter or electric car rental, parking may be your biggest frustration; spaces are few. Bike theft is also a substantial problem. A scooter tour of Pembroke Parish takes just a few hours, depending on the stops, which should include Fort Hamilton, the Bermuda Underwater Exploration Institute, and Admiralty House Park. Outside Hamilton, Pembroke has no ferry service, but buses serve various parts of the parish.

Hamilton and Pembroke are generally safe to walk. Take more caution after dark, as bagsnatchers have been a problem in quieter regions and the tourist-heavy areas around Pitts Bay and western Hamilton. North Hamilton's retail and residential areas are safe in the daytime; at night, avoid the area's remote streets, because visitors and locals have been accosted or robbed. Security cameras have been installed at numerous points for security.

City of Hamilton

Bermuda's capital since incorporation in 1793, Hamilton, or "Town" in island vernacular, borders the north shore of a long natural harbor at Bermuda's middle, making it the main port for cargo vessels that cross the Atlantic every week delivering the food, clothing, and other goods the island survives on. Until 2008, it was also the main port for cruise ships through the summer high season, but now most ships berth at the West End's Dockyard. The city's central location makes it the natural launchpad for explorations east and west through the parishes; no matter where you're staying, you will probably want to take a look around Hamilton first.

Strict building codes throughout Hamilton's history retained many of the old-time facades, though the late 1990s and early 2000s brought a plethora of contemporary office architecture and, for the first time, urban residential units. Global players in the island's international business industry are all based in Hamilton. Towers belonging to insurance companies have reshaped the city's profile from east to west, and while Hamilton's official borders have not expanded, many of its businesses have spilled west along Pitts Bay and east toward Crow Lane. The 2008-2013 global economic downturn brought an end to Hamilton's building boom, driving down corporate rents, but as Bermuda's economy recovers, this could change.

The previously novel concept (for Bermuda) of city living has taken root, though it's popular mostly with the unmarried and downsizing empty-nesters. Urban-style condominiums have pushed Hamilton north, providing apartment suites for Bermudians and expatriate city workers, as well as investment properties. No tourist accommodations fall within the strict city limits, although there are numerous lodgings in Pembroke, within a 15-minute walk from Hamilton's retail center.

The city is not difficult to navigate, with a straightforward grid system of streets running east-west (Front, Reid, Church, Victoria, Dundonald) and north-south (King, Court, Parliament, Burnaby, Queen, Par-la-Ville, Bermudiana). Several are one-way streets; look carefully at signs before entering on a scooter. The main flow of traffic comes back and forth via Front Street, or down Reid's one-way lanes up Queen and back out of the city via Church Street (also a one-way passage). The actual city borders are defined by King Street to the east, Parson's Lane in the north, Bermudiana Road in the west, and Front Street, along the harbor front, to the south. Within that space are two beautiful and well-used parks—Queen Elizabeth and Victoria—and numerous other attractions.

Aside from the nine-to-five weekday, shopping is what brings most people to Hamilton. Front Street—once the domain of Bermuda's white power bloc, whose key merchants were nicknamed the "Forty Thieves"—has today become a far more pluralistic thoroughfare. Gone are all but one of Front Street's old-money department stores; only A. S. Cooper & Sons remains. Smaller boutiques draw shoppers, while events like Harbour Nights, the Front Street Mile race, the Bermuda Day Half-Marathon, and the Christmas Boat Parade bring out residents from every parish to celebrate along the waterfront. Many Front Street retailers are geared to tourists, while Reid, Queen, and Church Streets remain major shopping destinations, connected by the rambling Washington Mall, which underwent a major expansion in recent years.

Don't restrict your visit to the city's most trafficked regions. Long denigrated as "back o' town," culturally vibrant North Hamilton has plenty to offer. Strolling around the region's streets, you can enjoy the West Indian architecture, with wooden verandas, brightly hued cottages, and walled gardens harking

City of Hamilton

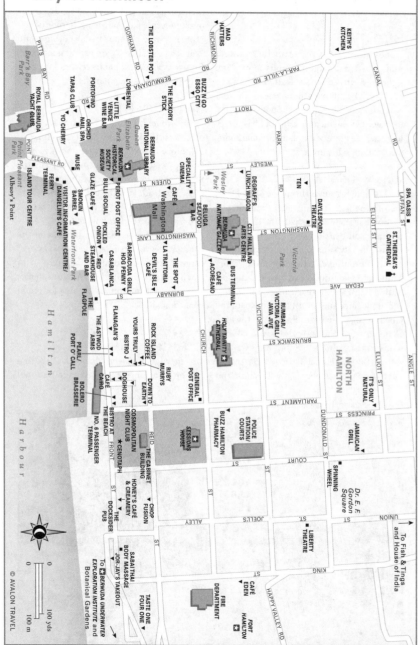

KEITH'S KITCHEN

MAD HATTERS

ST. THERESA'S CATHEDRAL

SPA OASIS

THE LOBSTER POT

BUZZ N GO ESSO CITY

TEN

DEGRAFF'S LUNCH WAGON

DAYLESFORD THEATRE

IT'S ONLY NATURAL

THE HICKORY STICK

L'ORIENTAL

BERMUDIANA

LITTLE VENICE WINE BAR

PORTOFINO

ORCHID NAIL SPA

TAPAS CLUB

YO CHERRY

BERMUDA NATIONAL LIBRARY

BERMUDA HISTORICAL SOCIETY MUSEUM

PEROT POST OFFICE

SPECIALTY CINEMA

CITY HALL AND ARTS CENTRE

BERMUDA NATIONAL GALLERY

BELUGA SEAFOOD

RUIMBAR/ VICTORIA GRILL/ JAVA JIVE

ROYAL BERMUDA YACHT CLUB

ISLAND TOUR CENTRE
Albuoy's Point

MUSE

GLAZE CAFÉ

BULLI SOCIAL

PICKLED ONION

RED STEAKHOUSE AND BAR

CAFÉ4

BAR

WASHINGTON LANE

THE SPOT

CAFÉ ACOREANO

BUS TERMINAL

SMOKIN BARREL

DANGELINI'S CAFÉ

BARRACUDA GRILL/ HOG PENNY

DEVIL'S ISLE CAFÉ

CASABLANCA

LA TRATTORIA

HOLY TRINITY CATHEDRAL

VISITOR INFORMATION CENTRE/

FERRY TERMINAL

THE FLAGPOLE

THE ASTWOD ARMS

FLANAGAN'S

YOURS TRULY

BISTRO J

ROCK ISLAND COFFEE

RUBY MURRYS

GENERAL POST OFFICE

PEARL/ PORT O' CALL

CAIRO

CAFÉ

DOGHOUSE

DOWN TO EARTH

BUZZ HAMILTON PHARMACY

POLICE STATION/ COURTS

BOLERO BRASSERIE

BISTRO AT THE BEACH

NO. 6 PASSENGER TERMINAL

COSMOPOLITAN NIGHT CLUB

THE CABINET BUILDING

CENOTAPH

REID

SESSIONS HOUSE

SPINNING WHEEL

JAMAICAN GRILL

HONEY'S CAFÉ & CREAMERY

CHOP FUSION

THE DOCKSIDER PUB

LIBERTY THEATRE

SABAI THAI BODY MASSAGE

JOE-JAY'S TAKEOUT

CAFÉ EDEN

FORT HAMILTON

TASTE ONE FOUR ONE

FIRE DEPARTMENT

To ★ BERMUDA UNDERWATER EXPLORATION INSTITUTE and Botanical Gardens

To Fish & Tings and House of India

Dr. D. E. F. Gordon Square

NORTH HAMILTON

Victoria Park

Wesley Park

Queen Elizabeth Park

Washington Mall

Waterfront Park

Bar's Bay Park
Point Pleasant Park

Hamilton
Harbour

PITT'S BAY RD
GORHAM RD
RICHMOND RD
PAR-LA-VILLE RD
CANAL RD
LAFFAN ST
ELLIOTT ST W
CEDAR AVE
BERMUDIANA RD
POINT PLEASANT RD
PLEASANT RD
QUEEN ST
PARK RD
TROTT RD
WASHINGTON ST
WESLEY ST
VICTORIA ST
BRUNSWICK ST
CHURCH ST
ELLIOTT ST
ANGLE ST
PRINCESS ST
DUNDONALD ST
UNION ST
BURNABY ST
PARLIAMENT ST
COURT ST
REID ST
FRONT ST
JOELL'S ST
ALLEY
KING ST
HAPPY VALLEY RD

0 100 yds
0 100 m

© AVALON TRAVEL

back to a quieter time in old Bermuda. Don't miss the neighborhood's retail bargains or popular eateries.

SIGHTS

Hamilton's small size means there are no vastly different neighborhoods to explore; sights and attractions are scattered throughout. North Hamilton is the only really distinct section, mainly because it has not been privy to major development to date and has therefore retained more of its quaint original architecture than other areas.

Albuoy's Point

Busy Albuoy's Point is the wedge of parkland behind the ferry terminal off Front Street. Mature baygrape trees shade the little patch of grass and benches surround the harbor front—the city's main boat pickup spot for day and evening charters, including snorkeling and glass-bottomed boat excursions, sailing trips, and festive cruises. Public toilets are located on Point Pleasant Road, the lane linking the park to Front Street, which also has a few souvenir shops and charter tour company offices. On the park's western side sits the salmon-colored **Royal Bermuda Yacht Club,** its members-only clubhouse and

marina the headquarters of the Argo Group Gold Cup match-racing competition and the biennial **Newport Bermuda Race,** now over 100 years old. Across the harbor is government-owned White's Island, during World War II a U.S. Coast Guard base and today the fireworks venue for public celebrations such as the Christmas Boat Parade.

Barr's Bay Park

From Albuoy's Point, a thin stretch of land on the north side of the Yacht Club links to Pembroke's **Barr's Bay Park,** another shady lawn for watching yachts come and go up the harbor. You can also access this park from Pitts Bay Road. Musical and other events are staged here throughout the year. A plaque and a sculpture by Bermudian Chesley Trott commemorate the 1835 landing site of the American slave ship *Enterprise,* whose human cargo won freedom through the courts in an emancipated Bermuda. Like Albuoy's, Barr's Bay is also a common pickup area for rental boat companies.

★ Bermuda Historical Society Museum

On the edge of Queen Elizabeth Park, in a trio of rooms inside the Bermuda National

Barr's Bay Park on the Hamilton waterfront

The Birdcage

Front Street's odd-looking blue-and-white "Birdcage," at Heyl's Corner, the junction with Queen Street, has become a beloved island symbol thanks to traffic police who have posed for thousands of holiday snapshots from the kiosk in their Bermuda shorts. The platform, which acts as a traffic island, *does* look like Tweety Bird's hangout, but it got its name from a former city official, Geoffrey Bird, who in the 1950s devised its design to keep the bobbies safe while directing traffic. It is just a tourist-pleasing gimmick in the 21st century, but the Birdcage remains a Hamilton icon, even celebrated in gold charm jewelry.

Library, is the charming little **Bermuda Historical Society Museum** (13 Queen St., tel. 441/295-2487 or 441/236-4193, apbermingham@logic.bm, 10am-2pm Mon.-Fri. May-Oct., 10:30am-1pm Mon.-Wed. and Fri. Oct.-Apr., free). The museum is run by knowledgeable volunteers, including some published historians, on behalf of the Bermuda Historical Society. Par-la-Ville, the 1814 building that now houses the library, was once a gracious Georgian homestead, like many that lined Hamilton's streets in the 19th century. Its wooden veranda today overlooks the crush of traffic on Reid Street. Outside, a landmark giant rubber tree also survives; it was planted in 1847 by the merchant William Perot, who built and lived in the house. The museum's prize artifacts include original Hogge money, 18th-century cedar furniture including a cradle and prayer chair, and silver flatware made in Bermuda. Be sure to take a look at the exquisite etched-glass hurricane shades in the dining room and the carved palmetto seats of the Queen Anne cedar chairs.

Queen Elizabeth Park

Formerly known as Par-la-Ville but renamed to mark the queen's Diamond Jubilee in 2012, this beautifully landscaped **Queen Elizabeth Park** (8am-sunset daily, free) is the city's most-used green space, popular with office workers for outdoor lunches in the spring and fall (summer's heat and humidity discourage anyone wearing a suit from leaving the comfort of air-conditioning for more than a few minutes). Mosaic pathways lead through the oasis, connecting Queen Street with Par-la-Ville Road, parallel to the west (there's a delightful moon-gate entrance on this side). A third entrance runs through the Par-la-Ville parking lot from Church Street, to the north. Rock gardens, flower beds, trellises, pergolas, and shady mature trees can be found throughout. The park was once the private garden of the Perot family, which included an island postmaster who designed Bermuda's first stamp, the circular Perot stamp, of which there are only 11 in the world today. Visit the quaint **Perot Post Office** (11 Queen St., tel. 441/292-9052, 9am-5pm Mon.-Fri.), still a working post office, on the park's eastern border.

Wesley Park

At the corner of Wesley and Church Streets, on the southwest corner of the City Hall parking lot, pocket-size **Wesley Park** pays tribute to a milestone civil-rights episode. The Theatre Boycott, by peaceful black activists in June 1959, protested segregation of the island's cinemas. The 10-day boycott was so successful it brought down racial barriers in churches, hotels, and other institutions. The park features a tall bronze sculpture by Bermudian artist Chesley Trott called *When Voices Rise*, depicting protesters. The park is a shady little stopping place with benches, brick pavers, palms, and a tamarind tree.

City Hall and Arts Centre

Hamilton's central landmark and public gathering spot, the simple lines and traditional features of the **City Hall and Arts Centre** (Church St., tel. 441/292-1234, www.cityhall. bm, 9am-5pm Mon.-Fri., free) are the masterpiece of legendary Bermudian architect Wil Onions, who was renowned for adapting cottage aesthetics to almost every project he undertook. Completed in 1960, the building, whose design is basically an oversize cottage with a slate roof and tower, was inspired by Stockholm's city hall. Its 90-foot tower supports a weathervane with a bronze rendition of the shipwrecked *Sea Venture.* Bronze statues by Bermudian sculptor Desmond Fountain depict children playing in fountains set in a water lily pond.

City Hall serves many functions. It is home to the offices of the Corporation of Hamilton on the ground floor, where portraits of mayors and Queen Elizabeth II hang in the stairwell. The main theater on the building's west side hosts performing arts, and the **Bermuda National Gallery** and the **Bermuda Society of Arts** are up the grand cedar stairs. Outside, public performances like choir recitals, Christmas marching band concerts, and occasional government press conferences are held on the steps.

★ Bermuda National Gallery

Home to a fine permanent collection of artwork, and host of regularly changing shows of work by contemporary local artists, **Bermuda National Gallery** (BNG, upstairs, City Hall and Arts Centre, Church St., tel. 441/295-9428, www.bermudanationalgallery.com, 10am-4pm Mon.-Fri., 10am-2pm Sat., $5 adults, free seniors and students) was created in 1992 to promote public education and art appreciation through its exhibitions and outreach programs. The original collection comprised works of European masters—Gainsborough, Murillo, Reynolds—gifted by Bermudian Hereward T. Watlington. The Watlington Collection has since been joined by African art, a provocative collection of black-and-white photographs by Bermudian Richard Saunders, and Hale Woodruff linocuts. The gallery hosts seasonal exhibitions, including the popular summerlong Bacardi Limited Biennial every two years. You may join a free tour of the gallery at 10am Thursday. The BNG also hosts a regular program of films, seminars, cocktail parties, and evening lectures by visiting curators and art historians.

City Hall is home to the Hamilton mayor's office and Bermuda National Gallery.

"Guilty-with an Explanation"

There can't be a more authentic slice of island life than a morning spent hearing the convoluted excuses, remonstrations, and final verdicts of Plea Court. The special session of **Magistrates Court** (Dame Lois Browne Evans Bldg., 58 Court St., tel. 441/295-5151, ext. 1230) is held at 10am Monday-Friday. Open to the public, it brings out every segment of the population to answer to accused crimes, both trivial and serious. Intoxication, shoplifting, handbag-snatching, assault, swearing in public—the litany of "summary only" offenses can rarely be tried in Supreme Court and must be dealt with by a magistrate.

One by one, defendants are called to enter a plea to their charges. If they choose "not guilty," the court adjourns the case for review or to fix a trial date. But it is the "guilty" pleas to trivial offenses that are most entertaining, when defendants creatively try to win a lighter sentence or fine before the magistrate's bench. "Guilty—with an explanation" is almost always the prelude to a hilarious yarn; it's met by anticipatory snickers all around. The presiding magistrate may join in the fun with snappy comebacks or personal anecdotes that delight the press box, lawyers, and even the other waiting defendants. Of course, a crotchety magistrate can just as easily put a damper on the jovial proceedings.

The proceedings used to evoke an almost Dickensian aura amid the old-time wood-paneled courtrooms of its former location on Parliament Street; now ensconced in contemporary headquarters, Plea Court has evolved—but the entertainment value remains.

★ Holy Trinity Cathedral

I was an adult before I climbed the 155 stairs to the top of "The Cathedral," as **Holy Trinity Cathedral** (Church St., tel. 441/292-4033, 8am-5pm daily, free) is called by Bermudians, but as soon as I'd reached its eye-popping view over Hamilton, I wished I hadn't waited so long. It's one of the best ways to get a sense of the city and its surroundings. To the north lie Government House, Pembroke Marsh, and the North Shore shipping channel; to the east the House of Assembly, King Edward VII Memorial Hospital, and the freight docks; to the west, City Hall, Hamilton's city grid, the Great Sound, and Dockyard; and to the south, Front Street, White's Island, and the harbor. The neo-Gothic Anglican church has stunning stained glass windows, flying arches, lady and warrior chapels, and a carved altar screen. Its first cornerstone was laid in 1844, though construction suffered numerous setbacks over subsequent decades, including an arson fire in 1884 that forced authorities to tear down the whole structure. Work began again in 1886, with imported stone from Nova Scotia, Scotland, and Indiana used in conjunction with Bermuda's own limestone. Plans by Scottish architect William Hay called for a spire above the 144-foot tower, but these were scrapped after various delays. The **cathedral's tower** (10am-4pm Mon.-Fri., $3 adults, $2 seniors and students, free under age 5) was finally completed in 1905. The climb—up a slightly claustrophobic spiral, followed by regular stairs to the terrace—is not for the completely unfit, but you can take breaks along the way on two spacious landings. Watch out for the piles of pigeon dung toward the end.

Victoria Park

Anyone interested in Bermuda botany should take a stroll through **Victoria Park** (8am-sunset daily, free), with shaded winding paths between beds of decorative flora and mature trees and shrubs. Scented gardenia bushes, golden acacia trees, even towering Norfolk pines thrive in this small park in Hamilton's northern section. On its main lawn is a cast-iron Victorian bandstand, which underwent a complete restoration in the United Kingdom in 2008. The park is bordered by Victoria Street, Dundonald

Bermuda's Black Culture and the Rebirth of North Hamilton

"Back o' town," as North Hamilton is known, was long castigated as a drug-ridden, crime-plagued neighborhood with nothing for travelers. That reputation is changing as the culturally vibrant neighborhood stakes its future on celebrating the island's black culture and its residents' own architectural, musical, and political achievements.

Court Street was the oft-troubled artery running up from the harbor—and rival Front Street—through the heart of North Hamilton. Its name became more than a geographical locator in the public imagination; for black Bermudians especially, it is symbolic of being ignored during decades of white control. For many white residents, the area is a complete enigma that was avoided.

In recent years, grassroots groups have worked to change perceptions, reinvigorating North Hamilton with cultural centers, public events, and new businesses, plus initiatives to encourage residents to preserve some of the most historic and beautiful architecture on the island. The area has been likened to New Orleans's French Quarter. Between King Street to the east, Parson's Road to the north, Cedar Avenue to the west, and Victoria Street to the south, North Hamilton boasts both a vibrant business center and quaint residential lanes, where gingerbread architecture, pastel homes, and quiet walled gardens have been largely undisturbed by the rampant development of the rest of Hamilton. Scores of clothing stores, salons, bakeries, nightclubs, and popular restaurants attract patrons for fresh fish and Caribbean cuisine.

"My roots are here—my grandfather built the First Church of God on Angle Street, so I do have a heritage that binds me to North Hamilton," says Elmore Warren, a neighborhood native who heads up a Court Street-based television station, Fresh TV, and runs an entrepreneurial company called Fresh Creations. "I grew up here and now I work here, so I have a self-interest in figuring out ways to bring value to this area." Court Street's stigma in recent history dates to 1977, when televised race riots included a showdown between crowds of fire-bombing black youth and armed police. But residents say North Hamilton's time for rejuvenation has come.

"This is the place where cultural tourism should begin," says Warren. "This is the place where revolutionaries were born—the black heroes of Bermuda, the ones who fought for equal rights and desegregation." A plaza at Union and Dundonald Streets is dedicated to the legendary E. F. Gordon, a firebrand lawyer and black-rights pioneer of the 1950s who rallied black Bermudians and sowed the seeds for the breakthrough Theatre Boycott in 1959, which saw segregation barriers fall in hotels, restaurants, churches, and public institutions. North Hamilton's **Pembroke Youth Centre** nurtured Bermuda's only Olympic medalist, boxer Clarence Hill. American social activist Marcus Garvey had an office on Angle Street. And the first black press, the historic **Bermuda Recorder,** was also based here.

Since the government declared North Hamilton an Empowerment Zone in 2005, entrepreneurs have benefited from a concerted effort to bolster the neighborhood via financial advice and management expertise—elements unavailable for many years to black businesspeople in Bermuda. One of the most innovative additions of the 2000s was the opening of **Chewstick,**

Street, Cedar Avenue, and Washington Street. There are public toilets here.

St. Theresa's Cathedral

An ornate contrast to its Anglican counterpart across town, Bermuda's Roman Catholic **St. Theresa's Cathedral** (13 Elliott St., tel. 441/292-0607 or 441/292-8486, sttheresas@ northrock.bm, 6:30am-7pm daily, free) was

built in 1932 and named for Saint Theresa of Lisieux, "The Little Flower." The church's tower was not finished until 1947, and 20 years later St. Theresa's became a cathedral when Bermuda was officially named a diocese. St. Theresa's boasts the largest weekly attendance of worshippers on the island, with numerous masses and evening services. The Portuguese Bermudian community's

A North Hamilton mural by artist Manuel Palacio pays tribute to Bermudian soccer stars.

a foundation launched by artist-musician Gavin Smith to heal racial divisions and inspire youth through the arts. The organization spent its formative years at the corner of Elliot and Courts Streets, attracting audiences to its Friday live bands or Sunday night open-mic sessions at its fire engine-red headquarters. Chewstick moved to Front Street, but its headquarters was destroyed by fire in 2016; it plans to reopen in new premises to showcase everything from rap and ballet to bagpipes and spoken word.

A visit to North Hamilton should include a tour of the architectural history of Angle Street, Elliott Street, Ewing Street, and Princess Street, where Victorian row housing, wooden verandas, and cute cottages can be found around every corner. Court Street between Victoria and Dundonald Streets is home to a wonderful array of fashion boutiques, music and shoe stores, and several food outlets. Visit the **Caribbean Food Market** (47 Court St., tel. 441/293-9260), where specialty items like cassava, yams, and green seasoning are available.

North Hamilton's culinary offerings alone are enough to tempt visitors. **Fish & Tings** (45 Angle St., tel. 441/292-7389) satisfies a craving for curried fish, barbecued chicken leg, or plantain. Crowds jam **Jamaican Grill** (32 Court St., tel. 441/296-6577) for jerk chicken, oxtail, and brown stew. Don't miss vibrant street markets and family fun days, with live music, arts and crafts vendors, and food stalls.

religious *festas*, which honor specific saints, use the cathedral for the colorful spectacles, including the procession of Santo Cristo, when hundreds gather at St. Theresa's on the fifth Sunday after Easter for a march through the city. The cathedral's **gift shop** (tel. 441/292-0416, 10am-2pm Mon.-Sat.) sells rosaries, cards, candles, and English and Portuguese books.

★ Sessions House

From the harbor, the **Sessions House** (21 Parliament St., tel. 441/292-7408, 8:45am-5pm Mon.-Fri., parliamentary sessions 10am-12:30pm and from 2pm Fri. Nov.-July, free) is the landmark Italianate-style building that defines Hamilton's skyline. Built in 1819, the tower was added decades later to celebrate Queen Victoria's Golden Jubilee.

Today, sitting atop Parliament Street, the Sessions House contains Bermuda's Supreme Court on its ground floor and the House of Assembly—one of the oldest parliaments in the world—upstairs. Parliament sits every Friday throughout the winter and spring, breaking for the summer and reconvening after November's ceremonious Throne Speech—when the governor reads the government's to-do list to Members of Parliament (MPs), dressed in their finest.

As in the British House of Commons, members of Parliament are seated according to political party, with opponents facing each other across the floor. A speaker, sporting a traditional black robe and wig, oversees the proceedings, which include at least a couple of all-nighters every year—there is no strict cutoff for debates nor time limits on speeches. Heckling opponents while they are speaking is called "interpolating" and is allowed, within reason, provided hecklers do it from their appointed seat. Famous debates have covered everything from whether to allow motorcars onto the island back in the 1940s (finally approved in 1946) to the Golden Arches in 1995 (a move to bring in fast-food franchises was voted down). Feel free to watch the frivolity from the public gallery during parliamentary sessions. You can also visit the empty gallery Monday-Friday to inspect its cedarwood, portraits, and the speaker's silver mace, when Sergeant-at-Arms Arnold Allen is happy to talk about the House of Assembly and show visitors around.

The Cabinet Building and the Cenotaph

South of the Sessions House sits the imposing two-story **Cabinet Building** (105 Front St., tel. 441/292-5501, 9am-5pm Mon.-Fri., free), where the "Upper House," or Senate, meets (10am Wed. Nov.-July). Completed in 1833, the building is home to the premier's office and headquarters of the cabinet ministers, whose navy sedans are usually parked outside.

The Cabinet Building lawn is the venue of the annual November Throne Speech, which the governor delivers before a packed crowd of dignitaries and MPs in hats, topcoats, and tails; Bermuda Regiment soldiers; and hundreds of onlookers and tourists. An imposing bronze statue depicts Sally Bassett, a legendary heroine of Bermuda's slavery days. According to folklore, the enslaved Bassett was implicated in the poisoning her master and his wife, and was publicly burned to death.

Sessions House

Along the lawn's south perimeter stands the 1920 Cenotaph, a limestone monument honoring Bermudian soldiers killed in the two world wars and other international conflicts. Next to it, on the southeast side of the Cabinet lawn, a polished black granite memorial lists more than 3,000 local war veterans. A solemn Remembrance Day ceremony is held here November 11, when surviving vets parade down Front Street; the occasion sees wreaths of symbolic poppies laid and a gun salute by the Bermuda Regiment. The day is a public holiday on the island, and hundreds attend the event.

ENTERTAINMENT AND EVENTS

Hamilton is the staging point for numerous big events throughout the year. The city also has a busy nightlife, particularly in summer, when visitors swell the bars and clubs. Winter can be quiet during the week, but you can usually count on Bermudians to party on Friday and Saturday nights. Tickets for all major events, as well as movies, can be purchased online at www.ptix.bm and www.bdatix.bm. Check out www.nothingtodoinbermuda.com for the most complete weekly and monthly listings. Highlight events are usually seen on billboards and lamppost banners throughout the city.

Bars

An urban vibe rocks **Beluga Seafood Bar** (Washington Mall III, 18 Church St. opposite City Hall, tel. 441/542-2859, 11:30am-2:45pm and 6pm-10pm Mon.-Sat., 5pm-9:30pm Sun.). Owner-manager Matteo Gilardoni and his team welcome newcomers as if they were regulars. In the mall's basement, the decor is Miami hip—glowing neon, nightclub chandeliers, and white lacquer complement the shots of Beluga Noble Russian vodka, fine champagne, and caviar hors d'oeuvres. **Red Steakhouse & Bar** (55 Front St., accessible entrance via Reid St., tel. 441/292-7331, www.redbermuda.com, 11:30am-late Mon.-Fri., 6pm-late Sat.-Sun.) serves up sophisticated

atmosphere, signature cocktails, an impressive wine list of more than a dozen by the glass, and VIP balcony seating overlooking Hamilton Harbour.

Toast a sunset with the cool crowd at Hamilton's loftiest drinks perch, the rooftop "sky bar" of **Muse** (17 Front St., opposite the ferry terminal, tel. 441/296-8788, www.muse.bm, happy hours 11am-3pm Mon., 11am-3pm and 6pm-10pm Tues.-Sat.). Among the inspired cocktails are the Ritz Fizz (champagne, amaretto, blue curaçao, and lime cordial). Lunch spot by day, **Bulli Social** (7 Queen St., tel. 441/232-2855, 11am-6pm Mon., 11am-8pm Tues.-Thurs., 11am-10pm Fri.-Sat.) is a post-work favorite for Wine-Down Wednesdays and Friday-night happy hours. A mixed-age crowd packs the park-side patio for live music.

Little Venice Wine Bar (32 Bermudiana Rd., tel. 441/295-3503, noon-2am Mon.-Fri., 6pm-10pm Sat.) is an offshoot of the popular adjoining restaurant, attracting a more mature crowd than other venues' twenty-somethings; fans of Little Venice come for fine wines, cosmopolitans, and other cocktails, plus tapas ranging from mini-burgers to dumplings, meat and veggie skewers, and a sampling of cheeses. Sit at tables indoors or out on the patio.

An intimate ambience can be found at the pocket-size bar inside **Barracuda Grill** (5 Burnaby Hill, tel. 441/292-1609, www.barracuda@irg.bm, noon-2:30pm and 5pm-11:30pm Mon.-Fri., 5:30pm-11:30pm Sat.-Sun.), where bartender Ryan Gibbons mixes masterly martinis and other classics amid the snug but stylish interior. Downstairs, landmark sister venue **Hog Penny** (5 Burnaby Hill, tel. 441/292-2534, www.hogpennypub.irg.bm, 11:30am-4pm and 5:30pm-11pm Mon.-Wed., 11:30am-4pm and 5:30pm-1am Thurs.-Sat.) is a well-loved British-style pub with draft pints, ciders, rum swizzles, and local craft brews, along with comfort staples like bangers and mash and Cornish pasties. During most of the year, live music is on tap.

With its liquid tiles, South Beach vibe, and

more than 100 rums on offer, Rumbar (29 Victoria St., tel. 441/296-5050, www.irg.bm, 4pm-close Mon.-Fri.) has been a hip addition to the local nightlife scene. It's located downstairs from Victoria Grill. Couches, an outdoor patio, and a raw bar serving ceviche (and no sushi for a change) attract happy-hour crowds. Corporate happy hour crowds pour off the street-side patios Friday evenings at the chic Port O' Call (87 Front St., tel. 441/295-5373, www.portocall.bm, 4pm-7pm daily). Mix with software engineers and private bankers over specials on wines, beers, and custom cocktails. Around the corner, up Chancery Lane, the restaurant owner's son has opened Bermuda's first speakeasy craft-cocktail bar, Yours Truly (2 Chancery Lane, tel. 441/295-0429, 5pm-1am Tues.-Thurs., 5pm-2am Fri.-Sun.). With just eight bar stools (no standing) and 12 tables, allowing a limited number of guests at a time, the pocket-size venue attracts lineups for its custom libations, featuring handmade ingredients from ginger beer to garnishes such as dehydrated watermelon and lemon rinds. Look for the red door.

The Doghouse (93 Front St., tel. 441/232-3644, 4pm-3am daily) draws large crowds with its lively street-side setting and ample well-priced drinks menu. The tongue-in-cheek tagline is "Come. Sit. Stay." Like its moniker, Ten (10 Dundonald St., tel. 441/295-0857, www.ten.bm, happy hour 4pm-7pm Mon.-Fri., 7am-3pm and 5pm-9pm Mon.-Fri., 7am-2:30pm Sat.) is Euro-cool, with floor-to-ceiling artwork, couch-and-cube seating, and an alfresco patio that has made it one of the city's favorite café-bars. Tucked away on a quiet block on the street level of a condominium building that blazed a residential trail into the city's northwest, it has a well-stocked wine cellar, elegant tapas, and award-winning cocktails that attract a full house for weekday happy hours.

Friday night happy hour brings regulars to Coconut Rock (Williams House, 20 Reid St., tel. 441/292-1043, 11:30am-10:30pm Mon.-Sat., 1pm-10:30pm Sun.), where a DJ or karaoke provide entertainment. Partake of

bleu cheese burgers and other menu items, or visit the Yashi Sushi Bar in the back. The Docksider Pub & Restaurant (121 Front St., tel. 441/296-3333, www.dockies.com, 11:30am-3am Mon.-Fri., 9am-3am Sat.-Sun.) is one of the hot spots among Bermuda's youth, who are attracted by reasonable drink prices, pizza, and pub grub. The popular sports bar opens for live games shown on its big-screen TVs weekend mornings, when the crowd consists largely of bleary-eyed expats eager to catch a British soccer showdown.

Lively happy hours, reasonable prices, and televised sports bring a full house to Bermuda Bistro at The Beach (103 Front St. at Parliament St., tel. 441/292-0219, www.thebeachbermuda.com, 10am-3am daily). On either side of Burnaby Hill, Front Street's Flanagan's Irish Pub (Emporium Bldg., 69 Front St., tel. 441/295-8299, www.flanagans.bm, 11am-1am Mon.-Fri., 9am-1am Sat.-Sun.) and Pickled Onion (53 Front St., tel. 441/295-2263, www.thepickledonion.com, 11am-1am daily) are popular among both locals and visitors for nighttime carousing, and both have panoramic terraces overlooking the harbor. Flanagan's is an especially good venue for viewing the finish line of January's Front Street Mile race. Flanagan's has an adjoining sports bar, Outback (from 5pm Mon.-Thurs., from 11am Fri.-Sun.), with 22 high-definition TV screens, including a 63-inch giant and individual screens with remote controls at each booth. Casey's Cocktail Lounge (25 Queen St., tel. 441/292-9994, 10am-10pm Mon.-Sat.) attracts a very Bermudian crowd, especially on Friday afternoons before public holiday weekends.

Old British pub culture returned to Hamilton when The Astwood Arms (85 Front St., tel. 441/292-5818, noon-midnight Mon.-Sat.) opened inside a former jewelry store in 2017. With its replica engraved Victorian oak sconces, bar-keep uniforms, and on-tap selections of Spitfire Kentish Ale, Shepherd Neame IPA, Kronenbourg, and Guinness, it feels genuine. Classic bar grub completes the illusion, with fish fingers ($11),

Scotch eggs ($8.50) and Cornish pasties ($12), a ploughman's lunch ($18), and fish-n-chips with mushy peas ($21). Seating is inside the cavernous pub, or streetside on the porch.

Clubs

Cosmopolitan Night Club (95 Front St., tel. 441/705-2582, 10pm-3am Fri.-Sat.) draws dancing crowds of late-night partiers year-round to its indoor-outdoor venue at Bermuda House Lane, linking Front and Reid Streets. R&B, soca, reggae, and hip-hop, along with some of the island's best DJs, make it a lively scene. **Café Cairo** (93 Front St., tel. 441/295-5155, cafecairo@northrock.bm, 5pm-3am Tues.-Sat.), has long been popular for after-hours schmoozing. While the venue has won raves for its Middle Eastern restaurant, it morphs into a club after 10pm, when the DJ arrives and devoted night owls hit the dance floor. North Hamilton's **Spinning Wheel** (33 Court St., tel. 441/292-7799, 3pm-3am Mon.-Fri., 8am-3am Sat.-Sun.) and **Place's Place** (43 Dundonald St. at E. F. Gordon Square, tel. 441/293-9268, noon-late Mon.-Sat.) are busy weekend hangouts.

Cinemas

Hamilton has two cinemas, both of which show major box-office releases, including 3-D blockbusters and the occasional Oscar-nominated indie. Twice-nightly showings, plus weekend matinees, keep movies around for a week or two. Tickets can be purchased at the door or online via the cinemas' websites or www.ptix.bm.

The Speciality Cinema and Grill (12 Church St., tel. 441/292-2135, www.speciality-cinema.bm, 11am-10pm Mon.-Sat., noon-8pm Sun.) has two cinemas within its complex, both with comfortable seating and surround sound, plus a café and deli where moviegoers buy tickets and popcorn and other snacks. You can have a cold drink or hot meal (roast beef, grilled chicken, fish sandwiches) before the show.

The Liberty Theatre (49 Union Square, between Victoria St. and Dundonald St.,

tel. 441/292-7296, www.libertytheatre.bm) is a larger venue with a regular-size screen, though the surroundings are not quite up to par with the average North American multiplex. After a good run at The Liberty, films usually head west to Dockyard for a second run at The Liberty's sister cinema, The Neptune.

Theater, Music, and Dance

Live performances are held in Hamilton throughout the year. Check www.nothingtodoinbermuda.com or *The Royal Gazette* to see what's going on. Schedules and online tickets are available at www.bdatix.bm and www.ptix.bm.

Daylesford Theatre (Washington St., opposite Victoria Park, tel. 441/292-0848, bar tel. 441/295-5584, bar hours 5pm-11pm Mon.-Fri., www.bmds.bm) is headquarters of the Bermuda Musical and Dramatic Society (BMDS), which stages regular plays throughout the year, as well as the popular Christmas pantomime at City Hall. The **City Hall and Arts Centre** (17 Church St.) is the island's major venue for theatricals and dance, theater, and orchestra, including many of the Bermuda Festival of the Performing Arts events.

Festivals and Events
BERMUDA FESTIVAL OF THE PERFORMING ARTS

The New Year brings the **Bermuda Festival of the Performing Arts** (tel. 441/295-1291, www.bermudafestival.org, Jan.-Mar.), a two-month cultural showcase of top international acts, from contemporary dance troupes and circuses to ballet and orchestral performances. Several venues are used, but most performances take place in the evenings at Hamilton City Hall and Arts Centre.

BERMUDA MARATHON WEEKEND

The mid-January **Bermuda Marathon Weekend** (tel. 441/737-8850, runbermuda@gmail.com, www.bermudaraceweekend.com) includes an international marathon, a half-marathon, a 10K run and walk, and the Front Street Mile. The 10K starts and finishes at Devonshire's Bermuda National Sports Centre, but the other events take place on Front Street, in Hamilton.

BERMUDA INTERNATIONAL FILM FESTIVAL

The March **Bermuda International Film Festival** (BIFF, tel. 441/293-3456, fax 441/293-7769, www.biff.bm) adds an unusual touch of bohemia to Hamilton's normally conservative ambience as black-garbed twentysomethings from the West Village and Hollywood wander around incongruously between screenings. The showcase has made a name on the world's celluloid circuit and draws not only award-winning indie directors but also international film financiers intrigued by Bermuda's offshore benefits. BIFF has also drawn celebrity visitors such as Michael Douglas, Jim Sheridan, Carrie Fisher, and Willem Dafoe.

HARBOUR NIGHTS

Harbour Nights (7pm-9pm Wed. May-Sept.) is a crowded street festival that includes arts and crafts stalls, bouncy castles and train rides for kids, alfresco food, and live performances by Bermuda bands and gombey troupes. The fun takes place on Front Street, which is closed to traffic between Parliament and Par-la-Ville Streets. Reid Street is also shut down for the evening.

BERMUDA DAY PARADE

The **Bermuda Day Parade,** on the last Friday in May, is the island's version of Caribbean Carnival. Following a half-marathon, which travels on alternate years from either the West or East Ends through Front Street's cheering crowds to a Pembroke finish, an hours-long parade of majorettes, gombeys, decorated floats, dance troupes, and other community performers winds through the city. Families stake out their seats the night before to get a good viewing spot, and then camp out on sidewalks most of the day.

OTHER EVENTS

In May, five classes of boats—J105, J24, Lasers, Etchells, and International One Designs (IODs)—race for honors in a hotly contested regatta organized by the Royal Bermuda Yacht Club, **Bermuda International Invitational Race Week,** and pitting visiting sailors against local counterparts in the Great Sound.

Co-managed by the Royal Bermuda Yacht Club, the **Newport Bermuda Race** (www.rbyc.bm, www.bermudarace.com), a bluewater sailing contest from Newport, Rhode Island, to St. David's, brings a fleet of maxiyachts to Hamilton and St. George's Harbours in June. The race is more than a century old and runs in alternate years as the Marion Bermuda Race, a contest from Buzzard Bay, Massachusetts.

The **Queen's Birthday Parade** in June brings colonial pomp and ceremony to Front Street to mark the British monarch's special day. A gun salute is followed by a marching parade featuring the Bermuda Regiment Band Company and Corps of Drums.

A trio of big-fish team events stretches through July as part of the **Bermuda Triple Crown Billfish Championship** (www.bermudatriplecrown.com), offering cash and prizes, including a top prize to the largest blue marlin catch. Events take place around the Hamilton Princess & Beach Club, Barr's Bay Park, and the docks of the Royal Bermuda Yacht Club.

For the **Labor Day March and Celebration** (tel. 441/292-0044), participants, including gombeys and majorettes, march to Bernard Park in Hamilton for a daylong festival honoring Bermuda's labor movement and organized by the Bermuda Industrial Union.

Argo Group Gold Cup (www.bermudagoldcup.com) is an international event in October that brings the world's top yacht match-racing competitors to vie in a showdown of spinnakers for the sport's oldest trophy, the King Edward VII Gold Cup, in Hamilton Harbour and the Great Sound.

The Dance of the Gombeys

Gombeys draw huge crowds on Front Street.

Bermuda's cultural ambassadors are the gombeys, a name meaning "drums" given to African-inspired dance troupes adorned in elaborate outfits featuring feathers, beads, and sequins. In kaleidoscopic costumes, gombeys have long been adored by their Bermudian fans, but only in recent decades have they been officially recognized by the government to represent the island at international events.

Gombeys derive from a grassroots tradition that borrows elements from Native American, British military, and Caribbean influences. Distinct family troupes evolved in the parishes over the centuries, and even today, gombey troupes consist of relatives and friends of specific families, and many include youngsters as young as two or three.

Their dance may appear to the uninitiated to be a free-for-all, but it is actually a structured art form with a beginning, middle, and end that dramatizes a popular Bible story or legend, such as that of David and Goliath. Gombey troupes used to appear mostly on Boxing Day (the day after Christmas), attracting crowds as they walked through parish neighborhoods, but they now perform at many cultural festivals through the year, including the Wednesday **Harbour Nights** in Hamilton. Tradition holds that spectators toss coins of appreciation on the ground, which are later gathered by a designated gombey.

The iconic dance is coupled with ornate costumes, which are works of art in themselves. Peacock feathers, beads, and sequins are painstakingly used to construct each outfit, with a mask attached to a tall, feathered headdress, and gloves, scarf, and boots. Accessories include drums, ornamental bows and arrows, braids, and tomahawks. Typically, the troupe's captain uses a whip or whistle to orchestrate dance routines and storylines, keeping the other members in line.

Bermuda gombeys have performed at major events such as the Edinburgh Tattoo, the Smithsonian Folklife Festival in Washington DC, and on the island with visiting Native American groups who hold strong familial ties with Bermuda's St. David's Island community.

Bermuda Heroes Weekend

Bermuda Heroes Weekend (tel. 441/400-4376, www.bermudaheroesweekend.com) bills itself as the ultimate summer fete, inviting sequin-bedecked merrymakers to "Come Play with Us." Styled after Rio de Janeiro, New Orleans, and Trinidadian soca carnivals, the island-wide mid-June extravaganza makes the most of a public holiday devoted to honoring Bermuda's local heroes.

The festival was launched in 2015 by soca DJ Jason Sukdeo (a.k.a. D'General), a proud Bermudian of Guyanese descent who parlayed his impressive following of fans into the type of support impresarios dream about. An estimated 8,000 merrymakers take part in a giddy five events over four days. In 2017 more than 700 visitors flew in for the occasion.

Some of the weekend's events are free to the public, while others have admission fees or package pricing. The festivities begin with a Friday night concert at the National Sports Centre in Devonshire, followed by a raft-up party at Shelly Bay, Hamilton Parish. Pan in the Park, featuring steel pan artists and bands at Victoria Park in the City of Hamilton is next. Hardy night owls enjoy the Super Hero J'Ouvert event, a glow-in-the-dark all-nighter at Bernard Park in Pembroke. The weekend wraps with a day-long Parade of Bands at Clearwater Beach, Southside, St. David's, featuring top DJs and a dance-off between thousands of participants decked out as feathered troupes. Food vendors and a cash bar cater to the crowds.

For the **Remembrance Day Parade and Ceremony,** the Bermuda Regiment and Band Company join war veterans in a solemn march down Front Street in the City of Hamilton on November 11, a public holiday.

In December, kids and parents pack Front and Church Streets for the festive **Santa Claus Parade,** which features colorful illuminated floats, parish majorettes, gombeys, and Santa riding on a vintage fire engine. Elves toss bags of candy to onlookers. The **Christmas Boat Parade** that traverses Hamilton Harbour is also a holiday must-see—it's a magical parade of yachts, barges, charter boats, and pleasure craft decked out in cleverly themed light displays, vying for prizes. The best viewing is from Front Street docks or restaurant terraces and along Harbour Road. An annual treat for children, the annual **Bermuda Musical & Dramatic Society Pantomime** (www. bmds.bm) takes place at Hamilton's City Hall and Arts Centre and features the island's amateur actors in a British-style theatrical extravaganza.

SHOPPING

The bulk of Hamilton's retail stores are found along the length of Reid, Front, Queen, Burnaby, and Church Streets, as well as Court Street in North Hamilton. There are also several malls linking these major thoroughfares. These include the **Walker Arcade** (between Front St. and lower Reid St.), which also connects to the **Old Cellar** (off Front St.); **Butterfield Walkway** (Front St. alongside Butterfield Bank); the **Emporium** (69 Front St., east of Butterfield Walkway); the **Bermudiana Arcade** (west of Queen St.); **Windsor Place** (east off Queen St.), and the **Washington Mall** (with several floors of shops extending between Reid St. and Church St.).

Most Hamilton stores open at 10am-5pm or 5:30pm, although a few open as early as 8:30am. Some Front Street, Queen Street, and Reid Street stores stay open later Friday in the Christmas season and Wednesday during summer Harbour Nights. Sunday afternoon shopping also happens occasionally in busy seasons. Virtually all retail stores, save a few smaller outlets, accept credit cards. Many carry store details and post special offers and promotional events on Facebook, and a few are also on Twitter.

Books

Bermuda Book Store (3 Queen St., near Heyl's Corner at Front St. junction, tel. 441/295-3698, www.bermudabookstore.com) embodies the best elements of a successful, independent book shop, from its wooden floors and rambling rows of carefully curated titles to owner-manager Hannah Willmott's precociously well-read staff. The store is housed in a historic building it has inhabited for decades. There's also a well-stocked section for kids and teens.

Brown & Co.'s **The Bookmart** (35 Front St., tel. 441/279-5443, www.phoenixstores.com) is a good place to find the latest best-seller, as well as Bermuda publications, and international magazines. Its well-stocked children's section is one of the island's best. Alongside it on the top level of the department store is a **Glaze Café** outlet, serving java, smoothies, wraps, sandwiches, and cool drinks. Take your snack out on the veranda, which has sweeping views of Front Street and the harbor. It's also a convenient place to wait for your ferry, located just across the street from the main terminal.

Clothing and Shoes

While many Bermudians beef up their wardrobes on overseas shopping sprees, there's still plenty to please fashionistas in Hamilton's stores. Some of Front Street's old-money department stores are gone, but smaller city boutiques draw shoppers.

Atelerie (9 Reid St., tel. 441/296-0280, www.atelerie.com) is small but well stocked, bursting with designer labels such as DVF, Rag and Bone, and Paige Denim. Artist-photographer Heather Macdonald has her finger on the pulse of what women *really* want. Cozy PJs, seamless lingerie, silk scarves, and jewelry galore make it a trove of endless treasures. Just up the street, **Modblu Boutique** (46 Reid St., tel. 441/405-3250, www.modblu-bermuda.com) curates an equally au courant collection of styles, including affordable jewelry, scarfs, shoes, and bags.

For that Pucci scarf or pair of Jimmy Choos, join high-end mavens at **Lusso** (51 Front St., tel. 441/295-6734, lusso@tess.bm), purveyor of the latest catwalk designs, including suits and swimwear, plus luxury labels such as Rebecca Minkoff and Ferragamo. Ask to be shown the sale products, including top designer shoes and bags, as discounts sometimes are unmarked. Its sister store,

Front Street's Heyl's Corner

Bermuda Shorts

If you really want to blend in, go native: There's no more Bermudian a uniform (for men, anyway) than Bermuda shorts. But you have to get it right. As one retailer opined, "a lot of people don't understand the difference between Bermuda shorts and shorts bought in Bermuda." Key to the shorts' authenticity is length, which should be no less than one inch above the knee, and cut in a particular way, stiffly creased down the front, and held up by a belt.

Fabrics can vary from Madras prints to lemon yellow and pastel pink, matched with same-color ties and knee socks if you *really* want to look the part. Don't worry about sticking out in such unusual hues; you won't. Look around Hamilton any weekday, and you'll find a rainbow sea of males parading up and down the busy streets as if there was nothing at all outlandish about wearing robin-red shorts, matching knee socks, a dress shirt, a natty tie, and blazer. The shorts are perfect attire for the hot, humid climate.

Genuine Bermuda linen-blend shorts can be found for under $60 at the **English Sports Shop,** which has branches in Hamilton, Somerset Village, and St. George's. **The Authentic Bermuda Shorts** sells its high-quality cotton twill styles at its Hamilton flagship store as well as shops including **A. S. Cooper** (which has branches in Southampton and the Dockyard in addition to Hamilton), **Luxury Gifts Bermuda** in Hamilton Parish, and **Pulp & Circumstance** at the airport. It also sells online.

Boutique C.C. (1 Front St. W., tel. 441/295-3935), is where locals shop for cocktail dresses, eveningwear, and suits at reasonable prices.

Find Italian knitwear at **Stefanel** (12 Walker Arcade at Reid St., tel. 441/295-5698). **A. S. Cooper & Sons** (59 Front St., tel. 441/295-3961, www.ascooper.bm) and British bastion **Marks & Spencer** (28 Reid St., tel. 441/295-5516) have more mainstream fashion offerings, including corporate and evening wear, shoes, and accessories.

Go-to men's stores are few but include **A. S. Cooper Man** (29 Front St., tel. 441/295-3961, www.ascooper.bm), **Gibbons Company** (21 Reid St., tel. 441/295-0022, www.gibbons.bm), and **Thirty Two 64** (15 Front St. tel. 441/400-5030). Genuine pink, yellow, and red linen-blend Bermuda shorts ($60) can be found at **English Sports Shop** (49 Front St., tel. 441/295-2672), along with linen and wool blazers ($250-275), Bermuda silk ties (sporting longtails, horse and carriage, and Hamilton's pastel skyline), and conservative women's fashions.

To find Bermuda shorts for both men and women, go to the flagship **The Authentic Bermuda Shorts** (TABS, Walker Arcade, 12 Reid St., tel. 441/704-8227, www.tabsbermuda.

com) founded by Bermudian Rebecca Hanson and selling high-quality cotton twill styles.

Bermudians head to **Calypso** (45 Front St., tel. 441/295-2112, www.calypsobermuda.com) every spring for their new bathing suits—everything from string bikinis to racing backs. Head upstairs for discounts on Eileen Fisher, Max Mara, and evening wear. Beach bums and surfer dudes also love **Makin' Waves** (Chevron Bldg., 11 Church St., tel. 441/292-4609, www.makinwaves.bm), a 3,000-square-foot store stocked with flip-flops and swimwear, stand-up paddleboards, scuba and snorkeling equipment, and accessories.

For shoes and handbags, **Perry Collections** (2 Reid St., tel. 441/296-0014) has the most coveted selection, with Badgley Mischka, Kate Spade, and Stuart Weitzman. For upscale European styles, visit **Voilà** (Butterfield Walkway, 67 Front St., tel. 441/295-2112, ext. 120, www.calypsobermuda.com). **Colosseum** (80 Reid St., tel. 441/297-2012, colosseumltd@yahoo.com) carries trendsetting shoes and bags from Italy, as well as Louis Vuitton bags on consignment. The Walkway **Nine West** (23 Reid St., tel. 441/295-0022) and **Trends** (22 Reid St., tel. 441/295-6420) stock a full range of shoes and bags. **W. J. Boyle & Son** (31 Queen St., tel. 441/295-1887) is the island's leading footwear chain, carrying a wide range of men's, women's, and children's styles; one of its Hamilton sister shops, **Sports Locker** (Windsor Place, 18 Queen St., tel. 441/292-3300), stocks Merrell hiking boots, Teva sandals, Sperry boat shoes, and sneakers. **Casual Footware** (40 Court St., tel. 441/295-9968) sells comfortable Birkenstock, Mephisto, and Hogan footwear.

Jeans purists, male and female, will love the racks of True Religion and Diesel styles at **Mambo** (Old Cellar Lane, Front St., tel. 441/295-3003), while teens and club-hoppers gravitate to the more affordable **Zig-Zag Boutique** (31 Dundonald St., tel. 441/295-0785).

For lingerie, **Women's Secret** (14 Reid St., tel. 441/295-2112, ext. 150, www.womensecret. com) and **Gibbons Company** (21 Reid St., tel. 441/295-0022, www.gibbons.bm) are the island's primary purveyors.

Perfume and Cosmetics

The Bermuda Perfumery's **Lili Bermuda** (Butterfield Walkway, 67 Front St., tel. 441/296-2885, www.lilibermuda.com) offers island-inspired fragrances. Several other stores sell designer perfumes and cosmetics. **MAC Boutique** (53 Front St., tel. 441/295-8843) is staffed by enthusiastic young makeup artists. The large department store **Gibbons Company** (21 Reid St., tel. 441/295-0022, www.gibbons.bm) carries most of the major cosmetics lines, at U.S.-competitive prices. Department store **A. S. Cooper & Sons** (59 Front St., tel. 441/295-3961, www.ascooper. bm) also has a large well-stocked floor of major brands, including Dior, Estée Lauder, and La Prairie. **Strands** (31 Reid St., tel. 441/295-0935, www.strands.bm, 8:45am-6pm Mon.-Wed. and Fri., 8:45am-8pm Thurs., 8:45am-5pm Sat.) carries Clarins exclusively, and its knowledgeable staff is able to offer product advice as well as on-site skin spa treatments. **Brown & Co.** (35 Front St., tel. 441/279-5524, www.brown.bm) stocks a full

range of most designer perfumes on its convenient Front Street level.

Gifts and Souvenirs

Pulp & Circumstance (4 Washington Lane, tel. 441/542-9586) is a mecca for soaps and bath products, stuffed toys, and locally designed greeting cards. **Urban Cottage** (11 Front St., tel. 441/296-3039) curates an eclectic mix of fashion, jewelry, kitchenware, and glassware, including Bermuda parish pillowcases and match-me-if-you-can prints. **Island Shop** (3 Queen St., tel. 441/292-5292, www. islandexports.com) carries artist Barbara Finsness's hand-designed tablecloths, ceramics, handbags, and linens, as well as gorgeous Venetian glass jewelry.

A Front Street landmark, the quaint little **Irish Linen Shop** (31 Front St., tel. 441/295-4089, www.theirishlinenshop.com) sells Madeira hand embroideries, table and bed linens, and handkerchiefs by Souleiado, Le Jacquard Français, and Yves Delorme. You can also find one-of-a-kind gifts here, including soaps, candles, and exquisite Bermuda cedar trays made by craftsman Jeremy Johnson. Proceeds from **Trustworthy Gift Shop** (Old Cellar Lane, 47 Front St., tel. 441/296-4164, www.bnt.bm), which stocks Bermuda books, arts, and crafts, help support Bermuda National Trust's historic homes and nature reserves.

Sporting Goods

Sportseller (Washington Mall, lower level, 9 Reid St., tel. 441/295-2692, sales@sportseller. bm) is the island's premier running and triathlon store, with shoes and apparel by Nike, Asics, and Under Armour, as well as yoga gear, racing suits and goggles, hiking packs, and accessories. You can register for local road race events at the shop. **Pro Shop** (17 Reid St., at Washington Lane, tel. 441/292-7487, proshop@ibl.bm) stocks soccer, tennis, and running gear, including Adidas, Reebok, and Umbro brands.

International Sports Shop (2 Church St., tel. 441/295-4183, www.issl.bm) carries

Best Souvenirs

There's always a T-shirt or paperweight to take home, but if you look around, you'll find far more interesting souvenirs of your trip to Bermuda.

Established in 1928, **The Bermuda Perfumery** (Stewart Hall, 5 Queen St., St. George's, tel. 441/293-0627, U.S. tel. 800/527-8213, www.bermuda-perfumery.com or www.lilibermuda.com) used to operate out of the rambling gardens of a historic estate in Hamilton Parish. When the land was sold in the late 1990s, the business moved to St. George, and today, the popular Lili line of fragrances, including perfume (0.5 ounces $95), soaps, body lotions, and bath and shower gel, is sold in stores island-wide, including **Lili Bermuda** (Butterfield Walkway, Hamilton, 67 Front St., tel. 441/296-2885). The scents—including Easter lily, jasmine, oleander, and passion flower—appear to have a fan base overseas. You can learn all about their production by visiting the perfumery and its pretty little garden, now housed at a historic Bermuda National Trust property.

There's nothing more Bermudian than cedar—the *Juniperus bermudiana* variety, of course. Cedar trinkets are sold around the island, but you can watch maestro craftsman Chesley Trott in person at the **Bermuda Arts Centre** (Royal Naval Dockyard, tel. 441/234-2809, www.artbermuda.bm) at Dockyard, working wonders out of a pile of gnarled silver twigs or tree trunks. Pull-toys and public-art sculptures are his specialty; all of Trott's works demand top prices. **Jeremy Johnson's Village Carpentry** (127 North Shore, Pembroke, tel. 441/292-2088) is an aromatic roadside workshop selling cedar animals and other hand-carved mementos. In Paget, high-polish cedar trays and goblets made by prison inmates and sold at the **Masterworks Museum of Bermuda Art** (Bermuda Botanical Gardens, 183 South Rd., Paget, www.bermudamasterworks.com) make gorgeous gifts.

Gosling's Black Seal Rum will ensure your enjoyment of black 'n' cokes and dark 'n' stormies long after you leave Bermuda. Bottles of rum (1 liter $13), as well as Gosling's and Horton's rum cakes, can be found at **Bermuda Duty Free** (Departures Hall, tel. 441/293-2870), the retail outlet at the international airport.

Island artworks are some of the nicest products to take home. The **Bermuda Society of Arts** (City Hall and Arts Centre, Hamilton, tel. 441/292-3824) holds regular shows, and its office stocks members' oils, acrylics, watercolors, and sculptures for sale. Artist Barbara Finsness's popular **Island Shop** (3 Queen St., Hamilton, tel. 441/292-5292; 49 Front St., Old Cellar Lane, tel. 441/292-6307) carries her designs on linen tablecloths and place settings, handbags, and ceramics. Gift shop **Pulp & Circumstance** (4 Washington Lane, Hamilton, tel. 441/292-9586) has greeting cards by Bermudian artists and photographers.

The General Post Office's **Philatelic Bureau** (Church St. and Parliament St., Hamilton, tel. 441/297-7807) sells collections of commemorative stamps featuring themes of cultural and historical significance to the island. Numismatists seek out the **Bermuda Monetary Authority** (43 Victoria St., Hamilton, tel. 441/295-5278, www.bma.bm) for boxed gift sets of Bermuda coins, including commemoratives such as 2005's gold and silver quincentennial issue and the island's distinctive new set of vertical notes, released in 2009.

And, of course, don't forget those **Bermuda shorts.**

soccer and other sporting gear and clothing and fitness equipment. **Sports R Us** (61 Church St., tel. 441/292-1891) is the island's largest sports store, with everything from equipment to running, golf, tennis, and competitive swim gear. There's also a large range of shoes, beach slippers, and waterproof slides.

Winners' Edge Bike Shop (73 Front St., tel. 441/295-6012, www.winnersedge.bm) stocks Trek, Gary Fisher, and Cannondale bicycles as well as gear, clothing, and accessories; an on-site shop does repairs. **Bicycle Works** (13 Tumkins Lane, tel. 441/297-8356, www.bicycleworks.bm) is the island's authorized dealer of Specialized brand cycles and carries accessories, clothing, and shoes. Repairs can be done on-site.

China and Crystal

Historic **Bluck's** (4 Front St., tel. 441/295-5367) is the island's oldest vendor of china and crystal, opened in 1844. The forest-green cottage-style building wedged between Front Street's financial and insurance blocks is famous for both classic and contemporary designs by Kosta Boda, Baccarat, and Royal Doulton. Department store **A. S. Cooper & Sons** (59 Front St., tel. 441/295-3961, www.ascooper.bm) carries major lines of china and crystal from Europe and around the world.

Jewelry, Watches, and Sunglasses

Treasures inside **Alexandra Mosher Flagship Store & Studio** (5 Front St., tel. 441/236-9006, www.alexandramosher.com) and **Washington Mall Boutique** (Washington Mall West, lower level, 7 Reid St., tel. 441/236-9009, 10am-5pm Mon.-Sat.) are handcrafted by the Best of Bermuda Award-winning artist in sterling silver and gold, her designs inspired by island flora and fauna—and many incorporating Bermuda's hallmark pink sand.

Another contemporary addition to Bermuda's jewelry scene, **Atlantic Jewellery Studio** (Washington Mall, lower level, 9 Reid St., tel. 441/542-1554, www.atlanticjewellery.com) features the work of gemologist and metalsmith Jacquie Lohan, who also blends island motifs and materials (beach sand) into her award-winning creations for men and women.

The island's two largest retailers for jewelry and watches are **Crisson** (55 Front St. and 16 Queen St., tel. 441/295-2351, www.crisson.com) and **Astwood Dickinson** (25 Front St., opposite the ferry terminal, tel. 441/292-5805, www.ascooper.bm). Bermuda-themed gold pieces featuring the local flora and fauna can be found at the latter, while both carry major brand names, including Rolex, Tag Heuer, and Mont Blanc.

Walker Christopher (9 Front St., tel. 441/295-1466, walkerchris@cwbda.bm) is known for its own designs in fine jewelry, especially a beautiful collection of sterling-silver

Christmas ornaments featuring Bermuda icons like gombeys and angelfish. A new edition is created each year. **Swiss Timing** (95 Front St., tel. 441/295-1376) specializes in European watch brands, including Zenith, Concord, and Certina.

Gem Cellar (Old Cellar Lane, 47 Front St., tel. 441/292-3042, www.gemcellar.bm) makes Bermuda charms and custom-designed pieces, and also does valuations and repairs. **E. R. Aubrey Jewellers** (101 Front St., tel. 441/296-3171, and 19 Queen St., tel. 441/295-3506, www.bermudaluckystone.com) manufactures and imports sterling silver and titanium jewelry and create-your-own designs.

Style mavens seeking eyewear will find good choices in Hamilton. Opened by actor Michael Douglas and reggae artist Collie Buddz, both Bermudians, **The Sunglass and Watch Shop** (13 Reid St., tel. 441/292-7933) stocks designer brands such as Gucci, Ray-Ban, and Maui Jim. **Eyes On Sail On** (Washington Mall West, lower level, 7 Reid St., tel. 441/295-0808) stocks Tory Burch, Gucci, and other major brands, along with Helly Hansen and Patagonia rain jackets and outdoor wear. **Makin' Waves** (31 Queen St., at Church St., tel. 441/292-4609, www.makin-waves.bm) has VonZipper and Oakley shades. Optometry specialists **Argus Sunwear** (Melbourne House, 25 Reid St.; 11 Parliament St., at Victoria St., tel. 441/295-7861) offers Oliver Peoples, Dolce & Gabbana, Coach, and Prada frames at its two boutiques.

Technology

All things technological cost substantially more in Bermuda than on the mainland, but there are ample retailers to keep you connected. For Apple products and accessories, visit authorized reseller **iClick** (Williams House, 20 Reid St., tel. 441/542-5425, www.iclickbermuda.bm), whose gurus can also help you with gadget cases, laptop backpacks, and Beats and Bose headphones. **P-tech** (3 Reid St., tel. 441/295-5496, www.ptech.bm) is a general electronics store, offering cameras and cell phone accessories from Nokia, Nikon, and Sony. An online prints and photo cards service is also located inside. **Computer Solutions** (7 Victoria St., tel. 441/297-3331, www.computersolutions.bm) stocks Toshiba laptops, HP desktops, disc players, and accessories.

Leisure Time (28 Queen St., tel. 441/296-4386, www.leisure.bm) has a full range of movies on DVD and Blu-ray disc for rent or sale, plus games for PlayStation, Xbox, and Wii, along with a bounty of movie munchies. Alongside Hamilton's bus terminal, **Audio-Visual Electronics** (4 Washington St., tel. 441/292-1354) deals in DVDs, players, and mobile phones, including Apple and Samsung brands.

For Kids

Several stores will interest kids and their parents. Favorites include **Treats of Bermuda** (Washington Mall, 7 Reid St., tel. 441/296-1123) for candy, Lego, and Thomas the Tank Engine; **The Annex** (upstairs in the Phoenix Centre, 3 Reid St., tel. 441/279-5410), with Lego, Barbie, candy, and toys; and **Pulp & Circumstance** (4 Washington Lane, tel. 441/292-9586), a treasure trove of stuffed animals and upscale baby gifts. **People's Pharmacy** (62 Victoria St., tel. 441/292-7527, www.peoplespharmacy.bm) has one of the best children's toy sections, with board games, arts and crafts, and candy and chocolate. **Gibbons Company** (21 Reid St., tel. 441/295-0022, www.gibbons.bm) has a large clothing and toys department for children and babies near its Church Street entrance, opposite the main bus terminal—including a Gap boutique and a wide selection of toys and accessories.

For stylish European clothes for kids, don't miss **Blukids** (Washington Mall, tel. 441/202-5065) and **Benetton** (24 Reid St., upstairs, tel. 441/295-2112), which stock fashionable shoes and well-made cotton and wool outfits. **The Irish Linen Shop** (31 Front St., tel. 441/295-4089) sells hand-stitched babies' layette sets, embroidered dresses, booties, and

other gift items. **English Sports Shop** (49 Front St., tel. 441/295-2672) also has a children's department, with preppy woolens, golf shirts, and turtlenecks, while its sister store **Marks & Spencer** (28 Reid St., tel. 441/295-0031) has a great selection of the UK brand's kids' clothes, including bathrobes, slippers, socks, and undergarments. The **W. J. Boyle & Son** (70 Church St. E., tel. 441/295-1887) outlet in eastern Hamilton is kid-focused, with socks, leather and outdoor sandals, boots, and sneakers.

SPORTS AND RECREATION

The **Island Tour Centre** (Albuoy's Point, 5 Point Pleasant Park, tel. 441/236-1300, www.islandtourcentre.com, 8am-6pm daily summer, 9am 1pm daily winter) acts as a centralized booking agent for all kinds of water-based and landlubber activities island-wide, including scuba dives, sailing charters, kayak and Jet Ski tours, flyboarding, powerboating, eco-expeditions, horseback riding, booze cruises, parasailing, and glass-bottomed boat tours. The center represents more than 20 vendors. Check out the wide assortment of brochures and flyers inside to choose your adventure, or view options online via the website. Payment is required when you reserve.

Scuba and Water Sports

No scuba operators depart from Hamilton; most water sports outfits are run out of Dockyard. But several sail and boat tours depart from Albuoy's Point or alongside the ferry terminal on Front Street and can be booked and paid either directly or through the adjacent Island Tour Centre. Albuoy's pickups can usually be arranged with private charters, even if their vessels are kept elsewhere. Some of the best are: catamaran cruises aboard the *Chelonia* (tel. 441/334-9771, www.cheloniabermuda.com), the *Restless Native* (tel. 441/531-8149, restless@logic.bm), and the 77-foot *Zara* (www.bermuda-yachts.com); sail charters on a 51-foot ketch run by **Sail Bermuda** (tel. 441/737-2993, www.

sailbermuda.com); and glass-bottomed boat tours aboard the *Reef Explorer* (tel. 441/535-7333, www.bermudareefexplorer.com).

Crewed charters offering full catering and water sports are run from Hamilton Harbour aboard the three "lady boats" of **Tam-Marina** (tel. 441/236-0127, www.ladyboats.com)—the motor-yachts *Lady Tamara* and *Lady Charlotte* and the sportfisher *Boss Lady;* Captain Dean DaCosta's 75-foot motor yacht *Spellbound* (tel. 441/236-6556 or 441/505-2628, www.spellbound.bm); and the sumptuous 100-foot *Venetian* (tel. 441/704-3000, www.diningbermuda.com), owned and run by the MEF restaurant group. Multiple Best of Bermuda Award winner *ÜberVida* (tel. 441/236-2222, www.ubervida.net, pickup from No. 1 Dock, Front St., east of the ferry terminal) is a 70-foot multiple-deck catamaran that has become a big favorite for its 90-minute Friday sunset cruises, with a DJ and cocktails; all-day excursions to Bermuda's northern barrier reef; and themed reggae, Cup Match, and Oktoberfest cruises. With room for 150, it's also a top choice for private parties, weddings, and charters.

Prefer to do your own thing? Popular rental boat company **Aquatic Bermuda** (tel. 441/236-2200 or 441/747-9443, www.aquaticbermuda.com) lets you be the captain, renting Beachcat pontoon boats with storage for picnics, snorkeling gear, and water toys—perfect for a whole-day or half-day of exploration. Hamilton Harbour, the Great Sound and its "Paradise Lakes" (tranquil bays between numerous islands), and the Sandys shoreline are perfect for this and all are accessible from a Hamilton starting point.

Tours

Walking is a great way to explore Hamilton's relatively small grid, peppered with historic and interesting sights like museums, churches, and the Parliament buildings. Hamilton Town Crier **Ed Christopher** (tel. 441/777-9738 or 441/292-1234, eschrist@logic.bm) impresses with his official uniform and feathered hat, as well as his local knowledge, in free weekday

walkabouts (10:30am Mon.-Fri. Apr.-Oct., by reservation Nov.-Mar.), starting at the City Hall steps on Church Street. His two-hour mosey explores much of North Hamilton's quaint streets and architecture.

Spas

Smartly positioned in the heart of the business district, **Orchid Nail Spa** (Vallis Bldg., 54 Par-la-Ville Rd., tel. 441/296-8696, www.orchidspabda.com, 9am-6pm Mon.-Sat., noon-5pm Sun.) is a Best of Bermuda Award winner for its mani-pedis ($40-110) for men and women. Other services include shellac, acrylic, and gel nail treatments. **Polished** (1 Reid St. at Queen St., tel. 441/232-6245, info@polishedbermuda.com, 9am-7pm Mon.-Sat., 9am-5pm Sun.) is stocked with London's Butter brand of polishes and offers manicures, pedicures, nail art and extensions, waxing, eyelash and eyebrow tinting, and party lashes.

La Serena Express Spa (A. S. Cooper & Sons, 3rd Fl., tel. 441/239-0184, laserenaspa@thereefs.bm) is the Hamilton offshoot of The Reefs resort's award-winning spa in Southampton, offering 30- to 45-minute sessions, including Fast and Fabulous facials ($79), Brief Bikini waxes ($40), and a Manicure in Minutes ($35). **Siam Thai Massage and Herbal Spa** (Williams House, 1st Fl., 20 Reid St., tel. 441/295-3999, siamspa.bda@gmail.com, 10am-8pm daily), located in the middle of Hamilton, offers massages with and without oil, herbal body treatments, and beauty services including facials, waxes, and mani-pedis. Favorites are the herbal compress massage (1 hour, $105) and traditional Thai massage (30 minutes $55, 120 minutes $195).

Just up the street, Hamilton hallmark **Strands** (31 Reid St., tel. 441/295-0353, www.strands.bm, 8:45am-6pm Mon.-Wed. and Fri., 8:45am-8pm Thurs., 8:45am-5pm Sat.) has a day spa with a full menu of Clarins skin treatments for men and women. **Sabai Thai Body Balancing Massage & Spa** (131 Front St., tel. 441/292-6456, www.thaimassagebermuda.com, 9am-9pm Mon.-Sat.) offers traditional Thai body massage and "Thai boxing" or sports massage. Online bookings should be made 36 hours in advance.

Farther from central Hamilton's bustle is Spa Oasis (14 Laffan St., off Cedar Ave., tel. 441/297-2347, www.spaoasis.bm, 9am-7pm daily), whose menu includes Thai, Balinese, Swedish, hot stone, and deep tissue massage, along with other treatments ranging from facials, waxing, and threading to pedicures (1-hour massage $89, 1.25-hour full-body mud wrap $119). The spa's calm rooms sit inside the gingerbread architecture of a traditional Bermuda cottage, located on a residential street behind St. Theresa's Cathedral.

FOOD

Hamilton's culinary scene is evolving, with gluten-free cafés, ice cream and frozen yogurt bars, contemporary small-plates lounges, new ethnic and vegetarian offerings, and a trend toward more sidewalk dining. Could the arrival of *Top Chef* star Marcus Samuelsson at Pembroke's Hamilton Princess be raising the bar? Maybe. Restaurateurs are displaying a new competitive energy, reaching out to foodies with digital come-ons, updated restaurant interiors, and more innovative menus that tap into locavore trends and put creative spins on Bermudian traditions. Look for fresh local produce and seafood—the catch-of-the-day ranges from Bermuda wahoo and tuna to rockfish, yellowtail, or grouper. Sushi is ubiquitous, either eat-in or take-out. All restaurants are nonsmoking by law. Most accept credit cards and have free Wi-Fi, and many promote daily specials on their Facebook pages. Restaurant dress code is generally smart-casual—so avoid wearing sneakers or T-shirts to dinner.

Seafood and Sushi

Multiple-award-winning ★ Beluga Seafood Bar (Washington Mall III, 18 Church St. opposite City Hall, www.belugabar. bm, tel. 441/542-2859, 11:30am-2:45pm and 6pm-10pm Mon.-Sat., 5pm-9:30pm Sun.) earns its kudos with what aficionados swear is Bermuda's best sushi, created by maestro Sammy Wong, a Malaysia native who trained in Japan. The sleek little venue, on the mall's lower level, is perfect for lunch or before heading out to the cinema in the evening. Don't miss the Japanese "pizza" (vegetable tempura, $11), guaca shrimp ($12), diamond dragon sushi roll, or number-one request, the Sammy roll ($18), named for its buoyant creator. Regulars sometimes let Sammy have free rein—ask him to make something special for you using the day's fresh fish arrivals, then watch him get creative.

Located upstairs at Port O' Call Restaurant, Pearl (87 Front St., tel. 441/295-9150, www. pearl.bm, noon-2:30pm and 5pm-10pm Mon.-Fri., 6pm-10pm Sat., $8-21) tops the wish lists of many serious sushi-lovers with its fresh ingredients and creative spins on classic dishes. A popular takeout lunch destination, Misaki (5 Burnaby St., tel. 441/296 7254) offers sushi with a "pick and mix" option, along with appetizers, rolls, and ramen bowls.

The Lobster Pot (6 Bermudiana Rd., tel. 441/292-6898, www.lobsterpot.bm, 11:30am-10pm Mon.-Fri., 5:30pm-10pm Sat., 6pm-10pm Sun., $30-38) has been a beloved fixture of this corner of Hamilton for decades, and it still has one of the island's most enjoyable bars, as well as an atmospheric dining room where you might as well be below deck on a sumptuous ocean liner. Fresh Bermuda or Maine lobsters and pan-fried rockfish, snapper, and grouper—and an award-winning version of Bermuda's traditional fish chowder—make this one of the island's best seafood venues.

North Hamilton's Fish & Tings (45 Angle St., tel. 441/292-7389, patrick_channer@hotmail.com, 11am-10pm Mon.-Thurs., 11am-11pm Fri.-Sat., $14-25) specializes in Jamaican dishes: fish curries, stews, and jerk everything.

Cafés, Diners, and Delis

Cafés, diners, and delis are located all over Hamilton, though a few catering to the corporate crowd are closed Saturday. An increasing number of licensed lounges have given Hamilton a hipper edge. There are plenty of places to drop in for a takeaway bite; a food court is located downstairs in the Washington Mall's Church Street section, and good delis are located in the larger supermarkets such the MarketPlace (Church St.), The Supermart (Front St.), and Miles Market (Pitts Bay Rd.).

One of the island's longtime local joints, ★ The Spot (6 Burnaby St., tel. 441/292-6293, 6:30am-10pm Mon.-Sat. summer, 6:30am-7pm Mon.-Sat. winter) is a landmark, at its present location for more than 60 years, and a Bermudian melting pot, remarkable for its customers of all races, ages, and backgrounds who come for great homemade dishes and the convivial atmosphere. The diner's longtime owner, businessman Ted Powell, sits down for a welcoming chat with visitors if he is on the premises. Try the soups (red bean, barley, split pea, $6), hot sandwiches with gravy ($15), thick shakes ($7), and pancakes-with-bacon breakfasts ($12). Takeout is fast, and the service is ultra-friendly (and kid-friendly). Don't leave without a hand of sweet Bermuda bananas, regularly sold from the checkout counter.

Perfectly placed for passing passengers, Dangelini's Café (8 Front St., next to the ferry terminal, tel. 441/295-5272, 7:30am-5pm Mon.-Fri., 7:30am-4pm Sat., $2-9) wins fans for its fresh-baked goodies, including gluten-free creations, as well as sandwiches, wraps, paninis, and gourmet coffee. Drop into Rock Island Coffee (48 Reid St., tel. 441/296-5241, www.rockisland.bm, 7am-6pm Mon.-Fri., 8am-1pm Sat.) for great java and one of the city's more interestingly mixed crowd of patrons. Dreadlocked "trustafarians"—trust-funded bohemians—linger over lattes, while lawyers and actuaries rush in for espresso and a chocolate-chip cookie. The staff roasts, grinds, and brews beans from Colombia, Kenya, Jamaica, and elsewhere. The artsy surroundings—a wood-floored cottage decorated in ever-changing local paintings and photography—add to the ambience of pure Bermudian bohemia. There's a garden out front with tables, umbrellas, and views of the cruise ships in the summer.

Cottage Café & Bistro (Washington Mall, 20 Church St., tel. 441/292-0880, breakfast 7:30am-11:30am daily, lunch 11:30am-4pm daily) is all about locally sourced and creatively concocted comfort fare, from its frittatas ($14) and blueberry waffle cake with lemon curd ($13) to black truffle mac and cheese ($13) and chicken and biscuit sandwich ($16).

Dishing out savory Middle Eastern cuisine from two locations, Casablanca (18 Washington St.; 61 Front St., tel. 441/295-9999, http://casablanca.bm, 11am-8:30pm daily) has a popular lunch buffet ($11 per pound) offering salads, hummus, falafels, pita bread, couscous, fish tagine, lamb shawarma, and other specialties.

You can get an authentic taste of Portuguese cuisine at Café Açoreano (Russell Eve Bldg., 2 Washington St., tel. 441/296-0402, 6am-8:30pm daily), where deep-fried *malasada* (doughnuts, $1.25) are a Bermudian breakfast favorite, among other sweet treats. Great coffee and a convenient location alongside the central bus terminal also make this tiny 20-year-old café worth a visit, along with its extended hours and hot deli items ($11 per pound) such as *frango a canarinho* (chicken leg), *feijao vermelho com chourico* (red beans and chorizo), and *bacalhau dourado* (codfish casserole).

At ★ Ten (10 Dundonald St., tel. 441/295-0857, www.ten.bm, 7am-3pm and 5pm-9pm Mon.-Fri., 7am-2:30pm Sat.), corporate coffee-breakers share space with hydrating gym rats and coffee klatches. The delicious light fare (falafel and salsa verde sandwiches $12, Asian noodle salad $8, evening tapas $9-13) is as good as the Euro-cool decor and snappy service by ShayJuan, Carrie, and the team. Enjoy quiche, pizza, or panini alfresco while people-watching from the patio in the warmer seasons.

Java Jive (29 Victoria St., tel. 441/296-5050, www.irg.bm, 7am-5pm Mon.-Fri., $3-12), a tiny offshoot of Victoria Grill at the same address, sells hot and cold coffees, breakfast wraps, fresh-baked muffins, croissants, salads, and daily panini specials. The friendly manager Glynis will make you feel at home. Take it out, or watch the corporate world go by from the patio.

Bulli Social (7 Queen St., tel. 441/232-2855, 11am-6pm Mon., 11am-8pm Tues.-Thurs., 11am-10pm Fri.-Sat.) tempts lunch-goers with nine different takes on the gourmet burger ($14-22)—from a classic with American cheese and pickles to Persian lamb with cumin on pita bread, chicken with brie and avocado, or shrimp with crème fraîche. All are served on a brioche bun with fries, slaw, and a choice of gluten-free bread. Hotdogs on croissants, "hangover" poutine, and the ultimate grilled cheese keep comfort addicts coming back. Take out, or sit on the terrace next to the cool green expanse of Queen Elizabeth Park.

Owned by the Flanagan's Irish Pub group, **The Snug** (Emporium Bldg., 69 Front St., tel. 441/295-8299, 7:30am-4pm Mon.-Sat.) is a tucked-away café in the ground floor of the same building, offering breakfast sandwiches ($11) and eggs Benedict ($15), as well as lunch soups, chili, sandwiches, and buffalo wings.

A favorite deli is ★ **The Hickory Stick** (Clarendon Bldg., 2 Church St., tel. 441/292-1781, 6:30am-3pm Mon.-Fri.), whose Dagwood-esque sandwiches are legendary. Locals and visitors traipse in for footlong subs stuffed with deli meats smothered in melted cheese. Deli sandwiches ($4-10) range from basic tuna to Cajun chicken and a grilled vegetable wrap. Salads, from coleslaw to Hawaiian, are $5-11. Cornish pasties, pies, and quiche ($8) and home fries ($3) are also served up daily. Staff set up a sandwich-making assembly line to efficiently serve long lines of customers snaking through the little eatery noon-2pm. Go early or late to avoid a wait. Farther inside the Washington Mall's ground-floor level, **Eateries** (tel. 441/295-5890, 7:30am-5pm Mon.-Fri., 8am-5pm Sat.) is a fast-service sandwich and "round-the-world" buffet outlet.

Family-run **Jamaican Grill** (32 Court St., tel. 441/296-6577, 6:30am-9pm Mon.-Thurs.,

24 hours Fri.-Sat., $7-18) attracts aficionados of Caribbean cuisine with a scrumptious menu of oxtail, jerk chicken and pork, brown stew, ackee and saltfish, and West Indian curries. Fast service and delicious meals keep crowds lining up at 5pm every Friday and Saturday for the outdoor jerk chicken barbeque. Order your meal as takeout or enjoy it in the atmospheric little diner, which has a cluster of tables downstairs and a few overlooking the jovial gathering.

Buzz (www.buzzcafe.bm) cafés around Hamilton serve clientele on the go with gourmet coffee, smoothies ($8-11), wraps and paninis ($12), quesadillas ($15), shakes ($8-12), and more. Locations are: **Buzz Washington Mall** (upper level, Washington Mall, Church St., tel. 441/295-1979, 7:30am-5pm Mon.-Fri., 9am-5pm Sat.); **Buzz Hamilton Pharmacy** (17 Parliament St., tel. 441/292-5160, 8am-4:30pm Mon.-Sat.); **Buzz AIG** (AIG Bldg., Richmond Rd., tel. 441/298-5333, 7:30am-4pm Mon.-Fri.); and **Buzz N Go Esso City** (37 Richmond Rd., at Par-la-Ville Rd., tel. 441/296-2390, 6am-midnight Mon., 24 hours Tues.-Sat.).

★ **Devil's Isle Kitchen & Bar** (16 Burnaby St., tel. 441/296-1129, www.devilsislecoffee.bm, 8am-10pm Mon.-Thurs., 8am-11pm Fri., 9am-11pm Sat., 9am-4pm Sun.) is a restaurant-bar in the heart of Hamilton with a takeout deli area. Breakfast, lunch, and dinner menus are very locavore-friendly, with a farm-to-table mission driving everything that comes out of the kitchen. Dishes include home-brewed coffees and a variety of breakfasts ($13-24), sandwiches and salads ($18-28) for lunch, and a creative dinnertime array of small or large plates ($12-36). Eat in the coffee house-inspired restaurant or outside on the sidewalk patio.

International

Winner of a Wine Spectator Award of Excellence, foodie favorite ★ **Barracuda Grill** (5 Burnaby Hill, tel. 441/292-1609, www.barracuda-grill.com, noon-2:30pm and 5:30pm-10pm Mon.-Fri., 5:30-pm-10pm

Sat.-Sun.) pleases with both a cutting-edge interior and outstanding seafood, steaks, and chops. Grilled artichoke figs ($16), bone-in ribeye ($46), seared Bermuda rockfish ($38), and gingerbread toffee pudding ($13) are among the favorites.

Red Steakhouse & Bar (55 Front St., wheelchair-accessible entrance via Reid St., tel. 441/292-7331, www.redbermuda.com, lunch 11:30am-3pm Mon.-Fri., dinner 6pm-10pm Mon.-Sat., bar 11:30am-2am Mon.-Sat.) brings cosmopolitan flair to a prime Front Street location. Its dinner menu offers faves like steak and lobster ($55), roasted rack of lamb ($40), and grilled mahimahi ($34), but beef is king here; all cuts of the filet mignon, T-bone, striploin, rib-eye, and cowboy are certified Angus beef and can be accompanied by decadent sides such as truffle mac and cheese. Enjoy sunset from the balcony and stay for the DJ after dessert.

Contemporary hip is the mood at **Muse** (17 Front St., opposite the ferry terminal, tel. 441/296-8788, www.muse.bm, 11am-3pm and 6pm-10pm Mon.-Sat.), which has an alfresco dining room balcony. The menu is French-Asian fusion made from fresh local produce. Creations include a seared rockfish with lemon and white wine sauce ($29), beef tenderloin in red wine sauce ($42), and quinoa wild rice bowl with chicken or shrimp ($26). A good selection of French and American wines complement the fare. Evening visitors will love the top-floor Skybar.

Tapas Club (12 Bermudiana Rd., tel. 441/296-3330, 4:30pm-midnight daily) serves up authentic hot and cold Spanish tapas, including dishes of garlic shrimp ($9), salted cod with aioli ($11), crispy fried chickpeas ($6), and manchego cheese slices ($7). Jugs of sangria and wine flights add to the festive ambience at tables inside or out.

Southern-style bistro **Victoria Grill** (29 Victoria St., tel. 441/296-5050, www.victoria-grill.com, lunch noon-2:30pm Mon.-Fri., noon-2:30pm and 5:30pm-10pm Mon.-Thurs., noon-2:30pm and 5:30pm-11pm Fri., 5:30pm-10pm Sat.) serves up comfort dishes in a sleek-but-cozy interior appropriate for both a power lunch and a family meal. Rave reviews pour in for the made-at-your-table guacamole appetizer ($11). The mains menu ($24-38) boasts rockfish, chicken, and steaks. The local kale salad is also a hit ($19). Finish it off with layered crepe cake or fried mango pie ($10). Outdoor seating on a terrace is also available in summer.

Run by the culinary talents behind the former Splendido restaurant at Paget's Horizons resort, **Angelo's Bistro** (Walker Arcade, 15 Reid St., tel. 441/232-1000, bistroangeleo@logic.bm, 10am-9pm Mon.-Sat.) occupies the arcade space between Reid and Front Streets, including a Mediterranean-style courtyard with a bubbling fountain. The menu also makes you feel as if you might have landed in Capri for the day: Thin-crust pizzas ($18), caprese salad ($14), chicken piccata ($27), and Bermuda fishcakes ($24) highlight lunch and dinner, and there are breakfasts of sweet rolls, omelets, and eggs Benedict. Takeout is available.

Sophistication, in both ambience and menu, distinguishes **Port O' Call** (87 Front St., tel. 441/295-5373, www.portocall.bm, lunch noon-2:30pm Mon.-Fri., dinner 6pm-10:30pm Mon.-Sat., $21-39), where you can dine inside or on the street-side terrace. Dishes such as grilled halloumi and heirloom tomatoes, tempura-fried shrimp, and pomegranate fennel lamb rack won't disappoint. A private dining room can accommodate special parties. Owned by the same restaurant group, tiny **Bistro J** (102 Chancery Lane, tel. 441/296-8546, www.bistroj.bm, lunch noon-2:30pm Mon.-Fri., dinner 6pm-10pm Mon.-Sat.) has a more relaxed charm, with blackboard menus offering a limited but tasty assortment of daily specials. Two courses are $25 and three courses $30.

With a European-themed cuisine, ★ **Bolero Brasserie** (95 Front St., entrance off Bermuda House Lane, tel. 441/292-4507, www.bolerobrasserie.com, lunch 11:30am-2:30pm Tues.-Fri., dinner 6pm-10pm Mon.-Sat.) not only has a prime Front Street dining porch but a consistently award-winning menu featuring an extensive wine list as well as vegetarian choices. Classic brasserie dishes have a contemporary twist: pork cheek and snail sauté ($33); squid ink linguine ($31); mahimahi, lump crab, and avocado ($36); and avocado fries ($9).

Lunch Wagons

Jovial husband-and-wife team Keith and Elaine DeSilva do a rip-roaring weekday lunchtime trade at their Best of Bermuda Award-winning **Keith's Kitchen** (48 Woodlands Rd. at BAA parking lot, tel. 441/295-1310, $5-7). Join the line of locals for hefty tuna sandwiches, BLTs, and straight-off-the-grill burgers at the landmark blue truck, which has spread out on this site over the years and now has attached shaded waiting areas and nearby picnic tables. Tucked inside the gates of the BAA soccer stadium, the truck is a five-minute walk north from Front Street up Par-la-Ville Road and across a small roundabout at the Serpentine Road junction.

Office workers line up weekdays at lunchtime for burgers, sandwiches, and friendly chitchat at **DeGraff's Lunch Wagon** (City Hall parking lot, tel. 441/799-3904, 9am-3pm Mon.-Fri., $5-6). **Jor-Jay's Takeout** (Front St., in the parking lot opposite Supermart, tel. 441/296-3114, 8am-3pm Mon.-Thurs., 8am-4am Fri., 11:30am-4am Sat., $3-6) is very popular with late-night revelers on their way out of town. The lunch wagon makes scrumptious homemade burgers, sandwiches, fries, and fish cakes, and although the wait is sometimes a half hour, it's worth it.

You can't miss Kemar Maybury's fire truck-red **Smokin' Barrel** (1 Waterfront Park, Front St., directly outside the ferry terminal, tel. 441/337-0211, 7am-11pm Mon.-Thurs., 7am-3am Fri.-Sat.). The hugely successful barbecue joint cooks up plates of Momma Slappin' wings ($10), jerk shrimp ($18), and burgers and ribs ($10-12). Maybury, son of a well-known Bermudian drummer, hopes to parlay his hit into a permanent Reid Street restaurant.

Pub Fare

Technically it's a bar, but the **Pickled Onion** (53 Front St., tel. 441/295-2263, www.thepickledonion.com, lunch 11:30am-10pm daily, $9-40) has a restaurant-caliber menu, with a variety of nicely presented appetizers, pastas, fresh fish, salads, steaks, and desserts. The live music and drinks are a bonus.

You couldn't find a more British-looking establishment than **Hog Penny** (5 Burnaby Hill, tel. 441/292-2534, www.hogpenny-pub.com, lunch 11:30am-3pm daily, dinner 5:30pm-10pm daily, bar until 1am daily, $10-37), where home-cooked staples like shepherd's pie and toad-in-the-hole are comfortable favorites. Its "crusted dinners" (beef wellington, scaloppini veal chop) are well liked.

Flanagan's Irish Pub (Emporium Bldg., 69 Front St., tel. 441/295-8299, www.flanagans.bm, 11am-1am Mon.-Fri., 9am-1am Sat.-Sun., $15-42) has a crowd-pleasingly extensive menu of steaks, burgers, fresh fish, daily pasta specials, and desserts. Don't miss the authentic codfish and potato breakfast on weekend mornings. **Bermuda Bistro at The Beach** (103 Front St., at Parliament St., tel. 441/292-0219, www.thebeachbermuda.com, 9am-midnight daily, $12-29) gets a full house for its paninis, burgers, pizza, seafood, and bar snacks.

All-day breakfasts, super sandwiches, pizza, and build-your-own burgers get top billing at **The Docksider Pub & Restaurant** (121 Front St., tel. 441/296-3333, www.dockies.com, 11:30am-3am Mon.-Fri., 9am-3am Sat.-Sun., $11-21), a crowded hangout all year round. Earlier opening hours accommodate soccer and rugby fans who come to watch live televised games.

Asian

L'Oriental (32 Bermudiana Rd., above Little Venice, tel. 441/296-4477, www.diningbermuda.com, noon-2:15pm Mon.-Fri., 6pm-10pm Sat., 6pm-9pm Sun.) has sushi and sashimi ($10-11), *teppanyaki* ($26-43), and main courses like broccoli beef ($30) and half aromatic crispy duck ($31).

Busy Chinese and Thai takeout Chop Fusion (88 Reid St., tel. 441/292-0791, www. bermudarestaurants.com, lunch 11:30am-2:30pm Tues.-Fri., dinner 5pm-10pm daily) is popular for eating in as well. The dramatically designed dining room allows for large parties or dinner for two, and service is efficient and friendly. Staples include fried rice ($10-19), pad thai ($15-22), and vegetable or meat chow mein ($13-18).

Indian

Outstanding Indian fare, equal to the caliber found in London or Toronto, is the strength of ★ House of India (Park View Plaza, 57 North St., tel. 441/295-6450, www.houseofindia.biz, lunch 11:30am-2:30pm Mon.-Fri., dinner 5:30pm-9:30pm daily), where a dedicated team of chefs turns out lunch buffets and nightly feasts of tandoori, *biryani*, and *balti* specialties. The award-winning chicken *passanda*, chicken and beef kormas, and chicken and lamb tikka masalas (all about $20) are particularly well done. Try warm fluffy naan breads in garlic or plain flavors, as well as stuffed *kulcha* varieties, and a wide selection of vegetarian dishes. Appetizers include *bhajiyas*, *pakoras*, and samosas. Service is very friendly.

Part of the Port O'Call restaurant group, Ruby Murrys (2 Chancery Lane, tel. 441/295-5058, www.rubymurrys.bm, lunch noon-2:30pm Mon.-Fri., dinner 5pm-10pm Mon.-Sun.) was a hit straight out of the blocks. Named for Cockney rhyming slang for "curry" (after a popular 1950s singer from south Belfast), the restaurant mixes traditional and modern Indian cuisine such as tandoori fish tikka ($21), *murgh lababdar* ($18), and beef madras ($19), plus a wide choice of naans and *kulchas*. Vegetarians will appreciate the mushroom *pulao, dal makhani, chana masala,* and other nonmeat choices.

Italian

Little Venice (32 Bermudiana Rd., tel. 441/295-3503, www.littlevenice.bm, noon-2pm and 6pm-close Mon.-Fri., 6pm-close Sat.) was the vanguard of Bermuda's lovefest with Italian cuisine back in the 1960s. Today, it's still going strong, and the restaurant's owners, Capri natives, have a dozen popular restaurants and a catering service that feeds the island's social scene. Little Venice was always the power-lunch venue, and it still attracts insurance-industry movers and shakers as well as occasional celebrities (Michael Douglas has dined here). Efficient, entertaining staff members keep the dining room buzzing. Appetizers like roasted octopus ($24), homemade pastas (gnocchi $28, spaghetti with clams $34), meat dishes like beef tenderloin with foie gras ($46), and lovingly crafted desserts make up the menu.

Just down the street, Portofino (20 Bermudiana Rd., tel. 441/292-2375, www. portofino.bm, 11:45am-2:30pm and 6pm-9:30pm Sun.-Thurs., 11:45am-2:30pm and 6pm-10:30pm Fri.-Sat.), one of the island's few Italian restaurants not owned by the Little Venice Group, has been wildly popular for more than 30 years. Speedy waiters, pastas ($12-27), tasty salads ($9-17) and meats ($22-37), and a cozy, red-checkered interior make Portofino a hit. Dinner reservations for groups more than two are recommended to avoid lining up down the street on summer weekend evenings. A fast, wide-ranging takeout service is offered alongside the main restaurant.

★ La Trattoria (Washington Mall, 22 Washington Lane, www.latrattoria.bm, tel. 441/295-1877, 11:30am-3:30pm and 5:30pm-10:30pm Mon.-Sat., 5:30pm-10:30pm Sun.) makes diners feel they've stepped into the terra-cotta courtyard of an eatery in Naples or Rome. The menu has always been a crowd-pleaser, with homemade pastas (orecchiette with sausage, $24), award-winning pizzas ($20-23) baked in the dining room's wood-fired oven, and great appetizers (*trio del mare*, $19), and desserts, including homemade gelato. La Trattoria's Caesar salad ($10) and cappuccino are arguably the best on the island. With the eatery's stellar service, nothing is perceived as a problem, least of all wailing children or ordering off the menu. Kids are well accommodated with crayons, balls of dough, cost-effective smaller platters, and even white pizzas. As a result, the place is full of families but also attracts couples and adult dinner parties.

Vegetarian and Vegan

It's the popular smoothie bar that brings folks all day long into **Down to Earth** (56 Reid St., tel. 441/292-5639, 9am-5pm Mon.-Sat.), but as you wait for your spinach-raspberry-almond butter-chia seed creation, many other healthful goodies will catch your eye. A little grocery store of vegan products—granola cereals, green teas, gluten-free pizza, nuts galore—it also stocks a full selection of vitamins and natural supplements.

Mother-daughter team Anjula and Ashley Bean cater to a phalanx of regulars with their vegan-friendly menu at **Juice 'n' Beans** (55 Court St., tel. 441/292-6454, 7am-6pm Mon.-Sat., deli $14 per pound). Hot deli offerings include a tofu-and-black bean breakfast, Indian curries, and changing daily specials. Nonvegans come for the delicious baked goodies, gourmet coffee, smoothies, and window seats that offer prime Front Street people-watching.

Vegans, vegetarians, and health nuts make a beeline to **Café Eden** (9am-4pm Mon.-Thurs., 9am-noon Fri.) inside **ABC Natural Foods** (Hamilton Seventh-Day Adventist Church, 41 King St., tel. 441/292-4111, 9am-5:45pm Mon.-Tues. and Thurs., 9am-6:15pm Wed., 9am-1:15pm Fri., 10am-1:45pm Sun.) for smoothies, veggie hot dogs and burgers, dried fruits, cereals and nuts, soy and dairy-free products, dairy-free ice cream, and organic juices.

★ **It's Only Natural** (8 Princess St., tel. 441/292-6617, itsonlynatural@onelove.bm) puts on a noontime vegan hot lunch every Wednesday and Friday, serving up tasty lentil or chickpea burgers, Asian tofu, split pea soup, and vegetable lasagna—until it runs out. Accountants line up with Rastafarians

and veggie-seeking tourists for a take-out or stay-put meal at a couple of tables inside the store. Pricing is determined by weight: $15 per pound.

My Sereni-Tea (Bermudiana Arcade, Queen St., tel. 441/296-2114, www.mysereni-itea.com, 8:45am-6pm Mon.-Fri., 9:30am-6pm Sat.) has a large selection of holistic hot and iced teas plus vegan-friendly soups and snacks, along with essential oils, books, and crystals as well as massage, acupuncture, and yoga treatments.

Ice Cream and Yogurt Bars

Meltdown Ice Cream (Old Cellar Lane, off Front St., tel. 441/538-0065, 11:30am-5:30pm Mon.-Sat.) is a pocket-size eatery offering the popular Bermuda Artisan Ice Cream brand in flavors such as rum swizzle and black rum and ginger. Owned and run by husband and wife Bruce and Sheree Lines, the little outlet calls to overheated passersby with its cool subway tiles, shady tables, and cheery flowerpots.

Yo Cherry (8 Bermudiana Rd., tel. 441/292-2020, www.yocherry.com, 11am-10pm Mon.-Thurs., 11am-12:30am Fri., 10:30am-12:30am Sat., 10am-10pm Sun.) is run by a Bermudian couple, Carlos and Regina Francis. It nabbed a Best of Bermuda Award for its daily flavors of self-serve fro-yo, such as chocolate custard, caramel sea salt, and red velvet, offered alongside sorbet, gelato, ice cream, and more than 50 toppings. Its location on Bermuda's Restaurant Alley and generous opening hours also make it a cure for after-dinner munchies.

La Trattoria Shop (22 Washington Lane, tel. 441/295-9499, 9am-4pm Mon.-Sat.) sells decadent homemade gelato from a little outlet opposite La Trattoria restaurant. **Honey's Café & Creamery** (Brunswick Mall, 119 Front St., tel. 441/292-6464, 11am-7pm Sun.-Tues., 11am-10pm Wed.-Sat. Apr.-Oct.) features 16 flavors, including dairy-free, sugar-free, sorbet, and soft-serve varieties. The venue incorporates local Bermuda honey in its toppings and smoothies, hence the name.

Grocery Stores

One of the island's best-stocked grocery stores, **The Supermart** (125 Front St., tel. 441/292-2064, www.supermart.bm, 7am-9pm Mon.-Sat., 11am-6pm Sun.) carries the British line of Waitrose products along with other UK lines. Its meat department, cheese boutique, and fresh Bermuda produce section are also excellent. There's a broad wine and liquor range, as well as an expansive hot and cold deli. Parking is on the street or opposite in the small parking lot.

Flagship of the island-wide chain, the **Hamilton MarketPlace** (42 Church St., tel. 441/295-6066, www.marketplace.bm, 7am-10pm Mon.-Sat., 9am-7pm Sun.) is a massive food emporium offering a full liquor store, a meat department, an enormous bakery, and a full-scale deli with hot and cold dishes and salad bars. Kids will enjoy the carts for family use and the remote-control train that runs on a circuit overhead tooting its horn. Parking is available outside and in a dedicated parking lot beneath the store.

The **Shopping Centre** (35 Victoria St., tel. 441/292-4545, 7am-10pm Mon.-Sat., 9am-7pm Sun.) is a MarketPlace branch that carries a much smaller selection of goods. **Arnold's Express** (135 Front St. E., tel. 441/292-4301, 6:30am-midnight daily), belonging to the successful island-wide grocery store chain, stocks essential sundries plus wine, beer, and liquor.

Liquor Stores

You can buy beer, wine, and spirits in most grocery stores, finally allowed in 2013 to sell liquor on Sunday, but there are also dedicated liquor merchants in Hamilton. Historic **Gosling Brothers** (33 Front St., at Queen St., tel. 441/298-7337, www.goslingsrum.com, 9:30am-6:30pm Mon.-Sat.) is famous for its Black Seal Rum and dark 'n' stormies but also supplies much of the island's fine wines, ports, and other liquors. Gosling's has a dedicated **Wine Shop** (9 Dundonald St., tel. 441/298-7368 or 441/298-7377, info@goslingsstore.com, 10am-5pm Mon.-Fri., 9am-5pm Sat.), a retail outlet that attracts serious wine-lovers.

With more than 1,000 bottles on sale from around the world, it has no equal in Bermuda. The store also stocks champagnes, liquors, and Riedel crystal glasses.

Front Street Liquors (57 Front St., just west of Burnaby St., tel. 441/292-6620, 9:30am-7pm Mon.-Sat.) sits opposite the Flagpole. **Burrows Lightbourn** (127 Front St., tel. 441/295-1554, 9am-6pm Sat.-Thurs., 9am-9pm Fri.) has an outlet alongside the popular Supermart grocery store. **Carousel Liquors** (137 Front St. E., tel. 441/292-2559, 8am-9pm Mon.-Sat.), next to Arnold's Express, sells wine, beer, and spirits.

ACCOMMODATIONS

There are presently no hotels or guesthouses located within Hamilton's boundaries, though many are nearby in Pembroke.

INFORMATION AND SERVICES

Visitor Information Centre (tel. 441/295-1480, 9am-4pm Mon.-Sat.) is located alongside the ferry terminal building on Front Street. Knowledgeable staff offers advice, information, and brochures on the island's tours, activities, attractions, and events, as well as bus and ferry tickets. The **Hamilton Police Station** (52 Victoria St. at Court St., tel. 441/295-0011 or 441/242-1704, fax 441/299-4589, www.police.bm) is located in a large modern building that also houses courtrooms and government offices. A reception desk handles walk-in queries or problems. The **Government Administration Building** (30 Parliament St., tel. 441/295-5151) houses numerous government departments, including the Department of Immigration, which deals with work permits and vacation extension requests.

Opposite the General Post Office is Bermuda's biggest travel agency, **Travel Edge** (35 Church St., tel. 441/292-3033, www.traveledge.bm, 8am-5pm Mon.-Fri.), offering expertise in cruises, seat sales, and flight queries. **Watlington & Conyers Travel** (Armoury Bldg., 1st Fl., 37 Reid St., tel. 441/295-3815, www.watlingtonandcony-erstravel.com, 9am-5pm Mon.-Fri.) is also an IATA-accredited agency.

Public toilets are located at the General Post Office; Point Pleasant Road at Albuoy's Point; at Waterfront Park opposite HSBC on Front Street; in Queen Elizabeth Park; and at banks and department stores. Quickie Lickie Laundromat (74 Serpentine Rd., tel. 441/295-6097) is a longtime fixture of the city. Located amid corporate office blocks, Just Shirts Launderers & Drycleaners (20 Bermudiana Rd., tel. 441/292-3063) caters to a lot of business clients.

ATMs are at all banking centers, inside A. S. Cooper & Sons and the Brown & Co. stores on Front Street, in the General Post Office (after 6pm, swipe any credit card at the door to enter), at the BIU gas station on Dundonald Street, inside the Windsor Place Mall on Queen Street, on the ground floor of the Washington Mall, and inside two gro-cery stores: The Supermart (Front St.) and Hamilton MarketPlace (Church St.).

Banks

HSBC (Harbourview Centre, 37 Front St.; 64 Church St.; Compass Point, 9 Bermudiana Rd.; tel. 441/295-4000, www.hsbc.bm, 9am-4:30pm Mon.-Fri.) also has branches in Somerset and St. George's. Butterfield Bank (65 Front St., at Burnaby Hill; Rosebank Centre, 11 Bermudiana Rd., at Richmond Rd.; Reid St.; tel. 441/295-1111, www.butterfield-bank.com, 9am-4pm Mon.-Fri., 10am-3pm Sat. at Rosebank Centre) has ATMs island-wide and branches on Pitts Bay Road and in Pembroke, Somerset, and St. George's. Clarien Bank (19 Reid St., tel. 441/296-6969, www.clarienbank.com, 8:30am-4pm Mon.-Fri., 9:30am-1:30pm Sat.) offers financial, in-vestment, and insurance services.

Pharmacies

Phoenix Centre (3 Reid St., tel. 441/279-5451, www.phoenixstores.bm, 8am-6pm Mon.-Sat., noon-6pm Sun. and holidays) is the island's largest general drugstore and flagship

of an island-wide chain of pharmacies. The Hamilton location also has a big toy store and carries international magazines and newspa-pers. Clarendon Pharmacy (31 Victoria St., ground Fl., tel. 441/295-9137, clarendon_dispensary@psl.bm, 8am-6pm Mon.-Sat.) carries chocolates, greeting cards, baby prod-ucts, and other drugstore items. Par-la-Ville Pharmacy (2 Church St., tel. 441/296-5510, www.pharmacy.bm, 8am-8pm Mon.-Fri., 10am-6pm Sat.) sits at the convenient busy in-tersection of Church and Par-la-Ville Streets, well-stocked with drugstore brands and snacks, and has an efficient pharmacy.

Hamilton Pharmacy (Parliament St., tel. 441/295-7004, 8am-9pm Mon.-Sat.) is a busy but friendly little store, complete with a dispensary, a Buzz Café outlet, toys, books, magazines, and stationery. It is conveniently located just a stone's throw from Parliament, the law courts, and the General Post Office. People's Pharmacy (62 Victoria St., tel. 441/292-7527, prescriptions tel. 441/292-9261, fax 441/295-0639, www.peoples.bm, 8am-8:30pm Mon.-Sat., 10am-6pm Sun.) is efficient and well stocked, with friendly staff and easy parking. The large modern store car-ries loads of drugstore products, but it also has magazines, a children's toy store and book sec-tion, greeting cards, and candy.

Post Offices

The General Post Office (56 Church St., at Parliament St., tel. 441/297-7893, www.bpo.bm, 8am-5pm Mon.-Fri., 8am-noon Sat.) sells stamps (including first-day covers and collec-tors' issues), has a mail drop, offers parcel and express post, has ATMs, and offers kiosks al-lowing free Internet access. Historic Perot Post Office (11 Queen St., tel. 441/292-9052, 8am-5pm Mon.-Fri.) is the only sub-post of-fice in Hamilton.

Internet Access

Hamilton has numerous wireless Internet hot spots, including at most cafés and res-taurants, which offer free Wi-Fi. There are also a few dedicated outlets that offer use of broadband-enabled PCs or wireless Internet. All post offices also offer free public Internet access.

The **Bermuda National Library** (13 Queen St., tel. 441/295-3104 or 441/295-2905, www.bnl.bm, 8:30am-6pm Mon.-Thurs., 10am-5pm Fri., 9am-5pm Sat.) offers free Wi-Fi and free Internet access (30-minute limit) on its five PCs. Printing costs $0.25 per page. **TeleBermuda International** (Victoria Place, 31 Victoria St., Hamilton, tel. 441/296-9000, www.telebermuda.com, 9am-4:30pm Mon.-Fri.) has a customer-care center in Hamilton offering Internet access via Wi-Fi and two broadband-enabled PCs.

Gas Stations
Bermuda Industrial Union Gas Station (22 Dundonald St., tel. 441/292-2726, 7am-midnight daily) has helpful staff and a convenience store selling hot dogs, cold drinks, snacks, newspapers, and candy. **Esso City Tigermarket** (37 Richmond Rd., tel. 441/295-3776, 24 hours daily) is the island's only 24-hour service station. Its busy convenience store stocks hot and cold snacks, including hot dogs, pies, coffee, and cold drinks.

TRANSPORTATION
Buses
The central bus terminal—the **Hubert W. "Sparky" Lightbourne Central Terminal** (Washington St. at Church St., tel. 441/292-3854)—is named for a longtime driver. It is the central hub for all bus routes running throughout the parishes. Tickets, tokens, and passes can be purchased here also.

Ferries
Hamilton Ferry Terminal (6:30am-8pm Mon.-Fri., 7:30am-6pm Sat., 8:30am-6pm Sun. and holidays), serving Paget, Warwick, Southampton, the West End, and the East End, is on Front Street, alongside Albuoy's Point. A ferry ride to Dockyard is a mere 20 minutes (scooters allowed), to the Town of St. George a scenic 45 minutes. Fares on the Blue (West End/Dockyard), Orange (St. George's), and Green (Rockaway Southampton) Routes are $5 adults, $2.75 ages 5-15, free under age 5, and on the Pink (Hamilton/Paget) Route $3.50 adults, $2.75 ages 5-15, free under age 5. Cash is not accepted; pay with tickets or tokens. For information, call **Sea Express** (tel. 441/295-4506 or 441/295-6575, www.marine-andports.bm).

Scooters and Bicycles
There are no scooter liveries within city limits, but there are two in neighboring Pembroke. One of the island's top bicycle stores rents road bikes to visitors out of its North Hamilton location: **Bicycle Works** (13 Tumkins Lane, off Woodlands Rd., tel. 441/297-8356, www.bicycleworks.bm, 8am-6pm Mon.-Fri., 9am-5:30pm Sat.) offers a variety of brands ($70-95 per day, discounts for longer periods).

Taxis
There are taxi stands along Front Street outside Brown & Co. near the ferry terminal and just west of City Hall on Church Street, alongside the city parking lot. Otherwise, use the **Hitch app** (www.hitch.bm) or call one of the cab companies to arrange a pickup: **Bermuda Industrial Union Co-op** (tel. 441/292-4476, cooptaxi@fkbnet.bm), **Bermuda Island Taxi** (tel. 441/295-4141, www.bermudaislandtaxi.com), or **BTA Dispatching** (tel. 441/296-2121, www.bta-dispatching.com). Typical average taxi rates from Hamilton to the airport are $40, to St. George's $55, to the Southampton beaches $30, and to Dockyard $60.

Pembroke Parish

From back o' town to Fairylands and everything in between, Pembroke encompasses a diverse world of Bermudian culture on the coattails of Hamilton, which sits within the parish. Encompassing the insurance towers of Pitts Bay, the grandiose old-money mansions of the harbor front, the salt-sprayed charm of Spanish Point, and the vibrantly scrappy chutzpah of the Marsh Folly community, Pembroke might be the best microcosm of Bermuda as a whole—the best, worst, richest, and least fortunate distilled into its coasts and valleys. Once the rural environs of Hamilton, Pembroke now is completely suburban, its once-tranquil neighborhoods now bearing the aural scar of roaring traffic.

Pembroke begins where Hamilton ends: all points west of Bermudiana Road, east of King Street as far as the Devonshire border, and north of Parson's Lane to the North Shore are part of the parish. The main routes include Pitts Bay Road, which winds out of the city into tony residential neighborhoods, all the way to Cox's Hill and St. John's Road, which connects with Spanish Point Road. North Shore Road runs along the northern edge of the parish as far as Mission Lane, when it enters Devonshire. East Broadway leads out of Hamilton along the harbor's edge to Crow Lane. Parson's, Palmetto, and Marsh Folly Roads are major thoroughfares through the parish north of Hamilton. Langton Hill and the dramatic Black Watch Pass cut north through the parish to the North Shore.

The variety of interesting neighborhoods makes for great explorations, from Spanish Point, a self-contained community steeped in maritime history, to Fairylands and Point Shares, where high pastel walls hide centuries-old waterfront spreads, and areas of North Hamilton, where West Indian cafés and local playgrounds reveal a totally different facet of Bermudian life.

SIGHTS

Pitts Bay Road is one of Bermuda's most scenic thoroughfares; lined by guesthouses, pastel mansions, and sprawling gardens, it is one of the island's wealthiest old-money districts. The serene residential enclaves of Fairylands, Point Shares, and Mill's Point contain centuries-old waterfront homes of Bermudian merchant families, many of whose descendants still live here. These are private property, of course, but a stroll down the network of neighborhood lanes is nevertheless peacefully revealing. In the early spring, many homes have gardens carpeted with freesias, and the sound of traffic is nonexistent.

Admiralty House Park

Once the site of an 1816 residence named Admiralty House and later a Royal Navy Hospital, **Admiralty House Park** (North

Admiralty House Park

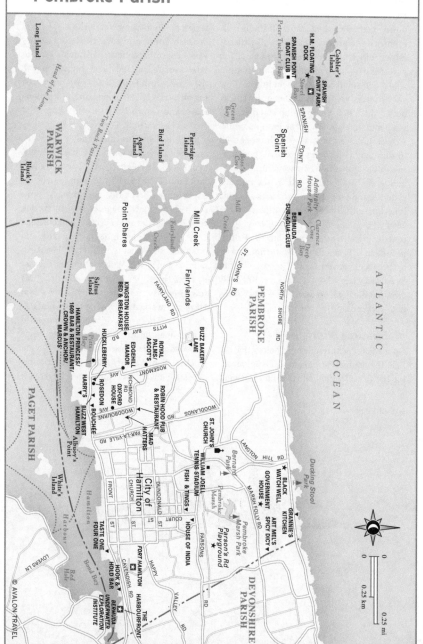

Pembroke Parish

Shore Rd. and Spanish Point Rd., sunrise-sunset daily, free) now belongs to the National Parks System. The former mansion, torn down except for a dilapidated off-limits ballroom, used to provide housing for British admiralty officers who worked at Dockyard. The graceful park has gorgeous old trees, nature trails, and small beaches, including shallow Clarence Cove, which, sheltered by a sturdy dock (which kids love to jump and dive off), is a popular neighborhood swimming venue. Across the cove, Deep Bay is also well used in summer, with young daredevils performing in-air stunts on their way into the turquoise depths. Notable also are the tunnels, galleries, and caves dug into the park's seaside limestone cliffs by the British military in the 1850s. The property was a Royal Navy signal center during World War II, but the British pulled out of Bermuda in 1951, turning it over to the island's government. The park tends to be packed when school is out and is especially crowded during Cup Match and other summer weekends.

★ Spanish Point Park

Situated on a picturesque promontory that defines the channel entrance for ships approaching the Great Sound and Hamilton Harbour,

Spanish Point Park (sunrise-sunset daily, free) is a delightful excursion—either for a quick visit and photos or a whole day's relaxation. Utterly peaceful, it sits at the tip of Spanish Point, a historic little community whose charming cottages and rambling tributaries evoke a long and direct connection with the sea. Spanish Point Road twists down past the offshoots of Doubloon Lane, Stormalong Lane, and Ocean Bright to the shorefront park at the bottom. The route is fringed by gingerbread architecture, candy-pink walls, and even a few rare wooden homes. One resident has labeled his property "The Home that Jack Built, 1924." Beside a parking lot, a beach edges Stovell Bay, a tiny harbor where pint-size fishing boats, dinghies, and storybook ruby sailboats sit at a collection of moorings.

At the bay's mouth lies a rusty hulk and pontoons, the remains of the H. M. Floating Dock. Launched in Woolwich on the Thames in 1869, the 47,000-cubic-foot dry dock was towed across the Atlantic by three Royal Navy steam frigates, arriving in Bermuda 39 days later. The largest dry dock in the world at the time, the structure was able to heave 10,000 tons and was used by the Royal Navy at Dockyard. By the early 1900s, however, it was outdated, unable to accommodate larger new

Spanish Point Park

vessels, and was sold and towed to Spanish Point to be dismantled. World Wars I and II intervened, and the effort was abandoned. Although it's an eyesore, the hulk today provides a sheltered harbor for local boats.

The park itself lies inside a tiny gate, its shady lawns, whispering pines, and baygrapes stretching along the finger of land bordered by the North Shore and Great Sound. There are picnic tables and benches, and a sprinkling of reefs and islets just a few yards off the North Shore side has created calm, shallow coves perfect for snorkeling. Walk to the end of the park that looks out over the shipping channel toward Dockyard—a good vantage point to watch the comings and goings of ocean liners and cargo ships. The park attracts locals who wash cars or play cards near the beach. There are public toilets near the parking lot.

Black Watch Well

Ignored by passing motorists, Black Watch Well sits at the sometimes chaotic three-way intersection of North Shore Road, Langton Hill, and Black Watch Pass, marked by a sign that explains the little structure's history. The well takes its name from the heroic Scottish soldiers of the 1st Battalion of the 42nd Regiment of Loyal Highlanders, who are forever remembered here as having come to the aid of the area's "poor and their cattle in the long drought of 1849." The limestone well they dug still bears its wooden roof, though its interior has been capped for safety reasons. Park at nearby C-Mart's parking lot, or across the road at the **Ducking Stool Park,** whose name refers to its history as a site like St. George's, where 17th-century public punishments, using a seat on a log to dunk sinners, were frequently staged. These days, it is a popular Cup Match campsite, with deep swimming holes off its scenic cliffs. The dramatic Black Watch Pass is also worth driving or walking through; its towering limestone walls, which were carved by hand in the 1930s, demonstrate a magnificent feat of engineering and show the crumbling geological strata of local limestone. The pass links North Shore Road with Marsh Folly and Palmetto Roads.

Government House

From the junction of Black Watch Pass and North Shore Road, you can also see the impressive lawns of Government House, whose Victorian towers overlook North Hamilton and the North Shore. Open days for public visits are held occasionally; the property is home to Bermuda's resident British governor, who holds numerous official functions here. Built in the late 1800s, the 30-room house sits on 33 acres of manicured lawns and gardens, tennis courts, an Olympic-length swimming pool, forests of cedar and spice trees, and mature plantings made over the years by previous British governors or royal visitors. The grounds are cared for by the Bermuda government's Parks Department. Queen Elizabeth and Prince Philip have stayed here, as have Prince Charles, Sir Winston Churchill, and President John F. Kennedy.

The property, which flies the British governor's flag when he's on the island, was tainted with a horrific crime in 1973, when then-governor Sir Richard Sharples was shot dead while walking his dog at night, along with his aide-de-camp, Captain Hugh Sayers. Two Bermudian men were convicted of the crime and hanged, and ensuing race riots marked the most bitter, turbulent episode in the island's modern history. The property is used for national and ceremonial functions, such as the Queen's Birthday cocktail party in June, held to honor Bermudians receiving lifetime achievement awards bestowed by Buckingham Palace.

St. John's Church

Built in 1621, the original **St. John's Church** (127 St. John's Rd., tel. 441/292-5308, free) was one of the island's first churches, a wooden structure with a thatched palmetto roof. It was destroyed less than a century later by a hurricane-fed fire and replaced by a stone church, which was demolished in 1821 and rebuilt to meet the needs of a larger congregation.

Numerous additions and renovations have been made since then, but the Anglican church remains a popular community landmark. The beautiful interior is notable for its stained glass, bell tower, and 2,418-pipe organ, rebuilt in 1989. The crowded graveyard contains historic family plots—stacked to make more room—interspersed with ancient cedars and other shady trees and shrubs. Funerals are held many weekday afternoons; there have even been graveside performances by colorfully garbed gombey troupes.

Pembroke Marsh Park

Used as the island's trash dump for the latter part of the 20th century, **Pembroke Marsh Park** (bordered by Marsh Folly Rd. and Parson's Rd., sunrise-sunset daily, free) bears the scars of longtime pollution that could take decades to erase. The good news is that process has already begun, with trash now disposed of at the North Shore incinerator, and the marsh today the focus of government plans to return it to public parkland. While scientists say pollution levels in the water are high, the area remains a popular birding site; egrets and herons are seen in the vicinity, along with endemic plantlife. Access is difficult and dirty, however. A public

playground, alongside the park on Parson's Road, is a popular attraction for children of all ages.

★ Fort Hamilton

Built in the 1870s, **Fort Hamilton** (Happy Valley Rd., off King St., tel. 441/292-1234, sunrise-sunset daily, free), like Fort St. Catherine in St. George's, remains one of the best examples of the island's historic fortifications. It's equally interesting to historians, gardeners, and sightseers, thanks to its awesome panorama of Hamilton and Pembroke, as well as the Paget shoreline. The fort served as the southern end of the Royal Navy's Prospect defensive line—intended to halt an enemy attack on Spanish Point and thereby protect the Royal Naval Dockyard and fleet anchored at Grassy Bay.

Managed by the Corporation of Hamilton, the fort is used today as a plant nursery, the reason for its meticulously landscaped gardens. Mosaic pathways lead among vibrant flower gardens, and benches are positioned on lower lawns and atop the ramparts, where cannons point out over Hamilton's streets below.

Fort Hamilton

A wooden drawbridge leads into the fort, where a guardroom sits at the entrance. Inside, steps near the entrance lead down into the circular moat garden, planted with gorgeous ferns, waxy elephant ears, orchids, bromeliads, and other shade-loving species. A skinny dirt path follows the moat completely around; despite the occasional mosquito, it is one of my favorite walks. Along the way, doorways lead into the fort's dungeons, which are worth exploring if you have time. The smell of thick, damp limestone permeates this network of subterranean galleries, which kids especially will find fascinating. The catacomb is usually well lit, and there are various entrances and exits, including one set of stairs that must number in the hundreds.

A caretaker's cottage is situated on the main lawn, and there are well-maintained restrooms here. Kilted dancers and drummers perform a bagpipe "skirling" ceremony (noon Mon. Nov.-Mar.) at the fort (tel. 441/292-1681 to confirm the schedule).

★ Bermuda Underwater Exploration Institute

The world's last frontier—the ocean—is the domain of the **Bermuda Underwater Exploration Institute** (BUEI, 40 Crow Lane, East Broadway, tel. 441/292-7219, tickets tel. 441/297-7314, www.buei.org, 10am-5pm daily, $15 adults, $12 seniors, $8 ages 6-17, free under age 6). You'll learn about the world's oceans through a small but interesting array of hands-on exhibits and eye-popping artifacts. The notable collection of early diving apparatus includes a diving bell, an exosuit, and a bathysphere replica of the famous metal pod in which William Beebe and Otis Barton descended a half mile down off Bermuda in the 1930s. The adventure starts with a simulated (and rather hokey) submersible dive to the 12,000-foot bottom of Bermuda's seamount.

The institute is a tribute to the career of the late Teddy Tucker, a world-renowned Bermudian diver who retrieved artifacts and dived on most of the island's 150 or more known shipwrecks. The **Tucker Shipwreck Gallery** features a map of wrecks and exhibits of their contents, including cannons, bottles, and clay jars. The **Treasure Room** displays Spanish gold and pirate booty collected from local dive sites, as well as a replica of the infamous Tucker Cross, which mysteriously disappeared from the Bermuda Maritime Museum (now the National Museum of Bermuda) just before Queen Elizabeth's visit in 1975.

Science at Sea uses interactive exhibits to teach visitors about the body's reaction to the pressures of the deep, and a wall of bioluminescent creatures down a darkened tunnel mimics the feel of the deep ocean. Kids will especially like the video-simulated shark cage that allows you to experience the charge of a great white. Upstairs, don't miss the **Jack Lightbourn Shell Collection,** showcasing some 1,200 of the Bermudian diver's own shells, including 1,000 different species, of which 110 are Bermudian.

Oceans Gift Shop sells marine-inspired books, games, and toys. A gourmet restaurant, **The Harbourfront,** is located on the site's waterfront.

BEACHES

Clarence Cove at Admiralty House Park off North Shore Road is a delightful little beach, tucked at the foot of the park and shallow enough for young children. Shady baygrape trees provide welcome cool. Nearby **Deep Bay** is best accessed farther down the North Shore (via unmarked steep stone steps cut into the hillside off North Shore Road near a bus stop). At low tide, there's a beach here, but it is most popular for diving and jumping into its deep swimming hole.

The coves and bays off **Spanish Point Park**'s North Shore edge are perfect for snorkeling or bathing when the wind's from the south (most of the summer). Shallow reefs here can be seen through clear water even from the shoreline. The route 4 bus comes by here from Hamilton, or you can come by scooter and leave vehicles in the small parking lot.

SPORTS AND RECREATION
Scuba and Water Sports

K. S. Watersports (Hamilton Princess & Beach Club, tel. 441/232-4155, http://kswatersports.com, 8:30am-6pm daily) offers Jet Ski Safaris (2 hours, May-Oct., $225 single, $245 double), plus kayak rentals (hourly $25 single, $30 double), 13-foot Boston Whalers (up to 4 adults, $185 for 4 hours, $340 for 8 hours), 23-foot pontoon boats (up to 12 people, with captain $600 for 4 hours, $1,200 for 8 hours) and stand-up paddleboards ($25 per hour). Rentals and tours can be booked online or by phone.

Based on the beach at the foot of the expansive park, **Admiralty Cove Adventure Park** (Admiralty House Park, tel. 441/336-7001, bermudaadventurepark@gmail.com, 10am-4pm Mon.-Thurs., 10am-3pm Fri. summer) rents kayaks, floats, and snorkeling gear and offers walking tours of the park as well as cliff-jumping expeditions from the area's coastline (a popular pastime for locals). Laser tag parties can also be arranged.

Bermuda Sub-Aqua Club (Admiralty House Park, tel. 441/292-9656 or 441/291-5640, www.bsac.bm) is a NAUI-registered training and diving organization. It arranges regular expeditions for its 150 members throughout the year. Club nights are held after 7:30pm Wednesday at the clubhouse, a pink building on the right as you enter the park. Visitors are welcome.

Fishing

Spanish Point Boat Club (Spanish Point Rd., tel. 441/295-1030) is one of the island's main sportfishing hubs, with docks and hauling equipment outside where boats land their record catches. A members' club, it nevertheless welcomes visitors.

Veteran sportfishing king Allen DeSilva runs **Mako Charters** (11 Abri Lane, Spanish Point, tel. 441/295-0835, www.fishbermuda.com) aboard his 56-foot air-conditioned Carolina sportfisher, *Mako,* the island's largest charter fishing vessel. DeSilva holds the current blue marlin record at 1,352-pounds

and boasts one-day hauls such as 44 yellow-fin tuna. Full-day (9 hours) charters for up to six people, beverages included, cost $3,000; a $500 deposit is required.

Tuna specialist Captain Kevin Winter operates **Playmate Charters** (4 Mill Point Lane, tel. 441/292-7131, cell 441/335-5172 or 441/799-8862, www.playmatefishing.com), offering full-day ($1,350), three-quarter day ($1,200), and half-day ($1,000) charters (maximum 10 people) aboard the 43-foot *Playmate,* a Torres Sports Fisherman outfitted with tournament tackle, a fighting chair, two fishing chairs, outriggers, downriggers, kites, and other accessories for modern game-fishing.

Soccer

Evening and weekend soccer games are held at the clubhouse field of the **Bermuda Athletic Association** (BAA, 24 Woodlands Rd., tel. 441/292-3161), an organization that has promoted a wide gamut of sports on the island—soccer, badminton, rugby, swimming, track and field—for over a century. Admission is usually free.

Tennis

Anyone can play at the government-owned **William Joell Tennis Stadium** (2 Marsh Folly Rd., at Cedar Ave., tel. 441/292-0105, 8am-10pm Mon.-Fri., 8am-7pm Sat.-Sun., $10 per hour). The busy facility, named for the Bermudian recognized for knocking down racial barriers in the sport, has eight courts (three clay, five hard courts), three of which are lit for night play and can be rented for an additional $8. Traditional tennis attire is required, and advance bookings are recommended. Peak times are after 5pm daily and Saturday morning. Private lessons (adults $70 per hour, juniors $60) are also available. The shop sells cold drinks and tennis balls and also rents rackets.

Spas

Inner Sanctum Spa & Salon (75 Front St. W., tel. 441/295-4808, www.bermudaspasandsalons.com) offers massage (25 minutes

Fort Hamilton's moat garden

the winter the water gets choppy. Shady trees, lawns for playing, and picnic tables make this a perfect family spot.

Don't miss **Fort Hamilton's moat garden and dungeons** (Happy Valley Rd., off King St., tel. 441/292-1234, 8am-sunset daily, free), one of the Hamilton area's best kid-pleasing attractions, or **Admiralty House Park**'s forested trails and rocky tunnels (North Shore Rd. and Spanish Point Rd., sunrise-sunset daily, free).

ENTERTAINMENT AND EVENTS

Weekly **skirling ceremonies** featuring the Bermuda Islands Pipe Band are held at Fort Hamilton (noon Mon. Nov.-Mar.). Dancers and drummers in kilts perform for the crowd atop the fort's panoramic ramparts. A weekend film series called **Bermuda Docs** (tel. 441/236-3870, www.bermudadocs.com) attracts aficionados on Sunday afternoons throughout the year to the Tradewinds Auditorium at the Bermuda Underwater Exploration Institute (BUEI). Tickets can be purchased from the **BUEI's Oceans Gift Shop** (tel. 441/294-0204) or online (www. bdatix.bm).

Nightlife

"Marina Nights" bring happy-hour crowds on Fridays to the harborside terrace of the **Hamilton Princess** (76 Pitts Bay Rd., tel. 441/295-3000, www.thehamiltonprincess. com, 5pm-9pm Fri. Apr.-Oct.). The big attraction is the elegant hotel's lobby bar and its alfresco terrace, perfect for schmoozing at sunset on the water's edge. Happy-hour drink specials (beers and rum cocktails $5) are offered. Rain or shine, there's a live band, a DJ, and a barbecue grill. The Crown & Anchor bar is open year-round (10am-1am daily). It has contemporary flair and world-class art, making for enjoyable evenings—the $12 martinis notwithstanding.

Many start the weekend early at nearby **Harry's** (The Waterfront, 96 Pitts Bay Rd., tel. 441/292-5533, www.harrys.bm, noon-10pm

$80), facials, body treatments, waxing, manicures (45 minutes, $60), and pedicures as well as hairdressing for men and women. **Exhale** (Hamilton Princess & Beach Club, 76 Pitts Bay Rd., tel. 441/298-6046, 9am-8pm daily) offers a full menu of fitness classes and treatments, such as facials (30 minutes, $100), flow massage (1 hour, $190), and scrubs, manicures, pedicures, waxing, or a combo with a Day of Restoration ($500).

For Kids

The government-run **Parson's Road Playground** is a popular attraction. Parents bring their kids after school at 3:30pm, and holidays find the swings, slides, tunnels, fort, and pirate ship crowded with happy youngsters. There's plenty of parking.

Spanish Point Park's tiny coves and quiet, shallow bays are just what children love, and kids can spend hours here exploring rock pools, snorkeling, and swimming. The park's North Shore edge, dotted with coves, is best when the wind is blowing from the south; in

Mon.-Sat.), where customers can enjoy special prices on martinis or sample the award-winning wines and champagnes in the popular spot's club-like atmosphere or on its waterside patio. Located on the ground floor of Bermuda's tallest corporate glass tower, Taste One Four One (141 Front St. E., tel. 441/292-0777, 8am-6pm Mon.-Thurs., 8am-9pm Fri.) is a contemporary watering hole with Friday-night happy hour.

Get local with a visit to the Spanish Point Boat Club (Spanish Point Rd., tel. 441/295-1030, 11:30am-midnight Sun.-Thurs., 11:30am-1am Fri.-Sat.), whose bar has a nightly gathering of neighborhood residents and local fishers who like the $3 highballs and beer. Like its sign says, the facility is a members' club, but visitors are welcome. Another waterfront drinking spot with authentically Bermudian ambience is the Blue Water Anglers Club's Hook & Hold Bar (28 E. Broadway, tel. 441/292-5529, 5pm-midnight Fri.), where Friday nights see a reunion of regulars who come for waterside sunset cocktails and DJ entertainment.

The Robin Hood Pub & Restaurant (25 Richmond Rd., tel. 441/295-3314, fax 441/292-9338, www.robinhood.bm, 11:30am-1am daily) has a lively sports-bar scene, including quiz nights and live soccer and ice hockey showdowns on big-screen TVs. It's a favorite stomping ground for British and Canadian expat residents.

SHOPPING

Jeremy Johnson's Village Carpentry (127 North Shore, tel. 441/292-2088 or 441/295-5370, villagecraft@northrock.bm, 8am-4pm Mon.-Fri.) has been a roadside institution since the 1960s. Today Johnson's aromatic workshop, spreading the scent of cedar along this stretch of North Shore, is worth a visit to get a glimpse of craftspeople at work. Johnson sells cedar trinkets, bowls, bookends, and other sweet-smelling mementos.

FH Boutique For Him/For Her (Hamilton Princess & Beach Club, 6 Pitts Bay Rd., tel. 441/298-6095, http://luxury.

bm, 9am-7pm Mon.-Fri., 10am-6pm Sat.-Sun.) offers carefully curated gifts and high-end fashion for men and women, including Thomas Pink, Pour les Femmes, and Camilla. Owner Miranda Conway's sister store, Resort Boutique, sits opposite FH Boutique, shares the same hours, and stocks elegant swimwear, fashionable towels, and kids' books and toys.

FOOD
Cafés, Pubs, and Takeout

One of Bermuda's best and most gargantuan fish sandwiches can be found at ★ Art Mel's Spicy Dicy (9 St. Monica's Rd., north off Marsh Folly Rd., tel. 441/295-3965, noon-10pm Mon.-Fri., noon-8pm Sat.), which, though tucked away in Pembroke's backstreets since the 1960s, is sought out by fish-lovers thanks to word-of-mouth praise. Named for the late Art Smith, the eatery is now run by his eldest son, Rockking, and other family members, cooking up its award-winning stacked sandwich ($17) with your choice of plain or toasted white, wheat, or raisin bread and coleslaw, cheese, or onions, along with melt-in-your mouth fries, crispy fish cakes on buns ($5), burgers ($6), and other fast food. Follow your nose—and the lines of people.

Grannie's Kitchen (113 North Shore Rd., opposite First Church of God, tel. 441/292-2914, 7am-5:30pm Mon.-Fri., 8am-5:30pm Sat., 8am-2:30pm Sun.) is the local go-to café for fish sandwiches and fish cakes, in particular, along with burgers and sandwiches. In-the-know tour guides make pit stops here to show off true "Bermy" cuisine. Chill to a contemporary vibe at Taste One Four One (141 Front St. E., tel. 441/292-0777, 8am-6pm Mon.-Thurs., 8am-9pm Fri.), where corporate types pull in en route to nearby offices for morning bacon-and-egg wraps. The seasonally inspired lunch menu ranges from salads ($11) to pasta (from $14) and quiche ($13).

Buzz West Hamilton (69 Pitts Bay Rd., tel. 441/295-1723, www.buzzcafe.bm, 6:30am-5pm Mon.-Fri., 8am-4pm Sat., 8am-5pm Sun.) is one of two Pembroke outlets of the busy coffee-and-snacks franchise, along with the more hidden **Buzz Bakery Lane** (19 Bakery Lane, off Serpentine Rd., tel. 441/292-2311, 7am-6pm Mon.-Fri., 8am-4:30pm Sat.).

Tasty pizzas ($13-25, including takeout) and loads of beer and pub grub get crowds to **The Robin Hood Pub & Restaurant** (25 Richmond Rd., tel. 441/295-3314, www.robin-hood.bm, lunch 11am-4pm daily, dinner 4pm-10pm daily, bar until 1am daily), where British soccer and Tuesday quiz nights entertain regulars. Breakfast sandwiches ($8), surf and turf ($28), pastas ($17), nachos ($111), UK staples like bangers and mash ($17), and Indian curries ($17) keep customers satisfied with big helpings and reasonable prices. Opening hours depend on scheduled live sports events, shown on TV.

International

In the elegant Rosedon guesthouse is ★ **Huckleberry** (61 Pitts Bay Rd., tel. 441/478-2256, www.rosedon.com, 8:30am-9:30pm daily), which offers breakfast, lunch and dinner in two parlors-turned-dining rooms as well as on the grand front porch. With an emphasis on fresh local ingredients parlayed into Southern-style comfort dishes, the restaurant has plenty for vegetarians and meat-lovers. Try an avocado crush ($15) or a *croque monsieur* or huevos rancheros (both $17) for breakfast. For lunch or dinner, there's the shrimp po'boy ($22), Southern-style corn hushpuppies ($10), fish tacos ($13), lamb meatball masala ($29), and blackened local rockfish ($37).

Marcus' (Hamilton Princess & Beach Club, 76 Pitts Bay Rd., tel. 441/295-3000, www.thehamiltonprincess.com, noon-3pm and 6pm-10pm daily), the 180-seat restaurant from celebrity chef and TV personality Marcus Samuelsson, has brought buzz and big exposure to the Pitts Bay neighborhood. The dapper Ethiopian Swedish star of TV's *Chopped* and *Iron Chef* series, who owns several award-winning restaurants in the United States and Sweden, makes occasional visits for special events and has won media acclaim for the elegantly boisterous ambience

and haute comfort-food menu. Included are dishes fusing fresh Bermuda fish and produce with Southern, West Indian, and Portuguese influences (fish chowder croquettes, dark 'n' stormy sorbet, jerk pork belly, cornbread madeleines). Main courses range from local catches ($36) to steak frites ($49) to signature classics like buttermilk-fried yardbird ($70). In a former gazebo with a veranda above the harbor, this is Bermuda's largest eatery. A Sunday champagne brunch is popular among locals, and DJs and live bands play on Thursday evenings.

The location brings swooning lunch, dinner, and happy-hour crowds to the 125-seat **1609 Bar & Restaurant** (Hamilton Princess & Beach Club, 76 Pitts Bay Rd., tel. 441/295-3000, www.thehamiltonprincess.com, 11am-10pm daily early spring-late fall), a large open bar and grill named for the date Bermuda's first 150 colonists made landfall after their ship wrecked. It stretches along the landmark property's state-of-the-art marina with breathtaking views of the harbor and Great Sound, serving a casual comfort-food menu that includes pizzas ($20), grilled local wahoo sandwiches ($20), roasted red snapper ($32), and steak frites ($38). With its contemporary glass walls and push-out shutters, there's perhaps no other local venue that quite screams "island life" so thrillingly. Savor a grapefruit cosmo in the balmy breeze while you watch spinnakers sail home and the sun melt over the West End.

Ask a local foodie and chances are they will name ★ **Mad Hatters** (22 Richmond Rd., tel. 441/297-6231, www.madhatters.bm, lunch noon-2pm Mon.-Fri., dinner 6pm-9pm Mon.-Sat.). Despite its rather humble though intimate appearance, a dining room and patio of the former Mariners Club sailors' home, it never fails to impress with stellar service and outstanding dishes that showcase the talents of British chef Ben Jewett. Fresh seafood, including flown-in mussels and oysters, highlights a menu that includes scallops and shrimp in saffron bouillabaisse ($42), Bermuda rockfish over vodka martini wilted spinach ($42), mussels in garlic cream sauce ($20), and rack of lamb ($44). Vegetarians can make requests to the chef. Inside, a collection of wacky hats speaks to the venue's *Alice in Wonderland* inspiration; in the spirit of British bonhomie that pervades the restaurant, diners can try these on or don a favorite bonnet for the night.

Multiple-award-winning restaurant **Harbourfront** (Bermuda Underwater Exploration Institute, 40 Crow Lane, E. Broadway, tel. 441/295-4207, www.harbourfront.bm, lunch 11:45am-3pm Mon.-Sat., dinner 6pm-10pm daily, happy hour 5pm-6:30pm Mon.-Fri.) is one of the island's best-patronized establishments, with a winning combination of fine service, a delicious menu—including a full sushi and tempura selection—indoor or dockside dining, and water views up the harbor. Whether you order an oyster carpaccio appetizer ($22), branzino with truffled white bean purée ($42), or a striploin steak ($44), you won't be disappointed. Maître d' Pierangelo Lanfranchi, a Lake Como native, makes all his customers feel like VIPs.

Named for bon vivant Harry Cox, the 20th-century patriarch of Bermuda's venerable Cox family, ★ **Harry's** (The Waterfront, 96 Pitts Bay Rd., tel. 441/292-5533, www.harrys.bm, noon-10pm Mon.-Sat.) is a gourmand's heaven on the harborside across from that other foodie mecca, Miles Market. The elegantly designed steak house boasts a 300-strong wine list, granite and dark wood finishes, and a menu that can't help but impress. Menu highlights include appetizers like steamed clams ($18) and entrées including a filet mignon ($43), veal scallopini risotto ($39), and roast lamb sirloin ($42), with must-have sides such as creamed spinach and house-cut fries with truffle oil. Don't miss the extraordinary urinal in the men's bathroom—designed like a giant lily.

Comfort meets cosmopolitan at **Bouchée** (75 Pitts Bay Rd., tel. 441/295-5759, www.bouchee.bm, 7:30am-2:30pm and 6pm-9pm Mon.-Fri., 6pm-9pm Sat.), where you will be made to feel at home with local regulars. The French-inspired menu includes breakfast fare such as omelets, crepes, pancakes, and eggs Benedict, along with a weekend-only codfish and potatoes ($19). For lunch ($15-22), tuck into *croques* and *crevettes,* quiches, *moules frites,* and croissant sandwiches. Dinner dishes include foie gras ($15), pan-seared duck breast ($26), and Bermuda fish chowder ($9).

★ **Ascot's** (Royal Palms Hotel, 24 Rosemont Ave., tel. 441/295-9644 or 441/296-0831, www.ascotsrestaurant.bm, lunch noon-2pm Mon.-Fri., dinner 6:30pm-9:30pm Mon.-Sat.) is where Northern Ireland's Edmund Smith cut his chef's teeth before winning international awards with his fresh take on Bermudian cuisine. Entrées include grilled salmon with black Chinese rice and braised leeks ($43), charred veal chop ($52), and pan seared snapper ($44). Lunch at **Just 24,** on the veranda of this 19th-century manor house, offers more casual dining with salads, burgers, and open-faced sandwiches ($11-29)—plus views of the gardens spilling with bougainvillea, shady poincianas, and citrus.

Tearooms

An over-the-top afternoon tea ($48 pp) is served daily in the lobby-area court of the expanded ★ **Crown & Anchor** (Hamilton Princess & Beach Club, 76 Pitts Bay Rd., tel. 441/295-3000, www.thehamiltonprincess.com, reservations required, 3pm-5pm Sat.-Sun.). A Best of Bermuda Award winner and repeatedly recognized as one of the top 10 afternoon teas in the world, the feast includes finger sandwiches, profiteroles, panna cotta, scones with jam and clotted cream, pastries, sorbets—and 14 teas, including several black varieties as well as green, herbal, and fruit teas.

Grocery Stores

To describe **Miles Market** (The Waterfront, Pitts Bay, tel. 441/295-1234, www.miles.bm, 7:30am-7pm Mon.-Sat., 11am-5pm Sun.) as a mere grocery store is an understatement. The specialty food store—owned by the Cox

Onion Nation

If you call someone on the island "a real onion," there can be no stronger endorsement of their genuine Bermudian-ness. "Onion" is a popular term of endearment among locals, and numerous businesses also use onion in their names, though none have anything to do with selling the aromatic vegetable.

Bermuda's fascination with onions dates back to the late 1800s, when crates of the pungent bulb grown by island farmers were shipped off to winter markets in New York and Philadelphia, along with potatoes, tomatoes, lilies, and arrowroot. Hamilton's docks were the major shipment hub for thousands of barrels and crates of produce. Red or white Bermuda onions—known for their mild, sweet taste—remained a major island export until cheaper produce from California and Florida, coupled with higher U.S. import tariffs, put an end to the trade in the early 1900s.

Bermuda still harvests onions, but not for export. Seek them out at farmers markets or roadside stands—their legendary taste will not disappoint. You'll also find onion tarts, jams, chutneys, and other dishes on many local restaurant menus.

family, to whom the entire surrounding waterfront complex belongs—Miles has been a fixture of the gourmet scene since 1862. Today, in a modern headquarters, it boasts professional staff and pretty much any foodstuff an epicurean could desire. Everything is expensive, but Miles's meat department is the island's best, with melt-in-your-mouth cuts and both wet-aged and dry-aged beef selections. Treats include cheeses from around the world; fresh croissants and *pain au chocolat;* a menu of olive oils and marmalades; ethnic sections; wines from France, Napa, and Lebanon; and organic everything. Miles also has a coffee bar, Café Godiva, so you can sip a latte or cappuccino while you shop. The Miles to Go deli offers takeout feasts (salads, fish cakes, polenta, grilled vegetables), and staff pack lunch boxes or gourmet picnics to order (tel. 441/295-1234, ext. 255, from $30) with smoked salmon, grilled chicken, fresh fruit platter, and a strawberry tartlet.

Garden Market (13 Serpentine Rd., tel. 441/292-7000, 7am-7pm Mon.-Thurs., 7am-8pm Fri.-Sat.) is a family business with friendly staff, vegetables from local farmers, and liquor. **Arnold's Family Market** (113 St. John's Rd., tel. 441/292-3310, 6:30am-midnight daily) is a bustling neighborhood hub that has morphed over recent years from a cramped grocery to a modern expanse.

There's a large liquor section, meats, produce, baked goods, and magazines. The place is a zoo on Friday and Saturday nights.

With ample parking on the stretch of North Shore leading east from Hamilton, **C-Mart** (96 North Shore Rd., at the corner of Black Watch Pass and Langton Hill, tel. 441/292-5332, 7am-6pm Mon.-Thurs., 7am-7pm Fri.-Sat., 8am-12:30pm Sun.) makes a convenient stop for snacks, newspapers, or liquor. The tiny outlet, a favorite with Cup Match campers who set up in the seafront park opposite, also sells fresh baked goods, hot pies, and dry and frozen goods. **Point Mart** (Cox's Hill, tel. 441/292-0342, 8am-9pm Mon.-Sat.) is tiny but well stocked. **Manuel Soares & Son** (Old House Lane, Spanish Point, tel. 441/292-1426, 7am-8pm Mon.-Sat.) is the only grocery store in the heart of Spanish Point.

Liquor Stores
Serpentine Liquors (15 Serpentine Rd., tel. 441/292-7842, 8am-8pm Mon.-Sat.) touts "the coldest beer around" along with a full wines and spirits selection.

ACCOMMODATIONS
$200-300
The quaint two-story **Oxford House** (20 Woodbourne Ave., tel. 441/295-0503, www.oxfordhouse.bm, $270 s, $290 d, including

breakfast) once sat in a quiet residential neighborhood on the edge of Hamilton but now faces a corporate invasion. The 12 small elegant rooms, each with an en suite bath and furnished like private residences, cater to those attending meetings within a few blocks, or visitors who want a central location that's not on a beach. Each dollhouse-like room has dressers, curtains, floral bedspreads, a coffee-maker, air-conditioning, cable TV, and free Wi-Fi. Continental breakfast is served in the lounge every morning.

Tucked into a residential lane off Pitts Bay, **Kingston House Bed & Breakfast** (5 Turnstile Lane, off Pitts Bay Rd., tel. 441/295-6597, www.bbbermuda.com, $179 s, $269 d) has won glowing reviews for Bermudian hosts Harry and Marlie Powell, who converted their 1921 two-story homestead into a B&B. The house's three units, all with en suite baths, boast an Endless pool and are surrounded by mature gardens. The elegant Palmetto Suite is the largest, with a queen bed and a sitting room with a fireplace and a balcony. The Bird of Paradise Room has twin beds that can be converted into a king and a balcony, while the Jacaranda Room has a queen bed. A light breakfast is served in the dining room or on the outside patio. The property's location on the edge of Hamilton allows easy access to ferries, bus stops, shopping, and city dining.

$300-400

Winner of TripAdvisor's 2014 Traveler's Choice Award for best hotel in the Caribbean, ★ **Royal Palms** (24 Rosemont Ave., tel. 441/292-1854, U.S. tel. 800/678-0783, Canada tel. 800/799-0824, www.royalpalms.bm, $320-499 d, including breakfast) is a former manor house on the edge of Hamilton set in a gorgeous English-style garden overflowing with birdsong, bougainvillea, and citrus trees. The sophisticated little hotel offers impeccable rooms, professional service, and relaxing surroundings. With its hallmark white shutters and wraparound veranda, the turn-of-the-20th-century property's other big draw is its standout restaurant, **Ascot's.** A total of 32

rooms and suites are decorated in European florals with high ceilings, classic moldings, and window seats overlooking the lawns. All have cable TV, air-conditioning, and high-speed Internet access. There's also a small but private pool. Not surprisingly, Royal Palms is usually fully booked by business visitors on weekdays, but it makes a perfect weekend escape for couples. A few mini suites have kitchenettes. Owned and operated by the Bermudian Smith family, it is one of the island's best small hotels.

Edgehill Manor (36 Rosemont Ave., tel. 441/295-7124, www.edgehill.bm, $250 s, $350 d) is a refurbished colonial-style mansion turned bed-and-breakfast. Seven large rooms—four upstairs with private balconies and splendid views—have air-conditioning, ceiling fans, private baths, cable TV, Wi-Fi, small fridges, microwaves, and safes. The property also has a large freshwater pool in the quiet garden. It's located in a pretty neighborhood just a seven-minute walk from central Hamilton.

Over $400

Fondly known locally as "The Princess" and often dubbed the "Pink Palace," the ★ **Hamilton Princess & Beach Club** (76 Pitts Bay Rd., tel. 441/295-3000, U.S. tel. 800/441-1414, www.thehamiltonprincess.com, $495-3,000) is a scenic 15-minute walk from Hamilton's center and has been a fixture of the Pitts Bay waterfront since Victorian times. The candy-pink hotel was built in honor of Queen Victoria's daughter, Princess Louise, who visited Bermuda in 1883, launching a tourism industry in her wake. During World War II it was an intelligence center where mail and radio communications were analyzed by more than 1,000 British "censorettes." The historic landmark property is currently enjoying an exciting renaissance, thanks to its 2012 purchase by the Bermuda-based billionaire Green family—although it's still managed by Fairmont Hotels & Resorts—and $100-million refurbishment that made it the place to stay during 2017's America's Cup. The massive makeover brought substantial upgrades to the hotel's lobby and retail space as well as to 69 guestrooms and suites, and construction of a state-of-the-art, 60-berth superyacht marina, large infinity pool with hot tub, private cabanas with bar and food service, and two new restaurants with eye-popping views—the open-air **1609 Bar & Restaurant** on the marina and **Marcus',** by celebrity chef Marcus Samuelsson. Rooms offer harbor views or a garden or pool outlook, and some have private balconies with views stretching up the Great Sound. Throughout its public areas the hotel also showcases a world-class art collection by the likes of Jeff Koons, Damien Hirst, and Warhol. Guided tours are offered at 10am Saturday or by appointment.

Rosedon (61 Pitts Bay Rd., tel. 441/295-1640, www.rosedon.com, $400-508 d) stands opposite the Hamilton Princess & Beach Club and is one of Pitts Bay's grand old mansions, built in 1906. Decorated like an English manor home in oak, mahogany, and redwood, the 44-room bed-and-breakfast is popular with business travelers as it's a short walk from Hamilton. Some rooms are in the main house, but most in an adjacent building next to the pool and have cable TV, air-conditioning, private baths, phones, fridges, coffeemakers, and Wi-Fi. "Royal Rooms" are a step up, with whirlpool tubs. Same-day laundry service is available. Guests have a choice of picnic lunches or poolside à la carte service, and staff serves a grand afternoon tea (4pm daily). The property also has the delightful Huckleberry restaurant, and offers wedding and honeymoon packages.

Owned by the harborfront complex that comprises Miles Market and several global business headquarters, **The Waterfront Residence** (11 Waterloo Lane, tel. 441/299-0700, hospitality@thewaterfront.bm, www.thewaterfrontresidence.bm) offers a total of six bespoke harborfront accommodations, three gardenfront condominiums ($400), and three with balcony and ocean views ($600). All are a five-minute walk into Hamilton, with easy access to nearby groceries, restaurants, and public transport.

INFORMATION AND SERVICES

Woodbourne Chemist (Woodbourne Ave., tel. 441/295-2663, 8am-6pm Mon.-Sat.) is Pembroke's only pharmacy, conveniently located near several hotels and guesthouses.

Gas stations around the parish include **Rubis East Broadway Service Station** (25 Crow Lane, tel. 441/296-7225, 7am-midnight Mon.-Sat., 8am-10pm Sun.); **Rubis St. John's Road Station** (61 St. John's Rd., tel. 441/297-5111, 7am-7pm Mon.-Sat., 10am-6pm Sun.); and **Rubis Waterfront** (2 Waterloo Lane, at The Waterfront, tel. 441/295-3185, 8am-6pm Mon.-Sat. Apr.-Oct., 8am-5pm Mon.-Sat. Nov.-Apr.).

Public toilets are in Spanish Point Park, Admiralty House Park, Fort Hamilton, hotels, and restaurants. **ATMs** are located at the **Butterfield Bank Waterfront Branch** (90 Pitts Bay Rd., tel. 441/294-2070).

TRANSPORTATION

The beauty of staying in Pembroke is that all points in Hamilton are walkable. Pembroke has no ferry stops, but the Front Street terminal is close by.

Buses

Numerous bus routes serve Pembroke, all departing from Hamilton's **central bus terminal** (Washington St. between Church St. and Victoria St., tel. 441/292-3854). To visit Spanish Point, take route 4 (every 20 minutes). Routes 10 and 11 (every 15 minutes) head north through Pembroke on their way to St. George's; route 10 takes North Shore Road (Black Watch Pass), and route 11 goes via Palmetto Road. Route 5 (hourly, or every 30 minutes at peak commuter times) travels to Pond Hill via Glebe Road. Route 9 (hourly) runs between Hamilton and Prospect, Devonshire. Route 2 (hourly) and route 3 (every half hour) head east out of Hamilton, route 2 along East Broadway (Bermuda Underwater Exploration

Institute) and route 3 along Cavendish Road into Devonshire (Fort Hamilton). Fares to Hamilton Parish and St. George's are $5, to all other areas on these routes $3.50 (exact change or tokens, tickets, or passes required), free under age 5, $2.75 ages 5-15.

Scooters and Bicycles

Oleander Cycles (15 Gorham Rd., tel. 441/295-0919, after-hours assistance tel. 441/236-5235, www.oleandercycles.bm, 8:30am-5:30pm Mon.-Sat.) rents standard single or double scooters. Rates ($55 standard, $65 double for one day, $225 standard, $266 double per week, $17 standard, $21 double per day after 7 days) include scooter delivery and pickup (or hotel pickup), the first tank of gas, a helmet, a lock, a basket, third-party insurance ($30), and island-wide roadside service for breakdowns. Prefer to pedal? Mountain bikes are $40 per day, $175 per week, $10 per day after seven days.

Smatt's Cycle Livery (74 Pitts Bay Rd., tel. 441/295-1180, www.smattscyclelivery. com, 8am-5pm daily) is directly outside the Hamilton Princess & Beach Club. The outlet rents single-seat ($55 per day) and dual-seat

($75) scooters ($225 single, $267 dual per week). Island-wide roadside assistance is part of the deal. Pedal bikes are also available, for $40 per day, $145 per week.

Taxis

There are taxi stands outside the Hamilton Princess & Beach Club. To order a cab, use the **Hitch app** (www.hitch.bm) or call the island's three main cab companies: **Bermuda Industrial Union Co-op** (tel. 441/292-4476, cooptaxi@fkbnet.bm), **Bermuda Island Taxi** (tel. 441/295-4141, www.bermudaislandtaxi. com), or **BTA Dispatching** (tel. 441/296-2121, www.btadispatching.com).

Electric Cars

Hamilton Princess & Beach Club (76 Pitts Bay Rd., tel. 441/295-3000, info@currentvehicles.com, www.currentvehicles. com, pickup 9am-4pm daily) has a fleet of two-seater electric Renault **Twizy** vehicles, and a growing number of resorts have Twizy charging and parking stations. A one-day booking costs about $100, including a $30 third-party insurance fee; discounts are offered for bookings over seven days.

Devonshire and Paget Parishes

Devonshire Parish 82   Paget Parish 92

Look for ★ to find recommended sights, activities, dining, and lodging.

Highlights

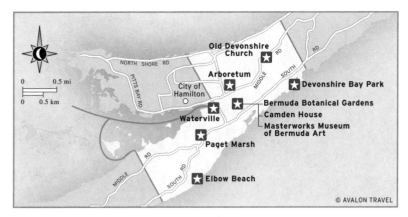

© AVALON TRAVEL

★ **Arboretum:** Quiet trails wind through fiddlewood forests and meadows, alive with bluebirds and cardinals (page 84).

★ **Old Devonshire Church:** Centuries old, this whitewashed pocket-size church is notable for its traditional architecture, cedar-fused interior, and quaint gardens (page 85).

★ **Devonshire Bay Park:** This bay encompasses a tiny beach that's great for kids, a small national park with a spectacular outlook on the South Shore, and the ruin of an early coastal fort (page 87).

★ **Bermuda Botanical Gardens:** Bermuda's favorite park has rolling lawns, mazes, and a scented garden (page 94).

★ **Camden House:** The premier's official residence is open for public viewing twice a week (page 95).

★ **Masterworks Museum of Bermuda Art:** This groundbreaking institution is the work of a nonprofit that repatriates Bermuda artworks by luminaries like Winslow Homer and Georgia O'Keeffe (page 96).

★ **Waterville:** Antiques and oils adorn the interior of this gracious waterfront homestead, headquarters of the Bermuda National Trust and representative of centuries-old Bermudian architecture (page 97).

★ **Paget Marsh:** Teeming with birdlife, this former peat marsh can easily be explored via a quaint boardwalk (page 99).

★ **Elbow Beach:** Walk from end to end and swim in the clear turquoise rollers of one of Bermuda's most famous pink stretches (page 100).

Located at the island's heart, Devonshire and Paget share common traits but occupy divergent places in the collective imagination.

With verdant valleys, rolling farmland, old estates, centuries-old churches, and nature reserves, the regions are fairly similar in appearance and incorporate a variety of geography, from coastal areas to inland farms. Like the rest of Bermuda, both are heavily residential and steeped in history—Paget's of the seafaring variety, Devonshire more military-minded. Both parishes have also borne the brunt of modern-day progress, and today serve as conduits for ever-increasing streams of traffic moving between the City of Hamilton and the island's other parishes.

Differences become more apparent spending time in each. Devonshire is deep country in the most laid-back sense, with deserted coast-view trails, quiet cedar-fringed farms, stables, and tucked-away family estates reminiscent of the English countryside. Its shoreline communities feature fishers' stalls and dry goods stores that belong to another century. Noisier, more developed Paget proffers a more suburban edge, as it gazes across the narrow foot of the harbor at the city, its coveted Harbour Road properties long owned by merchants and traders, yesterday's movers and shakers. Together these parishes encompass central Bermuda and, along with Pembroke, are generally considered the most desirable areas to live. They boast a massing of old money and convenient proximity to Hamilton, with fewer traffic jams than other areas en route to the city.

Devonshire's bucolic borders begin northeast of Hamilton, touching Pembroke at the junction of Spruce Lane and North Shore Road, and continuing south along Glebe Road to Paget's edge at Foot of the Lane. Devonshire's contents spill east, spreading between South and North Shores as far as Collector's Hill and Cable Hill. Undulating Middle Road rambles through the parish center, while North Shore and South Shore Roads hem its edges on both sides. Devonshire includes large tracts of farmland, including the lovely Orange Valley and Locust Hall Nature Reserve, owned and managed by the National

---

Trust, where acres of lilies and snapdragons spring from the earth during Easter season.

Paget, meanwhile, moves west from the quirkily named Happy Talk Drive, continuing past the Bermuda Botanical Gardens. Trimingham Hill, a highway hub from Hamilton, channels traffic westward through Paget via pretty, winding Harbour Road, central Middle Road, or South Shore Road, all of which connect with and continue through Warwick Parish after the north-south boundary of Cobb's Hill. Paget's north boundary includes islands in Hamilton Harbour: White's, where youth groups enjoy summer camps; large residential Hinson's, which has a ferry stop on the Paget-Warwick run; and smaller outcrops such as Doctor's and Burnt Islands.

PLANNING YOUR TIME

Unless you're ensconced in a resort, it's likely you will pass through the central parishes of Devonshire and Paget many times on your way to Hamilton, or moving between the East and West Ends. Both parishes provide a highly scenic passageway, as well as sights, restaurants, bars, and beautiful outdoor spaces. Buses run several regular routes through Devonshire and Paget, and ferries are a scenic way to explore Paget's harborside and beyond. The old tribe roads make interesting tangents; east-west main roads are linked via these skinny north-south divisions that travel past red fields of newly sown soil, schoolyards, and back gardens.

Devonshire, the more rural of the two, is mostly residential, with few shopping and no hotel options, and features historic family estates, tracts of farmland and forest, a marsh protected as a nature reserve, a popular little spa, and a golf course. Paget houses the island's major hospital, King Edward VII Memorial, with its expanding medical environs, as well as two major hotels, beaches, bars, and restaurants. Wrapped around the bottom of Hamilton Harbour, it's closely connected to the city.

Outdoor enthusiasts will find plenty to do thanks to numerous resort tennis facilities, a nine-hole golf course at Ocean View Golf Club, and walking, riding, and running trails, plus two of the island's most expansive public parks, the Arboretum and Bermuda Botanical Gardens. Stretches of the Railway Trail are great for exploring the countryside. Buy fresh-caught lobsters from roadside fishers, or sunflowers and honey from a farm stand on Saturday morning. Stop for a Foot of the Lane picnic along Pomander Road's harborside, or walk the Railway Trail from Barker's Hill, the glistening North Shore panorama laid out before you.

Devonshire Parish

As a born-and-bred Devonshire resident, I confess the bucolic, valley-dotted parish, infused as it is with childhood memories, is my favorite in Bermuda. You'll find yourself at the physical center of Bermuda and also in the heart of the island's "country" roots. Old gardens on rambling estates tumble down gentle hills and fenced meadows, North Shore cottages cluster in salt-sprayed pastels, the surf echoes on South Shore verandas, and lily fields and footpaths wind through fiddlewood forests. Historically, Devonshire (pronounced "DEV-on-sure," not "shyer," as North Americans are tempted to say) is named for the southwest corner of England, birthplace of William Cavendish, the first Earl of Devonshire and one of the prominent London investors behind Bermuda's early development.

With no operating hotels and no commercial center for shopping or dining, Devonshire is the least tourist-focused parish. Exceptions are in January, when Bermuda Marathon Weekend runners compete in an international

Devonshire Parish

City of Hamilton

PEMBROKE PARISH

PAGET PARISH

DEVONSHIRE PARISH

SMITH'S PARISH

ATLANTIC OCEAN

ATLANTIC OCEAN

Hamilton Harbour

Pembroke Marsh

Penhurst Agricultural Park

Robinson's Bay

Palmetto Park

Devonshire Marsh

Vickers Bay

Cox's Bay

Devonshire Bay

Roads and places:

- CHURCH ST
- COURT ST
- FRONT ST
- PARSONS RD
- PALMETTO RD
- FROG LN
- NORTH RD
- PARSONS RD
- ORANGE VALLEY RD
- BARKER'S HILL
- PAGET FINGER RD
- TRIMINGHAM RD
- BERRY HILL RD
- MIDDLE RD
- JUBILEE RD
- TEE ST
- VESEY ST
- SHORE RD
- Railway Trail
- SOUTH RD
- BRIGHTON HILL RD
- MIDDLE RD
- DEVON SPRING RD
- HERMITAGE RD
- VERDMONT
- COLLECTOR'S HILL
- ST MARK'S RD
- MIDDLE RD
- THE LANE

Points of interest:

- FORT HAMILTON ★
- WORLD RUGBY CLASSIC/ NATIONAL SPORTS CENTRE ★
- DEVONSHIRE RECREATION CLUB ★
- EMPIRE GROCERY
- MID-ATLANTIC BOAT & SPORTS CLUB
- SAMMY'S KITCHEN
- ARBORETUM
- POLICE HEADQUARTERS/ POLICE RECREATION CLUB
- King Edward VII Memorial Hospital
- BERMUDA BOTANICAL GARDENS
- MASTERWORKS MUSEUM OF BERMUDA ART
- CAMDEN HOUSE
- POST OFFICE
- Ocean View Golf Club
- WATER HAZARD ▼
- KALEIDOSCOPE ART FOUNDATION ★
- NATIONAL EQUESTRIAN CENTRE
- OLD DEVONSHIRE CHURCH
- GILLIAN'S
- J&J PRODUCE ▼
- LINDO'S MARKET/ LINDO'S PHARMACY
- BERMUDA SQUASH RACQUETS ASSOCIATION
- BUTTERLY GARDEN ★
- BELVIN'S VARIETY
- SEASIDE GRILL
- PALM GROVE GARDENS ★
- DEVONSHIRE BAY PARK
- THE BARN
- MID-ATLANTIC WELLNESS INSTITUTE (MAWI)
- BUZZ N GO ▼

0 0.25 km
0 0.25 mi

© AVALON TRAVEL

House Names

If a foreign postal carrier had been dropped into Bermuda not so long ago, he or she might have been totally perplexed by the island's archaic address system. Until the 1980s, Bermudians generally relied on identifying properties by house names, because private residences rarely had numbers. Letters, therefore, simply went to "Anstey," Middle Road, Devonshire; or "Windswept," Southampton. When giving a guest directions, you might refer to the house color—"the blue house with white shutters, second on the right." Making matters more confusing was that many of the more remote lanes and neighborhood roads had no names at all, at least not officially. The government changed all that in the 1990s, methodically giving all roads a title—though sometimes rather curious ones (Happy Talk Drive, Frolic Lane, Pain Lane, and Stepmother's Drive among the oddities)—and numbering every house. Today everything is clearly identified, but Bermudians still like to name their houses, and most homes have decorative nameplates prominently displayed.

10K, or November, when crowds pour in for the annual World Rugby Classic, both at the Bermuda National Sports Centre. But visitors will find many corners worth exploring. It might be said that Devonshire is a state of mind rather than a destination. It demands slowing down, kicking back, and soaking in a different time when rhythms of life were connected to the earth rather than the minute or the dollar.

SIGHTS

If you take Cavendish Road out of Hamilton continuing east via Middle Road (bus route 3), you'll end up in the heart of Devonshire. From here, you can explore the parish's diverse nooks and crannies, where many of the sights are the comings and goings of regular daily life. Montpelier Road and Frog Lane lead to North Shore Road, passing circuitous Happy Valley before climbing past the grand Bermuda National Sports Centre. Frog Lane connects with Dock Hill, a short, steep exit onto North Shore Road. Take time to hang out at the former military cargo port Devonshire Dock, now a public dock where dreadlocked fishermen gather in the afternoons to cut up their catch and sell fresh fillets of snapper, rockfish, and other sweet-meat specialties from roadside coolers. Many of the ancestral homes in this area—some with gingerbread verandas, gazebos, even a crenellated

tower—belong to the Dill family; they were built in the 1700s by privateers and merchants. All along the North Shore, far less affluent homes boast rich traditional features, including front-door fanlights, keystones, parapets, and welcoming-arms stairways.

Staying on Middle Road will lead you past farms, churches, and inland neighborhoods. Rolling Orange Valley, largely consisting of age-old family estates, connects to major Palmetto Road or switches back along delightfully rural Parson's Lane toward Devonshire Marsh and Jubilee Road, Old Devonshire Church, Locust Hall Nature Reserve, and Vesey Street's equestrian areas.

If you head east along the South Shore, you can stroll the gardens of Palm Grove or Devonshire Bay—another public park and swimming area where some of the best fresh fish is sold straight off the commercial fishing boats on Friday. Look for the hand-drawn roadside sign.

TOP EXPERIENCE

★ Arboretum

The **Arboretum** (Montpelier Rd., sunrise-sunset daily, free), a 19-acre expanse of meadows, palms, and fiddlewood forests, is one of Bermuda's best parks, comprising wild tracts of wooded hillsides, large soft lawns, and stands of more common plants and trees, including cedars, flowering golden acacias, avocados, and acres of mature Surinam cherry forest. Owned by the government since the British Army pulled out in 1951, it is an important bird sanctuary, with flocks of trilling cardinals and rare bluebirds feeding and nesting in meadows off Middle Road. A giant olive tree at the roadside spreads its dark foliage over the sidewalk, and gargantuan rubber trees with endless root systems and hanging tendrils bear testimony to the centuries-old age of the park. Also off Middle Road, an ornamental bridge crafted with rustic cedar planks and railings leads into the park, and two quarry gardens inside, one with tiny pools, are planted with interesting ferns and other shade-loving flora. Children will enjoy the mature grove near Fort Hill, Prospect, with poincianas that drop red carpets of petals in summer and giant rubber trees, their tendrils providing natural swings. There's also an exquisitely planted butterfly garden, attracting monarchs and other species year-round. Don't miss the nearby limestone buttery, topped by exotic night-blooming cereus flowers in summer. An exercise trail in a 0.5-mile loop includes sit-up benches and balancing bars. Running clubs use the park for afternoon workouts, and birders, families,

and dog-walkers come for the tranquil trails, grassy spaces, and birdsong.

★ Old Devonshire Church

Cute as a button, **Old Devonshire Church** (106 Middle Rd., tel. 441/236-3671, www.christanglicanchurch.bm, Mon.-Fri. by appointment, services 7:30am-2pm Sun., free), a pint-size whitewashed example of pure Bermudian architecture, dates to 1624, when the original structure was built. The first was thatched in palmetto and destroyed by the hurricane of 1715; the current version was rebuilt of limestone the following year. The church's construction demonstrates the same techniques employed by those who crafted ships of the era. Various enlargements were made, but the plain style beloved by early parishioners was kept. Centuries later, the old church suffered severe damage in a 1970 fire, but reconstruction was faithful to its original and very simple design—a marked contrast to the Gothic Revival of the nearby Christ Church, built by the parish in 1851 when the old church was too small to hold the growing congregation. Notable in the historic building's interior is a Bermuda cedar screen decorated with quaint hearts and fleurs-de-lis. The pulpit and pews are also of cedar. Outside is the graveyard

Old Devonshire Church

and an 1817 hearse house built in the style of the church. Surrounded by climbing roses, flaming poinsettia plants, and old cedars, the church is popular for candlelit weddings, and carol services are a holiday staple.

Kaleidoscope Art Foundation

Kaleidoscope Art Foundation (27 Jubilee Rd., tel. 441/542-9000, www.kaf.bm, 9am-5pm Mon.-Fri., 10am-2pm Sat., and by appointment, free) is tucked away in a rural corner just off Devonshire's main thoroughfare. Exhibitions by local and visiting artists are held throughout the year. The facility is used by studio artists and children who attend popular after-school and holiday camps.

Devonshire Marsh

Botanists and bug-lovers will want to visit **Devonshire Marsh** (sunrise-sunset daily, free), a protected wetland cradled in the Middle Road valley and once dubbed "Brackish Pond"—which became a popular nickname for the whole parish in centuries past. The **Firefly Nature Reserve** and the **Freer Cox Nature Reserve** form the Bermuda National Trust's 10-acre marsh and have been set aside as a special sanctuary for birds and other island fauna. Waterways meander through the marshland, leading past natural orchids and a wealth of insects and birdlife. Unlike Paget Marsh, it remains largely the realm of scientists and birders, as the ground is deep and boggy; to date, no boardwalks or educational signage have been erected to guide public visits. The grassy borders of the marsh are harvested for fodder for the island's dairy cows.

Palm Grove Gardens

Owned by the Gibbons family, the **Palm Grove Gardens** (38 South Shore Rd., tel. 441/295-0022, 9am-5pm Mon.-Thurs., free) is a beautifully landscaped 18-acre estate that stretches from the main road to the sea. It is private property but open to the public, and very popular for staging wedding photos thanks to its well-planted gardens and

a statue of the Greek god Pan, Palm Grove Gardens

statues, water lily ponds designed in the shape of a miniature map of the island, stunning night-blooming cereus, sago, coconut, and Canary Island palms, ivy-coated limestone huts (called butteries), and a traditional Bermuda moon gate—said to bestow good luck on newlyweds. There is also a tropical bird aviary with a collection of parrots. At the foot of sweeping lawns, rock pools sit before a reef-strewn shoreline.

Butterfly Garden at Brighton Nurseries

Budding naturalists will love a visit to the **Butterfly Garden at Brighton Nurseries** (2 Brighton Lane, Brighton Hill, tel. 441/236-5862, 8am-5pm Mon.-Sat.), where monarchs, red admirals, buckeyes, and other varieties, depending on the season, flutter among flowering plants in a specially created greenhouse.

Historic Military Buildings

A scattering of historic military buildings once used by the British Army can still be seen around the Fort Hill-North Shore area. At **Prospect,** former military barracks today belong to **Police Headquarters,** where the complex of buildings is used for offices and cadet training. An Edwardian officers' mess with views of Hamilton and the Great Sound is now the Police Recreation Club. On Fort Hill, the **Prospect Cemetery** contains the graves of soldiers posted on the island through the 19th and 20th centuries. Farther north, where Orange Valley meets Palmetto Road, an old military hospital, like the barracks displaying hallmark iron verandas, is now a government office building overlooking the North Shore.

BEACHES
Robinson's Bay
Below hilly Palmetto Park on North Shore Road (just west of the Palmetto Road roundabout), Robinson's Bay is a perfect place for a quick dip in the heat of summer, when parish children dive from the high rocky ledges into an azure natural swimming hole. With its rocky formations and reefy edges, there are several areas to swim and snorkel in the tiny bays amid yellowtail, butterfly fish, and striped sergeants major. As a child, I enjoyed many waterlogged birthday parties and after-school dips here. The property, now public and rather run-down, bears the telltale signs of British military use in years past: steps carved into the water at various points, natural stone bridges between rocky outcrops, and old changing huts made of thick limestone. Locals can often be found line-fishing off the rocks.

★ Devonshire Bay Park
Tucked away at the end of a narrow South Shore lane, Devonshire Bay Park is easy to miss, but this scenic little corner of Bermuda offers a perfect place to relax, swim, picnic, explore, and meet Bermudians who frequent a decidedly nontouristy venue. There's a clean beach fringed by baygrapes and palmettos, and the quiet bay is good for swimming, except on very windy days when surf rolls through the channel into the natural harbor. Nearby residents keep small boats here, as do fishers, who return to clean and sell their catch on weekday afternoons. Friday is usually a sure bet to find them chopping up fillets for a loyal crowd of customers. A hand-drawn sign is usually posted at the main road to advertise the catch.

One of Bermuda's many coastal fortifications, **Devonshire Bay Battery,** a rebuilt

Devonshire Bay Park

version of Brackish Pond Fort, as it was once known, is located here, on a promontory in the adjacent park. The original was built in the 1750s, a square-shaped redoubt with a parapet and a central magazine—what's left are now archaeological remains. Around the shoreline of the national park, bordered by boiler reefs, you can see the whole south coast and wade in pools where crabs, shrimp, and tiny jewel-like fish dart until high tide returns them to the ocean.

To get here, turn off South Road toward the sea on Devonshire Bay Road. Follow this hedge-lined residential lane a few hundred yards as it veers to a sharp right, then hugs the bay as it swings left again into a small parking area. From here, you can walk into the park.

SPORTS AND RECREATION

Devonshire has plenty to offer the active traveler, including a golf course, a spa that's become popular among locals, and several dedicated sports centers, but the parish is also full of outdoor spaces to exercise while enjoying nature.

Swimming, Diving, and Athletics

Site of the former National Stadium, the government's **Bermuda National Sports Centre** (65 Roberts Ave., off Parson's Rd., tel. 441/295-8085, www.bermudasportscentre.bm, pool 6:30am-7pm Mon.-Fri., 10am-5pm Sat.-Sun.) is the island's premier athletics and sporting venue, and has hosted numerous international events, including the 2012 CARIFTA Games and the NatWest Island Games in 2013. The South Field contains a 400-meter track, all-weather field hockey turf, a soccer pitch, and a 2,000-seat grandstand (Usain Bolt secured his junior world record title in the 200 meters—19.93 seconds—here in 2004). Usage fees for the main competition track are ($8 per day. The North Field hosts cricket, soccer, and rugby events. An aquatics facility offers a 50-meter eight-lane pool, 10-meter dive tower and springboards, and

lockers and changing rooms. Drop-in rates are $16 adults; passes are available. The nearby **Arboretum** provides perfect cross-country running terrain in a relaxing natural setting; you can make a workout of a track warmup followed by a few hilly loops of the park.

Railway Trail (Devonshire)

The Devonshire portion of the Railway Trail is one of the most panoramic stretches of this national park, with elevated, 180-degree views of the main shipping channel into the Great Sound and Hamilton Harbour. Much of the North Shore is visible, from Dockyard to Shelly Bay. It is a particularly good spot to watch cruise ships and tankers moving through the channel into port or back out to the open ocean. Starting at Barker's Hill (leave scooters in the roadside Ocean View Golf Club parking lot), you can trek a good mile along the shady tarmacadam path, past Loyal Hill Playground and historic Bermudian cottages such as Firefly Hall and through busy pastel-colored communities peppered with children, dogs, and clotheslines. The trail continues through Smith's, past more lush vegetation, all the way to Gibbet Beach and Flatts Inlet—an out-and-back run of about four miles to Barker's Hill, with a refreshing swim mid-route.

Golf

With a spectacular view of the North Shore channel, **Ocean View Golf Club** (2 Barker's Hill Rd., tel. 441/295-9092, bar tel. 441/335-2361, www.oceanviewgolfclub.com) is one of two government-owned courses, along with Port Royal. As a public course, it offers easier booking accessibility and lower pricing, as well as more opportunities for contact with locals. Well maintained, the nine-hole, 2,940-yard, par-35 course (with 18 tee positions for a double round) offers a leisurely though not challenging outing and is best suited to mid-handicappers. With a putting green, driving range, well-stocked pro shop (7am-6pm daily Apr.-Oct., 7am-5pm daily Nov.-Mar.), and a comfortable clubhouse with a well-run bar and restaurant, plus a panoramic terrace, the club offers friendly facilities close to Hamilton. All-day greens fees with a cart are $50, and club rentals (Nike, Callaway) are $25. Online tee time bookings are available, as are lessons with any of the four pros (1 hour $90, nine-hole lesson $200). The club offers reduced fees after 3pm. The dress code calls for collared shirts, Bermuda shorts or long trousers, and soft spikes.

Horseback Riding

With its relaxed country atmosphere, Devonshire is the perfect parish in which to go horseback riding, and it has a long equestrian history. The parish's wooded hills, paths, and valleys, as well as its scenic stretch of Railway Trail, provide rare peaceful paths for riding in Bermuda's overdeveloped environment.

Competitive harness pony racing is a popular event held most weekends September-May at the **National Equestrian Centre** (48 Vesey St., Bermuda Equestrian Federation president Michael Cherry tel. 441/234-0485, www.bef.bm, $6 over age 11, $4 seniors, free under age 12), headquarters of the Driving Horse & Pony Club of Bermuda. Formerly called the Vesey Street Racetrack, the center has an egg-shaped track, a few bleachers, restrooms, and a canteen open during races, which are held evenings (under lights) or Sunday afternoons and are usually advertised; days and times are posted on the federation's website. Horse shows are also held at the center, where local riders vie for honors in dressage, equitation, jumping, and show jumping. Weekend Bermuda Hunt Club events (minus the foxes) are also scheduled at various off-road venues through the winter.

Soccer and Cricket

Crowds flock to **Devonshire Recreation Club** (20 Frog Lane, tel. 441/292-5539), dubbed "Devonshire Rec," for evening and weekend soccer games (the resident team is the green-and-gold Cougars) throughout the fall and winter, and cricket showdowns all summer long. Few of the sports fans who party here may appreciate it, but the building that houses the club, with its billiards hall, bar, and canteen, is actually a historic Georgian structure, built in 1760 as one of the Dill family's ancestral homes.

Squash

Visitors can use the gym and play on any of four courts at the **Bermuda Squash Racquets Association** (111 Middle Rd., tel. 441/292-6881, www.bermudasquash.com, 10am-10pm Mon.-Fri., 10am-5pm Sat.-Sun.) for a 24-hour guest fee of $20. Contact the club if you need a partner. Lessons ($53 for 40 minutes during nonpeak hours) are available from club pros, including club director **Patrick Foster** (patrickf@bermudasquash.com), formerly on the pro squash tour. As well as showers, changing rooms, a show court with audience seating for 150, and a licensed bar, the club has a small air-conditioned gym with stationary bikes, ellipticals, and treadmills.

Spas

It looks like a roadside cottage, but in-the-know spa-goers choose **Gillian's** (14 South Shore Rd., tel. 441/232-0496, www.gilliansbermuda.com, 8:45am-9pm Mon.-Fri., 8:45am-5pm Sat.-Sun.) for its luxurious but low-key appeal. Inside, the ambience invites immediate relaxation: candles, soothing music, antique furniture, and heated neck collars upon arrival. Experienced therapists offer everything from hot stone massages (1 hour, $150) and detoxifying mud treatments (2 hours, $190), French manicures ($63), tanning, even teeth whitening. Pamper packages include a six-hour Pure Day of Heaven ($475) that might leave you never wanting to return to the real world.

ENTERTAINMENT AND EVENTS

Parish events are mostly of the sporting nature, including regular soccer and cricket matches at Devonshire Recreation Club, squash tournaments at the Bermuda Squash Racquets Association, and track and field and other events at the Bermuda National Sports Centre. Check *The Royal Gazette*, www.nothingtodoinbermuda.com, or www.gotobermuda.com for details of scheduled events.

Nightlife

Despite Devonshire's tranquility, there are a few parish bars, and all deliver very different nightlife experiences.

The Water Hazard bar at Ocean View Golf Club (2 Barkers Hill, tel. 441/335-2361, 11am-1am daily) is a friendly place to stop in to inhale the gorgeous North Shore view. Visitors are welcome at Police Recreation Club (Headquarters Hill, Prospect, bar tel. 441/299-4261, noon-11pm Mon., noon-1am Tues.-Sun.), where members of the Bermuda police service socialize after hours. Somewhat rowdier are Mid-Atlantic Boat & Sports Club (37 North Shore Rd., tel. 441/295-0172, happy hour 4pm-8pm Fri.) and the bar at Devonshire Recreation Club (20 Frog Lane, tel. 441/292-5539, 4pm-1am daily), with festivities peaking on Friday and Saturday nights.

World Rugby Classic

Launched in 1988, the popular World Rugby Classic (tel. 441/295-6574 or 441/278-1446, www.worldrugby.bm) attracts thousands to the Bermuda National Sports Centre at Prospect to watch a weeklong showdown of former top international players. Teams from around the world face off with stars such as Willie McBride, Matt Dawson, Olivier Roumat, and Joost van der Westhuizen; when she was living in Bermuda, Welsh-born actress Catherine Zeta-Jones used to turn up to support the Welsh team. Daily admission is $25, a five-day pass $100. VIP passes with access to hospitality tents where visiting players hang out and nonstop cocktail parties are hosted by corporate entities start at $175 per day. A five-day pass costs $700 pp or $1,200 per couple.

Bermuda Marathon Weekend

Hundreds of locals and visitors take part in this mid-January weekend's quartet of Bermuda Marathon Weekend (tel. 441/737-8850, runbermuda@gmail.com, www.bermudaraceweekend.com) events: an international marathon, a half-marathon, a 10K run and walk, and the Front Street Mile. Many competitors take on the Bermuda Triangle Challenge—"three races in three days." The 10K starts and finishes at Devonshire's Bermuda National Sports Centre; all other events take place on Front Street in Hamilton.

Other Events

Held at Bermuda Botanical Gardens during the last week of April, the three-day Bermuda Agricultural Exhibition (tel. 441/524-7469, www.theagshowbda.com) features equestrian events, acrobats, and school displays, and has become a beloved institution.

SHOPPING

With no central community or village, Devonshire is not a shopper's paradise. One quirky exception is The Barn (53 Devon Spring Rd., tel. 441/236-3155, 9am-2pm Tues., Thurs., and Sat.), a bargain hunter's treasure trove, spilling over with secondhand toys, collectibles, and an impressive stock of books, from vintage and just-released fiction to kids' mystery series from the 1970s and 1980s. Nothing costs more than a few dollars. The nonprofit facility raises funds for several island charities. Opposite the Barn stands Bermuda's other hospital, the Mid-Atlantic Wellness Institute, a psychiatric treatment facility.

FOOD
Cafés and Takeout

Sammy's Kitchen (Mid-Atlantic Boat & Sports Club, 34 North Shore Rd., office tel. 441/295-0172, kitchen tel. 441/296-2697, 11am-11pm Mon.-Sat., 8am-midnight Sun., $8-18) serves up chicken, burgers, and island comfort food like peas 'n' rice and macaroni 'n' cheese during the week and draws a loud, jovial bar crowd on Friday nights. But the roadside club is best known for its authentic Sunday-morning codfish and potatoes breakfasts, appreciated by club members and other regulars who gather here for a laid-back café-style spread at the popular social and boating club, a few feet from the water's edge. Be warned: Breakfast starts early and only lasts "until it's all gone."

Take in a bird's-eye view of the North Shore seascape at **Sunset Grill** (Ocean View Golf Club, 2 Barker's Hill Rd., tel. 441/335-2361, 8am-3pm daily, $7-16). The licensed club bar, Water Hazard, and the restaurant have a full breakfast menu (eggs, pancakes, meats) and a lunchtime offering of soups, salads, shrimp po'boys, and vegetarian wraps. Golfers, caddies, locals, and visitors also drop in for tasty nibbles such as popcorn shrimp, codfish balls, and conch fritters. The restaurant has an inside dining area, but the best tables are on the terrace overlooking the greens and the azure swath of ocean beyond. Locals swarm here for an out-of-town happy hour (5pm-8pm Fri.).

Perennial winner of Bermuda's "Best Fish Sandwich," **Seaside Grill** (81 North Shore Rd., tel. 441/292-1241, noon-10pm Mon.-Fri., 8am-1pm Sun., $6-16) has made a name for itself with a menu of fresh-caught turbot steaks, mahimahi sandwiches, and wahoo nuggets in a bright turquoise roadside takeout. Sandwich purveyors can choose wheat, white, or rye and select their choice of toppings. The taste is universally thumbs-up.

Esso Collector's Hill Tigermarket (65 South Shore Rd., next to Collector's Hill, tel. 441/236-6574, 6am-11pm daily) might qualify as the island's friendliest petrol stop. Cheery staff and a well-stocked convenience store make the facility a popular way station for motorists and neighborhood regulars. Along with corner store-style sundries, the store is also home to **Buzz N Go Collector's Hill**, serving a full menu of hot and cold deli items, including omelets, wraps, paninis, and specialty coffees. You can enjoy your refreshment on-site; grab a stool at the people-watching window counter.

If you want a taste of true Bermuda and better than anything imported into the grocery aisles, don't miss the Saturday farm stand run by **J&J Produce** (foot of Brighton Hill at South Rd., tel. 441/236-8616, 7:30am-4:30pm Sat.). Husband and wife Junior and Patty Hill's cornucopia of seasonal fruits and vegetables includes sweet Bermuda onions, bananas, pumpkins, kale, quail eggs, and goat, plus sunflowers, lilies, and snapdragons in the spring.

Grocery Stores

Belvin's Variety (1 Vesey St., tel. 441/236-6644, 6am-midnight daily) stocks beer, liquor, dry goods, and frozen goods, and also sells fresh-baked hot beef, chicken, and mussel pies. **Empire Grocery** (12 North Shore Rd., tel. 441/292-0277 or 441/295-2625, 8am-6pm Mon.-Thurs., 8am-8pm Fri.-Sat.) has been part of the North Shore community since 1927 when the DeSilva family first opened its doors. Relatives still run the friendly, efficient convenience store, packed with "as much as we can fit," says an employee. That includes liquor, beer, grocery products, and deli meats.

Lindo's Market (4 Watlington Rd. E., tel. 441/236-5623, www.lindos.bm, 8am-7pm Mon., Tues., and Thurs., 8am-8pm Wed., Fri., and Sat.) is the only major supermarket in Devonshire, and one of the island's biggest and best-stocked. Owned by the Italian Bermudian Zanol family, the modern floor space includes a harvest of organic foods and Bermuda-grown produce, cheeses from around the world, wine, magazines, and a good fish and meat department with fresh-caught Bermuda wahoo and tuna and traditional Bermuda codfish cakes. There is also a large hot and cold deli counter, serving up fish cakes, mac 'n' cheese, sandwiches, and other goodies Monday-Saturday.

ACCOMMODATIONS

Devonshire currently has no guest houses or hotels, although plans are perennially discussed to redevelop **Ariel Sands Resort** (34 South Shore Rd.), closed since 2008 and co-owned by actor Michael Douglas, a member of one of the island's oldest clans, the Dills.

INFORMATION AND SERVICES

Lindo's Pharmacy (inside Lindo's Market, 4 Watlington Rd. E., tel. 441/236-7732, pharmacy@lindos.bm, 8am-7pm Mon.-Tues. and Thurs., 8am-8pm Wed. and Fri.-Sat.) is a handy stop-in located inside the main grocery store, just left of the entrance.

Devonshire Post Office (2 Orange Valley Rd., tel. 441/236-0281, 8am-5pm Mon.-Fri.) has helpful staff. There is plenty of parking and free public Internet access. **ATMs** are located at Lindo's Market, on Watlington Road, and Esso Collector's Hill Tigermarket. **Public toilets** are located at the Bermuda National Sports Centre, the Arboretum, Robinson's Bay, and area restaurants.

TRANSPORTATION
Buses

Regular bus service runs every half hour through Devonshire between Hamilton and Grotto Bay (route 3) in Hamilton Parish via Middle Road, Devil's Hole, and the caves, making for convenient sightseeing transport. Other Devonshire bus routes include South Shore Road (route 1) between Hamilton and St. George's every half hour via Spittal Pond and the Tucker's Town golf courses, and North Shore Road (routes 10 and 11) to and from St. George's every 15 minutes via the aquarium and Bailey's Bay. Bus fare to Devonshire falls into the three-zone tariff ($3.50 adults, $2.75 ages 5-16, free under 5, exact change or tokens, tickets, or passes required). Transfers are free.

Ferries

There is no ferry service to or from Devonshire.

Taxis

With no taxi stands, hailing a cab in Devonshire is hard work. A better strategy is to order one online via the **Hitch app** (www.hitch.bm) or call one of the cab companies to arrange a pickup: **Bermuda Industrial Union Co-op** (tel. 441/292-4476, coop-taxi@fkbnet.bm), **Bermuda Island Taxi** (tel. 441/295-4141, www.bermudaislandtaxi.com), or **BTA Dispatching** (tel. 441/296-2121, www.btadispatching.com).

Scooters and Bicycles

There are no livery services based in Devonshire, but scooter rental companies provide a free shuttle service to their nearest outlets in Hamilton or Paget.

Paget Parish

Hemmed by the South Shore on one side and Hamilton Harbour on the other, most of Paget is in a band of land across the harbor from Pembroke and the city. On the outskirts of Hamilton, Paget is a bustling community that many commute through. The river of traffic has brought noise and congestion, but beyond the main thoroughfares, Paget's charm endures in the beauty of its historic places, family estates, nature reserves, beaches, and meandering harbor front.

Off the South Shore Road, for example, take a neighborhood lane and feel the traffic turbulence evaporate into the sound of blue surf instead. Take Middle Road, bordered by elegant old homes and their impossibly green gardens, or dawdle down narrow lanes that roll into valleys or over hills. There's plenty to occupy a visitor who wants to be busy in Paget—restaurants, bars, sports facilities, and events.

Named for William Paget, the fourth Lord of Paget, the parish has seen modern amenities built or improved in the last decade, and

Paget Parish

Balmont Golf Course

Hinson's Island

Spectacle Island

Doctor's Island

WARWICK PARISH

HARBOUR

MIDDLE RD

COBBS HILL RD

ORD RD

SOUTH RD

Railway Trail

Salt Kettle Bay

Salt Kettle

CORNER SHOP

NVEURIE EXECUTIVE SUITES

FOURWAYS COTTAGE COLONY

GREENBANK GUESTHOUSE AND COTTAGES

HODGSON'S FERRY

BEAU RIVAGE RESTAURANT AND BAR

NEWSTEAD RESORT & SPA

CHAPEL RD

SHORE RD

White's Island

Hamilton Harbour

PEMBROKE PARISH

City of Hamilton

PITTS BAY RD

FRONT ST

CHURCH ST

DUNDONALD ST

RUBIS PAGET SERVICE STATION

ST. PAUL'S ANGLICAN CHURCH

OLEANDER CYCLES

LOWER FERRY

PAGET MARSH

POST OFFICE

ICE QUEEN

PAGET PHARMACY

PARAQUET RESTAURANT

THYME

MODERN MART

GRAPE BAY DR

CORAL BEACH & TENNIS CLUB

ELBOW BEACH

ELBOW BEACH HOTEL/ ELBOW BEACH CYCLES/ CAFÉ LIDO/SEABREEZE LOUNGE/ MICKEY'S BAR & BISTRO

COCO REEF RESORT

GRAPE BAY COTTAGES

RENDEZVOUS COTTAGE

Grape Bay Beach

PAGET PARISH

STOWE HILL

THE BIRDSEY STUDIO

TRIMINGHAM RD

POMANDER RD

Red Hole

POMANDER GATE TENNIS CLUB

WATERVILLE

POINT FINGER ROAD PHARMACY

PINK CAFÉ

CLARIEN BANK

FT. FINGER RD

BERMUDA BOTANICAL GARDENS

CAMDEN HOUSE

King Edward VII Memorial Hospital

Crow Lane Park

BERRY HILL RD

MIDDLE RD

MASTERWORKS MUSEUM OF BERMUDA ART

ARBORETUM

HOMER'S CAFÉ

DEVONSHIRE PARISH

SOUTH RD

SHORE RD

TEE ST

Hungry Bay

ATLANTIC OCEAN

0   0.25 km
0   0.25 mi

© AVALON TRAVEL

today it has hotels, acclaimed restaurants, high-end spas, tennis courts, and an 18-hole golf course.

SIGHTS

★ Bermuda Botanical Gardens

Bermuda's most visited and historic park, the **Bermuda Botanical Gardens** (183 South Rd., bus routes 1, 2, and 7, tel. 441/236-5902, sunrise-sunset daily, free) encompass 36 acres of rolling lawns, horticultural halls boasting orchids and cacti, and myriad outdoor gardens planted with exotica (ficus, rubber, and cotton trees) and down-home varieties (medicinal herbs).

Opened in 1898, the original "Public Gardens" totaled just 10 acres. They were renamed and expanded to their current size in 1965, when the government bought the Camden estate to the east from the Tucker family. Since then, specimens from around the world have been gathered and planted here, making the property the biggest and best natural showcase of both endemic and nonnative flora on the island.

Highlights of the gardens in the North Gate area include a cacti hillside, with alien-looking aloes, agaves, and other succulents that occasionally sprout spectacular blossoms; a collection of subtropical native conifers, including Bermuda's own cedar; and a "blue garden" featuring plants with blue fruit, flowers, or foliage. Behind Camden House, a display developed in 2006 showcases a kitchen garden, with edibles and cut flowers; an economic garden, with tobacco, arrowroot, cotton, and indigo, which early settlers cultivated for trade; and medicinal herbs used in old-time Bermuda. This area also has aviaries with peacocks, ducks, and parrots, and a delightful walled rose garden, one of Bermuda's best.

Hilly lawns spill down from Camden to South Road, peppered with mature trees such as acacias and cedars. Bordering the top lawns are wide beds planted with colorful lilies, freesias, and dahlias. This was where John Lennon saw a freesia named "Double Fantasy" during a 1980 visit to the island, inspiring Lennon's album of that name.

The western section of the gardens contains a wealth of miniature environments, from butterfly and maze gardens to subtropical fruit and palm collections to mammoth rubber and ficus trees. There is also a lovely

rubber trees in the Bermuda Botanical Gardens

Camden House

An elegant landmark visible from South Road atop the Bermuda Botanical Gardens' rolling lawns, government-owned **Camden House** (183 South Rd., tel. 441/236-5732, noon-4pm Tues. and Fri., free) is worth a visit. The 18th-century mansion has an imposing wooden facade with a two-story veranda offering sweeping views of the distant sea. Camden House is sometimes described as Bermuda's counterpart to 10 Downing Street or the White House (and yes, it is white), but the head of government doesn't live here; the building is used for occasional public events and VIP receptions. Princess Margaret, Colin Powell, Margaret Thatcher, and Jesse Jackson have all dined here.

Camden House is an example of Georgian architecture, with some additions completed between 1714 and 1830. The first owner of the house, Francis Jones, died of yellow fever in 1795. The home was passed to the Tucker family, and Hamilton mayor Henry James Tucker lived here until his death in 1870. It was during this time that an arrowroot factory was opened in buildings behind the main house, now the headquarters of the Masterworks Foundation. In 1966, Camden House was sold to the government as part of the Bermuda Botanical Gardens; the huge facing property on South Road is still owned by Tucker descendants.

Camden's interior, including plumbing, upholstery, and woodwork—and mountains of cedar—have been refurbished. In the dining room, which features carved paneling that reportedly took a mid-1800s cabinetmaker 30 years to finish, ornate walls set off a stunning hand-carved Bermuda cedar table and chairs to seat 22; boîte-like powder rooms recall a gentler age of tea parties and parasols; and expansive drawing rooms and studies, accented by historic antiques, artwork, books, crystal chandeliers, and gilded mirrors, make this one of the finest restored homes. One special feature on carved panels is the bird's-eye cedar, prized for its eye-catching grain. The William and

walled "sensory garden" planted with rosemary, jasmine, and other scented flora, with a gurgling fountain in the center, and several slat houses containing orchids, bromeliads, ferns, and cacti. Another interesting feature nearby is a tiny whitewashed Bermuda cottage, built for the 2001 Smithsonian Folklife Festival to showcase island architecture. Thousands of Bermudians come to the gardens every April for the three-day **Bermuda Agricultural Show,** a cultural and agricultural fair that's one of the island's biggest events.

The gardens are maintained by the government's Department of Parks. There are four entrances: North Gate (Berry Hill Rd.), South Gate (183 South Rd.), Peace Lutheran Gate (opposite that church), and West Gate (pedestrians only, Point Finger Rd.) next to the King Edward VII Memorial Hospital's modern Acute Care Wing. The **visitors center** (9am-5pm Mon.-Fri.) has restrooms; it's near North Gate, but can be accessed from any entrance.

Painters in Paradise

Bermuda is a place "to hide and hush," wrote American painter Marsden Hartley after a 1917 visit—a sentiment that would have found favor with other art-world luminaries, including Winslow Homer, Georgia O'Keeffe, and Charles Demuth, who all found the island a calm and creative inspiration.

Scores of artists have made their way to Bermuda, finding respite from real-world challenges in the island's sea, sun, tropical colors, unusual light, flora and fauna, and human personalities. In the process, many found fresh energy to paint and draw, reviving stalled careers or launching new artistic avenues.

O'Keeffe recovered from a nervous breakdown during her 1933-1934 sojourns in Somerset, where she eschewed her typical explosive colors for charcoal sketches of banana flowers and banyan trees. Fauvist E. Ambrose Webster (1869-1935) was struck by the island's palette of purples, blues, and oranges, which he used to capture evocative landscapes as well as bold portraits of native Bermudians. And Homer, one of the most influential American painters of the 20th century, enjoyed exploring the coastline when he visited Bermuda in 1899 and 1900, recording his sightseeing in 21 known watercolors of the island, which he proclaimed "as good an example as I have ever done."

Today works made in Bermuda are being brought back to the island thanks to the Masterworks Foundation, a nonprofit connected to the Masterworks Museum of Bermuda Art that opened in Paget's Bermuda Botanical Gardens in 2008. Among the 1,000 artworks are two O'Keeffe charcoals; two of Homer's seascapes, *Inland Water* and *Bermuda (The S.S. Trinidad)*; an Andrew Wyeth street scene of St. George's (*Royal Palms*); Ross Sterling Turner's impressionist views of gardens and neighborhood cottages; and photographer Karl Struss's three-dimensional color record of a postwar island in the 1950s.

Mary cushion-molded mirror over the dining-room fireplace is also worth a close look.

★ Masterworks Museum of Bermuda Art

Opened in 2008, the **Masterworks Museum of Bermuda Art** (MMBA, Arrowroot Bldg., Bermuda Botanical Gardens, 183 South Rd., tel. 441/299-4000, www.bermudamasterworks.org, 10am-4pm Mon.-Sat., $5, free under age 12) is the brainchild of the Masterworks Foundation, an indefatigable nonprofit that repatriates Bermuda artworks by famous artists, including Winslow Homer, Georgia O'Keeffe, and Charles Demuth, among an impressive collection of more than 1,000 paintings, drawings, photographs, maps, and memorabilia, much of it now showcased in the $9 million museum. Housed in a former arrowroot-processing factory, the complex comprises three gallery spaces, a book collection, and the aptly named **Homer's Café.** Next to it, the **Arrowroot**

Gift Shop is one of the best places to find Bermuda cedar artifacts, such as goblets, trays, and other authentic Bermuda gifts. The museum features outdoor sculptures, including a life-size moose and a stylized steel tribute to John Lennon's 1980 Bermuda visit and his resulting album, *Double Fantasy,* named for a freesia in the park. Masterworks has become a showcase for contemporary Bermuda artists as well. The foundation has an active calendar of outreach and educational programs, including art camps for kids, painters' picnics, and openings for temporary shows; check the schedule on its website.

Crow Lane

Crow Lane Park (sunrise-sunset daily, free), at the foot of Corkscrew Hill near the parish boundary with Devonshire, has a small lawn tucked along the water side of Foot of the Lane, the bottom of Hamilton Harbour. It's a good place for picnics or watching the sunset. A multitude of small pleasure craft are moored here next to the mangroves. Despite the sunny surroundings, the park has a sordid history. In 1730, enslaved Sally Bassett was publicly executed by burning here after being accused of poisoning a slave-owning Sandys couple (her bronze statue now stands in the grounds of the Cabinet Building on Front Street). Her case was the most notorious of many so-called poison plots used as a form of rebellion by slaves who practiced the religious art of Obeah. Bassett has been remembered in island folklore, and the park is now one of the sights on the African Diaspora Trail through the island.

A bronze statue of **Johnny Barnes,** who died at age 93 in 2016, was erected while he lived to greets motorists driving into Hamilton, near the Crow Lane roundabout where he stood every morning, rain or shine, for close to three decades. Barnes became a beloved national icon for waving rigorously to passerby, shouting out loudly, "I love you!" While many thought Johnny was nuts when he first began his morning ritual in the 1980s, commuters came to expect and even look forward to his beaming face. The statue, a gesture by area citizens to honor his goodwill, was established in 1996 along the garden verge at the start of East Broadway.

★ Waterville

A rambling 1725 homestead set on parkland that curls around the foot of the harbor, **Waterville** (corner of The Lane and Pomander Rd., tel. 441/236-6483, www.bnt. bm, 9am-5pm Mon.-Fri., free) is the headquarters of the Bermuda National Trust (BNT). Its elegant Georgian proportions make for instant time travel back to the 18th century. Somber oil portraits grace the walls in the lounge and dining room near the trellised entrance, and antiques, china, and a grandfather clock carry visitors back to early Bermuda. Originally a private home, Waterville belonged to the prominent Trimingham family, dating back centuries. Waterville's gardens and surrounding park are even more stunning. The **Heritage Rose Garden,** established in 1988 by the Bermuda Rose Society and showcasing many old Bermuda varieties, lights up the front lawn. Waterville Park includes a Victorian-style wooden gazebo—perfect for a picnic—and Duck Island, a low mangrove-covered islet where herons and waterfowl nest and ducks alight on the boats moored at Foot of the Lane. Neighborhood boaters access their vessels via this park, making it a hive of activity on summer weekends. A dirt path winds

Waterville, the historic Bermuda National Trust headquarters

John Lennon in Bermuda

Bermuda has reestablished a fascinating connection with John Lennon's legacy. The former Beatle spent the final summer of his life on the island—a two-month sojourn in June-July 1980 that's been credited as a creative reawakening of the star who had stepped away from his career in 1975 to spend time raising his son. Lennon sailed to Bermuda from Newport, Rhode Island, on a storm-wracked sailboat, landing in St. George's before he rented a home in Fairylands, Pembroke. He began to write again, and during a visit to the Botanical Gardens, he was inspired by a flower bed sign bearing the fanciful name of a freesia—"Double Fantasy." The moniker would become the title of his comeback album, recorded in New York just three weeks before he was fatally shot on December 8, 1980.

"I thought, 'Double Fantasy—that's a great title!' because it's got so many meanings that you couldn't begin to think what it meant. It means everything you can think of," Lennon said in an RKO radio interview recorded the day he died. Bermuda-based journalist Scott Neil, author of a 2012 book, *Bermuda Fantasy: John Lennon's Island Journey,* said Lennon benefited from the laid-back ambiance of the island. "Here, he was to reignite his songwriting talent, finding inspiration in his new surroundings," says Neil. "He worked on and refined the last songs he would ever write." Sounds from Bermuda can be heard in a number of the songs on both of Lennon's posthumous albums with Yoko, *Double Fantasy* and *Milk & Honey,* including the lapping of waves on a beach in the track "Beautiful Boy," which also features steel drums.

In 2012, musician-entrepreneur Tony Brannon (www.doublefantasybermuda.com)—who saw Lennon when the rock star visited his nightclub, Front Street's 40 Thieves & Disco 40, during the singer's 1980 visit—staged a "Peace Concert" tribute in the Botanical Gardens' show ring on Peace Day, September 21. Filmmaker Michael Epstein directed *John Lennon: The Bermuda Tapes,* an interactive album app chronicling the 1980 visit that was released in 2013 to benefit a global antihunger campaign. The Masterworks Museum gave its own kudos in the form of a commemorative steel sculpture created by Bermudian artist Graham Foster that incorporates mirror images of doves, blossoms, and Lennon's distinctive profile. The circular 4,000-pound structure welcomes visitors into the museum at the gardens—just yards away from where Lennon spied the fateful freesia's name.

through thick cherry hedges along the waterfront and past an old horse-watering station to the main-road sidewalk.

Pomander Road

Meander by scooter or on foot along the quaint harborside edging Pomander Road, a one-way residential lane that slips off the bustle of The Lane into yesteryear. Ducks paddle past the mangroves and moored pleasure boats and grassy nooks invite roadside picnics.

Despite its tranquility, there are a few businesses along the loop back to Harbour Road. **Aberfeldy Nurseries** (3 Pomander Rd., at The Lane, tel. 441/236-2927), one of the oldest and largest plant retailers, is a good place to look at hundreds of the island's endemic and ornamental garden plants. Farther west along

The Lane is the waterfront Little Pomander Guest House. Opposite sits **Pomander Gate Tennis Club** (Pomander Lane, tel. 441/236-5400, www.pgtc.bm).

At the junction of Pomander and Harbour Roads is the **Royal Hamilton Amateur Dinghy Club** (tel. 441/236-2250, www.rhadc.bm), cosponsor of the biennial Marion Bermuda Race and home to hundreds of motorboats. Hugged by the serpentine main road, **Red Hole** is the name for the sheltered bay here, home to a working boatyard and a tiny beach where dinghies used to ferry boat-owners to their yachts are pulled up on the sand at low tide.

The Birdsey Studio

Anyone who met Alfred Birdsey (1912-1996) would not easily forget him. The prolific unassuming painter welcomed thousands of visitors over the years to his Paget studio, where he often treated them to tea and a chat, no matter whether any art changed hands. Renowned outside Bermuda, his impressionistic Asian-influenced brushstrokes of island landscapes, yachts, harbors, and backstreets revolutionized the way Bermuda was captured in art and caught the imagination of collectors worldwide. Today his daughter, Jo Birdsey-Linberg, carries on the family tradition at **The Birdsey Studio** (Rosecote, 5 Stowe Hill, tel. 441/236-6658, linberg@ northrock.bm, by appointment). Like her father, she breaks artistic conventions—and makes guests feel entirely at home. Her breezy watercolor landscapes and whimsical animal portraits—popular children's gifts—range $80-450; oils are $400 and up. The studio is located in the back garden amid roses, lilies, cacti, and pawpaw trees. Birdsey-Linberg, a Latin scholar and musician, can be found here most weekday mornings with her "assistant managers"—three miniature dachshunds.

★ Paget Marsh

A 25-acre natural wetland lying in the ample valley between the South Shore and Hamilton Harbour, **Paget Marsh** (Lovers Lane, off South Rd., sunrise-sunset daily, free) is jointly owned and managed by the Bermuda National Trust and Bermuda Audubon Society. A highlight on any island ecotour, the marsh was long neglected and inaccessible until 1998, when an innovative conservation project recreated the pond, rid the area of much nonendemic plantlife, and encouraged the return of birds. The entrance is on Lovers Lane near the South Road junction; head down the steep hill and park at the bottom, where banana groves and adjacent agricultural lands form a barrier against the nearby intersection. Renovated signage on birdlife and plantlife leads the way to a wooden boardwalk that winds through the mangroves into the marsh. Benches have been built into the walkway at intervals.

Paget Marsh is essentially a remnant from a previous era, with much of its interior virtually untouched. As a result, it is home to centuries-old stands of cedar and palmetto, ancient mangroves, native wax myrtles, and Bermuda sedge, unique to the island and found only in this reserve. All are sustained by a primordial anchor of peat, which also serves to keep down the mosquitoes. The marsh supports varied birdlife, including green and night herons, great egrets, kingfishers, moorhens, and yellow-throated warblers, which feed on the abundance of insects and larvae. The wetland is also a breeding ground for the giant toad, which was introduced to Bermuda in 1885.

The marsh consists of several interesting microhabitats. Ancient red mangroves overhang the first section, their distinctive boughs and prop roots creating a tunnel-like effect over the walkway. With the water glistening around their silver root tangle, they represent relics from an era when the marsh was a tidal saltwater pond. This first section of the marsh is flooded, and ducks and other waterfowl can be seen here gathering food. Moving forward, huge vine-covered cedars, rustling palmettos, giant ferns, and bulrushes create a thick forest wall on both sides, but as the creaky boardwalk turns a corner, there emerges an open area of sawgrass savannah, similar to the Florida Everglades. This is a seasonally flooded area, where heavy rains drastically raise water levels in the winter. The boardwalk's end, reaching into the belly of the marsh, brings you to forests of original cedars and palmettos—a scene not unlike what the first settlers would have encountered in 1612. In the shade of these trees grow cinnamon, royal, and sword ferns, along with southern bracken and rare sedge. Environmentalists constantly cull invasive species such as the guava, Brazilian pepper, and Chinese fan palm to preserve the reserve's important endemic populations.

Visible from Paget Marsh is the silver spire of **St. Paul's Anglican Church** (Middle Rd. at Valley Rd., tel. 441/236-5880), an area landmark. Inside the church are beautiful stained-glass windows, old wooden pews, and cedar accents; outside, a historic graveyard with cedars and bougainvillea contains whitewashed tombs.

Salt Kettle

The spirits of pirates and privateers inhabit the tidy pastel lanes of Salt Kettle, home to Bermudian mariners and merchants over hundreds of years. Turn off Harbour Road onto Salt Kettle Road and follow it down into the intriguing promontory, which is now laden with historic homesteads, waterside gardens, and picturesque bays, all invested with the island's maritime history. A guest property is located here, **Greenbank Guest House & Cottages.** The Paget-Warwick ferry stops regularly at the public dock at the farthest point.

TOP EXPERIENCE

BEACHES
★ Elbow Beach

Originally called Elba Beach, before the Elbow Beach Hotel opened its doors in 1908, this prime stretch of South Shore strand curves a good half mile, incorporates two other private beachfront properties (Coco Reef Resort and Coral Beach & Tennis Club) as well as a public section, accessible by Tribe Road 48. Signs point to the beach from the main South Shore Road. Since all Bermuda beaches are public below the high-tide mark, locals enjoy this one just as much as resort guests—joggers, swimmers, and snorkelers can use the entire length. Elbow is a popular site for kitesurfers when the wind swings around to the south, and beach tennis and volleyball tournaments are held on the sand near the public steps. Elbow's clean, soft sand, cerulean breakers, and mostly gentle surf (hurricane season notwithstanding) make it perfect for all swimming abilities, but there are no lifeguards at the public section. Even if you're not a guest at the Elbow Beach Hotel, you can purchase a day pass ($100), which provides two deck chairs, an umbrella, and waiter service from the beachside bar and bistro, Mickey's. There are also restrooms and an outdoor shower for guests at the hotel's beachfront.

SPORTS AND RECREATION

Paget is one of the sportiest parishes, packed with running trails, tennis galore, volleyball,

Elbow Beach

water sports like kayaking and kitesurfing, and a scuba and snorkeling outlet.

Railway Trail (Paget)

It's hard to get away from traffic in Bermuda, and Paget's busy, hilly, narrow roads—major thoroughfares to and from Hamilton—often lack sidewalks and are far from ideal for running and walking. The Railway Trail is a flat, shady footpath cutting through scenic neighborhoods. The Paget portion of the trail starts at the top of Trimingham Hill on South Road, where signs and a crosswalk lead to the entrance. Passing through a short tunnel and between thick limestone cuts in the hillside, the trail runs past Grape Bay, with wide-open views of Paget Marsh and the City of Hamilton's skyline beyond. Although the trail occasionally hits tarmacadam sections and has to cross a couple of main roads—be extremely careful of the blind-corner crossing just west of the Paget traffic lights near Modern Mart—it soon enters a long, wide, tranquil stretch that passes through thick cherry woods and past farmers' fields and spice forests, leading to Warwick and beyond. If you keep going, you can actually make it all the way to Mangrove Bay in Sandys.

Tennis

Paget resort properties have tennis courts that can be rented by nonguests at an hourly rate. There are five Plexipave hard courts at **Elbow Beach Hotel** (30 South Shore Rd., tel. 441/236-3535, tennis shop tel. 441/236-8737, www.elbowtennisbda.com, 9am-6pm daily); two of these have floodlights for night play. Resident pros include David Lambert—Bermuda's Davis Cup team coach—his wife, Barbara, and champion daughters Tara and Jackie, who all give lessons (1 hour, $85). The pro shop has a restroom and stocks balls, outfits, cold drinks, and snacks. Racquets can be rented or strung here. Court fees are $15 (1 hour) or $20 with lights. For competitive play, call to set up a game or hit-up session with available top local players (only court fees apply).

Coral Beach & Tennis Club (34 South Shore Rd., tennis shop tel. 441/239-7223, www.coralbeachclub.com) is a private club with eight Har-Tru courts monitored to ATP standards. Three courts have floodlights. Visitors who are not club members can book lessons ($100 per hour, $60 half-hour) or games with club members. The tennis shop stocks clothing emblazoned with the club's insignia, plus balls. Racquets can be rented. Note that all-white tennis attire is required. Several club pros give private or group coaching.

Tiny **Pomander Gate Tennis Club** (Pomander Lane, tel. 441/236-5400, www.pgtc.bm) is nestled in a quiet harbor-front neighborhood, with its clubhouse and five hard courts the headquarters for several annual local tournaments. Court fees are $35 per couple per week for nonmembers, allowing weeklong use of courts during nonpeak hours. Per-usage fees are $6 for a court rental, $7 with lights for night play.

Spas

The Spa at Elbow Beach (Elbow Beach Hotel, 60 South Shore Rd., tel. 441/239-8900, fax 441/239-8906, www.elbowbeachbermuda.com, 9am-6pm daily), is one of Bermuda's most luxurious resort spas. Six private treatment suites (four single and two for couples) offer granite soaking tubs, pebble-lined showers, and glittering ocean views from private balconies. Thai, Balinese, and Tibetan influences permeate the spa, located off the hotel pool area. Treatments include the Rum Swizzle Ritual—yes, the cocktail comes with it, along with a full body scrub, bath, and massage (3 hours, $435); the Ocean Body Wrap (1.5 hours, $125); and the Holistic Facial (2 hours, $229). Forty-eight-hour advance bookings are recommended.

With an elegant setting at the Newstead Resort & Spa on the Paget shore of Hamilton Harbour, **Newstead Spa & Salon** (27 Harbour Rd., tel. 441/249-7119, www.newsteadbelmonthills.com, 9am-6pm daily) has four treatment rooms, a couples suite, a wet room, a lounge, and a hair salon. Treatments

Home and Garden Tours

Sotheby's antiques. Mystery roses by the dozen. Art by Warhol, Rembrandt, and El Greco. These are the treasures to be found at the ancestral homes that welcome visitors every spring in the popular **Open Houses and Gardens,** organized by the **Garden Club of Bermuda** (tel. 441/234-2455, www.gardenclubbermuda.org) and showcasing different parishes whose elegant, sometimes extravagant properties provide a behind-the-scenes look at privileged Bermuda. A half dozen or so homes throw open their doors to the public one day a year to raise money for club scholarships given to Bermudians studying horticulture or the environment. The homes and gardens selected are usually in the same neighborhood, so visitors can walk easily among them. While centuries-old homes and no-holds-barred interior design make for eye-popping walkabouts, visitors will usually find the featured gardens no less spectacular. Feel free to photograph the flora and outdoor areas; no photography is allowed inside the homes. Check the club's tour brochures, distributed annually to hotels, guesthouses, and www.gotobermuda. com, for details. Private tours are also organized throughout the year ($100 up to 4 people, $25 per additional person).

include hot stone massage (1.5 hours, $219); Indian head massage (45 minutes, $99); and waxing, eyelash and eyebrow tints as well as mani-pedis for adults and kids. Half-day (4 hours, $550) and evening packages are also offered, with use of the steam rooms included.

ENTERTAINMENT AND EVENTS

Social butterflies will feel at home in Paget, home to numerous restaurants, bars, and popular cultural events.

Nightlife

An Ibiza-style party draws see-and-be-seen crowds to "The Big Chill" (www.the-big-chill. com) Friday nights at **Seabreeze Lounge** (Elbow Beach Hotel, 60 South Shore Rd., tel. 441/232-3999 or 441/236-9884, 5pm-midnight daily May-Oct.), where a panoramic terrace off the Café Lido complex offers views of Elbow Beach edged by coconut palms. DJ Felix Tod joins soulful vocalist Kassie Caines and guitarist TonyB at this tapas night-turned-dance party that provides a popular happy hour. Make a reservation days in advance or you won't get a seat.

On the beach below, **Mickey's Bar & Bistro** (Elbow Beach Hotel, 60 South Shore

Rd., tel. 441/236-9107, 10am-1am daily May-Oct., 10am-6pm Sat.-Sun. Nov.-Apr.) is a popular venue for a romantic glass of wine or a beachside hangout with friends.

Beau Rivage Restaurant & Bar (Newstead/Belmont Hills Golf Resort & Spa, 27 Harbour Rd., tel. 441/232-8686, http://beaurivagebda.com, 1pm-9pm daily) offers one of the best alfresco sunset-spying spots, with sweeping views of Hamilton Harbour beyond the resort's infinity pool.

The **Peg Leg Bar** (Fourways Inn, 1 Middle Rd., tel. 441/236-6517, www.fourways.bm, 6pm-midnight daily) is as irresistible as its name, with an authentically historic and snug British pub-like interior. It is often booked for private parties, so call ahead.

Bermuda Agricultural Exhibition

If you're planning a trip to the island in mid- to late April, don't miss the **Bermuda Agricultural Exhibition** (Bermuda Botanical Gardens, 169 South Shore Rd., tel. 441/524-7469, www.theagshowbda.com, 8am-6pm Thurs.-Sat., $10 adults, $5 seniors and ages 5-15, free under age 5), a truly local event and a highlight of the social calendar.

For more than a century, it was purely an agricultural competition, but the beloved "Ag

Show" has evolved into a broader cultural celebration showcasing island traditions, like kite-making and cedar craftsmanship, horticulture, culinary arts, and sports. Entrants compete for prizes for the best artwork, cakes, and roses, to name a few. Real animals—farmyard cattle, harness ponies, pet rabbits—are highlights for children, and a foreign troupe of dancers, clowns, or acrobats is usually invited to perform.

The three-day fair also offers a sampling of food stalls selling cotton candy, fish sandwiches, and other favorites. Everyone from the governor to buses of grandmothers comes out. For the fair at its best, go on Thursday; Friday brings schoolchildren, who get a special day off classes to attend, and Saturday is a complete zoo.

Other Events

Co-sponsored by Paget's Royal Hamilton Amateur Dinghy Club, the **Marion Bermuda Race** (www.rhadc.bm, www.marionbermuda.com), from Buzzard Bay, Massachusetts, to St. David's, is for amateur cruising yachts. Run in alternate years as the Newport Bermuda Race (from Newport, Rhode Island, to St. David's), each bring hundreds of competitors to the island.

SHOPPING

Arrowroot Gift Shop (tel. 441/236-2950, www.bermudamasterworks.org, 10am-4pm Mon.-Sat.) at the Masterworks Museum in the Bermuda Botanical Gardens sells postcards, quality cedar souvenirs (many made by prison inmates), china from the Masterworks Bermudiana Collection, vintage travel posters, and other Bermuda mementos you won't find anywhere else on the island. Its location used to be part of an arrowroot factory.

FOOD

Paget enjoys a thriving restaurant scene thanks to the plethora of hotels and guesthouses and its location on the outskirts of Hamilton.

Cafés and Takeout

With a quaint walled rose garden on one side of the French doors, and a cobblestone patio with shaded tables on the other, **Homer's Café** (Masterworks Museum, Bermuda Botanical Gardens, 183 South Rd., tel. 441/299-4001, 9am-4pm Mon.-Sat.) is a delightful spot to grab a light lunch bite with a glass of sauvignon blanc. The café serves baked goods, quiches, sandwiches, and other snacks along with coffee, beer, and wine. Relax outdoors in the courtyard or in Dobbie's Hideaway, the downstairs lounge furnished with couches and kids' activities. The café is wheelchair-accessible via an elevator and ramps.

The Pink Café (7 Point Finger Rd., ground fl., tel. 441/239-2057, 9am-3:30pm Mon.-Fri., lunch $9-12), inside the original King Edward VII Memorial Hospital building, is partly run by the facility's ubiquitous Pink Ladies and teenage Candy Stripers—volunteers from the Women's Hospital Auxiliary who, in their hallmark pink uniforms, work throughout the hospital aiding with patient care. Their much-loved little coffee shop serves up local favorites like fish cakes, black-eyed pea soup, and gingerbread to medical staff and hospital visitors. The hospital's **cafeteria** (1st floor, tel. 441/236-2345, breakfast 7:30am-9:30am Mon.-Fri., lunch noon-2pm Mon.-Fri., $5-12) is also open to the public and offers a truly local experience, complete with loads of well-priced comfort food like burgers, chicken legs, and macaroni and cheese.

Like its after-hours Hamilton counterpart of the same name, **The Ice Queen** (Rural Hill Plaza, South Rd., tel. 441/236-3136, 10am-5am daily, $3-15) sees lines out the door for its takeout cheeseburgers, chicken, and skinny fries when Hamilton bars close on Friday and Saturday evenings. Lunchtimes and early evenings bring a calmer clientele. Menu highlights are the delicious fish tenders and fish sandwich.

★ **The Paraquet Restaurant** (68 South Shore Rd., tel. 441/236-9742, www.paraquetrestaurant.com, 8am-midnight daily) is more public forum than restaurant, a welcome roadside drop-in that has been around for as long as most locals can remember, serving favorites like the delectably crusted fish cake on a bun ($8); hearty chowders and chilis ($7); breakfast specials like codfish and potatoes ($16); hot and cold sandwiches ($5-14); and cakes, pies, and caramel Cokes—plus more recent additions like rum-baked chicken wings, flatbreads, and salads. Kid specials include wahoo nuggets and grilled cheese. Special holiday menus are popular during the Easter, Christmas, and Thanksgiving seasons. The Paraquet's bakery offerings are also worth sampling: banana bread, gingerbread, rolls, and hot-cross buns (at Easter) are stacked daily on shelves near the entrance. Bermudians also bulk-order their Christmas cassava pies and Easter fish cakes (arguably the best on the island) from here. Opt for a stool at the foyer bars to get the full experience: Cabbies and other regulars hold debates on the political issues of the day here most afternoons.

International

For a casual setting and fare, step onto the terrace overlooking Elbow Beach, where the **Seabreeze Lounge** (Elbow Beach Hotel, 60 South Shore Rd., tel. 441/232-3999 or 441/236-9884, www.lido.bm, snacks 2:30pm daily, tapas from 5:30pm daily) serves tasty small plates, sushi, cocktails, and wine. Tapas ($9-19) include burger sliders, chicken satay and beef skewers, tapenade and hummus, and a full sushi menu. A custom gazebo allows all-weather outings; in winter, heat lamps, fire pits, and comfort dishes make it a cozy retreat. The popular Big Chill event on Friday nights through the high season turns up the energy level with a DJ, live music, and a dance floor.

Just below, ★ **Mickey's Bar & Bistro** (on the beach, Elbow Beach Hotel, 60 South Shore Rd., tel. 441/236-9107, www.lido.bm, lunch noon-3pm, snacks 3pm-5pm, dinner 6pm-9:30pm, bar service 10am-1am daily Apr.-Oct., $16-44) sits on a deck under an elegant custom canopy on the sand within a few

yards of the thunderous surf. The casual-chic eatery offers a modern Euro vibe and delicious salads, pastas, steaks, and seafood, including many vegetarian and gluten-free options. Service is stellar, the dishes beautifully concocted, and the alfresco surroundings utterly relaxing, even by Bermuda standards. Parents love it because kids can go build a sandcastle while they eat.

Tapas and 15 types of burgers are king at **Sanzibar** (Newstead Resort & Spa, 27 Harbour Rd., tel. 441/232-8686, www.beaurivagebda.com, 5pm-11pm daily). Tucked into the hotel alongside the full restaurant Beau Rivage, most of the tables at this bistro are within its crimson club-style interior, but a handful sit under umbrellas on the terrace, with spectacular pool and harbor views. Burgers run the gamut from chickpea patties ($17) to Kobe beef and foie gras ($80), and come with comfort staples like truffle fries, avocado, and fried egg. Seafood, meat, and vegetarian tapas range from $10 per serving to $85 combo platters.

Hidden away in the clubhouse of a residential condominium complex, **Thyme** (1 Cataract Hill, tel. 441/236-1379, www.thyme. bm, 11:30am-2:30pm Tues.-Thurs., 11:30am-2:30pm and 6pm-9pm Fri.-Sat., bar from 5:30pm daily) offers food with flair in an off-the-beaten path neighborhood. Bryden Pedro and chef Cameron Floyd took over the venue in 2017, adding more couch seating and changing the menu and wine list. After scaling the precipitous hill off South Road, you'll see the restaurant alongside the pool. Menu highlights include sandwiches and burgers ($12-17) as well as pizzas, including make-your-own options ($14-22), and satisfying desserts ($6-14) like lemon-blueberry-crumb cheesecake.

Fine Dining

Café Lido (beachfront, Elbow Beach Hotel, 60 South Shore Rd., tel. 441/236-9884, www. lido.bm, breakfast 7am-11am daily, dinner 6:30pm-9:30pm daily) is an elegant and sophisticated dining room adjoining the outdoor Seabreeze Lounge. With picture windows looking out to Elbow Beach and the surf just a staircase away, the restaurant oozes modern ambience with its terra-cotta and wood decor and professional service. The award-winning menu is outstanding, loaded with fresh fish and vegetarian options. Appetizers include tuna tartare ($20) and wild mushroom soup with chorizo ravioli ($12). Entrées offer a wide choice of seafood, filet mignon ($44), pastas ($18-38), and daily-changing desserts.

★ **Beau Rivage Restaurant & Bar** (Newstead Resort & Spa, 27 Harbour Rd., tel. 441/232-8686, www.beaurivagebda.com, breakfast 7am-10:30am, lunch 11:30am-2:30pm, dinner 6:30pm-9:30pm Mon.-Sat., brunch 11:30am-2pm Sun.) has both a commanding vantage point and impressive menu. Award-winning French chef Jean-Claude Garzia impresses diners with a harbor-front terrace with views of the city skyline and an infinity pool. Lunch features continental fare like niçoise salad ($25), *pan bagnat* ($16), and ham and brie baguette ($16), as well as wraps like a grilled vegetable and goat cheese ($14), burgers ($25), pizza ($17), and a kids' menu. An equally satisfying dinner menu includes breaded oysters ($23), rockfish fillet in champagne sauce ($40), grilled lamb chops ($48), and half roast chicken ($38). Happy hour on the infinity pool terrace is also dreamy.

Boasting a fabled 300-year reputation, **Fourways Inn** (1 Middle Rd., tel. 441/236-6517, www.fourways.bm, dinner 6:30pm-9:30pm daily, brunch 11:30am-2pm Sun.) offers history along with its gourmet menu. Built in 1727 by John Harvey of the Bristol Cream clan, Fourways has been a private home, a restaurant, and a guesthouse. Steeped in cedar and rife with antiques, narrow hallways, and low door frames, it retains a charming character and is a noted architectural landmark. The restaurant's award-winning kitchen has for decades garnered international accolades for offerings such as premium caviar, Wagyu beef carpaccio ($30), Colorado lamb chops ($54), broiled cured rockfish ($45), and Grand Marnier soufflé ($15), with a wine list to get lost in. Dinner for two with wine will cost at least $200. Patrons can choose to eat in the historic interior, where grandfather clocks and the Peg Leg Bar recall earlier times, or outside in the garden-fringed courtyard. Service is impeccable; the dress code is smart-elegant, jacket and tie optional. The popular Sunday brunch, themed for a region of the world, is a good way to sample Fourways's menu for lower cost: $50 adults, $25 under age 12.

Grocery Stores

Tucked behind Paget gas station, the small **A1 Paget Market** (Middle Rd. at Valley Rd., tel. 441/236-0351, 8am-10pm Mon.-Sat., 9am-7pm Sun.) is a convenient stopping place for liquor, fresh fruits and vegetables, deli meats, and baked goods. One of the stores in the MarketPlace chain, it is most popular for its rotisserie chicken and takeout chicken fingers, available near the back of the store. Staff are friendly and parking is easy.

The large, busy **Modern Mart** (104 South Shore Rd., tel. 441/236-6161, 8am-10pm Mon.-Sat., 9am-7pm Sun.) offers everything from groceries to foreign and local newspapers, and toiletries. The store's ample wine selection is worth a visit. Burrows Lightbourn's **Corner Shop** (30 Harbour Rd., at Manse Rd., tel. 441/236-0355, 9am-6pm Mon.-Sat.) is tiny but well stocked, with wines, spirits, and beer.

ACCOMMODATIONS
$200-300

For 50 years, Bermuda's Ashton family has run **Greenbank Guest House & Cottages** (17 Salt Kettle Rd., tel. 441/236-3615, www.greenbankbermuda.com, $190-300 d), a historic and picturesque property located on the water's edge at Salt Kettle, just a minute from the ferry dock. Basically furnished cottages and apartments, some with ocean, others with garden views, have kitchenettes, private entrances, and free Wi-Fi. Half the units sleep two people; several feature a kitchenette and two baths and sleep up to four. A pretty garden, serene neighborhood, access to public transport, and a prime vantage point for soaking up sunsets make it a favorite.

Fourways Cottage Colony (1 Middle Rd., tel. 441/236-6517, www.fourways.bm, from $275 d, including continental breakfast) has 11 cottages around a freshwater pool on a beautiful estate known for its historic restaurant, Fourways Inn. Each unit is simple but comfortable, with king beds, air-conditioning, flat-screen TVs, free Wi-Fi, and separate showers and baths. Suites have living rooms and private terraces. Children are welcome. With the famous dining room on-site, a gourmet dinner plan can be booked at a reduced rate. Guests also receive passes to the private Coral Beach & Tennis Club's stunning beachfront, with chairs, umbrellas, and drink service.

$300-400

Inverurie Executive Suites (1 Harbour Rd., tel. 441/232-5700, www.inverurie.bm, rooms $300, suites $500) target upmarket business travelers for extended stays. On a historic hotel site, it offers modern comforts and a breathtaking view of the harbor's blue expanse from every room's king bed. The adjacent ferry dock, Darrell's Wharf, allows easy access to Hamilton via a seven-minute ride. Five suites boast full kitchens, bedrooms, and lounges, while 10 single rooms have galley kitchens and baths. Top-tier amenities include Wi-Fi and flat-screen TVs. All rooms include daily housekeeping as well as coffee and tea amenities. Wooden decks front each of the rooms over the water.

For anyone seeking more solitude than a hotel or guesthouse can offer, ★ **Grape Bay Cottages** (Grape Bay Dr., off South Shore Rd., tel. 441/236-2515, www.gbcbermuda.com, 1-4 adults with up to 2 children $355 Apr.-Nov., $270 Nov.-Mar., 5-night minimum stay) may offer the perfect solution. Two cottages, Beach Crest and the beachfront Beach Home, each with two bedrooms, a kitchen, a living-dining area, and one bath, sit on exclusive, tranquil Grape Bay Drive, home to

millionaires and bigwigs, including the former premier of Bermuda. Especially popular in summertime, the cottages afford easy access to private Grape Bay Beach, and each has its own small garden and barbecue. Other amenities include cable TV, Wi-Fi, and air-conditioning. Owners Doug and Maria Frith make all their guests feel welcome.

Over $400

The 60-room ★ **Newstead Belmont Hills Resort & Spa** (27 Harbour Rd., tel. 441/236-6060, www.newsteadbelmonthills.com, from $470 d) offers harbor-front serenity in a contemporary setting. Basic 450-square-foot "Deluxe" suites are calmly inviting and have double beds, Bose sound systems, Wi-Fi, and views of the harbor, just feet away. "Studio Deluxe" rooms include king beds, small kitchens, and a waterfront balcony. One-, two- and three-bedroom suites have jetted tubs. The property's amenities include a spa, the gourmet Beau Rivage restaurant, two tennis courts, and a stunning infinity pool overlooking the harbor. Room and concierge service are also available, and a dedicated water taxi ferries guests back and forth to Hamilton morning and evening. Newstead guests are able to use the nearby Coco Reef Resort's pool and private beach on the South Shore, accessible via complimentary shuttle 8am-6pm daily; it can also deliver you to Newstead's sister property in Warwick, the 84-acre Belmont Hills Golf Club.

Another good choice on the same beach is **Rendezvous Cottage** (Grape Bay Dr., off South Shore Rd., tel. 441/234-0693, www.bermudagetaway.com, $415 Apr.-Oct., $325 Nov.-Mar.), with two bedrooms (one with a king, one with twin beds), a full bath, a living room, and a fully equipped renovated kitchen. Cable TV and Wi-Fi access are also provided, as well as an outdoor barbecue area and a washer-dryer. The nonsmoking cottage, which also comes with maid service, can accommodate four adults, or two adults and three children.

Owned by the Saudi Arabian royal family,

the 50-acre seafront **Elbow Beach Hotel** (60 South Shore Rd., tel. 441/236-3535, toll-free tel. 855/463-5269, http://www.elbowbeach-bermuda.com, from $775 d) remains one of Bermuda's premier properties. While only the lobby and conference rooms are operating in the landmark main building that awaits renovation, 98 boutique cottages and suites are in the gardens of the sprawling property. All have private sundecks, high ceilings with exposed beams, marbled baths with glass showers, goose-down bedding, air-conditioning, Wi-Fi, and broadband. The resort has a deluxe spa, five top-rate tennis courts, a climate-controlled pool, a fitness center, putting green, and a trio of beachfront restaurants. Three stand-alone cottages can also be booked. The beach is the property's crown jewel, stretching outside the hotel in a pristine half-mile arc linking to next-door Coral Beach. Between them, a public-access section makes this a popular spot in the summer. The hotel's beach facilities (deck chairs, umbrellas, showers, drink service, and changing rooms) are reserved for guests; day passes ($100) are available for nonguests.

Coco Reef Resort (3 Stonington Circle, South Shore Rd., tel. 441/236-5416, www.cocoreefbermuda.com, $365-500 d) is an oceanfront resort with 63 units (32 with ocean views, 31 beachfront). All are nonsmoking, each with a balcony or patio, cable TV, and wicker and floral furniture. The property includes a lobby with a 50-foot atrium and crystal skylight, a bar and restaurant, a gift shop, a library, and an outdoor dining area. With far fewer facilities or high-end amenities, the property isn't in the same league as neighboring Elbow Beach Hotel, but rates are lower and the beach outside is shared with the Elbow Beach Hotel. Coco Reef Resort has two free-use tennis courts and a heated swimming pool overlooking the ocean.

INFORMATION AND SERVICES

If you hear ambulance sirens in Paget, it's because the island's only emergency hospital is located here, near the Bermuda Botanical Gardens. Bermuda's main health-care facility, the **King Edward VII Memorial Hospital** (7 Point Finger Rd., tel. 441/236-2345), has an acute care wing with state-of-the-art emergency, dialysis, and diagnostic imaging departments. The original building, established in 1920, remains home to a cafeteria on the ground floor run by the Pink Ladies volunteer group, and a second cafeteria on the first floor. The hospital vicinity, along Point Finger Road, Berry Hill Road, and The Lane, is lined with doctors' offices and medical support services.

One of the island-wide Phoenix Stores chain, **Paget Pharmacy** (Rural Hill Plaza, 130 Middle Rd., tel. 441/279-5511, pharmacy tel. 441/279-5510, 8am-8pm Mon.-Sat., 10am-6pm Sun. and holidays) offers newspapers and magazines, makeup, beach supplies, postcards, and a prescriptions counter. **Island Health Pharmacy** (40 Point Finger Rd., tel. 441/236-8585, www.ihp.bm, 8:30am-5:30pm Mon.-Fri.) is inside a doctors' practice in this medical neighborhood, but non-patients welcome. Located farther north on the same road is **Point Finger Road Pharmacy** (16 Point Finger Rd., tel. 441/236-3859, www.pharmacy.bm, 8:30am-12:30pm and 1:30pm-5:30pm Mon.-Fri.), a full-service operation that offers free blood-sugar and blood-pressure testing.

Rubis Paget Service Station (65 Middle Rd., at Valley Rd., tel. 441/236-1691, 7am-9pm Mon.-Sat., 9am-6pm Sun.) is run by a friendly team. The on-site shop sells newspapers, cold drinks, and baked goods. **Clarien Bank** (Paget Plaza, 161 South Rd., at Point Finger Rd., tel. 441/296-6969, http://clarien-bank.com, 8:30am-4pm Mon.-Fri.), located in a corner shopping plaza, is the only bank branch in Paget and has full teller services and 24-hour ATM access. **ATMs** can be found at Paget Plaza, Rural Hill Plaza, Modern Mart, and the hospital. **Public toilets** are located at area restaurants and hotels, the Bermuda Botanical Gardens visitors center, and King Edward VII Memorial Hospital.

TRANSPORTATION

Buses

Paget is dotted with bus stops, making for easy public transport around the parish. Take the route 2 bus (hourly) through the parish center between Hamilton and Ord Road (north of Elbow Beach). To go to Sandys or the South Shore beaches farther west, hop on the route 7 bus (every 30 minutes) or route 8 bus (every 15 minutes), which take South Shore Road and Middle Road, respectively, to the Royal Naval Dockyard. Travel within Paget qualifies for the three-zone tariff of $3.50, $2.75 ages 5-16, free under age 5 (exact change or tokens, tickets, or passes required). Transfers are free.

Ferries

The quaint iron ferries *Georgia, Coralita,* and *Corona* on the Paget-Warwick route are worth experiencing, especially for the breezy harbor-hop to the ferry terminal in Hamilton. Paget has three very scenic stops along narrow Harbour Road, where you can either jump aboard or get off and explore. Farthest down the harbor is Lower Ferry (between Highwood Lane and Valley Rd.); Hodgson's Ferry opposite the Chapel Road junction is next, followed by Salt Kettle, at the foot of this charming old seafaring neighborhood. Corporate commuters use the service; in the mornings you can see suits, skirts, and heels scampering along serpentine Harbour Road to catch the vessels en route from the city's ferry terminal. If you board in Hamilton, the short circuit out and back takes about 30 minutes; ferries leave Hamilton every 30 minutes or less at commuter times, otherwise every 45 minutes. Fares are $3.50 adults one-way, $2.75 ages 5-15. For information, call **Sea Express** (tel. 441/295-4506, www.rccbermuda.bm) or check the schedules printed in the phone book.

Scooters and Bicycles

Paget is the headquarters for **Oleander Cycles** (6 Valley Rd., tel. 441/236-5235 or 441/236-2453, www.oleandercycles.bm, 8:30am-5:30pm daily), the island's largest scooter livery, with five other outlets around the island. Standard or deluxe (two-person) scooters can be rented by anyone age 16 or older; no driver's license is required, but instructors do a mini tutorial on Valley Road before letting visitors loose. Rates ($55 standard, $65 double per day, $225 standard, $266 double per week, $17, $21 per day after 7 days) include scooter delivery and pickup (or hotel pickup), the first tank of gas, a helmet, a lock, a basket, third-party insurance ($30), and island-wide roadside service for breakdowns. Pedal bikes can be rented for $40 per day, $175 per week.

Based at Paget's largest hotel, **Elbow Beach Cycles** (Elbow Beach Hotel, 60 South Rd., tel. 441/296-2300 or 441/296-8880, www.elbowbeachcycles.com) offers island-wide scooter delivery and pickup. Rates for gas scooters, from midsize to larger models able to transport two people, range $46-81 per day to $208-286 per week; electric scooters are $41 per day or $249 per week. Scooters and pedal bikes can also be rented here for as little as three hours. Check the website for deals, advance booking, and general information about touring Bermuda on two wheels. Midsize mountain bikes with 21 gears rent for $30 per day, $114 per week. Hybrid (battery-powered) electric bikes, allowing easier travel through Bermuda's hilly terrain, cost $35 per day, $129 per week.

Taxis

There is a taxi stand outside the main entrance of the Elbow Beach Hotel. Otherwise, book a taxi online via the **Hitch app** (www.hitch.bm) or call one of the cab companies to arrange a pickup: **Bermuda Industrial Union Co-op** (tel. 441/292-4476, cooptaxi@fkbnet.bm), **Bermuda Island Taxi** (tel. 441/295-4141, www.bermudaislandtaxi.com), or **BTA Dispatching** (tel. 441/296-2121, www.btadis-patching.com).

Warwick and Southampton Parishes

Warwick Parish 112   Southampton Parish 123

Look for ★ to find recommended sights, activities, dining, and lodging.

Highlights

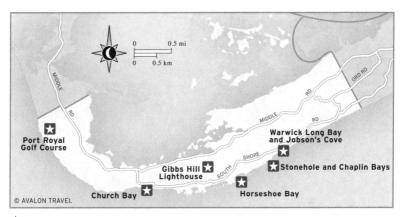

★ **Warwick Long Bay and Jobson's Cove:** Officially Bermuda's longest beach, this soft pink stretch is typically less crowded than those of nearby Horseshoe Bay, to which it's connected by trails through the dunes (page 116).

★ **Stonehole and Chaplin Bays:** Romantics—and families with small children—will appreciate this postcard-pretty retreat from the hubbub of neighboring Horseshoe Bay (page 116).

★ **Gibbs Hill Lighthouse:** Even Queen Elizabeth II deigned to stop here—and that was before gourmet meals were served. Today, a quaint restaurant, perched on the steep hilltop alongside the historic lighthouse, offers bird's-eye views and an inspired menu (page 123).

★ **Horseshoe Bay:** Bermuda's answer to Australia's Bondi Beach attracts crowds, but its beauty and access to miles of other beaches and coves make it worth a visit (page 127).

★ **Church Bay:** Boiler reefs located just a few yards from the rollers of this deeply soft beach make it one of the best snorkeling venues on the South Shore (page 128).

★ **Port Royal Golf Course:** Stunning ocean views and one of the greatest holes in golf (the 16th) have this course ranked among the world's best by *Golf Digest* (page 129).

Bermuda's most panoramically scenic parishes, with clifftop views of surf-tossed coastlines on one side and the Great Sound's archipelago on the other, Warwick and Southampton project the quintessential Bermuda experience.

The most recognizable images of the island are captured here. Full-blast Waikiki-esque fun in the sun? Check. Secluded azure grottoes? Check. Kitesurfing, golf, tennis, scuba, spas? Ditto. Beaches, water sports, and big-resort indulgences are the key draws for these parishes. Sprawling westward between Paget and Sandys, Warwick and Southampton encompass undulating terrain scattered with farmland, nature reserves, hotels, and national parks, to which the miles of south-facing beaches and coastal dunes belong. Meandering roads bearing soporific names like Sleepy Hollow Lane, Rose Glen, and Tamarind Vale.

When Bermudians talk about going "up de country," they mean heading west to Somerset through these parishes. There is a choice of routes: Harbour Road on its northern boundary is one of Warwick's main arteries, a wall-hugging sidewalk-free route meandering from the end of Hamilton Harbour around part of the Great Sound's southern rim. The serpentine journey poses a dilemma for scooter drivers: The scenery is alluring, but take your eyes off the road for a second and you might miss the next hairpin turn—a common occurrence, based on the number of patched holes in the road's low wraparound wall. Harbour Road represents one of the island's most sought-after addresses, hemmed by centuries-old mansions, coveted water views, and spectacular sunsets.

Near the Southampton border, Harbour Road connects via Burnt House Hill to Middle Road, which runs through the belly of the parish. The busy, low-lying route offers few pretty vistas but lots of local interest as traffic whisks Bermudians to and from sports clubs, grocery stores, schools, and residential neighborhoods. South Shore Road, with its wide curves and convenient hilltop pull-over areas, is the most dramatic vantage point to admire tumbling dunes, sweeping beach views, and

---

Previous: evening light over Warwick rooftops; Horseshoe Bay. **Above:** Gibbs Hill Lighthouse.

reef-dotted turquoise and midnight-blue ocean expanses. During the spring, migrating humpback whales—or at least their flukes and blowholes—are sometimes visible on the horizon beyond the inshore reefs.

South Shore Road continues west through half of Southampton before cutting north across the parish to Barnes Corner, where it ends at the harbor. From here, Middle Road becomes the only route west, running to Somerset Bridge in Sandys. Dissecting both parishes north-south are historic tribe roads—skinny, dead-straight, mostly pedestrian-only right-of-ways running shore to shore that were necessary for parish access before the days of larger thoroughfares and motorized vehicles. Early law dictated that the paths measured the width of a barrel to allow transport of rum, foodstuffs, and gunpowder. Parallel to the main east-west roads runs the scenic old Railway Trail, accessible via the tribe roads and signposted points off Middle Road.

PLANNING YOUR TIME

If you're staying at a hotel or guesthouse in Warwick or Southampton, you will find yourself close enough to the beaches or Railway Trail for early-morning dips and evening strolls any season of the year. Most Bermudians swim strictly June-October, but visitors will find the ocean's average 65°F winter temperature quite balmy. There are more than a dozen beaches, bays, and coves lining the southern side of both parishes. You can enjoy a different spot every day. Outdoors enthusiasts can enjoy diving, whale-watching in season, snorkeling, and horseback riding on the dunes or Railway Trail. The area is a magnet for golfers, with three courses in the two parishes, including the championship Port Royal Golf Course, which hosted the PGA Grand Slam of Golf 2009-2014.

Warwick and Southampton make convenient starting points for excursions to other parts of the island; they're well served by the island's transportation. If you're staying elsewhere on the island, you will definitely want to visit both parishes, if only for the views. Make day trips to swim and sunbathe, or visit some of the island's best-known restaurants and spas. Travelers heading west on excursions to Somerset and the Royal Naval Dockyard can make the most of the panoramic scenery, eateries, and sights en route.

Warwick Parish

Warwick, like the county in England, is properly pronounced WAH-rick, its silent, middle "W" confusing for American tongues. The parish was named for the Earl of Warwick, Sir Robert Rich, one of the original London investors in the colony in the 1600s and a key player in New World expansion during the Elizabethan Age.

Today, Warwick's residential areas are heavily populated and have suffered from crime and occasional gang violence. As in most other parts of Bermuda, high- and low-income neighborhoods are located cheek-by-jowl. Yet the parish also contains beautiful national parks and rambling historic estates.

Its key draws for are its wide assortment of accommodations within walking distance of the sand. For anyone whose chief aim is to relax, swim, and get a tan, there's no better area of the island. The 20-minute trip into Hamilton is hardly arduous.

SIGHTS

The best vistas can be appreciated by simply traveling along either **Harbour Road** or **South Shore Road** as you explore the parish; Middle Road is busier and less scenic. From the harbor, the expansive **Great Sound,** stretching from the harbor entrance to the fishhook of Dockyard, offers a pristine

Warwick Parish

SOUTHAMPTON PARISH

Black Bay

Spectacle Island

Perot's Island

Burgess Point

Jew's Bay

Riddell's Bay

South Shore Park

Fairmont Southampton

BURNT HOUSE HILL

SPICE

WARWICK CAMP

CLAIRFRONT APARTMENTS

WINDREACH RECREATIONAL VILLAGE

HAYWARD'S LIQUOR STORE/ WARWICK PHARMACY/ WARWICK LANES/ 13TH FRAME BAR/ IN THE POCKET LOUNGE

WARWICK ESSO TIGERMART

POST OFFICE

KHYBER PASS

MIDDLE RD

SOUTH RD

STONEHOLE AND CHAPLIN BAYS

WARWICK PLAYGROUND

WARWICK LONG BAY AND JOBSON'S COVE

Astwood Cove

Astwood Park

Stonehole Bay

Chaplin Bay

WARWICK PARISH

Sherwin Nature Reserve

Warwick Pond

LONGFORD RD

Little Turtle Bay

HARBOUR

Grace Island

Alpha Island

Beta Island

Gamma Island

Delta Island

Hawkins Island

HAWKINS

Nelly Island

Burt Island

Darrell Island

Ports Island

Zeta Island

Fern Island

Long Island

Lambda Island

Agassiz Island

Marshall Island

Bluck's Island

Irresistible Island

Head of the Lane

Gramaway Deep

Two Rock Passage

Hinson's Island

PEMBROKE PARISH

Hamilton

Hamilton Harbour

White's Island

GRANAWAY

BELMONT WHARF

DIVOTS

Belmont Hills Golf Club

BLU BAR & GRILL

LINDO'S FAMILY FOODS & PHARMACY

COBB'S HILL

SANDPIPER GUEST APARTMENTS

THE SWIZZLE SOUTH SHORE

RUBIS WARWICK GAS STATION/ GOLD COAST EXPRESS

FOUR STAR PIZZA/ WARWICK WORKMAN'S CLUB

WARWICK ACADEMY

COBB'S HILL METHODIST CHURCH

DARRELL'S WHARF

KEITH HALL RD

MORGAN'S RD

COBB'S HILL RD

ORD RD

Railway Trail

Salt Kettle Bay

HODGSON'S FERRY

LOWER FERRY

PAGET PARISH

ATLANTIC OCEAN

N

0   0.25 km

0   0.25 mi

© AVALON TRAVEL

panorama, its waters sprinkled with mostly private smaller islands where Bermudians live, keep summer cottages, or camp in August-September. Weekend yacht-racing and scheduled Bermuda dinghy-racing take place out here, as do impromptu public-holiday "raft-ups" of sometimes a dozen vessels or more, when local boaters anchor together for cocktails, picnics, and swims. Evening barbecue cruises to several islands can be arranged through Hamilton-based tour operators and boating outlets.

At **Darrell's Wharf,** the border of Paget and Warwick, ferries shuttle 15 minutes to Hamilton. This is a good spot to watch occasional cruise ships or weekly container vessels sail by, dwarfing the distant Pembroke shore and Hamilton skyline. While megavessels stay put at Dockyard, tugboats escort smaller ships through the narrow channel of Two Rock Passage in and out of Hamilton Harbour. Harbour Road's tony properties, with brick drives, pergolas, spilling bougainvillea, and freesia-carpeted lawns, are also eye-catching.

Wide viewing spots on South Shore Road allow scooter motorists or taxis to pull over at particularly scenic vantage points along the route. Populated by whispering pines, baygrape trees, and dramatic white-flowering Spanish bayonets, this route is also popular with local runners and walkers. Its high vantage point gives a spectacular aspect of the whole shoreline, as well as the boiler reefs, which lie exposed at low tide.

Cobb's Hill Methodist Church

Among Warwick's specific sights is the seemingly nondescript **Cobb's Hill Methodist Church** (off Cobb's Hill Rd. on Moonlight Lane, tel. 441/236-8586, http://cobbshillmethodist.com, services 9:30am Sun.). With a steeple and tiny sanctuary dating to 1827, the church "built by slaves in moonlight" holds a symbolic spot in the hearts of the island's black community. At a time when blacks were banned from worshipping in white churches, enslaved and free blacks of the early 19th

century constructed their own church in their spare time, including at night, using block from nearby quarries.

The church is a point of interest along Bermuda's African Diaspora Trail, but the building is open only during Sunday worship and Wednesday prayer evenings. Visitors are welcome to these weekly events. An addition to the building was erected in 1967 that now serves as the church hall. The most interesting section of the church is the old sanctuary, where cedar beams and limestone slate and block were used to build a simple but sturdy structure that has withstood natural tempests and changing political times.

Warwick Academy

Bermuda's oldest surviving school, the **Warwick Academy** (117 Middle Rd., tel. 441/236-1917, www.warwick.bm), lies west of Cobb's Hill. It was established in 1662 by early settlers on property designated as school lands since the colony's earliest days. Bermuda's 17th-century surveyor, Richard Norwood, was the first headmaster. Once government-owned, it is now one of several private schools on the island, with a long reputation for high academic standards and a racially diverse student body reflecting Bermuda's population. In 1962 Warwick was the first of the segregated white institutions to admit blacks. The original two-room schoolhouse remains visible in the current building, laid out around a small, shady quadrangle of palms. The cloakrooms, corridors, and curricula retain much of their British grammar-school roots, but Warwick Academy's International Baccalaureate graduates today go on to top colleges and universities in Britain, North America, and elsewhere. The school is open 8am-4:30pm Monday-Friday September-June. The office is open 9am-2pm on school holidays, including summer.

Sherwin Nature Reserve

The **Sherwin Nature Reserve** (Middle Rd., foot of Longford Rd., tel. 441/236-6483, www.bnt.bm, sunrise-sunset daily, free) stretches for nine acres along Middle Road. Its marshy ponds, farm fields, and woodlands lie in a wide central valley coated by endemic Bermuda cedars and allspice trees. Recognized as a wetland of international importance by the World Conservation Union, the pond was once part of a chain of wetlands through Bermuda's center, linking Southampton to Spittal Pond in Smith's. It is Bermuda's second-largest freshwater pond after Spittal and a sanctuary for resident and migratory waterfowl, including barn swallows in the fall, common snipes in winter, and mourning doves year-round. You might also spot resident roosters.

Formerly called Warwick Pond, the reserve was renamed in 2009 for the late Denis Sherwin, an ardent environmentalist. Interpretive signage along a circular path has made the reserve accessible to visitors, who can now appreciate the pond, marsh, and forest habitats along with varied flora and fauna—even educating themselves on endemics versus invasives along the way. The pond's fertile wetland borders are rented from the Bermuda National Trust by farmers for cattle grazing or agriculture. Warwick Pond's entrance is well marked by a sign on Middle Road at the turnoff to Tribe Road 3 (opposite Longford Rd.) and connects to the Railway Trail.

Khyber Pass

You can cut through this dramatically named access route to get from Middle Road to the South Shore. At the foot of the steep hill, near a landmark rubber tree outside Warwick Post Office, a memorial commemorates the island's enslaved people. Formerly the site of a local slave market, the corner today has been a staging area for craft markets in recent years. To reach the beaches, continue over Khyber Pass, bordered by soaring limestone quarries used for past building works. Spice Hill Road, on the other side, winds down to South Shore Road.

Warwick Camp

Warwick Camp (1 South Shore Rd. at Camp Rd., tel. 441/238-1045), the headquarters of the Royal Bermuda Regiment, covers a large property west of Warwick Long Bay and is opposite the entrance to Stonehole and Chaplin Bays. Although it's not generally open to the public, special tours or visits to the hillside site can be arranged. While the regiment itself was not formed until 1965, Warwick Camp was chosen in the 1870s as a base for the British military due to its strategic location, able to foil potential beach invasions. Today it comprises barracks, an officers' mess, a canteen, and a firing range. Regiment recruits conduct training exercises on the nearby dunes, allowing passersby the incongruous scene of soldiers playing war while beach-lovers frolic in the surf a short distance away.

TOP EXPERIENCE

BEACHES

Warwick is synonymous with beaches, and where the parish may lack in shopping or dining, it more than compensates with its glorious coastline. Beach tennis and volleyball enthusiasts will find all they need here. Lifeguards are posted at the most popular areas (including Horseshoe Bay) during summer, and Bermuda's Department of Parks ensures the soft, pink sand is combed of washed-up seaweed, jellyfish, and tar every morning. Watch for riptides, especially in pre-storm periods, and for Portuguese man-of-wars. Warning signs are clearly posted during hurricane season, warning off swimmers when approaching storms bring dangerous swells—a big attraction to daredevil kitesurfers.

Astwood Cove

Annually battered by storm surge, this little beach is beautiful but a little tricky to get to. Still, if climbing down clifftop trails isn't a problem, you will find privacy once you get down to this, Warwick's first public beach as you head west. Surrounded by agricultural land and a scenic seaside park that's a favorite for family picnics and wedding photographs, the beach itself sits at the foot of steep cliffs that have been badly eroded but continue to be important nesting sites for Bermuda longtails. High surf perennially claims the sand, leaving just a field of underlying rocks, though seasonal tides return it every year. In the summer and fall, however, the cove is a very private and perfect place to spend the day, with thick, soft sand and a scattering of offshore reefs just yards from the surf to snorkel over. You can also wander east along the coast, sprinkled with tidal pools containing trapped sealife and rock formations you can climb over. Picnic tables can be found in the park above, and ample parking is also available.

★ Warwick Long Bay and Jobson's Cove

Like neighboring Horseshoe, this is one of the island's most dramatic beaches, spanning a half mile of coast. The beach's thick, coral-sprinkled sand—perhaps Bermuda's pinkest—boiler reefs, and surrounding dunes and parkland make it a popular venue, yet it is never as crowded as Horseshoe, perhaps due to the lack of a café or shallow bathing areas.

A few steps west of Long Bay, connected via the dune trails, is Jobson's Cove, a tiny gem of a swimming hole nestled between cliffs and boasting swimming-pool-clear water. Honeymooners and children make a beeline for this beach, though, so you may find it busy later in the day, especially when cruise ships are in port. A horseshoe of tall limestone cliffs creates this perfect swimming hole, no more than 40 feet across. Shallow water near the sand, plus reefs encircling the foot of the cliffs, makes it good for novice or young swimmers and for snorkelers. Access Jobson's Cove via the signposted road down to Warwick Long Bay (park at the bottom and walk a few hundred yards along the west trail). Alternatively, you can go a little farther west on the main road and drive down the road to Chaplin and Stonehole Bays opposite Warwick Camp; a sandy dune trail leads east from Chaplin's equally beautiful setting to Jobson's Cove. Both also are an easy walk down from the main road bus stop.

★ Stonehole and Chaplin Bays

These twin coves lie just west of Long Bay, again connected by the South Shore's public park system and an easy trail through the dunes. Chaplin sits on the Warwick-Southampton parish border below Warwick Camp, and beachgoers may sometimes spot Royal Bermuda Regiment soldiers taking part

Jobson's Cove

Bermuda's "Pink" Sand

No need to don rose-colored glasses in Bermuda, at least on the beaches. The island's iconic pink sand is touted from brochures to bottled souvenirs. Most noticeable on the South Shore, especially on surf-heavy beaches like Warwick Long Bay, pink sand is the result of constant wave action on the nearby reef. Single-celled organisms called *Foraminifera,* or red foram, grow on the underside of Bermuda's reefs, their bodies peppered with holes through which they extend sticky threads to consume bacteria and other food. When they die, their bright red skeletons erode from the rock, drop to the seafloor, and wash up on beaches. Here they mix with white sand, composed of particles of shells, coral, seaweeds, mollusks, and other marine detritus.

The phenomenon happens in the Caribbean and at reefs in other parts of the world, but the result is most obvious on Bermuda's beaches, perhaps because the South Shore reef line is so close to the shore. The island's sand is mostly soft and fine, though some patches are made gritty with larger particles of shell, coral, and foram. Bermuda tourist trinkets have long incorporated the famous pink sand, and you can find tiny bottles of the stuff in souvenir shops around the island. Local artists and craftspeople also find inspiration in the beach sand, using it in souvenirs and artwork.

in military training exercises on the dunes. Chaplin, like so many coves with soft limestone cliff faces along this stretch, is a very good spot to watch Bermuda's magnificent white-tailed tropicbird (longtail); these seasonal seabirds make their spring-summer nests on beachside cliffs, offering up-close viewing as they repeatedly exit and enter their nooks. Both Chaplin and Stonehole offer good swimming and snorkeling areas and walkable access through dune trails to Horseshoe Bay in the next parish.

SPORTS AND RECREATION
Snorkeling

The coral reefs of the South Shore are among the most beautiful in the world, and close enough to shore to make them easily accessible. You don't even need to be a full-fledged scuba diver to enjoy them. Several beachside concessions, including an outpost at Warwick Long Bay during summer, rent masks, snorkels, and fins as well as the ubiquitous polystyrene "noodles," allowing for hours of easy floating over boiler reefs and sea grass beds and around the edges of sheltered coves and bays. Watch exquisitely multihued parrotfish nibbling on the reef, ethereal angelfish, anemones, speckled morays, cheeky sergeants

major, schools of jacks, and sometimes even endangered marine turtles.

Railway Trail (Warwick)

The Warwick portion of the Railway Trail stretches from the Cobb's Hill road crossing past Belmont Golf Club to Khyber Pass, a picturesque stretch of jasmine and fiddlewoods, towering limestone quarries, friendly neighborhoods, and rich farmland. It is frequented by runners, walkers, and cyclists, particularly in the evenings or weekend mornings. On Sunday morning, listen for the clanging of the bell at St. Mary's Church.

TOP EXPERIENCE

Golf

Belmont Hills Golf Club (97 Middle Rd., tel. 441/236-6400, www.newsteadbelmonthills. com), sister property to nearby Newstead, boasts 18 holes and 6,100 yards of intense bunkering, with artificial water hazards galore. Designed by Algie M. Pulley Jr., the course includes a waterfall and two lakes, turf to meet USGA standards, and a tee-to-green irrigation system. Handicappers call it a "shotmaker's course," thanks to tricky pin placements and challenging greens, but you have to wait until the 17th and 18th holes for great ocean views. Greens fees are $115, club rental $50, golf cart (mandatory until 3:30pm) $35. Players also receive a $20-pp golf or food voucher Tuesday-Friday. Lessons from the pro are $60 (30 minutes) or $100 (1 hour), and a 9-hole playing lesson is $250, 18 holes $400. Dress code is strictly club-style: collared shirts and slacks for men, "Bermuda-length" shorts for men and women accepted. Soft-spiked shoes are obligatory. You can replenish your energy at a food cart, snack shop, or the on-site **Blu Bar & Grill** or **Divots** restaurant. There is a ferry and private boat service to and from Hamilton from the Harbour Road dock.

Horseback Riding

Self-styled cowboy and former track star Michael Watson leads popular Western-style trail rides from **Watson's Stables** (24 Tribe Rd No. 2, Frithcote Lane, off Middle Rd., tel. 441/747-7433, www.watsonsbermudahorse-trailrides.com, 90-minute ride $90 for up to 6 people, private rides $150), opposite Belmont Hill Golf Club.

Bermuda Riding for the Disabled (WindReach Recreational Village, 57 Spice Hill Rd., tel. 441/238-2469, www.windreach-bermuda.org) provides therapeutic riding free of charge to children with special needs. The nonprofit group, funded by donations, has five horses and ponies and two full-time staff at a dedicated equestrian center complete with stables and show ring on the 3.75-acre site, which also has a petting zoo and sensory room. Visits and rides should be arranged well in advance.

Running and Walking

Walking enthusiasts will find plenty of off-road trails in Warwick, especially along the coast. On the dunes, twisting sand or dirt trails, hemmed by oleanders, baygrapes, prickly pears, and Spanish bayonets, are occasionally nosebleed-steep (one hill north of Chaplin Bay is dubbed "Kilimanjaro" by local runners). The trails are also pitted by knee-deep crab holes, so watch your step. **South Shore Road,** unlike many other major roads on the island, has ample grassy shoulders for safe walking and running.

Bowling

Warwick Lanes (47 Middle Rd., Warwick, tel. 441/236-5290, 6pm-midnight Mon.-Sat., 2pm-midnight Sun.) is one of two bowling alleys on the island and always attracts a crowd. The air-conditioned facility is owned by the Bermuda Bowling Club and has 24 lanes with

South Shore reefs

computerized scoring. A bar and restaurant, serving hamburgers, fried chicken, sandwiches and soups, are also on-site. Fees are a reasonable $6 per game, $4 children, $3.50 shoe rental.

For Kids

Children adore **WindReach Recreational Village** (57 Spice Hill Rd., Warwick, tel. 441/238-2469, www.windreachbermuda.org), a 3.75-acre oasis with an air-conditioned activity center, a petting zoo, a sensory trail, a campground, and a fully accessible playground and picnic area. The facility promotes activities for people of all ages with disabilities and special needs but has become a regular destination for all children on the island. The zoo, with its guinea pigs, goats, parrots, and miniature horses, is especially popular. The playground, a shady, treehouse-style setup of slides, swings, stairs, and ramps under a giant poinciana, is also a must-visit. Wheelchair-accessible restrooms are on-site. Tours and visits must be booked in advance.

Warwick Playground (South Shore Rd., east of Warwick Long Bay), one of a half dozen government-owned venues around the island, is a favorite. Run by the Department of Parks, the dog-free playground is well maintained, with soft white sand surrounding equipment suitable for kids of all ages, from infants to 10-year-olds. Swings, slides, tunnels, and a wooden fort and train are among the equipment. Kids also enjoy feeding and chasing the resident flock of chickens. A portable toilet and ample parking are available. A path on the playground's southern edge leads down to beachside parkland and Warwick Long Bay.

ENTERTAINMENT AND EVENTS

Warwick is weak on organized entertainment or events of any kind, and if you're staying in the parish, you will likely want to seek out nighttime activities at nearby hotels or head into Hamilton. There are a couple of bars, however, that attract crowds, mostly on Friday and Saturday.

Nightlife

Warwick Workman's Club (42 Cobb's Hill Rd., tel. 441/236-7470, noon-midnight daily except Christmas Day, happy hour 5pm-8pm Wed.) is a favorite with local cab drivers and construction workers as well as its 100-plus membership. Friday afternoons are boisterous, when, as in many parish bars, the weekend starts early, but the atmosphere is always cordial. **13th Frame Bar** (47 Middle Rd., tel. 441/236-5290, 6pm-midnight Mon.-Fri., 2pm-midnight Sun.) is inside the Warwick Lanes bowling alley. Friday happy hour starts at 4pm, and the bar also welcomes a busy Sunday-night crowd.

The Swizzle, South Shore (87 South Shore Rd., tel. 441/236-7459, www.swizzleinn.com, 11am-10pm daily), the Warwick branch of Hamilton Parish's landmark Swizzle Inn, draws crowds of devoted regulars, who come for the namesake drink but also the convivial party-like atmosphere, including live music on weekend afternoons and evenings. It offers a full menu of comforting pub grub (burgers, nachos, wings) as well as local seafood, pizzas, and veggie options.

SHOPPING

Shopaholics will find little retail in Warwick, other than tie-dyed T-shirts and other items sold from roadside stands. There is a sparse collection of convenience stores. **The Sports Source** (49 Middle Rd., tel. 441/236-9981, www.sportssource.bm, 9am-7pm Mon.-Sat.), a branch of the Hamilton store of the same name, is a rare exception, offering urban-wear shoes and fashions (Nike, Jordan, and Pepe) to a loyal following. Parking is easy in the small adjacent plaza.

FOOD
Cafés, Pubs, and Takeout

Gold Coast Express (Rubis Warwick Gas Station, 76 South Rd., tel. 441/232-2020, 6:30am-10pm daily) offers daily hot and cold buffets in this expansive, super-modern, and ultra-friendly gas station store. The fare includes specialty coffees (caramel iced

Summer Snowballs

Summertime lineups at small roadside stands near the South Shore beaches usually mean just one thing: snowballs. When temperatures soar and school's out, the crushed-ice-and-syrup confections sold June-September are a tempting way to cool off. Seasonal permit-holders—often students—set up carts daily to dole out the popular treat island-wide. Many choose spots along South Shore Road to catch traffic traveling to and from the beaches. After-work rush hour also sees a booming business, as locals snap up snowballs for the drive home.

Snowballs demand few tools or ingredients: ice cubes, an ice crusher, and special syrup, for which each vendor uses a different recipe of sugar and mix. Costing as little as $1, snowballs come in every flavor of the rainbow. If you want to taste the full gamut, ask for a Round the World—a combo of everything on hand, generally raspberry, strawberry, apple, cherry, and the all-time island favorite, ginger beer.

cappuccino $6) and breakfast sandwiches (bacon-and-egg croissant $8), a salad counter with Caesar and quinoa choices, and hot food specials (fried grouper on a baguette $10).

At Warwick Lanes, folks come to **In the Pocket Lounge** (47 Middle Rd., Warwick, tel. 441/799-4919, 6pm-11pm Mon.-Sat., 2pm-6pm Sun., $15-20) for the daily specials (fried chicken, Spanish rice, mashed potatoes) and the jovial goings-on around the bowling lanes. Special opening arrangements can be made for parties and group visits.

For a quick "greeze" (grease), as Bermudians call their soul-food lunches, drop in to **Four Star Pizza** (Warwick Workman's Club, 42 Cobb's Hill Rd., tel. 441/232-0123, www.fourstar.bm, 11am-10pm Mon.-Thurs. and Sat., 11am-11pm Fri., noon-10pm Sun., $8-22). Line up with the local crowd for pizzas, pastas, subs, and salads at this longtime café now run by the island-wide chain that operates an Indian-Chinese grill in the same complex, serving curries, vegetarian dishes, and appetizers.

Like its famous sister in Hamilton Parish, ★ **The Swizzle South Shore** (87 South Shore Rd., tel. 441/236-7459, www.swizzleinn.com, 11am-1am daily), serves up popular fare, including Portuguese red bean soup ($8), nachos (including a veggie version, $16), conch fritters ($13), and pub favorites, plus the infamous original Bailey's Bay Fish Sandwich—a huge grilled concoction with battered fish, melted cheese, and tartar sauce ($19). If you're not motoring, wash it down with a signature rum swizzle. Barbecues through summer weekends offer pork ribs and steaks galore.

Buzz N Go (66 Middle Rd., inside Warwick Esso Tigermart, tel. 441/236-3021, 6am-10pm Mon.-Sun.) serves up the chain's full range of paninis, quesadillas, iced cappuccinos, and smoothies.

International

★ **Blu Bar & Grill** (25 Belmont Dr., Middle Rd., tel. 441/232-2323, www.blu.bm, dinner from 6pm daily) commands panoramic views of the putting greens and Great Sound from the Belmont Hills resort's multistory clubhouse. Part of the Little Venice Group, which owns a half-dozen restaurants and runs the island's largest catering service, Blu draws a packed house year-round for its gourmet fare and comfort food. The stunning vantage point is also a major selling point: Its panoramic terrace was extended in 2017 to take advantage of America's Cup action in the Great Sound. The dinner menu features a full sushi selection and items such as a Thai calamari ($22), a fresh beet salad ($17), homemade pastas ($23-39), pizzas and flatbreads ($19-29), and grilled lamb chops ($60), as well a daily local fish special and numerous vegetarian choices. An outstanding wine list, with close to 100 well-selected California vintages, is another good reason to stop by.

A more casual restaurant on the same site, **Divots** (25 Belmont Dr., Middle Rd., tel. 441/434-8687, www.divots.bm, 11am-9pm Mon.-Wed., 11am-11pm Thurs.-Fri., 9am-11pm Sat., 9am-8pm Sun., snack hut 7am-3pm daily) also offers a panoramic view of the Great Sound. Drop in for a sunrise burrito ($12) or French toast ($8), beef and pulled-port sliders ($22), thin-crust pizzas ($14-20), as well as sandwiches. A kids' menu wins them over with grilled cheese, hot dogs, and fish-and-chips.

Grocery Stores

Bermudians flock to **Lindo's Family Foods** (128 Middle Rd., tel. 441/236-1344, www.lindos.bm, 8am-7pm Mon.-Tues. and Thurs., 8am-8pm Wed. and Fri.-Sat.), a large grocery that won a Best of Bermuda award in 2017 and is stocked with pretty much everything, including wines and liquors, baked and frozen goods, and a butcher department often offering freshly caught Bermuda fish. There's also a pharmacy. The adjacent **Hayward's Liquor Store** (49 Middle Rd., tel. 441/236-8610, 9am-9pm Mon.-Sat., 9am-6pm Sun.) is a handy stop outside Hamilton.

ACCOMMODATIONS

Warwick's residential neighborhoods hold numerous Airbnb and similar do-it-yourself rentals, and the parish also has a few tried-and-true guest houses.

Guests return again and again to ★ **Granaway** (1 Longford Rd., tel. 441/236-3747, www.granaway.com, $175-225, with continental breakfast), the elegant 1734 manor-turned-guesthouse that offers lush mature gardens, a large pool surrounded by shady palms, and eye-popping views of the Great Sound from its five main house guest rooms. While it fronts busy Harbour Road, serenity can be had in the English-style gardens. All rooms have private baths and air-conditioning, and breakfast is provided in the mornings. A separate cottage on the property (250-325, with breakfast), formerly slave quarters, has a well-equipped kitchen, bath, and private garden and patio with views of the sound. Granaway is about a 10-minute walk from the Belmont ferry stop on Harbour Road or the bus stop over the hill on Middle Road.

Clairfont Apartments (6 Warwickshire Rd., tel. 441/238-3577 or 441/334-8649, www.clairfontapartments.bm, $160-185) is spared the noisy main-road location of several of its competitors. The peachy complex, run as guest quarters for 30 years, sits high on a hill along a residential lane, a short walk from Warwick Long Bay, Jobson's Cove, and Warwick Playground. Six self-contained one-bedroom units and two studios include blow-dryers, voicemail, Internet, safes, and kitchen appliances. Spotlessly clean, modern, and airy, Clairfont offers an attractive alternative to pricier establishments that may have fewer amenities. Air-conditioning, maid service (except Sun.), cable TV, and a pool make guests feel pampered.

Sandpiper Guest Apartments (103 South Shore Rd., tel. 441/236-7093, www.sandpiper.bm, studio $166 d, one-bedroom $209) suffers from its proximity to the noisy main road, but with simple, airy rooms and a garden, pool, and hot tub, it's a good option for families, students, and anyone looking for affordable quarters near the beaches (it sits just a few minutes' walk from Astwood Cove). Fourteen rooms include five one-bedroom suites (with extra futons for additional guests) and studios with full kitchens. Barbecues are provided for poolside use.

A new high-end villa concept developed on one of the private Great Sound islands off Warwick could set a trend in the coming years. Billed as "Bermuda's private island," **Hawkins** (tel. 441/299-0700, hawkins@thewaterfront.bm, www.hawkins.bm) is the first of what could be a new trend in tourism here, along the lines of the Caribbean's Necker or Mustique. Owned and operated by the Bermudian Cox family trust, the 25-acre island covered by a lush woodland reserve offers villa rentals with a chicly designed main house and nearby guardhouse to accommodate up to 20 people. The island has a beach, a mile of walking trails, Wi-Fi, and a dock able to accommodate superyachts; a pool and more development are planned. Rates, available on request and on a case-by-case basis currently, include water sports equipment, all food and beverages, airport and boat transfers, a private chef, and on-site staff.

INFORMATION AND SERVICES

Rubis Warwick Gas Station (76 South Rd., tel. 441/236-4158, 6:30am-11pm daily) makes a convenient stop for gasoline, snacks, and a wide assortment of groceries, plus a large hot and cold deli, **Gold Coast Express.** The **Warwick Esso Tigermart** (66 Middle Rd., tel. 441/236-2595, 6am-10pm daily) is a super-size facility that includes a modern store with deli offerings, freshly baked pastries, and hot and cold snacks as well as magazines and toiletries. There's an ATM and restrooms.

Warwick Post Office (70 Middle Rd., just west of Khyber Pass, tel. 441/236-4071, 8am-5pm Mon.-Fri.) sells stamps and bus and ferry passes, and also offers free Internet access. **Lindo's Pharmacy** (128 Middle Rd., tel. 441/236-0010, rxd@lindos.bm, 8am-7pm Mon.-Tues. and Thurs., 8am-8pm Wed. and Fri.-Sat.), is located inside Lindo's Family Foods. **Warwick Pharmacy** (49 Middle Rd., tel. 441/279-5557, 7am-8pm Mon.-Sat., 11am-7pm Sun.) is a parish branch of the island-wide Phoenix group, offering a pharmacy, convenience store, and mini grocery, plus a small food court run by the popular Glaze, offering buffet-style hot dishes, a salad bar, and doughnuts daily.

Mix with the locals at **Warwick Laundromat and Dry-Cleaning** (15 Ten Pin Crescent, behind Hunt's Supermarket, tel. 441/236-5403, 6:30am-9pm Mon.-Sat., 6:30am-6pm Sun.). **Ord Road Laundry** (44 Ord Rd., tel. 441/236-8699) is the parish's other venue. **ATMs** are located at Lindo's Family Foods and at both Rubis Warwick Gas Station and the Warwick Esso Tigermart service station. **Public toilets** are located at Rubis Warwick Gas Station, Warwick Esso Tigermart, Astwood Park, and Warwick Long Bay, as well as in area restaurants.

TRANSPORTATION
Buses

Buses are a convenient way to get up and down the South Shore Road between resorts and beaches (route 7, every 15 minutes) and along Middle Road (route 8, every 15 minutes), though bus routes do not include the parish's pretty Harbour Road. The three-zone tariff for both routes is $3.50 adults, $2.75 ages 5-15, free under age 5 (exact change or tokens, tickets, or passes required). Transfers are free.

Ferries

Sea Express Ferries (tel. 441/295-4506, www.marineandports.bm) crisscross Hamilton Harbour throughout the day from the main ferry terminal in town to two stops in Warwick—Darrell's Wharf and Belmont Wharf. The scenic Paget-Warwick ferry route has kept its chugging iron-clad veterans, *Corona, Georgia,* and *Coralita,* quaint throwbacks to the days before the advent of the speedy, air-conditioned, quieter vessels now used on longer routes such as Hamilton-Dockyard. The Paget-Warwick ferries provide service every half hour at commuter times on weekdays, or every 45 minutes at other times, including weekends. Fares are $5 adults, $2.75 ages 5-15.

Scooters and Bicycles

Scooters, both single- and double-seaters, can be rented from livery outlets at major hotels, including Fairmont Southampton and The Reefs in Southampton, and the Elbow Beach Hotel in Paget, as well as from liveries in Paget and Hamilton. It's an easy way to beach-hop independently, if you are a confident biker. The cycle liveries also rent pedal bikes.

Taxis

Warwick has no set taxi stands, but many cabs move through the parish all day to serve Southampton's hotels. Use the **Hitch app** (www.hitch.bm) or call one of the cab companies to arrange a pickup: **Bermuda Industrial Union Co-op** (tel. 441/292-4476, cooptaxi@fkbnet.bm), **Bermuda Island Taxi** (tel. 441/295-4141, www.bermudaislandtaxi.com), or **BTA Dispatching** (tel. 441/296-2121, www.btadispatching.com).

Southampton Parish

Southampton lays claim to a close Shakespearean connection: Like the island's eight other parishes, it was named for one of the colony's original investors, in this case, the Earl of Southampton. Henry Wriothesley was a soldier and courtier as well as a patron of William Shakespeare; he had a poem dedicated to his generosity by the playwright, whose *The Tempest* was supposedly inspired by the 1609 shipwreck that led to Bermuda's colonization by the English. If he had actually laid eyes on the parish, Shakespeare would not have been disappointed. Southampton is Bermuda's most sweepingly scenic region, a crescendo of breathtaking seascapes, azure reef lines, heartbreakingly beautiful beaches, and top-of-the-world lookouts.

The parish is heavily populated with residential neighborhoods, many capitalizing on the unrivaled views and rugged coastline. It is also home to the large chain Fairmont Southampton hotel as well as award-winning smaller resorts, all claiming stunning beachfront properties or cliff-top real estate. South Shore Road through Southampton is reminiscent of California's Pacific Coast Highway, a curvaceous thoroughfare hugging the shoreline and hemmed by horizons worthy of a movie set.

Southampton extends west from Chaplin Bay on the South Shore and Riddell's Bay on the north side Great Sound as far as Tribe Road 6, which runs along the western edge of Port Royal Golf Course at the Sandys border. The parish's two main arteries are South Shore Road and Middle Road, the latter of which becomes, after exiting Warwick, a very scenic harbor-front drive to the Barnes Corner junction with South Shore Road.

From here, only Middle Road continues west through the parish.

Beaches, scuba diving, spas, tennis, golf, and hotel-based cuisine and entertainment make Southampton the premier parish for visitors of all ages and interests.

SIGHTS
★ Gibbs Hill Lighthouse

The main sightseeing attraction of the parish is 117-foot **Gibbs Hill Lighthouse** (68 St. Anne's Rd., tel. 441/238-8069 or 441/238-0524, www.bermudalighthouse.com, 9:30am-4:30pm Mon.-Sat., 10am-4:30pm Sun. and holidays except Christmas Mar.-Jan., $2.50 pp, free under age 5), good for a dedicated visit or a stop on your drive west. Built of prefabricated cast iron shipped from England, the historic landmark's 26-mile lamp was first lit on May 1, 1846, as a navigational marker for approaching ships. It was a revolutionary method at the time for diminishing the number of shipwrecks around the island's treacherous reefs; before its construction, some 39 vessels had foundered or sunk on the reefs, which extend 16 miles offshore in some areas. Ships now employ higher-tech navigation methods, but the lighthouse offers a backup. The flash of its light can be seen as far as 180 miles by planes flying at 10,000 feet or higher. For generations, lighthouse-keepers ran the property, but it is now operated electronically. At 10-second intervals, the light emits a two-second-long flash that is visible from most parts of the island. Its 1,000-watt bulb is housed within a revolving beehive lens.

The hillside is panoramic—Queen Elizabeth II visited in 1953 shortly after her coronation, and again in 1975; today a bronze

Southampton Parish

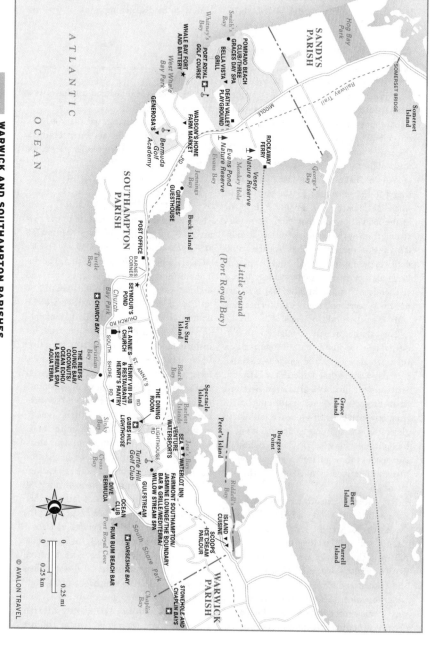

ATLANTIC

OCEAN

SANDYS PARISH

Hog Bay Park

Somerset Island

SOMERSET BRIDGE

Railway Trail

MIDDLE

Smith's Bay

Whitney's Bay

WHALE BAY FORT AND BATTERY

West Whale Bay Park

PORT ROYAL GOLF COURSE

POMPANO BEACH CLUB/THREE GRACES DAY SPA
BELLA VISTA GRILL

DEATH VALLEY PLAYGROUND

WADSON'S HOME FARM MARKET

GENEROSA'S

Bermuda Golf Academy

Vesey Nature Reserve

ROCKAWAY FERRY

Evans Pond Nature Reserve

Monkey Hole

Evans Bay

George's Bay

SOUTHAMPTON PARISH

GREENES' GUESTHOUSE

Jennings Bay

Buck Island

Little Sound
(Port Royal Bay)

Grace Island

Burt Island

Darrell Island

POST OFFICE

BARNES CORNER

Turtle Bay

SEYMOUR'S POND

CHURCH BAY

Bay Park

Church

CHURCH RD

Five Star Island

Black Bay

Spectacle Island

Peror's Island

Burgess Point

Christian Bay

ST. ANNE'S CHURCH

HENRY VIII PUB & RESTAURANT/ HENRY'S PANTRY

ST. ANNE'S RD

THE REEFS/ LOUNGE BAR/ COCONUTS/ OCEAN ECHO/ LA SERENA SPA/ AQUA TERRA

SOUTH SHORE RD

THE DINING ROOM

Barket Islands

Jew's Bay

Riddell's Bay

GIBBS HILL LIGHTHOUSE

SEA VENTURE WATERSPORTS

LIGHTHOUSE RD

FAIRMONT SOUTHAMPTON/ JASMINE LOUNGE/THE BOUNDARY BAR & GRILLE/MEDITERRA/
WILLOW STREAM SPA

ISLAND CUISINE

SCOOPS ICE CREAM PARLOUR

Sinky Bay

Turtle Hill Golf Club

GULFSTREAM

DIVE BERMUDA

OCEAN CLUB

Cross Bay

RUM BUM BEACH BAR

HORSESHOE BAY

South Shore Park

Port Royal Cove

Chaplin Bay

STONEHOLE AND CHAPLIN BAYS

WARWICK PARISH

0   0.25 km
0   0.25 mi

© AVALON TRAVEL

Inspiring Shakespeare's *Tempest*

There's a certain theme to Bermuda nomenclature that will gradually become apparent as you explore. In the city, one of the large reinsurance companies goes by the name of Ariel Re. In the old town of St. George's, there's a popular restaurant called Tempest Bistro. Over in Devonshire, the Dill family's resort, Ariel Sands (currently closed), sports a bronze statue of its namesake sprite leaping from the South Shore rollers. At least one home—Ross Perot's three-acre spread in Tucker's Town—is named Caliban. Various businesses carry stormy appellations (Tempest Employment Agency, Chubb Tempest Re). If you're starting to feel Elizabethan, you're on the right track—historians believe William Shakespeare's *The Tempest* has Bermuda to thank for its creation.

The violent 1609 shipwreck of the *Sea Venture* and its lucky castaways was chronicled in two contemporary accounts, one by crewman Silvanus Jourdan and one by passenger William Strachey, both of which circulated in London in 1610. *The Tempest* was first performed in 1611. It is known that descriptions of the disaster and the enchanting island whetted English enthusiasm for New World discoveries. Shakespeare undoubtedly would have been privy to the writings; among other connections, one of his major patrons was the Earl of Southampton, Henry Wriothesley, an investor in both the Virginia and Bermuda Companies. So experts believe it's no coincidence that his verse depicts a fanciful island, supposedly in the Mediterranean, but described in historically accurate terms for Bermuda as having "hogges of force and bignesse," "a pleasant drinke" made of cedar berries, and raucous seabirds whose tongues could "walke as fast as any Englishwomen's."

"The greatest writer of the English language was a bit of a literary pickpocket," notes Hobson Woodward, author of the 2009 book *A Brave Vessel: The True Tale of the Castaways Who Rescued Jamestown and Inspired Shakespeare's The Tempest*. Shakespeare's allegorical romance featuring characters Prospero, his daughter, Miranda, the elf Ariel, and savage Caliban happens to be launched by a monstrous storm whose "dreadful thunderclaps and sulphurous roaring" mirror the *Sea Venture*'s nemesis. "Enter Mariners, wet," the first act begins. Certainly the work's main themes—the roles of destiny and chance—also tie in appropriately to Bermuda's own story and its eventual Latin motto, *Quo Fata Ferunt* (Whither the Fates Carry Us).

plaque on the roadside below the lighthouse marks where she stopped to gaze over the Great Sound's scattering of islands. The best view is from the windswept balcony atop the structure's 185 stairs. The climb is not as tough as it might appear; eight floors, with mini exhibits that describe the tower's manufacture as well as general Bermuda history, provide resting platforms on the way up and down. Climb past the gargantuan lamp to the high-railed balcony with its 360-degree views to spy the South Shore horizons, the West End as far as the Royal Naval Dockyard, the Great Sound with Hamilton Harbour and the city in the distance, and the seascapes of Southampton and Warwick. The view reveals Bermuda's crowding of residential neighborhoods and the lack of substantial greenbelts. Alongside the lighthouse, in a former signaling station used by the British Army, is one of Bermuda's most distinctive restaurants, **The Dining Room,** and a gift shop selling souvenirs.

St. Anne's Church

A historic site responsible for the names of Church Bay (located opposite the church) and several vicinity streets, **St. Anne's Church** (13 Church Rd., tel. 441/238-1864, services 8am and 10:30am Sun.) makes a quaint stop on the way west. One of the original parish church sites, St. Anne's today stands where a cedar version, Port Royal Church, was built in 1620 by the first settlers. Structural additions over the years have incorporated some of the original cedarwood. The nave and chapel were built in 1716-1717, while the west-end tower was added in 1905. Its new bell, replacing one from 1780, could be heard as far away as Hamilton in those days. The old bell can

Sargasso Seaweed

Sargasso weed (*Sargassum*) washes up in piles on Bermuda's beaches year-round, depending on wind direction, and is either carried back out to sea by high tides or swept clean by fastidious bulldozers the next morning. These floating mats of brown seaweed are found in the Sargasso Sea, a vast area of the North Atlantic Ocean in which Bermuda is the only landmass.

Fed by the warm waters of the Gulf Stream, the seaweed got its name from Portuguese mariners of the Age of Discovery, who dubbed it *sargaco* or "grape" since its air sacs and structure resemble the fruit. The weed forms a self-sufficient food web that supports abundant small marinelife, including slugs, crabs, and shrimp as well as juvenile fish, eels, and turtles.

Oceanographer Sylvia Earle has called the Sargasso Sea "the golden rainforest of the ocean" because the two-million-square-mile area provides habitats, spawning areas, migration paths, and feeding grounds to an immense assortment of flora and fauna—including numerous endangered species.

In 2011, the United Nations Environment Programme threw its support behind an international effort to make the Sargasso Sea, like Australia's Great Barrier Reef or the Florida Keys, a Marine Protected Area (MPA)—a level of protection similar to a national park. The difference, however, is that the Sargasso Sea lies beyond any one country's legal jurisdiction or exclusive economic zone. Leading the lobby is the **Sargasso Sea Alliance** (www.sargassoalliance.org), a partnership led by Bermuda's government in collaboration with scientists and private donors, formed to fight for legislation to protect this critical ecosystem—and in doing so, to pioneer a path toward high-seas governance worldwide.

If successful, the group's campaign could win protective measures against environmentally harmful activities in the Sargasso Sea, including fisheries and seabed mining.

also still be seen in the vestry. The whitewashed building, one of the best examples of Bermudian ecclesiastical architecture, is surrounded by a picturesque graveyard that includes numerous tiny headstones marking the graves of infants and children. Park in the lot opposite the church on Church Road.

Seymour's Pond

Surrounded by marshland, with nearby pockets of woods and farm fields, tiny **Seymour's Pond** (sunrise-sunset daily, free) is tucked into the Barnes Corner junction of Middle and South Shore Roads. The half-acre reserve, owned and maintained by the Bermuda Audubon Society, is a natural freshwater pond, like Warwick Pond, and both belonged to the same connecting band of peat-marsh basins that once ran through Bermuda's central parishes. Described by Canadian biologist Martin Thomas as "the best example of a freshwater pond in Bermuda," the pond is known as a good place to find a wide variety of animals and plants. Bird-watchers

will see many resident and visiting species. Coots, ducks, and common moorhens make their home here, and herons can be spotted, usually sitting in trees and bushes around the pond edge. Dragonflies and damselflies swoop over the water, and diving beetles and other insects, including mosquitoes, hang out—though large numbers of the eastern mosquito fish, a freshwater guppy look-alike, keep their numbers in check.

Whale Bay Fort and Battery

Whale Bay Fort and Battery, in **West Whale Bay Park** (at the end of Whale Bay Rd., sunrise-sunset daily, free), makes a beautiful side trip. Once known as Fort Newbold for its commanding officer, Captain William Newbold, the half-moon-shaped fort was constructed in the mid-1700s, when several small coastal forts were built on the South Shore before the American Revolutionary War. Today its walls are gone, but the flagstone gun floor where the fort once stood remains a spectacular vantage point, overlooking West Whale

Bay and the dramatic sweep of ocean on the southern face of the island. Both the fort and nearby battery, built a century later, guarded the entrance to Hogfish Cut, a channel for small boats that was of value to local shipping as vessels traveled the western coast toward Dockyard. The battery's impressive walls, barracks, and underground magazine rooms are still standing and can be explored. Leave mopeds at the beach parking lot and climb the hill to the forts.

Evans Pond Nature Reserve

Access is difficult, but diehard naturalists will enjoy trekking around **Evans Pond Nature Reserve** (off Evans Bay Rd., sunrise-sunset daily, free), a small tract of private land containing one of the island's saltwater ponds that are connected to the sea by subterranean channels. The pond, nestled in woodland, is probably best viewed from a farm track off the busy main road. Fringed by black mangroves, this pond contains a rich ecosystem that often includes endemic species. Among the critters found here are giant toads, night herons, lizards such as the Jamaican anole, bonefish, bream, mullet, flatworms, sponges, seaweed, algae, and sea grass—though many of these are not immediately visible below the pond's surface. Eels and green turtles find their way to the pond occasionally, clambering overland. Turtles are only temporary visitors, though; while they feed as juveniles in Bermuda, they travel south to the Caribbean and Central America to breed.

Vesey Nature Reserve

Opened by the Bermuda National Trust and the local Audubon Society in 2013, this new reserve near the Southampton-Sandys parish border features two limestone quarries (inland and coastal), a natural limestone sinkhole, and a variety of habitats, from mangroves to woodland. The trust installed walking trails, interpretive signage, benches, and an observation deck from which you can survey the Great Sound. There's also a quarry exhibit showcasing an authentic five-foot-long quarry saw, once used to cut blocks to build island cottages (concrete blocks are used today).

BEACHES
★ Horseshoe Bay

The most-photographed beach in Bermuda, the various moods of **Horseshoe Bay** (94 South Shore Rd., opposite the junction with Horseshoe Rd.) appeal to diverse beach-lovers. Arguably Bermuda's number-one tourist attraction, it welcomes shiploads of tourists daily during the summer cruise season; often they're taxied here the moment their vessel makes port. As a result, weekday afternoons May-October see the half-moon-shaped bay packed with bodies soaking up the soft sand, balmy water, and picturesque surroundings. Flotillas of cabs descend to ferry them back to Hamilton's docks around 4:30pm every day.

Staffed by lifeguards May-October, the beach itself is alluring, but its on-site services allow for a full day's outing. At the entrance, **Rum Bum Beach Bar** (tel. 441/238-0088, 9am-10pm daily Mar.-Nov.) rents loungers ($18) and umbrellas ($15) from 8am. It's also where waterlogged beach bums can slake their thirst with dark 'n' stormies, frozen mojitos, prosecco, beer, sodas, and ice cream. The menu features fast-food meals, as well as late-night barbecue. Baby-changing facilities, showers, spacious sky-lit baths, and outdoor showers and faucets for washing sandy feet are provided.

Locals head to Horseshoe Bay year-round at dawn on Saturday mornings to swim, run, and walk, enjoying the serenity of the beach and its dune trails before the later crowds. Horseshoe is a favorite hangout of Bermudian teens and twentysomethings on Saturday afternoons, when night owls nurse their hangovers with pizza, cheeseburgers, and eyefuls of fashionistas.

Families with young children also choose Horseshoe for its cliff-sheltered ends, which offer shade and wading pools. Horseshoe's beach has less of a steep surfside drop-off than

Old Rattle and Shake

The onetime Bermuda Railway was a short-lived initiative that nonetheless offered a popular mode of transport in the years before private cars were allowed on the island.

Opened in October 1931, the train—nicknamed "Old Rattle and Shake"—carried passengers in first- and second-class carriages across the length of the island. At a time of racial segregation, the higher-priced sections were outfitted with wicker chairs and reserved for whites, while cheaper seats, for blacks, consisted of simple benches. Thirty-three bridges linked Bermuda's islands along the 22-mile line, an end-to-end journey that gave passengers accustomed to horse-and-carriage or boat travel a new perspective of the island.

The privately financed venture suffered from continual delays and breakdowns, running up large debts and eventually becoming unworkable. The train's iron construction was utterly incompatible with Bermuda's rust-inducing climate, and the cost of shipping diesel fuel to the island was prohibitive. The Bermuda government took over the line for a few years but finally closed it down in 1948, selling the parts to British Guyana.

The advent of automobiles in Bermuda marked the demise of the railway. After high-profile protests, including a petition signed by Mark Twain and Woodrow Wilson, both Bermudaphiles, led to a government ban on cars early in the 20th century, automobiles for private use and taxis were finally made legal in 1946. Legislators assumed that import duties and licensing would restrict vehicle numbers, but the once-peaceful crushed-coral roads were soon asphalted as locals enjoyed their newfound speed and mobility.

Neglected for decades, the old rail line was rehabilitated by the Bermuda government in the 1990s as a pedestrian walkway through the island as part of the public parks system. The Railway Trail has since become a popular route with joggers, horseback riders, and mountain bikers. Former railway stations in trailside cottages can be seen en route. Over the past few years, new interpretive signage has been erected, making the route easier to navigate. The project is sponsored by XL Catlin End-to-End (www.bermudaendtoend.bm), a nonprofit that hosts a springtime St. George's-to-Dockyard fundraising walk that attracts thousands of participants and, since 1988, has raised more than $5.5 million for island charities.

next-door Warwick Long Bay's, lessening the undertow and allowing for wading farther out. There is also a kid-perfect adjoining cove, officially named Port Royal Cove but unofficially dubbed the "Baby Beach," to the west of the main stretch. A turquoise swimming hole encircled by cliffs that keep its waters flat, this gem is a draw for those with toddlers or infants. Eastward, a handful of tiny sheltered coves dot the shoreline between Horseshoe and Chaplin Bay, offering utterly scenic, private retreats.

★ Church Bay

Rounding the last bend off South Shore Road as you head west, Church Bay's clifftop park (South Rd., opposite the junction with Church Rd.) dazzles with views of divinely turquoise vistas. The park makes a scenic stop for a picnic, while the reef-protected bay below is the best snorkeling spot on the island. Barracuda and parrotfish are commonly seen, and the fascinating architecture of the reefs themselves creates an underwater wonderland. Moreover, the beach's deep, pink sand and sheltered, sun-soaked nooks and crannies make it one of the island's best-loved beaches.

A timber boardwalk and fence lead down to the beach. The shady park at the top has a convenient pull-in and parking lot. Portable toilets are also on-site. You can rent snorkel gear from the nearby Dive Bermuda, based at the Fairmont Southampton.

West Whale Bay

Surprisingly under-visited **West Whale Bay** (end of Whale Bay Rd., off Middle Rd.) is one of the island's best beaches, offering pristine pink sand, clear turquoise water, safe coves, and a sense of undisturbed privacy for a public beach. Follow Whale Bay Road to a quiet parking lot at its end. A manicured lawn hemmed by pines leads to the beach, under towering cliffs. Dramatic boulders separate the beach into a string of shady private coves. Golfers can be seen down the distant shoreline, teeing off at the world-famous 18th green at Port Royal Golf Course. Portable toilets are located in the parking lot.

SPORTS AND RECREATION

Southampton is an outdoors enthusiast's nirvana, with great conditions and facilities for swimming, bodysurfing, kitesurfing, horseback riding, scuba, snorkeling, tennis, and golf. Parkland and the Railway Trail offer traffic-free space for walking, running, and mountain biking. Soccer (winter) and cricket (summer) fans can catch evening and weekend matches. Hotels have their own dive shops or liaisons with scuba outfits for dives off Southampton's reef line.

Scuba and Water Sports

Dive Bermuda (101 South Shore Rd., tel. 441/238-2332, www.bermudascuba.com, 8am-5pm daily summer) operates at the Fairmont Southampton, offering PADI certification and guided outings to wreck sites. Its shop rents snorkel and scuba gear, kayaks, floats, and airbeds and sells other gear. Staff have marked a "Snorkel Pathway" in Whaler Bay, noting points of interest such as corals and cannons with colored buoys.

Sea Venture Watersports (Fairmont Southampton, Waterlot Inn Dock, Jews Bay, Middle Rd., tel. 441/238-6881, www.jetskibermuda.com) offers an adrenaline-packed way to see Bermuda from the water by Jet Ski, water skis, wakeboard, or tube. Ski-boat charters with a captain-instructor cost $220 per hour. Personal watercraft rentals for drivers age 16 or older cost $125 (1 hour) to $330 (half-day), with higher rates for two- and three-person vehicles. Two-hour and

half-day personal watercraft tours around the West End, Great Sound, and myriad islands between can also be arranged. Reservations are advised.

Railway Trail (Southampton)

Southampton's stretch of the Railway Trail includes some of the route's most deeply forested stretches, tunneling through spice-tree and fiddlewood groves on a high ridge above Middle Road. It cuts across the Fairmont Southampton property and then meanders beneath Gibbs Hill Lighthouse (a tribe road cuts up from the trail to the lighthouse for easy access). A couple of breaks in the trail heading west mean you have to cross Middle Road and stay on the main road for a 0.5-mile section after Barnes Corner before a paved stretch of the trail picks up again, leading into the rural beauty of Sandys.

TOP EXPERIENCE

Golf

★ **PORT ROYAL GOLF COURSE**
Designed by Robert Trent Jones in 1970, the challenging, world-championship, 18-hole **Port Royal Golf Course** (5 Middle Rd., tel. 441/234-0974, www.portroyalgolfcourse.com, 7am-6pm daily, $180, forecaddie service $50 pp with 1-week advance booking) underwent a $14.5 million makeover to host the annual PGA Grand Slam of Golf 2009-2014. The 6,842-yard course is the island's longest, and with fairways that wind along dizzying clifftops and greens set against the ocean's dazzling turquoise, it was ranked one of the world's best public courses by *Golf Digest*. Greg Norman played here, Jack Nicklaus sang its praises, and actor Samuel L. Jackson chose Port Royal to host his celebrity tournament several years in the 1990s. The 2010 Grand Slam Champion Ernie Els called Port Royal's 16th hole—a crescent-shaped, 235-yard par-3, "the toughest hole I've ever played in my life." Proper golf attire is required (no jeans, T-shirts, beach attire, track suits, or sneakers). The **Bella Vista Grill** restaurant at Port

Royal's clubhouse serves lunch, dinner, and happy-hour cocktails.

TURTLE HILL GOLF CLUB

The executive 18-hole par-3 course at the **Turtle Hill Golf Club** at **Fairmont Southampton** (101 South Shore Rd., reservations tel. 441/238-8000, pro shop tel. 441/239-6952, golf.bermuda@fairmont.com, www.fairmont.com, 7am-6:30pm daily summer, 7am-5pm daily winter, $99 for 18 holes, includes cart) was designed by Ted Robinson, with a lofty palm-studded layout rambling over the South Shore property. Its 2,684 yards (the longest hole is 215 yards) include manicured hills, 60 bunkers, and three water hazards, making a course that takes an average 2.5-3 hours to play—appropriate for beginners or as a warm-up for longer courses. Unpredictable winds make it a challenging short course. Lessons, clinics, rentals, a practice putting green, and a pro shop offering lessons are on-site.

BERMUDA GOLF ACADEMY

The **Bermuda Golf Academy** (Industrial Park Rd., off Middle Rd., tel. 441/238-8800, www.bermudagolfacademy.com, 10am-10pm Mon.-Sat., 10am-9pm Sun.) is a good place for tuning up your tee game or simply having fun. The facility is home to an all-weather, 320-yard driving range featuring 40 practice bays, 25 of which are covered, and night lighting is offered. An 18-hole practice green, eight target greens, and a chipping-bunker play area also attract golfers, especially given the difficulty of landing tee times at favored clubs around the island. A bucket of 40 balls costs $6 daytime, $5 after dark. Private lessons ($80 per hour, $45 half-hour) can be booked with three PGA pros. Children and adults also love the facility's mini golf course, which has waterfalls, bridges, and Bermuda-style butteries. Mini golf costs $12 adults, $10 ages 10-16, $8 under age 10. The food truck **Generosa's Cuisine** (tel. 441/238-8580, generosascuisine@gmail.com, 11am-3pm and 5:30pm-9pm Tues.-Fri., 11am-8pm Sat., 10am-7pm Sun., $3-19), serving up Portuguese cuisine, is on-site.

Running and Walking

The wide, grassy shoulders of **South Shore Road** make it safe from traffic for walking and running. Fringed by spider lilies, goldenrods, and Spanish bayonets, the route sweeping high above the beaches makes for dramatically scenic territory. Down below, miles of

Port Royal Golf Course

Whale-Watching off the South Shore

Whale-watching has become a spring ritual off Bermuda's South Shore, the migration route for humpbacks as they travel from the Caribbean to North Atlantic feeding grounds. March-April, pods of humpback whales can be spotted even from shore; you may see a line of motorists pulled over to ogle the distant spouts or flukes beyond the reef line.

Most humpbacks follow regular migration routes. In the Atlantic, they tend to spend winters mating and calving in tropical zones, then move north to polar waters in the summer to feed. Unlike other species, they are highly acrobatic, breaching (throwing their whole bodies out of the water), swimming upside down with flippers raised in the air, or slapping the surface with their huge tails, called flukes. Scientists believe these may all be forms of communication between pod members, along with the species' characteristic singing.

Bermudian Andrew Stevenson has spent several seasons filming whales for his **Humpback Whale Research Project** (tel. 441/777-7688, www.whalesbermuda.com). His award-winning 2010 documentary, *Where the Whales Sing,* describes the humpbacks' journey through the eyes of his six-year-old daughter, Elsa. DVDs of the film are on sale at local bookstores and gift shops.

Several conservation-focused nonprofits and charter boat companies organize whale-watching tours in these months; half-day and full-day tours offer spectacular offshore encounters with the whales, which can sometimes be seen frolicking with calves. **Island Tour Centre** (tel. 441/236-1300, www.islandtourcentre.com) represents more than 20 vendors of ecotours and water sports. **Blue Water Divers & Watersports** (Robinson's Marina, Somerset Bridge, Sandys, tel. 441/234-1034, www.divebermuda.com) offers charters on request. **Bermuda Zoological Society** (tel. 441/293-2727, www.bamz.org) and **Bermuda Underwater Exploration Institute** (tel. 441/292-7219, www.buei.org) both offer whale-watching outings on their research vessels.

beach dunes with sandy trails through seaside vegetation are a great way to navigate on foot between coves, and also make for a challenging resistance workout away from main-road traffic for runners and walkers.

Soccer and Cricket

Soccer fans enjoy the weekend action at **Southampton Rangers Sports Club** (1 Middle Rd., tel. 441/238-0058) in winter. The same grounds convert to a cricket pitch May-September for the very competitive County matches that pit island teams against each other, drawing spillover crowds in summer.

Tennis

The **Fairmont Southampton Tennis Club** (Fairmont Southampton, 101 South Shore Rd., tel. 441/239-6950, mtminfo@gmail.com), has six Plexipave hard courts, three lit for night play. Daily court rental is $19 pp per day, $15 half-day. Private lessons are $115 for one hour for up to two players. The club shop

(9am-noon and 4pm-7pm Mon.-Fri., 9am-5pm Sat.-Sun.) stocks one of the island's best selections of Nike tennis gear along with other brands. Clinics are available.

Four all-weather tennis courts are run by the **Port Royal Tennis Club** (5 Middle Rd., tel. 441/238-9430), which leases the facility from the government. Located on the Port Royal Golf Course property, the courts are not pristine but are safe and playable.

Spas

The 15-room **Willow Stream Spa and Health Club** (Fairmont Southampton, 101 South Shore Rd., tel. 441/239-6924, www.willowstream.com, 6:30am-9pm daily, treatments 8:30am-8:15pm, salon 8am-7pm daily) is the island's biggest and most popular. Get spa treatments as well as basic sports, aromatherapy, and stress-relief therapies, facials, manicures, and pedicures. Terraced gardens, outdoor hot tubs with ocean views, and an indoor pool with waterfalls add to the facility's understandable allure. For nonguests, buying any treatment over $179 allows all-day use of all the facilities.

The 31,000-square-foot spa has devoted male patrons as well, offering den-like lounges, sports massage treatments, a Gentleman's Barber Facial, and a Power Pedicure. Have lunch in robe and slippers by the pool and hot tubs, or downstairs in the hotel's **Jasmine Lounge.** Specialties include the Hot Stone Massage (1.5 hours, $279), Couples' Side by Side (1 hour, $389), Stress Relief (1 hour, $189), and head and scalp massage or foot massage ($89). The spa offers a hair and nail salon, a steam room, a sauna, women's and men's lounges, and a couples' lounge and treatment room. The fitness center has a full range of Cybex cardiovascular and weight-training equipment and a personal trainer. Spa guests must be 18 years or older, and use of cell phones is not permitted.

With one of the island's most jaw-dropping views of the navy South Shore horizon from its floor-to-ceiling glass lounge, **La Serena** (The Reefs, 56 South Shore Rd., tel. 441/239-0184, www.thereefs.com, 8am-8pm daily) is a retreat away from the hubbub of daily life. Eight treatment rooms include a spa suite for couples' massage and a panoramic relaxation room. Choose treatments like Warm Bamboo Massage (1.5 hours, $209), Reiki (1 hour, $136), Super-food radiance facial (1.25 hours, $168), or Couples Massage (1.5 hours, $178). Special packages include daylong treatments with lunch at the resort restaurant ($299-479).

Three Graces Day Spa (Pompano Beach Club, 36 Pompano Beach Rd., tel. 441/234-0333, www.threegracesdayspa.com, 10am-7pm daily, 10am-3pm holidays) is an oceanfront spa, with two of its three treatment rooms overlooking the dizzying turquoise shallows of the West End coastline. Therapists provide an assortment of hot stone facials and massage, manicures, pedicures, waxing, and mud treatments. Some of the more intriguing are the Gommage Marine Massage with sea salt (30 minutes, $79) and a Total Indulgence

Package (massage, facial, lunch, manicure, pedicure, 5 hours, $399).

Tucked into a busy roadside plaza, **Nail Bar** (237 Middle Rd. at Heron Bay, tel. 441/232-0031, 10am-8pm Tues.-Sat., 10am-6pm Sun.) is a mini-spa, offering mani-pedis, facials, waxing, and massages. All treatments come with a glass of wine, juice, or tea while you get pampered.

For Kids

Southampton beaches are free nonstop attractions for children, with swimming, snorkeling, and bodysurfing. Horseshoe's main beach, its "Baby Beach," and shallow West Whale Bay a few miles west are all kid favorites. Don't forget the sunblock!

Its unfortunate name notwithstanding, **Death Valley Playground** (Middle Rd., opposite the Esso Terceira's Port Royal Station) is a fun, safe place for kids to let off steam on swings, slides, and activity structures for toddlers as well as older children. Shady benches and a picnic table sit alongside, and a large playing field lies adjacent. Located next to the busy main road, it's not quiet, but the little ones don't seem to mind. There is plenty of parking but no public toilets.

Gibbs Hill Lighthouse is also a fun trek for kids old enough to hike up the tower's 185 steps. There are platform breaks, so it's not too arduous for children ages five and older. At the top, they'll enjoy spying on all the white-roofed cottages and the panorama far below.

ENTERTAINMENT AND EVENTS
Nightlife

Several bars in Southampton hotels offer live entertainment throughout the week. The parish also has a couple of popular pubs and bars. At **Henry VIII Pub & Restaurant** (69 South Shore Rd., tel. 441/238-1977, www.henrys.bm, 6pm-1am daily), local musicians perform Friday-Sunday.

Guests of The Reefs cool their heels at the **Lounge Bar** (The Reefs, 56 South Shore Rd., tel. 441/238-0222, www.thereefs.com,

5pm-midnight daily), where 37 cocktails and a dance floor get the party started. Live entertainment is featured daily in high season. Likewise, the **Jasmine Lounge** (Fairmont Southampton, 101 South Shore Rd., tel. 441/238-8000, 7am-midnight daily) is a great way to kick off an evening out while enjoying a classic cocktail or glass of wine and live entertainment.

The Dock (Fairmont Southampton, 101 South Shore Rd., tel. 441/239-6623 or 238-8000, 5pm-10pm Thurs.-Sun. Apr.-Oct.) at The Waterlot Inn has become a popular waterside venue for a chic evening out. If you can draw your gaze away from the spectacular sunsets this western-facing bay commands, you'll enjoy the alfresco lounge's menu of hip cocktails, including the notorious Ridiculous Caesar and Bloody Mary Bar ($99) concoction that's delivered to your table with a ridiculous combo of add-ons: mini-burgers, grilled shrimp, a lobster tail, an oyster, wagyu striploin, and more on skewers. Or, create your own cocktail from à la carte options. Stellar service and tasty tapas bring crowds for Friday happy hour, when Bermudian Mike Hind plays his ukulele.

Boundary Sports & Grille (Fairmont Southampton, 101 South Shore Rd., tel. 441/298-8000, 5pm-midnight Mon.-Thurs., 5pm-1am Fri., 11am-1am Sat.-Sun.) brings a welcome high-end sports bar to the West End, with smoked-barbecue specialties and other pub favorites.

Festivals and Events

More than 200 players fly in for this prestigious seven-day test of bridge skill, the **Bermuda Regional Bridge Tournament** (kathleensharpekeane@gmail.com, www.bermudaregional.com), hosted by the Bermuda Bridge Federation and held in the last week of January at the Fairmont Southampton.

TEDxBermuda (www.tedxbermuda. com, Mar.) promotes "ideas worth spreading" with an annual slate of international and local speakers following the internationally popular TEDTalks on cutting-edge technology, entertainment, and design. The independently organized event is held at the Fairmont Southampton and attracts an audience of about 1,000 for the five-hour Saturday afternoon mind-fest.

The popular **Bermuda KiteFest** (www.gotobermudatourism.com) at Horseshoe Bay is an Easter weekend spectacle not to be missed. The event, held noon-3pm Friday, draws hundreds for a colorful showdown of kites both store-bought and homemade in traditional island styles. Kite-flying is practically an art form in Bermuda, where traditionalists turn tissue paper and sticks into kaleidoscopic flying contraptions, complete with tails and "hummers." Islanders come to check out the best designs in various categories, fly their own kites, enjoy kids' games and music, and share picnics of sticky hot-cross buns and codfish cakes. Kite-making demonstrations are often the highlight.

Beachfest (beachfestbermuda.com) celebrates Emancipation Day on the last Thursday of July, which also happens to be the kickoff to the island's biggest public holiday, Cup Match. The all-day beach party on Horseshoe Beach brings thousands of residents and visitors for dancing, drinking, and general merrymaking in the sun.

The **Canada Day Beach Party** (Warwick Long Bay, noon-5pm), organized by the Association of Canadians in Bermuda (ACIB), has become an annual tradition on the Saturday nearest July 1, with Molson beer served up along with rum swizzles and a barbecue of burgers and hotdogs—while a DJ blasts the sounds of Rush, Neil Young, Barenaked Ladies, and The Tragically Hip. Entrance is gained through a $20 membership in ACIB, which garners you drink and food tickets.

Horseshoe Bay is the site for the annual **Bermuda Sand Castle Competition** (tel. 441/505-7822, www.sandcastle.bm, 10am-4pm), held at the start of September. The creative contest is free to enter and fun for both entrants and spectators, with five categories open to children, adults, families, teens, and tourists. The competition has in the past brought in the talents of professional American sand sculptors whose incredible creations wow the crowds of spectators.

In December, the island's top golf clubs, including the Port Royal Golf Course, team up to host the **Bermuda Goodwill Golf Tournament** (tel. 914/239-3077, www.bermudagoodwillgolf.com), which brings golfers from the United States, Canada, and the Britain, with teams made up of one professional and three amateurs.

SHOPPING

Like Warwick, Southampton is not a shoppers' mecca, offering only hotel-lobby boutiques and the occasional souvenir outlet. Label-conscious travelers will appreciate Longchamp and Rolex at the **Fairmont Southampton** (101 South Shore Rd., tel. 441/238-8000), home to a microcosm of Front Street's top-end retailers. **The Reefs** also sells Bermuda-inspired gifts at a small boutique on its property.

The **Lighthouse Gift Shop** (68 St. Anne's Rd., 9:30am-4:30pm Mon.-Sat., 10am-4:30pm Sun. and holidays except Christmas Mar.-Jan.) is good for postcards and tacky Bermuda memorabilia like clay ferries, baseball caps, and pirate flags.

FOOD
Cafés and Takeout

For Bermudian favorites such as Sunday codfish breakfast, pan-fried rockfish, peas 'n' rice, and bread pudding, drop into ★ **Island Cuisine** (235 Middle Rd., tel. 441/238-3287, www.islandcuisine.org, 6am-9:45pm Mon.-Sat., 7am-2:45pm and 5pm-9pm Sun.). The bright blue roadside diner is run by mother-daughter team Audrey and Alicia Tucker, who offer affordable home-style all-day breakfast, beer, and wine. Breakfast specials include banana pancakes ($9) and omelets ($12). At lunch, choose anything from peanut butter and bacon sandwiches ($6) to one of the best burgers ($5) on the island. The dinner menu features meatloaf ($17) and a

fishcake dinner ($17). A menu for kids under age 10 offers grilled banana ($3) and peas 'n' rice ($5).

Right next door to Henry VIII Pub is **Henry's Pantry** (69 South Shore Rd., tel. 441/238-1509, 10am-7pm Mon.-Sat.), which sells cold drinks, snacks, and a few deli items like chicken legs, beef patties, and fish chowder, along with a full wine, beer, and liquor selection. Manager Anthony Faries will fill you in on all Bermuda's need-to-know intel before you buy the daily newspaper.

"Not your average food truck," **Generosa's Cuisine** (10 Industrial Park Rd. off Middle Rd., tel. 441/238-8580, 11am-3pm and 5:30pm-9pm Tues.-Fri., 11am-8pm Sat., 10am-7pm Sun., $3-19) likes to declare. Based at the Bermuda Golf Academy and named for family matriarch Generosa Rodrigues, it has delicious Portuguese regional dishes that satisfy with a takeout or eat-in menu. Charbroiled spare ribs, curry shrimp, and pork and beans with collard greens are favorites, along with lattes and beer. Patrons enjoy cooling out on the patio alongside.

Take a sweet timeout at **Scoops Ice Cream Parlour & Cupcake Café** (237 Middle Rd., Heron Bay, tel. 441/238-5382, noon-9pm Mon.-Thurs., noon-10pm Fri., 11am-10pm Sat.-Sun.) on the way between Dockyard and Hamilton. The bright orange building is hard to miss, and its ice cream flavors include peanut butter cup chocolate swirl, watermelon sherbet, and black-raspberry truffle. A delectable menu of cupcakes includes lemon, chocolate mint, red velvet, and apple strudel.

Pining for pizza? **Heron Bay Pizza House** (Heron Bay Plaza, next to Heron Bay MarketPlace, tel. 441/238-2753, 11am-10pm Mon.-Sat., 1pm-8pm Sun., slice $5, pies $12-26) serves up fluffy pizzas with toppings galore. **Rum Bum Beach Bar** (Horseshoe Bay, 94 South Shore Rd., tel. 441/238-0088, 9am-10pm daily Mar.-Nov., $12-15) rents beach gear and serves up burger, hot dog, and chicken combos. Enjoy the outdoor patio with tables and shady umbrellas, or picnic on the beach.

Tasty tapas-style lunch or dinner can be enjoyed in the air-conditioned comfort of a hotel lobby bar at **Jasmine Lounge** (Fairmont Southampton, 101 South Shore Rd., tel. 441/238-8000, www.fairmont.com, 11am-midnight daily), with all-day cocktails, gourmet sandwiches (steak ciabatta $22), an array of tempting tapas such as tamales and sushi ($18), Peruvian meatballs ($16), and flatbread pizzas ($19-24). Main courses served in the evenings include prime rib ($37) and a fresh catch of the day. Afternoon tea ($29) is offered 3pm-5pm daily.

International

Hugged by idyllic Sinky Bay, ★ **Marcus' on the Beach** (Hamilton Princess Beach Club, South Beach, tel. 441/295-3000 or 441/298-2028, www.thehamiltonprincess.com, lunch and snacks 10am-6pm daily Apr.-Oct., dinner 6pm-9:30pm daily Apr.-Sept.) indulges in the same swoon-worthy comfort food served up at Marcus Samuelsson's main restaurant in the Hamilton Princess Hotel in Pembroke. The beach and amenities are open only to hotel guests, but the seasonal restaurant allows nonguests to reserve Thursday-Saturday evenings. The menu matches the elegant setting and includes coconut crusted crab cakes ($21), jerk chicken ($35), burger served on Johnnie bread ($26), and creamy mac 'n' cheese ($10). Watching a crimson sun sink while sipping a pineapple crush or crisp pinot grigio—does it get any better?

Seafood shines at the beachside **Ocean Club** (Fairmont Southampton, 101 South Shore Rd., tel. 441/238-8000, www.fairmont.com, dinner 6pm-9pm daily high season). Located in the Fairmont Beach Club (accessible by hotel trolley), the seasonal restaurant overlooks the hotel's private beach and the South Shore breakers, its patio a perfect alfresco venue. The menu features fresh local catches (tuna, rockfish, wahoo), as well as Prince Edward Island blue mussels ($19), Maine lobster cocktail ($24), pan-roasted half chicken ($32), plus chowders, salads, and a few meat dishes.

Henry VIII Pub & Restaurant (69 South Shore Rd., tel. 441/238-1977, www.henrys.bm, lunch noon-3:30pm Mon.-Sat., pub fare noon-10pm Mon.-Sat., dinner 6pm-10pm daily, brunch noon-3pm Sun.) looks Tudor but has been a Southampton roadside fixture only since 1970. Permeated with the aroma of prime rib and spilled beer, the low-ceilinged eatery is Bermuda's best example of an English-style pub. A strong local following keeps the place lively even in the off-season, especially on Sunday nights when a raucous crowd enjoys dinner and live entertainment until 3am. The kitsch includes strolling minstrels in the dining room, and the menu is heartily enjoyable. Highlights are the Bermuda rockfish ($39), Chateaubriand for two ($79), and pastas ($22-31). There's also a sushi bar and 14 different ales. There's live entertainment after 9:30pm Friday-Sunday.

Coconuts (The Reefs, 56 South Shore Rd., tel. 441/238-0222, www.thereefs.com, noon-11pm daily, Apr.-Nov.) wins the hearts of alfresco diners and numerous awards for the island's best lunch venue, most romantic restaurant, and best table with a view. Set on a treehouse-style covered deck below tumbling cliffs overlooking the surf, lunch offers light but creative dishes like blue crab guacamole, quinoa salad, and baby back ribs. A typical dinner menu might include Bermuda snapper crab ($18), carrot and cardamom risotto ($22), or butterflied tenderloin ($40). No matter how scrumptious the food, it will always be eclipsed by the spectacular surf and glittering turquoise reef line just a few feet away. For ultra-romantic occasions, dinner can be served at candlelit tables set right on the beach (7pm-8:15pm, 5-course prix fixe, $125 pp).

With equally striking ocean views, **Aqua Terra** (The Reefs, 56 South Shore Rd., tel. 441/238-0222, www.thereefs.com, dinner 6pm-10pm daily Mar.-Dec., lunch noon-4pm daily Nov.-Jan.) offers craft cocktails and farm-to-table casual fare, from salt-crusted roasted beets ($12) and rockfish with kale ($38) to burgers ($22) and short ribs ($34).

Bermudian brunch-goers park bumper to bumper along South Shore Road outside The Reefs every Sunday for **Ocean Echo** (The Reefs, 56 South Shore Rd., tel. 441/238-0222, www.thereefs.com, noon-3pm Sun., $45 buffet, $55 on holidays, half-price ages 5-12, dinner 6pm-10pm daily), the hotel's window-walled curved dining room, which tantalizes taste buds while wowing guests with eye-popping horizons.

Mediterranean

Gulfstream (117 South Shore Rd., tel. 441/238-1897, www.dining-bermuda.com, lunch 11:30am-2:30pm Mon.-Wed., 11:30am-5pm Fri.-Sun., dinner 5pm-10pm daily) looks like a roadside diner, but its menu is more gourmet. Run by a European group, Gulfstream's creative menu has delicious pastas, pizzas, salads, and seafood. Appetizers include clams in white wine and garlic ($18) and roasted duck spring rolls ($16); main dishes run the gamut from lasagna ($22) and beef stir-fry ($28) to fish of the day. The extensive thin-crust pizza menu ($10-19) includes vegetarian options. Seating is in the coolly lit interior, or outside on the terrace.

Tucked into a historic cottage at the foot of Gibbs Hill Lighthouse, ★ **The Dining Room** (68 St. Anne's Rd., tel. 441/238-8679, thediningroom@northrock.bm, www.bermuda-dining.com, lunch 11:30am-3pm Fri.-Sat., dinner 5:30pm-10pm Tues.-Sun.) is another member of the Rustico group. Its unique location—with 360-degree views out the quaint cottage windows—makes for memorable meals, but the menu is also attractive. Inventive dishes include chickpea vegan meatloaf ($24), tuna poke bowl ($22), gorgonzola gnocchi ($26)), and pumpkin ravioli ($18). Lunch offers jerk-chicken and fish sandwiches ($16) and lamb burgers ($24), as well as salads, pizzas, and rum-doused fish chowder. There's a broad cocktails, beer, and wine list, including more than a dozen wines by the glass.

Mediterra (Fairmont Southampton, 101 South Shore Rd., tel. 441/238-8000, 6pm-9:30pm daily) serves up inspired European tapas and shared dishes such as hummus and tapenade ($21), seafood paella ($36), and whole-roasted sea bass ($35)—but not without a big dose of comfort. A baked chocolate tart ($12) with a dulce de leche martini, anyone?

Chef Livio Ferigo opened **Bella Vista Grill** (Port Royal Golf Course, 5 Middle Rd., tel. 441/232-0100, 10am-10pm Mon.-Thurs. and 7:30am-10:30pm Fri.-Sun. winter, 10am-10:30pm Mon.-Thurs. and 10am-11pm Fri.-Sun. summer, $20-64) following years of success at Dockyard's Bone Fish Grill and Café Amici. Culinary creations here are original, such as the Pernod-dipped escargots and Azores chorizo carbonara, and there are pastas, burgers, and surf-and-turf specials. In the summer, step out for a pre-dinner cocktail on the west porch; the venue overlooks Port Royal's panoramic back nine.

Fine Dining

Dating to 1670, the historic ★ **Waterlot Inn** (Fairmont Southampton, Jews Bay, Middle Rd., tel. 441/239-6623 or 441/238-8000, www.fairmont.com, dinner 6pm-10pm daily summer, 6pm-10pm Tues.-Sun. winter, brunch 11am-2pm Sun.) is a Bermuda landmark, beloved for its indulgent menu and resident ghost. Local lore says the spirit of pioneering owner Claudia Darrell still stalks the building that was home to generations of her seafaring ancestors, as well as a blacksmith shop and parish post office. In the early 1900s, Darrell inherited the house and converted it into an English-style tavern where she befriended visiting celebrities like Mark Twain, Eugene O'Neill, and Eleanor Roosevelt, becoming an island legend. Hamilton's flags flew at half-mast when she died in 1949. The cedar beams, thick limestone walls, and low ceilings have been converted to intimate dining rooms. Patrons often arrive by boat, and nothing is more bucolic than summer sunset cocktails and tapas at its updated waterside lounge, **The Dock.** An AAA Four Diamond Award winner, Waterlot aligns its menu with that of an upscale American steakhouse, despite its UK tavern appearance. Caesar salads are prepared tableside for two or more ($18 pp), or try oysters Rockefeller ($32), seared tuna ($39), and cedar-plank salmon ($34). The star attraction is the USDA steak ($45-68), aged a minimum of three weeks. Pick your accompaniments (seared foie gras, truffle butter, ginger beer sauce). Shared side orders such as garlic creamed spinach, truffled mac 'n' cheese, and hand-cut onion rings are worth splurging on. The dress code is "resort elegant."

Grocery Stores

Heron Bay MarketPlace (227 Middle Rd., at Heron Bay, tel. 441/238-1993, 7am-10pm Mon.-Sat., 9pm-7pm Sun.) is one of the larger of the MarketPlace chain, stocking a large array of foodstuffs and including a bakery on-site. A small mall attached to the grocery has a pizza restaurant, a florist, and other retail outlets.

Markets

Wadson's Home Farm Market (Wadson's Farm, 10 Luke's Pond Rd., tel. 441/238-1862, www.wadsonsfarm.com, 10am-6pm Tues.-Fri., 9am-1pm Sat.) is an organic mecca for area residents and anyone looking for some of Bermuda's best vegetables, lamb, chicken, pork, and sausages. Farmer Tom Wadson hails from a centuries-old Bermudian family and focuses his energies on all things chemical-free. His Southampton farm, a good example of a sustainable organic operation, offers tours to visitors by appointment.

ACCOMMODATIONS

Southampton is home to several high-end resorts. The parish also has cottage colonies, guesthouses, and Airbnb and VRBO rentals.

Greenes' Guesthouse (71 Middle Rd., tel. 441/238-0834, www.thegreenesguesthouse.com, $150 d, including full breakfast) is a family-run bed-and-breakfast in a panoramic property overlooking Jennings Bay and the Great Sound. Jane Greene and her son David have turned their very large house into comfortable modern accommodations with lounges, a home theater, and a large dining room for the full breakfast Jane cooks every morning (she also bakes gingerbread for afternoon tea). The six spacious rooms, each with a private bath, have air-conditioning, heating, phones, fridges, and cable TV. The main kitchen is open for guest use. While the sprawling property sits just a few yards off busy Middle Road, its rear side has serene lawns, patios, and a 40-foot pool overlooking the ocean. A public bus stop is just down the main road, though Jean often transports guests to nearby shops or the Rockaway ferry dock in her car. She hasn't raised her rates in many years.

Encompassing 100 acres, the ★ **Fairmont Southampton** (101 South Shore Rd., tel. 441/238-8000, toll-free reservations tel. 800/257-7544 or 506/863-6310, www.fairmont.com, $439-2,500 d) is the island's largest luxury resort hotel property and a major conference center. Built in 1972 on a ridge overlooking both the South Shore and Great Sound, the resort commands priceless views and easy access to South Shore beaches and the West End. A free ferry service shuttles guests across the Great Sound to Hamilton. Major upgrades over the past decade have refurbished the guest rooms and the multiple dining establishments. The resort's 593 accommodations include 11 basic suites, 23 one- and two-bedroom suites, 2 split-level penthouse suites, and 74 rooms; all have private balconies, in-room safes, air-conditioning, minibars, private baths, walk-in closets, cable TV, voicemail, Internet access, and blow-dryers. All but the first floor is nonsmoking. The resort has 10 restaurants, two bars, and the 31,000-square-foot **Willowstream Spa.** Recreational amenities include two swimming pools, both with hot tubs, an 18-hole par-3 golf course, 11 all-weather tennis courts, and a private beach. Other amenities include a cycle shop, a dive shop, Jet Ski rentals, and a year-round complimentary Kids Explorers Camp for children ages four and up.

★ **The Reefs** (56 South Shore Rd., tel. 441/238-0222, U.S./Canada tel. 800/742-2008, www.thereefs.com, $660-1,035 d) consistently rakes in international awards for privacy, professionalism, and the well-appointed property. Nestled in the cliffs above its own beautiful beach, accommodations range from guest rooms and suites, all with private balconies, to two- and three-bedroom Club Condos and cottages. Top-end point suites, with private outdoor hot tubs, have contemporary decor. **La Serena Spa** is among the amenities, along with an infinity pool, its horizon blending with the South Shore's. Meticulous landscaping makes every lawn and planted palm appear freshly scrubbed. Honeymooners, babymooners, families, and guests of every age bracket seem to enjoy the place equally. Wedding, honeymoon, and anniversary packages are offered. Three restaurants, a gym, a pool, kayaks, croquet, shuffleboard, and tennis courts make this a property you might never want to leave.

Named for the schools of long-finned surf fish that swim offshore, the 75-room **Pompano Beach Club** (36 Pompano Beach Rd., tel. 441/234-0222 or 800/343-4155, www.pompanobeachclub.com, $570-1,850 d, 4-night minimum stay in high season) commands one of the island's most dramatic seascapes, ensconced in the cliffs of the southwest shoreline overlooking an atoll-like bay where low tide allows you to wade out on a shallow sandbar, called Pompano Flats, to the surrounding reef line where sea turtles frolic. Winner of numerous hotel awards, Pompano is a family-owned property with a casual atmosphere, ultra-personalized service, and a high rate of repeat guests. Rooms have dated decor, with tiled floors, potted plants, floral prints, and pastel watercolors, but private balconies with uncommon surf views make up for it. Golf, honeymoon, and anniversary packages are offered. The resort has a spa, fitness center, game room, oceanfront heated pool, kiddie pool, hot tubs, six tennis courts, and a glass-enclosed 60-seat restaurant. A water sports outlet offers guests kayaks, paddleboats, sailboats, and windsurfing gear, and an exceptional golf experience can be had at the adjoining world-championship Port Royal Golf Course.

INFORMATION AND SERVICES

The parish has one mail drop at **Southampton Post Office** (2 Church Rd., off Middle Rd., tel. 441/238-0253, 8am-5pm Mon.-Fri.). Parish gas stations include **Terceira's Port Royal Service Centre** (31 Middle Rd., tel. 441/234-0090, 6am-10pm

Fairmont Southampton

daily), a busy outlet with pleasant staff, hot dogs, fresh pies, sodas, and fruit drinks; and **Rubis Raynor's Service Station** (217 Middle Rd., near Heron Bay, tel. 441/238-3492), which has a **convenience store** (6am-7pm Mon.-Thurs., 6am-8pm Fri., 7am-8pm Sat.) and 24-hour gas accessible via credit card.

ATMs are at Heron Bay MarketPlace (227 Middle Rd.) and Terceira's Port Royal Service Centre (31 Middle Rd.). **Public toilets** are located at Horseshoe Bay and at the major hotels, restaurants, and golf clubs. In addition, portable toilets are located at Warwick Long Bay and Church Bay.

TRANSPORTATION
Buses
Catch the route 7 bus (Hamilton-Barnes Corner-Dockyard via South Shore) to get to the beaches or the lighthouse, or route 8 (Hamilton-Barnes Corner-Somerset via Middle Road) for points along the parish's harborside; buses on both routes run every 15 minutes most of the day. The fare to all points in the parish is $3.50.

Ferries
Busy with weekday commuters, the fast **ferry service** (tel. 441/295-4506, www.rc-cbermuda.bm) stops near the parish border with Sandys at Rockaway, Southampton. This ferry stop is accessible off Middle Road, opposite the Port Royal Golf Course. Weekday service offers an express route (20 minutes) to Hamilton from Watford Bridge (7am), Cavello Bay (7:10am), and Rockaway (7:20am). The evening's last ferry leaves Rockaway at 6:40pm, arriving in Hamilton at 7:20pm. Ferries depart Hamilton every 15

minutes at peak commuter times, every 90 minutes at other times (no service Sun.). The fare is $5 adults, $2.75 ages 5-15, free under age 5. No cash or change accepted; tickets or tokens only.

Scooters and Bicycles
Smatt's Cycle Livery (Fairmont Southampton, 101 South Shore Rd., tel. 441/238-7800, www.smattscyclelivery.com, 8am-5pm daily) rents single-seat ($50 per day) and dual-seat ($55) scooters ($225 single, $267 dual per week). Island-wide roadside assistance is included. Pedal bikes ($40 per day, $145 per week) are also available.

Oleander Cycles (The Reefs, 56 South Shore Rd., tel. 441/239-0189, www.oleandersy-cles.bm, 9am-5pm daily) rents standard single ($55 per day, $225 per week, $17 after 7 days) or double ($65 per day, $266 per week, $21 after 7 days) scooters. Rates include scooter delivery and pickup (or hotel pickup), the first tank of gas, a helmet, a lock, a basket, third-party insurance ($30), and island-wide roadside service for breakdowns. Mountain bikes are $40 per day, $175 per week, $10 per day after seven days.

Taxis
Southampton's cabs can be found lined up outside the Fairmont Southampton entrance as well as at The Reefs and Pompano and down at Horseshoe Bay on busy days. You can also use the **Hitch app** (www.hitch.bm) or call to arrange a pickup: **Bermuda Industrial Union Co-op** (tel. 441/292-4476, cooptaxi@fkbnet.bm), **Bermuda Island Taxi** (tel. 441/295-4141, www.bermudaislandtaxi.com), or **BTA Dispatching** (tel. 441/296-2121, www.btadispatching.com).

Sandys Parish

Royal Naval Dockyard......... 145

Somerset Village............... 157

Around Sandys 161

The distinctive "fishhook" of Bermuda is the island's charismatic West End, Sandys.

It's an undulating patchwork of geography in which the rugged South Shore coastline on one side and the mirrorlike Great Sound bays on the other sandwich a rural bosom of onion fields, towering cedars, and loquat woods. The West End is all about peace and quiet; more than in any other parish, you can find loads of both. Winding country lanes littered in oleander petals invite leisurely strolls past red-earthed farms, avenued estates, and craggy islets where whalers once lived. You can watch old-time dinghies with billowing sails scoot across open ocean or hang out with fishermen as they clean their catch in the afternoon. The fact that Sandys is so detached from the rest of Bermuda—a 40-minute drive from the bustle of Hamilton—lends serenity to any time spent in the parish. No wonder that a traveler would encounter places called Tranquillity Hill, Pinkhouse Lane, and Daisyfield Drive.

The parish name may conjure a delightful image of nonstop beaches—which wouldn't be deceiving—but Sandys (pronounced "Sands") actually derives from Sir Edwin Sandys, one of the colony's first Virginia Company investors. The parish comprises an arcing string of five islands plus a chunk of mainland bordering Southampton at Port Royal Golf Course. From the west, the islands are Ireland Island North, Ireland Island South, Boaz Island, Watford Island, and—the largest—Somerset Island, which connects to the rest of the parish at its western tip via Somerset Bridge, the world's smallest drawbridge. Quaint Somerset Village on Somerset Island is a point of confusion when Bermudians talk about "Somerset." Sometimes they may mean the village itself, but they could be referring to the larger area. Locals tend to call addresses farther west than Somerset Bridge, including the other islands and Dockyard, "Somerset."

Steeped in both early colonial and British military history, Sandys has historically important fortifications, military cemeteries, and cultural heritage museums as well as two of Bermuda's most extensive national parks plus several smaller ones, as well as dramatic coastal landscapes and endless shallow reef systems you can spend full days exploring. Quintessential Bermudiana is everywhere—village verandas, cricket matches, and cottage-fringed lanes, and cheerful homespun

---

Previous: Commissioner's House; tranquil shallows at Hog Bay Park. **Above:** Watford Bridge.

Highlights

★ **National Museum of Bermuda:** The most visited Bermuda attraction, with the island's best view, this museum is housed inside the tall ramparts of the six-acre Keep, the Royal Naval Dockyard's citadel (page 147).

★ **Bermuda Fitted Dinghy Races:** Somerset Village is the best place on the island to witness this hugely popular spectacle throughout the summer (page 159).

★ **Somerset Bridge:** Drive or walk over the world's tiniest drawbridge, or just watch boaters navigate the skinny passage beneath its planks (page 162).

★ **Fort Scaur and Park:** With panoramic views of the Great Sound and Dockyard, this fort and surrounding parkland make a great stop for a picnic or photo op (page 162).

★ **Hog Bay Park:** The island's third-largest park is a serene paradise—38 acres of trails through farmland, woods, and coastal scrub plus, at low tide, a beach (page 163).

★ **Railway Trail (Sandys):** Arguably the finest stretch of Bermuda's old railway bed is this section between the former U.S. Naval Air Station Annex and Somerset Village (page 165).

★ **Cup Match:** This annual cricket extravaganza over the July-August cusp is an immediate initiation into island life (page 165).

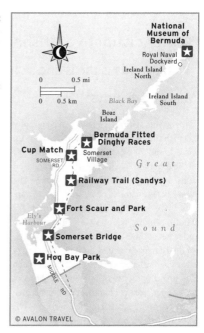

Sandys Parish

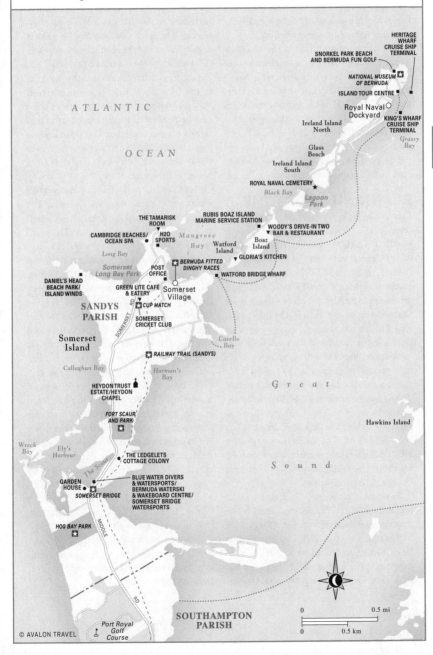

ATLANTIC

OCEAN

HERITAGE WHARF CRUISE SHIP TERMINAL

SNORKEL PARK BEACH AND BERMUDA FUN GOLF

NATIONAL MUSEUM OF BERMUDA

ISLAND TOUR CENTRE

Royal Naval Dockyard

KING'S WHARF CRUISE SHIP TERMINAL

Ireland Island North

Grassy Bay

Glass Beach

Ireland Island South

ROYAL NAVAL CEMETERY

Black Bay

Lagoon Park

THE TAMARISK ROOM

RUBIS BOAZ ISLAND MARINE SERVICE STATION

WOODY'S DRIVE-IN TWO BAR & RESTAURANT

CAMBRIDGE BEACHES/ OCEAN SPA

H2O SPORTS

Mangrove Bay

Watford Island

Boaz Island

GLORIA'S KITCHEN

Long Bay

Somerset Long Bay Park

POST OFFICE

BERMUDA FITTED DINGHY RACES

WATFORD BRIDGE WHARF

DANIEL'S HEAD BEACH PARK/ ISLAND WINDS

GREEN LITE CAFÉ & EATERY

Somerset Village

SANDYS PARISH

SOMERSET RD

CUP MATCH

SOMERSET CRICKET CLUB

Somerset Island

Cavello Bay

Callaghan Bay

RAILWAY TRAIL (SANDYS)

Harman's Bay

Great

HEYDON TRUST ESTATE/HEYDON CHAPEL

FORT SCAUR AND PARK

Hawkins Island

Wreck Bay

Ely's Harbour

THE SCAUR

THE LEDGELETS COTTAGE COLONY

Sound

GARDEN HOUSE

BLUE WATER DIVERS & WATERSPORTS/ BERMUDA WATERSKI & WAKEBOARD CENTRE/ SOMERSET BRIDGE WATERSPORTS

SOMERSET BRIDGE

HOG BAY PARK

MIDDLE RD

RD

SOUTHAMPTON PARISH

Port Royal Golf Course

© AVALON TRAVEL

0   0.5 mi

0   0.5 km

eateries. Like the other parishes, it is not without its social troubles—gangs and graffiti are particularly overt on sections of the main road here where idle groups of young people hang out—but visitors are rarely affected.

The center of attention is the awesome Royal Naval Dockyard, a combination of maritime endeavors, arts and crafts, beach fun, and food. The cruise ship terminals at Heritage and King's Wharves bring thousands of visitors weekly to the area throughout the high season. The surrounding parish—including the scenic old Railway Trail—should not be overlooked. Sandys has few places to stay, including one major resort.

PLANNING YOUR TIME

Ferries are a highly recommended way to travel to the West End, particularly if your vacation is a short one. The fast-ferry fleet of Sea Express is the way to go, zipping between Hamilton and Dockyard in a mere 20 minutes, making it possible to spend even a few hours in Sandys, which has much more to see and experience than Dockyard (the ferries, which carry scooters, also run to other points in the parish). If your schedule permits, spend one or two days exploring. If it's utter relaxation you're after, you could easily spend an entire day at Cambridge Beaches' Ocean Spa, or exploring Hog Bay Park, hiking, swimming, and snorkeling its pristine shoreline, where a little-known beach offers secluded beauty. Or soak in the small-town vibe of Somerset's country lanes, having lunch overlooking tranquil bays that have changed little in centuries.

In terms of must-sees, Dockyard is at the top of the West End's offerings, worth a few hours at least. Next is Somerset Village, with its charming shops, cafés, and picturesque lanes leading off Mangrove Bay. If you have time to explore farther afield, the parish has huge nature reserves (Hog Bay Park, Heydon

Trust Estate), one of the island's most scenic forts (Fort Scaur), ultra-Bermudian eateries (Woody's, Gloria's), and myriad water sports, including scuba dives at interesting shipwrecks. The Sandys Railway Trail is a major highlight—one of the most scenic and peaceful stretches of the old rail bed-turned-walking route, running from George's Bay Lane to the Somerset Police Station at Somerset Village, Mangrove Bay. Along the way, enjoy bucolic residential neighborhoods, tracts of farmland, soccer pitches, and trails leading down to quiet docks and picnic areas on the Great Sound (the very best stretch is from Somerset Bridge westward).

Dockyard is perfect for a family visit, with sights, attractions, and eateries. The Hamilton-Dockyard ferry run allows scooters on board, so it's easy to explore Dockyard on foot, then drive out to see Somerset Village and the rest of the parish. Alternately, you could take a one-way ferry from Hamilton, then ride the bus or drive a scooter back through the parishes. The bus ride to Hamilton takes about an hour, with numerous stops; if you're traveling by scooter, count on a 30- to 45-minute journey to the city. Or take the bus or drive out via Harbour Road or the South Shore beaches and ride the ferry back. Driving both ways makes for a lot of scootering. Another option is to go by ferry, explore, and then take a Dockyard bus as far as Somerset Bridge to catch the Green Route Sea Express back to Hamilton.

Middle Road is the main parish artery for vehicles, continuing from Southampton. Its name changes as it passes through Sandys, becoming Somerset Road after Somerset Bridge, Mangrove Bay Road at Mangrove Bay, Malabar Road after Watford Bridge, Cockburn Road until Cockburn's Cut, and finally Pender Road to the Clocktower buildings (take Pender or the wharf-side Freeport Drive on the way out).

Royal Naval Dockyard

The Royal Naval Dockyard on Bermuda's western point is crucial to understanding what shaped the history of Bermuda. It's also loads of fun to visit. The 24-acre area—the largest and best preserved of Bermuda's fortifications—is a functioning community with shops, restaurants, a marina, and working boatyards that embodies the maritime history of the island, including its 150-year Royal Navy connection. "Dockyard," as it's simply called by locals, sits on Ireland Island North, the westernmost of Sandys's five islands, its tip forming the entrance to the main shipping channel into the Great Sound. Towering stone pillars stand at its entrance on Pender Road, where the notorious, now abandoned Casemate Prison looms. As Bermuda's primary cruise ship port, Dockyard's waterfront is a hive of activity in summer, with ferries coming and going, tourists pouring off ships at King's and Heritage Wharves, and charter fishing, snorkeling, sailing, and glass-bottomed boat operators at the ready.

Two outlets of the **Island Tour Centre** located near Dockyard's ferry stop allow booking with 20 island-wide vendors for scuba, Jet Ski, horseback riding, ecotours, and more. Dockyard's sheltered marina hosts myriad marine businesses operating in historic former military buildings. Public restrooms and ATMs are located in the distinctive **Clocktower Building**, the air-conditioned home to a plethora of shops, a restaurant, and an ice cream bar. There are three **Visitor Information Centres** (open only when ships are in port) at both cruise ship wharves and near the ferry dock, along with rental scooters, tour trains, Segway tours, and buses for exploring the area.

Special evening festivals are held throughout the summer, with live music, gombey performances, and food and drink stalls. The 35th America's Cup event in 2017 spurred a massive nine-acre land-reclamation project at the Dockyard's entrance, creating an impressive event village for the regatta; its legacy is now a substantial waterfront area that may become a conference center, a sailing academy, or a venue for international sporting events.

HISTORY

On the heels of the American Revolution, Bermuda's role in the maritime geopolitics of the day gained new stature. With the loss of its chain of North American ports (other than Halifax), Britain urgently needed a winter anchorage in the event of war with the United States or France and to protect its political and trade interests in the Caribbean. Efforts were begun immediately to transform once-sleepy Bermuda into a well-fortified British naval base and dockyard. Royal engineers designed breakwaters, boat slips, barracks, wharves, and a fortified keep. Construction—including massive land reclamation—began in 1809 and continued through the 20th century. Initially, this construction work was carried out by enslaved African workers, but after emancipation in 1834, Britain shipped over thousands of convict laborers from England and Ireland. Housed in converted warships called prison hulks off Dockyard, convicts quarried the region's hard limestone and, block by hand-sawn block, built what eventually became a self-contained "Little England" of military barracks, a prison, a hospital, warehouses, and munitions storage buildings, encircled by massive bastions, gun placements, and ramparts.

The payoff was immediate for Britain. In the War of 1812 with the United States, Britain launched its attack on Washington from the Bermuda Dockyard, its ships successfully sacking and burning the city. Over the next century and a half, Dockyard's Grassy Bay anchorage and sheltered docks catered to Britain's greatest warships, which evolved from tall-masted men-of-war and ironclads

Royal Naval Dockyard

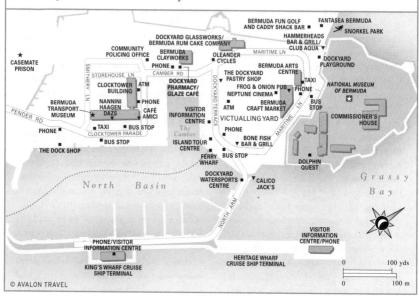

BERMUDA FUN GOLF AND CADDY SHACK BAR ■
FANTASEA BERMUDA
SNORKEL PARK

DOCKYARD GLASSWORKS/ BERMUDA RUM CAKE COMPANY ■
HAMMERHEADS BAR & GRILL/ CLUB AQUA ▼

COMMUNITY POLICING OFFICE ■
BERMUDA CLAYWORKS ■
OLEANDER ■ CYCLES
MARITIME LN
DOCKYARD PLAYGROUND ■

★ CASEMATE PRISON
PHONE ■ ■
CAMBER RD
BERMUDA ARTS CENTRE ■
DOCKYARD CYCLES

SMITHERY LN
STOREHOUSE LN
THE DOCKYARD PASTRY SHOP ■
TAXI ■

CLOCKTOWER BUILDING
ATM ■
DOCKYARD PHARMACY/ GLAZE CAFÉ ■
DOCKYARD TERRACE
FROG & ONION PUB ▼
NEPTUNE CINEMA ■
PHONE ■
NATIONAL MUSEUM OF BERMUDA ✚

BERMUDA TRANSPORT MUSEUM
NANNINI HAAGEN DAZS ★
PHONE ■
CAFÉ AMICI ■
VISITOR INFORMATION CENTRE ■
ATM ■
BERMUDA CRAFT MARKET ■
BUS STOP ■
COMMISSIONER'S HOUSE

PENDER RD
★ TAXI ■ BUS STOP
CLOCKTOWER PARADE
VICTUALLING YARD
The Camber
PHONE ■

PHONE ■
■ BUS STOP
ISLAND TOUR CENTRE ■
BONE FISH ▼ BAR & GRILL

THE DOCK SHOP ■
FERRY WHARF
■ BUS STOP
DOLPHIN QUEST ■
MARITIME LN

DOCKYARD WATERSPORTS CENTRE ■
CALICO JACK'S ■

North Basin

Grassy Bay

NORTH ARM

VISITOR INFORMATION CENTRE/PHONE ■

PHONE/VISITOR INFORMATION CENTRE ■

KING'S WHARF CRUISE SHIP TERMINAL

HERITAGE WHARF CRUISE SHIP TERMINAL

0   100 yds
0   100 m

© AVALON TRAVEL

armed with cannons to steam-driven dreadnoughts and diesel-turbine frigates bearing World War II torpedoes. The area also supported thousands of naval personnel and civilian staff.

The British operated an apprentice program at Dockyard in the 20th century, training a generation of Bermudians in the skilled trades of masonry, engineering, and electronics; some of these tradesmen are still alive today. The Royal Navy finally pulled out of Dockyard in 1951. Not until the 1970s and 1980s that a major renovation campaign transformed the Victorian military buildings into retail centers, restaurants, and artists' studios. Responsibility for the area now lies with the semipublic West End Development Corporation (WedCo), which has restored some of Dockyard's historic buildings, converting portions into residential lofts.

The National Museum of Bermuda, formerly the Bermuda Maritime Museum, located in the six-acre fortress Keep at Dockyard's westernmost section, was opened

in 1975. The museum's Commissioner's House, a landmark 1820s building made of limestone and prefabricated iron, was restored and opened in 2000 as a cultural heritage museum.

SIGHTS

With its historic wharves and restored military buildings, Dockyard is an attraction in itself, even without its shops and museum. Feel free to stroll around the area, where attractions sit next to working boatyards and sailmakers. Most of the shops and visitors services hug the waterfront along Clocktower Parade, the Camber Road, Maritime Lane, and Dockyard Terrace. You can watch glassblowing demonstrations, see ceramics being fired, and watch a cedar crafter work beauty from gnarled tree limbs.

Walk out along **King's Wharf** or **Heritage Wharf,** where scores of fishing craft and private yachts sit in a marina near giant cruise ships at the West End April-November. Opposite the entrance to the

National Museum of Bermuda is the 1831 **Cooperage,** a historic building where barrels for preserving foodstuffs in salt were manufactured. Today it houses the Frog & Onion Pub. Two forges are on display in the atrium by the cinema and craft market. On the other side of the atrium lies the **Victualling Yard,** where high walls protected the Royal Naval fleet's food and drink from theft. Today, picnic benches near the wide-open lawns make it a good lunch spot.

★ National Museum of Bermuda

Bermuda's largest and most visited attraction, the **National Museum of Bermuda** (The Keep, 15 Maritime Lane, northern point of Dockyard, tel. 441/234-1333, www.nmb.bm, 9am-5pm Mon.-Fri., 9:30am-5pm Sat.-Sun., last admission 4pm, $15 adults, $12 seniors, free under age 16) combines a spectacular property with historic buildings and fascinating exhibits, artifacts, and cultural heritage displays. Dolphin Quest is also based inside the property, allowing viewing of the dolphins even if you don't participate in its programs, which require advance reservations.

The museum's property was expanded from 10 to 15 acres and renamed in 2009 when the Bermuda government approved the transfer of the historic Casemate Barracks (a prison during the 1960s-1980s) and adjacent buildings and fortifications to the museum. The move restored the site's 19th-century military footprint, encompassing the dramatic Northwest Rampart, linking the Keep fortress with the Casemate area. The Casemate Barracks is currently closed for restoration, with no reopening date set as yet. Until then, the museum is in the Keep, a stronghold built to protect the Dockyard against attack by land or sea (though it never had to). The citadel has seven bastions and ramparts, reinforced by casemated gun emplacements with lines of sight sweeping the Great Sound and North and South Shores.

In the museum's lower grounds, the cavernous **Queen's Exhibition Hall,** where 4,860 kegs of gunpowder were once stored, tells the story of "Shipwreck Island," a compelling showcase of early shipwrecks, including artifacts from the *Sea Venture,* Spanish gold, and rare 17th-century ship rigging. The exhibit also explores life aboard ships and underwater archaeology. Across the lawn is the **Boatloft,** distinguished by its clock tower, where traditional Bermuda fitted dinghies are on display, along with other island craft. The famous pilot gig *Victory,* fully rigged, and the century-old racing yacht *Dainty* are prize maritime treasures. There are also exhibits on fishing and turtling, and children like to climb on the regal statue of Neptune, Greek god of the sea, out in the Keep Yard.

Kids will also love the **Museum Playground,** behind the Queen's Exhibition Hall, where a 21-foot lighthouse and slide—ensnared by a 70-foot green moray eel—will inspire pint-size adventures. An interactive playhouse with exhibits on local history encourages hands-on entertainment. Leading to the upper grounds from the ticket office is an intriguing exhibit inside the atmospheric **High Cave Magazine.** "Prisoners in Paradise" details the story of Dockyard's convict prisoners and Bermuda's Boer War prisoners, groups who left their legacies in the form of beautiful carved woodwork and stone artifacts.

The crown jewel of the museum, however, is **Commissioner's House,** on the upper grounds, the grand home of the Dockyard's civilian commissioner. It's a building unlike any other in Bermuda: The world's first cast-iron building, its girders, redbrick, and flagstones were shipped from England in the 1820s; while its three-foot-thick walls consist of hard limestone quarried from the Dockyard. Even if you're not interested in its exhibits, note that the house offers a spectacular vantage point: From the top-floor wraparound veranda, the sweeping panorama of the entire Dockyard is revealed, as well as the glistening turquoise seascapes of both the North and South Shores.

Three floors of exhibits fill the Commissioner's House, with rare Bermuda maps and historic Hogge money—the island's first currency. Other rooms explore the transatlantic slave trade and slavery in Bermuda, the Newport Bermuda Race, and the stories of Portuguese and West Indian immigrants. The second floor's dining rooms pay tribute to the British Navy and U.S. Navy in photographs and artifacts. Take a look also at the stunning 36-seat dining table in the Commissioner's Room, once a wartime mess hall, which now houses a collection of contemporary maritime art. Downstairs, a dozen interlocking rooms contain the exhibit "Bermuda's Defence Heritage," detailing the forts and cannons of the 17th century to Bermudian vets of World War II. A documentary film here includes interviews with local veterans. There's also the story of the famous "censorettes"—young Englishwomen headquartered at the Hamilton Princess Hotel who were trained to sift through incoming mail and telecommunications, checking for coded messages being sent to Germany. And don't miss a towering mural in Pillared Hall (containing the rear interior staircase), where Bermudian artist Graham Foster spent three and a half years recreating Bermuda's history in 1,000 square feet of floor-to-ceiling detail. Accessible from the first floor or ground floor, the hall is an artistic spectacle that has won rave reviews for Foster's prodigious talent and spawned a coffee-table book.

A major player in the island's heritage protection, the National Museum also has a conservation center where artifacts found on local shipwrecks and other sites are preserved. The museum coordinates with historians, archaeologists, and teams from abroad to organize joint field trips and dives throughout the year. Museum visitors can explore the historic windblown ramparts and gun placements around the Keep's perimeter, where Bermuda's only flock of sheep graze as natural lawnmowers. Museum admission also allows you to view the dolphins of **Dolphin Quest** (15 Maritime Lane, tel. 441/234-4464, www.

dolphinquest.org, 9:30am-5pm daily), located at the Keep Pond on the lower grounds.

Casemate Prison

Looming over the southern side of Dockyard is the now-closed Casemate Prison, or Casemate Barracks, built by convicts in the 1830s. The grim two-story structure is made of hard limestone, its thick walls and vaulted roof built to sustain enemy cannon and mortar fire. When the British Navy left Dockyard in 1951, "Casemates," as it's called locally, became the island's main prison, not closing until 1995, when a new prison facility, Westgate, was built just outside Dockyard on Pender Road.

Bermuda Transport Museum

Near the entrance to Dockyard, down one side of the Clocktower Mall building, the **Bermuda Transport Museum** (2 Smithery Row, tel. 441/799-2886, 10am-4pm Fri.-Sun., $5, free under age 12) relocated to larger West End premises in late 2017 after winning positive reviews inside a tiny Hamilton mall. The new space showcases 50-plus vintage Bermuda motorcycles and classic cars as well as a few carriages. Old Triumph and Zundapp bikes jostle with Hondas and Suzukis, but the focus is on Mobylettes and Cyruses—humble 50-cc specimens that were heavily modified by Bermudian youth in the 1970s. Train and boat exhibits are promised; there is already on display a huge foiling wing from Oracle Team USA's 2017 America's Cup catamaran, as well as a full mechanic's workshop and live engine displays.

BEACHES

Snorkel Park Beach (31 Maritime Lane, tel. 441/234-6989, www.snorkelparkbeach.com, 9am-6pm daily Apr.-Nov., $5, free under age 13), the Dockyard's only beach is through the limestone tunnel at the northwest corner of Dockyard, alongside the public playground and fountain. Rent snorkel gear, water toys, lounge chairs, and umbrellas, or eat and drink at on-site **Hammerheads Bar & Grill.** The beach is small but clean, and its waters offer good snorkeling at the foot of towering ramparts. Reef areas farther out in the shallow bay are also teeming with marinelife. Kids love the pontoons for jumping into the water. A **Fantasea Diving** outlet within the park offers learn-to-scuba (2.5 hours, $100 pp), rentals of pedal boats, snorkels, and kayaks, Jet Ski Safaris (1 hour, $150) and snorkel tours (Wed.-Fri., $39). Snorkel Park has large restrooms as well. Bermuda has plenty of pristine beaches offering back-to-nature serenity; this one is purely about social, noisy fun.

SPORTS AND RECREATION

Water Sports and Tours

Most water sports outfits are run out of Dockyard. Your first stop should be one of the two **Island Tour Centres** (tel. 441/236-1300, www.islandtourcentre.com, 8am-6pm daily summer, 9am-4pm daily winter), one at the pink hut adjacent to the ferry stop, and the other upstairs at the Island Outfitters building just across the street. Here you can book any type of water or land tour; the center acts as a one-stop shop for more than 20 vendors

island-wide for Jet Skis, paragliding, scuba, horseback riding, flyboarding, whale-watching, and ecotours. Most of the charter boats operating from Dockyard book tours through the center. Advance bookings can be made via the website. The **Dockyard Watersports Centre** is just a few yards away on the North Arm that connects Maritime Lane to both cruise ship wharves. Numerous vendors operate from this location and keep their vessels and water toys here; their services can be booked directly, or via the Island Tour Centre.

Fantasea Bermuda (Dockyard Watersports Centre, North Arm Dr.; inside Snorkel Park, tel. 441/236-3483, www.fantasea.bm, 8am-6pm daily May-Oct., www.fantasea.bm), the only PADI diving center in Dockyard, also offers snorkeling and sightseeing cruises, pontoon boat rentals, Railway Trail bicycle excursions, stand-up paddleboarding, and ecotours. Tours are typically 3.5 hours and range $75-85 adults, $55 children. Among the offerings are scuba diving trips to shipwrecks: *Sea Venture,* a decommissioned ferry sunk off Bermuda's coast in 2007, which brought the first English settlers in 1609; *Constellation,* a wooden American schooner that sank in 1943 after serving as a cargo ship in World War II; and *L'Herminie,*

ROYAL NAVAL DOCKYARD

kayaks and charter boats at Dockyard

Spirit of Bermuda

Bermuda sloop *Spirit of Bermuda*

In the "Age of Sail," Bermudians were renowned for innovative methods of boatbuilding and their sailing prowess. A nonprofit group has rekindled those talents in a new generation. The **Bermuda Sloop Foundation** (12 Wesley St., Hamilton, tel. 441/737-5667, www.bermudasloop.org) designed, built, and in 2006 launched an 85-foot (107 feet with the bowsprit) sail-training schooner, which now inspires maritime interest in young Bermudians.

The design of *Spirit of Bermuda* is based on the rig of an actual vessel that sailed out of Bermuda in the mid-19th century, with three heavily raked masts, the tallest in the middle, and a single boom on the mizzen. The main and foresail sheet like a jib, slightly overlapping the mast, and another jib is set forward on the schooner's long bowsprit. It has been adapted for safety reasons from the original Bermuda sloop design, which, while fast, challenged crews with its massive amount of sail—a huge, gaff-rigged mainsail and a square topsail. By contrast, *Spirit's* design is nimble but more akin to the Bermudian schooner hull, whose design evolved into the modern yacht. Noted for their speed and durability, cedar-made Bermuda sloops were the envy of the Atlantic in the 18th century, with many countries adapting the rig for trade, for privateering, and for pirating; they were often captured by pirates who coveted their getaway abilities.

Spirit of Bermuda was launched from a boatyard in Rockport, Maine, and now operates a full sail-training program for Bermuda youth. Berthed at Dockyard near the ferry dock, the ship is also hired out for private group charters (maximum 45 people). Various island stores also sell *Spirit*-monogrammed clothing and baseball caps.

a French wooden warship that sank in 1838, scattering cannons over the ocean floor. Dive instruction includes PADI Open Water certification ($600 for group session) as well as advanced courses. Two-tank ($169 pp) and one-tank ($119) dives are four-hour excursions; if you have your own BCD and regulator, you receive a 25 percent discount. Snorkeling passengers can tag along for great reef viewing ($75), or just come for the boat ride ($35).

Operating out of Dockyard, **Coconut Rockets/Bermuda Flyboard** (441/504-7197) lets you get airborne over the water. By way of boots and bindings, you're attached to a pressurized flyboard and propelled by a water jet pack up to 35 feet above the ocean surface.

Located on the grounds of the National

Museum of Bermuda, **Dolphin Quest** (15 Maritime Lane, tel. 441/234-4464, www.dolphinquest.org, 9:30am-4:30pm daily) is part of a U.S.-based for-profit group that also runs interactive dolphin encounter programs in Hawaii. Different programs are geared to various ages, including young children, and include programs where participants can get in the water and touch and swim with the boisterous mammals. The cost ranges from $219 for a 30-minute Dolphin Dip to $700 for a five-hour immersion as Trainer for a Day (age 10 and up). Reservations can be made two months in advance online or through its reservations office (tel. 540/687-8102 or 800/248-3316).

You can walk on the seafloor with **Hartley's Undersea Adventures** (tel. 441/234-2861 or 441/334-7607, U.S. tel. 866/836-3989, www.hartleybermuda.com, 9am and 1:30pm daily, $99 adults, $49.50 riders), which has a pickup point next to the moon gate at Heritage Wharf. Morning and afternoon trips of 3-4 hours aboard dive boat *Rainbow Runner* offer shallow-water helmet diving, allowing even nonswimmers to go beneath the surface to see reefs and marinelife wearing a helmet that gets fresh air pumped from the boat. No tanks, snorkels, or masks are needed, and you can even wear prescription glasses or contact lenses, as your head stays dry. Tame angelfish and grunts, familiar with the helmeted visitors, come out to be fed on these expeditions.

Based at Dockyard, award-winning ecotour company **Hidden Gems** (tel. 441/704-0999, bermyreefexplorer@gmail.com, www.bermudahiddengems.com, reservations www.islandtourcentre.com, over age 7, summer 7 hours $175 pp, winter 5 hours $100) offers year-round excursions to different parts of the island as well as charter tours and can pick up at the Fairmont Southampton and the Botanical Gardens south gate. Owned and run by former teacher Ashley Harris, the company offers a way to experience the "real" Bermuda, with an active itinerary that might include climbing to the top of St. David's Lighthouse, swimming in a crystalline cave, or literally jumping off a cliff. Harris provides each tourgoer with a backpack stocked with all necessary supplies, including snacks, water, a mask and snorkel, a flashlight, and an umbrella.

Other Tours

You can see Dockyard aboard a Segway with **Segway Tours** (tel. 441/236-1300, www.segway.bm or www.islandtourcentre.com, 10am-4pm daily May-Oct.). Look for the yellow double-decker bus parked at the Camber Road intersection with Dockyard Terrace; advance bookings also can be made online or at the Island Tour Centre outlets at Dockyard or Hamilton. A 90-minute tour includes a video and training session to help you master the electric self-balancing scooter. The cost is $80, with weight and age restrictions.

Mini-Golf

Commanding an acre of oceanfront property with 180-degree vistas alongside Snorkel Park is Best of Bermuda Award-winner **Bermuda Fun Golf** (tel. 441/400-7888, www.fungolf.bm, 10am-10pm daily summer, 10am-sunset Fri.-Sun. winter, $15 adults, $12 children). The mini-golf complex has become a mecca for fans of the sport thanks to its 18 carefully designed holes that masquerade as some of the world's best: Number 7 at Pebble Beach, the island green at Sawgrass, the Golden Bell at Augusta, and the Braid Bravest at Gleneagles—they're all here. Relax at the **Caddy Shack Bar** afterward.

For Kids

Dockyard's tiny-town feel is just right for kids. Getting there is half the fun. The Sea Express fast ferry from the Hamilton ferry terminal ($8 return adults, $4 ages 5-16, free under age 5) is a blast, even for grown-up kids. The 20-minute ride darts across the breezy Great Sound with boats, houses, and skylines to take in.

At Dockyard, exit the ferry and head right, following the main road around to the **National Museum of Bermuda** (15

SANDYS PARISH
ROYAL NAVAL DOCKYARD

Maritime Lane, tel. 441/234-1333, www.nmb. bm, 9am-5pm Mon.-Fri., 9:30am-5pm Sat.-Sun., last admission 4pm, $15 adults, $12 seniors, free under age 16), where kids can learn loads about pirates, shipwrecks, and gold treasure lost in Bermuda waters over the centuries. The lower floor of **Commissioner's House** appeals to young museumgoers with its cave-like maze of interlocking rooms, where exhibits feature giant cannons, forts, and local soldiers from the 1600s to the 1900s. Upstairs, kids can admire sweeping views of the entire North Shore from the building's upper balcony. Don't let them climb the railing! On the lower grounds, wrap up the visit with time at the **Museum Playground,** where a zippy slide curves out of a play lighthouse entwined within a giant moray eel structure. An interactive **Playhouse** will keep young children engaged in tactile activities.

Dolphin Quest (15 Maritime Lane, tel. 441/234-4464, www.dolphinquest.org) is located on the southern part of the lower grounds. The mutual appeal of dolphins and kids is adorable, and while actually swimming with the clever mammals is a wonderful experience, just watching them cavort in the Keep Pond is almost as much fun. It's free with admission to the museum. Reservations for dolphin encounters need to be booked in advance; use the website.

Outside, to the right of the museum gates, is the **Dockyard Playground** (free), complete with a pirate ship to scramble aboard, captain's wheels to turn, and a tunneled slide to descend, along with swings. In the heat of summer, it's grilling here by midmorning. If they get too hot, there's a fountain for youngsters to get soaked in.

Through the adjacent gate is **Snorkel Park Beach** (31 Freeport Rd., tel. 441/234-6989, Apr.-Oct.), a great little cove for kids, with tons of amenities and playthings. Rent a noodle, mask and snorkel, or a floating chair. Adults like the beachside bar, just a few yards from the water's edge. There are large restrooms and a restaurant serving hot dogs, burgers, and other lunchtime staples

sure to please waterlogged youngsters. Next door, **Bermuda Fun Golf** (tel. 441/400-7888, www.fungolf.bm, 10am-10pm daily summer, 10am-sunset Fri.-Sun. winter, $15 adults, $12 children) is a hit with hackers of all ages; children's parties are often held here.

Alternatively, the **Frog & Onion Pub** (The Cooperage, Maritime Lane, tel. 441/234-2900, www.frogandonion.bm) serves up hearty pub grub inside or under umbrellas on the outdoor terrace. There's a large games room in the back, with coin-operated video games and a pool table. Don't miss **Nannini's Häagen-Dazs,** a popular ice cream bar, or **Bermuda Fudge Company** (tel. 441/533-8343, www. bermudafudgeco.com) in the Clocktower Mall. Both are a hit with pint-size customers.

Finally, if the kids are still awake, **Neptune Cinema** (4 Maritime Lane, tel. 441/234-2923) occasionally shows children's matinees, mainly during midterm breaks and Easter and summer holidays. Get some popcorn and candy and relax in the small air-conditioned interior.

ENTERTAINMENT AND EVENTS
Nightlife

Laid-back resort by day, **Snorkel Park Beach** (31 Maritime Lane, tel. 441/234-6989, www. snorkelparkbeach.com, 10pm-3am Mon. and Wed.-Thurs. May-Oct., age 18 and over, $10 cover charge) turns nightclub when the sun goes down, attracting crowds of islanders and visitors with regular happy hours at its open-air **Club Aqua,** beach parties featuring top local DJs and live music, limbo dancers and gombeys, and special dance events that last until the wee hours and require smart-casual dress throughout the summer months.

Floating bar **Calico Jack's** (tel. 441/504-5225, 11am-1am daily summer) looks like a beat-up pirate vessel—and that's the whole point. The converted ferry now doubles as a booze-cruise private charter that sometimes crashes the party in Hamilton, or an all-day bar when moored near the moon gate outside Heritage Wharf. DJ nights and themes like

Thirsty Thursday and Sunday Rumday are popular, and although walking the plank is optional, many patrons swear jumping off the bow between rounds is the highlight.

Cinema

Neptune Cinema (The Cooperage, Victualling Yard, 4 Maritime Lane, tel. 441/292-7296) is the West End's only cinema; it usually gets movies after they have shown at Hamilton's Liberty Theatre. The friendly staff sells popcorn and candy, but don't expect an IMAX-style screening.

SHOPPING
Clocktower Mall

Clocktower Mall (9am-6pm daily summer, 10am-5pm daily winter) is the West End's main shopping center, with more—and busier—retail outlets than Somerset Village, particularly on weekends and during the cruise-ship season, when the mall gets swamped with passengers. Note that many stores here keep shorter winter hours, as the Dockyard reverts to quiet maritime enterprises once cruise season is over. There are ATMs, restrooms, and air-conditioning.

Beautiful kilim rugs, hanging lanterns, ceramics, shawls, and clothing from **Grand Bazaar** (tel. 441/234-4646, www.grandbazaarbda.com) are brought in from Turkey by husband-and-wife team Bulent and Teresa Ganal. Shipping to the United States, Canada, or Britain can be provided. Boyd and Muna Vallis also run a husband-and-wife operation, **Fair Trade** (tel. 441/234-5657), with carved wooden animals, wind chimes, jewelry, sarongs, and beautiful trinkets from Indonesia.

Bermuda Triangle, Littlest Drawbridge, and **Dockyard Linen** sell Bermuda T-shirts, cedar trinkets, ornaments, and other island souvenirs. **Carole Holding Studio** (tel. 441/238-7310, www.caroleholding.bm) carries the artist's painted mailboxes, postcards, cutting boards, and mugs based on her island watercolors. **Bermuda Fudge Company** (tel. 441/533-8343, www.bermudafudgeco.com) sells its own gluten-free fudge ($13 per half pound) in flavors from peanut butter crunch to mint chocolate swirl. West End branch stores of Front Street's **A. S. Cooper** (tel. 441/234-4156), **Crisson** (tel. 441/234-2223), **E. R. Aubrey Jewellers** (tel. 441/234-4577), **Davison's** (tel. 441/234-0959), and **Calypso** (tel. 441/295-2112) are also located here.

Calico Jack's floating bar

Camber Road

On Camber Road, just around the corner from the Clocktower Mall, **Makin' Waves** (tel. 441/234-5319, www.makinwaves.bm, 9am-6pm daily) has the West End outlet of its popular beach gear store. The large space is a surf shop with everything for fun "in, on, or under the water," including swimwear and shades by Maui Jim and Oakley; a full range of snorkeling equipment; souvenirs; casual wear brands like Billabong, Rip Curl, Roxy, and Quiksilver; sandals, flip-flops, and board shorts; and skim and body boards, as well as large stand-up paddleboards.

Jon Faulkner Gallery (7 Camber Rd., tel. 441/234-5116, www.jonfaulknergallery.com, 9am-6pm or later daily summer, 10am-5pm daily winter) has a floor full of bright ceramics for sale and worldwide shipping service. No reservations are needed for its popular paint-your-own pottery studio; prices ($16-48) include the cost of glazing and firing. Turnaround time is 7-10 days, and pieces can be shipped.

Maritime Lane

You can watch free glassblowing and flameworking demonstrations at **Dockyard Glassworks** (1 Maritime Lane, tel. 441/234-4216, www.dockglass.com, 9am-5pm daily summer, 9am-7pm when ships are in port, 10am-5pm daily winter), where artists create beautiful art glass in the Venetian tradition. An adjoining retail gallery sells a rainbow of glassworks, which make elegant souvenirs and gifts, including Christmas ornaments. Adjoining the little factory is the **Bermuda Rum Cake Company** (tel. 441/234-4216, www.bermudarumcakes.com, 9am-5pm daily summer, 9am-7pm when ships are in port, 10am-5pm daily winter). Sample nine different flavors of the island's favorite dessert, including black rum, rum swizzle, dark chocolate rum, and banana rum.

Opposite the entrance to the National Museum of Bermuda, the 20-year-old **Bermuda Craft Market** (4 Maritime Lane, tel. 441/234-3208, 9:30am-5pm daily summer, 10am-5pm daily winter) is a co-op that sells the work of more than 60 artists, a collection that includes cedar, candles, needlework, quilts, ceramics, and batiks. There's also a section full of rare Bermuda books and contemporary editions. Sample Bermuda food products like ginger beer or jam, and meet artists who give demonstrations of crafts such as banana doll-making or jewelry creation throughout the high season.

Next to the Bermuda Craft Market, with a cherry-red English phone box outside, is the **Bermuda Arts Centre** (tel. 441/234-2809, www.artbermuda.com, 10am-5pm daily, free), one of the key venues for showcasing island artists. Regular seasonal shows as well as a retail store and resident artists' studios give visitors a true sense of the vibrant local arts scene. Plein air watercolorist Christopher Marson and oil painter Chris Grimes keep working studios here, as does renowned cedar craftsman Chesley Trott. Drop into his sweet-smelling workshop, where rough boughs lie ready for transformation into polished works of art. Trott, who teaches in the prison system, has an impressive collection of cedar pull-toys, including crickets and frogs. His public artworks are somewhat larger—an eight-foot totem pole, intricately carved with Bermudian icons, sits in the arrivals hall of the airport. The venue is wheelchair-accessible.

Dockyard Terrace

Island Outfitters (tel. 441/238-4842, 9am-5pm daily, 8am-8pm when cruise ships are in port), located in one of the old two-story naval buildings just steps from the ferry stop, sells T-shirts, tanks, jewelry, and Bermuda souvenirs, including duty-free rum, sherry peppers, and pepper jam (must be ordered by 1pm the day your of cruise ship's departure). It's a popular Wi-Fi zone too, with tables outside for catching up on email, news, and social media.

FOOD
Cafés, Pubs, and Takeout

Frog & Onion Pub (The Cooperage, Maritime Lane, tel. 441/234-2900, www.

frogandonion.bm, lunch 11:30am-5:30pm daily, dinner 5:30pm-9:30pm daily, bar 11:30am-midnight daily) serves up much-loved pub grub. Starters include German pretzels ($10) and deep-fried pickles ($11). Salads are inventive, with Southwest chicken and blackened wahoo ($20). And old favorites never die: fish-and-chips ($25), bangers and mash ($19), steak and kidney pot pie ($21) and chicken balti curry ($20). The pub also offers quiz nights, happy hour specials, and live entertainment most evenings, plus kids' activities on Sunday afternoons (magic shows, free ice cream). The outside patio is a popular free Wi-Fi hot spot.

Situated in a former British naval officer's cottage, ★ The Dockyard Pastry Shop (12 Dockyard Terrace, entrance to Victualling Yard, tel. 441/232-2253, www.thedockyard-pastryshop.com, 9am-5pm daily) serves up cappuccino, pastries, desserts, gourmet sandwiches, quiche, and pies. Customers can enjoy lunch on the little patio, or head indoors to the upstairs room. It also serves beer and wine. Anglophiles can enjoy afternoon tea (2pm-5pm daily) with fresh-baked scones, clotted cream, and marmalade. No wonder it won a Best of Bermuda Award for "Best Place to Satisfy Your Sweet Tooth."

With its shady terrace overlooking a private cove, Hammerheads Bar & Grill (Snorkel Park Beach, 31 Maritime Lane, tel. 441/234-6989, www.snorkelparkbeach.com, 9am-6pm daily, bar 11am-3am daily Apr.-Oct., $11-17) is popular for its burgers, sandwiches, snacks, and cold drinks, including frozen alcoholic and virgin cocktails.

Nannini's Häagen-Dazs (Clocktower Mall, tel. 441/234-2474, 9am-6pm daily summer, 10am-5pm daily winter) has large premises at the mall's front entrance to accommodate eager crowds who flock here for frozen indulgence (waffle cone $5.50). Tables invite a welcome rest in the mall's welcome air-conditioning. It serves Starbucks coffee too.

Glaze Dockyard (Dockyard Pharmacy, 7 Camber Rd., tel. 441/279-5551, 8am-5pm Mon.-Fri., 9:30am-5pm Sat.-Sun.), one of several Glaze outlets throughout the island, is perfect for a takeout gourmet coffee, smoothies, cold drinks, sandwiches, chicken nuggets—and the all-famous doughnuts.

International

Pizza and pasta are king at Café Amici (Clocktower Mall, 5 Freeport Rd., tel. 441/234-5009, www.amicibermuda.com, 9am-10:30pm daily Apr.-Oct., 9am-5pm Sun.-Thurs., 9am-9:30pm Fri.-Sat. Nov.-Mar.), the West End's only Italian restaurant. The family-style eatery is located in the western corner of the Clocktower Mall. Chef-owner Livio Ferigo has created a comfort-food menu based on his childhood favorites, including pastas ($19-24) and pizzas ($16-23). He goes local for Sunday breakfast ($17), however, offering a spread of traditional Bermudian codfish and potatoes 9am-noon.

Sister restaurant Bone Fish Bar & Grill (6 Dockyard Terrace, tel. 441/234-5151, www.bonefishbermuda.com, lunch 11:30am-10:30pm daily, bar 10:30am-1am daily, $16-37) serves up a wide menu of Bermuda seafood, pasta, jerk chicken, salads, and sandwich specials. The front patio, just steps from the ferry dock, is a shady people-watching place in the afternoon, while the giant wooden deck commanding a large outside corner features live bands and DJs for nighttime entertainment, as well as salsa (Mon.), karaoke (Wed.), and reggae (Thurs.).

ACCOMMODATIONS

To date there are no lodgings in the Royal Naval Dockyard, though various historic buildings here have been converted to loft living spaces.

INFORMATION AND SERVICES

Dockyard has three Visitor Information Centres: Two operate in the cruise ship terminals (King's Wharf and Heritage Wharf) only when a ship is in port; the main outlet sits in Gazebo 2 near the ferry dock at Dockyard

Terrace (tel. 441/296-9400, 8am-4:30pm daily, 8am-8pm when ships are in port). Each sells bus and ferry tickets and passes, and provides information and advice on local tours and attractions. Dockyard's **Community Policing Office** (2 Sally Port Lane, North Basin, tel. 441/234-1010, 8am-8pm) was established in 2014 as an auxiliary police base in Sandys. The main police station is in Somerset Village.

At the area's only liquor store, you can find everything from cold drinks and coffee to fishing tackle and boating supplies. **The Dock Shop** (Pier 41, tel. 441/238-4141, 7am-7pm Mon.-Fri., 8am-6pm Sat.-Sun. summer, 8am-5pm Mon.-Fri., 9am-5pm Sat.-Sun. winter), located at the entrance to Dockyard on the waterside, has a marine gas station alongside; the facility provides berthing and bunkering services to vessels. **The Dockyard Pharmacy** (7 Camber Rd., tel. 441/279-5410, 8am-5pm daily) is a full-service pharmacy stocking prescriptions, international newspapers, beauty and fashion accessories, souvenirs, and a West End outlet of **Glaze Café.**

ATMs are outside the western entrance to the Clocktower Mall, on Dockyard Terrace, and at the Visitor Information Centres. **Public toilets** are located inside the Clocktower Mall, in a small building on Dockyard Terrace, outside Bermuda Craft Market, inside the National Museum of Bermuda's lower grounds, and on two upper floors of Commissioner's House. The whole of Dockyard is a **Wi-Fi** hotspot, though some areas such as restaurants and cafés may be better for getting online.

TRANSPORTATION
Buses
Bus service to and from Dockyard offers a scenic journey if you take route 7, which goes via the South Shore beaches (route 8 also travels between Hamilton and Dockyard via Middle Road). Buses leave Hamilton every 15 minutes for the West End. The 14-zone journey ($4.50) takes about an hour. Bus stops are located in front of the National Museum of Bermuda and in front of the Clocktower Mall.

Ferries
The **Sea Express** (tel. 441/295-4506, www. marineandports.bm) Blue Route operates regularly between Hamilton and Dockyard from morning (7:10am) to night (last ferry leaves Dockyard at 9pm summer, 4:30pm winter) Monday-Friday, with less-frequent service on Saturday, Sunday, and public holidays.

a courtesy shuttle in Dockyard

The service runs every half hour throughout most of the day. Most runs are Hamilton-Dockyard direct. Along the way, you'll see Front Street's facade; the lavish harbor-front mansions of Pembroke's Fairylands and Point Shares neighborhoods; landmark Two-Rock Passage, where ships come through; and the islands of the Great Sound. The breezy ride takes just 20 minutes. Sit up on the sunny top deck (with salt spray on windy days), or escape the heat in the main air-conditioned cabin. Cash is not accepted on ferries; buy tokens, tickets, or passes from the ferry terminal or Visitor Information Centres in Hamilton, St. George's, or Dockyard. Regular one-way fare to Dockyard is $5 adults, $2.75 ages 5-15, free under age 5; take your scooter on board for $4.50.

Scooters and Bicycles
Oleander Cycles (King's Wharf, Royal Naval Dockyard, tel. 441/234-2764, 8:30am-5:30pm daily) rents single- and double-seater scooters, as well as mountain bikes. Scooters can be rented by anyone age 16 or older. Rates ($55 standard, $65 double for 1 day, $225 standard, $266 double per week, $17 standard, $21 double per day after 7 days) include scooter delivery and pickup (or hotel pickup), the first tank of gas, a helmet, a lock, a basket, third-party insurance ($30), and island-wide roadside service for breakdowns. Bicycles can be rented for $40 per day, $175 per week.

Taxis
If cruise ships are in port, there are usually lots of taxis in and around Dockyard. Taxis stands can be found outside the gates of the National Museum at Dockyard, and in front of the Clocktower Mall. Some operators are qualified tour guides—look for the special Blue Flag sticker or flag.

Shuttles
The **Horseshoe Bay Shuttle** via mini-buses ($14 round-trip, $7 one-way) is run by the Bermuda government and West End Development Corporation. Buses travel throughout the day between the popular South Shore beach and King's Wharf terminal when ships are in port; the last shuttle back to Dockyard is at 7pm. Bermudian **Beau Evans** operates a blue-and-white free courtesy shuttle train that loops around Dockyard. Hop aboard for a ride between shops and restaurants.

Somerset Village

So small that you might whiz right by it if you're not paying attention, Somerset Village is a quaint, historic little community hugging picturesque Mangrove Bay. Mangrove Bay Road slopes through it to Dockyard. Pastel storefronts, wooden verandas, and the kind of old-time languor you thought the Internet had forever vanquished make Somerset a relaxing little community. Lanes like Tween Walls, which run off on either side of Mangrove Bay Road, are worth strolling. Take a swim in the palm-fringed bay, where the surface looks like a mirror when the wind is right, or from the public dock, where freight was once offloaded from ships onto horse-drawn carts. Like Flatts Village, Somerset was a key maritime port for trade and boating around the island in the days before roads linked the parishes. Illicit cargo was often taken to harbors like these to evade customs duties in Hamilton or St. George's. Today, Somerset doesn't seem capable of such energy. Sample the several eateries and mosey around the sleepy shops. As part of a West End tour, it only takes a few hours to experience the village.

BEACHES
Mangrove Bay Beach, with its line of coconut palms and pile of wooden dinghies, offers a taste of the way Bermuda used to be. Swim

Somerset Village

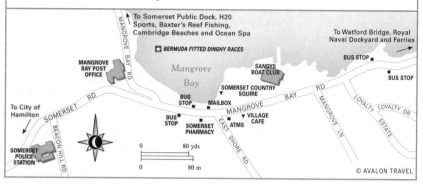

To Somerset Public Dock, H20
Sports, Baxter's Reef Fishing,
Cambridge Beaches and Ocean Spa

To Watford Bridge, Royal
Naval Dockyard and Ferries

BERMUDA FITTED DINGHY RACES

BUS STOP

MANGROVE
BAY POST
OFFICE

SANDYS
BOAT CLUB

BUS STOP

*Mangrove
Bay*

SOMERSET COUNTRY
SQUIRE

MANGROVE BAY RD

SOMERSET RD

BUS
STOP

MAILBOX

To City of
Hamilton

BUS
STOP

SOMERSET
PHARMACY

MANGROVE

BAY RD

VILLAGE
CAFE

ATMS

MANGROVE LN

LOYALTY ESTATE

LOYALTY DR

BEACON HILL RD

EAST SHORE RD

0   80 yds

SOMERSET
POLICE
STATION

0   80 m

© AVALON TRAVEL

in the shallow, clear bay where schools of fry jump at dawn. There's plenty of parking in front of the post office.

SPORTS AND RECREATION
Water Sports

Take to the water to explore by Jet Ski, kayak, sailboat, or motorboat from **H2O Sports** (30 King's Pt., Mangrove Bay, tel. 441/234-3082, www.h2osportsbermuda.com, 8:30am-7pm daily May-Dec.). Single or double kayaks ($25 per hour), stand-up paddleboards ($25 per hour), day-sailers ($80 1st hour, $10 each extra hour), Hobie Cats ($60 1st hour), and 17-foot sailboats and motorboats ($100 1st hour, $30 each extra hour) can be rented along with snorkel and fishing gear. It's a perfect way to explore the many tiny coves, beaches, islands, and islets around this part of the island. Pack a picnic and head to the reef-laden South Shore flats or around Mangrove Bay and the Great Sound coastline. Jet Ski Safari tours are $135 for 75 minutes.

Fishing

Baxter's Reef Fishing (tel. 441/234-2963 or 441/334-9722, www.bermudareeffishing.com, 8:30am and 1pm daily, $110 pp, $650 custom charters for up to 6, $85 under age 13) departs from Mangrove Bay public dock at the foot of Cambridge Road. Captain Michael Baxter

offers half- and full-day reef-fishing charters in his 32-foot Cape Islander, *Ellen B.* Typical catches are chub, grouper, triggerfish, snapper, porgy, shark, and barracuda; you can catch and release, or take your fish home for dinner. The boat can accommodate up to 10 people.

Spas

Cambridge Beaches' **Ocean Spa** (30 Kings Point, tel. 441/234-3636, www.cambridge-beaches.com) has seven rooms and offers a full menu of face and body treatments as well as massage therapy. The De-Stress Muscle Release (80 minutes, $220) and Marine Breeze Facial (60 minutes, $140) taps the fountain of youth. Packages combining a facial with a massage and manicure (Ocean Spa Sampler $293) allow use of the whirlpool, sauna, steam room, lockers, showers, robes, and slippers. Upstairs, Aquarian Baths, a luxurious indoor heated pool with a retractable roof, is also available. Half-day (10am-1pm or 2pm-5pm, $40) or full-day (10am-5pm, $65) passes are a nice way to experience the resort and chill out on vacation.

ENTERTAINMENT AND EVENTS
Nightlife

There's not much of a nightlife scene in Somerset, aside from a lively bar at one central village establishment, **Somerset Country Squire** (10 Mangrove Bay Rd., tel. 441/234-0105, 11am-1am daily).

★ Bermuda Fitted Dinghy Races

Mangrove Bay and its nearby shoreline provide some of the best vantage points from which to watch the Bermuda dinghy races. The much-loved tradition, featuring the island's trademark vessels vying for weekly honors amid mountains of sail and a flotilla of spectator boats, is one of the summer's highlights. Dinghy races are held every Sunday afternoon, alternating between different parts of Bermuda, namely St. George's Harbour, Granaway Deep in the Great Sound, and Mangrove Bay, where they sail from **Sandys Boat Club** (tel. 441/234-2248). The best part is when crewmembers jump overboard to lighten the load (they usually get rescued by passing friends or swim to raft-ups, where they can cheer on their boat with a beer or rum). Just around a few corners, on Watford Island, the **West End Sailboat Club** (tel. 441/234-1252) organizes the annual East-to-West Comet Race.

Non-Mariners Race

"Anything but a boat" is the battle cry of participants vying for honors in Mangrove Bay's annual **Non-Mariners Race** (tel. 441/234-2248). Organized by the Sandys Boat Club, the Sunday-afternoon affair on the weekend following Cup Match features teams of Bermudians gussied up as pirates or in top hats, trying to sail across the bay in assorted craft made from anything you might least imagine had the ability to float. Needless to say, most end up in the drink. It's a laugh, for participants and the crowd of onlookers, many of whom arrive by boat and form party-style raft-ups that remain the entire day. Check out their Facebook page.

SHOPPING

Knowledgeable, friendly staff make shopping a delight at **Somerset Pharmacy** (49 Mangrove Bay Rd., tel. 441/234-2484, sompharm@northrock.bm, 8am-6pm Mon.-Thurs., 8am-5pm Fri.-Sat., 11am-2pm Sun.), which also sells postcards, towels, and souvenirs. Its best items are the well-chosen toys for all ages, rivaling larger Hamilton stores. Major-brand dolls, action figures, arts and crafts, balls, board games, baby toys—it's a child's heaven.

Genuine linen-blend Bermuda shorts (pink, yellow, red, $60) can be found at the Somerset branch store of **English Sports Shop** (Somerset Rd., tel. 441/234-0770, 10am-5pm Mon.-Sat.), along with linen and wool blazers ($250-275), Bermuda silk ties (sporting longtails, horse and carriage, and Hamilton's pastel skyline), and conservative women's fashions.

FOOD
Cafés and Pubs

Home turf of yachties and other neighborhood regulars, the **Somerset Country Squire** (10 Mangrove Bay Rd., tel. 441/234-0105, lunch 11:45am-2:30pm Thurs.-Sat., noon-4pm Sun., dinner 5:30pm-9:30pm daily, $6-30) has a cave-like bar and dining room downstairs that's used throughout the winter, and an alfresco bar and terrace overlooking Mangrove Bay, where fish dinners, fresh lobster, burgers, steak and kidney pies, and filet mignon are popular summer fare. A children's menu is offered and live TV sports, including NASCAR and English soccer matches, draw a crowd.

Cambridge Beaches (30 Kings Point Rd., tel. 441/234-0331, www.cambridge-beaches.com) has two casual alfresco cafés: **Breezes** (lunch noon-3pm daily, dinner 7pm-9pm Thurs.-Sat. May-Oct., $9-55) is on Long Bay Beach; **Shutters** (noon-3pm daily year-round, $6-22) at the resort's poolside, is open for lunch.

Venette and her team run a tight ship at the pocket-size roadside **Village Café** (29 Mangrove Bay Rd., tel. 441/234-3167, 7am-4pm and 6pm-11pm Mon.-Thurs., 7am-3pm Fri., 9:30am-4pm Sat.), efficiently whipping up a tasty early-morning breakfast (bacon, egg, toast, coffee $10, omelets $11, Johnny bread $3) until 10:30am weekdays, before serving a wide-ranging lunch menu from burgers ($6) to Bermuda fish entrées ($17) to a lineup of locals. Pizzas are also popular, as either an 18-inch pie (from $18) or $5 slices.

Fine Dining

Candlelight dinners are served in ★ **The Tamarisk Room** at Cambridge Beaches (30 Kings Point Rd., tel. 441/234-0331, U.S. tel. 800/468-7300, www.cambridgebeaches.com, 7pm-9:30pm daily), where cedar-steeped surroundings, dark coral walls, and silver service make for a formal treat. Jacket and tie are optional for male guests, but "elegant-casual" is the suggested dress code. The gourmet five-course menu by chef Keith DeShields changes daily, along with recommended wine selections. Appetizers include spicy chicken and coconut soup ($12), while mains include local delicacies such as a garlic-baked half lobster (seasonal, $50), and more exotic fare such as a roasted rack of Kurobuta pork ($37). For dessert, try the chocolate martini ($17).

ACCOMMODATIONS

Dating back to the 1930s, **The Ledgelets** (6 The Ledgelets Dr., tel. 441/504-6962, www.theledgelets.com) is a slice of old-time Somerset. Owners John and Alison Young have refurbished the cluster of pink cottages that once belonged to his grandfather. Sitting in the quiet coastal community alongside one of the most scenic stretches of the Railway Trail, Sunrise Cottage ($750), with three bedrooms, three baths, and a separate living room and playroom, is perfect for a family getaway. The one-bedroom Pool House ($250) has a porch surrounded by lush gardens. Both are tastefully outfitted with beach and bath towels, toiletries, cable TV, surround-sound music, updated kitchen, free Wi-Fi, a barbecue, a washer-dryer, and a shared pool.

Historic ★ **Cambridge Beaches** (30 Kings Point Rd., tel. 441/234-0331, U.S. tel. 800/468-7300, www.cambridgebeaches.com, $434-1,300 d) is one of the island's premier cottage colonies—resorts in which units are arranged around a central clubhouse amid other facilities. The five-star, 30-acre resort has 94 rooms, four private beaches, a putting green, a croquet lawn, tennis courts, a water sports center, two restaurants, two bars, and a spa. A pool with an infinity edge and waterfall feature is a highlight of the property. In the main house, a paneled library and stuffed floral sofas conjure the ambience of a grand English mansion. Accommodations range from rooms to suites to a cottage with a private pool. Old-style rooms and suites in cottages, or contemporary condo-style units overlooking Mangrove Bay, are furnished in an island-chic mahogany, sisal rugs, rattan, and bold florals. Amenities include cable TV, Internet hookups, air-conditioning, and king beds. Bette Midler, Kenny G, and Natalie Cole have all stayed here over the years. A no-children policy (minimum age is 13) means it's a favorite for honeymoons, anniversaries, and other couples escapes. It also has a useful dine-around exchange agreement with other West End properties that allows guests to eat meals at The Reefs resort or Bella Vista at Port Royal Golf Course, with the only cost being transportation and beverages.

INFORMATION AND SERVICES

Mangrove Bay Post Office (55 Mangrove Bay Rd., tel. 441/234-0423, 8am-5pm Mon.-Fri.) offers snail-mail and Internet service. It is the island's most picturesque post office, in a restored historic building a few feet from the sand of Mangrove Bay Beach.

Somerset Pharmacy (49 Mangrove Bay Rd., tel. 441/234-2484, 8am-6pm

Mon.-Thurs., 8am-5pm Fri.- Sat., 11am-2pm Sun.), offers a pharmacy and regular drugstore items, as well as postcards, beach towels, and lots of toys. One of few independent pharmacies on the island, **Caesar's Pharmacy** (30-32 Somerset Rd., tel. 441/234-0851 or 441/234-0987, caesarpharm@tbinet.bm, 9am-7pm Mon.-Sat., 2pm-6pm Sun.) has an efficient pharmacy and all the drugstore basics in a small store.

Somerset Police Station (3 Somerset Rd., atop the hill entering Mangrove Bay, tel. 441/234-1010 or 441/234-1011, www.police.bm) is the regional detachment with responsibility for the West End. Two retail banks have branches in Somerset Village: **Butterfield Bank** (45 Mangrove Bay Rd., tel. 441/234-0048, 9am-4pm Mon.-Fri.) and **HSBC** (31 Mangrove Rd., tel. 441/295-4000, 9am-4:30pm Mon.-Fri.). **ATMs** are located outside both bank branches. **Bud's Wines & Spirits** (10 Mangrove Bay Rd., tel. 441/234-1740, 8:30am-8pm Mon.-Sat.), on the main village street alongside the Somerset Country Squire, stocks ice, cigars, bait, beer, and wine. **Public toilets** are available at restaurants, Mangrove Bay Post Office, and next to Somerset Police Station.

TRANSPORTATION

Buses 7 and 8, which travel every 15 minutes between Hamilton and Dockyard, serve the village. The Watford Bridge stop is the closest to Somerset Village, served by the Sea Express Blue Route **ferries** with five scheduled stops throughout the day. The one-way fare is $5 adults, $2.75 ages 5 to 12 (tokens or tickets required, no cash or change accepted).

Oleander Cycles has an outlet at Cambridge Beaches (30 Kings Point Rd., tel. 441/234-0331), renting single- and double-seat scooters.

Around Sandys

The environs of Somerset Village and points east as far as the Southampton border encompass a wonderful array of places to leisurely pass time. Swim at the countless little coves, hike through the several beautiful parks, and ogle spectacular ocean views on both shores. The region is best seen in a flexible time frame; even a day on a scooter or walking the Railway Trail will give you a truer sense of real life "out West."

SIGHTS
Lagoon Park and the Royal Naval Cemetery
Beyond Dockyard's gates and over one-vehicle-wide Grey's Bridge on Ireland Island South is **Lagoon Park** (sunrise-sunset daily, free), a large, quiet chunk of parkland that has a spectacular islet-sprinkled coastline on the Great Sound. Named for the central lagoon, which attracts birdlife, insects, toads, and frogs, the park has lots of picnic tables and grassy lawns, as well as coves and bays for swimming. Nestled alongside the parkland is a large meadowy valley that contains the Royal Naval Cemetery, with intriguing headstones and above-ground cemetery plots, where the lives and often unfortunate deaths of naval officers, crewmen, and their families are honored with touching inscriptions. Easter lilies pop up in spring, and wildflowers are scattered over the hillside.

Somerset Long Bay Park
Lovely **Somerset Long Bay Park and Nature Reserve** (Daniel's Head Rd., off Cambridge Rd., sunrise-sunset daily, free) is co-owned by the Bermuda National Trust and the Bermuda Audubon Society. This coastal mangrove area is a sanctuary for resident and migratory birds. A plot of adjoining private land was purchased to expand the protected zone, which now includes a stretch of pristine coastline. Restoration of the reserve included

culling invasive species and replanting endemics, as well as clearing garbage. Located on a quiet stretch far from the noise of road traffic, the grassy park, equipped with a playground set, is a shady place to relax, and the shallow beach, with turtle grass and reefs just a few yards out, is a good spot for snorkeling. It's also a popular local beach for picnics and swimming in summer.

★ Somerset Bridge

The smallest drawbridge in the world, **Somerset Bridge** (Somerset Rd. at Robinson's Marina) has become a quintessential Bermuda icon, featured on postcards and the island's banknotes for almost a century. The bridge's central plank can be raised just wide enough to permit a yacht's mast to be eased through by someone standing above, thereby allowing vessels to pass between the Great Sound and Ely's Harbour (though this is a rare occurrence in modern times). Built in the 17th century, the structure is one of the most historic points in the parish, connecting Somerset Island to the mainland. A roadside park sits alongside the bridge, a good place for a picnic while watching boats pass through the waterway. The park also connects to the Railway Trail.

★ Fort Scaur and Park

One of the region's loveliest views can be had from a quiet bench atop **Fort Scaur** (Scaur Hill, Somerset Rd., sunrise-sunset daily, free), overlooking the Great Sound and Dockyard. A telescope allows you to see as far as Fort St. Catherine and St. David's Lighthouse. The West End fort and its surrounding 22 acres of parklands are one of the island's most scenic and well-preserved fortifications. Built in the 1870s, the fort was intended to guard the crossing at Somerset Bridge and a landward enemy approach toward the Dockyard. It was used through the 1920s; later the American 52nd Coast Artillery mounted two eight-inch railway guns here. The fort, with ramparts, cannons, and gun placements, is surrounded by a defensive ditch that extends the length of Somerset Island. A steep trail leads eastward through the woods to the Railway Trail on the shoreline below. You can also walk into the galleries flanking the hillside and go through the sally port into the ditch, itself an impressive feat of engineering. Picnic tables and lawns invite relaxation in the adjoining park.

On the left as you descend the other side of Scaur Hill, heading out of the West End,

Fort Scaur

cherry forests around the property. The land is a noted birding location.

★ Hog Bay Park

One of Bermuda's most spectacular wild parks, government-owned **Hog Bay Park** (sunrise-sunset daily, free) comprises 38 acres of open space, leading from a roadside parking lot on Middle Road to the coast. Between are undulating shady dirt trails that lead past an ancient limekiln near the entrance, rise past numerous tracts of agricultural fields and cherry, loquat, and spice trees, and descend to seaside trails past prickly pears and the silvery skeletons of Bermuda cedars. While it is Bermuda's third-largest park, and one of its most untamed, Hog Bay is underused; you can find remarkable solitude exploring it in any season, although the steep hills require you be fit. Follow the main trail down to the shoreline, where there's a beach area at low tide and a beautiful spot for swimming. Sea grass attracts turtles here, and rock pools contain crabs and sergeants major. You can actually explore a long section of the coastline, with the wide-open horizon of the South Shore flats stretching out as far as you can see. At low tide, the shallows extend for about 1,000 feet, good for snorkeling.

The park, which is used occasionally for cross-country races and mountain biking, is named for Bermuda's wild hogs, which roamed the island when the first settlers arrived in the early 17th century. It's believed that in years prior, passing mariners had offloaded the animals to multiply and create a natural larder at Bermuda that might feed castaways wrecked on the island's treacherous reefs. The former Hog Bay, where settlers found a large herd of the swine in the West End, is now called Pilchard Bay.

BEACHES

The West End's **Glass Beach,** on Ireland Island South, is a repository for washed-up sea glass of all shapes and colors. So much is piled up that you can't even see the underlying sand. That wind chime-like tinkling

trail to the beach at Hog Bay Park

is **The Parapet,** the mustard-colored home where artist Georgia O'Keeffe stayed during her visit to Bermuda in the early 20th century. O'Keeffe was recovering from depression at the time, but her charcoal drawings of a banyan tree and banana flowers helped restore her creative energies.

Heydon Trust Estate

Open to the public, the privately owned, 22-acre **Heydon Trust Estate** (Heydon Dr., off Somerset Rd., sunrise-sunset daily, free) is a natural enclave of protected woodland, farmers' fields, a couple of private homes, and the charming **Heydon Chapel** atop the hill. Turn in off the main road and follow the country lane all the way to the tiny whitewashed building, which overlooks the Great Sound. It dates to a 1616 survey of Bermuda, and today is still used for religious services. Nearby, a walled rose garden contains numerous chinas, teas, and other species; it's considered one of Bermuda's best collections. There are also trails rambling through the extensive you hear as you approach is the glass pieces being turned over by gentle waves rolling in. The beach, not signposted, is located on the southwest shoreline (not the Great Sound side) outside the pillars at the bridge leading into Dockyard. Follow Cochrane Road back from Cockburn's Cut about 650 feet, and you'll find a trail through the casuarina woods (look for the historic stone tower). The beach is at the foot of the trail.

Black Bay, also on Ireland Island South, opposite the Royal Naval Cemetery, has a gem of a beach that appears only at low tide. Night herons can sometimes be seen standing like statues on the coastal rocks—until they dart for crabs in the shoreline rock pools. Throughout most of the summer, it's a good place for a shallow, calm swim, and there are picnic tables nearby.

Somerset Long Bay (turn off Somerset Rd. onto Cambridge Rd., which leads down to the park and shoreline) is the perfect place to cool off, far from traffic and the crowds who frequent the larger South Shore beaches (including Warwick Long Bay) most weekdays. On weekends and public holidays, Somerset Long Bay sees local families come for picnics and swimming.

Daniel's Head Beach Park (turn off Somerset Rd. onto Long Bay Lane, then left along the shore to the end of Daniel's Head Rd.), comprises 17 acres of coastal green space, including two public beaches with pristine bays perfect for snorkeling, kayaking, or stand-up paddleboarding. Vendors are on-site in summer, along with a café. Just offshore is the *Vixen* shipwreck, a fish magnet that's a mecca for snorkelers.

SPORTS AND RECREATION
Water Sports
Blue Water Divers & Watersports (Robinson's Marina, Somerset Bridge, tel. 441/234-1034, www.divebermuda.com) has been leading dive expeditions for more than 30 years. Its qualified guides lead a two-tank dive ($130) at 9am daily, followed by a single-tank dive ($90) in the afternoon. Scuba enthusiasts often want to do both, with a soup lunch at the marina in between. Dive packages can also be arranged. There are numerous interesting shipwreck dives off the West End, many in shallow reef-laden waters, including the 1881 *North Carolina,* the 1943 *Hermes,* and the *Maria Celestia,* a U.S. Civil War blockade-runner that sank in 1864 (the vessel's paddle wheels remain intact).

jet skiing under Somerset Bridge

Bermuda Waterski & Wakeboard Centre (Robinson's Marina, Somerset Bridge, tel. 441/234-3354 or 441/335-1012, www.islandwindsbermuda.com) is run by Bermudian über-athlete Kent Richardson, an accomplished triathlete and expert skier. He gives group or individual water-ski and wakeboarding lessons (1 hour $200, up to 6 people) aboard his *Ski Nautique* in the Great Sound or off the West End, depending on the weather. Richardson also offers cliff jumping and snorkel tours aboard his speedboat.

Somerset Bridge Watersports (Robinson's Marina, Somerset Bridge, tel. 441/234-0914, www.bdawatersports.com, 8am-7pm daily Apr.-mid-Oct.) rents 13-foot (2 hours $95, 4 hours $145) and 15-foot Boston Whaler motorboats, kayaks ($25 single, $30 double per hour, 4 hours $60 single, $75 double) and Jet Skis (1.25 hours single $125, double $135). All three options are great for exploring the West End by water.

Island Winds (Daniel's Head, tel. 441/234-1111 or 441/705-1111, www.islandwindsbermuda.com) is based at this beachside peninsula where Canadian Forces kept a military base until the 1990s. Today, it's a favorite destination for water sports enthusiasts. Glenn Mello's enterprise rents and sells equipment and offers lessons on stand-up paddleboarding (board rental $30 per hour), windsurfing (lessons $200), kayaking, and kiteboarding.

★ Railway Trail (Sandys)

The Railway Trail in outer Sandys Parish is one of the nicest stretches to walk of the whole island, with a flat shady trail passing farmlands, residential neighborhoods, forts, and dramatic seascapes. Get on at George's Bay Road, at the former U.S. Naval Air Station Annex; the trail leads all the way to Mangrove Bay. From the former Somerset Bridge ferry stop westward, the trail hugs the Great Sound shoreline, with wonderful views and tributaries that allow you to break off to swim or visit sights like Fort Scaur. Be careful of speeding motorbikes along the tarmacadam sections;

local residents are allowed to use motorized vehicles on the trail.

ENTERTAINMENT AND EVENTS

TOP EXPERIENCE

★ Cup Match

Bermuda's favorite public holiday is held Thursday and Friday in late July or early August; it celebrates **Emancipation Day,** marking the freedom of Bermuda's slaves, followed by **Somers Day,** in honor of island founder Sir George Somers. With the weekend tacked on, Cup Match makes for a four-day extravaganza loosely revolving around a historic and hotly contested cricket match. Cup Match takes place every other year in Sandys, alternating with St. George's. For over a century, St. George's and Somerset Cricket Clubs have battled for victory—and major bragging rights—in a two-day tournament that draws thousands of spectators to either end of the island (teams take turns playing host).

But Cup Match is so much more than cricket. Many attend the game at **Somerset Cricket Club** (6 Cricket Lane, tel. 441/234-0327), whose team colors are red and navy, or St. George's Cricket Club (navy and baby blue) simply to socialize over mussel pie, fish sandwiches, and peas 'n' rice sold from stalls dotting the grounds. Others come to try their luck at Crown & Anchor, an old British Navy dice game, during the only two days of legal public gambling. The weekend presents a who's who of Bermuda and a slice of true island life, making it imperative to experience if you're vacationing here at that time.

FOOD

Cafés, Bars, and Takeout

Tucked behind the legendary Somerset Cricket Club (home of Cup Match every other year), **Green Lite Café & Eatery** (15 Cricket Lane, tel. 441/234-1211, 8:30am-9pm Mon.-Thurs., 8:30am-11pm Fri.-Sat., 10am-7pm Sun., $3-10) is a rarity in Bermuda—a vegetarian and vegan establishment. Shawnette

Rules of Cricket

Cricketers in action at Cup Match

More popular even than Christmas among Bermudians, Cup Match is a two-day public holiday celebrating cricket, held on a Thursday-Friday in late July or early August. Cup Match incorporates Emancipation Day, marking the end of slavery in Bermuda in 1834, and Somers Day, the founding of Bermuda by English admiral Sir George Somers. Many Bermudians take the midsummer break to go camping, boating, and beaching, but the focus of holiday fervor is the annual cricket showdown between the east and west ends of the island.

For weeks leading up to the match, residents flaunt their team's colors—baby blue and navy for St. George's (east), navy and red for Somerset (west). The match is held in alternate years at Somerset or St. George's Cricket Club, drawing crowds of thousands. Attendees often spend both days at the cricket grounds, soaking up the food, fashions, and festive atmosphere—not to mention the game itself.

For those unfamiliar with the intricacies of Bermuda's national summer sport, a few basic insights:

· The game is played between two sides, each with 11 players; as in baseball, each team takes turns hitting and pitching a ball (called "batting" and "bowling"), and the team with the most runs wins.

· Each side has a captain who nominates his players before a coin toss; if a captain wins the toss, he chooses whether to bat or bowl first.

· A match can last one or two "innings" (when a team bats).

· The team batting tries to score as many runs as possible up and back a narrow 22-yard "pitch" between batter and bowler, while hitting the ball around the oval field.

· The team bowling (always overarm) can get the batsman out by catching the ball or knocking two wooden "bails" from the top of the "stumps" with the ball; stumps are three vertical wooden posts making up the "wicket," situated at each end of the pitch.

· To novices, cricket is best known for its arcane terminologies—oddities such as "googly" (a screwball pitch designed to fake out the batter), "double century" (an individual batter's score of 200 runs or more), "chinaman" (a left-handed spin bowler), "maiden over" (six pitches in which no runs are scored), "leg-break" (a pitch that breaks into a batter's body off the bounce), and "sticky wicket" (a field that is partly wet and dry, causing uncertain bounce conditions that confuse batters).

Simmons Smith's brainchild is attracting a loyal following of healthy eaters eager for lentil and chickpea burgers, spinach lasagna, breaded broccoli, stir-fried cabbage, apple crumble, split pea soup, and a salad and smoothie bar.

You'll find Gloria Smith cooking up a storm at **Gloria's Kitchen** at West End Sailboat Club (Watford Island, tel. 441/234-1252 or 441/234-2523, lunch 11am-3pm Mon.-Sat., dinner 5pm-10pm Fri.-Sat., $9-14), including loads of fresh fish, chicken, salads, and peas 'n' rice. Standing on the edge of a harborside inlet where convict laborers were once jailed, popular local watering hole **Woody's Drive-In Two Bar & Restaurant** (1 Boaz Island, tel. 441/234-2082, tel. 441/234-6526, 11am-1am daily, $7-17) offers typical Bermudian comfort food. Most popular are its wicked fish sandwich (one of the island's best), fish cakes, and burgers. The outdoor bar attracts locals.

Four Star Pizza (65 Somerset Rd., tel. 441/234-2626, 7am-11pm Mon.-Thurs., 7am-midnight Fri.-Sat., 7am-10pm Sun., $8-22) has a wide-ranging menu of takeout or delivery subs, Indian curries, and Asian rice dishes, in addition to its popular pizza. **Misty's Takeout** (54 Main Rd., tel. 441/234-2449, 11am-10pm Tues.-Sat., 9am-5pm Sun., $5-9) is popular for its fish sandwiches and burgers—ideal for an authentically Bermudian lunchtime picnic.

Right next door, alongside the busy road, **De Island Shack** (56 Main Rd., tel. 441/777-7422, 6am-6:30pm Mon.-Fri., 7am-6pm Sat., 11am-5pm Sun.) has an enthusiastic social media following and a delicious daily menu of fresh-baked scones, pumpkin muffins, and apple crumb pie, as well as coffee and herbal teas. You can find local favorites such as gingerbread, cinnamon buns, and Bermuda-made sherbet, as well as gluten-free treats.

Grocery Stores

The aroma of whole rotisserie chicken draws folks to the **Somerset MarketPlace** (48 Somerset Rd., tel. 441/234-0626, 8am-10pm Mon.-Sat., 9pm-7pm Sun.), the area's largest grocery store and part of an island-wide chain. A full array of frozen and dry goods are sold, along with wines, beer, spirits, dairy, meat, and deli products.

Arnold's Supermarket (41 Somerset Rd., tel. 441/234-2237, 7am-10pm Mon.-Sat., 7am-midnight Sun.) is just down the road east of MarketPlace but offers a much smaller selection of goods. The next-door **Arnold's Liquor Store** (tel. 441/234-0963) does a roaring trade. **Maximart** (42 Middle Rd., tel. 441/234-1940, 6:30am-midnight daily) is a small modern supermarket with lots of parking and all the basics, including fresh fruits and vegetables.

ACCOMMODATIONS

Outer Sandys doesn't have much lodging, although there are numerous short-term rental units on www.airbnb.com, www.vrbo.com, www.bermudarentals.com, and www.bermudagetaway.com. Just across the Southampton-Sandys border at Caroline Bay, plans are under way for a **Ritz-Carlton Reserve** (8 Caroline Bay Rd., tel. 441/234-4900, http://www.carolinebaymarina.com) with 84 rooms and 147 residences on the former site of a U.S. military base; it's slated to open by 2020.

Garden House (4 Middle Rd., tel. 441/234-1435) is a true gem, tucked up a limestone drive just footsteps from Somerset Bridge. For more than three decades, owner Rosanne Galloway has rented a two-bedroom, two-bath cottage ($200 d) and a poolside studio unit ($115 d). Both have full kitchens. The three-acre property's manicured gardens surround the home. Persian carpets, antiques, TV, and private phones make guests feel at home.

INFORMATION AND SERVICES

Rubis Robinson's Marine Service Station (178 Somerset Rd. at Somerset Bridge, tel. 441/234-0709, robinsons1@logic.bm, 6:30am-10pm Sun.-Thurs., 6:30am-10:30pm Fri.-Sat.) is a year-round hub of visitor and local activity. The small station shop sells shades, fishing supplies, and snacks. The plaza outside is home to several water sports outfitters and deep-sea fishing operations, and the dock is also used by area anglers.

Rubis Boaz Island Marine Service Station (28 Malabar Rd., Boaz Island, tel. 441/234-0128, 6:30am-8:30pm Mon.-Sat., 7am-7pm Sun. summer) sells cold drinks, cookies, potato chips, and some canned goods. There is also a marine service area on the waterfront for boat fuel refills. **Sandys Esso Service Station** (37 Somerset Rd., tel. 441/234-1542, 6:30am-8pm Mon.-Sat., 8am-5pm Sun.) is a handy outlet on the main road into the West End.

Two laundries within a half mile of each other are **Sandys Laundromat** (MarketPlace Plaza, off the main road, tel. 441/238-3200) and **Somerset Laundromat** (57 Middle Rd., tel. 441/234-3361). **ATMs** are located outside Maximart and Somerset MarketPlace grocery stores. **Public toilets** are located at Hog Bay Park and at area gas stations and restaurants.

TRANSPORTATION
Buses

Routes 7 and 8 run via Middle Road through Sandys every 15 minutes throughout the day, with the first bus leaving Hamilton at 7am and the last departing Dockyard at 10:20pm Monday-Friday; on Saturday the first bus is at 9:30am and the last departs Dockyard at 11:59pm. Sunday and public holidays, schedules run every half hour 9:30am-6pm.

Ferries

The **Sea Express** (tel. 441/295-4506, www.marineandports.bm) Blue Route runs between Hamilton and Watford Bridge and Cavello Bay in the early morning, late afternoon, and evening. While Hamilton-Dockyard service operates every half hour, ferries travel to these outer parish stops only during commuter periods. The 6:30am ferry from Hamilton stops in at Dockyard before returning to the city. One-way fare is $5 adults, $2.75 ages 5-15, free under age 5 (no cash or change accepted; tickets or tokens only).

Smith's and Hamilton Parishes

Smith's Parish.................. 172   Hamilton Parish............... 182

Look for ★ to find recommended
sights, activities, dining, and lodging.

Highlights

★ **Spittal Pond Nature Reserve:** Explore this sprawling 34-acre bird sanctuary—the island's premier nature reserve—via rolling coastal trails with unparalleled outlooks over the South Shore (page 175).

★ **John Smith's Bay:** A family favorite, this small half-moon bay is good for a day's retreat or just a dip (page 178).

★ **Bermuda Aquarium, Museum & Zoo:** This waterfront facility's lush grounds and modern exhibits offer an up-close look at the island's diverse marinelife, plants, and conservation projects, as well as intriguing creatures from around the world (page 184).

★ **Blue Hole Park and Walsingham Nature Reserve:** Head to this forest reserve with winding trails through cherry bushes, mangroves, and sunken caves where fish and turtles can sometimes be seen (page 185).

★ **Crystal Cave and Fantasy Cave:** See two spectacular examples of a honeycomb that riddles the parish (page 187).

★ **Shelly Bay Beach and Nature Reserve:** Nothing is more beautiful on a summer day than the mirror-flat turquoise shallows of this roadside beach (page 189).

© AVALON TRAVEL

With some of Bermuda's most rugged scenery, Smith's and Hamilton Parishes appeal to outdoors enthusiasts seeking Bermuda's less-manicured facets, along with birders, beachgoers, history buffs, and families.

Two beautiful bodies of water shape the contours of these parishes—Harrington Sound and Castle Harbour. Each is ringed with stunning homes, often hidden from the main road, and a honeycomb of limestone caves, including two open for public tours. Both parishes feature sections of the South and North Shores, scenic stretches of the Railway Trail, wide farmland tracts, beaches, swimming coves, nature reserves, historic sites, and must-see attractions.

There are several routes to travel through the two parishes, the most scenic being South Shore Road and Harrington Sound Road. In Smith's, South Shore Road leads east from Collector's Hill, up McGall's Hill, and past the wooded splendor of Spittal Pond Nature Reserve to John Smith's Bay and Mangrove Lake, Bermuda's largest saltwater pond. Continuing east on the South Shore, a small chunk of Hamilton Parish is cushioned by the undulating greens of the world-famous Mid Ocean Club. Briefly crossing the parish boundary into Tucker's Town, St. George's, it's necessary to cut through Paynter's Road to return to Hamilton Parish via picturesque, serpentine Harrington Sound Road.

From the eastern reaches of Hamilton Parish, you can take the Causeway into St. George's or explore North Shore neighborhoods, such as Coney Island, Bailey's Bay, and Crawl. North Shore Road also hugs the cove-sprinkled coast through Smith's to the border of Flatts Village, before linking to a narrow, postcard-pretty stretch of Harrington Sound Road—another pleasant way east, particularly on dead-calm days when the North Shore horizon looks like a lake, and arriving cruise ships can be seen following the distant channel into the Great Sound. Middle Road is a third route through Smith's, traversing the parish's residential interior, with schools, a riding stable, and grazing pastures. Interconnecting roads like precipitous

Harrington Hundreds, St. Mark's Road, farm-dotted Verdmont Road, and Knapton Hill, with its moon gates and modern middle-class spreads, are also worth meandering.

PLANNING YOUR TIME

Both Smith's and Hamilton Parishes are full of historic, eco-oriented, and recreational attractions. You could spend several days' exploring this region, with the Bermuda Aquarium, Museum & Zoo, Spittal Pond Nature Reserve, Crystal Cave and Fantasy Cave, and beaches. Any of these could also be visited as part of a drive east to St. George's, since all are easily accessible from the main roads. Cafés, restaurants, and ice cream parlors, like those at Flatts Village, Collector's Hill, Crawl, or Bailey's Bay are en route. Kayak and sailboard rentals, scuba, snorkeling, and sailing charters can also be arranged through several operators here.

Beginning in Flatts, a whole day's outing could be tailored to a circuit of Harrington Sound, encompassing visits to Bermuda Aquarium, Museum & Zoo, the caves, parks, beaches, or historic sites like Holy Trinity Church. Shopping and organized entertainment in both parishes, however, are few, with mostly tiny stores inside large attractions. Hotel and guesthouse accommodations are also few, so it's likely you would venture here from other parishes. Mopeds, taxis, and buses are efficient ways to get around; well-marked bus stops are outside most sights.

As elsewhere, the Railway Trail offers lovely out-of-the-way views, coastal serenity, and glimpses of genuine Bermudian life, though the trail is interrupted by main roads at a couple of points. Several of Bermuda's best swimming areas are located in these parishes, a mixture of South Shore's surf and sand and North Shore's calmer, sometimes rocky coves, snorkeling areas, and deep swimming holes.

Smith's Parish

The dramatic lookouts, diverse plants and animals, and the coastal trail of Spittal Pond Nature Reserve are enough to make Smith's worth visiting, but the parish has much more, including a historic, some say haunted, house that's now a museum, beautiful beaches on both shores, panoramic stretches of the Railway Trail and Harrington Sound, and a few good restaurants. Smith's is largely residential, with a busy community hub at Collector's Hill offering a grocery, a pharmacy, restaurants, gas, and ATMs.

The parish also has substantial parcels of land producing onions, strawberries, carrots, and other seasonal produce. A dairy farm, one of just two on the island, sits next to Spittal Pond Nature Reserve. Smith's is home to many Portuguese residents, some of them newly arrived Azorean contract workers, others naturalized immigrants; many more are families that have been here for generations.

Driving through the rolling parish, you can't help but be wowed by spectacular views of all kinds: Longtails arching from sheer cliff faces, red dawn lifting over the glass-like surface of Harrington Sound, sapphire depths of a favorite swimming hole that maintain the rural modesty of Bermuda as it used to be.

SIGHTS
Verdmont Museum

High on a hill overlooking the South Shore, **Verdmont Museum** (6 Verdmont Lane, off Collectors Hill, tel. 441/236-7369, www.bnt.bm, 11am-2pm Wed., 10am-4pm Fri., $5 adults, $2 ages 6-18, or $10 combo ticket for 3 BNT museums) is a historic home that offers a glimpse of old-time colonial life as well as a ghost legend. Flanked by sentry-like palmettos and surrounded by rambling lawns and rose beds, this treasure of the

Smith's Parish

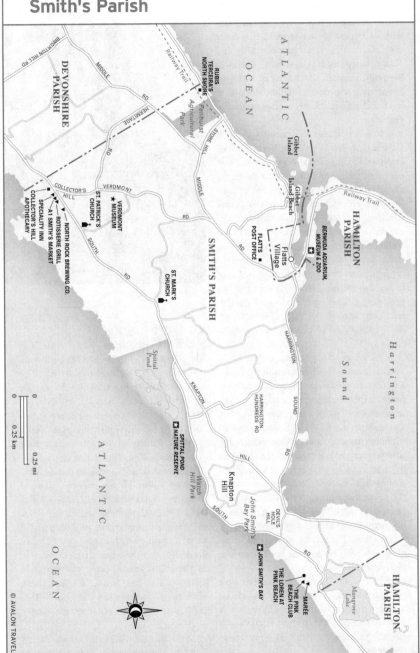

© AVALON TRAVEL

Bermuda National Trust sits at the end of a quiet lane off heavily trafficked Collector's Hill. The home's distinctive architecture, with four grand chimneys and a fine cedar staircase, incorporates elements of 17th- and 18th-century building design. Unlike most Bermudian houses, which typically exhibit a hodgepodge of structural add-ons, Verdmont has remained structurally unchanged for 300 years.

Historians guess Verdmont was built around 1710. The home's English-influenced layout includes a formal drawing room and parlor on the ground floor and a charming nursery at the top of the house, displaying a rocking horse, Victorian dollhouse, and other timeworn toys. The home's collection of furniture, assembled by the trust in the 1950s, includes fine Bermuda cedar cabinets, desks, and a Chippendale-style tallboy with marching legs. Several imported furnishings were brought to the island by early sea captains, including Chinese porcelain and English hurricane shades. Portraits of several former Verdmont owners hang throughout the house.

Some believe the phantom of one 1930s resident, Spencer Joell, remains in the house. Several tour guides over the years have reported experiencing strange feelings, finding furniture inexplicably moved around, and sensing an odd chill in various rooms, including the attic nursery. Visitors often ask whether the house is haunted. One incident involved a New Jersey couple who took a snapshot of the nursery in 1976, and later mailed the photo to Verdmont's then-curator. The room was empty, they said, when they took the picture, yet the photo showed a man sitting at a table. The curator recognized the figure immediately because she had known him well—it was Joell.

In recent years, archaeological digs have been carried out on the property and exhibits added to interpret the story of Verdmont's enslaved residents. The gardens are also worth exploring, peppered with herbs, roses, and fruit trees.

historic St. Mark's Church

St. Patrick's and St. Mark's Churches

Along South Road in the McGall's Hill area, the Portuguese influence is strong. The large circular Roman Catholic church, **St. Patrick's** (23 South Shore Rd., tel. 441/236-9866, stpats@logic.bm) incorporates Portuguese elements into readings and songs of its 9am Sunday service. Gardens carefully planted with Easter lilies, vegetables, or brilliantly hued flowers speak to the community's agricultural legacy, and the names of so many neighborhood residents—Moniz, DeSilva, Cabral, Furtado—reflect the waves of Portuguese immigration over the past 150 years. Azoreans were brought to the island in the mid-1800s to help spur a farming revival. By the 1870s, annual exports of Bermuda onions (70,000 barrels and 350,000 crates), arrowroot, potatoes, and tomatoes to U.S. East Coast cities had revitalized the island's economy.

At the top of McGall's Hill sits **St. Mark's Church,** a quaint parish landmark built in

1847 whose spire can be seen down the valleys on both sides. Inside, its cedar altar and pulpit are good examples of Bermudian workmanship. The graveyard, draped with riotous bougainvillea at certain times of year, is also worth a wander.

TOP EXPERIENCE

★ Spittal Pond Nature Reserve

The rugged, 34-acre **Spittal Pond Nature Reserve** (sunrise-sunset daily, free), co-owned by the Bermuda National Trust and the government, has two entrances along South Shore Road. Both have parking lots and lead to the circuitous trail around the park, though the eastern entrance offers more direct access to some of the most dramatic viewing spots. This is the island's premier nature reserve and includes a valley cradling the large brackish pond, several freshwater ponds, and surrounding marsh and woodland through which meandering trails climb to spectacular outlooks over the South Shore.

The reserve's varied habitats provide a refuge for resident and migratory birds, including woodland cardinals, finches, mallards, turnstones, sandpipers, cliff-nesting longtails,

blue herons, white egrets, occasional visiting hawks, and the ubiquitous yellow-crowned night herons, which devour crab populations throughout the island.

The park's highlights include the Portuguese Rock—a historic carving on an exposed rocky cliff face, believed to have been left by Portuguese mariners before the island's colonization. The inscription, now cast in bronze, includes letters that look like "RP" (possibly for *Rex Portugaliae*, referring to João III, Portugal's monarch) and the date 1543. Historians believe the markings were the work of 32 castaways who escaped their shipwreck off Bermuda that year and spent time on the island fashioning a new vessel from cedar timber. Up here, atop cliffs tumbling down to frothy boiler reefs below, the flat rock face surrounded by a cedar fence gives a breathtaking view of the whole southern coastline. Assorted contemporary graffiti has been carved in the outlook's limestone.

Just down the trail from Portuguese Rock is "Jeffrey's Hole," a cave with an overhead entry hole; the cave, according to local lore, once served as a temporary shelter for an escaped enslaved person. Another oddity, at the western end of the park, is the Checkerboard—a large, flat square rock surface near the water's

Spittal Pond Nature Reserve

Bermuda's Portuguese Heritage

On November 6, 1849, a sailing ship made port in Hamilton carrying the first 58 Portuguese immigrants to Bermuda. "We sincerely trust this importation of laborers will answer the end contemplated," read a dispatch in *The Royal Gazette*, "and we hope they will be the means of inducing the cultivation of the wine more extensively than at present."

Vineyards never became a thriving enterprise in Bermuda, but those first farm workers from the island of Madeira were the vanguard of waves of Portuguese immigration. Thousands of Portuguese followed, mostly from the remote Azores Islands, filling a dire need for agricultural expertise. The export of onions, arrowroot, tomatoes, and other products became an economic generator for the island in the late 19th century.

Bureaucratic and societal discrimination relegated Portuguese immigrants to the status of second-class citizens into the 1960s and 1970s. Strict government regulations attempted to bar the immigration of whole families and restricted job classes to menial labor. Like blacks until desegregation in the 1960s, the Portuguese were banned from many of the island's social clubs. But established Portuguese helped new immigrants find their footing and lobbied for their rights. In the 1980s, the Portuguese-Bermudian Association pressed the case of long-term residents of Portuguese descent who had been born in Bermuda but had no legal right to stay on the island. The group finally nudged the government to grant long-term residency to people of various nationalities who made significant contributions to Bermudian society. Today, Portuguese Bermudians make up 25 percent of the population.

The **Vasco da Gama Club** (51 Reid St., Hamilton, tel. 441/292-7196), is a longtime social and political hub for the community. Portuguese is now considered a second language on the island, and in recent years, government and some businesses have begun to provide services in Portuguese. The **Portuguese Cultural Association** promotes traditions by teaching dance, cooking, and other arts performed at events such as the Bermuda Day Parade in May.

Religious *festas* also make colorful public spectacles throughout the year, with ornate costumes and processions on carpets of petals to celebrate Roman Catholic saints. In the procession of Santo Cristo, held the fifth Sunday after Easter, hundreds gather at St. Theresa's Cathedral in Hamilton for a solemn march through the city's streets to seek miracles for the sick and needy. In June, Portuguese Bermudians celebrate the **Festa do Espiritu Santo** (Festival of the Holy Spirit) in King's Square, St. George. An elaborate pageant paying tribute to the legendary charity of Queen Isabel includes a feast for participants who are served bowls of *sopa* (soup) and *pão dolce* (sweet bread).

The **Portuguese Consulate** (Melbourne House, 11 Parliament St., Hamilton, tel. 441/292-1039) is headed by Honorary Consul Andrea Moniz-DeSouza, who works as a liaison between the Bermuda and Portuguese governments and the local Portuguese community.

---

edge bearing crosshatch markings. Experts can't decide whether it was crafted by human hands or the sea, which sprays over the edge and pounds the rock on stormy days.

Descending from Spanish Rock, follow a skinny coastal trail edged by prickly pears and baygrapes to a wind-battered promontory where parrotfish can sometimes be seen nibbling the reef edges. Turning inland past a small pond with egrets and ducks, the woodland trail is laced with banks of bright-green flopper plants, a succulent whose lantern-like flowers bob by the hundreds over assorted ferns and wild blossoms. Continuing past fiddlewood groves, aromatic spice trees, and sugarcane, the trail leads past a dairy farm to the western parking lot; exit onto South Shore Road and follow the grassy verge east for about 150 feet until a set of wooden steps leads under a hedged arch back into the reserve. The woodland trail continues around the large pond's northern rim back to the east parking lot.

Hurricanes periodically send towering

waves over the cliffs into the valley and pond, the salt leaving a swath of dead vegetation. Hurricane Fabian's terrific storm surge ate away chunks of the South Shore limestone cliffs in 2003, and the erosion from this and other tempests is still evident. The Department of Parks crews continually cull invasive species and replace them with hardy endemics like palmettos and cedars.

The park's steep trails and hour-long circuit restrict access to the able-bodied, but good views of the South Shore can be had from the wooded trailhead alongside the eastern parking lot. There is a portable toilet here too.

Watch Hill Park

Just east of Spittal Pond, looking out over one of Bermuda's most dramatically spectacular stretches of coastline visible from the main road, tiny **Watch Hill Park** (sunrise-sunset daily, free) offers a peaceful stopping place for a picnic or rest while heading east. Anglers come here after work and on weekends, casting their lines for pompano and "good-eating" reef fish like snapper, rockfish, triggerfish, and hogfish. The park is located on a peaceful stretch of South Shore Road, where traffic is generally very light. The main road east from here is the quintessential "scenic route," leading far from rush-hour destinations—to leisurely Tucker's Town and its private golf courses.

Penhurst Agricultural Park

When actor Michael Douglas's late mother, Diana Dill Darrid, a Bermudian, married President Nixon's former Treasury chief of staff Donald Webster in 2002, the bride and groom asked guests to donate toward the preservation of **Penhurst Agricultural Park** (Middle Rd., west of Store Hill, sunrise-sunset daily, free) in lieu of wedding gifts. They held a publicized ceremony to plant cedar saplings on Christmas Eve inside the 14-acre reserve, which rambles from Middle Road down across the Railway Trail to North Shore, encompassing farm fields and dense woodland

that few Bermudians have explored. Visible from the park entrance area are the communications tower and giant satellite dish on the next-door property of Cable & Wireless, on which the lion's share of Bermuda's telecommunications depends. The park gives easy access to the Railway Trail in Smith's; south of the trail, it descends to a grassy spread where a bench overlooks the North Shore. Bluebirds, cardinals, mourning doves, and finches can all be seen and heard here, amid the fiddlewoods, palmettos, and cedars. Department of Parks crews have culled invasive species, such as Mexican pepper bushes, and planted replacement endemics.

Harrington Sound

This inland sound, favored by boaters and anglers, is considered by naturalists to be biologically unique in the world because of its necklace of underwater caves, tidal currents, submerged notches, and the abundance of marinelife. Calico clams, black mussels, purple urchins, harbor conches, squid, and spiny lobsters can all be seen, not to mention rays that occasionally lift out of the water like speckled stealth bombers before coming down in a loud splash—a heart-pumping experience for any nearby swimmer.

Measuring three square miles, the sound is 80 feet deep in some places and ringed by steep cliffs and sheer shores, the highest point being Abbot's Cliff in Hamilton Parish. Below these, numerous caves provide fascinating exploration for cave divers, kayakers, and snorkelers, though the mouths of some, such as Green Bay Cave on the western shore, lie underwater. (Inside this particular cave, stalactites hang from the ceiling above the surface.) Another example is Shark Hole Cave, in the emerald-hued southwest corner, which extends under the traffic of Harrington Sound Road. Swimmers can often feel patches of cool water throughout the sound, as seawater from the outer shore enters through hundreds of fissures.

Scattered around the sound are various private islands (Rabbit Island, Cockroach

Island) where Bermudians keep summer cottages. Sporting events such as Zoom Around the Sound (a run, walk, and cycle event), the Round the Sound Swim, and the Trunk Island Swim also take advantage of the sound's scenic loop and its mostly calm waters in the summer and fall. You can take a summer evening boat tour of the sound via **Discovery Tours** (6pm-7:15pm daily May-Sept., $45 pp), conducted by educator Robert Chandler and naturalist Jennifer Gray. Boats leave from the Bermuda Aquarium dock. Flatts Bridge is a great vantage point to view most of the sound, and swimming is popular off the rocks at Shark Hole—the only soft landing is a small beach at the property of the Palmetto Gardens condominiums, at the three-way junction of North Shore, Middle, and Harrington Sound Roads. But the high cliffs and private properties encircling much of this body of water prevent easy access, except by boat.

BEACHES

TOP EXPERIENCE

★ John Smith's Bay

The lifeguard station posted at this crescent-shaped cove attests to its popularity, particularly among families with children. Nestled between two promontories, the beach—named for pioneer Captain John Smith of the Virginia Company, which administered early Bermuda—is usually fairly protected from high waves and winds and has an adjoining little park. Ample parking, toilets, and a friendly daily lunch wagon that doles out drinks, burgers, fish cakes, and fries to hungry swimmers make John Smith's a top choice to avoid the beach crowds of Warwick and Southampton.

Coconut palms and baygrapes frame the beach, where jutting rocks have created convenient mini coves that provide a measure of privacy even when the beach gets busy. Tucker's Town's sweep of surf along the private Windsor and Mid Ocean Beaches can be seen in the distance. On Sunday mornings,

the beach attracts a group of recreational swimmers who meet for spiritual gatherings at dawn throughout the year. Easter Sunday also sees a special beachside religious service.

Gibbet Island Beach

The beauty of Gibbet Island and its idyllic facing coves belies an ugly past: Its name refers to the gallows that once stood on the island, where enslaved people and criminals were hanged, their bodies on public display as a warning to passing maritime traffic. Such history remains a sore spot in the ongoing effort to foster harmonious race relations more than 170 years after slavery ended in Bermuda. Today, the property is owned by a private family trust, so the beach is officially off-limits, though the public Railway Trail runs through the land to Flatts Inlet, which also offers a refreshing dip. Here, a bridge once carried the train on to Shelly Bay and points farther east; eight massive stone pylons remain in the inlet. To rejoin the trail, you need to retrace your steps, walk through Flatts Village and around the inlet, and follow North Shore Road into Hamilton Parish.

SPORTS AND RECREATION

Railway Trail (Smith's)

The Smith's Parish portion of the Railway Trail is short in comparison with stretches in Paget, Warwick, and the West End, but it offers views of the North Shore, a shady fairyland of forest, and easy access to the Penhurst Agricultural Park. Banks of nasturtium and asparagus fern line the muddy path, hemmed by steep limestone walls where the trail was cut through the hillside. This stretch of trail is a popular route for equestrians on their daily outings from nearby Hinson Hall Stables. Enter halfway up Store Hill. You can walk west to adjoining Penhurst, or about 0.5 mile east to Gibbet Island, where the trail breaks at the water's edge. Follow North Shore Road east and pick up the trail again in Hamilton Parish. For a longer excursion, experience the other two-thirds of the western North Shore stretch by starting in Devonshire, where the trail can be accessed from Barker's Hill or Palmetto Road. Try an out-and-back walk from here, returning for lunch at Ocean View Golf Club.

Spas

Opened in 2017, **The Spa at the Loren** (116 South Rd., tel. 441/493-1602, www.theloren-hotel.com, 9am-7pm daily Apr.-Oct., 10am-6pm Nov.-Mar.) is operated by Three Graces Day Spa, the managing group behind successful spa-salons at Paget's Newstead Resort and the Pompano Beach Club in Southampton. In the cool, contemporary setting are hair and nail salons, dry heat wood saunas, relaxation spaces, and treatments rooms. Come for curated combos such as a hot stone massage and classic pedicure (2 hours, $299), a facial (45 minutes, $119), or a signature massage (1 hour, $189).

ENTERTAINMENT AND EVENTS

Athletes take to the waters of scenic Harrington Sound for the charity marathon **Round the Sound Swim** (tel. 441/293-8333, ext. 1906, or 855/447-6886, www.aquamoon-adventures.com) in mid-October. The event is competitive, with staggered starts beginning at 10am for five distance categories ranging 0.8K-10K. The joint finish is at the private Palmetto Bay Beach on Harrington Sound Road. The event awards trophies for speed, position, and money raised from pledges, and visitors to the island can participate by simply paying the entry fee. Kayaks with paramedics and police are on hand.

FOOD
Cafés and Pubs

The Collector's Hill neighborhood at the intersection of South Road and Collector's Hill has a handful of busy eateries. A local favorite, friendly ★ **Speciality Inn** (4 South Shore Rd., tel. 441/236-3133, speciality@ northrock.bm, 6am-10pm Mon.-Sat.) serves up home-style comfort food, including the creamiest mac 'n' cheese, in a casual cafeteria-style diner. Lori Woolfe cajoles the clientele with "Dahlin'" and "Sweetheart." The down-home ambience brought Clint Eastwood here during a golfing holiday in 1996, as well as Jimmy Carter and his son Jack, a former Bermuda resident; all appear on the wall of fame. Grab a barstool in front of the grill for a quick Bermudian-style breakfast (bacon, egg, and cheese on a coffee roll, $6) or M&M

John Smith's Bay

pancakes ($9). The wide-ranging lunch and dinner menus offer everything from burgers ($5) served on freshly baked rolls to wraps and sandwiches ($4-15) and pizzas (from $11), and there's a separate kids' menu ($9 special). A full sushi menu is also available, prepared at a separate bar by dedicated sushi chefs. Home-baked loaves of banana bread and gingerbread are sold at the checkout counter. Breakfast is served until 4pm. The only thing missing is a liquor license.

Roadside diner **Rotisserie Grill** (8 South Rd., tel. 441/232-7444, 11am-10pm Mon.-Sat., 7:30am-8pm Sun., $13-22) does a roaring trade with its comfort-food menu of pasta, pizza, local fish, and family-size dinners of roast chicken or ribs, with biscuits and sides of mashed potatoes. Eat in or take out, including Sunday-morning breakfast.

Named for the rocky outcrop located 10 miles off Bermuda's North Shore, Bermuda brewpub **North Rock Brewing Co.** (10 South Shore Rd., tel. 441/236-6633, lunch 11am-3pm daily, dinner 6pm-9:30pm daily) is a British-style pub, complete with a dark-hued interior, booths, and a bar. The menu is pricier than a corner pub, but it's varied, with local craft beers and staples like steak-and-ale pie ($23), bangers and mash ($19), and fish-and-chips ($22), along with burgers, sandwiches, pastas, and ribs. Bermuda fish and lobster are offered in season.

International

Marée (The Loren at Pink Beach, 116 South Rd., tel. 441/293-1666, www.thelorenhotel. com, 5:30pm-9pm Tues.-Sat.) is a pricey curated culinary experience. A four-course "dining experience" ($125) offers an immersion in fresh local fare, from micro greens and rockfish to Bermuda onions and goat cheese. Start with teenage carrots and fennel salad, followed by lobster gnocchi or grilled eggplant. Main dishes include *sous vide* snapper and duo of beef with short rib and New York strip. Lemon olive oil cake trumps the desserts.

The casual **Pink Beach Club** (The Loren at Pink Beach, 116 South Rd., tel. 441/293-1666, www.thelorenhotel.com, 7am-9pm daily), just yards from crashing surf, makes you feel as if you're on the deck of a ship, refreshed by the elements. All-day menus encompass breakfast, Sunday brunch, and dinner. Gaze at blue horizons with healthy comfort food: smashed avocado flatbread ($18), caprese panini ($20), chimichurri rubbed skirt steak ($36), and, for dessert, chipwiches ($12).

Groceries

At a crossroads, **A1 Smith's Market** (10 South Shore Rd., at Collector's Hill, tel. 441/236-8763, www.marketplace.bm, 8am-10pm Mon.-Sat., 9am-7pm Sun.) is a little grocery that stays stocked with most of the basics and Bermudian bakery items, a full dairy and butcher's counter, fresh fruit and vegetables, and a well-priced wine selection. Cheerful checkout clerks make it a busy neighborhood stopping place.

Serving the billionaires of Tucker's Town and the nouveaux riches of Knapton Hill, **Harrington Hundreds Grocery & Liquor Store** (99 South Shore Rd., opposite Spittal Pond's east entrance, tel. 441/293-1635, www. harringtonhundreds.bm, 8am-8pm Mon.-Sat., 9am-6pm Sun.) is a foodie oasis with a selection of Bermuda-grown fruit and vegetables (sweet strawberries, ripe on-the-vine tomatoes, melt-in-your-mouth melons) and a wide selection of organic fare, including vegan and gluten-free items. The store carries a good wine selection from California and Europe, fresh-baked stick loaves, and Ben & Jerry's ice cream.

Corkscrews (5 Park House, Middle Rd. at Verdmont Rd., tel. 441/293-0656, 10am-9pm Mon.-Sat., 10am-3pm Sun.) makes a convenient stop for wine, beer, and liquor. Teetering halfway up Flatts Hill, **Belvin's Variety** (5 Middle Rd., tel. 441/292-4583, 6am-midnight daily) would be easy to miss if not for all the truck drivers and cabbies angling for parking outside. The pocket-size convenience store is perfect for picking up a newspaper, a cream bun, and other basic necessities.

ACCOMMODATIONS

The parish is attracting its share of press since the 2017 opening of the island's first boutique hotel in a decade. Bought by developer Stephen King, **The Loren at Pink Beach** (116 South Rd., tel. 844/384-3103 or 441/293-1666, www.thelorenhotel.com, $920-3,600) is on the historic 13-acre site of the former **Pink Beach Club,** a cottage colony dating to 1947 that went bankrupt in 2013. Bucking the longtime country-club floral aesthetic of Bermuda's hospitality tradition, the Loren has injected sleek urban style into this already ritzy section of coastline. Perched above a breathtakingly beautiful stretch of the South Shore, the hotel has 45 oceanfront rooms and suites, along with 3,300-square-foot duplex villas, two restaurants (The Marée and Pink Beach Club), a gym, and a spa. Glass, gray tones, natural wood, turquoise, and red accents lend a modern vibe. Rooms offer high-speed Wi-Fi, Sferra linens, private balconies, room service, and five-piece marble baths with walk-in rain showers, freestanding tubs, and Malin and Goetz products. Outside, guests can enjoy amenities like poolside cabanas, a library, two oceanfront heated pools, and beach access from the pool deck. There is also a business center. The stunning shorefront restaurant space and pool deck often host wine tastings and other events.

INFORMATION AND SERVICES

Collector's Hill Apothecary (7 South Shore Rd. at Collector's Hill, tel. 441/279-5513, prescriptions tel. 441/279-5512, www.phoenixstores.com, 8am-8pm Mon.-Sat., 11am-7pm Sun.) is well stocked with makeup and toiletries, snacks, toys, magazines, and a large pharmacy with online refills.

Smith's has just one gas station, with a small convenience store attached: **Rubis**

Terceira's North Shore (2 North Shore Rd., tel. 441/292-5130, 6:30am-8pm Mon.-Sat., 9am-4pm Sun.). **Flatts Post Office** (65 Middle Rd., next to Whitney Middle School, tel. 441/292-0741, 8am-5pm Mon.-Fri.) is a tiny parish landmark. **ATMs** are located outside **Collector's Hill Apothecary** (7 South Shore Rd., at Collector's Hill) and at **Harrington Hundreds Grocery** (99 South Shore Rd., opposite Spittal Pond's east entrance).

TRANSPORTATION

There are no scooter rental outlets or ferry services in Smith's. Scooters can be rented elsewhere and are a good way to scoot around the parish, especially off the main thoroughfares. Buses are also an efficient way to travel the main arteries of Smith's. Bicycles, rentable from hotels and liveries, are great for exploring the Railway Trail.

Taxis

To arrange a pickup, use the **Hitch app** (www.hitch.bm) or call one of the main cab companies: **Bermuda Industrial Union Co-op** (tel. 441/292-4476, cooptaxi@fkbnet. bm), **Bermuda Island Taxi** (tel. 441/295-4141, www.bermudaislandtaxi.com), or **BTA Dispatching** (tel. 441/296-2121, www.btadispatching.com)

Buses

Buses travel all three routes through the parish. Take route 1 for South Shore Road destinations (Hamilton-Grotto Bay and St. George's; buses run every half hour). Take route 3 for points on Middle Road (Hamilton-Grotto Bay and St. George's, every half hour); it also travels through Flatts Village and along picturesque Harrington Sound Road. Routes 10 and 11 ply North Shore Road (Hamilton-St. George's, every 15 minutes). Fares from Hamilton are $3.50 adults, $2.75 ages 5-15, free under age 5. Exact change, tokens, tickets, or passes are required.

Hamilton Parish

Though it carries the same name as Bermuda's capital, Hamilton Parish is distinct from the City of Hamilton, about six miles away in Pembroke Parish. The two Hamiltons are not named for the same person; the parish, like the other eight, took the name of an early investor, in this case, James Hamilton, the second Marquis of Hamilton, while the city was named for Governor Henry Hamilton nearly 200 years later. The Bermudian lexicon distinguishes clearly between the two: When someone says, "Let's go to Hamilton," they mean "Town," the city. Hamilton Parish locations are described by their neighborhood ("Bailey's Bay," "Crawl," "Harrington Sound"). Historically, Hamilton Parish was known as Bailey's Bay by most islanders, since the North Shore community was a hub of trade and boat travel around the island in its early days.

Today, Hamilton Parish, a half-doughnut around Harrington Sound, is largely residential, with mostly hidden waterfront homes, as well as several public parks, a large resort, and popular attractions such as the Bermuda Aquarium, Museum & Zoo and the caves. Unless you are staying in St. George's, from the airport you'll travel through Hamilton Parish to reach any other part of the island.

SIGHTS
Flatts Village

Flatts Village (North Shore Rd.), or "Flatts" as the general vicinity is known, has enjoyed a renaissance in the 2000s, with a tasteful renovation of its smattering of shops and architecturally interesting cottages, as well as the addition of new restaurants, much-needed sidewalks, and a revamped marina. The tiny community lies on the eastern band of Flatts Inlet, a finger of shallow-edged turquoise harbor that links Harrington Sound to the ocean. Directly opposite Flatts on the inlet

is the Bermuda Aquarium, Museum & Zoo, the area's main attraction. Aside from the few restaurants, there's virtually nothing to do in Flatts Village except ogle the tide sweeping in and out of the pristine sound, the two-knot current creating the nearest thing to river rapids for white-water kayakers. Sport anglers return to port at sunset, and others simply cast their lines over Flatts Bridge and nearby docks when weather permits. Fishing off island bridges is supposedly illegal, but the rule is widely ignored and rarely enforced. Line fishing is allowed from the rocks beneath the bridge, however, and containers for disposing of old fishing line—a hazard for turtles and other marinelife—have been installed here. Jumping and diving off the bridge into the rushing tide is a favorite summertime activity for daredevil youth. In the early mornings or evenings, spotted eagle rays and larger manta rays can be seen swooping beneath as they commute between the sound and the shore beyond.

The area is historically important as one of Bermuda's earliest and busiest settlements in the 17th and 18th centuries, when travel and communication between the parishes was primarily by boat. Like other sheltered harbor settlements, including Crow Lane, Ely's Harbor, and Riddell's Bay, Flatts became a center for trade and a refuge for smugglers fleeing customs duties levied at Hamilton and St. George's. "Later, when Bermudians turned to shipbuilding and overseas trading, these villages took on the significance of home ports," wrote historian William Zuill in his 1946 *Bermuda Journey*. The sleepy whimsy formerly found in Flatts has mostly been lost in the noise and speed of today's nonstop traffic, which flows through the village via North Shore Road—as well as summer's marine rush hour at day's end in the inlet.

Hamilton Parish

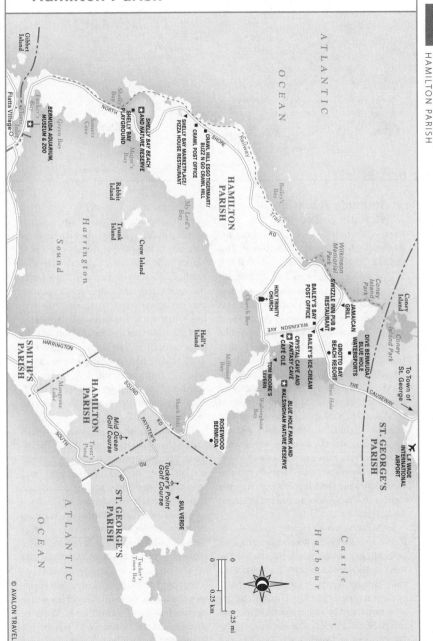

© AVALON TRAVEL

Flatts Village

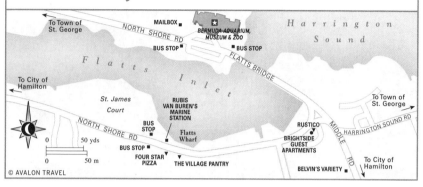

★ Bermuda Aquarium, Museum & Zoo

Bermuda's best-known attraction, the **Bermuda Aquarium, Museum & Zoo** (BAMZ, 40 North Shore Rd., tel. 441/293-2727, www.bamz.org, 9am-5pm daily except Christmas Day, last admission 4pm, gift shop 10am-4pm, $10 adults, $5 seniors and ages 5-12, free under age 5) sits opposite Flatts Village on the shore of Flatts Inlet. Supported by the nonprofit Bermuda Zoological Society (BZS), the facility is government-owned and attracts both public and private funding. BAMZ is a hub for research and conservation programs protecting marine turtles and coral reefs. BZS educators offer marine and terrestrial field trips, school visits, and environmental education outreach programs. BAMZ works to raise awareness about fragile oceanic islands—not only Bermuda but also the delicate flora and fauna of Australasia, the Caribbean, Madagascar, and other threatened ecosystems.

BAMZ, which is wheelchair-accessible, offers an up-close look at Bermuda's marinelife, especially its precious coral reefs—some of the most northerly in the world. The aquarium's main hall displays large moray eels, schools of silver minnows and squid, spiny lobsters, an octopus, and 200 other species of fish and invertebrates. The pièce de résistance is the 140,000-gallon North Rock Exhibit—the first living coral reef exhibit of its scale in the world. Occupying the whole western side of the main building, two interlocking tanks are naturally lit from above, cleverly mimicking North Rock, a reefy outcrop some 10 miles north of the facility on the North Shore. Inside the smaller front tank, tiny jewel-like reef fish dart among anemones, queen angelfish sway like ballerinas, and sponges, corals, and sea fans all can be seen up close. Behind this, the larger tank offers floor-to-ceiling viewing of sharks, barracudas, schools of pompano, and golden-frilled triggerfish. Benches are provided, and children—even babies and toddlers—can commune at floor-level with the various curiosities.

The lively seal exhibit, with western Atlantic harbor seals, is located near the entrance. Watch feedings at 9:30am, 1:30pm, and 4pm daily. Beyond the aquarium's front entrance, in an outdoor pool next to the bus stop, swim a collection of green turtles.

The on-site Natural History Museum explores the geology and biodiversity of Bermuda with audiovisual and interactive exhibits, as well as lab-style drawer displays of preserved animals. Outside, the zoo contains more than 300 birds, mammals, and reptiles in exhibits that aim to teach about the habitats found on oceanic islands. Redbrick paths, rest areas, lookouts over Harrington Sound, and beautifully landscaped gardens featuring some of Bermuda's most exotic flowering plants and trees encourage a leisurely visit that can easily span a couple of hours. A flock of pink flamingos lives in a large open area at the zoo, where the birds have reproduced successfully.

The Australasia Exhibit recreates the humid interior and landscape of a rainforest for the menagerie of wallabies and a boa constrictor that live here. Parrots squawk loudly in the cliff-style rock faces above them. In the Caribbean Exhibit, birds dart freely among bamboo and other tropical forest plants, along with pairs of golden lion tamarins. The monkeys are part of an international conservation program, the Species Survival Plan (SSP), which links Bermuda to an organized effort to boost the populations of endangered animals. Bred in captivity, many tamarins are released back into the Brazilian rainforest. You will also see scarlet ibises, a red-rumped agouti, chachalaca, and endangered Haitian sliders (terrapins) in this exhibit.

"Madagascar: Land of Mystery and Wonder" features a predatory catlike fossa as well as a troupe of ring-tailed lemurs that leap around a large free-flight area featuring a waterfall and rock formations. There are also exhibits showcasing the vibrant beauty of tiny tomato frogs, chameleons, and leaf-tailed geckos. The Bermuda Zoological Society shop sells eco-friendly items, and has a licensed on-site café, Azu Beastro, with views of lovely Harrington Sound.

★ Blue Hole Park and Walsingham Nature Reserve

This vast property (sunrise-sunset daily, free), held largely by a private family trust but open to the public, incorporates coast and forested land from Blue Hole Park to Tom Moore's Jungle, as Walsingham Nature Reserve is more frequently called. Of the whole area, government-owned Blue Hole Park is the only designated public park, with the best access and more parking. Although each area of interest can be accessed by its respective entrance—a half mile or so apart—all are linked and can be explored on foot from any entry point.

Tom Moore's Jungle (Walsingham Lane, off Harrington Sound Rd.) is a tangle of Surinam cherry forests, crystalline caves, and mangroves surrounding Tom Moore's Tavern, a four-star restaurant housed in a 1652 waterfront inn. Both the tavern and forest take the name of Thomas Moore, an Irish poet and bon

a reptilian highlight of the Bermuda Aquarium, Museum & Zoo

vivant whose mediocre romantic verse during a brief stay as court registrar (Jan.-Apr. 1804) managed to keep him very much alive in local legend. A highlight of the so-called jungle are the swimming grottoes, fed via subterranean tunnels by the tides of Castle Harbour; turtles and fish can often be seen in the turquoise depths. The Castle Harbour coastline here is also perfect for snorkeling, with shallow bays, reefs, and mangroves. Bird-watchers will enjoy spotting not only the herons that stalk crabs on the shore but also finches, cardinals, and doves. Caves honeycomb the woodlands. Part of this chunk of land, the 1.25-acre Idwal Hughes Nature Reserve, is owned by the Bermuda National Trust and contains indigenous palmettos and cedars, along with unique geological formations.

The region is also riddled with underwater caves, including the most famous, Crystal Cave and Fantasy Cave, open to the public. Tom Moore's Jungle connects to Blue Hole Park through a woodland trail leading under elfin bush archways. Blue Hole Park can also be accessed directly via Blue Hole Hill, the main road leading to the airport; its turnoff is tucked in to the right just before the busy Causeway that crosses Castle Harbour to the airport and St. George's. Home to a popular dolphin show in the 1970s, the park is honeycombed with caves, including a cave mouth called Causeway Cave and caverns along the shoreline filled with seawater. One, dubbed the "blue hole" due to its exotic aquamarine hue, has become a popular jumping in spot for adventure tour groups. A small, picturesque beach with mangroves sits near the park's entrance and car park. Bermuda's oldest rock, a very hard limestone estimated to be 800,000 years old, can be found at the surface in the Walsingham area.

Bermuda's most famous tree, a calabash, is located here. Tom Moore sat in its generous shade to compose his poems, and on November 4, 1844, members of the nascent Royal Bermuda Yacht Club held their first meeting and a celebratory lunch under its branches; the iconic club has celebrated

Blue Hole Park and Walsingham Nature Reserve

key anniversaries at the spot ever since. Unfortunately, Hurricane Emily in 1987 nearly destroyed the tree, but cuttings were replanted and it has now sprouted to several feet in height. Follow the trail left of the tavern about 200 yards to a clearing, where you will see the surviving sapling.

Holy Trinity Church

With a picture-perfect setting, **Holy Trinity Church** (Trinity Church Rd., off Harrington Sound Rd. or North Shore Rd.) also happens to be historically important. The current building, or at least part of the nave, dates to 1660-1670, but historians believe there was an even earlier stone structure on the site that bore a palmetto-thatch roof. Regardless, Holy Trinity is one of the oldest church buildings in the western hemisphere, having survived hurricanes, storm damage, and numerous alterations and additions over the centuries.

Perhaps the church's most notable feature is its array of 28 stained glass windows, most of them English and installed since

Into the Deep with Beebe's Bathysphere

In August 1934, Bermuda made global headlines when two scientists achieved a pioneering feat that captured the public imagination: They descended a record 3,028 feet (a nautical half mile) off the island encased in a steel contraption called a bathysphere. Naturalist William Beebe, a former assistant curator of birds at the New York Zoological Society, and bathysphere inventor Otis Barton had spent several years here, establishing the Bermuda Oceanographic Expedition in 1928. The island made an ideal laboratory thanks to its biodiversity, year-round mild climate, and easily accessible depths. The pod was lowered by a steel cable from a ship at the surface, the two men curled up like spiders and staring out a glass porthole at the wondrous specimens.

"Here I was privileged to peer out and actually see the creatures which had evolved in the blackness of a blue midnight which, since the ocean was born, had known no following day," later noted Beebe in his 1934 book, *Half-Mile Down*. Electricity and a phone line were run into the bathysphere, allowing Beebe's observations to be relayed to an artist at the surface who made fantastic drawings of the iridescent fish, silvery eels, flying snails, and mists of crustaceans for the world to ogle. "We are still alive," was his comment to the anxiously waiting team at the surface when the pair dipped for the first time to a depth of a quarter mile.

Beebe, who had switched his scientific focus from birds to tropical studies in the 1920s and begun his diving quest with a homemade helmet, had an uncanny ability to describe the eerie netherworld of the deep in a way that was entirely factual, yet read like science fiction. "To the ever-recurring question, 'How does it feel?' I can only quote the words of Herbert Spencer: I felt like 'an infinitesimal atom floating in illimitable space,'" he noted. "No wonder my sole contribution to science at the time was: 'Am writing at a depth of a quarter of a mile. A luminous fish is outside my window.'"

Beebe continued his research in Bermuda through World War II, carrying out scores of dives in the submersible chamber. He also wrote numerous popular works on his discoveries with detailed descriptions of "the last frontier." Life-size replicas of his 5,000-pound bathysphere—which measured just four feet, nine inches in diameter—can be found at both the Bermuda Aquarium, Museum & Zoo and the Bermuda Underwater Exploration Institute.

the 1890s. Five of these were designed by Sir Edward Burne-Jones, a noted pre-Raphaelite artist who designed for the William Morris Company. Experts have declared the quintet the best collection of his work anywhere in the world. Holy Trinity's furnishings are also impressive, including its mahogany pulpit, the 200-year-old Bevington-built organ, and a bronze baptismal font made in the 1970s by a resident sculptor (the original 1840s stone font can be seen in the churchyard). The church's silver collection is valuable, with the oldest piece, a handsome tankard, dedicated to "the church of Hambleton Tribe, 1677." Outside, wander through the churchyard with its roses and royal palms as well as gravestones. The church is open on Saturday while it is being cleaned and during services (10:30am Sun.), but contact the parsonage (tel. 441/293-5366 or 441/293-1710) to arrange a visit at another time.

★ Crystal Cave and Fantasy Cave

While the group tour experience can sometimes be kitschy, the actual geological phenomena visible in these two dramatic caves is worth the price of admission. Superstar Beyoncé loved them so much during a 2008 visit that she chose to stage a fashion shoot inside the caverns. While **Crystal Cave and Fantasy Cave** (Wilkinson Ave., tel. 441/293-0640, www.caves.bm, by guided tour only, 9am-5pm daily, last tour 4:30pm) are but two of hundreds of caverns around Harrington Sound and Castle Harbour, they are the largest and most elaborate. Guided tours are carried out every 20-30 minutes throughout

Saving Bermuda's Sea Turtles

In the summer of 2005, a handful of baby turtles hatched from eggs on an East End Bermuda beach and laboriously wobbled their way down to the nearby surf. Not so exceptional, perhaps, for waters frequented by marine turtles, except for the fact that it was the first time in almost a century that eggs had actually been laid and successfully hatched on the island. The phenomenon was celebrated by local naturalists involved in the **Bermuda Turtle Project** (www.conserve-turtles.org), one of the world's longest-running tagging and research programs, established in 1968, which today partners with the Sea Turtle Conservancy.

While the baby turtles in question were loggerheads, the Bermuda Turtle Project is mainly focused on the critically endangered green turtle (*Chelonia mydas*), once so plentiful on the island that colonists would gather hundreds of eggs at a time and capture 40 adults per boat per day. The species diminished almost immediately; as early as 1620, the Bermuda Assembly moved to prevent turtle killing. Modern threats, despite legal protection, are no less severe. Turtles fall victim to boat collisions as well as to ocean debris such as plastics, Styrofoam, tar, and balloons, which fatally clog their digestive tracts. Entanglement in fishing gear, including discarded nets and lines, also kills marine turtles.

The Bermuda Turtle Project, through the Bermuda Zoological Society and the Bermuda Aquarium, Museum & Zoo, works to educate Bermudians about these dangers. Green turtles are carried by ocean currents for the first years of their lives, until they mature enough to bottom-feed at inshore habitats. Bermuda's green turtles spend up to 15 years in this developmental stage, grazing on lush sea grass beds amid the coral reefs in the island's surrounding atoll. Once adult and averaging 300 pounds, green turtles migrate south to foraging and mating grounds.

Ultimately, the Turtle Project hopes to encourage a return of nesting populations on the island. In the 1970s, more than 25,000 green turtle eggs were brought to Bermuda from Costa Rica and buried on isolated beaches. Some 16,000 turtles hatched and swam away. Since turtles are known to return to nest at the beach where they were born, scientists hope that when these offspring reach maturity (age 50 in green turtles, whose lifespan reaches a century), they will come back to Bermuda.

Green turtles tagged or recorded in Bermuda have been traced back to origins in Costa Rica, Florida, Mexico, Suriname, and Venezuela, showing the vast ocean ranges covered by the species. Unfortunately, the size of its habitat poses dangers: Many turtles mature safely in Bermuda only to be slaughtered in the Caribbean or Central and South America. Each summer, the project invites students, scientists, and resource managers from turtle-visited countries such as Costa Rica, Nicaragua, Panama, and the United States to take part in a 10-day field course. Participants visit sea-grass beds on the Bermuda platform and net turtles who feed there to learn methods of gathering data—including turtle growth rates, movement patterns, and even the genetic composition of turtles found around Bermuda. Project scientists are also teaching the use of satellite telemetry to track movements of turtles.

the day; in the winter, when visitor numbers dwindle, you might be lucky enough to get a private viewing. Admission is $22 adults or $30 for both caves, $10 ($12) ages 5-12, free under age 5. If you visit just one, Crystal Cave is the most eye-popping and features a greater variety of formations.

Island folklore tells how Crystal Cave was discovered in the early 1900s by two boys playing a game of cricket. When they lost their ball down a hole, they found a subterranean wonderland beneath their feet. A 25-minute tour leads 80 feet down into the earth by way of a steep set of stairs cut into the limestone. At the bottom, the well-lit series of caverns opens up to expose a sapphire-bottomed lagoon, some 55 feet deep, over which a "floating trail" of pontoon bridges has been erected. Walk across the water, past soaring stalagmites and spear-like stalactites dripping incessantly into the pool. Swimming is not allowed.

A brief "nature walk" leads through an avenue of royal palms and down a redbrick path through the estate gardens to Fantasy Cave. Avocado trees, sprawling Indian laurels, and mature cherry groves nearly drown out the traffic at the busy intersection beyond. This cave's 88 steps wind down to another subterranean wonder, an open area dense with crystalline columns and more stalactites and stalagmites. Narrow walkways allow you to explore various underground nooks and crannies before climbing back to the surface, a 30-minute adventure.

The property has picnic tables under awnings; a popular café; a gift shop selling imported gemstones, rock crystal, and quartz; and pristine public restrooms.

Crawl, Bailey's Bay, and Coney Island

A trio of North Shore neighborhoods leads from Shelly Bay to the Causeway in Hamilton Parish. Peppered with gospel halls, a rainbow of cottages, and essential local services like gas stations, variety stores, and laundry, they lack visitor attractions or restaurants, but all give a good sense of regular island life. The Railway Trail is the perfect way to traverse the area via the rocky coastline. Bicycles, scooters, and mopeds also allow easy exploration, and the area has a main bus route.

Crawl is a hillside neighborhood leading up past Shelly Bay as you head east. Artist Otto Trott's gallery is here, and Dub City Variety stocks snacks and sundries. The Railway Trail leaves Shelly Bay, following the coastline to Burchall Cove, before leading past craggy limestone formations, inlets, and bays into Crawl. This is one of the trail's most beautiful sections, exposing seaside cottages and charming old butteries as it hugs the ocean on its way to the dramatic island-dotted seascape of Bailey's Bay. While the noisy main road runs parallel nearby, the thick limestone walls of the railway create tranquility. Crawl ends at Bailey's Bay, a sheltered harbor for small boats surrounded by hilly residential pockets and farmland. Eastward around the corner, turn into Coney Island Park, a rugged peninsula incorporating parkland, beach coves, a cricket club, and various government outposts such as the Fisheries Department. There's a Jamaican Grill restaurant here, and usually a cricket match on summer weekends.

BEACHES

North Shore Road's rocky shoreline throughout Hamilton Parish—from Flatts Inlet to Coney Island—provides plenty of quiet coves, fishing spots, and swimming holes. The beauty of this shoreline is the lack of beach crowds, as there are few beaches. Instead, deep pristine water falls away from low rocks, from which the daring can dive. The shoreline, calmest when the wind is blowing from the south, is blanketed in reef life, making it ideal for snorkeling or kayaking.

★ Shelly Bay Beach and Nature Reserve

Incorporating a lovely beach, a first-rate playground, a cricket pitch, soccer fields, and a protected nature reserve, this chunk of coastal Hamilton Parish invites hours of recreation. It is a favorite spot for locals on weekends throughout the spring and summer months.

The soft white sand and gentle slope of the beach make it a perfect spot for small children or weak swimmers. Although the busy North Shore Road is too nearby, the beach is beautiful on a summer morning despite the traffic noise. Due to its easy access, the beach is also a magnet for windsurfers when the breeze swings around to the northwest. Picnic tables are on the grassy lawns east of the beach. Bordering the park is a nature reserve, home to biodiverse mangroves.

Shark Hole

A dock at the ominously named Shark Hole (there's virtually no risk of the toothy creatures) allows easy access to swim or snorkel in the emerald waters of this corner of the sound. Encircled by cliffs and bypassed by a hairpin section of Harrington Sound Road, the inviting grotto is also the site of a cave that extends beneath the main road. If you venture inside, you can hear the passing traffic above.

SPORTS AND RECREATION

Hamilton Parish offers a world of outdoor spaces and organized underwater tours, trails, and parks. Soccer fields and cricket pitches are at Shelly Bay Beach Park and the charming Sea Breeze Cricket Oval on Coney Island, both good for watching island teams and mixing with avid local fans, who are usually happy to explain the complexities of the games.

TOP EXPERIENCE

Scuba and Water Sports

Get your blood racing with a wakeboarding outing aboard John Martin's **AXIS Adrenaline Projects** (Flatts Inlet, tel. 441/537-1114, www.axisadrenaline.com, $230 per hour groups up to 10, five 1-hour shred sessions $1,100). Armed with Ronix and Radar gear aboard his custom Tige RZ2 speedboat, he'll calmly teach you the basics—then let you jump the wake and fly. Based in Flatts Inlet, he can pick up island-wide.

Dive Bermuda (Grotto Bay Beach Resort, 11 Blue Hole Hill, tel. 441/293-7319, www.bermudascuba.com, May-Sept.) is a five-star PADI dive center with 30 years' experience, offering certification and advanced courses, instructor development, night dives, one-tank ($95) and two-tank ($150) dives, and private charters to many East End dive sites, including the Spanish shipwreck *Cristóbal Colón* and the popular "Cathedral," a towering coral reef preserve you can swim through, just off the St. David's Island shore. Equipment rental is $15 each for a buoyancy control device, a wetsuit, or a regulator.

Perhaps the island's most stunning snorkeling site is at **North Rock,** about nine miles off the North Shore, where an area of extremely shallow (4- to 30-foot deep) reef extends from a rocky outcrop that supports a large beacon warning off approaching ships. Swim down through wide avenues of reef, populated with giant sea fans, corals, anemones—and crowds of every kind of Bermuda fish species. The site inspired a 140,000-gallon tank exhibit by the same name at the Bermuda Aquarium. To protect the reef, just two moorings are located here and several operators take trips throughout the summer. One great expedition is organized by the **Bermuda Zoological Society** (tel. 441/293-2727, see www.bamz.org or

Dive Bermuda boat

www.islandtourcentre.com for details), which schedules four-hour weekend afternoon outings to North Rock and back ($60) aboard its research vessel, *Endurance*. Trips depart from the Bermuda Aquarium dock in Flatts Village.

Blue Hole Water Sports (Grotto Bay Beach Resort, 11 Blue Hole Hill, tel. 441/293-2915 or 441/293-8333, ext. 37, www.blueholebermuda.com) has a wide assortment of stress-free ways to explore the turquoise calm of Ferry Reach and Castle Harbour, including sit-on-top kayaks ($20 per hour), paddleboards ($30), Sunfish sailboats ($35), and small motorboats. Thirteen-foot Boston whalers are $120 for two hours and $300 for eight hours. Snorkel gear is also available.

Ana Luna Adventures (Grotto Bay Beach Resort dock, tel. 441/504-3780, http://analunaadventures.com) runs sailing charters May-August aboard its 45-foot French-built catamaran, including afternoon snorkel outings ($79), glow-worm tours ($69), sunset champagne cruises ($79), and 24-hour all-inclusive tours ($1,950 for 2 people). All departures are from the Grotto Bay Beach Resort dock.

Railway Trail (Hamilton Parish)

Pick up the Railway Trail in Hamilton Parish on North Shore Road after crossing Flatts Bridge and passing the Bermuda Aquarium, Museum & Zoo. Rounding the next corner as you head east, pull in on the left and park your scooter looking out toward the ocean. Access to and through the Shelly Bay is easy and scenic thanks to a boardwalk linking the Railway Trail with the beach, 0.5 miles away. The wooden walkway is a safe nonmotorized coastal path parallel to busy North Shore Road.

The trail continues through a protected nature reserve, northeast of Shelly Bay's picnic park, which contains mangrove-fringed tidal pools and many indigenous plants. Continue on the trail through the Crawl neighborhood, hugging the craggy coastline with a beautiful marine view and a glimpse of Bermudian life. The Bermuda government and a nonprofit, Friends of Bermuda Railway Trail, reconnected the Crawl trail with its Bailey's Bay continuation in recent years with several wooden bridges across the water via the original stone pylons. The project allows pedestrians and bicyclists to avoid the busy main road and keep to the shore-based trail instead, all the way to Coney Island.

Spas

Just walking into **Prospero's Cave Spa** (Grotto Bay Beach Resort, 11 Blue Hole Hill, tel. 441/293-8333, U.S. tel. 855/447-6886, www.grottobay.com) is soothing enough, thanks to the sound of water falling onto an impossibly turquoise lake beneath floating wooden walkways. A spa treatment amid such a natural setting is a true indulgence. Massage treatments ($90-320) are offered, along with waxing, threading, manicures, and pedicures.

ENTERTAINMENT AND EVENTS

Runners, walkers, and cyclists turn out for the Bermuda Zoological Society's **Zoom Around the Sound** (tel. 441/293-2727, ext. 130, volunteers.bzs@gov.bm), a 7.2-mile circular course around Harrington Sound via Harrington Sound Road and North Shore Road. Held in March to raise money for the Bermuda Aquarium, Museum & Zoo, the race starts and finishes at BAMZ. The entry fee is $30, refreshments are served, and T-shirts and goody bags go to all participants. In the **Round the Sound Swim** in October, open-water swimmers compete in 10K, 4K, 2K, and 0.8K swims in scenic Harrington Sound (tel. 441/293-8333, ext. 1906, U.S. tel. 855/447-6886, www.aquamoonadventures.com).

Free admission days, kids' story time (11:30am Fri. except holidays Sept.-June), yoga classes, lectures, and themed events are held regularly at **Bermuda Aquarium, Museum & Zoo** (40 North Shore Rd., Flatts, tel. 441/293-2727, www.bamz.org).

SHOPPING

Hamilton Parish shopping is limited to small gift and souvenir stores inside several of the main attractions and restaurants, including the Swizzle Inn, the caves, the Grotto Bay Beach Resort, and the Bermuda Aquarium, Museum & Zoo. The latter is probably the most interesting, with its eco-friendly inventory, such as stuffed toys and quality animal toys for kids, including dinosaurs and endangered species; classical and world music CDs; and a good collection of Bermuda books, including the comprehensive coffee-table edition of *The Natural History of Bermuda,* by Canadian biologist Martin Thomas, and diver-photographer Ron Lucas's *Bermuda Reef Portraits,* both published by the Bermuda Zoological Society.

You can find Bermuda shorts at **Luxury Gifts Bermuda** (60 Tucker's Point Dr., tel. 441/298-6095, http://luxury.bm, 9am-7pm Mon.-Fri., 10am-6pm Sat.-Sun.).

FOOD
Cafés and Pubs

Families and other zoogoers love **AZU Beastro** (Bermuda Aquarium, Museum & Zoo, tel. 441/296-2429, www.bamz.org, 9:30am-4pm daily, happy hour and barbecue 6pm-9pm Fri. summer, $7-11) for baked goods, sandwiches, paninis, and wraps. Burgers, hot dogs, and grilled cheese keep the young ones satisfied. Licensed for beer, wine, and liquor, moms and dads can rest while the little ones keep busy in the nearby zoo playground.

Pizza House Restaurant (Shelly Bay MarketPlace, North Shore Rd., tel. 441/293-8465, 11am-10pm daily, $5-26) is one of a three-outlet chain offering pizza slices, pizza trays for parties, sandwiches, subs, burgers, and salads. **Buzz N Go Crawl Hill** (Esso Tigermart gas station, tel. 441/293-0777, www.buzzcafe.bm, 6am-10pm daily) is the Hamilton Parish branch of the successful chain of delis, offering sandwiches, paninis, salads, smoothies, and specialty coffees. The Coney Island outlet of **Jamaican Grill**

(1 Duck's Puddle, tel. 441/293-8899, 11am-10pm Mon.-Wed., 7am-10pm Thurs. and Sun., 7am-midnight Fri.-Sat., $10-13) serves up West Indian favorites like jerk chicken, coconut fish, and cocoa bread.

★ **Café Olé** (8 Crystal Cave Rd. off Wilkinson Ave., tel. 441/293-7865, 9am-4:30pm daily) attracts taxi drivers and other locals with breakfast and Sunday opening hours. Service is super-friendly and fast, the restaurant spotless, and the menu tasty. Breakfast includes eggs, bacon, or a combo sandwich, while the lunch menu has local fresh fish sandwiches ($14) and hamburgers ($7), as well as hot dogs, cookies, and other snacks. Stop for lunch while heading east. Quaintly tiled, powder room-style restrooms are located a few steps from the café.

A local institution, the ★ **Swizzle Inn Pub & Restaurant** (3 Blue Hole Hill, tel. 441/293-9300, www.swizzleinn.com, 11am-1am daily, $14-30) is as much a Bermudian hangout as a tourist magnet thanks to its lively social calendar, satisfying menu that includes all-day breakfast, and deadly pitchers of rum swizzle. The Swizzle's caloric masterpiece, the Bailey's Bay Fish Sandwich (chunks of battered local fish fillet topped with melted cheese, tartar sauce, lettuce, and tomato stuffed precariously inside white toast, $19), has reached legendary proportions, and visitors stop for lunch on their way to the airport, just a few minutes away. The swizzle, made from an artful combination of Gosling's Black Seal Rum, Gold Rum, and fruit juices, makes it dangerous to get on a scooter afterward: Take a cab to lunch instead. Nightly entertainment includes live bands, trivia nights, and Mardi Gras, St. Patrick's Day, and U.S. Thanksgiving celebrations. The on-site Swagger Out Gift Shop is popular for hangover souvenirs, accessible online.

Bailey's Ice-Cream (2 Blue Hole Hill, tel. 441/293-8605, noon-7pm daily) is a hot spot, thanks to its 40-odd flavors of Bermuda-made award-winning ice cream, yogurt, and sorbet. In summer, people wait in long lines for chocolate-chip cookie dough, butterscotch crunch,

Oreo sweet cream, and mango-passion fruit—all available by the tub in island supermarkets. Sit in the air-conditioned interior or outside on the brick patio. The 20-year-old eatery also serves snacks, sandwiches, hot dogs, and chili.

Bermuda's only pizza-delivery chain, **Four Star Pizza** (6 North Shore Rd., Flatts Village, tel. 441/292-9111, www.fourstar.bm, 11am-10pm Mon.-Thurs. and Sat., 11am-11pm Fri., noon-10pm Sun., $10 minimum order, $2 delivery charge) delivers deep-dish, low-carb, and 10- and 14-inch specialty pizzas, calzones, sub sandwiches, salads, chicken wings, desserts. Dine-in is also available. If you're accustomed to North American fast food, you might be shocked by the steep prices ($25 for a 14-inch pizza).

International

Having relocated in 2016, **Rustico** (36 North Shore Rd., Flatts Village, tel. 441/295-5212, www.bermuda-dining.com, lunch 11:30am-3pm, dinner 5pm-10pm daily) now has roomy outdoor space and a renovated bar on a busy corner, with take-out or eat-in service. Lovers of Mediterranean cuisine will not be disappointed, with a well-chosen wine list and lamb shank osso buco ($35), shiitake and sausage *ragù* over truffle polenta ($28), pastas ($16-24), thin-crust pizzas (from $14), and vegetarian dishes incorporating vine-ripened tomatoes, lots of garlic, and porcini and portobello mushrooms. Devotees swear by the efficient service and carefully crafted dishes.

Opened in 2017, ★ **Village Pantry** (8 North Shore Rd., tel. 441/478-2300, http://villagepantry.bm, 8am-10pm Mon.-Fri., 9am-10pm Sat.-Sun.) is owned by the thriving Devil's Isle group, owners of Buzz cafés around the island. Located at the former site of Rustico, now a few hundred yards down the street, the restaurant is wildly popular for Sunday brunch and creatively sourced and prepared lunch and dinner fare. Appetizers include lamb lollies ($17) and poke bowls with Korean gluten-free kelp noodles in two sizes ($15 and $27). Main courses range from fresh grilled wahoo ($34) to strip steak ($35)

to Alsatian-style flatbreads ($14-18), veggie tacos ($18), and Brazilian seafood stew ($38). A cheese board for two is $20. Wash down with the famous coffee, smoothies, signature cocktails, or a selection from the impressive wine list.

Fine Dining

★ **Tom Moore's Tavern** (Walsingham Lane, off Harrington Sound Rd., tel. 441/293-8020, www.tommoores.com, lunch by appointment, dinner 6:30pm-10pm daily Feb.-Dec. except Cup Match Thurs. and Christmas Day) is a AAA Four Diamond restaurant in a historic setting deep in the forested Walsingham Nature Reserve. The intriguing waterfront building, an old homestead built in 1652, became an inn during the 19th century and is named for Irishman Thomas Moore, who lived on the property briefly in 1804 and penned a collection of love poems beneath a calabash tree. The restaurant, colloquially referred to as "Tom Moore's," still inspires romanticism; its silver service, elegant multicourse menus, and hushed interiors make it a favored spot for very special nights out. If you pine for a $1,600 bottle of Château Lafitte-Rothschild 1999, a $110 glass of dessert wine, or fountains of Armand de Brignac champagne, general manager Bruno Fiocca will make it happen. In addition to Prince Charles, who ate lunch here on a 1970 visit to the island, the restaurant's celebrity guests have included oil magnate Ross Perot, former New York City mayor Michael Bloomberg, and former Italian prime minister Silvio Berlusconi, all three of whom own homes in Tucker's Town.

Canadian executive chef Robert Nicolle's menu has appetizers like caramelized sea scallops ($22), carpaccio of the day ($19), and rum-soaked fish chowder ($12); main courses range from blue cheese-stuffed pork tenderloin ($36) to slow-roasted salmon ($38), a fish of the day ($41), and vegan options such as wild mushroom and couscous parfait ($28). Desserts include a dark chocolate tart ($12) and banana mousse cake ($13).

Ports, cognacs, and liqueurs are available. Your pocketbook will undoubtedly groan (a 17 percent gratuity is added to your bill), but the experience is memorable. The restaurant seats up to 160 in five rooms on two floors. Special events are not limited to the dinner-only schedule. In recent years, Tom Moore's has followed the island trend and relaxed its strict dress code to "elegant-casual," with no jacket required.

Groceries

Long checkout lines evenings and weekends are the only downside of **Shelly Bay MarketPlace** (110 North Shore Rd., tel. 441/293-0966, 8am-10pm Mon.-Sat., 9pm-7pm Sun.), a superstore with everything you could want for food or drink, as well as toys, kitchen supplies, towels, and coolers.

Ways Market (202 North Shore Rd., tel. 441/296-2967, 8am-9pm daily) is a small convenience store perfect for picking up a newspaper, wine, bakery items, or other basic necessities.

ACCOMMODATIONS

Family-run **Brightside Apartments** (38 North Shore Rd., Flatts Village, tel. 441/292-8410, brightside@link.bm) has been a fixture of Flatts since 1979, commanding the southwest portion of so-called Lazy Corner—the busy junction of Middle Road, North Shore Road, and Harrington Sound Road—that now houses the popular Rustico restaurant. Guest units, all with basic decor, range from a basic double room ($150) and studio with kitchen ($180) to cottages (2-bedroom $380, 3-bedroom $420-600), and are cushioned by beautifully landscaped gardens. There's a large swimming pool in the center of the complex. All rooms have a microwave, fridge, coffeepot, phone, cable TV, free Wi-Fi, and air-conditioning. The location is handy to the aquarium, the caves, St. George's, restaurants, beaches, and bus routes.

The 21-acre **Grotto Bay Beach Resort** (11 Blue Hole Hill, tel. 441/293-8333, U.S. tel. 855/447-6886, www.grottobay.com, minimum 3 nights, waterfront suites $339-585) covers a lush hillside above the Causeway, with panoramic views of Castle Harbour, Coney Island, Ferry Reach, and the airport, less than a mile away. The resort's many yards of coastline encompass sheltered coves, an east-facing main beach, and a dock with a water sports center. The property is riddled with crystalline caves; one is open for walking, and another, Prospero's Cave, is home to the resort's stunning spa, where treatments can be enjoyed beneath the cool ceiling of stalactites. On landscaped grounds, the resort has a pool with a swim-up bar, four tennis courts, two lit for night play, and a sheltered beachfront where vendors rent paddleboards, kayaks, and motorboats as well as sailing and scuba excursions. Many of the 201 suites, outfitted in tropical prints, are somewhat boxy, with tiny baths, but have lovely views of the bay below. Rooms on upper (2nd and 3rd) floors afford the best views, and all have private patios (on the ground floor) or balconies. Free Wi-Fi is offered throughout the resort. The casual atmosphere, playground, and children's program during high season make it a good choice for families.

The large Great House lobby is reminiscent of a hunting lodge or a Polynesian loft, with open-beamed ceilings, solid oak floors, knotty pine columns, a cozy winter fireplace, and nooks for reading or meeting friends. Two dining rooms—one formal, the other laid-back tropical—are located off the lobby, and the hotel's Sunday brunch is a big draw for locals. A pergola over the water is available for private four-course dinners ($499 per couple).

The hotel is the only one in Bermuda offering an all-inclusive option ($114 adults, $84 ages 3-16, on top of the room rates), which covers food and beverages, except premium-brand liquor, wine, and champagne, all gratuities, tennis, nonmotorized water sports, and an unlimited public transportation pass. Other variations on meal-plan packages are also available.

INFORMATION AND SERVICES

Hamilton Parish has three gas stations: **Rubis Van Buren's Marine Station** (3 North Shore Rd. at Flatts Village, tel. 441/292-2882, 7am-9pm daily); **Crawl Hill Esso Tigermart** (North Shore Rd. at Crawl Hill, tel. 441/293-6491, 6am-10pm daily); and **Rubis Causeway Service Station** (15 Blue Hole Hill, tel. 441/293-0621, 6am-10pm Mon.-Fri., 7am-10pm Sat., 8am-8pm Sun.).

Hamilton Parish has one post office, **Crawl Post Office** (42 Radnor Rd., tel. 441/293-1400, 8am-5pm Mon.-Fri.). ATMs are located outside **Four Star Pizza** (6 North Shore Rd.), **Rubis Causeway Service Station** (15 Blue Hole Hill), **Shelly Bay MarketPlace** (110 North Shore Rd.), and **Crawl Hill Esso Tigermart** (North Shore Rd. at Crawl Hill).

TRANSPORTATION
Buses

Buses are an easy way to travel through Hamilton Parish, with frequent well-marked stops, including at the Bermuda Aquarium, Museum & Zoo, Shelly Bay, the caves, and Grotto Bay Beach Resort. Take route 1 (via South Shore Road, Tucker's Point, and the caves) every half hour, or route 3 via Harrington Sound Road every 15 minutes (both run from the City of Hamilton-Grotto Bay and St. George's). Buses 10 and 11 travel North Shore Road (via the aquarium and Shelly Bay) every 15 minutes, between City of Hamilton and St. George's. Fares to the parish $4.50 from Hamilton.

Scooters and Bicycles

Oleander Cycles (Blue Hole Hill, next to Grotto Bay Beach Resort, tel. 441/293-1010, www.oleandercycles.bm, 8:30am-5pm daily) rents standard single ($55 per day, $225 per week, $17 after 7 days) or double ($65 per day, $266 per week, $21 after 7 days) scooters. Rates include scooter delivery and pickup (or hotel pickup), the first tank of gas, a helmet, a lock, a basket, third-party insurance ($30), and island-wide roadside service for breakdowns. Mountain bikes are $40 per day, $175 per week, $10 a day after seven days.

Taxis

There are taxi stands at Grotto Bay Beach Resort, and cabs can also be found in the parking lots at Crystal Caves and Swizzle Inn. Use the **Hitch app** (www.hitch.bm) or call one of the cab companies to arrange a pickup: **Bermuda Industrial Union Co-op** (tel. 441/292-4476, cooptaxi@fkbnet.bm), **Bermuda Island Taxi** (tel. 441/295-4141, www.bermudaislandtaxi.com), or **BTA Dispatching** (tel. 441/296-2121, www.btadispatching.com).

St. George's Parish

The Old Town of St. George.... 201
Around the Old Town.......... 213

St. David's Island and Southside... 222

Bermuda's old-time soul can be found in St. George's Parish, landing point of the first settlers and home to the oldest permanent English town in the New World.

Wandering the shady backstreets, where peeling pastel walls and hidden gardens invite soporific afternoons, visitors get a sense of traditional island life a world away from bustling corporate Hamilton. Both the parish and the 400-year-old town are called St. George's, seat of Bermuda's government for two centuries and a UNESCO World Heritage Site, along with the nearby fortresses. The parish encompasses parkland and residential areas, plus the airport, Southside, St. David's, and Tucker's Town, all on an amalgam of islands joined by bridges to form the eastern chunk of Bermuda's mainland—the so-called East End. The town and its environs, as well as Ferry Point National Park, sit on St. George's Island. The parish's other main islands are St. David's, attached to a former U.S. military base, now called Southside, and Cooper's, a former NASA site and now a nature reserve with seven pristine beaches. Scattered offshore islets include Smith's, Paget, Hen, and Governor's Islands in St. George's Harbour, and Nonsuch and Castle

Islands spanning the channel into Castle Harbour.

Exploration of the parish should begin in the old town, whose tangle of skinny streets, including the original town grid of the early 1600s, juxtaposes immensely historic sites with the contemporary homes of St. Georgians. In a nation where consumerism is king, St. George's stands apart as an anachronistic getaway. A stroll around its harborside square evokes the rowdy days of American Civil War smugglers, whose latter-day counterparts are laid-back yachties on their way to a winter in the Caribbean. The old town is the kind of place where one can idle away the hours without achieving more than some serious people-watching and enjoying an ice cream cone.

An interactive World Heritage Centre on the harbor-front at Penno's Wharf highlights the area's fascinating history. Other key attractions include Tobacco Bay, Fort St. Catherine, and Ferry Point National Park, a national reserve where Easter lilies and

---

Previous: Cooper's Island Nature Reserve; State House, the colony's first stone building. **Above:** St. David's Lighthouse.

Look for ★ to find recommended
sights, activities, dining, and lodging.

Highlights

★ **World Heritage Centre:** Any tour of St. George's logically begins here, where modern exhibits and informed guides explain Bermuda's history (page 203).

★ **St. Peter's Church:** Visit the oldest continually used Protestant church site in the New World (page 205).

★ **Fort St. Catherine:** Explore exhibits and peer over the ramparts at the very stretch of ocean the first castaways saw after escaping the shipwrecked *Sea Venture* (page 214).

★ **Cup Match:** St. George's and Somerset Cricket Clubs battle for victory in a tournament that draws thousands of spectators and provides an immediate initiation into island life (page 219).

★ **Cooper's Island Nature Reserve:** The newest addition to Bermuda's public parkland, this 44-acre peninsula comprises pristine beaches, coastline, and woodlands (page 223).

★ **Carter House:** This 300-year-old home-turned-museum tells the intriguing story of St. David's, from its whaling days to the advent of the U.S. military base (page 223).

St. George's Parish

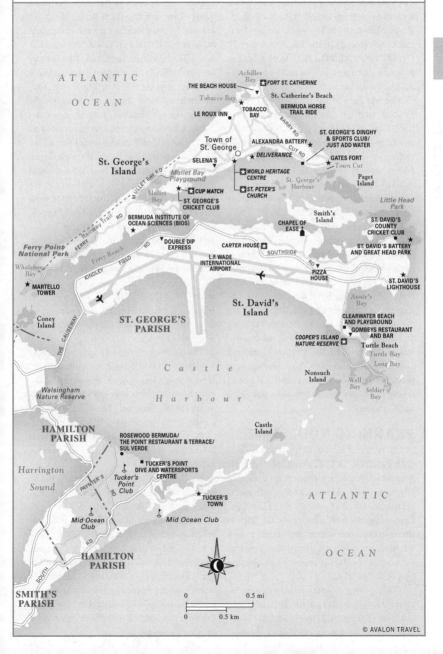

ATLANTIC
OCEAN

Achilles Bay

THE BEACH HOUSE   ★ FORT ST. CATHERINE
St. Catherine's Beach

Tobacco Bay   BERMUDA HORSE
TRAIL RIDE

LE ROUX INN   TOBACCO BAY

St. George's
Island

Town of
St. George

ALEXANDRA BATTERY   ST. GEORGE'S DINGHY
& SPORTS CLUB/
JUST ADD WATER

SELENA'S   DELIVERANCE   GATES FORT
Town Cut

Mullet Bay
Playground   WORLD HERITAGE
CENTRE   St. George's
Harbour   Paget
Island

CUP MATCH   ST. PETER'S
CHURCH

ST. GEORGE'S
CRICKET CLUB   Smith's
Island   Little Head
Park

CHAPEL OF
EASE   ST. DAVID'S
COUNTY
CRICKET CLUB

BERMUDA INSTITUTE OF
OCEAN SCIENCES (BIOS)

Ferry Point
National Park   DOUBLE DIP
EXPRESS   CARTER HOUSE   SOUTHSIDE RD   ST. DAVID'S BATTERY
AND GREAT HEAD PARK

Ferry Reach   L.F. WADE
INTERNATIONAL
AIRPORT   PIZZA
HOUSE   ST. DAVID'S
LIGHTHOUSE

Whalebone
Bay

MARTELLO
TOWER   St. David's
Island   Annie's
Bay

Coney
Island   THE CAUSEWAY   CLEARWATER BEACH
AND PLAYGROUND   GOMBEYS RESTAURANT
AND BAR

ST. GEORGE'S
PARISH   COOPER'S ISLAND
NATURE RESERVE   Turtle Beach

Castle   Nonsuch
Island   Turtle Bay
Long Bay

Walsingham
Nature Reserve   Harbour   Well
Bay   Soldier
Bay

HAMILTON
PARISH   Castle
Island

Harrington
Sound   ROSEWOOD BERMUDA/
THE POINT RESTAURANT & TERRACE/
SUL VERDE

PAYNTER'S RD   TUCKER'S POINT
DIVE AND WATERSPORTS
CENTRE

Tucker's
Point
Club   ATLANTIC

Mid Ocean
Club   TUCKER'S
TOWN

Mid Ocean Club   OCEAN

HAMILTON
PARISH

SMITH'S
PARISH

0   0.5 mi
0   0.5 km

© AVALON TRAVEL

cherry hedges line the eastern stretch of the Railway Trail. St. David's is a quirky community long detached from the rest of Bermuda; it remains quite unto itself. Once home to enslaved Native Americans whose descendants trace their lineage to the Pequot people, St. David's swirls with tall tales from a heyday of whaling and pirating, its residents still innately tied to the sea.

The air pervading St. George's harks back to another time. It was only during the Victorian era that the parish was finally linked to mainland Bermuda by a half-mile causeway—and even that connection has proven tenuous at times. In 2003, Hurricane Fabian's surges swept over the winding roadway, killing four people, and St. Georgians were confined to the parish.

Despite perennial problems with youth gangs and petty crime, neighbors generally know everyone's business and the rhythms of life invite small-town generosity, candid opinion, and an utterly fatalistic humor. After decades of promised hotel developments, the East End is finally getting a St. Regis, a luxury property slated to open by 2020 overlooking St. Catherine's Beach, north of the town—where shipwrecked *Sea Venture* castaways rowed to safety in 1609. The development promises a massive rejuvenation for the area, whose retail and restaurants have struggled in recent years.

PLANNING YOUR TIME

St. George's may be your first point of contact with Bermuda, as L. F. Wade International Airport is located here, cruise ships occasionally berth in the old town, and private yachts are required to clear customs at the East End. Cruise passengers in summer and fall flock to the town's beaches; winter visitors tend to seek out the town's forts, museums, churches, and parks. In a few days it's easy to combine the best of both worlds.

The old town is worth a full day's exploration to visit its landmark buildings and stroll intriguing backstreets and the landmark forts. Exploring on foot is the best

strategy. Within the town, the *Deliverance* replica, St. Peter's Church, the State House, Tucker House, and the Bermuda National Trust Museum's Rogues & Runners exhibit are vital to understanding the colorful past of St. George's. Grand Fort St. Catherine and its beach should not be missed, and along the way are Alexandra Battery and the compact Gates Fort, teetering over the pencil-thin Town Cut, where liners pass, sometimes precariously, into St. George's Harbour from the open sea. Tobacco Bay's unique volcanic structures and busy beachside café make it one of Bermuda's best places to snorkel, though it's packed with crowds in summer. With more time, expand your tour with a hike through Ferry Point National Park—home of the 1820s Martello Tower and two other forts, a lovely beach, and a scenic stretch of the Railway Trail—and a visit to St. David's and Cooper's Island. You can get to St. George's by fast ferry from Hamilton (45 minutes), by scooter (25 minutes from the center of the island), or several bus routes from the capital (1, 3, 10, and 11). In addition to two area resorts, there are several well-run bed-and-breakfasts plus self-catering apartment rentals.

The old town revamped itself after obtaining UNESCO World Heritage status in 2000. New signage was posted, and many of the most historic streets were bricked over to enhance the old-time feel. The World Heritage Centre on historic Penno's Wharf is a logical starting place for any tour of the parish, with interactive exhibits, informational booths, and helpful staff.

St. George's has haunted history tours, walking tours, historical reenactments, and beach parties. Town markets on Sunday afternoons bring out arts and crafts and local entertainment. St. George's is a festive place over the end-of-year holidays; the Bermuda National Trust Christmas Walkabout in early December—a buzzing Friday night street festival attended by thousands—is one of Bermuda's favorite events. On New Year's Eve, you can watch a mammoth onion drop into King's Square.

The Old Town of St. George

Bermuda's first capital, St. George's has remained a living town from its earliest days. Never ruined or relocated, like Virginia's Jamestown, it has retained the look and feel of its 17th-century origins, representing an impressive 400 years of domestic, religious, and military architecture. Because the town was the island's major port and capital for nearly 200 years, the story of St. George's is essentially the story of early Bermuda and the island's drastic reversals of fortune that alternately shaped St. George's as a boomtown or backwater.

HISTORY

The town was named for England's patron saint and dragon slayer, Saint George, by an English admiral who claimed Bermuda for the Crown in 1609. Sir George Somers headed the English relief fleet, which in July 1609 was crossing the Atlantic with supplies for James Fort, Virginia, when it was hit by a hurricane. The flagship *Sea Venture,* carrying Somers and 150 men, women, and children, wrecked off St. Catherine's Beach. Miraculously, no one perished in the disaster, nor did the ship sink. Wedged on reefs, the *Sea Venture* and its cargo were salvaged by the survivors, who spent the next 10 months as castaways, fashioning two new ships, *Deliverance* and *Patience,* of island cedar. The wreck's remains eventually sank and today are buried beneath sand.

All but three men continued their journey to the New World in 1610, Somers among them. But when the admiral later sailed back to Bermuda to gather more supplies for the starving Virginia settlers, he died, purportedly after eating contaminated meat. His body was returned to his birthplace, Lyme Regis in Dorset, England—now also a World Heritage Site and the sister city of St. George's since 1996. The admiral's heart was buried in what is now the site of Somers Garden, near the town center.

The physical town began as a collection of palmetto-thatched wooden huts built by the first official settlers, who sailed from England in 1612 aboard the *Plough.* Erected around a market square, the community was dubbed New London. The colonists had to learn how to adapt to life in the tropics and improvise building methods and materials; by the close of their first century, colonists' huts had been replaced by sturdier limestone buildings and bridges linking Bermuda's main islands.

More than half of Bermuda's 90 fortifications were erected here, surviving virtually intact as the earliest English masonry forts of the New World (most in the Americas were constructed of timber). Bermuda never actually came under enemy fire, however. Today, the UNESCO site comprising the town and surrounding forts is considered "a place of cultural heritage of the greatest importance for humanity."

Economic stagnation interspersed with periods of immense prosperity characterized the development of the old capital and Bermuda as a whole. In the 1700s, whaling, shipbuilding, piloting, privateering, and maritime trade built a thriving economy as St. George's became a bustling port. At the end of the 18th century, the old town finally lost its status as capital when Hamilton was officially incorporated; authorities wanted a more central port, and after 200 years, the seat of island government was moved to Pembroke Parish.

The U.S. Civil War (1861-1865) brought boom times back to St. George's, which became a strategic port for the transshipment of goods between Britain and the Confederacy. While the island, like Britain, was officially neutral, Bermudian sympathies lay heavily with the South. Cotton ("white gold") was carried by Southern blockade runners to the island, where it was traded for British munitions and European luxury goods.

The Old Town of St. George

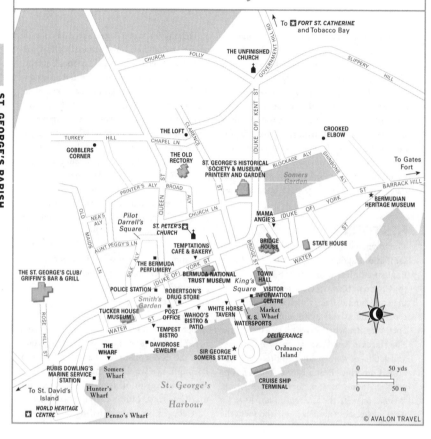

To **FORT ST. CATHERINE** and Tobacco Bay

THE UNFINISHED CHURCH

CROOKED ELBOW

To Gates Fort

THE LOFT

GOBBLERS CORNER

THE OLD RECTORY

ST. GEORGE'S HISTORICAL SOCIETY & MUSEUM, PRINTERY AND GARDEN

Somers Garden

BERMUDIAN HERITAGE MUSEUM

Pilot Darrell's Square

ST. PETER'S CHURCH

MAMA ANGIE'S

BRIDGE HOUSE

STATE HOUSE

TEMPTATIONS CAFÉ & BAKERY

THE ST. GEORGE'S CLUB/ GRIFFIN'S BAR & GRILL

THE BERMUDA PERFUMERY

BERMUDA NATIONAL TRUST MUSEUM

TOWN HALL

King's Square

POLICE STATION

ROBERTSON'S DRUG STORE

VISITOR INFORMATION CENTRE

Smith's Garden

TUCKER HOUSE MUSEUM

POST OFFICE

WHITE HORSE TAVERN

Market

K. S. Wharf

WAHOO'S BISTRO & PATIO

WATERSPORTS

TEMPEST BISTRO

DELIVERANCE

THE WHARF

DAVIDROSE JEWELRY

SIR GEORGE SOMERS STATUE

Ordnance Island

RUBIS DOWLING'S MARINE SERVICE STATION

Somers Wharf

To St. David's Island

Hunter's Wharf

St. George's Harbour

CRUISE SHIP TERMINAL

WORLD HERITAGE CENTRE

Penno's Wharf

0   50 yds
0   50 m

© AVALON TRAVEL

Tourism proved a boon for St. George's in the 20th century, with the development of ritzy Tucker's Town and the arrival of the first liners and flying boats to Bermuda. Later, World War II brought a land-lease deal between Britain and the United States that transformed the islands of Castle Harbour into a U.S. Naval Air Station, whose air base later became Bermuda's civilian airport. The U.S. military pulled out in 1995, and the East End base lands were renamed Southside and opened for public use. Beaches, an emergency medical center, and sports areas are on the land, which has also been used for affordable housing.

SIGHTS

The old town has a plethora of public museums and historic sites open most of the year, but shops, banks, and houses are historically significant as well. Scores of pre-1800 structures are scattered throughout the town, and many are marked with their own World Heritage plaques. These include **Stockdale,** a private home on Printer's Alley; **Esten House** on King's Square, now home to an art gallery and shops; **Stiles House,** HSBC's branch on Water Street; the postcard-pretty **Fanny Fox's Cottage** at the top of Duke of Clarence Street; and many others that are unmarked.

★ World Heritage Centre

A tour of St. George's should begin at the wheelchair-accessible **World Heritage Centre** (19 Penno's Wharf, tel. 441/297-5791, www.sgf.bm, 10am-4pm Mon.-Sat., museum $5 adults, $2 children, free under age 5), where audiovisual exhibits, knowledgeable staff, and information on history and attractions in the area can be found. The ground-floor orientation gallery provides an entertaining walk through Bermuda's early history, including comparisons between St. George's and Jamestown, the tale of the *Sea Venture,* and the island's key role in the Revolutionary War and the U.S. Civil War. Also detailed is the story of whaling along with eye-catching dioramas and models of the early town. Voices of key characters in St. George's history help explain milestone events. A children's area covers life in early Bermuda with hands-on exhibits and a dress-up section where they can mimic soldiers, sea captains, and colonists.

In the lobby, get maps and brochures on attractions and tours. A "time-tree" highlighting historic episodes guides visitors upstairs, where changing exhibits relating to the Island's East End heritage are on display, and a short film introducing the old town's attractions and history plays. Computer touchscreens and interpretive panels detail the story of St. George's, St. David's, and their fortifications. A charity shop in the building, Second Hand Rose, sells books, CDs, jewelry, china, and other trinkets.

King's Square

King's Square has long been the hub of community life. Emblazoned with the town crest, the **Town Hall** (tel. 441/297-1532, 9am-4pm Mon.-Fri., free) is the meeting place of the officials who represent the Corporation of St. George's (whose offices are housed in modern premises on Ordnance Island). The building is furnished in cedar, and its walls pay tribute to past mayors, their portraits gazing down on visitors. On the northern edge of the square, you can't miss a couple of **stocks** and pillories—used in the past to publicly shame citizens for minor transgressions such as petty theft and adultery. You can pose for photos to mimic 17th-century citizens, who would have been pelted with rotten fruit or eggs by a rowdy crowd. Near the water's edge, the historic **ducking stool** was for dunking women accused of being "nags and gossips." Popular 15-minute reenactments are held several times a week for the amusement of visitors.

Attached to the square by bridge is **Ordnance Island,** once the British military's storage place for munitions as well as a gallows, now home to a cruise-ship wharf and a small harbor-front park, where a bronze statue of Bermuda's founder, *Sir George Somers,* by Bermudian sculptor Desmond Fountain, throws its arms to the sky in apparent relief at reaching land here 1609.

Deliverance

Ordnance Island is also home to a replica of the *Deliverance* (www.sgf.bm, 10am-4pm Mon.-Sat., $3 adults, $2 ages 5-16)—the ship built by Sir George Somers and the other shipwrecked *Sea Venture* castaways in order to sail on to Jamestown, Virginia. The life-size model, with cabins and stairways that demonstrate the claustrophobic nature of life aboard such vessels, underwent a complete renovation of its woodwork and rigging before it reopened in 2009 with audiovisual exhibits telling the 40-foot vessel's dramatic story. Included are interpretive panels about "The Ship That Saved America" as well as an animatronic figure of William Strachey, a 17th-century Englishman who survived *Sea Venture*'s crash landing; his detailed diaries describing the epic shipwreck and survival were widely read in London and inspired a contemporary—William Shakespeare—to write his last play, *The Tempest.* Exhibits describe the epic hurricane that wrecked the *Sea Venture,* the castaways' ingenious survival on Bermuda, and their escape aboard two hand-hewn ships, one of which was *Deliverance,* to Jamestown—where food supplies they had

African Diaspora Trail

Bermuda's black heritage and the 200-year legacy of slavery on the island are remembered through a chain of monuments and museums. The African Diaspora Trail belongs to an international group of heritage sites by the same name, all officially designated UNESCO Slave Route Projects. There are a dozen points of interest on the island, each marked by a bronze plaque. Six of these are located in St. George's. If you dedicate a full day, you could begin at the National Museum of Bermuda at Dockyard in Sandys, then take the fast ferry to St. George's and bus or scooter back through the central parishes. Some of the key sights and points of interest along the trail:

The West End's **Commissioner's House,** at the National Museum of Bermuda, contains exhibits and compelling artifacts detailing the island's part in the transatlantic slave trade, as well as slavery in Bermuda. Ships carrying enslaved people often smashed on Bermuda's reefs, leaving artifacts such as iron manacles, glass beads, and cowry shells belonging to the human cargo. Many Bermuda families can trace their roots to enslaved people who worked as farmers, ship pilots, whalers, or carpenters on the island before slavery was abolished in 1834.

Warwick Parish's **Cobb's Hill Methodist Church** was built by enslaved and free blacks, who often toiled "by moonlight" in the after-hours allowed by their masters. A Chief Justice permitted a piece of land to be released for the project, and the church was finished in 1827. Today, it is located on Moonlight Lane, and its congregation includes descendants of those who labored to build it.

Barr's Bay Park, on the City of Hamilton waterfront, is included on the trail, as it was the place where an American schooner named the *Enterprise* landed in 1835. Sent off course by a storm, the ship was carrying a cargo of 78 enslaved people—an illegal activity in Bermuda a year after abolition. Local officials refused to clear the vessel, and members of a Bermuda Friendly Society took the captain to court. The enslaved people eventually were allowed to choose whether to stay in Bermuda or return to the United States. All but one woman and her five children opted to remain on the island; the descendants of those 72 people can still be found in Bermuda.

A Bermuda National Trust property (although not open to the public), **Verdmont Cottage,** alongside the historic house in Smith's Parish, was once a slave quarter. Slaves would have helped build the main house, living in the outroom and buttery. Later, they worked as laborers or domestic help. Verdmont Cottage was the property's original kitchen, and archaeologists believe it also served as slave quarters.

Site of a dedicated graveyard for enslaved people, **St. Peter's Church** in the Town of St. George hosts a special ceremony each Emancipation Day (late July or early Aug.) to remember Bermuda's enslaved. Inside the church, a gallery on the western end was built in the early 1700s to allow free and enslaved blacks to attend services in the segregated society. The graveyard is located outside the gallery, separated from the main gravesite of many of the early town's white citizens. An interesting artifact in the church is a baptismal register for 1834, in which a line drawn at the month of August indicates when blacks no longer had to be entered as "slave" or "free."

Opened in 1994, the **Bermudian Heritage Museum** in the Town of St. George celebrates achievements of black Bermudians, including personalities in music and sports, the gombey tradition, and members of Friendly Society lodges who helped blacks adjust to life after emancipation.

For more information on the African Diaspora Trail, contact the **Department of Cultural Affairs** (tel. 441/292-9447), or Bermuda's Visitor Information Centres throughout the island.

gathered on the island helped starving settlers hang on to America's first colony. Children, particularly, will enjoy experiencing history on this climb-aboard monument, which also makes for great photo ops of the surrounding old town.

State House

On a hilltop over King's Square stands the distinctive white **State House** (King St. and Princess St., 10am-4pm Wed. except holidays, free), the 17th-century colony's first stone building and only surviving structure

St. Peter's Church

public ceremony in the town square every spring, attended by the governor and the Bermuda Regiment.

★ St. Peter's Church

One of Bermuda's most famous hallmark buildings, **St. Peter's Church** (Duke of York St., tel. 441/297-0216, www.stpeters.bm, 10am-4pm Mon.-Fri., 11am-3pm Sat., service 11am Sun.) is a busy venue for local weddings and funerals, where attendees crowd into the cedar-packed interior. The original church on this site was made of wood and thatched in palm fronds by the first settlers in 1612. The first meeting of the fledgling Assembly was held on August 1, 1620, two years before the State House was built as the government's dedicated headquarters. Among the items on that inaugural agenda: a ban on both "idle and unprofitable persons" and the slaughter of turtles. St. Peter's is built on the same site, qualifying it as the oldest Protestant church in the New World, rebuilt in stone in 1713; its tower was added in 1814. Inside, its exposed cedar ceiling beams and pews, cedar communion table, and dole cupboard (used to store donations of bread for the parish poor) are all excellent examples of early craftsmanship; the furniture is believed to be the oldest on the island. St. Peter's collection of communion silver is also notable: The St. George's Chalice was given to the church by the Bermuda Company in 1625, while the communion set bears the royal arms of William III, who had it made and sent to St. Peter's in 1697. On its 400th anniversary in 2012, the old royal title "Their Majesties Chappell," given to authorize the chalice's delivery to the island, was restored to St. Peter's. There is also a rare piece of 1616 Hogge money on display, one of the island's earliest coins, decorated with the iconic image of the wild pigs that roamed Bermuda in the early years of settlement.

The church graveyards are almost as fascinating. In the eastern graveyard, notable townsfolk are buried alongside modern VIPs. Under the shade of coconut palms, a second graveyard holds the bodies of enslaved and

of the period. Built in 1622, it was used as a munitions storage depot, a courthouse, and home of the world's oldest parliament outside Britain. For 200 years, the State House was the seat of government for the colonial General Assembly's meetings. It is constructed of sturdy limestone blocks set in a mortar of turtle oil and lime; it's believed that some of the island's first enslaved Caribbeans may have helped to build it, introducing new methods at a time when cedar-framed structures were the norm. An original third story used for holding gunpowder was removed during 1730 renovations and restored in 1969.

Most notoriously, the State House was the venue for more than two dozen witch trials during the colony's first century, which, as in Europe and the United States, resulted in the public hanging, burning, and torture of women. Since 1816, the State House has been rented for the annual sum of a single peppercorn by Bermuda's oldest Masonic lodge, St. George No. 200 of the Grand Lodge of Scotland. The paltry rent is paid at a colorful free blacks. Even after the abolition of slavery in 1834, Bermuda's black and white societies remained divided until official segregation was outlawed in the 1960s. A solemn walk and ceremony is held at this site every year on the eve of Cup Match, whose Thursday public holiday in late July or early August celebrates Emancipation Day.

The Bermuda National Trust Museum

Few Americans realize the strategic role tiny Bermuda played in the U.S. Civil War (1861-1865). **The Bermuda National Trust Museum** (Globe Hotel, King's Square, 32 Duke of York St., tel. 441/297-1423, 10am-1pm Tues., 10am-4pm Wed., 11am-2pm Sat., $5 adults, $2 ages 6-18, free under age 6) tells the dramatic story of blockade runners, spies, and international subterfuge when the town was a hotbed of Confederate sympathies, Union authorities, and British cotton smugglers. Four years of war activity brought unprecedented wealth to St. George's, marking its heyday. The Globe Hotel dates to around 1700, when the island's governor, Samuel Day, sparked a bitter court battle when he tried to claim it; he later died in prison. The building became headquarters of Confederate agent Major Norman Walker, who lived here with his wife Georgiana and their three children while he masterminded the flow of guns and war supplies through Union blockades. The museum's exhibit "Rogues & Runners" details the complex web of loyalties in Bermuda in that era and how the town became a major port for Southern captains and a transshipment center for UK-bound cotton. Included in admission is a brief film about Bermuda and St. George's. The museum shop sells Bermuda books, souvenirs, and arts and crafts. A ticket to all three Trust museums (the others being the Tucker House and Verdmont Museums) is $10.

Bermudian Heritage Museum

A tribute to black Bermudian history, the **Bermudian Heritage Museum** (Samaritans Lodge, Duke of York St. and Water St., tel. 441/297-4126, 10am-3pm Tues.-Sat., $3 adults, $2 children, free under age 5) opened in 1998 in the historically relevant 19th-century lodge that belonged to the Grand United Order of Good Samaritans, one of the largest Friendly Societies, groups that aided newly freed blacks before and after emancipation in 1834. The museum records the story of slavery and these societies, as well as related symbols and other folklore, such as the gombey tradition and the origins of Cup Match. One of the recommended stops on the African Diaspora Trail, the museum highlights historical milestones of black pride, notably the 1959 Theatre Boycott, a protest by black moviegoers that brought about the end of official racial segregation in restaurants, hotels, and schools. Black entrepreneurs, sporting figures, and politicians are also honored.

Tucker House Museum

Built as a merchant's house, this simple whitewashed building takes its name from Henry Tucker, one of the colony's most important figures as president of the Governor's Council. Walking through its elegant interior takes you back to the time of candlelit chandeliers, brick ovens, and four-poster beds. **Tucker House Museum** (5 Water St., at Barber's Alley, tel. 441/297-0545, 10am-12:30pm Mon., 11am-3pm Wed., $5 adults, $2 ages 6-18, free under age 6) is a treasure trove of priceless antiques, including English mahogany and Bermudian cedar furniture, family portraits by American artist Joseph Blackburn, hand-sewn quilts, and kitchen utensils. On the lower floor, visit the archaeological display, which chronicles recent excavations and the artifacts found below the cellar floor. Also notable is the kitchen, where Joseph Hayne Rainey, a freed South Carolina slave and later the first black member of the U.S. House of Representatives, operated a barbershop for several years. The adjoining **Barber's Alley** pays tribute to Rainey and Susan Rainey, his seamstress wife, who both escaped to Bermuda during the U.S.

Civil War and set up successful businesses before returning to the United States. Off this alleyway, there is a pocket-size public garden, Smith's Garden, which Princess Anne officially opened in 1991. A ticket to all three Trust museums (the others being The Bermuda National Trust Museum and Verdmont Museum) is $10.

Somers Garden

For a tranquil break between museum tours or a shady lunchtime picnic, visit Somers Garden (sunrise-sunset daily, free), the town's largest public park. A fine collection of palms amid manicured lawns and flowerbeds is bounded by Duke of York Street, Shinbone Alley, Blockade Alley, and Duke of Kent Street. Teddy bear picnics and art-in-the-park events are sometimes held here. The oasis is named for Sir George Somers; his heart is buried here, commemorated by a stone monument in the park's center.

St. George's Historical Society & Museum, Printery, and Garden

Tucked away in the backstreets, the headquarters of the St. George's Historical Society (Featherbed Alley, tel. 441/297-0423, 10am-4pm Mon.-Sat., $5 adults, $2 under age 12) is home to an intriguing little museum, a historic printery, and a pretty garden. The building itself is an 18th-century gem, complete with a traditional "welcoming arms" stairway. Like Tucker House, interesting possessions give a sense of life long before email, television, and motorized transport. The building's lower floor is especially historic: It was the site of the island's first printing press, operated by the King of England's printer, Joseph Stockdale, to produce the colony's original newspaper. Inside is a working replica of a 15th-century Gutenberg printing press, like the one Stockdale used.

The Old Rectory

The Old Rectory (Broad Alley, behind St. Peter's Church) is a Bermuda National Trust property that serves as a private home. With one of the most photographed facades on the island, the quaint homestead featuring rose-dotted gardens is one of Bermuda's oldest buildings, dating to 1699. It once belonged to an infamous Bermudian pirate, Captain George Dew, and later to Parson Alexander Richardson, who was nicknamed the "Little Bishop."

The Unfinished Church

Like Gaudí's unmistakable Sagrada Familia Cathedral in Barcelona, Bermuda's Unfinished Church (Government Hill Rd., top of Duke of Kent St., free) is a story of half-done architectural artistry. Leased by the Bermuda National Trust, the Victorian Gothic structure was the victim of financial problems, infighting among its congregation, and a series of vicious storms. When construction began in 1874, the church was intended as a grand replacement for St. Peter's Church but was never completed. The structure's soaring arches, cruciform shape, and imposing—but roofless—tower give a hint of the grandeur the architects hoped to achieve. Entry was declared off-limits in 2011, until it can be renovated for public safety.

SPORTS AND RECREATION
Scuba and Water Sports

Water sports outfitters mostly moved to Dockyard with the advent of the mega ships, but some still operate from St. George's Harbour. You can also rent kayaks, sailboats, motorboats, and snorkel equipment from Hamilton Parish outfits to explore the many bays, coves, and islands of the East End—from St. George's Harbour to Castle Harbour, Ferry Point to Coney Island. Traveling by water brings a whole new perspective, even for Bermudians. Paddling a kayak is a particularly good way to get around; the wildlife, including turtles, is least disturbed this way, and you'll see things the Jet Ski speed demons won't. You can book excursions island-wide through the Island Tour Centre outlets at

Dockyard and Hamilton, or book in advance (www.islandtourcentre.com).

K. S. Watersports (8 King's Square, tel. 441/297-4155, http://kswatersports.com, 9am-6pm daily) offers Jet Ski Safaris (2 hours, May-Oct., $225 single, $245 double), plus kayak rental (hourly $25 single, $30 double), 16-foot Boston Whalers (up to 6 people, $195 for 4 hours, $350 full day), 23-foot pontoon boats (up to 13 people, $600 for 4 hours, $1,200 full day) and stand-up paddleboards (1 hour, $25). Rentals and tours can be booked online or by phone.

Tours

Take part in one of the spooky **Haunted History Tours** (tel. 441/705-1838, www. hauntedhistorybda.com, 60-75 minutes, 8:30pm Thurs. Apr.-Oct., $35 pp, $25 under age 16 and over age 65) through the old town's twisting streets, led by St. Georgian Kristen White. The tour starts at **Long Story Short** (Tucker House Basement, Water St.), which she owns. Tickets are available at the bookstore, online (www.ptix.bm), or on the night, if available.

Crystal Woolridge of **Bronco Stables Horse & Carriage Co.** (35 Barry Rd., tel. 441/297-8395 or 441/704-7840, cmp-70@ hotmail.com, www.broncostablesbermuda. bm, $100 for 1 hour) gives horse-and-carriage tours of the town and surrounding neighborhoods. She and her beloved horses, Maggie and Max, take visitors on entertaining explorations of the northeast coastline, including stops at two forts and a glass beach.

Spas

Tranquil Hair and Beauty (Somers Wharf, tel. 441/297-0026, 10am-7:30pm Wed.-Thurs., 10am-2pm Fri.-Sun.) offers well-priced face and body treatments, including massages (1 hour, $95), pedicures ($55), and waxing and hair services.

ENTERTAINMENT AND EVENTS
Festivals and Events

Top hats and bonnets come out amid full pomp and regalia for the annual **Peppercorn Ceremony,** held in mid- to late April. The tradition dates to 1815, when the seat of the island's government moved to the new capital, Hamilton. As a conciliatory gesture, the Assembly, which was vacating its long-time home at the State House, symbolically passed the building to officials of the new Corporation of St. George. The yearly rent

The Unfinished Church

requested for Bermuda's oldest Masonic Lodge, St. George No. 200 of the Grand Lodge of Scotland, was one peppercorn. Every year, dignitaries drive to the East End en masse to join the governor, who, in feathered helmet, presides over the official handover ceremony in King's Square. A 17-gun salute heralds the governor's arrival, and the Bermuda Regiment's Band Company and Corps of Drums also performs. The 45-minute spectacle, watched by curious crowds, includes the high-decibel proclamations of the town crier of St. George's, who rings his bell and yells loudly enough to command immediate silence. The peppercorn is presented on a velvet cushion laid out on a silver platter. For upcoming ceremony dates, contact the **Corporation of St. George** (5 Ordnance Island, tel. 441/297-1532).

Held the first Friday evening in December, the Bermuda National Trust's **Christmas Walkabout** has become a calendar institution. Thousands pour into old town St. George after work to sip cider and meet old friends while strolling the historic streets, strung with festive illuminations. Stores stay open late, candlelit museums offer free admission, and carolers fill King's Square with song. For information, contact the **Bermuda National Trust** (tel. 441/236-6483, www.bnt.bm).

Other holiday events in the town include the annual **Santa Claus Parade,** with majorettes, elves, and St. Nick, and the **New Year's Eve** celebrations at King's Square, complete with live music, a festival atmosphere, and the dropping of a giant (fake) Bermuda onion. In the high season, **Old Towne Market** (Water St., 2pm-6pm Sun. Apr.-Oct.) events are held. Crowds meander along a festive walkway of local food and arts and crafts, as well as a peddlers' market selling everything from old china to jewelry.

Pretend you're a 17th-century plebeian at the weekly **ducking stool reenactments** (King's Square, noon Mon.-Thurs. and Sat. high season). The bellowing town crier calls everyone to order at 11:45am before the volunteer "wench" gets her due in the harbor, to the delight of onlookers, at the stroke of noon. The 15-minute demonstration harks back to the days when women were punished for gossiping and nagging.

SHOPPING

St. George's has few shops compared to Hamilton, and many are branch stores, but several new boutiques have opened in recent years. Shops around King's Square sell T-shirts, perfume, and souvenirs, while Water and Duke of York Streets offer clothing, shoes, toys, and a bookstore. Somers Wharf, west along Water Street, has a quaint shopping complex on the waterfront.

The Bermuda Perfumery (Stewart Hall, 5 Queen St., tel. 441/293-0627, www.lilibermuda.com, 9am-5pm Mon.-Sat. summer, 10am-4pm Mon.-Sat. winter) is located in history-steeped Stewart Hall, a Bermuda National Trust property. The quaint building, with pocket-size garden, houses a production center and retail outlet, where the world-famous White Oleander, Frangipani, Pink, and newer perfume varieties such as SunKiss, South Water, and Mary Celestia are bottled. There are also talcum powders and body creams in the hallmark scents. Free tours are given on how the fragrances are made. The Bermuda Perfumery also serves afternoon tea.

Designer perfumes can be found at **Peniston Brown** (6 Water St., tel. 441/297-1525, 10am-4pm Mon.-Sat.), many of them at U.S. prices. Guerlain makeup is also sold here.

Stunning harbor views from floor-to-ceiling windows mirror the decor at **Davidrose Jewelry** (20 Water St., tel. 441/293-7673, www.davidrose.bm, 10am-5pm Mon.-Sat. summer, 10am-5pm Tues.-Sat. winter, or by appointment). The fashionable turquoise boutique is owned and run by Bermudian David Zuill and his wife Avrel Rose, who met as university students in Toronto. Diamonds, gemstones, and precious metals are used to fashion bridal and engagement jewelry, statement pieces, custom creations, and a luxury silver line that includes Bermuda-themed pendants.

Spanish for "heron," La Garza (Block House, 5 Bridge St., behind the Town Hall, tel. 441/705-2787, www.lagarzabermuda.com, noon-4pm Mon.-Fri., by appointment Sat.-Sun.) carries 12 creative collections of handmade jewelry inspired by natural Bermuda and crafted by environmental designer Tara Cassidy. Her work features pink sand, shells, coral, lionfish, juniper, even colorful beach plastic.

Mother-daughter team Kelli and Roseclair Thompson are behind Saltwater Jewellery (29 Water St., tel. 441/519-9906, 10am-4pm Mon.-Sat., noon-3pm Sun.), where they have transformed their love of Bermuda sea glass into one-of-a-kind bracelets, necklaces, and earrings. The pair also work Venetian glass, freshwater pearls, and semiprecious stones into their creations.

Enjoy a glimpse of island panache inside Gregory Nelmes Interior Design (8 York St., lower terrace level, tel. 441/704-7740, 11am-4pm Mon.-Sun.), where the award-winning Bermudian designer displays some of his hallmark shelter treasures for sale—lamps, vintage bottles, blue-and-white crockery, artworks, Bermuda-themed cushion covers, traditional furniture with contemporary upholstery. The array is so tempting, you might have to arrange for shipping some home.

Bermudian glassblowers create colorful works of art for sale at Dockside Glass (3 Bridge St., tel. 441/297-3908, www.dockglass.com, 9am-6pm daily). Vases, exotic glass fish, and plates—all featuring a swirling rainbow of hues—can be purchased here. Rum cakes (www.bermudarumcakes.com) in nine flavors and three sizes are also for sale. Well-known Vera P. Card (22 Water St., tel. 441/295-1729, vcard@ibl.bm, 11am-4pm Mon.-Sat. Apr.-Oct, 11am-4pm Mon.-Fri. Nov.-Dec., by appointment Jan.-Mar.) is an elegant retail shop on Water Street alongside the Tempest Bistro, carrying fine jewelry, watches, crystal, clocks, and china by Lladro, Swarovski, and other brands. Long Story Short (Tucker House Basement, Water St., tel. 441/297-0448, noon-5pm Mon., Thurs., and Sat.) stocks fiction, classic literature, coffee-table editions, gift books, and a small kids' section. The standing-room-only space, squeezed beneath Tucker House Museum, also carries a selection of Bermuda books.

Aside from the expected toiletries and candy, Robertson's Drug Store (24 York St., St. George's, tel. 441/297-1828, pharmacy tel. 441/297-1736, 8am-7:30pm Mon.-Sat., 2pm-6pm Sun.) stocks a wonderful array of toys, beach gear, children's and Bermuda books, magazines, newspapers, and children's art supplies. A branch of its popular Hamilton stores, The Island Shop (Somers Wharf, tel. 441/297-1514, www.islandexports.com, 10am-5pm Mon.-Sat.) carries beautiful ceramic and linen products designed by local artist Barbara Finsness. It is the perfect place to find Bermuda-inspired gifts, all with colorful tropical themes like butteries and Bermudiana blooms.

Cigar-lovers will want to seek out Churchill's (27 Duke of York St., tel. 441/297-1650, churchills@myoffice.bm, 8am-9pm Mon.-Sun.), home of fine Cuban cigars and a good selection of wines, spirits, and gift items, including an array of wine-bottle openers and other bar essentials.

FOOD
Cafés, Pubs, and Takeout

A proper afternoon tea is served in the delightful walled garden at The Bermuda Perfumery (Stewart Hall, tel. 441/705-2390, sweetpbermuda@hotmail.com, www.lilibermuda.com, 1pm-4pm Wed. and Sat., $30, cash only). Dig into finger sandwiches, petits fours, and scones served with local honey, jam, and chantilly cream. The delicately indulgent spread is served with a choice of fine teas.

At the foot of the stairs leading up to St. Peter's Church, Temptations Café & Bakery (31 York St., tel. 441/297-1368, 8:30am-4pm Mon.-Sat.) serves up decadent treats in its simple interior, including cakes, pastries, and muffins, as well as sandwiches, hot soups, and coffee. Sit at banquettes with views out to Duke of York Street, or farther inside at tables. Be careful when you step outside, though; the sidewalk is so narrow, you risk falling into the busy thoroughfare's traffic.

Mama Angie's (48 Duke of York St., opposite Somers Garden, tel. 441/297-0959, 8am-2:45pm Mon.-Sat.) is the kind of place where time slips effortlessly away. Tucked into the busy main street, the tiny eatery serves up java and Western omelets, sandwiches, macaroni 'n' cheese, fish cakes—and lots of local atmosphere. Try the juicy homemade burgers ($5).

White Horse Tavern (8 King's Square, tel. 441/297-1838, www.whitehorsebermuda.com, breakfast 11am-5pm Mon.-Fri., lunch 11am-5pm daily, dinner 5pm-10pm daily, $11-29) is a waterside sports bar offering a codfish breakfast on Sunday. It specializes in pub and seafood dishes, and takeout is available.

The Wharf (14 Water St., tel. 441/297-3305, www.thewharf.bm, lunch 11:30am daily, dinner 5pm daily, $20-45) provides a perfect spot to sit outside on the harbor's edge and watch visiting yachties load provisions or work on their boats. The menu offers local specialties like fish chowder and grilled wahoo as well as pub favorites such as burgers, cottage pie, and fish-and-chips. There are vegetarian and children's menus, plus takeout service.

The view is the main attraction at **Griffin's Bar & Grill** (St. George's Club, 6 Rose Hill, tel. 441/297-4235 or 441/297-1200, www.stgeorgesclub.bm, noon-10pm Mon.-Wed. and Fri., 10:30am-10pm Sat., 11:30am-3:30pm Sun., $20-31), a lively sports bar-style restaurant with a popular Sunday brunch buffet.

★ **Sweet SAAK Bakery** (16 York St., tel. 441/297-0663, www.sweetsaak.com, 8:30am-3pm Tues.-Sat.), run by siblings, is a super-popular bakery that whips up cupcakes, scones, cinnamon buns, cakes, marshmallow chocolate chip cookies, and other decadent treats.

Mediterranean

★ **Wahoo's Bistro & Patio** (36 Water St., tel. 441/297-1307, www.wahoos.bm, 11:30am-9:30pm Tues.-Sun.) wins high ratings for its scrumptious menu; dine inside, in a bistro-style dining area, or out on the harborside deck or terrace. For lunch, try Austrian owner-chef Alfred Konrad's award-winning fish chowder ($8), caprese or cannellini bean salad ($12), or curried fishcakes ($13); dinner choices include fresh rockfish ($37), Bermuda lobster when in season, cowboy steak ($42), wiener schnitzel ($26), and daily pasta specials. Named for Bermuda's deliciously meaty gamefish, the restaurant devotes an entire section of its menu to wahoo specialties—wahoo pâté, chowder, nuggets, tacos, even a wahoo burger.

Chinese

Wong's Golden Dragon Restaurant (13 Duke of York St., tel. 441/297-0408, 11:30am-10pm Mon.-Sat., $10-14) offers a range of Mandarin and Szechuan specialties, including fried rice and noodles, lo mein, foo young, chop suey, and sweet-and-sour beef, chicken, and pork, as well as many vegetable dishes.

Fine Dining

★ **Tempest Bistro** (22 Water St., tel. 441/297-0861, lunch 11:30am-2pm Wed.-Sun., dinner from 6pm Mon. and Wed.-Sat.) brings contemporary culinary flair to an 18th-century wharf-side building once used as a warehouse. Vaulted ceilings, exposed brick, and wooden floors in the main dining room, coupled with an inspired locavore menu by chef Christopher La Placa and service by maître d' Mark Turner, make meals here a special treat. There is also the option of eating alfresco on the harborside veranda. The former carriage house was brought back to buzzworthy life by the folks who run the award-winning Mad Hatter's in Pembroke, and it fast became the go-to for St. George's gourmands. Start with duck prosciutto ($17) or a plate of mussels in a dijon cream sauce ($18) before moving on to mains such as shrimp and scallop bourguignon ($35), lamb rack ($41), or roasted herbes de Provence chicken ($29). Inventive specials using fresh seasonal local ingredients are offered daily.

Grocery Stores

Owned by Hamilton's Supermart group, **Somers Supermart** (41 York St., tel. 441/297-1177, www.supermart.bm, 7am-10pm Mon.-Sat., 8am-6pm Sun.) has been at the same busy intersection for decades, the only grocery store in town. The small store offers all the basics.

ACCOMMODATIONS

A number of reasonable family-run bed-and-breakfasts and self-catering apartments offer inexpensive comfort. Also check www.airbnb.com, www.vrbo.com, www.bermudarentals.com, and www.bermudagetaway.com, which list several St. George's rentals, including a few in historic town buildings.

St. Georgian Susan Oatley has been provides travelers with a comfortable, cost-effective place to stay in the old town in a studio apartment attached to her home, **Gobblers Corner** (1 Turkey Hill, tel. 441/297-2519 or 441/335-3429, oatley@northrock.bm, $120), with a queen bed, a large bath with a shower, air-conditioning, cable TV, free Wi-Fi, a washer and dryer, and a kitchen with a fridge, stove, and microwave. A private backyard has a barbecue for guest use. Located just two minutes from the town center in picturesque backstreets, the apartment is handy for travelers not seeking resort-style amenities.

Architectural technologist Philip Seaman restored a 200-year-old carriage house owned by his family into a guest property he called **The Loft** (7 Duke of Clarence St., tel. 441/232-2243 or 441/537-7337, $175), which has won praise from guests who adore the quaint structure with modern amenities such as a full kitchen with stainless appliances, a modern bath, and a sleeping loft with a double bed. Seaman won an award from the Bermuda National Trust for his careful transformation of the building. On the same property, he went on to restore a one-bedroom he calls **The Ruin** ($170) and two-bedroom **The Cottage** ($185).

It's worth staying at **Crooked Elbow** (5 Shinbone Alley, tel. 441/297-0898, www.

bermudagetaway.com, $165 d) for the address alone. Resident Anne Rowe rents out the lower apartment of her historic home, which has a private entrance. Included are an air-conditioned bedroom with a queen, a living room, a full kitchen, a bath, and a dining room, plus free Wi-Fi.

The St. George's Club (6 Rose Hill, tel. 441/297-1200, www.stgeorgesclub.com, 1-bedroom $495, 2-bedroom $620) is a cottage complex time-share facility that also offers short-term rentals for travelers, space permitting. Cut into the hillside, the resort's 25 air-conditioned one- and two-bedroom cottages, all with cable TV and fully equipped kitchens, have spectacular views of the old town. Guests enjoy use of a private beach club, three freshwater pools (one heated), an on-site convenience store, three tennis courts, and a putting green. There is also a business center with Internet access, a photocopier, and FedEx services.

INFORMATION AND SERVICES

Created in 1995, **The St. George's Foundation** (15 Duke of York St., tel. 441/297-3370, www.sgf.bm) is the nonprofit that drove the UNESCO campaign; since then, it has raised funds and orchestrated capital improvements to the old town. The group works to stimulate tourism in the area and encourage educational projects and has partnered with overseas entities, including the Colonial Williamsburg Foundation, the Jamestown/Yorktown Foundation, and the Historic Charleston Foundation.

The old town's **Visitor Information Centre** (7 Market Wharf, King's Square, tel. 441/297-0556, stgeorgesvic@bermudatourism.com, 10am-4pm Mon.-Sat., depending on cruise ship schedules) is a key stop to get your bearings and gather information about the East End. Manager Phillip Anderson provides tour, transportation, and general information, and sells ferry and bus tokens and tickets. **St. George's Post Office** (11 Water St., tel. 441/297-1610, 8am-5pm Mon.-Fri.) is housed in a historic building near the center of town.

St. George's Esso Service Station (2 Rose Hill, tel. 441/297-1622, 7am-7pm Mon.-Sat.) is near the entrance to town, on the drive leading up to the St. George's Club. **Rubis Dowling's Marine Service Station** (12 Water St., tel. 441/297-1914, 7am-9pm Mon.-Fri., 7am-7pm Sat., 8am-5pm Sun.) is along the harbor next to Tavern by the Sea.

HSBC (tel. 441/297-1812, 9am-4:30pm Mon.-Fri.) and **Butterfield Bank** (tel. 441/297-1277, 9am-4pm Mon.-Fri.) are conveniently located near each other at King's Square and the junction with Water Street. **ATMs** are at bank branches on King's Square and Water Street. **Public toilets** are on King's Square and at area restaurants.

TRANSPORTATION
Buses and Ferries

Several bus routes from Hamilton serve St. George's Parish, and a few daily fast ferries from Hamilton via Dockyard provide the scenic option of getting there by water. **Buses** 1, 3, 10, and 11 travel between the capital and the Town of St. George daily. Bus 1 runs every half hour, the other routes every 15 minutes.

Sea Express (tel. 441/295-4506, www.marineandports.bm) runs daily Hamilton-Dockyard-St. George's ferry trips April-October (leaving Dockyard at 9:30am, 11:30am, 2:15pm, 4:15pm, 6:15pm Mon. and Wed.-Thurs., and 9:30am, 11:30am, 1:30pm Tues. and Fri.) on its Orange Route. From Hamilton or Dockyard, one-way fares cost $5 adults, $2.75 ages 5-15, free under age 5. Buy tickets, tokens, or passes in advance at the ferry terminal or select stores, as cash is not accepted on board.

Scooters

Oleander Cycles (26 York St., tel. 441/297-0478, www.oleandercycles.bm, 8:30am-5:30pm daily) rents single- and double-seater 50-cc scooters and mountain bikes. Scooter rental rates start at $55 standard or $65 double per day. Major credit cards are accepted.

Taxis

There is a taxi stand outside the White Horse Tavern in King's Square, but it may be necessary to call for pickup in winter; there are always cabs at Bermuda's nearby airport, so wait time should not be excessive. Use the **Hitch app** (www.hitch.bm) or call one of the cab companies to arrange a pickup: **Bermuda Industrial Union Co-op** (tel. 441/292-4476, cooptaxi@fkbnet.bm), **Bermuda Island Taxi** (tel. 441/295-4141, www.bermudaislandtaxi.com), or **BTA Dispatching** (tel. 441/296-2121, www.btadispatching.com).

Around the Old Town

Except for the forts, St. George's Parish beyond the old town is not part of the World Heritage Site, but its parkland and neighborhoods are worth visiting and can be covered in a day's visit. A circular loop north and east of the town heads up Cut Road and along Barry Road, incorporating three important fortifications—Gates Fort, Alexandra Battery, and Fort St. Catherine. Continuing on, Coot Pond Road meanders past Achilles Bay and Tobacco Bay (a prime snorkeling spot) on the North Shore, then back to the town's exit via Government Hill Road.

West of the town, past Mullet Bay, is the extensive Ferry Point National Park, home to a nature reserve, hiking trails (including a scenic stretch of the Railway Trail), and three forts—the Martello Tower, Ferry Island Fort, and Burnt Fort. Across the Swing Bridge, explore the large St. David's and Southside communities. There's also a section of the parish completely removed from the rest;

crossing Longbird Bridge and the Causeway into Hamilton Parish, a chunk of St. George's lies west of Shark Hole on Harrington Sound, encompassing most of the golf-coursed splendor of the exclusive Mid Ocean Club and Rosewood Bermuda. Tucker's Town continues east along South Road past mansions and private beaches to the tip of Frick's Point, where Castle Island, Nonsuch Bay, and other rocky guardians of Castle Harbour lie in a chain all the way back to St. David's.

SIGHTS
Gates Fort and Alexandra Battery

Two easy-to-visit forts that belong to the World Heritage Site are Gates Fort and Alexandra Battery (sunrise-sunset daily, free), located within a few hundred yards of each other along Barry Road, on the easternmost flank of St. George's Parish. Perched on the picturesque **Town Cut**—the main shipping passage into the harbor—sits tiny Gates Fort, named for Sir Thomas Gates, a key figure aboard the ill-fated *Sea Venture* who went on to become deputy governor of Virginia. The original fort was built in the 1620s and rebuilt in 1700 as a parapet for guns. Down the road, Alexandra Battery overlooks Frobisher's Bay,

where Gates supervised the construction of the ship *Deliverance* in 1610. The fort was built in the 1840s, though various subsequent reconstruction efforts created a concrete emplacement for four guns.

TOP EXPERIENCE

★ Fort St. Catherine

If you only see one fort in Bermuda, **Fort St. Catherine** (15 Coot Pond Rd. at St. Catherine's Point, tel. 441/297-1920, 9am-4pm Mon.-Fri., $7 adults, $5 seniors, $3 ages 5-15, free under age 5) should be it (Fort Hamilton is a close second). Fort St. Catherine's well-preserved interior, exhibits, and artifacts make it worth an hour's stop. On the northern tip of St. George's Island, the fort stands above St. Catherine's Beach on one side and Achilles Bay on the other. Built during settlement in 1612, its ramparts gaze over the stretch of ocean where the *Sea Venture* hit reefs in 1609, causing England to finally claim Bermuda. Enter by a wooden drawbridge over a dry moat to a reception area and ticket office. Inside the lobby, interpretive exhibits detail the fort's evolution, and how it fits into Bermuda's chain of forts. Guides point the way down steps and tunnels

Fort St. Catherine

leading into the bowels of the fort, where magazines have displays and uniformed mannequins to illustrate the mechanisms of military life. Other rooms have replicas of the Crown Jewels as well as swords, muskets, pistols, and giant rifled muzzle-loaders weighing 18 tons each. The fort saw military use through World Wars I and II, when local forces were trained here. Fort St. Catherine's main terrace—a lofty plateau rimmed by ramparts overlooking the parrotfish-nibbled reefs below—has been the setting for several theatrical displays, the most notable by Hollywood's Charlton Heston in a 1950s production of *Macbeth*.

Bermuda Institute of Ocean Sciences (BIOS)

Located on the north shore of Ferry Point, and visible from Kindley Field Road, the **Bermuda Institute of Ocean Sciences** (BIOS, 17 Biological Lane, tel. 441-297-1880, www.bios.edu, free tour 10am 1st Wed. of the month) was established in 1903 in Flatts. Scientists from Harvard and New York Universities, together with the Bermuda Natural History Society set up a marine research facility here due to its balmy climate, biodiverse reefs, and relatively easy access to ocean depths of 12,000 feet. The BIOS has been at its present location since 1932, after receiving an endowment and facilities provided by the government and the Rockefeller Foundation. Today, it is a world-renowned nonprofit center that regularly hosts visiting scientists and students who join local counterparts in research projects. The station also runs a popular year-round Road Scholar (formerly Elderhostel) program for senior travelers, who get an inside look at "Science in Bermuda Shorts" going on around the station and island.

The Wednesday tour gives visitors a look inside the station's many laboratories, where they can meet international scientists who have achieved breakthrough discoveries here, in fields such as pharmaceutical research and climate studies. When in port, the BIOS research vessel, RV *Atlantic Explorer,* a live-aboard deep ocean marine laboratory, features onboard labs, high-tech machinery, living areas, and captain's bird's-eye views. Scientific lectures and a marine science open house are held throughout the year.

The atmosphere at BIOS these days is akin to a college campus; in effect, the facility acts as one. Undergraduate and graduate internships, distance-learning programs, and a panoply of research projects are all carried out here, along with summer courses and workshops. The station is one of two centers for studies on the impact of the ocean on climate change, and in 1998 it established the International Center for Ocean and Human Health. Under that program, scientists are involved in a range of cutting-edge research, including studying marine uses in pharmaceuticals. The Risk Prediction Initiative, a partnership with the global reinsurance industry, is also based here.

Ferry Point National Park

For hikers and history buffs, **Ferry Point National Park** (Ferry Rd. off Mullet Bay Rd., sunrise-sunset daily, free) is one of Bermuda's treasures, named for its westernmost tip, Ferry Point, where a boat transported passengers before the Causeway bridge was built. The stretch of the Railway Trail here is one of the most remote, far away from main-road traffic and the hustle of residential neighborhoods. The trail runs beside the North Shore, bordered by a nature reserve, mangroves, and a brackish pond called Lovers Lake. Easter lilies and silver cedar skeletons pepper the landscape, and on stormy days sea spray washes across the dirt path. In the western section of the park, three forts—**Martello Tower, Burnt Point Fort,** and **Ferry Island Fort**—belong to the World Heritage Site. Visits to the tower can be arranged through the Department of Parks (tel. 441-236-5902) or by calling park rangers at Fort St. Catherine (tel. 441-297-1920), who will open the tower. You can cross the small drawbridge and climb up the 1820s structure, made of hard Bermuda

Nonsuch Island and the Return of the Cahow

Its evocative name is alluring enough, but what the East End's Nonsuch Island represents in the environmental world is akin to a scientific miracle. The island is the largest of several that sit off Castle Harbour, including Governor's Island, Castle Island, and Southampton Island. In 1951, Nonsuch and the other islets won world renown, and immediately were declared protected nature reserves, when they were found to be the last nesting habitats of the cahow, or Bermuda petrel.

Gadfly petrels are specific to a single oceanic island or group of islands—in the cahow's case, Bermuda. In the 1500s, the nocturnal birds were so abundant that their high-pitched courtship calls scared off passing mariners, who believed the islands inhabited by devils. Fossil remains indicate that up to a half-million pairs were nesting on Bermuda, inhabiting rock crevices or burrows on the forest floor. Castaways and wild hogs deposited on the island by passing ships nearly destroyed the cahow population. By the time colonists arrived a century later, with rats and domestic animals, they fed off the tame birds in such large quantities that, according to historical reports, cahows were almost nonexistent within a decade.

In January 1951, after an absence of more than 300 years, seven breeding pairs were discovered by Robert Cushman Murphy, curator of birds at the American Museum of Natural History, and Bermudians Louis S. Mowbray and David Wingate. "It was kind of like rediscovering the dodo," remembers Wingate, a 15-year-old student at the time, who made the cahow his life's work. After graduating from Cornell University, he returned to Bermuda, where he was named the island's first conservation officer in 1966, a post he held until he retired in 2000. He was almost solely responsible for the cahow's return, creating a living laboratory of endemic species at Nonsuch Island, as well as overseeing cahow nests on other isolated islets and even creating artificial burrows to encourage nesting. Wingate—whose daughter Janet recounts life as a 12-year-old on the island in her 2005 memoir, *Nonsuch Summer*—recreated pristine wetlands, mangroves, cedar, and palmetto forests, as well as shoreline coastal habitats and bird-viewing areas.

Today, another Bermudian, Terrestrial Conservation Officer Jeremy Madeiros (cahowman@yahoo.com), continues the work. Cahows are now reaching record numbers of breeding pairs, including some at an established nesting colony on Nonsuch, complete with successfully fledged chicks. Madeiros has been painstaking in his efforts to ensure such a comeback, hand-feeding chicks when necessary to keep survival rates high.

Cahows have been the subject of documentaries and media coverage in recent decades, including a feature-length 2006 film, *Rare Bird,* by Bermudian filmmaker Lucinda Spurling. Conservationists are confident that if protective measures continue, they will flourish again. Most notably, a project teaming videographers with the Cornell Lab of Ornithology set up live streaming video (www.nonsuchisland.com) of a cahow nest that depicts chicks and parents in action during the summer nesting season.

Ecotours to Nonsuch are sometimes organized by the Bermuda Zoological Society or Bermuda Institute of Ocean Sciences. Special visits can also be arranged by appointment with the **Department of Environment & Natural Resources** (tel. 441/236-4201).

limestone. Inside, exhibits detail the tower's military importance and the daily lives of the British garrison soldiers who staffed it. Burnt Point Fort is older, built in the 1600s to defend the western approach to Bermuda. Ferry Island Fort, built in the 1790s, is named for the boat service that used to carry St. Georgians to the mainland at Coney Island, before bridges linked the parish to the mainland.

Tucker's Town

Created in the 1920s when 500 acres of land were forcibly expropriated from a rural black community, Tucker's Town quickly became the enclave of the rich and famous. The exclusive Mid Ocean Club demands an initiation fee of $30,000, and members include those who own multimillion-dollar homes on the manicured peninsula dubbed "Billionaire's

Row": Texas billionaire Ross Perot, former Italian prime minister Silvio Berlusconi, and former New York mayor Michael Bloomberg among them. Of course, what lies here is off-limits to visitors, including the breathtakingly beautiful Windsor and Mid Ocean Beaches (a guarded roadblock forbids nonresidents). But you can visit the public dock on Tucker's Town Bay to get a view of the upscale neighborhood—and Bloomberg's lavish spread on an opposite hillside. The dock is a nice picnic spot, and you can even swim in the sheltered bay, where area boaters keep their craft moored. Take Paynter's Road to cut through the Rosewood Bermuda property, an enclave of palm-flanked golf course, then follow Harrington Sound Road through Hamilton Parish to its junction with North Shore Road. Once this meets the Causeway, you have once again entered St. George's Parish.

BEACHES

St. Catherine's Beach and Achilles Bay and **Tobacco Bay** are the three main beaches of St. George's, all located north of the town. St. Catherine's is the largest, a stretch of white sand below the fort. Tiny Achilles Bay is good for snorkeling. But if you want to party, head to **Tobacco Bay** (9 Coot's Pond Rd., tel. 441/297-2756, http://tobaccobay.bm, 10am-6pm Mon.-Fri., 10am-9pm Fri.-Sun.), where a beach bar and restaurant have become one of the East End's top-ranked attractions. Natural stone columns rising from the bay make it a unique snorkeling spot, and trails up and around the beach provide scenic lookout points. The popular bar serves up frozen cocktails, beer bucket specials and rum swizzles, while the café menu (burgers wahoo nuggets, barbecue specials and ice cream) attracts a local lunch crowd. Lockers, showers, changing rooms, and complimentary Wi-Fi are also available. The bay offers rentals of canopy loungers throughout the park, as well as kayaks ($25), waterbikes ($40) and sea scooters ($50) by the hour.

Farther afield, **Whalebone Bay** at Ferry Point National Park also has good sea glass collections, depending on tides and currents. Its shallow water, glassy calm when the wind is blowing from the south, is good for children and novice swimmers.

SPORTS AND RECREATION
Water Sports

Launched in 2014 at the dock of the old town's yacht club, **Just Add Water** (St.

Tobacco Bay

George's Dinghy & Sports Club, 24 Cut Rd., tel. 441/707-5000, 8am-8pm daily Apr.-Oct., 9:30am-5pm Wed.-Mon. Nov.-Mar.) promises freewheeling adventures for all ages—from ATX paddleboard and kayaking expeditions (1.5 hours, $70) and Jet Ski tours (1.5 hours, $120) to cycle and snorkel tours (3 hours, $90) and cost-effective motorboat rentals (4 hours, $195), along with other water sports. The company's shop sells UK surfer brand Animal as well as T-shirts, hats, and accessories.

You don't have to be a guest to use the Rosewood Bermuda's **Tucker's Point Dive & Watersports Centre** (tel. 441/298-4050, watersports@tuckerspoint.com, www.divinginbermuda.com, 8:30am-5pm daily), which rents kayaks, sailboats (Hobies and Snarks), and motorboats (2 hours $140, half-day $445) that come equipped with snorkel equipment, towels, snacks, and water. Reservations are recommended, especially on summer weekends.

Sailing

Both local and out-of-town yachties congregate at **St. George's Dinghy & Sports Club** (24 Cut Rd., tel. 441/297-1612, www.stgdsc.bm). The club is far smaller than its Hamilton cousins, the Royal Bermuda Yacht Club and the Royal Hamilton Amateur Dinghy Club, but it is very involved in the area's sailing scene and acts as local host for several international events, including a cruising rally from Virginia.

Railway Trail (St. George's)

This parish's section of the Railway Trail in Ferry Point National Park is far removed from main roads or even large residential neighborhoods, lending it a deep serenity not found on the trail's other stretches. It is also very scenic, with a mile-long stretch of unpaved trail running parallel to the North Shore, high above spray-washed rocks and azure bays. An outand-back route allows for a swim at pretty Whalebone Bay. Tangents along the way can lead you past mangroves, through steep casuarina forests, or into historic sites such as

graveyards and forts. The only modern disturbance is the occasional jet leaving the nearby airport directly overhead, but luckily there are only a handful of takeoffs each day.

TOP EXPERIENCE

Golf

The crème de la crème of Bermuda golf courses, the revered **Mid Ocean Club** (tel. 441/293-0330, www.themidoceanclubbermuda.com, greens fee $250 pp), a highly challenging 18-hole championship course, is *the* place to play. PGA great Ben Crenshaw called it one of the best small courses in the world. Guests of club members are allowed to play on Monday, Wednesday, and Friday, including guests of several hotels on the island (check with your concierge to see if arrangements can be made). Designed in 1921 by Charles Blair Macdonald, one of the world's top designers, the course was altered slightly by Robert Trent Jones in the 1950s. It boasts spectacular views of the reef-dotted ocean, its rolling greens and immaculately maintained fairways teetering over the South Shore cliffs. You might run into Jack Nicholson or Catherine Zeta-Jones at the Colonial-style clubhouse. Over the years, players have included Babe Ruth, Dwight Eisenhower, Winston Churchill, the Duke of Windsor, and George H. W. Bush. The annual PGA Grand Slam of Golf was held here in 2007 and 2008. The club atmosphere is very formal: Jacket and tie attire is expected for dinner.

Tucker's Point Golf Club (Rosewood Bermuda, golf pro shop tel. 441/298-6970, www.rosewoodhotels.com, greens fees $150 Mon.-Fri., $180 Sat.-Sun., $100 seniors), like Mid Ocean, is an 18-hole championship course open to guests of members and guests of certain island hotels. Great vistas, a par-70 course with TifEagle greens and high elevations over Harrington Sound and Castle Harbour, plus bells-and-whistles service make playing here memorable. Walking is discouraged. A state-of-the-art pro shop offers shoe-cleaning, well-kept locker rooms, and coffee and orange juice stations. There is also a driving range, a 10,000-square-foot practice putting green, and a short-game area. The hilltop clubhouse houses the popular Grille Room & Bar, which serves lunch to players daily.

Horseback Riding

Bermuda Horse Trail Ride (Moran Meadows, 7 Salt Spray Lane, tel. 441/537-0400, www.bermudahorsetrailride.com, bdatrailride@gmail.com, ages 9 and over, Mon.-Sat.) is one of only three horseback-riding operations on the island, and the only one near the East End. Mark and Natalie Moran operate personalized tours along the northeast coastline (1 hour $130, 1.5 hours $180, 2 hours $230) for groups of two or three, along coastal routes near Fort St. Catherine, Tobacco Bay, and the St. George's Club golf course, as well as along the St. George's parish beaches in winter.

Running and Walking

The parish has perhaps more open space than any other for enjoying runs or long hikes. Ferry Point National Park and Cooper's Island Nature Reserve offer tens of acres of both trails and paved roadways set amid stunning natural scenery.

For Kids

Mullet Bay Playground (southern edge of Mullet Bay Rd., leading into St. George's) is a popular stop for children. In a grassy park near the moored boats of Mullet Bay, the playground has a wide assortment of climbing frames, swings, and slides, usually well maintained. There is a parking lot at the site. **Fort St. Catherine** is also a must-see for its labyrinth of tunnels, climbable cannon, and spectacular vantage points for pretend pirates.

ENTERTAINMENT AND EVENTS
Nightlife

Tobacco Bay (9 Coot's Pond Rd., tel. 441/297-2756, http://tobaccobay.bm, 10am-6pm Mon.-Thurs., 10am-9pm Fri.-Sun.) is the liveliest East End venue, with sunset socials, weekend beach flow yoga, Friday sunset bonfires, Saturday lounge parties, and super soca Sundays.

The Beach House (Fort St. George, 6 Rose Hill, next to Fort St. Catherine, tel. 441/297-1400, www.stgeorgesclub.com, noon-9pm Tues.-Sun. Apr.-Nov.) is a perfect place to while away the sunset hours after a day of snorkeling in Achilles Bay below. Owned by the St. George's Club, it is one of Bermuda's few beachside bars.

The handsome **Tucker's Bar** (Rosewood Bermuda, 60 Tucker's Point Dr., tel. 441/298-4010, 11am-11pm daily) adjoins The Point Restaurant & Terrace at the resort. Overlooking the pool, it makes for a sophisticated pre-dinner cocktail or post-golf refreshment.

★ Cup Match

Thousands pour into St. George's every other summer for the cricket showdown and carnival atmosphere of **Cup Match** (www.bermudacupmatch.com). The island's favorite holiday sees club teams from both ends of the island, St. George's and Somerset, meet for a two-day contest, held alternate years at each club's headquarters. The **St. George's Cricket Club** (56 Wellington Slip Rd., tel. 441/297-0374, www.stgeorgescricketclub.com) welcomes the masses, who fill bleachers and enjoy a festival of local food and drink provided by vendors selling island favorites like mussel pies, conch fritters, and rum swizzles. Gambling, in the form of Crown & Anchor game tables, is legalized for the occasion, and tens of thousands of dollars change hands at the so-called "Stock Market"—along with gallons of rum and other spirits. Amid the blazing heat, Cup Match draws everyone from politicians to schoolchildren to celebrate the century-old festival.

Other Events

The island's top golf clubs, including the Mid Ocean Club and Tucker's Point Golf Club, team up to host the **Bermuda Goodwill Golf Tournament** (tel. 914/239-3077, www.bermudagoodwillgolf.com) in December, bringing golfers from the United States, Canada, and Britain, with teams made up of one professional and three amateurs.

FOOD
Cafés and Pubs
Tobacco Beach Bar & Grill (1 Coot Pond Rd., Tobacco Bay, tel. 441/297-2756, http://tobaccobay.bm, 10am-6pm Mon.-Fri., 10am-9pm Fri.-Sun., $10-20), serves up a full menu of fish sandwiches, burgers, frozen cocktails, and DJ entertainment to crowds who pour in daily to the popular swimming hole.

Beach House (Fort St. George, 6 Rose Hill next to Fort St. Catherine, tel. 441/297-1400, www.stgeorgesclub.com, lunch noon-4pm and dinner 6pm-9pm Tues.-Sun. Apr.-Nov.) serves up pub grub such as Cannon Balls (jumbo scallops, $14) and conch fritters ($12), as well as entrées such as a seafood platter ($23) and rack of lamb ($32).

Mediterranean
★ **Sul Verde** (Rosewood Bermuda, 60 Tucker's Point Dr., tel. 441/298-6983, www.rosewoodhotels.com, lunch noon-3pm daily, dinner 6pm-9pm daily, bar 11am-10pm daily) is an unabashedly Italian family-style restaurant, and an elegant one, with a magnificent antipasti buffet (focaccias, cold cuts, housemade pickles, $20 appetizer, $27 main course), a mozzarella bar ($15), a full selection of pizza and pasta ($22-28), an extensive wine list, and substantial mains, from meatballs with spaghetti ($26) to pork tenderloin medallions ($32). The setting, the upper floor of the Rosewood Bermuda resort's grand golf club, overlooks the velvet golf course—appropriately, its name translates as "on the green"—and blue horizons of Castle Harbour, making it a great choice for family gatherings. The dress code is smart casual.

Fine Dining
With its elegant steakhouse atmosphere,

★ **The Point Restaurant & Terrace** (Rosewood Bermuda, 60 Tucker's Point Dr., tel. 441/298-4010, jackets suggested for men, hours vary by season) is fashioned after New York's award-winning Gramercy Tavern. Low lighting, fireplaces, plantation shutters, and vintage oil-on-canvas murals once owned by Pan American Airlines and depicting the major ports of the world lend an aura of old-school quality. The menu is designed to impress, boasting appetizers like crispy duck egg ($17) and lobster and swordfish carpaccio ($21), and entrées such as Berkshire pork ($38), Amaretto-crusted lamb loin ($40), and goat cheese and a trio of vegetarian tarts ($31). A prix fixe "360 Menu" offers a 5-, 7-, or 10-course gourmet journey ($85-135) created by Chef Guido Brambilla and inspired by destinations depicted in Gerard Henderson's murals—Beirut, Canton, Istanbul, and Rio de Janeiro. With a fireplace and floor-to-brick-vaulted ceiling backdrop of 3,000 bottles, the Wine Room offers an unforgettable private dinner party setting within the restaurant.

On Mullet Bay Road
Many Bermudians swear by the fish cakes at **Selena's** (123 Mullet Bay Rd., tel. 441/297-2979, 11:30am-9:30pm Tues.-Sat., 9am-7pm Sun.), where the fast food is deliciously homemade. Burgers, fried chicken, baked goods, daily soup specials, oxtail, and barbecued ribs are also on the menu. The restaurant is run by Selena Minors, who serves up her goodies daily to a full house, including takeout, with efficient and friendly style.

Friendly **Cousins Variety** (123 Mullet Bay Rd., tel. 441/297-1752, 8am-10pm daily) is located in the same building as Selena's on the north side of the winding main road out of town. Hands of freshly picked Bermuda bananas and baked goods, including gingerbread, are among its best offerings.

ACCOMMODATIONS
Accommodation choices in St. George's Parish are sparse. Check sites such as www.airbnb.com, www.vrbo.com, www.bermudarentals.

com, www.bermudagetaway.com, and http://justaddbermuda.com for other options. The government has had longtime plans to develop a former Club Med site overlooking St. Catherine's Beach, but that project will take years to happen.

Mike and Debi Montgomery's **Le Roux Inn** (14 Secretary Lane, tel. 441/292-9212 or 441/338-2952, monty@logic.bm, $150 d) was indeed a "ruin" when they bought the property, hence the play on words. Today, guests find home-style comfort in the refurbished cute-as-a-button cottage, where almost every need has been thought of. Games, linens, and a library of Bermuda books have been provided since 2001. The studio-style cottage, which sits apart from the main house, has a high open-beamed ceiling; Mexican-tile floors; air-conditioning; heat for winter; a kitchenette with small fridge, toaster oven, hot plate, and microwave; a queen bed; a bath with A shower; an eating area; and a grill. Only cash and traveler's checks are accepted.

★ **Rosewood Bermuda** (60 Tucker's Point Dr., tel. 441/298-4010, www.rosewoodhotels.com, $900-6,200 d) is situated on a stunning coastal property that was home for decades to the historic Castle Harbour Hotel, later a Marriott. The site has a championship golf course and high-end fractional ownership residences. Perched on a forest-covered hilltop overlooking the horizons of Castle Harbour on one side and Harrington Sound on the other, it offers a total, utterly relaxing escape. The hotel incorporates a 2,000-square-foot spa and fitness center, two 25-meter infinity pools, four tennis courts, a croquet lawn, a water sports center, a 5,000-square-foot conference center, a five-star restaurant and

bar, and 88 guest rooms, including 68 deluxe rooms (poolside units come complete with daybeds) and 20 elegantly outfitted suites, all boasting dramatic views, Kohler baths, wet bars, gilt mirrors, walk-in closets, Persian rugs, and English-manor decor. Accommodations range from rooms with balconies to one- and two-bedroom suites and villas, some waterfront or poolside; all have flat-screen TVs, Egyptian linens, twice-daily housekeeping, and panoramic views of either Castle Harbour or Harrington Sound. The building's cedar-steeped interiors include marble surfaces and fireplaces at every turn, lush carpeting, retail spaces with resort-wear and jewelry, chandeliers, "view corridors," and a giant spiral gold staircase leading up to the eye-popping spa terrace, whose chalet-style treatment rooms overlook carefully landscaped gardens with yoga areas and jasmine-covered pergolas, forested hillsides, and the turquoise horizons of Harrington Sound. Free Wi-Fi and VoIP telephone service are offered throughout the property. Guests also have access to the golf, beach, and tennis clubs. The beach club, with a surfside restaurant, infinity pool, and gorgeous reef-dotted South Shore strand, is located a mile away on the exclusive Tucker's Town peninsula next to the Mid Ocean Club, with shuttles running throughout the day.

INFORMATION AND SERVICES

The **Airport Mail Facility** (2 Kindley Field Rd., tel. 441/293-1767) is a handy post office for passengers at L. F. Wade International Airport. The **Airport Police Station** (tel. 441/293-1940) services L. F. Wade International Airport.

St. David's Island and Southside

"You got your passport?" locals jokingly rib Bermudians who stray from other parishes into the distinctive neighborhood of St. David's—for fresh lobster, sightseeing, or rum-rich nights out at the parish's single tavern. Indeed, St. David's, like its southwest Wales counterpart, stands out for feeling utterly apart from the rest of Bermuda, with a quirky sense of individuality, stoic humor, and catchy turns of phrase. Maybe it's because the island was disconnected from the main part of Bermuda until the 1930s. Today a perimeter road leads off airport-hugging Kindley Field Road, past Southside, and finally into the serpentine collection of country lanes that bear curious names such as So Far Drive and Tranquility Lane, where the sea-swept hillsides are peppered with pastel homes.

St. David's begs one to slow down, linger, hang out, and ease into the community mindset. For those who look beyond the tatty surface, the rewards are rich. It is the people who make St. David's a unique community, and they have fueled the folklore and legends of the original 500-acre island. Far-fetched tales—and everyone here has one—sometimes turn out to be completely true. St. David's folk love to share their neighborhood with "outsiders," whether in the form of a fish sandwich or a tall tale about their ancestors. Either way, sit back, relax, and soak it in; there's every chance you'll never stumble upon such an unusual community again.

With Carter House, St. David's Lighthouse, St. David's Battery, and Great Head Park, you could easily while away a day here, but an afternoon suffices. Take bus route 6 from the Town of St. George, or transfer from any of the Hamilton-St. George's routes (1, 3, 10, and 11) onto route 6 after Kindley Field Road.

HISTORY

Named for the patron saint of Wales (though there's no trace of Welsh culture here), St.

David's swirls with maritime legends traced back to the community's immersion in whaling, boatbuilding, fishing, and piloting—the practiced art of guiding ships into port safely through the skinny channels between reefs. There's the story of Tommy Fox, who climbed into a whale's belly to prove he could. Or the tale of "wreckers" who cheered a "turtle in the net"—their euphemism for luring ships onto reefs with coastal fires in order to plunder them. Residents believe to this day that some of that treasure is buried beneath the soil of farmers' fields in the neighborhood. Lily farming was a major industry here in the late 19th and early 20th centuries, when the fragrant white blooms were shipped overseas by the thousands at Eastertime.

St. David's also stands apart due to its Native American links. People from various indigenous nations were shipped to the island as slaves, starting in the 17th century. Many ended up living in St. David's, marrying Bermudians and gradually becoming part of the social and ethnic mix of the area. Today, many St. David's residents claim Native American family roots, particularly among the Pequot people of New England. Over the past decade, the St. David's community has made strong efforts to revive these links, forging cultural alliances with U.S. Native American groups whose members have visited the island several times to attend festivals and exchange genealogical history.

But World War II would change St. David's drastically, in both physical and less tangible ways. The island's original size was expanded by 150 acres when the U.S. Army descended in 1941 to undertake a gargantuan project: obliterating Cooper's Island, Longbird Island, and a large part of St. David's Island to form Fort Bell and Kindley Field, later called Kindley Air Force Base and then U.S. Naval Air Station Bermuda. The Severn Bridge, which had linked St. David's to the mainland in 1934, was dismantled, and once again, St. David's, tucked behind the new sprawling foreign entity, was separated from the rest of Bermuda.

The lands were returned to St. David's in the late 1990s and renamed Southside. In 2008, the adjoining Cooper's Island peninsula was declared a national park and nature reserve and opened to the public. Part of this impressive open space was used as a NASA tracking station from 1960 until 2000. One of NASA's 18 radar and telemetry outposts around the world, it provided vital communications links to astronauts on space missions. The European Space Agency used the site in 2011, and NASA returned to Cooper's Island in 2012 to deploy a temporary mobile tracking unit used to support satellites in low-earth orbits and monitor rockets launched from Wallops Flight Facility in Virginia.

While St. David's belongs to St. George's Parish, its separate identity is recognized by the fact it claims its own electoral constituency.

SIGHTS

Until 1995, the large tract of St. David's land now called **Southside** belonged to the U.S. Naval Air Station and was not open to the public. When the U.S. military pulled up stakes in 1995, locals finally got access to the lands bordering L. F. Wade International Airport. While the whole area still has the look and feel of a military base (wide concrete avenues, military-style construction) rather than a typical Bermudian aesthetic, Southside offers much-needed recreational space. It's home to a bowling alley, a launderette, and a fast-food restaurant, but locals come for Clearwater Beach and Turtle Beach, recreational areas with noisy go-karting clubs, and for Clearwater Playground.

★ Cooper's Island Nature Reserve

The Cooper's Island Nature Reserve, long a birding habitat, is a must for anyone who appreciates pristine beaches, coastline, woodland, and a serene outdoors hike in any

season. A former NASA site, it was opened to the public as a nature reserve in 2008. The 44-acre park is an important nesting site for the endangered Bermuda petrel, called the cahow, and in 2005 scientists discovered one of the beaches was a nesting ground for at least one loggerhead turtle.

Spend a day on beautiful, usually empty, beaches. Four additional beaches now join Clearwater and Turtle Beaches on the park's outskirts: Turtle Bay and Long Bay face south, while Soldier Bay and Well Bay sit on the edge of Castle Harbour. Much of Bermuda's marine and terrestrial wildlife can be found here: Breeding pairs of long-tailed tropicbirds, or longtails, nest in cliffs and can be seen swooping over the bays. Spotted sandpipers dart along the beach, and great blue herons and snowy egrets are birder favorites. Goldfinches, catbirds, and white-eyed vireos nest in the woods. Rare land hermit crabs make their homes on the coastline. Sea grass beds in the coves support juvenile turtles, black grouper, spiny lobsters, yellowtail snappers, and queen conch. No private transport is allowed inside the reserve; park at the gate and walk in. Park rangers patrol.

★ Carter House

The oldest dwelling in St. David's, **Carter House** (Southside Ave., tel. 441/293-5960, http://carterhousemuseum.org, 10am-4pm Tues.-Thurs. and Sat. summer, 10am-4pm Sat. winter, $2 adults, free under age 12) is believed to have been built around 1640. With its sloping limestone roof, original hand-cut cedar beams, buttresses, and "welcoming arms" stairs, the whitewashed cottage looks completely out of place amid the sterile development of the former base lands. It was built by the descendants of Christopher Carter, a member of the Sea Venture crew who stayed behind in Bermuda when the other colonists continued on to Virginia. Carter's descendants lived in the home for centuries, and as was custom in rural areas, many were buried on the land. When the U.S. military took possession of the property, these graves were exhumed and moved to the Chapel of Ease church in St. David's. Carter House was used as a home for military officers, but after the base was closed, it was renovated and returned to the community. Today, it's run by the St. David's Historical Society as a museum to celebrate the history of the unique community, including traditions of whaling, piloting, fishing, boatbuilding, and farming.

Chapel of Ease

Down the pretty lane bearing the same evocative name, the **Chapel of Ease** (near Tranquillity Lane, tel. 441/297-1231, 9am Sun.) captures the maritime history of this East End community. The simple Anglican church is decorated with stunning stained glass windows, and the whitewashed graves outside hold the remains of sailors, soldiers, and maritime pilots with the surnames of centuries-old Bermudian families—Lamb, Fox, Hayward, and Pitcher.

St. David's Lighthouse

Like its Gibbs Hill counterpart in Southampton, **St. David's Lighthouse** (Lighthouse Hill Rd., tel. 441/236-5902, 7:30am-4pm daily, free) is a landmark to guide ships safely past the island's treacherous reef line. Built in 1879, the structure rises 55 feet to a fixed-light lantern. It was purportedly erected here as a foil against St. David's "wreckers"—nefarious locals who would purposely lure ships onto the reefs to loot their cargoes. If you think the view from its base is good—overlooking the windswept pastel cottages of St. David's—wait until you climb the 85 steps to the top.

St. David's Battery and Great Head Park

St. David's Battery at Great Head Park (southeast end of St. David's Island, off Battery Rd., sunrise-sunset daily, free) commands one of the most dramatic vantage points in Bermuda—and for good reason. The clear sightlines from this clifftop park, with views across the entire East End, were chosen so that this 1910 fortification could help defend the Narrows Channel in conjunction with Alexandra Battery across St. George's Harbour. The last major fortification to be built in St. George's Parish, the battery was used for coastal defense until 1957, including stints during World War II. Four large gun emplacements, with two British breech-loading guns still in situ pointing out to sea, sit above magazines and storerooms, which

Carter House

Forts and Guns

Anyone touring Bermuda's surviving forts can trace the rise and fall of the British Empire. Built from 1612 through the 1950s, the structures tell us about Bermuda's changing role over the centuries and the evolution of global superpowers. The chain of defense also reflects the evolution of warfare. Bermuda once counted a total of 90 fortifications, but today many of these exist only as buried remains or are inaccessible due to overgrown vegetation or trash-dumping. Over the past decade, the Department of Parks has gradually restored some of these historic sites to their former glory, enhancing cultural tourism in the process.

A dozen impressive examples of forts are in good condition and open to visitors. From the east, around the Town of St. George, these include: Fort St. Catherine, Alexandra Battery, and Gates Fort. At nearby Ferry Reach, the Martello Tower, Burnt Point Fort, and Ferry Island Fort are worth visiting, as is the park where they are located. In St. David's, the dramatic St. David's Battery, with its cannon and cliffs, makes a panoramic place for a picnic. In Hamilton, don't miss a visit to Fort Hamilton, one of the best-kept forts, with moat gardens, dungeons, and a plateau of lawns overlooking the city. Farther west, Whale Bay Fort and Battery commands views of the South Shore's turquoise horizons, while Fort Scaur's benches give a peaceful vantage point over the Great Sound. At Bermuda's westernmost point, the island's largest fortress—the cannon ramparts, casemates, magazines, and bastions of the Royal Naval Dockyard, including the six-acre Keep of the National Museum of Bermuda—are the island's most notable historical landmarks.

A couple of the early forts built on the outer islands of St. George's are immensely valuable in heritage terms. Fort Cunningham, on Paget Island in St. George's Harbour, and King's Castle on Castle Island, at the entrance to Castle Harbour, are accessible by boat, though a tour boat and guide are advised, since Castle Island is very difficult to land at, and Fort Cunningham can only be reached via a tunnel (flashlight required). Southampton Fort and Smith's Fort lie on protected nature reserves and are therefore out of bounds. A handful of other forts, including Fort Victoria in St. George's and Fort Prospect in Devonshire, are in disrepair and are therefore currently inaccessible, but that may change if restoration continues.

The first forts were small limestone constructions, most of them built on outer islets of St. George's Parish in the 1600s. They were intended primarily for local defense (against pirates, for example), since Bermuda was not considered valuable property from a 17th-century geopolitical perspective. That changed radically, however, after the U.S. Revolutionary War (1783), when Britain lost all her U.S. ports between Halifax and the Caribbean. Bermuda became a strategic possession, and fortifications were considered vital for Britain's empire-building. Fortified commands were put up the length of the island, and the Royal Naval Dockyard was built as a mid-Atlantic hub for the British fleet. By the mid-1800s, "Fortress Bermuda" had become a bastion of the British Empire.

"The 'enemy' up to the first decade of the 1900s was the United States," writes Edward C. Harris, past director of the National Museum of Bermuda, in *Bermuda: Five Centuries*. "With [one exception], all the great forts built in the 19th century were intended to hold Bermuda from an American conquest. That the Americans ended up assuming the coastal defense of Bermuda forts 1941-1945 is perhaps the greatest military irony of our history."

The impressive legacy of Bermuda's fortifications includes gun placements, historic cannons, and other artillery. St. David's Battery, for example, was built in 1910 and kept in use as late as 1957, when the British military finally pulled out of the colony. Today, a pair of 1890s rifled breech-loader guns manned in both World Wars still point out to sea—a telling tribute to the importance of the island's coastal defenses even in modern times.

unfortunately have been marred by modern graffiti and garbage. The 9.2-inch guns had a range of about seven miles, easily capable of stopping an enemy vessel before it ventured too near the island. Despite the neglect, the park, towering over the eastern cliffs where you can watch longtails soaring over the reefs, remains a top-of-the-world place for a picnic or a photo opportunity. A bronze memorial to Bermudians lost at sea is here; the 16-foot-tall monument, by Bermudian sculptor Bill "Mussey" Ming, depicts an upturned rowboat attached to symbolic sea-related items—a life jacket, a paddle, an hourglass, and nautical dividers (navigational plotting instruments).

BEACHES

Clearwater Beach and adjacent Turtle Beach are highly recommended for swimmers of all abilities, including children. This is one of a handful of beach areas with government lifeguards on duty throughout the summer season. The wide bay of Clearwater is shallow and usually calm throughout the summer, its long arc of white sand facing southeast toward the islets guarding Annie's Bay. Just across the lawn, Clearwater Playground has boldly colored climbing frames, ropes, tunnels, swings, and slides that make it a hit with kids. The on-site concession, Gombeys Restaurant and Bar (193 Cooper's Island Rd., tel. 441/734-0858, from 10am daily), rents out snorkeling gear as well as kayaks, paddleboats (1 hour $30), and umbrellas.

Walk through the gates of the new Cooper's Island Nature Reserve to four more lovely beaches: Turtle Bay, Long Bay, Soldier Bay, and Well Bay. A lifeguard is posted at Long Bay, and there are restrooms next to Turtle Bay. Because access is only on foot, these beaches tend to remain quiet, even during the busy summer season. Boating access is also restricted, keeping out noise and overcrowding, and protecting the peninsula's reefs and sea grass beds.

SPORTS AND RECREATION

Cricket is a big passion in this neighborhood, home of the loftily named Lords Oval at St. David's County Cricket Club (52 Great Bay Rd., tel. 441/297-0449). Located on a plateau below Battery Park, where the ocean breeze whips in from the cliff, the club welcomes visitors to watch hotly contested games before a knowledgeable crowd during the sport's summer season. County cricket tournaments

Turtle Beach

against rival island clubs are exciting to watch, even if you're not familiar about the ins and outs of the game.

Four asphalt tennis courts compose the **Kindley Community Tennis Courts** (Southside, northeast of the Clearwater turn-off, tel. 441/295-0855, free), which formerly belonged to the U.S. military and are now public. There's an adjacent basketball court as well.

Strykz Bowling Lounge (tel. 441/297-2727, strykz@live.com, 4pm-10pm Wed.-Thurs., 4pm-midnight Fri., 2pm-midnight Sat., 2pm-8pm Sun.) attracts local fans with its 10 lit lanes of bowling, projector screens, and a café serving pizza, burgers, hot dogs, and chicken wings.

ENTERTAINMENT AND EVENTS
Nightlife

Gombeys Restaurant and Bar (193 Cooper's Island Rd., tel. 441/293-5092, from 10am daily) is a licensed bar, drawing a late party crowd on weekends in high season, plus special events year-round, including a New Year's Eve party.

FOOD
Cafés and Pubs

Near the busy junction of Kindley Field Park, Swing Bridge, and St. David's Road, **Double Dip Express** (1 Kindley Field Rd., tel. 441/293-5959, 10am-11pm daily summer, 11:30am-9pm daily winter) does a roaring trade, selling ice cream ($3 a scoop) of all flavors, fish cakes ($6), and hot dogs ($4), as well as baked goods and other short-order treats.

The canteen at **St. David's County Cricket Club** (52 Great Bay Rd., tel. 441/297-0449, $6-15) serves a small menu of fresh fish sandwiches, fish cakes, and burgers during cricket tournaments, soccer games, and other community events on the panoramic oceanfront field. Call the club for schedule information.

At the site of a U.S. Naval Air Station McDonald's franchise that closed when

the U.S. forces left Bermuda in 1995, **Pizza House** (106 Southside Rd., tel. 441/293-5700, 10:30am-9pm Mon.-Wed., 10:30am-10pm Thurs.-Sat., noon-9pm Sun.) serves pizza by the slice or box ($4-26) and burgers ($5), as well as fries and soft drinks. **Gombeys Restaurant and Bar** (193 Cooper's Island Rd., tel. 441/293-5092, from 10am daily, $6-14) has burgers, hot dogs, fish sandwiches, chicken wings, and conch fritters for hungry swimmers. It is also a licensed bar, drawing a late crowd on weekends.

INFORMATION AND SERVICES

Southside Police Station (2 Stokes Point Rd., tel. 441/293-2222) services the whole parish. The **Lamb Foggo Urgent Care Centre** (1 Hall St., tel. 441/298-7700, 4pm-midnight Mon.-Fri., noon-midnight Sat.-Sun.) offers medical treatment for minor injuries or illnesses. The friendly staff, easy access, and community-friendly hours make **Southside Laundromat** (103 Southside Rd., tel. 441/297-3419, 7am-9pm daily) a well-used service in the area. **St. David's Variety** (tel. 441/297-0475, 6am-10pm Mon.-Sat., 8am-8pm Sun.) is the area's mini grocery-cum-corner store.

TRANSPORTATION

Exploring different parts of St. David's and Southside is best done by scooter, given the distances between points of interest. Visiting St. David's Lighthouse and Cooper's Island Nature Reserve, for example, takes a while by bus. If you're planning to spend the whole day at Southside beaches, however, a bus trip from Hamilton or St. George's is more practical, saving the cost of a rental when most of your time will be spent swimming or sunbathing.

Scooters

The St. George's outlet of **Oleander Cycles** (26 York St., tel. 441/297-0478, www.oleander-cycles.bm, 8:30am-5:30pm daily, $55 per day) rents single- and double-seater 50-cc scooters.

Buses and Ferries

Routes from Hamilton include bus routes 1, 3, 10, and 11; they travel between the capital and the Town of St. George daily. The number 1 bus runs every half hour, the other routes run every 15 minutes. Bus number 6 runs between the old town and St. David's (including Southside); a transfer lets you board another bus at Southside's first gate to travel to Clearwater Beach and back every half hour.

Sea Express (tel. 441/295-4506, www. marineandports.bm) runs daily Hamilton-Dockyard-St. George's ferry trips April-October (leaving Dockyard at 9:30am, 11:30am, 2:15pm, 4:15pm, 6:15pm Mon. and Wed.-Thurs., and 9:30am, 11:30am, 1:30pm Tues. and Fri.) on its Orange Route. From Hamilton or Dockyard, one-way fares cost $5 adults, $2.75 ages 5-15, free under age 5. Buy tickets, tokens, or passes in advance at the ferry terminal or select stores, as cash is not accepted on board.

Background

The Landscape 230

Plants and Animals 237

History 250

Government................... 257

Economy 260

People and Culture 268

The Landscape

An archipelago arranged as a fishhook, Bermuda comprises more than 100 islands encircled by a collar of coral. Wary Spanish mariners of the 16th century dubbed them *Las Islas de Demonios* (Islands of Devils), while the English preferred the more benign moniker "The Summer Islands." Today, eight of the largest islands—St. George's Island, St. David's Island, Bermuda Island, Somerset Island, Watford Island, Boaz Island, Ireland Island South, and Ireland Island North—are connected by bridges and a causeway into a single entity that locals simply call "The Island." Within the many picturesque harbors, bays, and sounds are scatterings of smaller islands and islets, some public, others privately owned, many just rocky uninhabited outcrops lacking structures or vegetation. The main island is relatively small at 21 square miles (22 miles end to end, and never more than two miles wide), with the hook's western third curling around to the northwest. But due to its varied and hilly—though not mountainous—terrain, Bermuda from the ground is rather deceptive, leading one to believe that, just around the next corner, there might be more than the sum of its compressed vital statistics. An aerial view is more revealing: As you descend to land at the airport, sweeping from violet deep-ocean across reef-dotted aquamarine shallows, the island appears almost fragile in its entirety—a geographically isolated oceanic oddity.

Bermuda's unique, seemingly contradictory characteristics have long intrigued scientists. A subtropical island about 650 miles from the nearest mainland (Cape Hatteras, North Carolina), it bears little resemblance to its Caribbean cousins in climate, biota, or geology. Instead, Bermuda is bathed by the balmy Gulf Stream, which exerts a moderating influence on its climate, just as the easterly trade winds do down south. Yet, unlike the tropical Indies, Bermuda's winters are damp and storm-wracked. There is no typical wet or dry season; indeed, the island's weather habits are so capricious that a thunderstorm can let loose on one parish while sparing all the others.

Geologically, despite its volcanic origins, the island's core is soft white limestone. There are no rivers, lakes, or streams. The topography is neither towering nor dangerously low (Town Hill in Smith's Parish is the highest point of land at 259 feet elevation). And though tiny, Bermuda's landmass holds an astonishingly diverse range of natural habitats—from marshland to sand dunes and cedar woodland—that support an equally varied ecology.

Visitors, of course, are tantalized by such offerings. Bermuda's geologic permutations have left a place characterized by mostly welcoming temperatures; by floral eye candy found throughout the island's undulating length; by soft, rosy-hued beaches and turquoise swimming holes; by saltwater sounds that provide perfect natural harbors; by pastel homes hewn from the very rock they sit on; and by a necklace of biodiverse coral reefs—the most northerly in the world.

Except for the ferocity of its storms, including seasonal hurricanes, Bermuda's environment is indeed charmed. Immune to natural disasters such as earthquakes, volcanoes, mudslides, or floods, devoid even of dangerous plants or animals, its appearance conjures a manicured country garden rather than a mid-Atlantic atoll.

Previous: a weathered cedar fence; bougainvillea.

GEOGRAPHY

Bermuda lies at 32°17' N, 64°46' W, along the latitude of Savannah, Georgia. The nearest point of land is Cape Hatteras, North Carolina, 650 miles to the northwest. Roughly the size of Manhattan, Bermuda is 2,100 miles west of the Azores and 910 miles north of the Bahamas. There are no distinct topographical regions on the island, but rather a variety of natural habitats, all of which can be found in most of the nine parishes.

Bermuda consists of a limestone cap sitting at the pinnacle of a submerged volcanic seamount. Its geological origins can be traced back 110 million years to the Mid-Atlantic Ridge, a volatile, mostly submerged division between the divergent American and European tectonic plates. Scientists believe "Mount Bermuda" was the byproduct of a massive volcanic eruption just west of the ridge, which moved slowly westward over the next 80 million years. A second eruption caused the volcano to enlarge into the Bermuda Seamount, incorporating a trio of peaks: the Bermuda Pedestal (on which the island now sits), Challenger Bank, and Argus Bank. Of these, only the 13,000-foot Bermuda Pedestal now extends above sea level. The seamount moved an additional 500 miles west in the following 30 million years, leaving the island currently situated in a stable area of the earth's crust.

The seamount's limestone cap was formed biologically over the last million years as seaweeds, algae, corals, and other shallow-water marine organisms laid down deposits. A 350-foot-deep layer of calcium carbonate was formed, and as sea levels fell, about 100,000 years ago, this layer was exposed to air. The result was the formation of many tons of sand, which wind blew across the island to form rolling dunes that eventually hardened into what geologists term aeolian limestone, meaning "created by wind." Remnants of these old dunes, sometimes even dunes atop dunes, can be seen along the shoreline of Bermuda or in road cuts such as the dramatic Blackwatch Pass in Pembroke. Soft, porous limestone rock now makes up Bermuda's entire surface and has been quarried over the centuries for roof slate and building blocks used for Bermuda's characteristic island homes.

The porous nature of the limestone helped shape Bermuda's geological identity. It allowed rain to soak into the surface rock, deterring freshwater runoff that would have created streams, rivers, and lakes. Instead, rainwater burrowed deep into the earth, forming a network of twisting underground tunnels, caverns, and caves, which still honeycomb certain parishes and give Bermuda one of the highest concentrations of caves in the world. Some are found underwater, becoming refuges for rare species. In the best-known, you can find stalactites and stalagmites, columns, flow stones, and soda straws.

Bermuda's biological history begins about 800,000 years ago—the date of the oldest terrestrial fossils, belonging to a petrel (a tube-nosed seabird), found in Hamilton Parish. But climatic changes and the dramatic rise and fall of sea levels over time created havoc for the habitats, animals, and plantlife that may have lived on an ancient Bermuda far larger than its current form. As Canadian research scientist Martin Thomas points out in his book *The Natural History of Bermuda,* observations from deep-ocean submersibles examining the Bermuda Pedestal have revealed former beaches at a depth of 315 feet—a fascinating clue about the island's previous life. It was not until about 10,000 years ago that rising sea levels stabilized and Bermuda took its present shape. Marine and terrestrial organisms then arrived as larvae, spores, or adults, transported by wind or carried on debris propelled by the powerful Gulf Stream. Against big odds, these first forms of life would slowly spawn the rich environment to which Bermuda is home today.

CLIMATE

Bermuda's climate is subtropical and influenced by two major factors: the Gulf Stream and the Bermuda-Azores High. Like a giant

The Bermuda Triangle

If there's one thing most everyone knows about Bermuda—even if they've never set foot on the island—it's that the archipelago lies in the maw of a spooky phenomenon dubbed the "Bermuda Triangle." Bermudians who live or travel overseas get peppered with questions about the popular myth, and it is a favorite topic of discussion among tourists, but locals tend to dismiss it with humor and skepticism. Despite the Triangle's perennial appearance in books and science-fiction TV series, scientists agree it is nothing more than an enduring legend fueled by deadly coincidence.

Conspiracy theorists have devoted seas of ink to explaining why ships and aircraft have sunk, caught fire, or vanished without a trace within an area of Atlantic Ocean spanning Bermuda; San Juan, Puerto Rico; and Miami, Florida. Some believe these were the victims of paranormal occurrences, blaming malevolent sea creatures, time warps, aliens, and the lost city of Atlantis. Others speculate that natural sources such as fog fields, magnetic anomalies, or methane bubbles popping up from the sea floor might have caused planes' instruments to malfunction or vessels to sink.

Empirical data suggests a far simpler explanation—that such "mysteries" aren't really mysterious at all. Given the fact that many Triangle incidents took place during raging storms or in the 1940s and 1950s before the advent of high-tech navigation equipment such as global positioning satellites, basic human error or the whims of Mother Nature could easily account for the disasters. In fact, Lloyd's of London accident records have shown that the Triangle's geographic area is no more dangerous than any other part of the ocean—a conclusion confirmed by the U.S. Coast Guard.

Yet the world's fascination with the Triangle continues, particularly with the story of Flight 19, the unsolved disappearance of five Avenger torpedo bombers on December 5, 1945. The Triangle's best-known tale describes how the aircraft left Fort Lauderdale, Florida's Naval Air Station on a routine practice mission with 13 student pilots, accompanied by their commander, Lt. Charles Taylor. The flight plan called for a test bombing run followed by a triangular course east and north, a distance of 120 miles. But about 90 minutes after leaving the base, the squadron found itself in trouble. Taylor sent a radio transmission reporting that his compasses were malfunctioning, and it soon became clear he was hopelessly disoriented. As night fell and a storm approached, communications faded and finally stopped, presumably when the planes ran out of fuel and plunged into the sea.

One of two Martin Mariner search planes that went to look for the missing squadron also disappeared; there were reports of an explosion after it took off, and airplane debris was spotted nearby. Nothing was seen of Flight 19, however. The Navy, pressured by Taylor's family, cited "causes or reasons unknown" for the disaster, rather than pilot error. In subsequent decades, the story of Flight 19 became the focus of Triangle speculation, which heightened after Charles Berlitz's sensational bestseller of 1974, *The Bermuda Triangle.* Flight 19's planes and pilots even enjoyed a reappearance in Steven Spielberg's 1977 UFO classic, *Close Encounters of the Third Kind.*

One of the most lauded books on the Triangle attempts to lay such fantasies to rest. *The Bermuda Triangle—Solved* was written by Arizona librarian Larry Kusche, who in 1975 decided to investigate claims put forward by the plethora of articles and books on the Triangle's unsolved mysteries. Digging into contemporary accounts and other primary sources, he discovered factual material other writers had overlooked or ignored, much of it pointing to entirely rational explanations for unusual events. His book catalogs his findings, offering in-depth detail about some of the myth's highlights and ultimately refuting many claims.

Surprisingly, Bermuda has never made much of the legend, even as a potential tourist attraction. Eponymous cocktails took the name, and several island companies pay tribute to the folklore with Triangle monikers. Yet some tourism stakeholders feel the island should be marketing the Triangle to the world at large.

storm off Bermuda's shore

Officially, Bermuda has two seasons—summer and winter—which have defined the tourism industry. Summer, the high season for visitors, runs April-October, while winter, once snubbed as the "off" or "low" season, runs November-March.

Most Bermudians, however, would argue the island actually does enjoy four seasons like its mainland counterparts. Locals can immediately discern the first breath of fall in the second week of October, when temperatures dip from the torpor of summer, or the sweet calm of spring in early April after the windy barrage of New Year storms.

The island has no rainy season; instead, rain tends to be spread throughout the year, with January being the wettest month on average, with six inches of rain. Typically, even torrential rainstorms peter out after an hour or two, and rare are the days when the sun does not make a single appearance. The hour-by-hour changes can prove challenging to packing clothes for a Bermuda holiday in any season; choose a mix of outfits and layers to accommodate the unexpected.

True summer can be counted on May-September, with temperatures peaking in July-August. Relative humidity, ranging 75-85 percent all year, but occasionally spiking to 90 percent in midsummer, makes Bermuda feel uncomfortably like a greenhouse, draining energy—and buckets of sweat—in the summer. Hydration is key to doing anything active in these months, and swimming is the most refreshing way to cool off. October-December marks one of the most pleasant times of the year, when cool breezes prevail, but the sun can be hot enough that you'll want to swim. The windy season usually takes control after Christmas, bringing storms, cold winds, rain, and damp days and nights January-March; this is, perhaps, the most unpredictable season, often with long spells of sunshine amid the tempestuousness. Ignore the euphemistic descriptions on tourist brochures, though; it can get *very* chilly by Bermudian standards,

security blanket, the Gulf Stream flows northeast from the Gulf of Mexico—from which it takes its name—through the Straits of Florida to an area northeast of Bermuda, channeling warm equatorial water northward on its journey. The Gulf Stream moderates temperature, bringing mild weather throughout the year and preventing Bermuda from getting as hot or cold as mainland areas of the same latitude. Frost is not found here, though winter gets the occasional hailstorm.

The Bermuda-Azores High is a high-pressure zone that also exerts a welcome influence on Bermuda's climate. In the summer, the zone lies east of Bermuda, bouncing storm systems north of the island and causing light southerly winds throughout the season. In winter, though, the high sits too far southeast to make a difference, allowing northerly gales to pummel the island with cooler temperatures. Unlike the Caribbean, Bermuda has no trade winds or monsoons, and its isolated position brings a lower risk of hurricanes.

Preparing for a Hurricane

Bermudians can reel off the dates and names of worst-offending hurricanes like a list of wayward relatives they would have preferred had not visited: Emily, a category 1 hurricane that caught the island off guard on September 24, 1987, causing $35 million in damage; 1995's Felix, which swept away surfside restaurants and swiped the island back and forth three times; and Fabian, a category 3, which scored a rare "direct hit" on Bermuda on September 5, 2003, killing four people, closing several hotels, knocking out power for several weeks, and causing an estimated $300 million in damage. In one instance, two hurricanes—Fay and Gonzalo in mid-October 2014—made landfall at Bermuda within the space of just a few days.

While most hotels and guesthouses make safety and logistical arrangements for guests in the event of a hurricane, it helps to be prepared if you're staying in a private home or renting a property. A hurricane checklist should include canned goods (including pet food for any animals you may be taking care of), candles, flashlights, propane lanterns, batteries, a battery-powered AM-FM radio, a propane stove, a tarpaulin (in case roof slate blows off), and a bucket and rope for hauling freshwater from the tank. Secure all moveable objects from the garden or yard (garbage cans, barbecues, garden furniture). Secure storm shutters, and tape or board up windows. Clear out roof gutters and put strainers in downspouts to keep debris out of drinking water. Make sure pets are kept indoors. Stock up on emergency supplies, including medications. Fill the bathtub to enable flushing of toilets. Make sure vehicles have full gas tanks.

Storm updates and news are provided by the Government Emergency Broadcast Facility on 100.1 MHz FM. The national Emergency Measures Organisation (EMO), comprising first responders along with key government ministers and utility representatives, gathers in a "war room" to coordinate response and communication during the worst of the storm. Occasionally, in the event of very high winds, the St. George's Causeway—connecting St. George's Island to the mainland near the airport—is temporarily closed.

Bermuda uses the American Saffir-Simpson Hurricane Scale to judge the strength and property-damage potential of approaching storms:

- **Category 1:** winds 74-95 mph; minor damage

- **Category 2:** winds 96-110 mph; roof, window, vegetation, and small-craft damage

- **Category 3:** winds 111-130 mph; structural damage to homes, vegetation

- **Category 4:** winds 131-155 mph; extensive damage

- **Category 5:** winds 155-plus mph; catastrophic damage

During a storm, do not go outside, and stand clear of the windows in case flying debris smashes the glass. If you must go out, watch for falling branches and power lines. When the eye of the storm passes over the island, the weather will calm down dramatically, but do not assume that the hurricane is over. Remain inside, because the storm will resume from the opposite direction.

After the storm, report any fallen trees or downed power lines and do not drive unless absolutely necessary. To save food for as long as possible, try not to open the fridge or freezer for long periods. Call 911 for an emergency, or 955 to report a power outage.

and many homes and hotels have no heating, aside from fires and electric heaters. Remember, too, that a modest 60°F can feel downright frigid if you happen to be driving a scooter on a windblown winter's night; wear gloves like Bermudians do. Spring signals a drop in winds and a resulting rebirth in garden growth and blossoms, as calm, sunny weather prevails and temperatures begin their inevitable rise toward the end of May. Bermuda Day, on the last Friday in May, is the traditional first day of summer, though islanders usually refuse to swim until at least a month later.

Temperatures

Bermuda's summer and winter temperatures differ considerably, though the yearly average is a balmy 76°F. Monthly variations are more telling: Average temperatures range from 66°F in February to 85°F in August, the effects heightened considerably by summer's humidity. Annual lows and highs normally range from 55°F to 95°F.

Seawater temperatures hover around 65°F in the winter but warm to a bath-like 83°F by August. It's more than possible to swim and scuba dive year-round, however.

Rainfall

Bermuda's rainfall is fairly evenly distributed throughout the year, with no true rainy season, though rain is more likely to intrude on outdoor activities if you visit January-March. Even then, Bermuda rainfall tends to come in the form of a quick downpour rather than daylong drizzle, so barring a hurricane, weather rarely ruins a Bermuda vacation. Indeed, it's possible to have torrential rain in Paget while St. Georgians simultaneously bask in the sun.

Hurricanes

The hurricane season officially runs six months, June-November, but Bermudians consider themselves safe until the seawater temperature hits 85°F, usually in July, and after it starts to dip again, by mid-October.

Bermuda escapes most of the annual storms due to its tiny landmass, though severe storms have scored direct hits—on average every six years. More common are huge storm swells off the beaches, which whip up surf and prohibit swimming, and heavy rain and wind when hurricanes are in the vicinity. Storms have also spawned tornadoes that twist across isolated areas of the island, ripping off roofs before vanishing out to sea.

Hurricane near-misses, when these violent vortexes sideswipe the island, have occurred some seasons; very rarely, hurricanes bounce back eastward after first careening toward the U.S. East Coast. Particularly after the fury of Fabian, however, Bermudians are highly aware of a hurricane's destructive force and monitor the track of every single storm during this season, no matter how large, small, or apparently distant.

The government and media communicate details of approaching storms, and Bermuda's Emergency Measures Organisation is well prepared to orchestrate recovery and cleanup in the event of severe damage. After Fabian killed four Bermudians, the government implemented stricter storm preparations, including closing the mile-long Causeway to St. George's when big storms draw close. Yet, Bermuda is generally more resilient than Caribbean islands in the event of a direct hit, thanks to its sturdy limestone and cement-block buildings, well-developed infrastructure, and modern communications system. Most householders stock up every summer with hurricane supplies (tarps, flashlights, batteries, and buckets).

The **Emergency Measures Organisation** (tel. 441/295-0011) broadcasts police, government, and media alerts via 100.1 FM; other stations are often knocked off the air during power outages. Weather warnings, including marine forecasts, are broadcast by the **Bermuda Weather Service** (tel. 977, www.weather.bm) or via Bermuda Harbour Radio (tel. 441/297-1010, www.marineandports.bm). During hurricane season, both the **U.S. National Weather Service** (www.nws.noaa.gov) and **The Weather Channel** (www.weather.com) track developing storms and their movements through the Caribbean and Atlantic with satellite images and forecasts.

Bermuda storm folklore includes stories about the predicting power of shark oil, which islanders used to extract for homespun meteorological indicators. Even in the 21st century, orthodox science sometimes takes a backseat to these traditional barometers—sealed bottles of fatty hydrocarbons extracted from a shark's liver. Some Bermudians still hang shark oil in a sheltered spot outdoors and check its contents to predict a storm's ferocity. While younger generations now turn to television, old-timers swear the bottle's contents turn cloudy during disturbances, and if a hurricane actually looms, a spiraling plume will be visible inside.

ENVIRONMENTAL ISSUES

Bermuda may look like a pristine paradise, but pollution, pesticides, and overdevelopment are wreaking havoc on the island's ecosystems.

Warning signs are causing scientists to become alarmed; they note that reductions in plant and animal species, as well as the ebbing health of some species, are important barometers of environmental degradation. Since 1997, the island's sea grass beds—vital habitats for conch, sea urchins, rockfish, turtles, and spiny lobsters—have drastically declined; marine biologists say 20 percent of the 5,100 acres have been eradicated in the last decade alone. Leaching cesspits and dredging are blamed for the loss, and authorities promise sea grass beds will be added to the list of protected areas of the island.

Residents catch rainwater on white roofs that channel it into underground storage tanks.

Disposal of waste, including sewage, is one of Bermuda's biggest problems and one of the most prominent on the minds of environmentalists, who have worked in recent years to make sustainable development a public debate. The island burns its garbage at an incinerator constructed for $64 million in 1992; its tower, at Tynes Bay, Devonshire, is visible along the North Shore. Sewage waste, dissolved and pumped out to sea, has caused a growth surge in marine weeds that choke slower-growing corals—an ecological imbalance scientists are monitoring.

Pollutants in ponds and nature reserves—evident in the resulting populations of deformed toads—are also raising concern. A large part of the problem may be the lackadaisical attitude Bermudians have long held toward pesticides. For decades, householders liberally sprayed bug-killers such as Baygon and Raid, and environmental organizations now push for the use of less-toxic alternatives.

Even Bermuda's air quality is susceptible to modern contaminants. Large numbers of high-emission motorbikes, as well as cars, have raised air pollution to dangerous levels in some areas around the City of Hamilton, even exceeding annual readings of some European cities, scientists report. These are issues Bermudians must grapple with and find solutions to as island development, traffic, and population—along with their ugly fallout—seem only certain to increase.

Water Conservation

Rainwater is at a premium on an island, as households depend on it as their main source of freshwater—at least to run faucets, showers, baths, and toilets, if not for drinking. Large water tanks are built under every home, and rain is caught as it has been for centuries—on traditional white limestone slate roofs, whose pipes and gullies channel it to a subterranean tank. From there, water is pumped into domestic plumbing systems. There are also large public water-catchments for government use. Not surprisingly, water conservation is the rule amid chronic droughts, and water shortages are common. Conservationists have sounded warnings about the problem of increasing water consumption on the island, particularly the pressure it exerts on underground lenses, which supply larger private users, such as hotels, as well as the City of Hamilton. Bermuda residents consume an estimated 1.58 billion gallons of water annually; each cruise ship consumes up to 50,000 gallons daily in port. The island has just one reverse-osmosis plant, to supply the hospital and offset shortages, but experts argue several more plants are needed to avert future crises.

Cruise Ships

The extent to which the cruise industry benefits Bermuda has generated much debate on the island, but perhaps even more controversial is the question of whether Bermuda's infrastructure can support the advent of far bigger ships. The world's cruise liners are estimated to have nearly doubled in size every decade. Panamax, and larger post Panamax vessels, are named for an enlarged superstructure design that fits the maximum lock dimensions of the Panama Canal. Such ships can carry upward of 5,000 passengers, double that of standard ships. Critics question whether Bermuda can absorb so many cruise visitors without a negative impact on other tourists and residents. Larger ships have already caused transport issues, forcing the government to ensure more buses, ferries, and taxis are available. Other concerns include pressure on garbage, sewage, and water systems, given that ships in port make liberal use of those services. Heritage Wharf, alongside King's Wharf at the Dockyard, has been the docking spot for mega-vessels since it was built in 2009. Far smaller and, typically, older ships make port in Hamilton, with occasional stops in St. George's.

Plants and Animals

HABITATS

The island's habitats are not as numerous or exotic as those found in pure tropical regions like the Caribbean and Central America. Yet Bermuda's ecosystems are interesting in their more subtle variety, as well as in their increasing fragility due to rampant development. The main habitats are the rocky shore; beaches and dunes; inland forest; marshes, ponds, and mangroves; karst and caves; sea grass beds; and coral reefs. All these areas can be seen and explored at sites around the island. Interpretive displays complete with audio are found at the Natural History Museum (part of the Bermuda Aquarium, Museum & Zoo) at Flatts, in Smith's Parish, and describe habitats and common species found in each.

The Rocky Shore

Some of the most impressive aspects of wild Bermuda are its rocky shore and coastal environments. Climbing up and down the spray-bashed coast, where biodiverse tide pools are often large enough to swim in, you can imagine the natural setting that greeted the castaways who reached Bermuda's shores. When the first humans arrived on the island's shore in the 1500s, they encountered a reef-necklaced oasis of endemic cedar forests and palmetto palms, both of which were beneficial to survival in myriad ways: for timber to build huts and ships, for roof thatch, for berries to mull wine, and for hearts of palm, which shipwreck survivors roasted or baked.

The rocky shoreline is home to a wealth of plants and animals, a unique bridge between marine and terrestrial environments. Algae, lichens, and rockweeds drape the intertidal zone, where they have adapted to a hybrid environment with features such as attachments, or "holdfasts," to the rock. The band between the lowest tide and the spray zone is darkened and made slippery by blue-green bacteria, which provide a larder of food for other animals. Among the various species found here, rainbow-hued parrotfish can be found grazing, gnawing on reef and rock with their hallmark beaked mouths. Crabs, snails, urchins, anemones, and seaweeds also thrive. The banded West Indian top shell (*Cittarium pica*) can sometimes be found; it's a protected species, and removing this creature is illegal. Growing profusely atop the wind- and sea-eroded limestone shore are hardy, salt-resistant succulents, such as the sea purslane, coast spurge, and seaside oxeye, whose vibrant yellow flowers dot the landscape. Prickly pears, spiky Spanish bayonets with luxuriant towers of white blossoms, baygrape brushes, fennel, and fields of seaside goldenrod, waving feathery butter-colored wands, cover areas above the tidal shore.

Beaches and Dunes

Sand dunes harbor a similarly tough variety of plants, whose growth effectively serves to anchor the dunes and prevent sand masses from shifting too far. Dune vegetation is peppered with the types of bright blossoms that are so striking in desert environments, although here, they are totally different varieties; these include the purple-flowered vine, seaside morning glory, wild stock, sea lavender, and the buttercup-like seaside evening primrose. Land crabs dig long burrows in dune areas to escape the prying beaks of hunting night herons; be careful when hiking the dunes not to twist your ankle in their exit holes.

Inland Forest

As a result of residential and urban development, Bermuda's original woodland, comprising endemic cedars, palmettos, and olivewood, has been whittled down over four centuries to mere remnants. Today, true remains of the old forest are almost nonexistent, since woodland is now dominated by introduced species. Many have proven detrimental to endemics; the Mexican pepper, whispering pine or casuarina, and the Chinese fan palm have successfully competed for space and nutrients with cedars and palmettos. Yet inland forests covering uplands and interior valleys contain dense evergreen coverage, providing vital breeding and nesting areas for birds, insects, and other species.

Surviving native trees include the Bermuda cedar (*Juniperus bermudiana*), the palmetto (*Sabal bermudiana*), the yellow wood, olivewood, and hackberry. Nonendemic fiddlewoods, allspice, Surinam cherry, and Indian laurel trees are much more common and can be found in forested hillsides and valleys and in the woodland tracts of most nature reserves. The East End's Nonsuch Island Nature Reserve, which can be visited through special tours, is the only area of the island where endemic forest has been totally restored over the past three decades. The government's Department of Parks has embarked on an island-wide restoration effort in many other protected areas to replace invasives with endemic and native saplings, a program that will take many years to achieve maturity.

Marshes, Ponds, and Mangroves

Peat marshes, freshwater and salt ponds, and mangroves are some of the most fascinating natural environments for amateur or professional biologists to explore. Such wetlands provide a vital feeding ground for bird species and also nurture insects, toads, lizards, and other animals. Bermuda's mangrove swamps—wet forests that can tolerate saltwater—are the Atlantic's most northerly.

Red and black mangrove trees, with a dense tangle of roots, many submerged, thrive in coastal swamps such as Hungry Bay on the South Shore, Blue Hole Park, and Ferry Point National Park. There are also brackish pond mangroves at Spittal Pond and Walsingham Nature Reserves. Bees and other insects are attracted to the yellow or white flowers of mangroves. Black mangroves have air-breathing roots, which rise like alien fingers from the water. These atmospheric environments are home to numerous species of snail, mollusk, and crab, as well as lizards, crab spiders, large hurricane spiders, dragonflies, tiny whistling frogs, and giant toads. Birdlife includes herons, kiskadees, migrating warblers, and waterfowl. The only plant to avoid when exploring nature reserves, particularly swamp forests, is poison ivy (*Rhus radicans*), a red-veined crawling vine that can leave a nasty rash after contact with skin.

Karst and Caves

Scientists have discovered diverse plant and animal life inside the island's honeycomb of marine and terrestrial caves. Most are located in Smith's and Hamilton Parishes, where karst scenery is characterized by limestone terrain containing sinks, underground caves, and pinnacle rock. The dark, still, and isolated environment inside caves has fed interesting biological adaptations and fostered endemic forms of life, some of which may have evolved from deep-sea creatures that inhabited Bermuda's seamount in prehistoric times. Unusual crustaceans, similar to shrimp, have been found in marine caves, and numerous more common biota, including sea squirts (sea cucumbers), sponges, and mollusks, also make their homes here. Cave mouths on land have helped keep alive many endemic species and are populated by ferns, herbs, and mosses.

Sea Grass Beds

Many of Bermuda's bays and shallow offshore areas are covered by sea grass beds, which are prime nurseries and feeding grounds for fish, turtles, invertebrates, and other species. Flounders, crabs, and crustaceans—and protected green turtles—can be spotted feeding on sea grass. The mud underlying sea grass beds is home to marine worms and other species. Snorkeling over sea grass beds can be fascinating, but watch out for spiny sea urchins if you put your feet down in these shallow areas.

Coral Reefs

The marine equivalent of rainforests, coral reefs are precious ecosystems whose rich biodiversity of plants and animals supports a complex web of interdependence. Coral reef organisms, including hard and soft coral species, construct their own environment and thrive in areas near the equator that receive even temperatures and sunlight year-round. Fed by the warm Gulf Stream, Bermuda's coral reefs are the world's most northerly; thanks to legislative protection, they have not been destroyed like so many in other regions.

Bermuda's coral reefs take various forms. Rim reefs encircle the island inside a shallow plateau that drops off beyond to the deep ocean. This reefy necklace, the bane of ships over the centuries, lies fairly close to the South Shore coastline, several hundred feet off in places; on the North Shore, by contrast, rim reefs are located about 10 miles out. Patch reefs are scattered across the shallow plateau, covering some 290 square miles around the island. Boiler reefs are "micro atolls"—wineglass-shaped structures that rise from the sea floor and harbor coral-based ecosystems in miniature. They are particularly visible just a few yards off the entire length of the South Shore and West End. At low tide, boiler reef rims can sit just above the surface. At high tide, you can actually swim down inside these mushroom-like formations to investigate various plants and animals within.

Bursting with life, coral reefs are continually decaying and rebuilding naturally, as organisms such as stony corals create the framework that other limestone-skeletoned creatures like forams, sea mosses, and bristle worms cement together. Anemones, sea fans, and soft corals then fill in the gaps—in turn, providing food on which other creatures come to graze. Boring clams, sponges, and barnacles undermine the reef structure in the meantime, a process that sees honeycombed chunks break off, providing fresh surfaces for new growth.

PLANTS

Bermuda's manicured environs are the product of its hothouse climate, a subtropical mixing bowl of high humidity, loads of sunlight, and brief, torrential rainfall that makes green thumbs of even neophyte gardeners. Not much is difficult to grow here,

The Bermuda Cedar

The Bermuda cedar (*Juniperus bermudiana*) is a symbol of survival for islanders, who have depended on the sturdy evergreen from the first days of human habitation. The endemic cedar, along with the palmetto and olivewood, covered the island in thick woods during the 1500s and early 1600s, and later sustained generations of English colonists. They used its timber for constructing homes, churches, and forts after colonization in 1612. They chose cedar for building light, rot-resistant Bermuda sloops—vessels that fueled a whole maritime industry for over a century in the 1700s. The cedar tree's aromatic red-hued wood was much sought-after for crafting cabinetry and fine furniture, including chests, tables, and four-poster beds, much of which graces modern Bermudian homes. Early Bermudians even produced liquor by fermenting the cedar's blue-gray berries and had medicinal uses for its dark-green foliage and hairy bark.

With salt-tolerant foliage and long roots anchored in the island's limestone-rich soil against hurricanes, cedars were so abundant that islanders squandered the wood, burning cedar forests in vain attempts to rid the island of rats. Colonists also shipped it carelessly overseas in the form of expendable crates to hold exports. Bermuda cedar was soon in such short supply that it became immensely valuable. Indeed, by the 18th century, island properties were valued by the number of cedars growing on them. Protection laws enacted over the years bear testimony to the iconic worth of the beloved cedar.

Bermuda's landscape changed drastically in the 1940s, when an environmental tragedy nearly wiped out the cedar. An invasion by two scale insects, the oystershell scale and the cedar scale, spread a virulent form of cedar blight that eradicated 90 percent of the island's cedar trees within a decade. As the infestation continued, Bermudian officials tried to curb the pests with introduced species such as the ladybug, but efforts were ineffective and too late. Silvery hillsides of skeleton trunks—some of which remain—underscored the enormity of the outbreak; by the time authorities had a handle on the problem, just 1 percent of the original forest remained.

It has taken the species decades to recover, but the cedar is slowly making a comeback, thanks

and garden clubs and horticultural societies devoted to raising roses, orchids, cacti, island endemics, and other dedicated plant varieties have flourished as a result. Yet, while gardens thrive, Bermuda's wild spaces are few. More than 75 percent of the island's landmass is developed; of that, over 10 percent is covered by concrete, roads, and buildings. Open space in the form of nature reserves and national parks makes up just 7 percent of all of Bermuda's land and is therefore strictly protected. It is in these reserves that various habitats, including inland forest, mangroves, and coastal zones, can be witnessed as they have existed for centuries. But mixed-use areas such as agricultural land, hotel properties, forts, and golf courses—though designed for different purposes—are also important breeding and nesting areas for bluebirds and other species and are home to many different types of both wild and planted flowers, bushes, and trees.

Flora bloom throughout the year (there is no autumnal fall of leaves), infusing the island with deep color and scent. Lanes lined with the prolific oleander (*Nerium oleander*) turn pink with perfumed petals starting in June. Midsummer carpets of flaming royal poinciana (*Delonix regia*) splash the landscape red in July. Riotous magenta bougainvillea vines paint parks and gardens showily year-round, while waxy frangipani trees (*Plumeria rubra* and *Plumeria alba*) and lady-of-the-night turn evenings sweet with fragrant flowers throughout the summer. Morning glory vines laden with blue-violet blossoms creep over walls and fences, and banks of red, yellow, and orange nasturtiums hem the roadsides. Trumpet lilies tumble onto sidewalks in October like golden goblets. And hedgerows of ubiquitous hibiscus to strong reforesting efforts by the island's Department of Parks and conservation services, using insect-resistant trees. Every September, Bermudian schoolchildren are encouraged to gather the tree's bluish-green berries to grow cedar saplings for dispersal around the island. The government is also pushing ahead with a long-range program to replace invasive species with cedars and palmettos in national parks—an effort to reclaim the look of Bermuda's first forests.

Cedars still hold a special place in Bermudian hearts. Planting a cedar tree on your property remains a popular wedding tradition, symbolizing the growth of the bride and groom's relationship. Bermuda cedarwood is coveted in the construction industry for doors, window frames, and beams—though it is now so hard to get, and therefore so expensive ($42 per board foot), that many homeowners opt for Virginia cedar instead. Indeed, cedar trees are in such demand, they have been illegally cut down and stolen from nature reserves.

Bermuda cedar

Visitors can find carved cedar trinkets for sale around the island, either in stores or from outdoor vendors (at Dockyard, for example). But the best examples of Bermuda cedar are found at auction. Check the daily paper; if your visit happens to coincide with one of the annual major auctions of contents from grand island homes, exquisite cedar heirloom chests or coffee tables will no doubt be among the offerings. Be prepared to put your pocketbook up against those of local aficionados, however; genuine Bermuda cedar treasures may appear the epitome of rustic beauty, but they cost the crown jewels.

(*Hibiscus rosa-sinensis*), hillsides of February freesias (*Freesia refracta alba*), and Bermuda Easter lily (*Lilium longiflorum*) fields stretching as far as the eye can see are iconic to the landscape.

Bermuda has 17 surviving endemic plant species; some 150 native species; 1,000 introduced species; and an estimated 900 cultivated plants. Such abundance has always entranced visitors. Former Beatle John Lennon was so taken by a particular species of yellow freesia he encountered in the Bermuda Botanical Gardens during a June 1980 sojourn—six months before his murder—that he gave his last album the same name: *Double Fantasy*. (Staff later planted a lily, suitably named Strawberry Fields Forever, where the freesia had once grown, though, predictably, the sign noting this vanished almost immediately.)

Much of Bermuda's plantlife can be seen without special visits to nature reserves—it's found along city streets, hemming roadways, and on public properties and attractions. The island's 130 miles of roadsides alone offer an eclectic mix of most island plants, from wildflowers to aloes and agaves, from bamboo thickets to herbs and exotic trees. Similarly, Hamilton's streets are lined with ornamental trees, including flamboyantly hued varieties such as the lilac jacaranda (*Jacaranda mimosifolia*), the cassias (golden and pink showers), and the African tulip tree. Reid Street's parade of sweet-smelling black ebony sends down cascades of fragrant powder-puffs in early summer. Outside the Bermuda Library on Queen Street, a centuries-old Indian laurel welcomes visitors to Queen Elizabeth Park; it looks like a tree from a storybook, thanks to its vast canopy, wide-stretched limbs, and gnarled spread of roots. In Flatts, a similarly historic mahogany tree stands at the junction of Middle Road and Harrington Sound, while a gargantuan banyan tree spreads over nearly an acre of land at the Southlands property in Warwick. Many of these landmarks are protected by law. Hamilton's Victoria Park and Fort Hamilton properties are also beautifully planted; the latter's highlight is a circular moat garden accessed through limestone dungeons and boasting a bedded jungle of towering ferns, sprawling vines, locust and wild honey (or "Swiss cheese") plants, elephant ears, bromeliads, life plants or "floppers," and other shade-loving species.

Bermuda's natural harvest of wild fruit is just as impressive. At different times throughout the year, roadsides, reserves, gardens, and trails are littered with abundant piles of fruit, lots of it collected by locals and used for making preserves—or eaten on the spot. Surinam cherries, produced twice a year, in the spring and fall, can be seen thick on evergreen bushes bordering many properties; the fruits are good to eat, though more sour than most North American cherry varieties. Loquat trees are heavy with fat, yellow fruit in January-February—a favorite after-school treat for passing children. Guava plums and prickly pears, though difficult to pick from

Bermudiana

In springtime, carpets of purple wildflowers cover rocky hillsides and sandy shores around the island. Bermuda's national flower, the Bermudiana (*Sisyrinchium bermudiana*), is also known as Bermuda iris or blue-eyed grass. It grows wild in dry, sunny, windswept, seemingly harsh areas such as Spittal Pond Nature Reserve. Standing about eight inches high, its slender stem and leaves are waxy and grasslike, its small flowers sporting violet petals and yellow centers. Though related to North American species, the Bermuda variety is endemic—it does not grow wild elsewhere.

thorn-infested plants, are commonly eaten or boiled for jams. Bay grapes ripen in the autumn on their waxy-leafed coastal bushes. Summer storms shake down plump avocados en masse. Towering pawpaw trees, palmlike in appearance with large, round yellow fruits that are good for baking and renowned as a meat tenderizer, can be found everywhere. Local bananas also grow abundantly; small and thin, they are sweeter than imported counterparts.

the Bermudiana national flower

Roses

Bermuda's British inclinations are nowhere so beautifully on display as in the parishes' many rose gardens. Indeed, the island has been proclaimed "a living museum of roses" by one garden historian, with more than 140 different varieties noted. Tea roses, Chinas, bourbons, noisettes, hybrid musks, climbers, ramblers, and miniatures—old garden roses are prolific on the island. Perhaps the most intriguing group is the so-called mystery roses, whose original names and provenance are not known. Instead, these sometimes-unusual blooms have been given the name of the place or owner of the garden where they were found, and most commonly are simply labeled "Bermuda roses."

Roses have been part of the Bermuda landscape since early settlement. In 1639, a visiting Spaniard noted that many gardens were full of roses, and since then, numerous references point to the popularity of the rose here through the centuries. The **Bermuda Rose Society** (P.O. Box PG 162, Paget, PG BX, www.rosesinbermuda.com), founded in 1954, today is affiliated with similar societies in Britain, North America, Australia, and New Zealand and is a member of the World Federation of Rose Societies. Its 100 members work to encourage the cultivation of roses, conserve old garden roses, and import others suitable to the island's climate and conditions.

Society members propagate hundreds of rose bushes for sale every year and also care for several dedicated rose gardens around the island, where all varieties can be appreciated free of charge. These include the rose garden at the Bermuda Botanical Gardens in Paget; another at the Heydon Trust Estate in Sandys; and the Heritage Rose Garden at Waterville in Paget, the Bermuda National Trust headquarters. Old garden roses can often be found in sheltered church gardens, too, such as Old Devonshire Church or St. Peter's in St. George's. Somers Garden in St. George's is another showcase for almost two dozen types of Chinas, teas, and mystery roses. The flowering season for most roses in Bermuda is October-May; depending on weather conditions, some varieties bloom throughout the year.

Interestingly, through the exchange of cuttings between society members and overseas colleagues, Bermuda roses such as the Smith's Parish, Emmie Gray, Miss Atwood, St. David's, and Bermuda Kathleen have taken root around the world, including several U.S. locations: Huntington Botanical Gardens in San Marino, California; the Antique Rose Emporium in Brenham, Texas; and the Brooklyn Botanic Garden in Brooklyn, New York.

Medicinal Plants

Island folklore has enshrined the healing and nutritive value of many Bermuda plants. The practice of herbalism dates back to the colony's earliest days, including the use of poisonous species as a form of revolt by enslaved people against their owners. Nontoxic plants also fueled a plethora of uses: The large red leaves from match-me-if-you-can bushes were soaked in whiskey or vinegar and wrapped over the body to relieve measles and fevers; plantains were believed to heal sexually transmitted diseases; allspice leaves were used as antioxidants; a bath of chicory and herbs could combat eczema and diabetes; the raw pulp of prickly pears was said to stop diarrhea; and cedar berry syrup was a common cold remedy.

A small medicinal garden, planted next to the kitchen beds behind Camden House, can be found at Bermuda Botanical Gardens. Herbalist Juliet Duncan lectures and writes on the therapeutic value of local plants. Her publication, *Historic and Edible Herbs & Berries of Bermuda,* can be found at some related retail outlets, including **Brighton Nurseries** (12 Brighton Lane, Devonshire, tel. 441/236-5862, brighton@logic.bm).

ANIMALS

Like any isolated oceanic island, Bermuda is a biologist's nirvana, not because of the number of species or habitats (there are fewer than on many Caribbean islands), but for the interesting way its ecology has evolved. Separated from natural competitors and predators that wiped out mainland counterparts, numerous marine and terrestrial species that arrived in Bermuda thousands of years ago have weathered the ages and today count as precious endemics, unique to the island.

The island has long drawn scientists to its mid-Atlantic location, unique marine habitat, geological phenomena, mild climate, coral reef accessibility, and unusual forms of marine and terrestrial plant and animal life. The island lays claim to more than 8,300 known species, half of which are marine. About 3 percent are endemic. Bermuda's biologically isolated ecology has posed intriguing questions to naturalists, particularly those interested in the development and survival of endemic species.

By its very geography, separated from the mainland by vast stretches of ocean, Bermuda's biological character is unique. From its earliest days, the Gulf Stream acted as a massive conveyor belt, carrying seeds, plantlife, and marinelife to the limestone-covered former volcano; animals able to swim or fly from mainland habitats also arrived, and life gradually took root. Cut off from predators and other factors that shaped the evolution of mainland counterparts, plant and animal life, along with the habitats they clung to, survived or developed differently. Before humans arrived on the island in the early 1500s, abundant turtles, cahows (Bermuda petrels), and fish made the archipelago an idyllic natural larder. Rats and hogs arrived with the first passing sailors, who, it is believed, offloaded swine to multiply for future provisioning. Rodents, domestic animals, cockroaches, and other pests multiplied with the waves of English colonists who followed, from 1612 onward, setting loose a domino effect of natural destruction that has continued into the 21st century.

Today, Bermuda's wildlife remains under the international microscope. The **Bermuda Zoological Society** (BZS, tel. 441/293-2727, info.bzs@gov.bm, www.bamz.org) and the **Bermuda Institute for Ocean Sciences** (tel. 441/297-1880, www.bios.edu) attract world-class scientists who use the island as a laboratory for global investigations, including studies on climatological risk prediction and the use of certain species, such as sea sponges, in pharmaceuticals. The Bermuda Zoological Society also funds conservation research projects on endangered creatures such as seahorses, turtles, and toads. The Bermuda Biodiversity Project, established through BZS in 1997, has generated important baseline studies of the island's species and habitats, with a focus on those considered critically endangered. Among other aims, its scientists work to record data on caves, coral reefs, and other special habitats; define major threats to the island's ecosystems; and develop education and public awareness programs.

Birds

Bermuda's fearsome early reputation as a haunted "Isle of Devils" is blamed on the eerie cry of the nocturnal cahow (*Pterodroma cahow*), or Bermuda petrel, which populated the island in the 1500s. Sailors heard the plaintive call of the large oceanic birds and believed the island was home to supernatural creatures. Unfortunately, the endemic cahow's placid nature and lack of agility when not in flight made it so easy to catch that early colonists were able to literally pluck the birds from nests by the thousands, pushing cahows to the brink of extinction within a scant decade of their 1612 settlement.

While the cahow is undoubtedly Bermuda's most famous avian resident, the island claims 22 breeding bird species (3 of which are seabirds, not year-round residents). Migrants and vagrants bring the tally to 360 species, though only an estimated 132 are commonly seen, according to author Andre Raine in his 2003 *Field Guide to the Birds of Bermuda*. Birdwatching enthusiasts will find plenty to marvel over. The gracious longtail, or white-tailed tropicbird (*Phaethon lepturus*), is Bermuda's national bird, featured on the local quarter; it

Protecting Vanishing Species

Bermuda has a checkered past when it comes to protecting its natural heritage. Destruction of habitats and species began as soon as humans began arriving in the 16th century. The "Isle of Devils" was actually a lifesaving larder for castaways and passing mariners, who feasted on everything from turtles and cedar berries to fat petrels, or cahows, that were captured and killed to the point of near-extinction. Hogs that had been previously set ashore to multiply foraged the early forest floor, while rats, cockroaches, and domestic animals brought disease and destruction.

After settlement, legislative measures were taken as early as 1615 to control the exploitation of species such as the green turtle, and later, the native Bermuda cedar (*Juniperus bermudiana*), a staple for shipbuilding and furniture. In later centuries, cultivation, overdevelopment, and pesticide use have had a severe effect on the island's fragile ecosystem. Human efforts to intervene have more often than not resulted in a spectacular comedy of errors. Such was the case with the Jamaican anole, a lizard brought to Bermuda in 1905 to combat the Mediterranean fruit fly. The anole quickly adapted but preferred ladybugs to fruit flies, setting off a destructive domino effect. A belated attempt in the 1950s to control the lizard with the great kiskadee was similarly disastrous; the raucous birds may have nibbled on reptiles, but they also attacked the nests of bluebirds and other natives.

The Bermuda government took decisive action in 2003 to protect and restore disappearing species and habitats, passing the Protected Species Act, which created a recovery plan and made it a crime to harm or capture certain listed plants and animals. The legislation is vital to endangered species, particularly those that live outside national parks and have never been protected. Those with special status include the white-tailed tropicbird (Bermuda's graceful harbinger of spring, also called a longtail), the skink (a rarely seen lizard), the land hermit crab, and the cahow, whose fragile population is being nurtured with special nesting habitats on off-lying islands.

Hurricane Fabian drove home the importance of encouraging endemic species. After 120-mile-per-hour gales blasted the island for 24 hours on September 9, 2003, flowering trees and ornamental plants were ravaged, while areas of sturdy cedars and palmettos stood virtually intact. As residents stocked up on tarps, roof slate, and generators in the aftermath, they also began investing in more down-to-earth gardening choices: cedar saplings and palmetto berries.

The Department of Environment and Natural Resources works with resident and visiting scientists to protect island species and habitats. Successful initiatives include installing moorings at popular dive sites to minimize anchor damage on coral reefs, and erecting canisters at coastal fishing areas so that anglers can properly dispose of nylon line—a major killer of sea turtles.

Bermuda's conservation organizations actively work to protect vanishing species, manage nature reserves, preserve open spaces and landmark buildings, and educate the public, particularly students. The **Bermuda Zoological Society** (16 North Shore, Flatts, tel. 441/293-2727, membership.bzs@gov.bm) supports the Bermuda Aquarium, Museum & Zoo and related education and species conservation programs. The **Bermuda National Trust** (BNT, Waterville, 2 Pomander Lane, Paget, tel. 441/236-6483, fax 441/236-0617, www.bnt.bm) preserves historic homes and buildings, manages nature reserves, and raises funds to buy tracts of undeveloped land for public use. The **Bermuda Audubon Society** (P.O. Box HM 1328, Hamilton HM FX, tel. 441/238-8268, www.audubon.bm) keeps several nature reserves, runs birding tours, educates on birdlife, and works to protect wildlife habitats. **Greenrock** (tel. 441/747-7625, www.greenrock.org) is an energized nonprofit focused on lobbying for green lifestyles and sustainable development. **Keep Bermuda Beautiful** (P.O. Box HM 2227, Hamilton HM JX, tel. 441/295-5142, www.kbb.bm) organizes annual trash cleanups and education campaigns.

can be seen swooping elegantly from nests in South Shore clifftops throughout the spring and summer. The raucous kiskadee, whose yolk-colored chest and bossy behavior makes it perhaps the most noticeable local bird, is entertaining to watch. Pairs of melodic northern cardinals or redbirds (*Cardinalis cardinalis*) frequent gardens and parks; the male's crimson plumage with tufty crest is unmistakable, as is its repetitive trilling song (females are smaller and more brown than red, but both have red beaks). Another treat is a shy beauty, the eastern bluebird (*Sialia sialia*). The only other endemic species is the small greenish-yellow Bermuda white-eyed vireo, whose chirpy song mimics its nickname, "chick-of-the-village." Common sparrows, barn owls, mourning doves, sandpipers, finches, moorhens, herons, and numerous species of waterfowl can all be frequently spotted. Most originated from the eastern and central United States, as well as the Caribbean.

Spring and fall are the most popular birding seasons. Thousands of migratory species travel north in the spring and south in the fall in these months, either using Bermuda as a convenient stopover or wintering on the island. Migrants can be seen as early as February. The aftermath of storms and hurricanes sometimes finds more exotic species from farther afield, having been carried off course by prevailing wind patterns. After the frantic 2005 season, for example, when Hurricane Katrina wreaked havoc on the U.S. Gulf Coast, scores of large frigate birds were suddenly spotted gliding high over the island—a species rarely found in the area.

Sadly, the bluebird—which flashes vivid cornflower as it flits between trees—is becoming something of a rare treat. Sightings usually occur near shady lawns or meadow areas of quiet parks such as Devonshire's Arboretum or Ferry Point National Park in St. George's. It also feeds and nests around golf courses. Flocks of bluebirds were once common throughout the island, nesting in cedar trees. In recent decades, Bermudians have rallied to protect the declining species (an estimated 500 birds remain), which has fallen prey to domestic and feral cats, has lost vital habitat to development, and has had to compete with the more adaptable sparrow for food and nesting sites. A widespread campaign distributes wooden bluebird nest boxes, with entry holes small enough to deter larger intruders, such as the pushy starling or kiskadee. Bluebird nest boxes can be seen island-wide in gardens and parks and along trails at hotels and golf courses.

Some of the island's best bird-watching locales include Spittal Pond Nature Reserve in Smith's Parish, whose range of habitats attracts diverse species from oceanic birds to waterfowl; Hog Bay Park in Sandys, a large tract of isolated land that includes coastline, wooded hillsides, and agricultural areas; Paget Marsh, with its endemic cedars and palmettos; and the undulating Arboretum. The **Bermuda Audubon Society** (P.O. Box HM 1328, Hamilton, HM FX, tel. 441/238-8268, www.audubon.bm) leads birding field trips, including sea-watching tours, throughout the year at parks and nature reserves. Check the society's website for tour details. *A Birdwatching Guide to Bermuda* (2002), by society president Andrew Dobson, is another good source of information on Bermuda bird species.

Insects and Spiders

The island has a robust population of creepy-crawlies, with more than 1,200 insects and over 1,000 other arthropods. Some are irksome, like mosquitoes, fleas, and mites, but none are very dangerous—though one rarely seen spider, the brown widow, is venomous.

The cockroach is one of the more conspicuous local insects. Bermuda has 11 species, including the large American cockroach (*Periplaneta americana*). They're harmless and can be found absolutely everywhere—from garbage dumps to the swankiest homes, where they fly in on summer nights like a bizarre windup toy.

Bermuda's butterflies are perhaps not so exotic as those of more tropical areas, but there are some beautiful varieties that frequent flower-packed gardens throughout the island. The gulf fritillary, cloudless sulphur, buckeye, cabbage white, and monarch are all fairly common. Some 200 moths seen on the island include the great gray sphinx or frangipani hawkmoth, whose large red-and-black caterpillars feast on the fragrant frangipani trees.

Beekeeping is popular in Bermuda, and honeybees are found buzzing in gardens and park beds—though their numbers have declined in recent years along with bee populations worldwide. Delicious Bermuda honey is sold in supermarkets and at the weekly winter farmers market in Hamilton. Other common insects include beetles, wasps, dragonflies, damselflies, grasshoppers, ladybugs, church worms, and centipedes—the largest of which is the St. David's centipede, or giant centipede, which can grow to a foot in length.

Some 59 different spiders can be found on the island. Of these, the colorful, spiny-bellied orb weaver, or crab spider—beloved by children for its clown-like red spines and black polka-dots—can be seen in trees and bushes. More dramatic is the golden silk spider, or hurricane spider, a hand-size bright yellow creature that drapes diaphanous webs in woodland areas. Island folklore says that when these webs are spun close to the ground, a hurricane is imminent.

Frogs, Toads, and Lizards

Bermuda's tree frog, the common whistling frog (*Eleutherodactylus johnstonei*), came from the Lesser Antilles in the 1800s. A second whistling frog species that also arrived from the Caribbean has not been seen in recent years, and scientists believe it may now be extinct. Tree frogs are delicate creatures, less than an inch long, with large black eyes and suction pads on their toes. Hidden away in damp areas of forests or gardens during the day, they emerge on balmy nights or during rainstorms, singing loudly, their echoing call aptly described by naturalist Martin Thomas as "a bell-like 'gleep-gleep.'" It is one of the most distinctive sounds of Bermuda.

Whistling frogs are among the two amphibians and eight reptiles, all introduced species, that now inhabit Bermuda. The giant toad, also called the cane toad or Surinam toad (*Bufo marinus*), is an iconic resident of all parishes, and unfortunately often is seen splayed on the macadam as roadkill. Both whistling frogs and Surinam toads are insectivores. Declining numbers of frogs and toads

Bermuda has four common lizard species.

have worried scientists over the past two decades; amphibians are considered barometers of environmental health, as their permeable skin allows contaminants to pass through. Tissue samples of both frogs and toads indicate the creatures are absorbing significant amounts of metals, pesticides, and petroleum hydrocarbons from Bermuda wetlands. The Bermuda Amphibian Project, sponsored by the Bermuda Zoological Society, is now trying to determine the source of these contaminants and their general risks to the environment.

Four lizard species live in Bermuda, including the critically endangered skink, or rock lizard, which has been on the island so long that it is now considered endemic. The bronze skink is easily recognizable, with shiny, scaled skin and clawed feet, but its numbers have been so drastically reduced that you may never see one. Just a few decades ago, skinks were found in most coastal and wooded areas but are now confined to remote sections of the shoreline with low-lying vegetation, such as the islets of Castle Harbour or forested parks like Spittal Pond Nature Reserve. They are also found in larger numbers on Nonsuch Island. Skinks do not climb trees like other lizards; by contrast they scramble along coastal rocks or underbrush, burrowing and feeding on fruit and arthropods, including beetles, spiders, and crustaceans. The reasons for their demise are not completely known, though cats and kiskadees are considered major culprits, along with overdevelopment and the impact of humans on their habitat. Roadside trash, for example, creates lethal traps for the clawed skinks, who crawl into empty bottles and soda cans but cannot escape the slippery interiors. An education campaign funded by the Environment Ministry and geared toward educating Bermudians about skinks appears to be succeeding, and scientists hope these efforts—plus the animal's protected status, established in 2003—will help halt any further deterioration of skink populations.

Among the other three lizards, all originally from the Caribbean, is the blue-green Jamaican anole, which was brought in to control the insect infestation of cedar trees but soon moved on to other prey like bluebird eggs and ladybugs. Males put on a decorative courtship display, each extending a large orange lobe from his throat while bobbing on walls and tree trunks. The yellow-green Barbados anole, at a maximum length of 14 inches, is the island's largest lizard, and its numbers are increasing; the aggressive creature feeds on bird eggs and insects. The coppery Antiguan anole is far more shy, preferring deeply shaded areas.

Whales and Dolphins

Humpback whales migrate north to the U.S. East Coast and Canada in the springtime. Their pods can sometimes be seen from land along the South Shore on a clear day. Ecotours run by the Bermuda Institute of Ocean Sciences (BIOS), the Bermuda Zoological Society (BZS), the Bermuda Underwater Exploration Institute (BUEI), and charter boat companies take passengers out on whale-watching expeditions in March and April. Check the daily newspaper for advertisements, or the websites of **BIOS** (www.bios.edu), **BZS** (www.bamz.org), and **BUEI** (www.buei.org) for details. The **Humpback Whale Research Project** (www.whalesbermuda.com), started by Andrew Stevenson in 2007, films and gathers research on humpbacks as they migrate past Bermuda. Pilot whales, sperm whales, minke whales, and Cuvier's beaked whales are also seen in local waters. Wild dolphins occasionally are found offshore, including the common ocean dolphin, but rarely venture within the reef line to beaches or bays.

Marine Turtles

There's nothing more magical, when kayaking around West End sea grass beds or dropping anchor in the sheltered chain of bays between Great Sound islands, than hearing a turtle flipper slap the surface or catching the glint of its shell in the sunset as it dives back down again. Turtle populations are now a fraction of what they were in centuries past, before human exploitation for meat and shells devastated nesting populations, particularly those of the green turtle. Today, all species of marine turtle in Bermuda waters are protected under law.

Five species are found here; the most common are the olive-brown green turtle, which grazes on sea grass beds, and the smaller, ornately shelled hawksbill, which feeds on reef sponges. The large reddish loggerhead, which lives in the Sargasso Sea for its first years of life, occasionally ends up in coastal waters; by contrast, the deep-diving leatherback never ventures into shoreline areas, but Bermuda happens to lie on the edge of its oceanic migratory route and breeding ground. Kemp's ridley, a rare and critically endangered species usually found in the Gulf of Mexico, occasionally makes its way to Bermuda waters.

Tragically, motorboats have killed and maimed numerous turtles in recent years, though some injured animals have been rehabilitated and released back into the wild by staff at the Bermuda Aquarium, Museum & Zoo and Bermuda Zoological Society.

Sharks and Sportfish

Bermuda's waters are spawning grounds for several larger fish, including commercial species such as yellowfin tuna, white marlin, blue marlin, wahoo, dolphin fish, and swordfish, making the island a popular deep-sea fishing destination. Of all the gamefish, marlin and swordfish are the most powerful speedsters, able to exceed 70 miles per hour (faster than a cheetah). Slashing their pointed bills to stun schools of fish, they pass Bermuda on annual summer migrations.

More than 20 shark species, including tiger sharks and dusky sharks—and docile whale sharks, the world's largest at 40 feet long—have been recorded off Bermuda, though divers do not usually see them. Sharks tend to frequent the reef platform at night, though many stay in deep ocean beyond the reef line. They are rarely seen inshore or off beaches, although old or sick sharks seeking easy meal pickings occasionally have followed cruise ships into port. Shark attacks in Bermuda, however, are all but unheard of. Since 2005, the **Bermuda Shark Project** has gathered valuable data via satellite tagging of tiger sharks off the Bermuda reef platform; research to date has demonstrated the sharks, the top predator in Bermuda's marine ecosystem, routinely travel thousands of miles between the island, the Caribbean, and points around the mid-Atlantic.

Other Fish, Shellfish, and Reef Life

Bermuda is renowned for its coral reefs and abundant fish and crustacean species. More than 430 marine species have been recorded from the island, and simply donning a mask and snorkel reveals the rich diversity of fish. Spend a few hours floating over reefs, and you will discover a symphony of shapes and colors, from jewel-like wrasses and tangs to elegant blue angelfish and spotted butterfly fish, iridescent turquoise parrotfish, gliding silver barracudas, and inquisitive bee-striped sergeants major. Amid the delicate beauty of sea fans, corals, and anemones, you will frequently see trumpetfish, clown-like cowfish, moray eels (green and spotted varieties), groupers, snappers, red hinds, triggerfish, hogfish, spiny lobsters, and many more varieties.

Prized for its sweet meat, the Bermuda rockfish is a reef inhabitant and a staple of local seafood menus. The longsnout sea horse used to be another common reef-area inhabitant, but its numbers have declined recently. You may see it, tail wrapped like an anchor around seaweed or sea grasses. Sheltered bays are home to peacock flounders, odd-looking puffers, balletic squid, urchin-eating porgy, Bermuda chub, grunts, and bottom-feeding bream. Spotted eagle rays, some measuring six feet in length, make for a dramatic sight as they sweep under Flatts Bridge into Harrington Sound. And common, but no less breathtaking, are the schools of thousands of tiny "fry" or minnows, which leap in unison to create silver arcs as they try to evade predators. Fishers typically set nets to catch fry for bait.

Portuguese man-of-wars are probably the most dangerous species you'll encounter. Warnings are posted on some South Shore beaches when onshore winds are bringing in large numbers of these long-tentacled jellyfish. Look out for their distinctive blue-purple balloons, with purple tentacles attached, washed up on the tideline. Where there is one, there are usually lots more in the water, being blown in from the same high-seas area.

After a severe decline in fish stocks over the 1970s and 1980s, the Bermuda government slapped a ban on the use of fish pots, which succeeded in increasing threatened populations. Spearfishing within the reef line or with scuba gear is also banned. Lobster fishing is restricted to the months of April-September. You can see examples of most local fish species in the fascinating tanks at the Bermuda Aquarium, Museum & Zoo in Hamilton Parish.

History

Bermuda's history is the story of unlikely survival—and remarkable economic success—against daunting odds. Geography was the first immense hurdle for this tiny speck of land isolated from the rest of the world by 650 miles of ocean. Perhaps as a result of such distance from the North American mainland, Bermuda had no indigenous people; its first inhabitants were shipwrecked English colonists of the early 17th century. Although Spanish mariners discovered Bermuda more than a century before the English ever set foot on the island, it was the English who eventually claimed the island. Bermuda's destiny and heritage could have been far different had the Spanish considered the island useful enough to colonize.

How did Bermuda evolve from such a minuscule mid-Atlantic outpost into one of the world's wealthiest countries? A mixture of very good luck and islanders' ability to take advantage of any and all opportunities. Living by their wits, Bermudians dabbled in piracy and privateering, benefited from the conflicts between larger warring nations, developed successful export farming, and later traded on their small landmass's natural beauty and offshore tax laws. Bermuda's course through 500-plus years of history, from discovery through the first decade of the 21st century, was not without failures, periods of pestilence, or turbulent growing pains. But the society, economy, and standard of living that resulted are today one of the globe's most envied. Bermudians are well aware of their collective serendipity and unique identity.

THE AGE OF DISCOVERY

Bermuda's early reputation was that of a fearsome devils' haunt, likely owing to tropical storms, animal shrieks, and the necklace of treacherous reefs. Yet those who did manage to make it safely ashore were uniformly surprised by what they found: a peaceful paradise with a rich supply of seabirds, turtles, fish, fruit, and wild hogs—believed to have been set ashore by passing mariners as food for castaways. "All the island and keys are covered with cedar forests and tufted palmetto palms," noted Spain's Diego Ramirez in 1603 after his galleon ran aground. "There are great droves of hogs in the island which have overrun it and trodden wide paths like well-traveled roads to the watering places."

After Italian pioneer Christopher Columbus forged the way to the New World in 1492, numerous mariners began traveling back and forth between Europe and the Americas on state-funded voyages. It was one such captain, Spaniard Juan de Bermúdez, who happened upon Bermuda by accident in 1505 and gave his name to the island.

The Legacy of Juan de Bermúdez

Bermuda's discovery date has long been a point of intrigue and uncertainty among historians, and the man who discovered and lent his name to the island is just as much an enigma. What is known is that Spanish seafarer Juan de Bermúdez was a pioneer during the Age of Discovery, a golden era of exploration and colonization by Spain and Portugal throughout the 1500s. Bermúdez, born in 1449 in the port of Palos on Spain's east coast, came from a seafaring family. Though he did not participate in the iconic 1492 voyage to the Americas by Christopher Columbus, he was a seasoned navigator who distinguished himself even among other mariners of the time through the sheer number of his pioneering transatlantic voyages. Between 1495 and 1519, he made 11 crossings back and forth between Europe and the West Indies; in ship records, he is named in expeditions of 1495, 1498, 1502, 1503, 1505, 1509, 1511, 1512, 1513, and 1519, when he finally died in Cuba.

It was on one of his journeys that Bermúdez first spotted Bermuda and named the island—but all concrete evidence ends there. The date of the milestone is unclear, though historians have recently tried to nail it down through a process of elimination. The mystery owes much to the fact that so little is known about Bermúdez himself. Like many mariners of the time, he was probably illiterate and left no letters, diaries, logbooks, or written testimonials—at least none that have been found. Nor does there exist a portrait, written description, or any physical image of the man to whom Bermuda owes its name.

Historians in the United States, Britain, and Bermuda now lean toward 1505 as the most likely date of discovery. Using Spanish sources, experts have analyzed the dates of Bermúdez's transatlantic crossings, matching them with the voyages of one particular vessel, La Garza. It was this ship, a caravel, of which Bermúdez was said to have been captain when he sighted the island—and 1505 was the only year he sailed the vessel. A telling clue comes from a 16th-century courtier, Gonzalo Fernández de Oviedo y Valdés, who wrote the first history of the West Indies. "I sayled above the island Bermuda, otherwise called Garza," he wrote in *La Historia General y Natural de Las Indias*, "being the furthest of all the islands that are found at this day in the world." Unfortunately, although Oviedo noted Bermúdez had given his name to the island, he failed to provide a date.

Bermúdez would have been 56 in 1505, and in the prime of his career. It is thought he stumbled on Bermuda by venturing too far north during a return voyage to Europe. While Bermuda did not appear on a map until 1511, the island became a key navigational marker for homeward-bound mariners throughout the rest of the century.

Spanish and Portuguese castaways, and at least one Englishman, landed on the uninhabited island during the 1500s, but no one claimed Bermuda for another 100 years. Historians attribute the paucity of interest to the island's lack of freshwater and natural resources, compared to the allure of gold and silver in other parts of the New World. Bermuda's reef line also posed daunting navigational challenges, which, coupled with superstitions of the time, earned it the nickname "Isle of Devils." It was not until 1609 that Admiral Sir George Somers recognized the colony's potential, after shipwrecking en route to Jamestown, Virginia. Before long, the tiny outpost would become one of Britain's most valued possessions.

Although Bermúdez is not known to have actually landed, several subsequent transatlantic captains and crews did, by accident or necessity. During the 1500s, mariners usually made every effort to avoid Bermuda, the "Isle of Devils." England's maritime hero Sir Walter Raleigh noted his Spanish counterparts feared fictitious spirits and "durst not adventure [there] but called it *Demoniorum Insulam*."

"It almost always rains there, and thunder is so frequent, that it seems as if heaven and earth must come together . . . the waves as high as mountains," wrote French explorer Samuel de Champlain in 1600. Gradually, after Ramirez's account filtered back to Spain, the archipelago became better known as a useful stopover for provisions by anyone who dared land there. Bermuda was also used as a navigational landmark for ships homeward-bound to Europe; vessels would venture north from the Americas and the Caribbean until they spotted the island, then veer east, carried home by prevailing winds.

Ramirez's false assumption that Bermuda's waters were rich in pearls raised the island's allure. Yet its lack of natural resources such as freshwater or gold made Bermuda far less attractive to conquistadors of the time than the wealth-laden territories farther west. As a result, Bermuda sat virtually untouched until 1609, when the first English colonists arrived—and then only by profound accident.

THE FIRST COLONISTS

"We found it to be the dangerous and dreaded islands of Bermuda . . . the Isle of Devils, and are feared and avoided of all sea travelers alive, above any place on earth," commented Englishman William Strachey, secretary-elect of Virginia and a passenger aboard the ill-fated *Sea Venture*. The 300-ton, 108-foot vessel, flagship of the Third Supply relief fleet to Jamestown, became separated from the rest of the fleet after encountering a ferocious hurricane off Bermuda. Its crew and passengers battled the storm for several days until it drove the ship onto rocks less than a mile off the island's East End, at the point now called St. Catherine's Beach. Admiral Sir George Somers and Sir Thomas Gates orchestrated the safe escape of all 150 survivors: men, women, and children who had left behind middle-class lives in southern England to live out New World dreams.

The castaways stripped the *Sea Venture* of rigging, weapons, food supplies, and timbers, something settlers would continue to do until the wreck sank from sight many years later. They fended for themselves over the next 10 months, building temporary shelters and constructing two new ships of Bermuda cedarwood to continue the voyage they had originally planned. "The Bermooda is the most plentiful place that I ever came to, for fishes, hogs and fowl," Sir George Somers would write. After much bickering among

the group, all but three left Bermuda in 1610 aboard the newly built *Deliverance* and *Patience* for Jamestown, where the supplies they'd gathered from the island proved salvation for the American colony's starving residents. Sir George returned to Bermuda for more goods but died here later in 1610. His heart was buried in St. George's.

It was not until 1612 that England's first official settlers arrived aboard the *Plough*, after a decision by the Virginia Company to include Bermuda among its American enterprises. London-based investors, called "Adventurers," realized that the new acquisition, with its safe harbors and lack of inhabitants, might prove advantageous for their New World exploits. Sixty people arrived at Bermuda, among them a carpenter named Richard Moore, selected by the Virginia Company to be Bermuda's first governor. Bermuda was dubbed "Virginiola" and, later, the "Somers Islands" or "Summer Islands," after Sir George Somers as well as its balmy climate. The first settlement was initially called "New London," but its name was later changed to St. George's. The fact that Jamestown fell into ruin and did not endure makes St. George's the oldest surviving English town in the Americas.

The first settlers laid the foundations for a colony that would develop into one of England's key possessions over the next 400 years. They fashioned palmetto huts and dug wells, creating a community around a market square at the East End, which, despite the subtropical setting, was as English as any in the motherland. The colony's laws and government were English, along with its judicial system, Church of England religious beliefs, education methods, and loyalty to King James. Great pressure was laid on Moore and the settlers to produce riches like pearls, silk, tobacco, and ambergris (a highly prized substance derived from whales' intestines and used in medicines and fragrances) to send back to the London investors, little of which ever materialized. Instead, the Virginia Company, and later the Crown, had to support the struggling colony with constant shiploads of food and supplies for most of the century.

Ironically, Bermuda's inhabitants were restricted from becoming self-sufficient by a monopolistic regimen; they were forced to trade only with Virginia Company ships and were barred from whaling or shipbuilding. Forts and bridges were built, and the main island was divided into "tribes," or privately owned parishes, creating Bermuda's first infrastructure. But the colonists felt stifled by the oppressive rules laid down by the company, and as a result, they rebelled. Finally, in 1684, trade restrictions were lifted when the company of investors was dissolved and Bermuda became a genuine Crown colony. Commercial independence was encouraged, and Bermudians looked to the sea to forge a lucrative livelihood that would endure for the next 200 years.

MARITIME TRADITIONS

Bermuda's residents quickly forfeited lackluster farming efforts to undertake all things maritime instead. Shipbuilding, piloting, whaling, and trade with nations to the south and east allowed entrepreneurial talent to flourish in the 1700s, and the colony finally began to thrive. In an era of constant wars among European nations, Bermudian privateers had the approval of the island's royal governors to prowl shipping lanes in search of enemy vessels to capture. Many of the island's most prominent families—Frith, Trimingham, Cox, Durham, Joell—were engaged in privateering, though sometimes their attacks on foreign vessels were simply in defense of shipping interests.

Native cedar was used to innovatively craft speedy sloops that became the envy of larger maritime nations. The vessels were heavily used for seaborne commerce; of Bermuda's 8,000-strong population in the early 1700s, a third of local men were constantly at sea. Unlike refuges in the Caribbean and Far East, Bermuda never became a hotbed of pirates, though it's easy to argue that Bermudians exhibited more than a modicum

of buccaneering behavior in many of their pursuits. "Wrecking," for example, was a nefarious pastime in which islanders would lure passing ships onto reefs with strategically placed fires aimed at disorienting them; salvagers would then row out to plunder the stricken vessels. The island also boasted a handful of homegrown bandits who became notorious for committing wicked deeds in other regions.

Most maritime ventures were aboveboard, however. Salt production and trade from the Turks and Caicos Islands became a major industry for Bermudians and their ships in the 1800s. Bermudian captains would journey south for summers in the Turks, then spend the winter trading their haul of salt for grain, tobacco, or meat in American ports. Whaling was a tough but profitable enterprise of the period, one that demanded talented seamanship. Humpback and sperm whales were hunted offshore for their "sea beef," oil from blubber, and occasional ambergris.

Bermuda became a marine hub of utmost importance to the British after the empire's defeat in the American Revolutionary War stripped the Crown of a string of ports between Halifax and the Caribbean. Britain decided Bermuda was a strategic location for a Royal Naval Dockyard—a fortified harbor where the royal fleet could anchor and reprovision. Work began on the facility at Bermuda's West End in the early 1820s and continued for several years, using mostly convict labor brought from Ireland and England. Forts throughout the island were enhanced or added to over the century, and the fortified Dockyard, a penal station for 40 years, became a military gem nicknamed "Gibraltar of the West." The Royal Navy remained there until 1951.

SLAVERY IN BERMUDA

Slavery existed in Bermuda for some 200 years, beginning in the early days of colonization—when blacks and some Native American enslaved people were brought from the Caribbean and the Americas—and lasting until the Slavery Abolition Act took effect in 1834. It evolved from the insidious roots of indentured servitude into full legal enslavement. Though the culture of Bermuda slavery differed greatly from the plantation system of the Americas' sugar and cotton economies, the prejudices that allowed its existence were the same. Enslaved people frequently rebelled against their owners, staged revolts, and ran away in protest.

Bermuda's enslaved were natives of the Caribbean, Central America, and Africa who arrived at the island through various circumstances. Some were sold off by sea captains to pay debts when they made port. Most were brought from the Caribbean. Enslaved women were generally kept busy with domestic work, including the care of children of white families; enslaved men commonly worked as house servants, gardeners, or farmers. Enslaved families were housed in cottages or cellar-like quarters attached to the main houses of Bermudian estates. Enslaved people were also master artisans and crafters. Notably, many of Bermuda's ship crews were black—whether enslaved or free men, they worked in overseas maritime trade, or as pilots trained to guide ships through reef-lined channels. Sometimes, enslaved people who excelled at such work were granted their freedom in exchange. After emancipation from slavery was legally established in 1834, many formerly enslaved people continued to work in maritime trades, running their own businesses and participating in the Atlantic trade network.

In the 1700s, draconian laws were laid down to control Bermuda's enslaved people, who by then made up a third of the population. Banishment to other islands was not uncommon for certain crimes, including any form of rebellion, and men, women, and children were sold, hanged, and punished at public venues such as King's Square in St. George's.

Due to its geographical location, Bermuda was intimately tied to the transatlantic slave trade. The island's reefs are a graveyard of ships, including those of slavers traveling from Africa's Gold Coast via the infamous Middle Passage. In recent years, items found at these wreck sites have included shackles used to restrain captives on voyages and beads and other artifacts used for barter in the slave trade. Many of these are now on display at heritage institutions such as the National Museum of Bermuda, which also serves as a site on the island's African Diaspora Trail.

By the 1800s, blacks had established their own churches, graveyards, and schools, some of which were run by Methodist missionaries who came to the island. Britain abolished the slave trade in 1807, and after a massive humanitarian lobby effort by the Anti-Slavery Society, finally outlawed slavery itself in 1833. Bermuda followed suit the next year, and the island's blacks celebrated Emancipation Day on August 1, 1834. Freedom brought its own challenges, however, and blacks heavily relied on their communities' "Friendly Societies" as a social network to help raise funds, facilitate lending, and encourage education and arts. Long after slavery ended, racial friction and legal segregation continued in Bermuda until the 1960s—still a sore point in black-white relations.

BACK TO THE EARTH

Emancipation was the final nail in the coffin of Bermuda's dependence on maritime activities. The island had lost control of the salt trade in the Caribbean, along with its monopoly on the carrying trade after conflicts between Britain and America eased and North American traders were allowed back into West Indian ports. The advent of steam power in the 19th century also helped to put Bermuda's sloops out of business. When slave labor dried up, it was time for Bermudians to find another way of life.

Agriculture, long abandoned in favor of nautical pursuits, became the new focus. Progressive governors advocated that immigrants from farming societies in Madeira and the Azores revitalize local farming in Bermuda. From 1849 onward, the arrival of Portuguese, with their strong work ethic and generations of agricultural know-how, changed the face of Bermudian society and the direction of its economy. Potatoes, arrowroot, tomatoes, and the world-famous Bermuda onion fast became lucrative exports to winter markets in New York and other East Coast centers. Over the second half of the 1800s, farming drove Bermuda's fortunes. The Easter lily also became a popular crop, and springtime harvests of the waxy white bloom were shipped overseas for sale.

Farming exports began to decline at the start of the 1900s, thanks to protectionist American tariffs and new competition from mainland farmers. Exports collapsed, though small-scale sales of lilies continued into the 20th century. Once again, Bermuda needed to reinvent itself.

TOURISM TAKES OFF

The island's saving grace came in the form of tourism, as wintering Victorian visitors proved the vanguard of a whole new industry. Travel as a recreational pursuit was a fairly new idea, but the island's quiet beauty attracted artists, writers, and the rich and famous, who traveled to the island for months at a time to escape the snowbound East Coast. Mark Twain, Woodrow Wilson, Babe Ruth, Winslow Homer, Georgia O'Keeffe, the Rockefellers, and the Vanderbilts lent cachet to the tiny island that sat just a few days' steamship cruise from New York. "What a contrast to the icy mountains and valleys of drifted snow," enthused early American visitor Julia Dorr after an 1883 sojourn. Over the first decades of the 20th century, Bermudian merchants set about investing in new hotels, restaurants, golf courses, and tennis courts, and the seeds of a century-long industry—as well as a new way of life for Bermudians—were sown. The era also brought the novelties of electricity, telephones, and elevators, technology that Bermuda embraced to improve the visitors' experience.

Bermuda forged agreements with major steamship lines to bring foreigners to the island through the 1920s and 1930s, when the industry truly came of age following the close of World War I. Bermuda was marketed as an upscale paradise. During the era of Prohibition in the United States, Bermuda was "one continual carousal," according to one British visitor. The advent of air travel and luxury cruises following World War II dramatically opened Bermuda to the masses; on the island, the motor car was finally permitted for residents, and new technology like televisions, record players, and washing machines became must-haves in Bermudian homes as islanders embraced "the American Dream." Tourism would continue to drive the economy nearly exclusively through the late 1980s, when international business took over as the primary economic generator for the remainder of the century. Tourism never recovered its heyday, but today business travelers contribute heavily to overall visitor numbers.

MILITARY INFLUENCES

The British and American militaries have played a large part in Bermuda's evolution, security, and economic success over the centuries. The Royal Navy ran its business at Dockyard through the first half of the 20th century, pouring a welcome sum into the island's coffers. British military forces operated island defenses during both World War I and II, though an attack on Bermuda never came. Bermuda's own militia groups, divided by race, also took part in fighting overseas in both conflicts. In World War II, some 500 local men and women left the island to join British, American, and Canadian forces in fighting around the world. Bermuda became a bastion of Allied defense in these years also, when the government signed a 1941 deal to provide the United States with 99-year leases for two base lands—one in the East End, the other in Southampton. A massive land reclamation project by the U.S. Army created a military airfield and naval base in these areas. Antiaircraft artillery were installed, and antisubmarine patrols used the island as a base from which to scour the Western Atlantic. Bermuda also became a headquarters for the British Imperial Censor in the war years, as "censorettes" intercepted coded Nazi messages.

After the Royal Navy and British Army garrison pulled out of Bermuda in the 1950s, the American and Canadian militaries continued to operate from the island. During the Cold War, Bermuda became a refueling station for U.S. nuclear bombers, and U.S. forces carried out aircraft missions from the island. Americans remained on the island until budget restrictions forced the bases' final closure in 1995.

TURBULENT TIMES

Despite its peaceful facade, Bermuda has suffered its share of social and racial conflicts. In the 20th century, women led a decades-long campaign for equality, seeking specifically the freedom to vote. Suffragettes, like their American and British counterparts, held rallies, marches, and protests in a bid to force lawmakers to grant them voting rights, which, in an archaic island system, were restricted to male owners of land of a certain value. While British women won suffrage in 1919, their Bermudian sisters had to battle old-fashioned notions for another quarter of a century. When island women finally won their fight in 1945, their victory opened the door for universal adult suffrage in Bermuda later in the century, though black Bermudians had a long fight for full social and economic equality ahead of them.

The first labor union, formed by black teachers in 1919, was the vanguard of a bitter civil-rights struggle that would last many decades. Activists, including labor hero E. F. Gordon, spent the 1950s and 1960s agitating for change, inspired by the rhetoric of Malcolm X, Martin Luther King Jr., and the black civic-lobby campaigns in Britain and North America. Bermuda's white establishment continued to hold the bulk of power and wealth, and black resentment built to a boiling point. The black-led Bermuda Industrial Union took shape in the late 1940s, representing the rights of mostly black blue-collar

workers for the next several decades. In 1959, blacks staged the "Theatre Boycott," a successful stand against racial segregation in cinemas, which also spread to restaurants, hotels, churches, and schools. As a direct result of the protest, discriminatory racial practices gradually ended, and blacks finally won the right to vote in 1963. However, black Bermudians continued to be largely shut out of economic power-sharing until the 1980s and 1990s.

Riots in 1965 and 1968 underscored the racial unrest, as did the violent upheavals of the 1970s, when Governor Sir Richard Sharples and his aide-de-camp, Hugh Sayers, were assassinated in 1973 on the grounds of Government House. Two black Bermudians were convicted and hanged, sparking an overflow of racial tensions in the form of violent street riots in 1977, and British forces were brought in to quell the disturbances. Capital punishment remained on the island's law books until 1999, though no one was ever hanged again.

The national crisis took a toll on Bermuda—financially, and in far more lasting ways—but change, while slow, did result, along with government promises to heal the island's social wounds. Royal commissions looking into the unrest pointed to gross racial inequality and recommended better housing, education, and more support for black businesses. Bermuda evolved into a more democratic and inclusive society, though members of the black community argue that it will take many more decades to achieve true economic equality.

MODERN PROSPERITY

From the 1980s until the global recession of the late 2000s, Bermuda enjoyed economic boom years fueled by international business, and to a far lesser degree, tourism. A six-year economic downturn was followed by recovery in 2014-2015 that saw gross national product return to positive growth. Overall, the island has been able to retain an enviable standard of living, with per capita income—in 2015 per capita GNP tallied $96,000—ranking among the world's highest, according to the World Bank. Bermudians of different races and backgrounds travel overseas frequently; attend top universities in the United States, Canada, the United Kingdom, and elsewhere; and benefit from Bermuda's need for highly skilled labor in the island's law firms, accounting practices, banks, insurance brokerages, and reinsurance, fund, and trust companies, among other fields.

As an international financial center that has won respect from global regulators, Bermuda plays an important role in worldwide economies. Yet, beyond business, Bermudian professionals scattered around the globe also achieve success in other careers, from British Premier League soccer to music and medicine. While social pressures continue—ironically, some of which are aggravated by the island's own success—the island prides itself on being a progressive, peaceful, and stable democracy.

Government

Politically stable and mostly self-governing, Bermuda has the oldest Westminster-style government outside Britain. Established by the island's English governor and colonists in the 17th century, the first legislative assembly met on August 1, 1620; among the 15 laws passed in its inaugural session was a ban on "idle and unprofitable persons" being shipped to the colony—a credo that has paved the way for Bermuda's capitalistic pursuits ever since.

One of the last remaining British Overseas Territories, Bermuda nevertheless manages most of its own affairs—including the passage of all laws. Despite the island's significant autonomy on national matters, the Queen of England remains the titular head of state, and responsibility for Bermuda falls to the Foreign & Commonwealth Office in London, which appoints a resident governor, approved by the queen. British diplomat John Rankin began his tenure in December 2016. As the Crown's voice on security, defense, and international issues, the governor—who lives in Bermuda at Government House, a grand rambling old property with a towered mansion on the North Shore in Pembroke—acts as a liaison between the Bermudian and UK governments. He also appoints the judiciary and police service, though these positions are really selected by the government; the governor's signature, over the last century at least, has been nothing more than a rubber stamp.

While many of the governor's day-to-day duties are purely ceremonial, he is a key diplomatic figure as a go-between for Bermuda and London.

Bermuda participates in the United Nations through British delegations, and the Bermuda government is consulted on all international decisions affecting the island—though relations between Government House and the perennially pro-independence Progressive Labour Party (PLP) have been frosty at times. Bermuda's interests in the United States are represented by the United Kingdom via its Washington DC embassy and a Bermuda government DC office, but the U.S. Consul General in Bermuda is also very active in the area of United States-Bermuda diplomacy. Mary Ellen Koenig, a career diplomat in the U.S. Foreign Service, has held the post since 2015.

For almost a half-century, the island has had an elected government formed under a two-party system. The Bermuda Constitution was drawn up on June 8, 1968, and updated in 1989 and 2003. In the Westminster tradition, the government is three-pronged, with executive, legislative, and judicial branches. The executive hierarchy is headed by the Queen of England, whose role is carried out by the governor; the governor is followed by a premier—leader of the party winning the most seats in a general election—and an 11-member cabinet nominated by the premier from among members of parliament. The 36-seat Legislature or Parliament has two legislative chambers: the House of Assembly, whose members are chosen by eligible voters in general elections held at least every five years, and the appointed 11-member Senate, or upper house of Parliament. All laws must be passed by the House of Assembly and approved by the Senate and the governor. The Senate's members, who represent political parties or are independent, are named by the governor, the premier, and the leader of the opposition.

Bermuda's legal system is its own, dating to 1612, though it is based on English common law. The judiciary, which enforces laws, is three-tiered: Magistrates Court, or lower court, rules on lesser criminal offenses; Supreme Court, or high court, decides more serious criminal cases, as well as civil issues; and the Court of Appeal hears appeals of Supreme Court decisions. Judgments have the right of final appeal to the Judicial Committee of the Privy Council in London. A chief justice, appointed by the governor, heads the Supreme Court, where English tradition goes full-tilt with judges in robes and powdered wigs. All judicial entities are based in Hamilton, with the largest Supreme Court room and the House of Assembly occupying separate floors of the Sessions House on the hill overlooking Parliament Street. The Court of Appeal sits here also. Magistrates Court is just down the block, in the modern Dame Lois Browne Evans Building on Court Street. A Commercial Court, a division of Supreme Court, sits inside the Ministry of Finance in the Government Administration Building on Parliament Street, opposite the House.

The political parties represented in Parliament are the Opposition One Bermuda Alliance (OBA) and the governing Progressive Labour Party (PLP). The PLP returned to power in a decisive 24-12 election victory in July 2017, after a five-year term by the OBA. Bermuda's government is the island's largest employer, with an estimated 15 percent of the population working in its various ministries and departments.

Bermuda has nine parishes—St. George's, Hamilton Parish, Smith's, Devonshire, Paget, Pembroke, Warwick, Southampton, and Sandys—each further divided for electoral purposes into 36 single-seat voting districts (Pembroke North, Devonshire South, etc.) that each elect a Member of Parliament (MP). These constituencies measure roughly half a square mile and hold about 1,000 voters each. The Corporations of Hamilton and St. George's largely run the affairs of their respective municipalities, based in Pembroke and St. George's, and parish councils act as local advisory groups. All Bermudian citizens over the age of 18 have the right to vote.

British-style pomp and pageantry accompany the official convening of a new Parliamentary session every fall (typically November, as MPs break for three months over the summer). MPs decked out in lounge suits and Ascot hats ascend the steps to the Sessions House for the reading of the Throne Speech—a rundown of the government's policy plans for the coming year. Visitors can visit Parliament every Friday when in session (upstairs in the House, at Parliament St. and Church St.) to watch island politicos harangue each other over issues ranging from serious (gang violence, government debt, poor public education standards) to purely trivial (whether to allow personalized vehicle license plates). In a society where appearance tops nearly all else, the latter motion was easily passed.

POLITICAL PARTIES

Although it went 35 years without winning an election, the **Progressive Labour Party** (www.plp.bm) is Bermuda's oldest political party, formed by black activists in May 1963 with a mandate to improve quality of life for the island's blacks. While its socialist-leaning platform called for better health care, education, and housing, the PLP's main target was electoral reform and the eradication of racial discrimination. Until the late 1960s, voting rights in Bermuda were restricted to property owners, which eliminated the majority of the black community, as well as most women of both races.

Equal voting and universal adult suffrage finally came about on May 22, 1968, when Bermuda's first election was held. The now-defunct United Bermuda Party, founded in 1964 and loosely based on the British Conservative party, formed the first government under the island's new constitution, winning 30 of 40 seats. The party held on to power for eight successive electoral victories, finally losing to the PLP in 1998 in a landslide 26-14 defeat. With a founding power base of old-family white merchants, the UBP was long perceived as a party dedicated to representing the interests of Bermuda's whites; indeed, Bermudians only half-jokingly refer to the virtual "cabinet meetings" held in the Royal Bermuda Yacht Club, a whites-only male bastion comprising Front Street's "Forty Thieves"—wealthy shopkeepers who shaped the island's destiny. Such history proved hard to shake—despite the fact that in later decades the party's ranks were bolstered by middle-class blacks, women, and conservative Portuguese, and two of its leaders were black. In 2011, an unpopular UBP was finally forced to merge with the Bermuda Democratic Alliance, a new party composed of many UBP defectors. The new entity relaunched as the One Bermuda Alliance, or OBA (www.oba.bm).

Given the emotive path of party politics, the PLP's decisive 1998 victory, which claimed 54 percent of the popular vote and catapulted the party into power for the first time, was a euphoric milestone for Bermuda's 60 percent black majority population. The election result also won support from whites who believed democratic change would help heal long-held racial frictions. Yet, under four successive leaders, the PLP government was increasingly criticized by both whites and blacks for overspends that pushed up the island's national debt. The PLP was reelected in 2003 and 2007, but in 2012 lost to OBA supporters anxious for an economic turnaround amid increasing job losses and an elongated recession. The OBA helped spur gradual economic regrowth, with fiscal policies geared to encouraging foreign exchange and trimming debt, including a civil-service hiring freeze. It also ended restrictive immigration policies such as six-year term limits on work permits that had been highly unpopular in the international business sector, and created two private-public agencies: one to run tourism, the other to pursue proactive business development for the island. Winning hosting rights of the 2017 America's Cup sailing regatta for Bermuda was another major achievement that helped spur infrastructural investment in new hotels, superyacht marinas, and public works.

Yet, despite economic gains, the OBA lost public support due to being widely perceived as lacking collaborative politics or public engagement, and being particularly out of touch with working-class Bermudians. A highly controversial new airport project (that eventually went ahead) and proposed immigration and citizenship reform led to public protests and marches through the City of Hamilton, with one incident culminating in police officers using pepper-spray to disperse a standoff outside Parliament. That, coupled by a slicker, more cohesive PLP election campaign with a digital prowess that attracted many new, and younger, voters, resulted in a decisive change of government in 2017. Thirty-eight-year-old David Burt, a George Washington University graduate, entrepreneur, and father of two, was sworn in as Bermuda's youngest Premier.

Bermudians love talking politics, and everyone from the multinational CEO to the taxi driver has a viewpoint, which they usually are more than eager to share. Tune in to Bermuda talk radio daily to hear what Bermudians feel about the issues of the day. Gang crime, affordable healthcare, sustainable utilities, and systemic problems in public education continue to be the most substantial national problems facing the government.

THE REGIMENT AND POLICE

As a British territory, Bermuda's security is the domain of the United Kingdom in the event of serious civil disturbances, terrorism, or other external factors. When street riots erupted in 1977, for example, Britain jetted in 250 Royal Regiment of Fusiliers soldiers, who quickly put an end to the visible chaos. Similarly, Scotland Yard police officers are sometimes called upon to investigate serious crimes on the island.

In most circumstances, however, the island's part-time army and police forces handle internal security issues. Since its establishment in 1965, the 600-strong Bermuda Regiment has held a mostly ceremonial role, marching with its Band Company and Corps of Drums in "Beating the Retreat" displays and other traditionally British events, such as the Queen's Birthday Parade, Remembrance Day, and Parliament Throne Speech. One area in which it has been more hands-on is hurricane relief after debilitating storms; inshore maritime patrolling is also proposed as a useful role in the future. Its policy of conscription—under which males ages 18-25 were recruited for three years of compulsory part-time service—was discontinued in 2014, and was to be official ended under the PLP government elected in 2017. With the governor acting as commander-in-chief, the battalion currently has 27 full-time staff, and service is voluntary. Back in the 1960s, the regiment's inception brought an end to racial segregation of local forces by amalgamating a white rifle corps and a black militia. Today, it is affiliated with Canada's Lincoln & Welland Regiment, as well as several in the United Kingdom.

The Bermuda Police Service, established in 1879, has nearly 500 officers, including plain-clothes detectives, marine patrols, and narcotics and forensics teams. Headquartered in Prospect, Devonshire, ever since the British Army garrison withdrew in 1958, the police force has stations in Hamilton and Somerset, as well as at the airport and marine detachments in Hamilton.

As gangs and gun crime increased through the 2000s, some Bermuda Police units on patrol began carrying guns for the first time. By contrast, their old-time ties remain steadfast; officers sometimes wear traditional British "Bobby" hats—to the amusement of North American visitors—as well as flat-capped versions, with both caps emblazoned with the force's silver crest and royal cypher. One of the island's most photographed sights is the Front Street "Birdcage"—a blue-and-white-spoked kiosk in the center of the road at Heyl's Corner, near the Queen Street junction, where an officer is occasionally posted to direct traffic, and also to pose for innumerable snapshots.

Economy

If Bermuda's wealth of past centuries was generated in large part by pirates and privateers, today's pursuit of capitalistic rewards from these 21 square miles is no less ambitious. Bermuda's per-capita GDP sits at around $96,000, and it remains a society of entrepreneurial spirit; islanders, no matter their job field, are ever ready to grasp shifting opportunities or run with a good idea. Necessity is the mother of invention, however, and much of that motivation comes from the fact that island life is comparatively expensive, with restaurant tabs, groceries, rent, retail, and transport generally costing more than in mainland centers. Practically all goods must be imported—food, clothing, household wares, animals, machinery—and prices reflect high government customs duties, pushing the cost of living in Bermuda to among the world's highest. That is despite the fact Bermuda has no traditional sales, income, or capital gains taxes, though the government levies a payroll tax split between employer and employee that slides between about 6.5-19 percent, depending on salary range and annual company payroll.

Bermuda's economy in the second half of the 2010s is on the rise, thanks to inward investment, new high-end hotels and corporate startups, a comeback by tourism, and gradual quarterly and year-on-year GDP growth. Some of that positive momentum is attributed to the 35th America's Cup, the historic sailing regatta held successfully in Bermuda's Great Sound in May-June 2017. The event, and its two-year run-up, attracted new residents (including the AC25 teams, their families, and big-brand sponsors), brought in thousands more visitors, and focused unprecedented media attention on the island via global media coverage. An impact study post-event found Bermuda's winning bid to host the Cup, along with a World Series qualifier in 2015, generated $250 million of economic activity and projected a further $90 million in legacy tourism.

It was a much-needed boost for Bermuda's economy, which continues to recover from a five-year recession that began in 2008 and brought a sobering end to decades of boom times. Through the late 1970s to the 1990s, the island had enjoyed a near-constant influx of capital-rich companies, and tourism hit its peak, fueling unbridled GDP and job growth. When the downturn came, the economy suffered sharp declines in international business, hotel and restaurant spending, and construction, and Bermuda's population lost an estimated 2,000-5,000 (mostly foreign) residents. By 2014, things had stabilized, and foreign investment gradually began to return. GDP growth by 2017 was on the rise, up 1.6 percent in the first quarter, with the international business sector remaining the primary driver of GDP, while tourism accounted for about 5 percent, but had a larger share of employment.

Bermuda's national debt—estimated at $2.5 billion by mid-2018—together with its annual servicing costs, remain a critical economic concern, outstripping other government expenditures. Austerity measures and stimulus initiatives, such as America's Cup, were the focus of five years of One Bermuda Alliance government; the new Progressive Labour Party administration elected mid-2017 pledged to keep economic growth atop its agenda, including support of international business, as well as diversification efforts to create more opportunities for working-class Bermudians.

Global business based on the island directly employs over 4,000 Bermuda residents and creates another 6,100 jobs in supporting industries, driving at least 60 percent of all economic activity. Sectors that support international companies, such as financial and legal services, IT, audit and accounting firms, have fared best, even amid tougher markets. Unlike domestic businesses, Bermuda's international sector has sustained a longtime labor shortage requiring thousands of foreign workers to fill often highly specialized white-collar jobs in the finance, funds, IT, or reinsurance industries. As the market matures, however, more Bermudians are filling senior roles in the sector; a 2015 study by the Association of Bermuda International Companies (ABIC) found nearly 40 percent of "IB" companies were managed by Bermudian executives. Bermuda-based corporations also provide a wealth of opportunities for young Bermudians, from multiple-year scholarships that pave the way to attend overseas universities to summer internships, and even jobs upon graduation.

From a historical perspective, Bermuda remains a textbook example of unbridled economic success—all the more impressive given its geographic remoteness. From tobacco farming to shipbuilding to the sale of winter vegetables, the island's economy moved from one pursuit to another over three centuries. In the 1900s, Bermuda reinvented itself twice. With no exportable natural resources, no heavy industry, and few viable exports other than onions, the island cashed in on its physical beauty, launching an enviable tourism industry in the early 20th century that became

Real Estate on "The Rock"

Bermuda has long claimed some of the priciest real estate in the world, equivalent to North American urban centers such as New York or Los Angeles. The global recession of the early 2010s, which saw thousands of expatriate workers leave the island over five years, cooled both Bermuda's sales and rental markets, though these were bolstered again by corporate growth and new incorporations, plus a substantial influx of new residents during the years leading up to and during America's Cup 2017. Size, location, and amenities, as always, determine prices but "executive" rentals today start around $7,000 monthly and can go upward of $16,500, with the average executive home renting for $9,000 in 2017, according to Coldwell Banker Bermuda Realty. A single-family, two- to three-bedroom cottage routinely costs up to $1.3 million, and two-bedroom condominiums sell for around $660,000.

Condos remain popular options for Bermudians looking to buy a piece of "The Rock," and numerous landowners have cashed in to develop properties for income. Hotels have led the trend, building luxury time-share villas for foreign clientele. Foreign purchase of Bermuda property has always been restricted to highest-valued properties, starting at about $2.5 million on houses ($450,000 for condos) offered to non-Bermudians, plus license fees, closing costs, and taxes.

Real estate market ups and downs notwithstanding, the island's perennial housing crunch has caused pressures of many kinds—social, economic, environmental—as politicians grapple with how to make local housing affordable. While real estate prices may now be more achievable for young couples or fresh graduates, for example, many Bermudians still hold out little hope of buying property unless they inherit or are helped by family members.

its economic pillar. An even more dramatic economic makeover was to follow: After the end of World War II, Bermuda simultaneously began to attract foreigners interested in the island for its offshore business benefits—and a behemoth second fiscal mainstay was born. Thousands of "captive" insurance companies, trusts, mutual funds, and most importantly, multibillion-dollar insurance and reinsurance firms have flocked to the island since the 1970s, turning Bermuda into a blue-chip financial center. International business quickly surpassed tourism as Bermuda's major economic pillar, and today the island is known as a top-tier international financial center, with its commercial reinsurance sector ranking as the world's second biggest hub, after London.

The resilience of "Bermuda Inc."—as the number-one industry is dubbed—is reassuring to all Bermudians because its multiplier or ripple effect sustains an entire economy. Yet the gap between those who benefit directly from corporate largesse, and those who do not, is wide, supporting a two-class system that feeds racial rifts and social pressures.

Undereducated young black men, particularly, feel shut out of the prosperity enjoyed by the international business sector.

Such fragility of the island's economy, and the fact that the sector's labor shortage in specialized financial fields means it is largely driven by non-Bermudians, are the downsides of what, on the surface, seems a win-win scenario. But Bermudians appear determined to encourage the wave of corporate opportunity for as long as possible. Notably, the government and the public-private Bermuda Business Development Agency (BDA) are focused on supporting stake-holding companies already located here, as well as attracting more of them, with fresh investment and employees to boost the population. Created in 2013, the BDA has engaged in proactive, highly targeted business development efforts in Europe and the Americas and has been successful in wooing new companies, particularly captive insurers, global law firms, and big-name investment managers. Its focus includes newer industries too, such as life sciences, insurtech, blockchain, and other technology start-ups, intended to diversify the island's economy and keep it globally competitive.

INTERNATIONAL BUSINESS

Insurance derivatives trader. Reserving actuary. Catastrophe modeler. Structured finance credit analyst. The arcane job descriptions for international business posts on the island fill most of the employment pages in the daily paper—a visible testament to the extent of the island's economic mainstay.

What brings so many foreign companies to the island? One of the most business-benign, responsive, and agile regulatory environments in the world, along with a tax-neutral environment, political stability, and a top global reputation are the main attractions, along with a handy location that's connected to key urban centers like New York, London, and Toronto via daily direct flights. "Exempt" or "permit" corporations—which differ from local companies in that they can be owned by non-Bermudians as long as their business is overseas—are not taxed on their worldwide earnings, and there are no taxes on interest, dividends, unearned income, or capital gains. The island also offers a wealth of world-class talent, with accountants, auditors, financial advisors, IT specialists, actuaries, lawyers, brokers, underwriters, and fund administrators all working within the few square blocks of the City of Hamilton. Additionally, the Bermuda market has a sophisticated commercial infrastructure, access to major capital and world financial markets, and cutting-edge telecommunications.

The island nonetheless has been vigilant about the types of companies it allows to establish here, and as a result has managed to hone its reputation as a respected, transparent offshore financial center, untarnished by the money-laundering, corruption, or dubious banking secrecy that plague many actual tax havens. In 2009, the island became the first offshore jurisdiction to be put on the white list of the Organisation for Economic Cooperation and Development (OECD). Indeed, Bermuda

has been fastidious about signing cooperative international partnerships and tax treaties, and has adopted stringent standards to keep pace with global anti-terrorist-financing criteria and other regulatory compliance demands. However, the specter of European Union or U.S. Congressional crackdowns on offshore companies poses a persistent challenge—along with local headaches like xenophobic attitudes toward expats.

Bermuda's international business sector comprises heavily capitalized reinsurance companies (firms insuring insurance companies' underwritten loss), the world's largest number of insurance captives (offshore subsidiaries offering insurance within a parent company or mainland group), long-term (life and annuity) insurers and reinsurers, financial services firms, mutual and hedge funds, private equity, trusts and private-client business, family offices, investment management, shipping and ship-management corporations, and commercial traders. Bermuda-registered jets, ships, and yachts are key contributors to the local economy, and two public-private authorities governing those registries are counting on the momentum of the America's Cup—which brought a plethora of superyachts and private jets to Bermuda, many for the first time—to add more private vessels and aircraft to their mostly commercial rosters. Aside from registries, actual visits by superyacht traffic also generates lucrative on-island spending; a study commissioned by the Bermuda Tourism Authority in 2017 found an 80-meter vessel with guests and owners on board spends an estimated $127,000 per week in port.

The largest class of new company registrations since 2009 has been "special purpose insurers" such as insurance-linked securities (ILS) firms; these entities leverage sophisticated financial instruments like catastrophe (cat) bonds and collateralized reinsurance to allow investment in insurance risks, uncorrelated to the trends of flighty capital markets. The influx of "alternative capital" has drastically softened reinsurance and insurance

Risky Business

Bermuda engineered the unlikely pairing of scientists and insurance companies in the mid-1990s, when the Risk Prediction Initiative (RPI) was established at the East End's Bermuda Institute of Ocean Sciences. The program brings together the latest scientific findings on climate change, weather patterns, and disasters with corporations whose business it is to insure the risk of hurricanes, tornados, tsunamis, and earthquakes.

The benefits work both ways: Scientists at top institutions around the globe receive funding for research on destructive weather phenomena while sponsor companies get cutting-edge data that allows them to better value and package risk as a commercial commodity. Weather research helps provide insurers with more accurate estimates of the probability and path of future catastrophes. In return, scientists see their study help communities in practical ways. Days before Hurricane Katrina's arrival on the U.S. Gulf Coast in 2005, for example, hurricane forecasters, including members of RPI, had pinpointed its trajectory and most likely point of impact, allowing corporations and government agencies to brace for the onslaught. "Those of us watching felt an intense dread because the hurricane was by then a recipe for disaster," noted the RPI's Kerry Emanuel, a professor at the Massachusetts Institute of Technology.

Among other projects, RPI scientists have developed a computer program that uses current and past data to plot trends and make predictions on the likelihood of weather phenomena striking particular locations around the globe. Their data is also being used to assess whether such catastrophes are the result of global warming or chance. Bermuda remains a perfect forum for such synergy between science and commerce, given its reinsurance juggernaut and its location in hurricane alley. Workshops held on the island bring together the two fields to discuss their findings and new areas for further research.

markets worldwide, including Bermuda's, where close to $25 billion, or three-quarters of worldwide ILS capacity, was listed by 2017 on the Bermuda Stock Exchange (BSX), a fully electronic offshore securities exchange. All "Big Four" accounting firms—PricewaterhouseCoopers, Deloitte, KPMG, and Ernst & Young—have major offices in Hamilton. Banking, investment, and management services; media companies; computer and data consultants; and many other Bermudian-owned businesses also support and benefit from international businesses here.

Reinsurance Juggernaut

The commercial insurance and reinsurance market has been king in Bermuda since the mid-1980s and plays a vital role in the global economy by contributing billions of dollars in financial relief through claims paid after major disasters. Creating the second-largest hub after London, 13 of the world's top-40 reinsurers hold licenses on the island,

employing some 40,000 people worldwide. Bermuda-based reinsurers provide about 35 percent of capacity for Lloyd's, and since 1997 have contributed a combined $200 billion in catastrophe payouts to U.S. clients. That includes nearly 10 percent of 9/11 insured losses; close to a third of claims following Gulf Hurricanes Katrina, Wilma, and Rita; 16 percent of liabilities after 2012's Hurricane Sandy; and a quarter of damage payments following 2017's devastation in the Caribbean and Florida by Hurricanes Harvey and Irma. Ratings agencies such as Fitch and A. M. Best rate the Bermuda market well prepared to meet claims from future catastrophic events, due to its ready pool of capital and claims-paying track record.

The industry's capital strength comes via diversification: By pooling premium from around the world, reinsurers spread risk so insurers are not overexposed in any one market. The end result is lower consumer and business premiums. The concept was born in Bermuda in the mid-1980s, when a critical shortage of capacity threatened the U.S. commercial liability sector. Led by J. P. Morgan and Marsh & McLennan, some of America's largest Fortune 500 companies invested a few hundred million dollars to capitalize two new ventures in Bermuda. XL and ACE (now Chubb) covered high-severity, low-frequency losses, providing critical excess coverage. Successive waves of company formations in Bermuda followed in subsequent decades, these in response to high demand in the property-casualty sphere. So-called "big cats" were set up after Hurricane Andrew, 9/11, and Gulf Coast hurricanes, causing a paradigm shift that shaped analytics, modeling, pricing, and quantitative analysis. Bermuda's corporate environment allowed the straightforward formation of companies, quick raising of capital, and resulting speed to market.

Today, the sector is changing rapidly, and, along with recent global regulatory challenges, has experienced economic pressures as the lines between traditional reinsurance and the capital markets collide. This phenomenon has seen billions of dollars in third-party "convergence capital" pumped into the market by alternative reinsurance companies such as pension- and hedge fund-backed reinsurers and insurance-linked securities (ILS), driving down rates while allowing new capital to take on underwriting risks to diversify their portfolios. Innovative risk-transfer mechanisms are revolutionizing conventional reinsurance models, forcing established companies to evolve and changing the fundamental ways in which catastrophe reinsurance is transacted. The pace of technology—fueling insurtech, fintech, regtech, and other distributed-ledger (blockchain) derivations—also poses significant challenges for an industry characterized by legacy systems and analog, not digital, internal operations.

Islanders depend heavily on international businesses in Bermuda, particularly the reinsurance sector. An economic impact survey released by the Association of Bermuda Insurers & Reinsurers (ABIR) in 2017 found its companies contributed almost $900 million annually to the island, through a combination of business services, transport, entertainment, real estate fees, charitable giving, and payroll tax for more than 1,600 employees, of which 67 percent were Bermudians, their spouses, or long-term residents. Together with captive companies, life and annuity insurance, and ILS, there are more than 3,000 insurance-related jobs on the island.

Companies stoke the economy in other ways, too, supporting nonprofits, such as museums and art galleries, and funding social programs like summer camps and health and housing initiatives. The good news for Bermuda is that although perennial problems such as work-permit controversies and U.S. tax crackdowns—plus the politically divisive ramifications of independence from Britain—have the potential to drive international business to competing jurisdictions like Switzerland, Dubai, Dublin, or Singapore, the future for now appears to be business as usual.

TOURISM
Golden Years

Missionaries and military officers were Bermuda's first visitors, their impressions of the island ranging from euphoric descriptions of an earthly paradise to indictments of a disease-ridden backwater. It was not until the late 19th century that the concept of travel as "vacation" was born. It took the 10-week winter sojourn of Queen Victoria's daughter, Princess Louise, in 1883, to officially launch tourism in Bermuda. Following glowing media coverage of her visit, America's elite—politicians, socialites, artists, and writers—began to travel to the island to escape North American winters. Woodrow Wilson, Rudyard Kipling, Mark Twain, and Frances Hodgson Burnett were among the most celebrated early visitors, and as hotels and clubs sprang up to accommodate tourists like them, Bermudian officials marketed the island as a lotus land for wealthy urban Americans. In 1911, the first guidebook extolled the offerings of Bermuda as "Nature's Fairyland" and the "Isles of Rest"—euphemisms that fixed the island in foreign imaginations as a romantic escape from the real world.

That image—of candy-pink cottages, blossom-sprinkled lanes, and private azure bays—has been Bermuda's calling card ever since, a magnet that made the island the private playground of the super-rich and gradually built a significant industry. The timing was perfect, as Bermuda desperately needed an economic lifeline. Agriculture in the early 1900s was starting to wane, and the chance for a makeover through tourism was welcomed. Early visitors attended garden parties, dances, and military displays, traveling around by bicycle or horse-drawn carriages on unpaved roads (cars were banned until after World War II). Croquet, tennis, and golf became popular, as well as the popular new pastime of swimming.

Gradually the island became both a winter and summer resort, with ocean liner service to and from the U.S. East Coast, whose residents made up 85 percent of the trade. A steady influx of year-round visitors began to pour into the island. Critics worried the influx would spoil Bermuda's quaint character, but there was no stopping it. Between the two world wars, the tourism industry became more developed, and Bermuda's appeal, especially to the glitterati, grew. Visits by Vincent Astor, William Vanderbilt, Charlie Chaplin, and playwright Eugene O'Neill underscored the island's self-perpetuated image as a place for the rich and famous.

Tourism's heyday came in the post-World War II years, thanks to the new civilian airport, built during the war by the U.S. military. The airport opened the island for the first time to large numbers of mainstream visitors. Bermuda was no longer the realm of the elite. The island had modernized too, allowing private cars and investing in large new hotels. By the mid-1960s, some 200,000 visitors were traveling to the island annually, including many thousands on cruise ships during the summer season. The industry's golden years throughout the 1970s and 1980s saw that figure catapult to a peak of 630,000 in 1985. Tourism employed thousands of Bermudians

and represented not only the country's economic lifeblood, but also its sense of identity and national pride.

Rising costs and competing destinations, especially bargain resorts in the Caribbean, triggered a slow but steady slump in the industry through the 1990s and turn of the millennium, spelling the death of several major hotels. Some went bankrupt; others were sold and leveled to make way for corporate offices and condominiums.

Recent Developments

Visitor numbers began to recover in the 2000s until the global recession of 2008. After ups and downs since then, the tourism tide appears to be finally turning—with consecutive years of rising visitor numbers. A record number of visitors, 693,000, traveled to the island in 2017. The upswing over consecutive recent years includes a younger demographic, airline seat capacity growth, and major sports tourism events. Also driving fresh hopes for tourism's rebirth is the advent of several new brand-name hotel properties.

Positive developments are happening at existing Bermuda hotels too. The boutique Rosewood Bermuda (on the historic former Marriott Castle Harbour property in Tucker's Town, St. George's) came out of receivership in 2017 after being sold to Miami-based Gencom, which promised a further $25 million investment in the property. The Bermuda-based Green family completed a $100 million upgrade of the Hamilton Princess in 2017. The Greens also developed the former Sonesta site on the South Shore as a beach club for Princess guests, with restaurant and tennis courts. Notably, they also announced plans in late 2017 for a 9,500-square-foot casino at the Princess; pending licensing, the Hamilton Princess Casino would be Bermuda's first gambling establishment, opening the door to what some believe could be a lucrative new trend that could grow jobs and reinvigorate tourism.

Fresh energy was stoking Bermuda tourism's revival even before the America's Cup.

The Bermuda Tourism Authority, created in 2012 as the official destination-marketing organization for the island, has focused on developing home-grown ideas by Bermudian entrepreneurs, overseeing the vacation rental market, encouraging group travel, superyacht tourism, and a "beach economy," reaching out to a younger visitor demographic with high-energy outdoor activities, and generally promoting Bermuda more robustly, particularly via digital channels. Its efforts have paid off: vacation air arrivals were up 17 percent at the end of 2016 (cruise passenger arrivals grew 5 percent), with more than three- quarters of growth found in the under-45 age bracket.

Tourism remains Bermuda's second-largest industry, after international business, and to a large extent both are codependent on each other. Increasing numbers of business conferences on the island attract attendees who need accommodations, attractions, as well as visitor-geared recreation, and many return on vacations with their families.

Modern Tourism

Most of Bermuda's 646,000 annual tourists in 2016 were cruise passengers (61 percent in 2016), followed by air arrivals (38 percent), and travelers aboard yachts (1 percent). The majority of visitors generally hail from the United States (86 percent of cruise passengers, and 75 percent of air arrivals), with lesser numbers from Canada (4 and 10 percent, respectively). The rest are made up of visitors mostly from Britain and other parts of Europe.

Generally, Bermuda visitors of all nationalities are affluent (making at least $100,000 a year) and many are repeat visitors. The island has always enjoyed a solid market of Bermudaphiles who come year after year for decades. Leisure travelers make up 67 percent of air arrivals, business visitors 18 percent, and those who come to visit families and friends who live and work on the island account for 13 percent. Shopping, soft adventure, cultural pursuits, and the more typical beach experience have long been the norm.

In recent years, air connections to U.S. East Coast cities has improved, with American Airlines connecting Bermuda to Philadelphia year-round in 2016, and JetBlue increasing service to and from New York. Having evolved from a winter resort to a midsummer escape in the 20th century, Bermuda is today a year-round destination challenged to offer attractions and events that appeal to visitors looking for more than sunburns and rum swizzles.

In the past few years, Bermuda has focused on developing bespoke cultural, experiential, events-oriented tourism. Sports tourism is also on the upswing; in addition to the America's Cup, for example, the island is attracting big-name events such as the International Triathlon Union World Triathlon Series (2018-2020). Outdoor markets and other events help bring a buzz to the UNESCO World Heritage Site of St. George's. At the island's other end, the handicrafts of Bermudian artisans—including cedarwork by inmates at the nearby prison—are sold at weekly Heritage Nights that showcase everything from cricket to gaming. North Hamilton has also caught the celebratory spirit, holding occasional street festivals where local cuisine, games, and music create a family atmosphere. And the City of Hamilton's Wednesday Harbour Nights through the summer months have evolved into an impressive showcase of Bermudian entrepreneurship.

Indeed, islanders are being encouraged to pitch their ideas for innovative new tours, activities, and events to appeal to visitors. Ecotourism is another facet of the industry with largely untapped potential, though there has been growing interest in activities such as whale-watching trips, reef snorkeling, birding tours, and other outdoor pursuits.

People and Culture

Bermudians grapple with their national identity, which, combining British colonialism, American capitalism, West Indian roots, and dashes of Portuguese and Native American culture, is sometimes incredibly difficult to pin down. Aside from the complicated ethnic and cultural mix, there's the deeper question of how to characterize islanders as a people—stuck somewhere, physically and philosophically, between the sophistication of the world we belong to and the insular self-complacency engendered by living on a remote island.

If generalizations can be made, Bermudians represent a rather quirky combination of small-town vice (islanders love nothing better than to gossip, and everyone knows everyone) and cosmopolitan sophistication (most have traveled overseas, many have attended well-known colleges and universities). As survivors in the broadest sense—of the sea, of hurricanes, of economic fragility and an unlikely history—Bermudians have evolved as an enigmatic and sometimes contradictory breed, both greedy and freely giving, open-minded and terribly bigoted, standoffish and disarmingly friendly. They are also an assimilation of many people and cultures over the centuries, creating a diverse society.

The perennial debate over political independence has strong social overtones for Bermudians as a people. If we cut our ties to Britain, do we lose or gain? Would Bermudians then have a stronger sense of identity? Can such a small society so far removed from others make it alone . . . and should we try? While many Bermudians would gladly keep hold of the motherland's apron strings, others feel ready to take the leap. Whatever's decided, it's fair to say that the Bermudian character—stoic, proud, ultimately charming, and resilient through many storms—will remain intact.

DEMOGRAPHICS

From its earliest days, Bermuda has been a home to immigrants. Unlike many Caribbean nations, there were no indigenous people when the first English colonists arrived in the early 17th century, likely due to the island's isolated position in the mid-Atlantic. Since then, empire-building, more than two centuries of slavery, and labor shortages have brought waves of immigration to the island—notably large numbers of British whites, West Indian blacks, and Azorean Portuguese. The official language has always been English, though Portuguese is spoken within a limited community.

According to the 2010 census, the population stands at roughly 64,000, of which 60 percent is black. Sixty-seven percent of the population is Bermuda-born, while 29 percent is foreign-born. UK immigrants made up 25 percent of the immigrant population, Americans 20 percent, Canadians 15 percent, Caribbean 12 percent, and Portuguese and Azorean nearly 10 percent. Until a cap on immigration in the latter half of the 20th century, the most recent immigrants were British teachers, police officers, pharmacists, and nurses in the 1950s and 1960s. Caribbean immigration began arriving en masse in the late 1890s when citizens of Jamaica, St. Kitts, Barbados, and Trinidad were fleeing economic depression. Development of the Royal Navy Dockyard demanded the region's skilled workers, and many West Indian Bermudian families can trace their roots back to this period. More Caribbean workers were recruited in the 1920s to build the Bermuda Railway, and later Caribbean police were sought to help balance the racial mix of Bermuda's police force. Portuguese have also had a large impact on Bermuda's demographics and culture since the first Azoreans were brought to the island in 1849 to revitalize agriculture. In the past 20-plus years, Bermuda's Asian- and

African-born community has developed; this is partly due to a high demand for Filipino guest workers as housekeepers, nannies, and caregivers, as well as demand for Indian, Indonesian, and Thai nationals by restaurants seeking cheaper labor than Bermudians are willing to provide. Even today, though immigration laws are far stricter, Bermuda depends on foreign labor to survive, and inevitably many expatriates marry locals and end up living on the island forever.

RACISM AND SOCIAL TENSIONS

The island's mix of races, cultures, and immigrants has not developed without bitter tensions. Slavery—from the earliest record in 1616 to emancipation in 1834—along with its socioeconomic fallout have proven the most divisive and emotionally fraught issue among Bermudians, right up to the current day. Slavery in Bermuda was domestic in nature, and very different in scale from the plantation system of the Caribbean or U.S. South—mainly because the islands had no sugarcane or cotton. Bermudian colonists used enslaved people to farm their land, crew their ships, and look after their homes and children. In a system of conflict and compromise, island whites and blacks influenced each other's lives heavily and shaped the culture and look of modern Bermuda—the generally lighter skin color of Bermudians compared to Caribbean or African blacks is an obvious example.

It took until modern times, the 1980s and 1990s, for Bermudians to start openly discussing race and racial tensions in their society. That is largely due to the fact that racial segregation here ended just a generation ago, in the early 1960s. One of the biggest issues for the black community remains the ongoing struggle to achieve economic equality, after decades in which even getting a mortgage from a white-owned bank was impossible. Racist views still exist in Bermuda, though with a large and growing black middle class, and increasing Bermudian youth receiving

higher education in multiethnic urban centers, it continues to recede. If racist sentiments are expressed, they are often subtler than in the United States. "Bermuda's blacks and whites mix very well nine-to-five, and at big community events," comments Charles Barclay, former editor of *Bermuda Business Visitor* magazine. "But among some in the older white community, there flourishes what might be described as a benign bigotry; a casual, condescending bias that one could laugh off as the folly of a fading era—were it not for the fact that they retain significant wealth and power."

Complicating the situation is the influx of "expats"—mostly white expatriate workers, many of whom are hired at higher salaries than Bermudian counterparts, black or white. Common resentment against foreign workers is difficult to separate from the issue of race, though more often than not, economic factors are to blame.

Regardless of color or salary, there is a definite pecking order in Bermudian society, according to tongue-in-cheek pundits. At the top of the heap are "Born Bermudians," though those with 300-year-old families rather than first-generation status are deemed *more* Bermudian, despite equality on paper. Next come the spouses of Born Bermudians, who are accorded respect almost grudgingly, although after 10 years of marriage, they qualify for Bermudian status. So-called "Paper Bermudians"—foreign-born individuals who have won their status, sometimes as long-term residents—are next down on the list. Finally come foreign workers, the expats. They have no voting rights, their children born in Bermuda are not granted citizenship—and they even have to stand in a different line than Bermudians at the airport when returning to the island.

Thanks to Bermuda's work-permit system—which allows one-year or three-year permits to workers in most categories, excluding key personnel at large companies—the expat population remains a largely silent one, at least publicly. Most foreign residents prefer not to speak out on issues of any kind, let alone controversial topics like race or political independence. Some Bermudians feel many foreigners consider the island a place to make money with little care for its people or culture. Yet within the corporate sector, for example, an easy gelling of local and overseas talent and socializing is the norm. As a visitor, you will mostly be unaware of such complicated social undercurrents, but they do exist and affect daily life for all residents.

RELIGION

Bermuda is often cited as the place that has more churches per square mile than anywhere else in the world, something that will readily become apparent as you spot innumerable places of worship around the parishes—from Anglican spires and Roman Catholic grandeur to African Methodist Episcopal congregations and simple gospel halls. Some churches stand on the site of 17th-century origins; others are modernist creations of the new millennium. Baptists, Seventh-Day Adventists, Christian Scientists, Lutherans, Ethiopian Orthodox, Jews, Evangelicals, even nondenominational churches—they are all well represented. The "Religion" pages in the Saturday edition of the *Royal Gazette* or the "Churches" listing in the phone book are proof of the island's deep religious roots, as well as the substantial power wielded by church lobby groups.

Visiting Bermuda's churches, either when they're empty or during services, is a fascinating lesson in local history and social studies. Most churches are open to the public at different times during the week. Check the schedules with the church offices.

LANGUAGE

As a British Overseas Territory, with 400-year-old links to the motherland, Bermuda's official language is English. Portuguese is a runner-up, as it is used or recognized by many of the population's 10 percent who trace their heritage back to Azorean immigration. As a result, Portuguese is taught in some schools and courses, and banks and public services sometimes produce signage, advertising, or instructions in both languages.

As the island's resident population grows more multicultural, one can hear any number of languages and dialects on the streets of Hamilton, from Spanish, Swedish, and Japanese to Mandarin and Punjabi. But these are a minority, and whether it be in corporate or social environments, English is the natural go-to. A small number of translation and interpreting services are available on the island; an example is **Bermuda Executive Services** (tel. 441/296-5627, www.bermudaemployment.com).

The actual Bermudian accent is unique, derived from the island's mid-Atlantic melting pot of Caribbean, English, North American, and Portuguese influences. The pronunciation and cadence of Bermudian English take some getting used to, and certain idioms are so distinctively homespun they're understood only by islanders. Many are captured in a pocket-size slang dictionary of local lingo called *Bermewjan Vurds,* by island comedians Peter Smith and Fred Barritt. First published in 1984, its perennial updates can be found in bookstores. Among the gems, "Wopnin" (what's happening?), "Greeze" (a large meal usually of the comfort food variety), and "ax" (ask).

Essentials

Transportation................. 272

Visas and Officialdom.......... 283

Recreation..................... 285

Food 291

Accommodations.............. 293

Conduct and Customs 296

Health and Safety.............. 297

Travel Tips..................... 304

Information and Services 309

Transportation

GETTING THERE
Commercial Airline

Bermuda has no shortage of direct flights from major cities on the U.S. East Coast, as well as from London and Toronto. Seven commercial airlines fly regular round-trips from 13 destinations in 2017.

Bermuda's **L. F. Wade International Airport** (BDA or TXKF, 2 Kindley Field Rd., St. George's, tel. 441/293-2470, www.bermudaairport.com) honors former Progressive Labour Party leader L. Frederick Wade, who died three years before his party formed the government for the first time in 1998. The airfield, built by the U.S. military in 1941, is located in the East End, in St. George's Parish, which is linked by a half-mile causeway to the rest of the island. It's a half-hour drive to central hotels.

Travelers flying back to the United States from Bermuda benefit from Bermuda's long amicable relationship with Uncle Sam: Since the 1970s, U.S. Customs preclearance at Bermuda's airport allows passengers to be treated as domestic arrivals once they reach a U.S. airport, avoiding the long lines at U.S. Immigration and Customs.

Construction of a new $267 million airport passenger terminal is underway, to be completed by 2020. Built by the Canadian Commercial Corporation, it will contain presecurity concessions, lounges, and duty-free shops, as well as security screening. Until then, the current terminal has several cafés, bars, and retail and duty-free shops in all departure areas, as well as on-site ticket purchase. Free Wi-Fi is offered throughout the airport's departure lounges, and powered seating allows passengers to charge electronic devices. Porters are on hand to help with luggage, and an executive lounge is located in U.S. Departures.

RESERVATIONS AND FARES

Bermuda tourism's toughest challenge has long been the high cost of air travel to and from the island. Industry officials and locals recognize cost as the biggest single hurdle to increasing visitor numbers over recent decades and have worked to find ways to bring flight prices down. The issue can be attributed to geography and supply-and-demand economics; since Bermuda is not a major urban center, airlines serving the island wield complete monopolies on the various gateways. As a result, Bermuda has become something of a cash cow for carriers; the island rates among the highest-yield destinations in the world, and the Bermuda government has to pay out in weak travel years under minimum revenue agreements with airlines.

Luckily for travelers, including Bermuda residents, more airline and gateway choices are emerging—including money-saving options. JetBlue launched increased service from New York's JFK airport in 2017, supplementing seasonal service from Boston. Discount airline WestJet has upped the competition for Air Canada, meaning lower fares to Toronto. Fare sales remain the most cost-effective way for leisure travelers to get to Bermuda, particularly in the peak summer season.

Seat availability diminishes and prices rise during the peak summer months and over Christmas, when Bermudians fly home en masse from London, Toronto, and U.S. East Coast cities. Generally, though, you will pay more April-October than during the quieter November-March off season. Midweek

---

Airlines

- **Air Canada:** tel. 441/293-1777 or 888/247-2262, www.aircanada.com
- **American Airlines:** tel. 441/293-1420 or 800/433-7300, www.aa.com
- **British Airways:** tel. 441/293-1944 or 44-844/493-0787, www.ba.com/bermuda
- **Delta Air Lines:** tel. 800/221-1212, www.delta.com
- **JetBlue Airways:** tel. 441/293-3608 or 800/538-2583, www.jetblue.com
- **United Airlines:** tel. 441/293-3092 or 800/864-8331, www.united.com
- **WestJet:** tel. 441/293-0550 or 888/937-8538, www.westjet.com

For airport information, including lost and found, call L. F. Wade International Airport (tel. 441/293-2470, 9am-5pm Mon.-Fri.). For U.S. Customs and Border Protection, call 441/293-8127. For the Bermuda Department of Civil Aviation (8:30am-5pm Mon.-Fri.) contact 441/293-1640 or bcaenquiries@gov.bm. For Bermuda Immigration, call 441/293-2542; for HM Customs, call 441/293-2424. Check www.bermudaairport.com for arrivals and departures, cancellations, and flight numbers.

fares are also less expensive than weekend options, as demand is higher Friday-Sunday, especially holiday weekends, when North American travelers tend to fly to the island for brief doses of subtropical R&R. Prices from the same city can vary dramatically, depending on all these factors. A ticket on American Airlines from New York City to Bermuda, for example, can range anywhere from $250 (during a seat sale) to well over $1,000.

The Bermuda airport's code is BDA (IATA) or TXKF (ICAO); it's the island's only airport. If you search for fares online, try checking different departure airports to win a cheaper fare. If you plan to travel from Britain and don't mind stopping, for example, fares from London via New York are sometimes cheaper than Gatwick-Bermuda direct.

You must have a return ticket to fly into Bermuda. Airlines normally will not sell one-way fares to foreign countries without proof of residency, and if you land here, you will not be permitted through Bermuda Immigration without proof of return. A valid, machine-readable passport is also required.

A $35 departure tax is charged to all air passengers to Bermuda, both visitors and residents. The charge is incorporated into the airfare and collected in advance. Children younger than two are exempt.

Two local travel agencies, both based in Hamilton, are **Travel Edge** (35 Church St., tel. 441/292-3033, fax 441/292-3205, www.traveledge.bm, 8am-5pm Mon.-Fri.) and **Watlington & Conyers Travel** (Armoury Bldg., 1st Fl., 37 Reid St., tel. 441/295-3815, http://watlingtonandconyerstravel.com, 9am-5pm Mon.-Fri.). Both are IATA-accredited agencies.

FROM THE UNITED STATES

There are five commercial airlines serving Bermuda from the United States. **American Airlines** flies direct from New York (JFK), Philadelphia, and Miami daily. **Delta Air Lines** offers daily direct flights from Boston, New York (JFK), and Atlanta. **United Airlines** has a direct flight from Newark. **JetBlue** offers daily service from New York (JFK) and Boston.

FROM CANADA

Air Canada and **WestJet** fly daily to Bermuda direct from Toronto.

FROM THE UNITED KINGDOM

British Airways flies direct to and from London's Gatwick airport Tuesday-Friday and Sunday. A British Airways Executive Club is located in the International Departures Lounge.

FROM OTHER COUNTRIES

New York, Boston, Atlanta, Miami, London, and Toronto are key cities for connecting flights to Bermuda from other U.S. and Canadian destinations, the Caribbean and Latin America, continental Europe, Africa, Asia, and Australasia.

Private Aircraft

Bermuda has seen its fair share of private jets during the 1990s and 2000s, mostly attributable to corporate traffic. Some island-headquartered companies own executive aircraft, while others opt for lease arrangements, "air shares," or other forms of joint ownership.

Noncommercial passengers are checked through Customs and Immigration in a small, separate private jet terminal at L. F. Wade International Airport in an efficient operation run by a private company, **Cedar Aviation Services** (tel. 441/232-3327 or 441/293-3892, FBO@cedaraviation.com).

A Bermudian company, **Longtail Aviation** (tel. 441/293-5971, www.longtailaviation.com) holds the only Bermuda Aircraft Operating Certificate (AOC), offering 24-7 executive charter flights aboard Bermuda-registered aircraft based on the island. Established in 1999, the company runs flights worldwide aboard its managed jets, including a transoceanic Falcon 900EX and an 18-seat Boeing Business Jet (BBJ).

Cruise Ship

Cruising to Bermuda has been a popular mode of getting to the island since the wintering elite used to journey here aboard elegant steamships from snowbound U.S. cities in the late 1800s. Today, cruise ship passengers to Bermuda are typically American budget travelers, and the season has long switched to summer (avoiding the North Atlantic's fierce winter storms—though hurricane season can still make for turbulent passages). Due to the efficiency of Hamilton-based port agents **Meyer Group of Companies** (35 Church St., Hamilton, HM 12, tel. 441/295-4176 or 441/296-9798, www.meyer.bm) and the well-organized slate of shore excursions, cruising is a good way to experience Bermuda's highlights in just a handful of days.

Cruising is popular, as it offers an all-inclusive package vacation, with transport, meals, and lodging included in a single price. Passengers sleep on board the ship during their Bermuda stopover, and most also eat on board—though flexible dine-around programs are now offered. The cruise ship industry contributes an estimated $90 million to the Bermuda economy through government taxes, on-island purchases by passengers and crew, and shore excursions.

Most excursions from U.S. ports take the form of weeklong cruises, with 3.5 days spent in Bermuda. Cruise ships visiting the island have hailed from dozens of different ports in recent years, including Baltimore, Boston, New York, Charleston, Fort Lauderdale, the Azores, Cuba, Puerto Rico, and other Caribbean islands. Of these, a few serve Bermuda weekly through the summer season, though ships and schedules change each year.

Most cruise ships visiting Bermuda berth at Dockyard's Heritage Wharf and King's Wharf terminals, built in 2009 to accommodate the trend toward larger vessels.

In 2016, a total of 398,000 cruise ship visitors traveled to Bermuda, 86 percent from the United States. Regular contract ships included: *Summit* from Cape Liberty, New Jersey (Celebrity Cruises, www.celebrity.com); *Explorer of the Seas* from Cape Liberty, New Jersey, and *Grandeur of the Seas* from Baltimore (Royal Caribbean International, www.royalcaribbean.com); and *Norwegian Breakaway* from New York and *Norwegian Dawn* from Boston (Norwegian Cruise Line, www.ncl.com). Ships such as *Veendam* (Holland American Line, www.

hollandamerica.com), along with cruises by the Premium Ocean Cruises line, Luxury's Regent Seven Seas Cruises and Silversea Cruises, MSC Cruises, Princess Cruises, and Carnival Cruise Line were all scheduled to make occasional visits with smaller ships, docking in Hamilton or St. George's.

Numerous other cruise ships, many of them European vessels sailing transatlantic voyages or 10-day or two-week excursions to or from the Mediterranean, schedule briefer stops at Bermuda, typically a one-day or overnight call. These occasional visitors have also included ships of American lines. For updated cruise schedules, with information on specific ships and ports of call, check with the **Bermuda Maritime Operations Centre** (www.marops.bm or www.marine-andports.bm) or contact **Bermuda Tourism Authority** (tel. 800/237-6832, www.gotobermuda.com).

Regularly visiting cruise ships arrive in Bermuda on either Monday or Tuesday morning and depart on Thursday or Friday afternoon. Technology has automated the Customs and Immigration checks; these departments receive the passenger manifests in advance and electronically review them before ships make port. Upon the ship's arrival, Customs officials board for a 30-minute inspection process, including a walk-through with drug-sniffing dogs, before passengers are free to go. Passengers need their ship's identity card—also usable as a credit card and cabin key on some vessels—plus personal ID, such as a driver's license, to reboard the ship.

Shore excursions (including golf, kayaking, snorkeling, yacht charters, walking tours, and bus tours to the Bermuda Aquarium, Museum & Zoo and Crystal Cave) may be booked online via cruise ships' websites or arranged after boarding through vessels' shore excursion desks. Alternatively, visitors can independently book tours and activities when they disembark at Bermuda, including sports or sightseeing options that may not be available on the ship's prearranged slate. If you prefer doing your own thing, this is the best way to go, but be warned: If you have not prebooked your excursions, you run the risk of sold-out tours and no available tee times.

Private Yacht

Bermuda is a strategic port for private yacht traffic between North America and the Caribbean; some 4,000 visitors arrived this way in 2016. Boats head south from all points on the Eastern Seaboard in the early fall, in preparation for key industry boat shows in St. Thomas, Tortola, Antigua, and other islands, and the start of the winter-long charter season in the West Indies. A similar migration occurs in the spring, when yachts return en masse to North American harbors from Florida to Nantucket for the summer. Bermuda is a convenient halfway point on both annual journeys for refueling, provisioning, making repairs, and taking on crew.

The America's Cup in 2017 attracted unprecedented superyacht traffic to several new marinas around the island, and Bermuda plans to use that momentum to keep megavessels returning. Hundreds of yachts descend on the island for international races held between May and July, either annually or every other year. These include the Charleston Bermuda Race (Charleston, South Carolina, to Bermuda) in May of odd years; the Bermuda Ocean Race (Annapolis, Maryland, to Bermuda) in June of even years; the Newport Bermuda Race (Newport, Rhode Island, to Bermuda) in June of even years, and the Marion Bermuda Race (Marion, Massachusetts, to Bermuda) in June of odd years. The Argo Group Gold Cup in October and International Race Week in June also attract scores of yachters for world-class match racing and International One Design events. Skippers of boats visiting the island during these times but not involved in any of these events should make advance arrangements for berthing and other needs.

Anyone traveling to the island by yacht needs to be acutely aware of ocean safety for the Atlantic crossing and also well attuned to the particular dangers of Bermuda's

Offshore Safety

The **Maritime Operations Centre,** managed by the government's **Marine and Ports Department** (www.gov.bm), advises all ocean-going yachts to stow the following safety equipment onboard:

- An emergency position-indicating radio beacon (EPIRB), preferably one that operates on frequency 406 MHz

- A VHF radio-telephone transceiver capable of 25 watts power output

- A single sideband (SSB) radio-telephone transceiver operating on medium and high frequencies, or satellite telephone

- An ocean-ready life raft designed to hold the total number of crew aboard your vessel, and a survival or "panic" bag containing prepacked rations and other essential items

- A radar reflector

- Parachute rockets, smoke flares, and dye markers

- Some form of auxiliary power

- Sufficient battery power to keep navigation and communication systems operating for several days to cover engine or generator failure

reef-strewn waters. Centuries of shipwrecks attest to the dangers of the area's tricky channels and necklace of reefs, which, extending up to 10 miles north of the island, are not taken lightly even by veteran mariners.

MAPS AND COMMUNICATIONS

British Admiralty Hydrographic Office charts for the Bermuda area are available from yachting supply or map and travel outlets in the United States and Canada. On the island, contact **PW's Marine Centre** (37 Serpentine Rd., Pembroke, tel. 441/295-3232, www.pwmarine.bm). All charts have been revised and electronically aligned so that satellite positions can be plotted. At the very least, all mariners should have charts depicting offshore beacons and reef areas, as well as major eastern approaches (the Narrows Channel and St. George's Harbour).

The island has one marine radio communications facility. **Bermuda Maritime Operations Centre,** which encompasses the Rescue Coordination Centre (RCC Bermuda) and Bermuda Radio/ZBR (tel. 441/297-1010, fax 441/297-1530, www.

marops.bm, INMARSAT C AOR [East] 581-431010110, or INMARSAT C AOR [West] 584-431010120). Duty officers are in 24-hour contact with the U.S. Coast Guard and other sea-air rescue centers in North America, Europe, and the Caribbean, and they maintain a continuous listening watch on international distress frequencies of 2182 kHz, 4125 kHz, marine VHF Channels 16 and 27, and digital selective call frequencies 2187.5 kHz and Channel 70 VHF.

Bermuda Radio also broadcasts navigational and weather warnings and information by voice and Navtex to an internationally published schedule. Radio broadcasts are initially broadcast on 2182 kHz and Channel 16 VHF, before switching to 2582 kHz and Channel 27 VHF. Continuous weather information is also available on VHF Weather Channel 2 (WX 02), frequency 162.4 MHz. Channel 16 VHF is reserved for distress calls, or call and reply. Be sure to stay off VHF Channels 12 (used by piloted ships), 10 (port operations), 22 (Bermuda Marine Police Section), and 70 (digital selective calling). There are no VHF radio-telephone link calls from Bermuda.

ARRIVING IN BERMUDA

During an approach to Bermuda, all vessels should make and maintain radio contact with Bermuda Radio beginning at 30 miles from the island; duty officers can assist when necessary. Buoys and beacons mark Bermuda's channels, in keeping with international marking systems. Port Hand markers are even-numbered green can buoys, which flash green when lit. Starboard Hand markers are odd-numbered red conical buoys, which flash red when lit.

Private vessels arriving at Bermuda have to obtain clearance (available 24 hours) from **Customs, Immigration, and Health** (eastern end of Ordnance Island, St. George's, tel. 441/297-1226, VHF Channel 16) in St. George's Harbour before venturing to any other part of the island. Fly code flag Q (the yellow quarantine flag) until Customs clearance is granted. The Customs boarding officer, who caters to all three departments, brings aboard all necessary clearance documents and collects a passenger tax of US$35 pp. A valid machine-readable passport is required.

ANCHORING AND BERTHING

There are safe anchorages in both St. George's and Hamilton Harbours; Bermuda Radio will provide anchorage and berthing instructions, and clearance must be given to shift berth or sail. The **St. George's Dinghy & Sports Club** (24 Cut Rd., St. George's, tel. 441/297-1612, www.stgdsc.com) can accommodate up to a dozen 100-foot yachts berthed in a Mediterranean mooring style (stern to dock), offering water, electricity, showers, laundry, Internet access, and garbage and waste oil removal. Yachts anchoring in St. George's Harbour are also offered full access to club facilities and can come alongside to fill water tanks ($0.15 per gallon). **Bermuda Yacht Services** (9 Ordnance Island, St. George's, tel. 441/297-2798, info@bdayacht.com) offers berthing and mooring arrangements along with full concierge services. In Hamilton and the West End, modern

facilities, plus water, ice, electricity, and trash disposal are offered by **King's Point Marina** (Dockyard, tel. 441/234-0300); **Caroline Bay** (Morgan's Point, Southampton, tel. 441/234-4900, www.carolinebaymarina.com), which has 2,300 feet of dock space to accommodate 30 superyachts berthed Mediterranean-style; the **Royal Bermuda Yacht Club** (Albuoy's Point, Hamilton, tel. 441/295-2214, www.rbyc.bm); **The Waterfront Marina** (96 Pitt's Bay Rd., Pembroke, tel. 441/295-1233); the **Royal Hamilton Amateur Dinghy Club** (25 Pomander Rd., Paget, tel. 441/236-2250, www.rhadc.bm); and the 59-berth **Princess Marina** (Hamilton Princess, dock manager David Carey, tel. 441/705-7431, david.carey@fairmont.com), which offers integrated pump-out facilities, custom-metered electrical service, and water distribution for vessels from 30 to 75 feet. Trash pickup can also be arranged through the Corporations of **Hamilton** (tel. 441/292-1234, docks manager Earl Francis) or **St. George's** (tel. 441/297-1532).

MARINE SERVICES AND INFORMATION

Having arrived safely at Bermuda, you will find a wealth of marine services in the ports of Hamilton, St. George's, and Dockyard. Harbour Radio can arrange for emergency repairs. **Fuel** (diesel or gasoline/petrol) is easily available at several waterfront marinas, including **Rubis Dowling's Marine** (1 Penno's Dr., St. George's, tel. 441/297-1914), **Rubis Boaz Island Marine** (Boaz Island, Sandys, tel. 441/234-0128), and **Rubis PW's Waterfront Marine** (Barr's Bay, Hamilton, tel. 441/295-3185). For bulk fuel orders, contact **Rubis of Bermuda** (tel. 441/297-1577, www.rubis-bermuda.com) to supply duty-free fuel via dockside pipeline or tank truck to its all-weather bunkering facility at Ireland Island, Sandys. Canvas repairs are done by **Dockyard Canvas Co.** (Royal Naval Dockyard, tel. 441/234-2678) and **Ocean Sails/Doyle Sailmakers Bermuda/Ocean Electronics** (60 Water St., St. George's, tel.

441/297-1008, www.oceansails.com). Rigging is handled by Triangle Rigging (tel. 441/297-2155, www.trianglerigging.com). Engine and other repairs can be handled by West End Yachts (10 Smithery Lane, Royal Naval Dockyard, Sandys, tel. 441/234-1303 or 441/703-1307, www.westendyachts.com), PW's Marine Centre (Pembroke, tel. 441/295-3232, www.pwbda.com), Bermuda Marine Supply & Services (72 Pitts Bay Rd., Pembroke, tel. 441/295-9950, www.marinelocker.bm), Anfossi Marine (17 Mill Creek Rd., Pembroke, tel. 441/292-8001, anfossimarineltd@ibl.bm), Offshore Yachting & Maintenance (83 Harbour Rd., Red Hole, Paget, tel. 441/236-9464, www.oymbermuda.com) and Mills Creek Marine (17 Mill Creek Rd., Pembroke, tel. 441/292-6094, www.millscreekmarine.bm).

Bermuda Yacht Services (Mark Soares, 9 Ordnance Island, St. George's, tel. 441/297-2798, www.bermudayachtservices.com) offers a 24-hour offshore emergency service and is also a one-stop shop sought out by visiting sail and motor yachts for arranging everything from marine salvage, towing, and yacht-sitting to fuel-brokering or provisions, plus visas, crew transfers, and work permits for technical contractors; check its website for anchorage charts, weather forecasts, and pre-arrival questionnaires for download.

The Customs clearance center for yachts on Ordnance Island in St. George's provides four-day forecast charts, tropical warnings, and Gulf Stream analysis. Pre-sail weather briefings can be booked from the Bermuda Weather Service meteorologist (tel. 441/293-5067). For emergencies in port, contact Bermuda Radio or call 911 for police, fire, or ambulance services. A detailed outline of marine regulations and resources can be found in Ralph Richardson's *Bermuda Boater,* published in 2004. The Bermuda Tourism Authority (tel. 441/296-9200, www.gotobermuda.com) also publishes a comprehensive resource booklet for private yacht travelers.

GETTING AROUND

"This is one of the last refuges now left in the world to which one can come to escape such persons," read a 1908 petition against allowing cars (and their drivers) in Bermuda. The petition was signed by Mark Twain and Woodrow Wilson, among other Bermudaphiles, who staged a successful lobby against the noisy onslaught of 20th-century transport. Alas, such quaint hopes for tranquility are long gone from Bermuda's now-frantic roads. The influence of celebrity visitors managed to keep out automobiles until as late as 1946, but since then, Bermudians have proven as hungry for four-wheeled convenience as anyone else. There are certain restrictions, including a limit of one car per household and a maximum vehicle size. Until 2017, the island outright denied car rentals to visitors, and even now they're limited to two-seater electric vehicles. Larger families or those traveling with babies or small children still face transport challenges getting around Bermuda, although public transport via buses and ferries is comfortable, safe, and mostly efficient around the major routes.

Taxis

Your first experience with Bermuda-style transport will most likely be a taxi ride from the airport. Taxi drivers have all airport flights covered, so there is rarely a problem getting a cab to where you need to go. When you exit Customs, you will be directed through glass sliding doors to the Arrivals Hall, where taxis line up outside at the curb. (If a resident is collecting you, he or she will be waving at you from the small corral at Arrivals, parked through the door from the hall on the right.) All taxis are metered; the government sets the rates, which are as steep as anything else on the island. A 45-minute ride to the hotel-peppered parish of Southampton, for instance, will set you back close to $50. A tip of 15 to 20 percent of the fare is appreciated—and expected, if there's heavy luggage to schlep. Rates are held by law at $7.90 (for up to 4 passengers) or $9.95 (5-7 passengers) for the first mile and $2.75 (or $3.50) for every additional mile. There is also a surcharge of $1 per piece of luggage. Fares are between 25 and 50 percent higher between midnight and 6am and all day Sunday and public holidays.

Bermudian taxi drivers are friendly and knowledgeable for the most part, and usually fastidious about cab cleanliness. They also have the lowdown on local politics. Some drivers are specifically registered as official tour guides (look for a blue flag atop the vehicle or in its front window, or make a special request from a taxi company or your hotel concierge). For travel to business meetings, the airport, dinner reservations, or any other time-sensitive appointment, prearranging rides hours in advance, or the night before an early flight, is advisable. Taxis can take a while to arrive for last-minute reservations island-wide, particularly when it's raining or during peak periods such as Friday-Saturday nights. If you need a taxi in parish extremities such as St. George's or Sandys, calling early is wise.

The island's taxi industry agreed to the installation of global positioning systems (GPS) in vehicles back in 2005, but some companies and cabs have since reneged. Technology, however, is gradually transforming the industry and providing efficiency and convenience for customers: increasing numbers of cabs are cashless, accepting credit cards via chip and pin, swipe, or tap technology. Uber doesn't exist in Bermuda, but the island's taxi-booking app, **Hitch** (www.hitch.bm), is popular; it uses regular cabs rather than independent drivers, but otherwise works the same way, allowing passengers to create an account, order a cab, split fares, and process transactions electronically.

If you are touring the parishes, hailing cabs along roadsides rarely succeeds, because most of the ones passing you will already be on calls. Flagging down a passing taxi in Hamilton is more rewarding, and there are also specific cab stands in the city (along Front St. and Church St. outside City Hall) and at King's Square in St. George's in the busy season. Major hotels always have taxis on hand, and Hamilton's Bermudiana Road, Bermuda's "Restaurant Row," is a sure bet for cabs on Friday and Saturday evenings.

The major cab companies include **Bermuda Industrial Union Co-op** (tel. 441/292-4476, cooptaxi@fkbnet.bm), **Bermuda Island Taxi** (tel. 441/295-4141, www.bermudaislandtaxi.com), and **BTA Dispatching** (tel. 441/296-2121, www.bta-dispatching.com). For special tours, ask for a qualified "Blue Flag" taxi operator.

Buses

Aside from perennial complaints about a few drivers' unfortunate lack of people skills, the island's bus service generally wins positive reviews from visitors and is also well used by locals, including resident schoolchildren, who can ride free. Routes cover the main roads and neighborhoods of the entire island, and vehicles are well maintained and air-conditioned. Strollers can be stowed in a rack at the front, and drivers are usually more than willing to alert you to your desired stop.

The candy-pink diesel fleet operates from the **Hubert W. "Sparky" Lightbourne Central Bus Terminal** (Washington St. at Church St., Hamilton, tel. 441/292-3851, 7:15am-7pm Mon.-Fri., 8am-6:30pm Sat., 8:30am-5:30pm Sun. and holidays), where passes, tokens, and books of tickets, plus routes and fare information, can be found. From here, buses travel east and west with numerous stops along the way. If you want to save time, opt for the fast ferries instead; buses take an hour between Hamilton and Dockyard, for example, compared to a breezy 20-minute journey across the Great Sound. But buses offer a slice of workaday Bermudiana you won't necessarily find on customized tours or taxi rides. Local custom demands Bermudians boarding the bus call out an all-inclusive "Good morning!" or "Good afternoon!" to the driver and seated congregation as they choose their seat. Students in their various school uniforms pile on board later in the afternoon, as buses take them home or to Hamilton. And views of the South Shore beaches and other scenic areas are worth the long journeys and sometimes-lurching movement as buses stop and start their way through the parishes. For more peaceful trips, avoid the rush hour and travel between 9am and 3pm or after 5:30pm.

For foreigners confused by the island's drive-on-the-left rule, bus stop poles offer color-coded clues to let you know which side of the road to stand on. Neon pink poles indicate a route inbound to Hamilton; the electric blue ones mean passing buses are headed out from the city. One rule all drivers enforce: Exact fare (coins only) is needed, so no change is given. Passes, tokens, and tickets are more economical if you plan to make frequent use of the bus or ferry to get around during your stay. The useful Transportation Pass is available for one day ($19), two days ($31.50), three days ($44), four days ($48.50), seven days ($62), one month ($69), or three months ($169) of unlimited use, allowing you to get on and off buses and ferries as many times as you wish. These are also sold at the ferry and bus terminals, and other authorized outlets.

There are 11 routes covering the island, on most of which buses run every half hour throughout the day. Morning start times vary according to route, but service begins as early as 6:15am and generally runs until around 6:30pm Monday-Friday. The exceptions are routes 7, 8, and 11, serving Southampton, Dockyard, and St. George's, which keep running until 10pm or 11pm. There are curtailed schedules and fewer buses on weekends and holidays. Fares are based on 14 zones and priced accordingly (each zone is about two miles long). Fares are either $3.50 or $5 (for Hamilton to Dockyard, St. George's, or Hamilton Parish), or $2.75 all zones ages 5-16, but special passes and books of tickets cost less per ride. Children under five, resident seniors, and local school students ride free. Routes, fares, schedules, and running times can be found on the government website (www.gov.bm/bus-routes-and-maps), in public transport

brochures available at Visitor Information Centres, or the **Public Transportation Board (PTB)** (26 Palmetto Rd., Devonshire, DV 05, tel. 441/292-3851 Mon.-Fri.). **Tours and group charters** (tel. 441/292-6704, prowland@ptb.bm) can also be arranged.

Ferries

Bermuda's ferry service, **Sea Express** (www.marineandports.bm), is fast and efficient, encouraging a large number of locals to use the boats to commute to work. Four "fast ferries"—two-tier air-conditioned, hovercraft-like vessels—practically fly over the Great Sound to Dockyard and along the North Shore to St. George's. For the nostalgic, the clunky old iron black-and-white ferries, *Georgia, Corona,* and *Coralita,* still chug along the Hamilton-Paget-Warwick route, while the veteran *Deliverance* and *Patience* make occasional scenic milk runs along the Somerset shore several times a day in summer.

The four ferry routes are divided by color: The popular and busiest Blue Route (which also takes scooters aboard) runs between Hamilton and Dockyard; the Pink Route serves the quieter stops of Paget and Warwick; the Green Route, an express service geared mainly to West End commuters, serves Rockaway, Southampton; and the Orange Route travels between Hamilton, Dockyard, and St. George's. The Orange Route is a wonderfully scenic—and hassle-free—way to do a day trip to the East End April-October (it doesn't operate over the winter period).

The cost of a single fare varies by route; an adult one-way fare to St. George's (via Dockyard) or from Hamilton to Dockyard is $5 (tokens $4.50), and across the harbor to Paget and back it's $3.50 (tokens $2.75). As with the buses, cost-saving transportation passes ranging from one day to three months offer unlimited ferry use. Books of 15 tickets ($25) are also cost-effective for longer vacations. While buses accept exact change, as well as tickets, tokens, or passes, ferry passengers will not be able to board using cash; purchase tickets, tokens, or passes in advance. Children under five and resident seniors ride free. Information, advice, schedules, tokens, tickets, and passes are available at the **Hamilton ferry terminal** (8 Front St., tel. 441/295-4506, 6:30am-8pm Mon.-Fri., 7:30am-6pm Sat., 8:30am-6pm Sun. and holidays). Passes, tickets, and tokens are also sold at the central bus terminal in Hamilton, and at sub-post offices, hotels, and guesthouses.

Scooters and Mopeds

They are fun, fast, and offer the utmost freedom to explore, but you should not underestimate the very real dangers associated with renting mopeds and scooters. Every year, visitors end up in the hospital's emergency room for treatment of grazes and gashes—"road rash" in local parlance—which can ruin a vacation. More serious injuries, such as broken limbs and head and back injuries, even fatalities, also occur—on average there is one death every month, and five people a day end up in the hospital's emergency department following road traffic collisions. The problem is such that cruise ships no longer recommend rental scooters to passengers for liability reasons, though livery reps continue to offer their services dockside.

For visitors who choose to rent motorized bikes, note the minimum age requirement is 18 years, though children can sit on the back as passengers—a highly risky proposition for youngsters. All scooter drivers and passengers are required by law to wear safety helmets securely fastened at all times.

Most gas stations are open 7am-7pm daily, though some remain open later. The only 24-hour gas station is **Esso City Tigermarket** (37 Richmond Rd., Hamilton, tel. 441/295-3776).

RENTALS

There are three liveries. The largest, **Oleander Cycles** (6 Valley Rd., Paget, tel. 441/236-5235, www.oleandercycles.bm, 8:30am-5:30pm daily), has several satellite locations: 15 Gorham Road, Hamilton (tel. 441/295-0919); The Reefs Hotel & Club, South Shore Road,

Southampton (tel. 441/238-0222); King's Wharf, Royal Naval Dockyard (tel. 441/234-2764); Blue Hole Hill, next to Grotto Bay Beach Resort (tel. 441/293-1010); and 26 York Street, St. George's (tel. 441/297-0478). **Smatt's Cycle Livery** (74 Pitts Bay Rd., outside the Hamilton Princess, tel. 441/295-1180, www.smattscyclelivery.com, 8am-5pm daily) has two other outlets—at the Fairmont Southampton (tel. 441/238-7800) and Rosewood Bermuda (tel. 441/298-4085). **Elbow Beach Cycles** (Elbow Beach Resort, 60 South Rd., tel. 441/296-2300, www.elbowbeachcycles.com) is based in Paget, but offers scooter delivery and pickup anywhere on the island, including Dockyard's cruise ship wharves.

All liveries offer a free shuttle between their outlets and locations where visitors are staying, and also pick up clients left stranded by broken-down vehicles. They usually have representatives at wharves in Dockyard and St. George's when cruise ships are in port. All scooters and mopeds have 50-cc engines with electric start and automatic gears. Rates vary, usually starting at around $50 per day, with special rates for longer rentals, but prices are fairly competitive between the companies and include delivery and pickup, a basket accessory, mandatory third-party insurance ($30 for up to 30 days), and the all-important helmet and lock.

Electric Cars

Given Bermuda's ever-increasing congestion, it was understandable the island had always denied car rentals to visitors. That changed in 2017, when Parliament passed legislation to allow the licensing and operation of minicar liveries. A fleet of two-seater electric Renault **Twizy** vehicles was launched from the **Hamilton Princess** (76 Pitts Bay Rd., tel. 441/295-3000, info@currentvehicles.com, www.currentvehicles.com, pickup 9am-4pm daily), with a growing number of resorts installing Twizy charging and parking stations, including Rosedon, Mid Ocean Club, The Loren at Pink Beach, Inverurie Executive Suites, Royal Palms, and Rosewood Bermuda.

Scooter Safety

Road traffic accidents (RTAs) are far too common in Bermuda, affecting both locals and visitors. Before you end up a victim of "road rash"—painful grazes after skimming macadam—or far worse, consider these basic safety tips.

- Drive on the *left,* and remember the left-hand rule when turning into junctions and navigating city streets. (Roundabouts, or traffic circles, routinely confuse the uninitiated; to negotiate them without a problem, be sure always to give way to traffic approaching on your right.)

- Wear the helmet provided with your scooter rental. It's the law, but it may also keep you alive in an accident. If you forget, as visitors sometimes do, you will notice locals flagging you down, waving their arms, and pointing at your bare head.

- Bermudians rarely do this, but keep to the speed limit of 35 kilometers per hour (about 22 miles per hour). Take corners especially carefully, and drive defensively at all times: You never know when a local is about to cut across a lane of traffic or throw a car door open in your path. Look out for blind entrances and sharp turns.

- Do not turn around to look at motorists or sights behind you. In a group of scooters touring together, let the slowest driver go in front.

- When it rains, take extra care, as mopeds and scooters skid and slide easily on slick roads. Drive slowly and brake gradually in these conditions, touching the rear brake first. The same goes for areas with sand or oil on the road.

- Many scooter and motorbike riders suffer bad calf burns because their legs touch the muffler. When you dismount your scooter after driving, stay clear of the muffler, which becomes dangerously hot; you should also avoid those of parked scooters when walking between bikes.

- Secure all possessions either inside the scooter compartment or tied with a bungee cord on the rear basket. Bag thefts from bikes are one of the most common island crimes, and you provide an easy target for thieves on bikes if your belongings are not obviously strapped down.

- Park only in legal spaces and lock the scooter, both with its ignition lock and the wheel lock provided. The rental rate insures against accidents, but not theft (though visitors generally do not get nailed for stolen bikes).

- If you do come off and suffer scrapes, Dr. Edward Schultz, head of Bermuda's Emergency Department, recommends treating road rash as you would a second-degree burn: Cleanse gently with saline or clean water, then use cream dressings, changed frequently. Don't use Vaseline or leave wounds open and dry. Swimming, long considered by Bermudians to be a healing factor, actually risks infection, says Schultz. Keep injured areas out of the sun, as the skin is more prone to damage.

The novelty has appealed to individuals and visiting couples. The greater safety factor, alone, compared to scooters, has made Twizys a very popular option.

Twizy drivers must be 25 years old and have a valid license. The minimum rental period is 24 hours, with a drop-box option for returning vehicles after-hours. A one-day booking costs about $100, including a $30 third-party insurance fee; discounts are offered for bookings over seven days. At press time, vehicle collection and drop-offs were only available at the Hamilton Princess, but Fairmont Southampton has been installing facilities to become a second hub, and there's an expanding network of free charge points around the island.

Bicycles

Bicycles up the adventure quotient for travelers who want exercise with their sightseeing. Increasing numbers of visitors are exploring Bermuda by bicycle, including off-road enthusiasts who enjoy the ever-popular Railway Trail. **Bicycle Works** (13 Tumkins Lane, Hamilton, tel. 441/297-8356, www.bicycleworks.bm) has road bikes (Felt 95, $70 one day, $250 seven days). All the liveries also rent pedal bicycles and hybrid electric bikes.

Train Tours

Bermuda lost its railway in the 1940s, but you will still see trains tootling around on tires on the main roads. **The Bermuda Train Company** (6 Valley Rd., Paget, tel. 441/236-3130, www.bermudatrain.com), owned by Oleander Cycles, uses colorful mini-trains to conduct tours around the City of Hamilton and the Royal Naval Dockyard April-November, though almost exclusively for cruise ship passengers. Bookings can be made via your ship, or independently through Oleander. Open-air carriages allow great sightseeing. Private tours for a minimum of eight passengers may also be booked, depending on schedule availability.

Visas and Officialdom

Air passengers arriving at L. F. Wade International Airport must pass first through Department of Immigration and then Customs controls. There are three separate lines—for Bermudian status-holders, Bermuda residents, and arriving foreigners—all of which can be long and tedious. Patience, a friendly demeanor, and the correct paperwork will help get you through. Know that the island's authorities and its legal system do not differentiate between drug dealers and those who carry small amounts of banned substances for personal consumption; for those who are caught, the penalties are stiff.

DOCUMENTS AND REQUIREMENTS
Passports and Visas

Travelers to Bermuda need a valid, machine-readable passport and a return or onward ticket, or other proof of transportation off the island to a country where right of entry has been granted. Open returns may have a time limit imposed on their length of stay by island Department of Immigration officials. Women traveling under a married name, but with identification documents stating a maiden name, should also bring a marriage certificate or certified copy.

Know the name of your hotel or guest-house, or the street address of the private home where you'll be staying. Keep the name and address of your accommodations handy for officials. If you are staying at a private residence, don't be surprised if the Department of Immigration officer personally knows your host. As you'll soon find out, the island is a *very* small place.

In 2014, the Bermuda government removed the need for entry visas or visa waivers, assuming visitors carry multiple-reentry visas (MRVs) for the United States, Canada, and Britain where needed. The change has made for a far smoother immigration process for tourist and business visitors of all nationalities. Check www.gov.bm/department/immigration or www.gotobermuda.com for updates.

Traveling Children

As well as the relevant travel documents, children who are not traveling with their parents must show a letter from their parent(s) authorizing the child to be accompanied by another adult. Parents traveling with adopted children should bring proper documents for their adopted children. Children entering Bermuda for adoption must carry Department of Immigration paperwork.

Length of Stay

The maximum amount of time a visitor may stay in Bermuda is six months, but only through exceptional circumstances; the standard limit is 90 days. If you wish to extend your length of stay (for example, owners of timeshare or fractional ownership properties), you must apply in person either to Secondary Immigration Control upon arrival at the airport, or to an Immigration Inspector at the **Department of Immigration Headquarters, Government Administration Building** (30 Parliament St., Hamilton, tel. 441/295-5151, 9am-noon Mon.-Fri.). Travelers cannot enter Bermuda to live, work, or look for work without work permits or other official documentation, nor will they be allowed in for an indefinite period, nor without a return ticket. For more information, check www.gov.bm/department/immigration.

TAXES AND CUSTOMS

All visitors must fill out a Customs Traveller Declaration (CTD) Form 98, citing any goods and gifts that will be left in Bermuda. Duty is payable on any goods not covered by the island's duty-free allowance. Once you pass through Immigration and collect your baggage, there may be long lines of visitors waiting to clear Customs, especially when several flights arrive at similar times or when crowds of Bermudians are carting back suitcases full of foreign purchases. Make sure you have completed your declaration form. A uniformed officer will either give you the all-clear and wave you through to the exit and ground-transportation stands, or will direct you to the baggage inspection desk.

Taxes

Residents and visitors are equal under Bermuda's Passenger Tax Act, passed in 1972. Passenger taxes are $35 for all air travelers (included in the airfare) and yacht passengers, and $20 per 24-hour period for every departing cruise ship passenger (collected in advance by cruise lines). Children under the age of two are exempt in both cases.

Duty Free

Visitors are allowed to enter the island with personal clothes and belongings, including sports equipment, cameras, golf bags, 50 cigars, 200 cigarettes, 500 grams (17 ounces) of tobacco, one liter of liquor, one liter of wine, and $30 worth of gifts. Duty of 25 percent will be levied on more than 20 pounds of meat and other foodstuffs brought into the island. There are strict rules governing the importation of plants, fruits, and vegetables, and these require an import permit. Live marine animals are not permitted, but fresh, frozen, or cooked fish or shellfish may be brought in, as long as it contains no algae or seaweed. For more information, visit www.gov.bm/department/customs.

Animals require proper documentation or they will be returned to their point of origin, since there are no quarantine facilities on the island. They must be accompanied by an import permit issued in advance by the **Department of Environment & Natural Resources** (tel. 441/236-4201, www.gov.bm/importing-animals-bermuda), as well as a health certificate issued within 10 days of the visit by a licensed vet in the animal's home country. For more details on document requirements, contact the department.

Returning Home

Bermuda visitors are allowed to take home duty-free merchandise purchased on the island. U.S. Customs has a pre-clearance facility at L. F. Wade International Airport, so declaration forms must be filled out in Bermuda before your journey home. Forms are available at airlines and travel agencies. **U.S. citizens** (www.cbp.gov) are usually permitted $800 goods allowance after 48 hours, including 200 cigarettes and 100 cigars. The allowance is renewed every 30 days. **Canadian citizens** (www.cbsa.gc.ca) are allowed $50 after 24 hours, $400 after 48 hours, or $750 after seven days. **UK citizens** (www.hmrc.gov.uk) can take back £390 worth of purchases from non-EU nations.

Different countries have varying rates of duty on goods carried back above the duty-free limits. Plants should not be taken back without permission from your own country.

FOREIGN CONSULS

Since Bermuda remains a British dependency, no foreign embassies are located here. Instead, relevant business is conducted through **British Embassies** in Washington DC (3100 Massachusetts Ave. NW, Washington, DC 20008, tel. 202/588-6500) and other centers. British nationals seeking their country's assistance can contact **Government House** (11 Langton Hill, Pembroke, HM 13, tel. 441/292-3600).

The **United States Consulate in Bermuda** (Crown Hill, 16 Middle Rd., Devonshire, tel. 441/295-1342, for life-and-death emergencies duty phone 441/278-7512 or 441/278-7514 during regular hours, or 441/335-3828 after hours or Sat.-Sun., http://bm.usconsulate.gov, 8am-4:30pm Mon.-Fri. except Bermuda and U.S. public holidays) serves Americans living in and visiting Bermuda, as well as Bermudians and foreign nationals who wish to visit the United States. Valid photo identification is required to enter the consulate. A small parking lot is located on the adjacent property.

An **Honourary Canadian Consul** (73 Front St., 4th Fl., Hamilton, tel. 441/292-2917, http://travel.gc.ca) was being appointed in 2017. Bermuda-related matters are also handled by the **Consulate General of Canada in New York** (1251 6th Ave., New York, NY, 10020-1175, tel. 212/596-1628, http://international.gc.ca).

The **Portugal Consulate** (Melbourne House, 11 Parliament St., Hamilton, HM 12, tel. 441/292-1039, hamilton@dgaccp.pt) is headed by Honorary Consul Andrea Moniz-DeSouza, an associate lawyer who works as a direct liaison with Lisbon, processing passport renewals, ID cards, and paperwork authentication. An estimated 10 percent of Bermuda's population is of Portuguese origin, most born in the Azores or to Azorean immigrants or guest workers. Many of Bermuda's Portuguese are children who were born in Bermuda but lack Bermudian status (citizenship) because their parents are not Bermudian—a quandary that confronts any child born on the island to non-Bermudian residents. There is also a steady stream of Azorean contract workers coming to Bermuda, as well as Portuguese Bermudian families on the island who maintain strong links to relatives in the Azores, Madeira, and Portugal.

Eighteen other nations, including Norway, Ireland, Belgium, Austria, Germany, France, Italy, Ghana, Mexico, and Jamaica, are represented by honorary consuls, who maintain diplomatic links with Bermuda via Britain's Foreign & Commonwealth Office. Honorary consul positions are awarded to resident Bermudians who are natives of or have strong links to represented countries.

Recreation

Bermuda is a recreational playground thanks to its temperate year-round climate, well-maintained sports facilities, organized clubs, and spectacular outdoor spaces. Bermudians are devout fans of every sport and hobby—from triathlons to bowling to motocross to soccer, along with newer activities like stand-up paddleboarding, wakeboarding, and beach tennis.

BEACHES

In Bermuda, you're never far from shore. Although some of its world-renowned beaches are officially private, belonging to resorts or restricted neighborhoods, most are open to the public sunrise-sunset.

Those responsible for most of the rave reviews are located on the South Shore, where sweeping tracts of coral-tinted sand are pounded by turquoise surf populated by iridescent parrotfish and schools of pompano and amberjack. The surf is relatively gentle, thanks to the protection of reefs that lie a stone's throw from shore (a mere few yards in some areas) on this side of the island.

The North Shore, including areas of the Great Sound and St. George's, though less of a tourist attraction, is just as beautiful for swimming, snorkeling, kayaking, and scuba diving. In contrast to the sand and surf of the South Shore, this side of the island is punctuated by small rocky coves and azure bays, some without beaches at all, and there is no surf. Local youngsters practice their high-diving here, and deep grottoes invite you to take a plunge. The reef line exists but, since it sits 10 miles offshore, is barely visible, and divers need a boat to get out there.

All the island's beaches are covered in the same white or pinkish sand, scattered with shells and seaweed, but with none of the pebbles or dark grit of Caribbean volcanic islands such as Montserrat or Guadeloupe. In the winter, prevailing northeast winds can make the North Shore choppy, but throughout most of the summer northern horizons are as calm as a lake.

You can swim all year round (though Bermudians don't). Water temperatures in summer can reach a balmy 85°F or more; winter temperatures dip to an average 65°F. The first official beach day is Bermuda Day, the last Friday in May, when boaters take to the water to kick off the season, but most locals wait until June or July to make their first beach foray. Midsummer's Cup Match holiday is the ultimate beach extravaganza, with practically every inch of shoreline occupied by family outings and elaborate seaside camping parties. Hundreds of residents celebrate the morning of Christmas Day at the water's edge with champagne picnics at Elbow Beach; some don Santa hats and bring miniature trees, complete with ornaments, for the festive occasion and, depending on the weather, a few hardy souls take a dip.

In recent years, the Bermuda Tourism Authority has worked to bolster the island's "beach economy" and increase services by encouraging entrepreneurs to operate from certain beaches. Lifeguards and concessions—for umbrellas and chairs, boogie boards, noodles, masks and snorkels, hair-braiding, and refreshments—can now be found at several public beaches, including Horseshoe Bay, Tobacco Bay, Clearwater Beach, Shelly Bay, John Smith's Bay, and Admiralty Park. The first two offer the most comprehensive facilities with liquor licenses, along with the privately-run Snorkel Park at Dockyard, attracting crowds in the summer months.

Bermuda's rollers are usually not large enough for hard-core surfing, hurricane season excepted, but there are a few practitioners. Kitesurfing—in which a rider, hooked by harness to a power kite, skims waves on a board—is more popular among local thrill-seekers. The far more sedate passion for stand-up paddleboarding (SUP) has also taken off in recent years, and you can rent boards from several outlets. There are no nude or topless beaches, and baring all on this conservative island will only win tut-tuts of disapproval and perhaps even land you in trouble with the law.

Be careful of riptides and undertow on the South Shore, especially during hurricane season, when swells propelled by approaching storms surge against the coast. Flags and notices are posted on key beaches during these periods.

PARKS AND NATURE RESERVES

Bermuda's open spaces give a fascinating opportunity to enjoy outdoor exercise while viewing eye-popping surroundings and wildlife. National parks and nature reserves throughout the island, owned by the Bermuda National Trust (BNT, tel. 441-236-6483, www.bnt.bm) and Bermuda Audubon Society (tel. 441-292-1920, www.audubon.bm), offer ocean scenery, woodlands, farm tracts, birdlife, insects, and geology. Contact either of these groups for seasonal information on birding tours and other ecotour schedules. Public parks are open dawn-dusk and demand no permits or admission fees. Remember to take only pictures, not plant or animal samples. For more information, contact the **Department of Parks** (tel. 441/236-5902).

TOUR OPERATORS

Bermuda has numerous tour operators that help you explore its landscape, marinelife, and skies. Here are some tour operators providing island-wide options.

If you're considering any type of land or marine tour or activity, your first stop should be the offices or website of the **Island Tour Centre** (Albuoy's Point, 5 Point Pleasant Park, Hamilton, tel. 441/236-1300, www.islandtourcentre.com, 8am-6pm daily summer, 9am-4pm daily winter, plus two outlets in the Royal Naval Dockyard). The center operates as a centralized booking agent for scores of activities island-wide, from scuba to horseback riding to party cruises and parasailing. Check out the assortment of brochures and flyers at its three outlets, or book online.

Byways Tours (tel. 441/535-9169, www.bermudafootsteps.com) is run by Heidi Cowen, a fifth-generation Bermudian and granddaughter of a lighthouse keeper. Accompanied by her spaniel, Buddy, in a mini-bus that can transport eight, she offers all kinds of explorations, including an end-to-end Island Tour with picnic lunch and a beach or park stop (about 5 hours, $100 pp, $50 for kids 6-10, lunch included, cash only). Family tours, history tours, and a Bermuda flora tour are other favorites (1.5-2 hours, $50 pp); many include stops for snacks or photos at places only a true Bermudian would know. She posts her daily observations on Facebook.

Antiques dealer, natural history buff, and former schoolteacher Tim Rogers of **Bermuda Lectures & Tours** (tel. 441/238-0344, timrogers852@msn.com) takes visitors on custom tours around the island. The UK native, a Bermuda resident for 30-plus years, is knowledgeable about Bermuda's architecture and cultural history, plants, animals, and geology. He often uses the Railway Trail for tours to explore all these topics. He creates bespoke experiences for individuals or small groups, depending on preference, with a standard hourly fee of $60 for up to four people.

Educator Robert Chandler and naturalist Jennifer Gray of **Discovery Tours** (tel. 441/335-4944, rkchandler@ibl.bm, or tel. 441/332-2966, jmermaidgray@gmail.com, 2 hours, $45 adults more than 3 people, $80 per hour under 4 people) lead island-wide guided walking tours, flora and fauna tours of national parks, cultural tours, and custom tours by request. With an environmental focus, their tours include Hog Bay Park, Blue Hole Park, and the South Shore beaches and dunes as favorite sites.

Don't forget that much of Bermuda's biodiversity is marine, not terrestrial; half-day and full-day marine tours can be arranged through several museums, conservation groups, and respected outfitters. The **Bermuda Zoological Society** (tel. 441/293-2727, ext. 2138, http://bamz.org) offers whale-watching and turtle-spotting tours, nighttime glowworm outings, and boat trips to North Rock and other spectacular seamount reefs for snorkeling.

Take to the air for a thrilling perspective of the entire island aboard **Blue Sky Flights** (tel. 441/516-3305, www.blueskyflights.bm, year-round 9am-sunset, half-hour "Discover" flight $250, 50-minute Sightseeing Tour $450-500 for 2 adults or 1 adult and 2 children). Canadian manager and pilot Heather Nicholds's love of flying shows as she cruises over the South Shore reefs, dips down to Dockyard and coasts back over bays and neighborhoods for a closer look. The plane can carry three passengers with a combined weight of 450 pounds.

For details on individual scuba and snorkeling operators, see the **Bermuda Tourism Authority**'s website (www.gotobermuda.com).

GOLF

Bermuda is one of the world's most golf-dense destinations, thanks to its seven courses—many boasting breathtaking ocean views and championship layouts. For eight years (2007-2014), the island hosted the PGA Grand Slam of Golf, but you don't have to be a world champion to enjoy the game. Balmy temperatures year-round bring golfers of every breed, and even duffers can enjoy the emerald fairways, turquoise horizons, and postgame rum swizzles in history-steeped clubhouses. Renowned golf-course architect Robert Trent Jones designed four of Bermuda's courses, including Tucker's Town's premier **Mid Ocean Club,** a par-70, 6,666-yard course over ocean bluffs that's rated one of the world's best links. It was here that Babe Ruth was said to have lost a dozen golf balls attempting to hit a tee shot over Mangrove Lake on the infamous fifth hole, a 433-yard par 4.

While just two of the courses are public, hotel concierges usually have no problem securing tee times for nonmembers at the island's private clubs. Lessons, for adults and kids, can also be arranged. The island also has a couple of driving ranges, plus a 10,000-square-foot practice putting green and short-game area at the tony **Tucker's Point Golf Club** at Rosewood Bermuda.

Greens fees at Bermuda clubs range $80-200 and can be higher. Proper golf attire is required, including shirts with collars and sleeves. Women's and men's right- and left-handed golf club sets are available at all courses; balls start at $40 per dozen. Use of golf carts is mandatory at some clubs or on weekends and holidays; caddies are available only at Mid Ocean. Visit www.gotobermuda.com to tour links, learn about tournaments, arrange vacation packages, or schedule a tee time up to a year in advance.

DEEP-SEA FISHING

Bermuda lies in the path of migrating schools of many species of fish, including tuna and wahoo. More than 27 varieties of game fish, including yellowfin and blackfin tuna, mahimahi, wahoo, great barracuda, amberjack, shark, and marlin can be found in local waters. June-September, blue and white marlin are plentiful; blues can range up to a whopping 1,350 pounds. Wahoo tend to run early (May), while schools of marlin and tuna arrive later (Sept.-Oct.).

Located off the island's southwest end, Argus and Challenger Banks are remnants of volcanic peaks that formed Mount Bermuda millions of years ago. The sides of these banks, dropping from 30 to 600 fathoms in just a few hundred feet, create a plentiful fishing ground, particularly the shallow plateaus where small baitfish come to feed—attracting larger fish seeking prey near the edges of the banks. Weather and tide action determine the type of fishing here, but bottom fishing, trolling (with depth sounders and "fish finders"), and drift fishing are all practiced. One of the more unusual fishing methods is blue-water fly-fishing, in which flying fish bait is rigged to a kite, popping the fish in and out of the water—a tempting lure for tuna.

Numerous sport-fishing vessels operate in Bermuda. Details can be found in the **Bermuda Yellow Pages** (www.bermudayp.com), or through the **Bermuda Tourism Authority** (www.gotobermuda.com), the **Bermuda Sportfishing Association** (tel. 441/295-2370), **Seahorse Anglers Club** (David Pantry, tel. 441/236-8451, www.seahorseanglers.com), **Blue Water Anglers Club** (28 E. Broadway, tel. 441/292-5529), or **Bermuda Anglers Club** (tel. 441/293-0875, www.bermudaanglersclub.com). Three events in July, the **Bermuda Billfish Blast** (www.bermudabillfishblast.com), the **Bermuda Big Game Classic** (www.bermudabiggameclassic.com), and the **Billfish Tournament** (www.bermudatriplecrown.com) bring scores of fishing buffs to the island thanks to trophies and cash prizes.

Local sportfishers support tag-and-release programs for sharks, tuna, and billfish. Restrictions control minimum weights and lengths for pelagic species like tuna and marlin. Longline fishing is currently not permitted, though the government has suggested it might be in the future. Fish pots are banned; protected species such as turtles, rockfish, and certain grouper cannot be taken; and recreational fishers may not sell fish or lobster. For more information, contact the **Department of Environment & Natural Resources** (tel. 441/236-4201).

You can also line-fish off the rocks on the North or South Shores, or with a rod and reel, though anglers agree there are fewer "big ones" now than there were just decades ago. Bait is also sold at a few waterfront gas stations, including Robinson's Marina at Somerset Bridge and the marina at Flatts Village.

SAILING

Sailing is an age-old tradition in Bermuda, and young islanders continue to make their mark in international competitions every year. Local associations for different boat types stage regattas and races featuring International One Designs, Fitted Dinghies, Lasers, Optimist Dinghies, Etchells, Bytes, Comets, J-24s, and J-105s March-November in Hamilton Harbour and the Great Sound. Hundreds of foreign and local yachts also race to Bermuda—from Newport, Rhode Island, or Marion, Massachusetts—on alternate years in a pair of historic events. International Race Week in June attracts top skippers from all over the world. The Argo Group Gold Cup in October brings professional sailors to compete for the oldest match-race trophy in the world in an exciting weeklong showdown.

A lasting legacy of the 35th America's Cup in Bermuda is the AC Endeavour Program, a youth education and community sailing initiative that taught hundreds of students to sail in 2017, with plans to continue similar outreach in the future. As well as practical sailing skills, the program exposes youngsters to math, engineering, technology, and arts through STEAM career pathways projects.

Local yacht clubs include the **Royal Bermuda Yacht Club** (tel. 441/295-2214, www.rbyc.bm), the **Royal Hamilton Amateur Dinghy Club** (tel. 441/236-2250, www.rhadc.bm), the **St. George's Dinghy Club** (tel. 441/297-1612, www.stgdsc.bm), and **Sandys Boat Club** (tel. 441/234-2248, www.sandysboatclub.com). For details on races, contact any of the clubs or the **Bermuda Sailing Association** (tel. 441/295-7935, http://sailing.bm).

HORSEBACK RIDING

Horseback riding through parkland, tribe roads, and across beaches can be a leisurely way to see Bermuda.

In the East End, Natalie and Mark Moran's **Bermuda Horse Trail Ride** (Moran Meadows, 7 Salt Spray Lane, tel. 441/537-0400, www.bermudahorsetrailride.com) offers private rides for small groups.

For harness-racing excitement, visit the **National Equestrian Centre** (48 Vesey St., tel. 441/234-0485, www.bef.bm) in Devonshire on Sunday afternoons through the winter season, when pony-trap owners vie for bragging rights.

Former track star Michael Watson's other love has always been horseback riding, specifically Western saddle, and he appears regularly at island equestrian competitions in full cowboy regalia. His tours, through **Mike Watson's Performance Horses** (tel. 441/747-7433), take visitors along the Railway Trail and through the maze of beach dunes in South Shore National Park.

TENNIS

Bermuda boasts more than 100 clay and hard-surface tennis courts, making the sport a true national pastime. Indeed, Bermudian Mary Outerbridge went down in the history books for introducing the game to America in 1874; she took a racquet, balls, a net, and a rulebook with her on a visit to New York and was allowed to design a tennis court on the grounds of the Staten Island Cricket Club, the first such court in the nation.

Most Bermuda hotels have courts, many lit for night play, as well as resident pros who offer clinics and private lessons (average rate is $50 per half hour). Proper tennis attire is required at most courts. Racquets can be rented and restrung at several centers.

Players will find September through June to be the best months for play, as heat and humidity make midday play, at least, debilitating throughout the summer. A panacea might be beach tennis—a fast-paced combo of tennis and volleyball played out on the sand—which made its island debut in 2008, with international stars competing and demonstrating the sport.

The government-owned W. E. R. Joell Tennis Stadium in Pembroke is a popular venue for lessons, games, and local tennis championships. For more information, contact the **Bermuda Lawn Tennis Association** (tel. 441/296-0834, www.blta.bm).

ATHLETICS AND TRIATHLONS

Running clubs took root in Bermuda in the 1970s, and the sport has been going strong ever since. On an island where some sports tend to split the population by race, it is also one of the few whose events have always brought together Bermudians of all ethnic and socioeconomic backgrounds. Visitors are always welcome. Road races are held September-June, usually on Sunday mornings, most of them sanctioned by the **Bermuda National Athletics Association** (BNAA, 15 Brunswick St., Hamilton, P.O. Box DV 397, Devonshire, tel. 441/296-0951, www.athleticsbda.com), an affiliate of the International Association of Athletics Federation (IAAF). Race dates and details are posted on the websites of the Bermuda National Athletics Association (BNAA), as well as the **Mid-Atlantic Athletic Club** (MAAC, www.maac.bm), which also organizes evening and weekend fun runs, and **Bermuda Timing Systems** (tel. 441/236-9586, www.racedayworld.com).

Bermuda runners comprise all abilities, from joggers seeking a sociable outing to former elite Olympic Trials competitors. Many take part in major events overseas, including the Boston, New York, Marine Corps, Chicago, Toronto, and London marathons, and ultra-distance events.

The highlight of the racing calendar is January's **Bermuda Marathon Weekend** (www.bermudaraceweekend.com), which incorporates a Friday mile event on Front Street, followed by a Saturday 10K race and a Sunday half-marathon and marathon.

Triathlon is also a highly popular sport in Bermuda, with weekend events throughout the fall and spring, kids training clubs, and local athletes competing in Ironman events worldwide. Two Bermudians, Tyler Butterfield and Flora Duffy, are also currently competing on the world pro circuit; Duffy won both the 2016 and 2017 International Triathlon Union World Triathlon Series. The Bermuda Tourism Authority signed a three-year contract with the ITU to hold Series events in Bermuda, with the first race in April 2018. For more information on events, contact the **Bermuda Triathlon Association** (www.bermudatriathlon.com).

SPECTATOR SPORTS

Even if you don't participate in Bermuda's recreational scene, you're spoiled for choice as a spectator. From road races to cycling, fitted dinghies to pony-racing or kitesurfing, you can enjoy any number of sporting events from the sidelines year-round. The island's truly "national" sports are soccer and cricket, and you can savor the essence of Bermudian life at any weekend game, where a festive atmosphere prevails.

Sports fans can check out www.islandstats.com for information and results about local teams in a panoply of sports, including basketball, squash, volleyball, netball, athletics, cricket, soccer, field hockey, darts, softball, rugby, and mountain biking. Bermuda Tourism Authority's website (www.gotobermuda.com), www.bermuda.com, and www.nothingtodoinbermuda.com all carry updated calendars of monthly events.

Cricket matches featuring local teams are played on weekends April-mid-September all over the island. The highlight, of course, is the annual Cup Match, played over two days in July or August since 1902. For more information, contact the **Bermuda Cricket Board** (tel. 441/292-8958).

Introduced by British military garrison soldiers in the 1800s, the game of **soccer** (football) has become the island's winter obsession. Matches are played on weekends and some weeknights in season (Sept.-Apr.). Contact the **Bermuda Football Association** (tel. 441/295-2199, www.bermudafa.com) for details.

Rugby (Bermuda Rugby Football Union, tel. 441/338-2952, www.brfu.bm) is also a highly popular sport, and weekend matches are well attended. The not-to-be-missed World Rugby Classic every November features former top players from around the world playing in 11 international matches.

The **Bermuda Bicycle Association** (tel. 441/291-5435, www.bermudabicycle.org) organizes road races, mountain bike trail races, time trials, and other special events throughout the year. Amateurs and visiting professionals compete in September's Bermuda Grand Prix, with a weekend of events including a time trial, circuit race, and criterium.

For a more leisurely spectator experience, drop by Elbow Beach in Paget or Shelly Bay Beach in Smith's on a windy day and watch daredevil **kitesurfers** catching air in apparent slow motion as they crisscross the rollers for hours on end.

Food

BERMUDIAN CUISINE

Is there a true Bermudian cuisine? Gourmands might snigger at such a proposition, but Bermuda has claimed its repertoire of hallmark dishes—usually a melting pot of items from other places adapted for local menus. The amalgam of British, West Indian, African, and Portuguese cultural influences has created an eclectic collection of local dishes. Many are pure comfort food, not the best for waistlines or arteries, but they are usually delicious. British cuisine has donated fish-and-chips, shepherd's pie, steak pies, and teatime desserts like scones, pound cake, trifle, and lemon meringue pie. Slavery's legacy is seen in dishes once rejected by Bermudian white society for their poor-man simplicity but now embraced in the fanciest restaurants; these include cassava and farine pie (made from root vegetables), peas 'n' rice and johnnycakes (common in the Caribbean), fried chicken legs, fried fish sandwiches (made with local catches like grouper or rockfish), butter-baked lobster, macaroni 'n' cheese, and sweets like macaroons, gingerbread, and coconut cake. The immigration of Azoreans over the past 150 years has entrenched certain dishes and snacks into the island's culinary lexicon. Portuguese *chourico* (spicy sausage) and *malacadas* (deep-fried doughnuts) are the most common examples, found island-wide at corner stores where hot snacks are served.

Restaurants dedicated to these assorted nationalities are good places to sample such dishes. Café Acoreano (Hamilton) is owned and staffed by Portuguese Bermudians. Jamaican Grill (with branches in Bailey's Bay and North Hamilton) is a popular family-run café-style eatery with jerk meats and West Indian curries. For the ultimate in British fare, head for any of the numerous pubs throughout the island—Henry VIII Pub & Restaurant, in Southampton, and Hog Penny, in Hamilton, set the standard—or attend an afternoon cream tea served at tearooms like Crown & Anchor at the Hamilton Princess, Pembroke, or Lili Bermuda Perfumery, St. George's. Down-home Bermudian restaurants are becoming sparse these days as upscale eateries take over, but holdouts like The Spot (Burnaby St., Hamilton) or Mama Angie's Coffee Shop, off the town square in St. George's, are still going strong.

Top chefs are adapting favorite local ingredients and everyman dishes into a more innovative interpretation of Bermudian cuisine on the pricier menus. As a result, there are few top-notch restaurants nowadays that don't serve a gourmet version of Bermudian fish cakes, banana or loquat chutneys, onion tarts, or rum cake. A recent example is star chef and author Marcus Samuelsson, of Harlem's Red Rooster fame, who is incorporating his twist on iconic island dishes into the menu of his panoramic restaurant inside the Hamilton Princess.

Bermuda fish is excellent, from the sweet fillets of snapper and rarer rockfish to the steaks of fresh-caught tuna, wahoo, and swordfish. Lobsters (the spiny variety) are in season September-March; fishing laws are strict, so you'll see only imported lobster on the menu over the summer months—at least in restaurants. There are no local shrimps, oysters, mussels, clams, or conch, so any of these on local menus have been imported. Under an environmental culling-meets-culinary program, "Eat it to Beat it," lionfish, an invasive species whose spines make it very tricky to catch and handle, is fast-becoming a comparable substitute for rarer rockfish or hogfish.

Fresh local produce is worth seeking out in season, mainly because imported fruit and vegetables can't compare with straight-from-the soil versions sold in grocery stores and roadside stands. Large bananas imported from the United States and Central America, overripe by the time they arrive, can't compete with Bermuda's own tiny sweet hands of fruit. Similarly, Bermuda carrots, tomatoes, and potatoes are well worth buying if you're staying in a self-catering unit or want to try the local harvest.

Wild fruits are also popular, namely the Surinam "Bermuda" cherry (a sour cherry), which has several harvests throughout the year, and the loquat, which hangs heavy on trees throughout the island in January-February.

Help yourself to a taste from trees in local parks or on public land along the Railway Trail. At the height of cherry or loquat season, you often see drivers pulling over to gather a roadside haul or schoolchildren dangling out of trees as they collect a fresh snack. Similarly, Bermudians gather bags of avocadoes to share among friends when the local trees drop their heavy harvests.

In the supermarkets, there has been a growing movement among some local farmers to supply organic fare, including organically raised chickens, vegetables, and salad greens. Locally grown products can be found in most large groceries, particularly The Supermart, on Front Street in Hamilton, and Tom Wadson's farm store in Southampton. Saturday roadside stands in most parishes are also well stocked with fresh fruit and vegetables in season.

Fishers sell their daily catch, including spiny lobsters in season, at roadside stands island-wide. Sometimes, this is simply a guy with a cooler. The best places are at the foot of Scaur Hill in Sandys; Devonshire Dock and Devonshire Bay in Devonshire; Blue Hole Hill in Hamilton Parish; and at the top of Trimingham Hill in Paget, leading out of Hamilton.

The best occasions, outside of restaurants, to sample Bermudian cooking and specialties are public festivals and holidays such as Cup Match, when alfresco gatherings or street fairs usually have food stalls selling fish sandwiches, fish cakes, homemade pies, and other goodies.

RESTAURANTS

Eating out is a favorite island pastime, and many residents, particularly those who work in Hamilton, and especially young expatriates, frequent local bars and restaurants several evenings a week. With Bermuda's steep tabs, that can add up; like everyone else, restaurants have to import the majority of their ingredients, a reality reflected in menu prices. Almost all charge an automatic 17 percent gratuity that's included on the bill. If you *really* enjoyed the food and service, you can leave an extra 10 percent, but otherwise the built-in surcharge will suffice. Check your tab to make sure it's included.

Bermudians would admit the quality of fare, even at the priciest restaurants, is inconsistent, and food and service do not always compare with the offerings of similarly priced establishments in urban centers such as New York or London. But generally, the standard is fairly high, with menus created by award-winning Bermudian and foreign-born chefs. Many Bermuda restaurants now connect with their clientele via Facebook, Twitter, and other social media.

BARS

Bermudians love to drink—there was even a song with that title released by a local artist in 2005. They also love to drink and drive, though media pressure and police crackdowns in the past 20 years have somewhat curtailed the habit. Don't be tempted to hop on a scooter after a few black rums or Elephant beers; many visitors (and locals) have been killed or badly injured over the years doing just that. But *do* enjoy Bermuda's bars; they must rank among the most lively in the world, particularly in the busy crush of summer. Happy hours are prevalent, with cheaper drink prices offered for a couple of hours after work, usually on Friday. A full wine list and a good choice of beers, cocktails, and liqueurs can be found at most drinking establishments and licensed restaurants. National favorites Black 'n' Coke (black rum—preferably Gosling's Black Seal—and Coca-Cola) and Cockspur 'n' Coke are party staples.

Accommodations

Island travelers can opt for luxury resorts, quaint cottage colonies, guesthouses, bed-and-breakfasts, as well as Airbnb and VRBO accommodations around the parishes. The range of accommodations is only matched by the vast price range, extending from about $200-10,000 per night for boutique suites. Most of the resort hotels offer average rooms in the $400-500 price bracket, compared to the $250 range of smaller independent properties. Summer's high season rates (Apr.-Oct.) are higher than winter's (Nov.-Mar.). A renaissance in Bermuda's hospitality industry ignited by the America's Cup saw a $100 million refurbishment of the historic Hamilton Princess & Beach Club, and a buyout of Rosewood Bermuda, with major reinvestment planned. The first new boutique hotel in a decade, The Loren at Pink Beach, opened in 2017, and five more are to follow by 2020, including a Ritz-Carlton, St. Regis, and other ventures. A 25-acre private island, Hawkins, in the Great Sound, is also a first; accommodating groups of up to 20 guests on a lush woodland reserve, it sets the stage for the type of exclusive rental that could drive a new demographic to Bermuda.

The key to choosing a place to stay in Bermuda lies in recognizing the type of vacation you want and can afford, as well as the style of accommodations you prefer. Because it's easy to cover the whole island, regional preferences are perhaps less important than, say, whether you plan to spend every day on the beach or shop till you drop. Most established Bermuda properties are on Facebook, or have their own websites featuring photos of rooms and amenities, rates, and full descriptions of facilities.

Reservations

Early reservations are strongly recommended for all accommodations. Popular hotels and resorts book quickly in the summer months, especially thanks to the phenomenon, typical for Bermuda, of repeat visitors who stake a claim on their accommodations up to a year in advance. Smaller properties or tiny

Camping Out

Crowds of locals lounging under roadside tarpaulins, blasting their stereos and barbecuing four-course meals—no, it's not squatters or a sudden outbreak of homelessness, just the start of camping season, Bermudian-style.

The island may lack North America's natural drama and absolute serenity of the great outdoors, but camping is a beloved summer ritual nonetheless. True, it's difficult to retreat far from the madding crowd on an island with so little undeveloped land, but for islanders, that's not really the point. Bermudians simply enjoy the change of scenery and routine, coupled with the camaraderie of outdoor living, even if they do take all the comforts of home with them—everything including the kitchen sink. "I saw one guy with his laptop and a 52-inch TV, which he was running from the battery of his dump truck," recalls Craig Burt, of the Department of Parks. "Bermudians don't like to leave anything behind."

Come July-August, particularly during the four-day Cup Match public holiday that falls between these months, Bermudians set up camp all over the island—in public parks, on roadsides, and along the South Shore dunes. At the height of camping season, virtual tent villages sprawl along the North Shore waterfront, along Kindley Field Road at Ferry Reach, between Warwick Long Bay and Horseshoe Bay, and everywhere in between. Whole families turn out, with camping accoutrements and picnic fare galore, to swim, rest, spend time with friends and relatives, wave to passing traffic, and generally enjoy time off work.

Camping is, however, restricted to Bermuda residents; all island visitors must be registered at a local hotel, guesthouse, cruise ship, or private residence—though, perhaps, if a visitor is staying with locals at a private residence, they could partake in this beloved ritual and join the bevy of tents under the subtropical stars.

rentals with just one or two rooms also get booked up quickly. For large properties, you may encounter better deals, including air-and-hotel package options, online; family-run properties with just a few rooms are best contacted directly. Check the Bermuda Tourism Authority's website (www.gotobermuda.com) and www.bermuda.com for full listings of most of the island's major hotels and guesthouses.

Rates

Rates go up during the high season (Apr.-Oct.), typically by a third, but sometimes are double the winter rates (Nov.-Mar.). With smaller properties, check whether quoted rates are double occupancy or per person. Beyond the quoted room rate, expect to pay a government tax of 9.75 percent and a 10 percent gratuity or a housekeeping or service charge. Other extra fees might include an extra-person charge, if you're adding a bed, or an extra charge for children, though most kids sleep free. Properties have different deposit requirements and cancellation policies; make sure you know the details before booking. All resorts and major hotels, and most guesthouses, accept major credit cards. Some private residences or apartment rentals only accept cash or traveler's checks.

ACCOMMODATION TYPES
Resort Hotels

Bermuda's major resort hotels are almost all beachfront or harbor-front—or, at the very least, have impressive views of the ocean. Most offer pools, tennis courts, retail, putting greens, spas, beauty salons, social desks or concierges, multiple restaurants, room service, porters, nightclubs, entertainment, scuba and water sports centers, and kids activity clubs during the high season. Some have a golf course on-site, or rights at sister properties. Failing all else, the concierge can arrange pretty much anything.

Bed-and-Breakfasts

A very cost-effective way to enjoy a Bermuda vacation, bed-and-breakfasts are usually a room in a private home or a historic property, with either a private or a shared bath. Breakfast is included in the rate and ranges from continental croissants to "FEB" (full English breakfast; for example, bacon and eggs). Eating out is normally required for other meals, so this type of lodging is best suited for short stays.

Private Residences

This is the way to see Bermuda if you are want to live like the locals. Staying on someone's private property, whether it's a studio apartment beneath the main house or a separate cottage across the lawn, gives a real sense of living like a local that you don't get to experience in resorts. More residents are placing their properties for hire on **Airbnb** (www.airbnb.com) and **VRBO** (www.vrbo.com), including long-term rentals to visiting businesspeople. By 2017, Airbnb counted more than 250 listings across the island, as Bermudians joined the worldwide trend to rent out rooms, attached apartments, separate cottages or second homes. Well-managed guest accommodations range from private villas with swimming pools to pullout-sofa studios.

Currently, most renters are not supervised by the Bermuda Tourism Authority (only properties with six or more units require government inspection and licenses), but new legislation to help regulate standards is due to update this in 2018. Don't be surprised to find properties with pools, waterfront docks, beautiful gardens, or historic legacies. Like the larger hotels, these nearly always offer amenities such as air-conditioning (a must in the summer months), Wi-Fi, self-catering kitchens, barbecues, ironing boards, and cable TV.

Apartments and Cottages

The island has numerous apartment and private cottage rentals that are located away from the owner's property, thereby offering total privacy. Some are stand-alone cottages located on estates in tony neighborhoods—upscale rentals in the $500 range for summer double occupancy. Others are less expensive, with several apartments arranged around a pool. All are self-catering, with kitchens and barbecues, but maid service is usually included.

Inns and Guesthouses

Bermuda has many inns and guesthouses, some in historic or picturesque neighborhoods, others on the water or featuring a pool. Doubles with king or queen beds and private baths inside a large homestead are the norm. Some allow for self-catering with kitchenettes (mini-fridge, microwave, toaster oven, and hot plate); others allow guests to share kitchen facilities. Breakfast, baked goods, and afternoon tea are sometimes served.

Cottage Colonies

These quaint throwbacks to the elegant vacations of the 1950s and 1960s are fast disappearing. The successful ones are upscale properties, with on-site spas, pools, putting greens, beaches, dining rooms, and concierge services. They feel almost like a private club and often lay claim to beautifully manicured estates dating back many decades. The more casual, cost-saving variety are regrettably a thing of the past.

Small Hotels

Repeat visitors swear by the island's small hotels, which often seem to offer as much in the way of luxurious amenities as their bigger counterparts. Spas, high-end restaurants, and designer baths are slowly becoming the norm for many of these. Yet they retain an intimate feel and connection with staff and other guests, which many visitors to the island like to experience.

Conduct and Customs

ATTITUDES AND ETIQUETTE

Perhaps due to its British past, the island projects an air of entrenched conservatism, at least on the surface. Loud public demonstrations, liberal sentiments, and overly revealing clothing—or a lack of adequate clothing altogether—do not go down well with most Bermudians. Men and women, black and white, tend to project a polite reserve upon initial contact—until they've sized you up, anyway. Like their iconic onions, they prefer to reveal themselves gradually.

Generally, things tend to change slowly in Bermuda, including attitudes and the adoption of new ideas. Outsiders are suspect—at least at first. A certain pace and ritual is expected in social encounters: The omission of a requisite "Good morning" or "Good afternoon" (passkeys to any conversation with locals) can mean the difference between terse unhelpfulness and beaming cooperation. Indeed, there's a darkly humorous local joke that describes how (fictitious) Bermudian air-traffic controllers let a plane crash because the pilot forgets to greet them properly as he makes his descent.

Mostly, playing by the rules goes a long way toward really fitting into the island's sometimes oddball environment—just don't expect Bermudians to consistently do the same. They can be flagrant scofflaws, and nowhere is that more apparent than on the island's roads. Local drivers break speed limits, double-park to have a chat or grab a takeout, dump trash out their car windows, and overtake on blind hairpin bends at 70 miles per hour. These are the same folks who'll shake their heads and tut-tut in disapproval if someone tells a bawdy joke too loudly in a restaurant or happens to walk down the street in a bikini top.

Punctuality is not as big a problem in Bermuda as it is in more laid-back island nations to the south, but, aside from the corporate circles of Hamilton, locals often tend to avoid being overly fastidious about time. Nor are they too worried about returning phone calls or emails immediately, turning up when they said they would, or delivering what was promised. Yet jobs get done, people make a living, and the economy ticks along. But when 5 o'clock tolls, Bermudians head for the door. Don't try to achieve anything important toward the end of a workday afternoon, particularly in bureaucratic environments. That goes triple if it's a Friday afternoon before a public holiday weekend. Islanders *love* their holidays, and it really doesn't matter whether it's Christmas or Cup Match (although the latter sees Bermudian frivolity at the extreme). Driving through Hamilton at such times reveals a free-for-all, a cheerful camaraderie that reverberates through "Town," as people wave, shout, honk their horns at each other—and load up on groceries as if Armageddon were about to arrive.

FESTIVALS AND EVENTS

Bermuda hosts numerous festivals and throughout the year. Some of the most notable celebrations include:

- **Bermuda Day:** Enjoy watching this public holiday's bike race and half-marathon, followed by a carnival-style parade with dancers and marching bands through Hamilton, or dinghy racing in St. George's Harbour. Bermuda Day, the last Friday in May, also marks the official first day of summer boating for Bermudians.

- **Bermuda Fitted Dinghy Races:** Traditional dinghies vie for weekly honors throughout the summer. Races (www.rhadc.bm) take place every Sunday afternoon in St. George's Harbour, Mangrove Bay, and Granaway Deep.

- **Bermuda Heroes Weekend:** Held over a long weekend in June and marking different

Public Holidays

New Year's Day	January 1
Good Friday	late March or April
Bermuda Day	last Friday in May
National Heroes Day	mid-June
Cup Match	last Thursday and Friday in July or 1st Thursday and Friday in August
Emancipation Day	last Thursday in July or 1st Thursday in August
Somers Day	last Friday in July or 1st Friday in August
Labour Day	first week of September
Remembrance Day	November 11
Christmas Day	December 25
Boxing Day	December 26

Public holidays falling on a weekend result in public closures of shops and offices on the following weekday. Government offices are closed on public holidays and weekends. For more information on public holidays, contact the **Bermuda Employers Council** (tel. 441/295-5070).

island heroes in history, "BHW," as it's dubbed, has mushroomed into one of the year's biggest signature events (tel. 441/400-4376, www.bermudaheroesweekend.com). A series of events planned through the year but held throughout the weekend attracts thousands to take part in a dawn-to-dusk multiple-day soca carnival at different venues through the island.

- **Cup Match (Emancipation Day and Somers Day):** This two-day holiday in August honoring both the abolition of local slavery and Bermuda's founder, Sir George Somers, stages a historic showdown between St. George's and Somerset Cricket Clubs, complete with island-wide campouts, boating raft-ups, and parties galore.

Health and Safety

With one of the highest standards of living anywhere, Bermuda poses none of the health risks found in many exotic destinations, particularly those in the Caribbean or Latin America. Notably, the island is free of the Zika virus plaguing that region; the government confirmed there was no known local transmission of the virus on the island.

Sanitary standards are excellent in Bermuda, and health care is modern and professional. The island's freshwater, rain caught on the limestone-coated roofs and channeled into tanks below every home, is nearly always potable—except after hurricanes and severe storms, when consuming water that's been exposed to rotting foliage and other debris in the tanks can lead to stomachaches and intestinal problems. Bottled water is available in all grocery stores, gas stations, drugstores, and restaurants. Bermuda is subtropical and therefore has no common tropical diseases, such as malaria. Vaccinations are unnecessary.

Bring all prescription medications you may need with you, including enough for an extra day or two in case flights are canceled or travel is delayed for any reason. Wear a medical-alert bracelet if you have a health problem, to help medical staff treat you properly in an emergency. Eyewear prescriptions and meds, left in their original containers for easy passage through customs, are best packed in carry-on luggage in case bags go missing.

TRAVEL AND MEDICAL INSURANCE

Any industry veteran will tell you travel insurance—while often deemed unnecessary—is a prudent investment, particularly if your regular health insurance does not cover overseas expenses or treatment. As well, primary insurers can sometimes take up to two weeks to verify a patient's policy details—an unworkable delay in an emergency. Bermuda's hospital cannot treat overseas patients who are not covered by insurance, unless they are able to pay on the spot. In an emergency, traveler's health insurance avoids logistical nightmares, allowing for confirmation of an overseas hospital bed and immediate air-ambulance transport. Take time to review your health-care plan before leaving home to find out exactly what is covered, as well as any restrictions that might affect the choice of hospital in an emergency. Remember, it's not just the patient who may need help in an emergency but also relatives or companions who may have to find lodging or make other travel plans while a patient is in the hospital.

MEDICAL SERVICES

Good medical services are provided by the island's main health center, **King Edward VII Memorial Hospital** (7 Point Finger Rd., Paget, tel. 441/236-2345, www.bermudahospitals.bm), which was modernized with a $300 million Acute Care Centre in 2014. The hospital provides round-the-clock emergency care and island-wide ambulance service; it is equipped with maternity facilities, a children's ward, a hyperbaric recompression chamber for divers and diabetics, and intensive care, dialysis, oncology, OR, ER, and cardiac diagnostic units, as well as other specialty services. Emergency air-ambulance service, organized by the hospital, provides access within 24 hours to U.S. and Canadian cities for treatment of serious conditions, including severe burns and spinal, neurological, and coronary problems. The hospital's East End clinic, the **Lamb Foggo Urgent Care Centre** (1 Hall St., Southside, St. George's, tel. 441/298-7700, 4pm-midnight Mon.-Fri., noon-midnight Sat.-Sun.) treats minor injury or illness.

A second local hospital, the **Mid-Atlantic Wellness Institute** (formerly St. Brendan's Psychiatric Hospital, 44 Devon Springs Rd., Devonshire, tel. 441/236-3770, www.bermudahospitals.bm), offers professional counseling and treats patients suffering from mental disorders.

Well-stocked pharmacies and drugstores are located throughout the island. Pharmacists can issue a maximum five-day refill of a prescription, including a one-cycle pack of birth-control pills, providing they approve that the medications and doses are accurate. If a longer supply is needed, you'll have to visit a local doctor who can write a new prescription. Pharmacies do not accept prescriptions from overseas doctors, so any phone call to Bermuda that your home physician might make on your behalf would be wasted. If you need to see a doctor, appointments can be made via your hotel, guesthouse, or host. Most major resorts and hotels have a physician on call who can arrange treatment or phone prescriptions directly to a pharmacy, sometimes without an office visit. Cruise ship passengers can visit local pharmacies, but it's usually simpler to contact their ship's doctor, who can write a five-day prescription, fillable at an island pharmacy by the ship's agent.

MEDICAL EMERGENCIES

King Edward VII Memorial Hospital has an effective protocol in place for emergency treatment of visitors who may need to be flown off the island for specialized treatment—as

Emergency Contacts

Ambulance, Fire, Police, and Marine	911
King Edward VII Memorial Hospital	441/236-2345
King Edward VII Memorial Hospital Emergency Room	441/239-2009
Bermuda Police Service	441/295-0011
Fire Services Headquarters	441/292-5555
Electricity Power Outage	955
Telephone Repair Service	441/295-1001
Harbour Radio	441/297-1010
Weather Forecast	977
Women's Resource Hotline	441/295-7273
Physical Abuse Hotline	441/297-8278
Crime Stoppers (calls are anonymous)	441/800-8477
Government Emergency Radio Broadcast	100.1 MHz FM

long as health insurance or upfront funds are provided. An air-ambulance journey from Bermuda to the U.S. East Coast costs $10,000-15,000. Keep on hand your information about any preexisting medical condition, as well as the name and contact number of your primary doctor, so that if air-ambulance transport is necessary, hospital staff can arrange for your doctor to be the receiving physician at the destination.

Among their myriad tasks, "Pink Ladies" and "Pink Men" volunteers (whose title refers to their rosy uniforms) help families find emergency lodging if a relative or traveling companion ends up having to stay in the hospital. Many island hotels and guesthouses also try to accommodate visitors during emergencies.

Patients who have been checked into the hospital need a "fit-to-fly" document signed by a local doctor in order to leave. The other possibility is for patients or their families to sign an "against medical advice" form, or AMA, but departure from the island's airport under such circumstances ranges from difficult to impossible. For cruise ship passengers checking out of the hospital, doctors will confer with the ship's physician to ensure all necessary equipment (oxygen, for example) is aboard the vessel before it leaves port.

The U.S. Consulate General (Crown Hill, 16 Middle Rd., Devonshire, tel. 441/295-1342, for life-and-death emergencies duty phone 441/278-7512 or 441/278-7514 during regular hours, or 441/335-3828 after hours or Sat.-Sun., http://bm.usconsulate.gov, 8am-4:30pm Mon.-Fri. except Bermuda and U.S. public holidays) can aid American citizens when things go awry, particularly those lacking travel insurance.

HEALTH PROBLEMS
Sunburn and Dehydration

Bermuda's high humidity, coupled with blistering summer temperatures—in the high 90s for much of July and August—can lead to severe sunburns, dehydration, and sunstroke. Regardless of your skin tone, wear sunscreens with high SPF content; some brands, such as Australia's Bullfrog, make waterproof sunblock of SPF 50 or higher, which protects your skin from harmful UVA and UVB rays for hours, even if you're sweating or in the water.

If you're not accustomed to the heat, cover up. Wear light clothing of natural fibers like cotton or silk that covers easy-to-burn or overexposed areas. Arms, hands, and shoulders can burn while driving a scooter, and even moped passengers end up sporting lobster-red knees and feet after sitting in the same position under scorching skies. Protect your face, including eyes and lips, with shades, a sun hat, and lip balm with sunblock. If you do get too much sun, slather on aloe creams or place paper towels soaked in vinegar on the affected region (an island remedy to draw the heat out). Then try to skip a day or two's beaching to let your skin recover; visit a museum or go shopping instead.

Stay hydrated in hot weather by drinking lots of water throughout the day, especially if you're exercising. Bermuda's humidity, regularly in the 80-90 percent zone, can make it feel like you're moving around inside a greenhouse. Dehydration's onset—including heavy sweating, cramps, and dizziness—means it's time to get out of the sun to let your body rest. Heat stroke, a potentially fatal condition, happens when the body's self-regulating thermometer shuts down completely. Symptoms include severe headaches and delirium. Get emergency aid and keep heat-stroke patients as cool as possible. Bermuda's hospital emergency department has intravenous treatment to speedily rehydrate and reenergize heat-stroke victims with electrolytes and water.

Keep children well protected from the sun, especially toddlers, who are often oblivious to the sun, or youngsters who may not complain about burns until the damage is done. Reapply sunscreen often, particularly if you are swimming, and take a large water bottle to the beach. Many adults and kids in Bermuda wear UV-protective clothing, including hats, bodysuits, and long-sleeved, high-necked tops made of swimsuit fabric to guard against months of destructive sun exposure at the beach or on the water. One local company, **Groovy UV** (tel. 441/232-0527), operated by Bermudian sailors Debbie and Adam Barboza, offers a full range of colorful outfits for all ages, including UV goggles and board shorts.

Sexually Transmitted Diseases

An estimated 300 people were living with AIDS/HIV on the island in 2016, and 767 have been diagnosed since the first reported AIDS case in Bermuda in 1982, according to the Department of Health. Less severe sexually transmitted diseases such as gonorrhea, syphilis, and genital warts are also the focus of periodic public health campaigns. Condoms can be purchased in all the island's drugstores. Confidential HIV screening and counseling are available at the **Communicable Disease Control Clinic** at the Hamilton Health Centre (67 Victoria St., tel. 441/292-6777, 8:30am-4:45pm Mon.-Thurs.). The Hamilton Health Centre also offers information regarding **sexual health services** (tel. 441/278-6442 or 441/236-0224, ext. 229 or ext. 242, 2pm-4pm Mon.-Fri.).

Insects and Poison Ivy

Bermuda has no truly dangerous wildlife—no scorpions, snakes, nor even sharks close to shore. (Sharks do frequent local waters but are seen rarely inshore. As a result, there has not been a reported shark attack in more than 50 years.) The few hazards that do exist are not serious, and mostly of the insect variety.

Mosquitoes are irritating outdoor pests on summer evenings, and during the day in areas where they breed. Wear a repellent in areas near ponds or marshland, for example, and after dark when the insects are prevalent. Bermuda's subtropical climate is also conducive to flea infestations; responsible pet owners treat cats and dogs regularly with prescription flea-killers that stop the little parasites from infestation. Bermuda has no ticks.

American cockroaches (the large, flying type)—euphemistically dubbed "palmetto bugs" in Florida—can be seen everywhere at night throughout the hot summer months, even on the walls inside elegant homes. They are rather frightening apparitions upon first encounter, but they are harmless; window screens usually serve to keep them outdoors. Savvy scooter riders appreciate shades or, better still, helmets with visors to keep wayward flying insects from face collisions.

Ants by the thousands are a byproduct of summer and are especially apparent after severe storms or hurricanes. Again, they are harmless, but a nuisance. To keep their numbers down, avoid leaving dirty dishes around, including pet bowls, and conquer invasions with a simple household tool: the vacuum cleaner. Some also swear by lemon sprays and baby powder.

The St. David's centipede, or giant centipede, which can grow to a foot in length, is rarely seen these days, but it can inflict a mild bite, so avoid it if you happen to spot one.

Poison ivy *(Rhus radicans)* grows wild in parks and brush areas of the island, including off-trail parts of Paget Marsh and other nature reserves. Stay on boardwalks or main trails to avoid it. Rash, blisters, and itchiness break out once you have been exposed to the plant, but they usually disappear without treatment within a couple of weeks. Use cool compresses or an antihistamine to soothe the itching.

BEACH HAZARDS
Rip Currents and Undertows

Other than the risk of scooter accidents, the sea poses the greatest danger to Bermuda visitors, particularly rip currents and undertows found off the South Shore beaches. Drownings are infrequent—and often caused by neither phenomenon. Bermuda has very few "dangerous surf" days, except around hurricanes, which tend to occur at the season's end in September and October. But inexperienced swimmers should check beach conditions carefully before entering the water and know what to do if they encounter risks.

Rip currents, also called riptides (though they are not tidal), are found at the world's surf beaches, such as those on Bermuda's South Shore. They occur as water dumped by breakers at the shoreline returns to the deep sea, "ripping" past natural structures such as rocks, reefs, or sandbars. They are intensified by onshore winds coupled with storm conditions. A rip current is recognizable as a sandy stream of fast-moving water flowing seaward, sometimes splashing as it hits incoming waves. It moves at right angles from the beach—a bottleneck of water stretching up to 200 meters. Swimmers trapped in its movement feel helpless as the surge carries them away from the beach. If you find yourself in a rip current, the number-one rule is: Keep calm. Swimming against the outward-flowing water is exhausting and unproductive, even for strong swimmers. Instead, try to swim across it, parallel to the beach. Rip currents aren't very wide, so a swimmer can usually reach the current's edge, escape its pull, and then swim back to safety. If you can't, don't panic. The current will eventually release you and will not pull you under.

Undertows or "runbacks," sometimes mistakenly called rip currents, occur by contrast in the rolling surf at the edge of steep beaches, posing a risk to weak swimmers. As a wave is about to break, water from the beach edge is sucked back beneath it. The force of gravity can be strong enough to sweep swimmers off their feet and beneath the crashing surf. The cycle repeats as more waves break, disperse, and break again. The phenomenon, intensified by the angle of a beach, can make even practiced bodysurfers feel a sense of lost control. If you get swept into a series of waves, try to stand up, climb out, or call for help.

May-October, lifeguards are stationed 10am-6pm daily at a few popular and family beaches around the island, including Horseshoe Bay in Southampton, John Smith's Bay in Smith's, and Clearwater, Turtle and Long Beach in St. George's. They are on the lookout for swimmers in trouble; wave an arm or call out if you need help. Avoid swimming alone or in rough conditions or storm swells; bodysurfing in hurricane surf, for example, can cause spinal fractures and other injuries. Warning signs and flags are posted in particularly stormy conditions at popular beaches, including Horseshoe Bay and Warwick Long Bay. A yellow flag crossed by a black diagonal stripe is a warning: See on-duty lifeguards or read information boards posted at the beach entrance. A red flag, for example, around a hurricane's approach and aftermath prohibits swimming. A flag atop the lifeguard tower indicates that a lifeguard is on duty.

Cliff-Diving

Shallow water and submerged rocks near favorite swimming holes have over the years left Bermudians paralyzed, in comas, or dead. While cliff-jumping has become extremely popular, especially at well-known points such as Admiralty House Park in Pembroke, diving headfirst from any points around the island where you are not entirely sure of water depth or the possibility of concealed reefs, sunken objects, or other hazards is ill-advised.

Portuguese Man-of-Wars

A translucent, frilly-edged, violet balloon, the jellyfish known as the Portuguese man-of-war might be considered exquisitely beautiful—if it wasn't such a menace.

This invertebrate marine animal (*Physalia physalis*) has a gas-filled purple-blue float topped by a crest that catches the wind and carries the organism over the ocean. But what you see at the surface is just a fraction of the creature, whose severely poisonous tentacles stretch many feet below. Found in the Gulf Stream and in tropical oceans worldwide, Portuguese man-of-wars travel in schools of hundreds or thousands and can be a swimming hazard on Bermuda's South Shore year-round, depending on wind direction and other conditions. Onshore winds blow them in. Look for their balloons washed up on the beach (they are difficult to spot on the sea surface) before you enter the water.

Avoid getting stung by the man-of-war's clinging blue tentacles, which can cause intense pain and occasional blistering, and leave red welts on the skin. The impact is rarely more serious, though small children, the elderly, and those with allergies face a greater risk of severe reaction. Notably, the jellyfish is not only harmful when intact, but also when its myriad tentacles are broken into particles by the surf, causing rashes and irritation. Out of the water, the sting is no less severe, so don't be tempted to pick one up.

The best remedy if you do get stung? Treatment and opinion among medical professionals has evolved over the past 20 years, advising everything from meat tenderizer to urine, and there is still no absolute consensus. The key, says Dr. Edward Schultz, director of Bermuda's ER, is to deactivate the venom-firing cells, called nematocysts, released by tentacles on to the skin. Schultz recommends that jellyfish victims:

- Remove any visible bits of tentacle (wipe off with a towel or gloved hand).
- Rinse with seawater.
- Soak the area in vinegar (acetic acid soothes pain and reduces inflammation).
- Shave the affected area to remove stinging particles.
- Apply a warm compress or immerse in hot water.

Lifeguards on Bermuda beaches will assist you with first aid if you get stung. While a hospital visit isn't usually necessary, go to the ER immediately if you have difficulty breathing, feel lightheaded or weak, or if the rash spreads. For emergency aid, call 911.

Fire Coral

Fire coral (Cnidaria phylum), a reddish-brown spongy-looking mass on the island's reefs, can deliver a stinging, burn-like sensation. Related to the jellyfish rather than the coral family, it can also scrape the skin. Rule of thumb on the reefs: Don't touch anything—for your comfort, as well as the reef's longevity (real corals can die when touched).

Other Marinelife

Fish to avoid include the porcupine-like lionfish, a poisonous species usually found in Australasia, but which has infiltrated Bermuda's waters in recent years. The fish usually avoids human contact, but if touched it releases venom from its puncturing spines.

The great barracuda's menacing profile is deceptive; despite its ugly, toothy grin, this large fish is usually harmless, though barracudas have been known to snap at shiny metal objects, so keep watches and jewelry out of sight. Moray eels may look fearsome, but they mostly avoid human contact—unless you shove a hand into one's lair.

Do not touch the flat red bristleworm or the related fireworm; their needles leave a rash. Most corals, sea anemones, and jellyfish deposit a poisonous zap on human skin, so try not to touch them. Spiny sea urchins hidden in sea grass also pose a hazard; wearing fins or surf slippers helps avoid such dangers, as well as nasty reef scrapes and coral cuts.

CRIME

Against Bermuda's bucolic backdrop, the specter of crime—even the petty variety (handbag snatches, break-ins)—may seem out of place. But it is an unfortunate reality of modern life. Every parish has its share of neighborhoods plagued by perennial drug problems, the catalyst for most of the island's criminal activity; gangs and drug abuse appear to be the biggest factors driving an increase in violent crime in modern Bermuda. For the visitor, this flip side of local life is usually barely visible, but it is there nonetheless, and sensible measures should be taken to guard against opportunistic crime.

Closed-circuit surveillance cameras are installed in several Hamilton locations, including North Hamilton's Court Street and Pembroke's Pitts Bay Road—two economically divergent neighborhoods, yet both areas where police have recorded a high number of crimes, ranging from bag-snatchings to assaults and drug-related incidents. Cameras in other parts of the city have reduced the number of bike thefts, bag snatches, and public nuisances.

Bag-Snatching

Protect your belongings and use the same street sense and practical judgment you would anywhere else in the world. The most common crime is bag-snatching, from beaches, scooter baskets, or, on rare occasions, from scooter riders wearing bags over one arm—sometimes leading to traffic accidents and injuries. Visitors are not the only victims; Bermuda residents are also targets, though most have learned to lock away handbags, knapsacks, or shopping items in compartments attached to the back or under the scooter seat, or to strap down belongings in a rear basket with bungee cords looped through bag handles. Thieves have also targeted tourists strolling through Hamilton's streets at night, notably in quiet, seemingly safe, upscale neighborhoods, where numerous hotels and guesthouses are located.

Take cabs at night if you are traveling alone. Be aware of your surroundings, keep wallets or purses out of sight, and wear long-strapped bags across your body, or hold them firmly to avoid becoming easy prey. On beaches, don't leave belongings unattended, or if you do, don't carry valuables and money. It is not unusual for swimmers to come back from a swim to find belongings gone or bags missing contents.

Break-Ins

Break-ins and home burglaries do occur throughout the parishes, and again, Bermudian householders face a similar risk. Indeed, although leaving doors unlocked was the neighborhood habit of decades past, residents rarely leave their homes unlocked anymore when they're out. Most locals also lock doors and windows overnight when they're sleeping. Tourist properties, particularly guesthouses and rental cottages outside the more secure confines of a hotel, are frequently targeted. Thieves know that windows and sliding-glass doors at holiday properties are often left open through ignorance or to let in the breeze if there's no air-conditioning. Easy-to-cut screens are no deterrent. Thieves commonly break into rooms and residences when inhabitants are sleeping, though break-ins have rarely turned violent. Use hotel property safes to store valuables, and lock your room or house at night and when you're not around.

Motorcycle Theft

Scooters are favorite targets of thieves, who usually go for joyrides or scavenge for spare parts before dumping the remains on the roadside. Lock up your scooter or moped whenever you leave it. Scooters sometimes have both an ignition lock and a U-lock to place on the back wheel. It's a drag to have to fiddle with several times a day, but well worth the effort. Other bikes are safe as long as the ignition key is removed. If your rental scooter or bike is stolen, contact the livery, which will usually collect you if you're stranded and notify the police.

Harassment

Travelers tired of harassment in the Caribbean will appreciate being left alone in Bermuda; rarely are drugs offered or sold in public, and purveyors of services such as hair-braiding generally do not actively solicit clients, foreigners included. In recent years, Hamilton has experienced a minor problem with panhandling, but those who beg are typically harmless and less dogged than in many other places.

SMOKING

Smoking is banned in Bermuda's enclosed public places and work areas under a 2006 law that included bars, restaurants, shops, cinemas, or any enclosed workplace—in line with similar rulings in North America and Europe. The law also prohibits cigarette vending machines on the island and the sale of cigarettes to anyone under age 18. Penalties for smokers who defy the law are $250, or $1,000 for repeat offenders.

Travel Tips

WHAT TO PACK

Bermuda's summer heat demands flip-flops, leather sandals, or boat shoes for comfort. Breathable fabrics such as cotton or silk are recommended for all seasons; layer up when it gets chilly. A waterproof, windproof anorak is always useful. Hats and shades are a must. Waterproof sunblock is also necessary, and mosquito repellent is advised.

BUSINESS HOURS

Most Hamilton offices follow their North American and English counterparts, with an official eight-hour workday Monday through Friday. Staff in retail outlets start winding down at 4:30pm, in readiness for a prompt 5pm exit. The "rush hour"—a misnomer, since it is more a motorized crawl through the parishes—typically runs 7:30am-9:15am weekday mornings and 5pm-6:15pm evenings, as residents make their way to and from Hamilton en masse. Traveling to and from the East End in these hours is usually not too difficult. Try to avoid being caught up in the western flow of traffic, however; all three arteries to and from Hamilton (Harbour Rd., Middle Rd., and South Shore) are crammed bumper-to-bumper with cars, and scooters zip down the center line to get ahead.

Major Front Street stores stay open during the summerlong Harbour Nights street festival (7pm-9pm). Stores throughout Hamilton usually keep longer Friday hours (until 9pm) during the Christmas period.

As a conservative, religious society with

more churches per square mile than nearly anywhere, Bermuda has been slow to embrace Sunday shopping. The law was amended in the late 1990s, and since then, most supermarkets are open 1pm-6pm, and hardware stores and some department stores are following suit. Alcohol was finally allowed to be sold 8am-9pm in grocery and liquor after a legislative amendment was passed in 2014. Most bars stay open until 1am, though nightclubs and a few private after-hours clubs wait to shut their doors until 3am.

TIME

Bermuda is on Atlantic time, one hour ahead of the Eastern time zone (Toronto, New York, and the U.S. East Coast) and four hours behind Greenwich mean time. Daylight saving time is observed, with clocks jumping forward an hour each spring and back in the fall. Daylight saving time was aligned with U.S. energy-saving measures in 2007, starting in mid-March and ending in early November. Dawn ranges 6:15am in summer to 7:30am in winter, and dusk falls between 5:15pm and 8:30pm.

MEASUREMENTS

Although Bermuda adopted the metric system for measurement in the second half of the 1900s (just as it went decimal in its currency), the conversion was far from universal on the island. As in Britain, imperial measures are found just as commonly in Bermuda as metric ones, both in private and government use, though United Nations reporting guidelines are typically followed by public agencies. Therefore, you'll see ubiquitous references in both official literature and local conversations to the island's size of 21 square miles or 21-mph speed limit, police reports describing individuals' height and weight in feet and pounds, newspaper ads for 10K running races, trade statistics in kilograms, and pool lengths by the meter. In this guidebook, the imperial system is used for measurements.

ACCESS FOR TRAVELERS WITH DISABILITIES

Bermuda is far from ideal as an accessible destination for travelers with disabilities, of whom arrive on cruise ships. But improvements have been made in recent years. Many more attractions, city sidewalks, restaurants, nightclubs, and public buildings have been made wheelchair accessible. However, many places, including retail stores and restaurants, and even some cruise ship ramps, pose great physical challenges. While the fast ferries and ramp-fitted ferry terminal are a breeze, public buses are not at all equipped for disabled access. Lobby groups have also complained that too few taxis accommodate wheelchairs.

The **WindReach Recreational Village** (57 Spice Hill Rd., Warwick, tel. 441/238-2469, www.windreachbermuda.org) is a nonprofit community group located on a quiet chunk of rural property surrounded by agricultural fields and residential neighborhoods. It offers special-needs services and activities, including a petting zoo, a wheelchair-accessible playground, and a fully accessible camping area with wheelchair-accommodating cabins, baths, and shower facilities. Located on the same property, **Bermuda Riding for the Disabled** (tel. 441/238-7433, http://brd. free.bm) provides therapeutic riding lessons and programs for children and adults with disabilities.

The **Bermuda Physically Handicapped Association** (Summerhaven, South Shore Rd., Hamilton Parish, tel. 441/734-8260, summerhaven@northrock.bm) is located on a quiet stretch of South Shore Road, opposite scenic John Smith's Bay.

The **Bermuda Red Cross** (Charleswood, 9 Berry Hill Rd., Paget, tel. 441/236-8253, www.bermudaredcross.com) rents equipment such as walkers and wheelchairs. Other resources include the **Association for the Mentally Handicapped** (tel. 441/292-7206); **Bermuda Islands Association of the Deaf** (tel. 441/238-8116, biad@therock.

bm); and **Bermuda Society for the Blind** (Beacon House, 3 Beacon St., Hamilton, tel. 441/292-3231).

TRAVELING WITH CHILDREN

There's no end to child-friendly fun in Bermuda, and, best of all, a lot of it is absolutely free. Beaches, public playgrounds, gombey dances, and the serenade of tree frogs—kids fall in love with the island even faster than their parents. Traveling to Bermuda poses no special health risks; the island has a standard vaccination program for infants and children, so there are few serious communicable diseases. Bermuda is also rabies-free, and water from the taps is usually safe. The short flight from U.S. East Coast cities—a few short hours—is doable for kids; flights from London are about seven hours. Many of the major hotels have special kids' camps during the summer high season; inquire about their activities and age restrictions when you book accommodations. Some hotels and guesthouses can also arrange babysitting.

Most child-care products are easily available on the island at drugstores and supermarkets, including diapers, wipes, sunblock, and children's pain relievers. The majority stock North American brands, except for The Supermart's popular English Waitrose grocery line; if you're traveling from Europe and will miss a favorite product, you might want to bring it with you. There are numerous toy stores and kids' clothing outlets, though prices generally run at least a third higher than in the United States. Generally, local eateries are more than willing to try to make young diners happy, with kids' menus, high chairs, and cheery waitstaff.

The best public playgrounds are located at Mullet Bay in St. George's; Shelly Bay in Hamilton Parish; Parson's Road in Pembroke; South Shore Road in Warwick (just east of the entrance to Warwick Long Bay); Death Valley, Middle Road, in Southampton; and inside the National Museum of Bermuda at Dockyard.

All are equipped with regulation climbing frames, tunnels, swings, and slides for both toddlers and older children.

WOMEN TRAVELING ALONE

Women will find Bermuda a far more benign traveling environment than many places in the Caribbean, Central America, or even a typical North American city. Bermudians pride themselves on the safety of their island, and violent, arbitrary crime is extremely rare. Female travelers should nevertheless use common sense and practical measures to keep safe, especially at night and if alone or in more remote areas. The Bermuda Police Service advises women traveling alone to choose well-lit routes and areas, to protect purses and other possessions against crimes of opportunity, and to carry a cell phone, flashlight, or warning device such as a small air horn. Mace and pepper spray are illegal in Bermuda. When socializing out at bars or restaurants, keep your drink in sight and don't accept drinks from strangers; date-rape drugs have been used on the island. Do not accept rides home from strangers, even if calling a cab may entail a longer wait.

Women need not expect to encounter unwanted harassment, either, although Bermudian men have the odd habit of issuing a surreptitious hiss to catch your attention. Whether you smile, wave, or have no reaction, there's rarely any further approach. The exception may be on the beaches, where local men sometimes try to chat up foreign women.

Should you need help or advice, the **Women's Resource Centre** (25 Point Finger Rd., Paget, tel. 441/295-3882, 9am-5pm Mon.-Fri., 24-hour crisis hotline 441/295-7273, www.wrcbermuda.com) is the island's prime advocacy group; its services include emergency response, counseling, assistance for victims, and a crisis intervention hotline. Other women's support and networking resources include a Bermuda group of the global 100 Women in Finance (http://100women.

org), Women in Reinsurance (http://www.wirebermuda.com), and the **Business & Professional Women's Association of Bermuda** (tel. 441/238-3685, bpwabermuda@yahoo.com).

SENIOR TRAVELERS

Bermuda has long been a favorite destination for older travelers, particularly in the wintertime, when golf, ecotours, and cultural programs take center stage. While scores of substantial discounts—on public transport, museums, and groceries—are offered to resident seniors, unfortunately these are not available to visitors. However, the island's moderate temperatures, easygoing lifestyle, and numerous accessible leisure activities make it popular among senior travelers, and costliness is often not a deterrent to this increasingly active and well-heeled demographic.

The best dedicated program for senior travelers to the island is Road Scholar, educational adventures created by the nonprofit Elderhostel. Based at Grotto Bay Beach Resort and Spa in Hamilton Parish, the program includes accommodations, dining, field trips, lectures, and evening entertainment for less than $350 a day. Weeklong courses range from a study of Bermuda birds to local history and heritage to an inside look at the cutting-edge global "science in Bermuda shorts" that goes on at the world-famous Bermuda Institute of Ocean Science (BIOS), encompassing topics such as the ocean's influence on climate change. All participants should be able to walk at least a mile, enjoy a long bus tour, and feel comfortable on short, smooth boat trips. To register or find out more, contact **Road Scholar** (tel. 877/426-8056, www.roadscholar.org).

The November-March period offers a program of daily events geared to visitors of all ages, though these are particularly popular with seniors. Included are glass-blowing demonstrations, bagpipe skirling ceremonies, gombey revues, guided walking tours of Hamilton, St. George's, and Somerset Village, and historical reenactments in St. George's. In any season, older travelers who wish to steer clear of scooters should opt for a multiday transportation pass that allows unlimited use of ferries and buses within the designated time frame. One-day, three-day, seven-day, and monthlong passes can be purchased at Visitor Information Centres and the Hamilton bus or ferry terminals.

GAY AND LESBIAN TRAVELERS

While Bermuda has a general tolerance for gays and lesbians on a grassroots level, politically, the island lags far behind North American and European societies. Gay sex was illegal in Bermuda until 1994, when Parliament decriminalized sexual relations between men after a private bill was introduced that year. No former law had outlawed lesbian sex.

More recently the island's gay community, led by grassroots lobbyists and supported by Amnesty International (Bermuda), battled for human rights legislation that would prevent discrimination based on sexual orientation. In 2013, Bermuda's Parliament voted in favor of landmark legislation, the Human Rights Amendment Act, that finally added sexual orientation to the list of prohibited grounds of discrimination.

In 2017, the island's Parliament voted against allowing same-sex marriages, but a landmark case effectively legalized same-sex marriages later that year after a gay couple took their case to the Supreme Court and won; the court ruled any ban on such a union was discriminatory and violated human rights. The island's first same-sex wedding was conducted at the Registry-General a month later. By year's end, however, an effective roll-back of marriage equality occurred under a new PLP government when the Parliament passed the Domestic Partnerships Act. The new law prevents any new same-sex marriages, offering fewer rights under domestic partnerships. LGBTQ couples who married elsewhere after same-sex marriages were banned on the

Tie the Knot

Planning to say "I do"? Bermuda is a top wedding destination, thanks to its heart-stopping scenery, proximity to North America, and relatively easy marriage requirements. The island dotes on long-held wedding traditions, including romantic moon gates (kiss beneath one and a long marriage is assured), horse-drawn carriages, his-and-hers gold and silver cakes, and locations like historic churches, public gardens, clifftops, and beaches that promise highly memorable nuptials.

Scores of visitors get married in Bermuda every year, so everyone—from local wedding planners to clergy and hotel staff—is ready to ease prospective brides and grooms (unfortunately, same-sex marriages are not currently legal in Bermuda) through the process. Many guesthouses and hotels have special **wedding packages,** churches offer chaplains for off-site locations, and even Bermuda's sometimes burdensome bureaucracy has honed the business of getting married into a painless to-do list.

Couples must have their "Notice of Intended Marriage" published in Bermuda's newspapers. You can download the form from www.gotobermuda.com (must be printed on white legal-size paper, 8.5 by 14 inches) or request one from the **Registry General** (Government Administration Building, 30 Parliament St., Hamilton HM 12, tel. 441/297-7709 or 441/297-7707, www.gov.bm/getting-married-bermuda). No blood tests or health certificates are needed, but copies of divorce decrees or death certificates must be submitted with the completed form, along with a cashier's check or bank draft for $368. After the notice is published, a license to marry is granted. It is valid for three months and can be collected from the Registry General office.

Civil ceremonies can be performed weekdays (10am-noon and 2pm-3:30pm) or Saturday mornings (10am-11:30am) in the Registry's Marriage Room for $245. Since new legislation passed in the fall of 2016, the Registry has also been to perform civil ceremonies outdoors on government properties such as scenic parks and beaches ($450). For more information, contact the Registry's Kim Minors (kminors@gov.bm). Justices of the Peace cannot perform marriages in Bermuda. You must have two witnesses over the age of 18 to any wedding ceremony; these can be provided by the Registry General's office Monday-Friday only.

Churches can be booked for a fee, and officiating clergy can be arranged to perform the ceremony on-site or elsewhere. **Catholic churches** in Bermuda will marry nonresident Catholics if baptismal certificates and other documents are provided in advance (for details, visit www.romancatholicbermuda.bm). Couples seeking marriage blessings or renewal of vows need to provide copies of their original Catholic marriage certificate.

Bermuda has several top-rated wedding planners, who efficiently coordinate details, from flowers and photographers to accommodations and catering. Among the best: **Bermuda Bride** (tel. 441/295-8697, www.bermudabride.com); **Das Fete** (tel. 441/400-5048, dasfete.com); **Bermuda Event Solutions** (tel. 441/236-9469, www.weddingsolutions.bm); **The Bridal Suite** (tel. 441/292-2025, www.bridalsuitebermudaweddings.com); and **To Have and To Hold Wedding and Event Planning** (tel. 441/236-7473, www.tohaveandtoholdbermuda.com).

One of the best resources to help prospective brides and grooms pull together all the details of their big day is the Bermudian Publishing Company's *Bermudian Weddings* magazine website (www.bermudianweddings.com). It carries advice from wedding planners; contacts for flowers, fashions, cakes, and rentals; bridal blogs sharing useful resources; plus photo features on real Bermuda weddings.

island are to be considered domestic partnerships in Bermuda.

Gay tourists will probably not experience any overt discrimination, but it's useful to recognize the island is a very conservative society, and open displays of affection even among heterosexuals are unusual, so subtlety is valued. Religious viewpoints drive public sentiment against same-sex relationships and marriage.

Bermuda hotels and guesthouses are noted for being welcoming and respectful to gay guests include the Fairmont Southampton and Hamilton Princess, The Reefs, and Royal Palms, among others.

VOLUNTEERING

Bermuda's charities and nonprofit organizations depend heavily on volunteers to carry out much of their day-to-day workload. Very often, unpaid volunteers are retired or wealthy Bermudians, or the spouses of expatriate workers who don't hold work permits and are looking for social and professional interaction. From walking the canine residents of the SPCA to providing CPR instruction to staffing the front desk at an art gallery, volunteers keep the island running smoothly. If you are visiting Bermuda for an extended period and would like to get involved, check the charities' listings in the Bermuda Yellow Pages (www.bermudayp.com), or contact the **Centre on Philanthropy** (Sterling House, 16 Wesley St., Hamilton, tel. 441/236-7706, www.centreonphilanthropy.org) to find out which organizations are in need of extra help.

Information and Services

TOURIST INFORMATION

The website of the **Bermuda Tourism Authority** (www.gotobermuda.com) offers a well-researched rundown on immigration rules, wedding resources, daily activities, seasonal events, island-wide accommodations, and group and incentive tours, along with a mechanism to book trips online, including air-and-hotel packages. The **BTA** (22 Church St., Hamilton, tel. 441/296-9200, contact@bermudatourism.com, U.S./Canada tel. 800/BERMUDA—800/237-6832, email travel@bermudatourism.com) is based in Hamilton.

Once on the island, a first stop should be any of three **Visitor Information Centres,** open year-round to provide free maps and brochures. They can also advise on day trips, tours, shows, and other activities. Opening hours vary:

- **City of Hamilton** (Front St., next to the ferry terminal, tel. 441/295-1480, 9am-4pm Mon.-Sat. year-round)
- **Royal Naval Dockyard** (Gazebo 2, Terrace Pavilion, in front of ferry dock, tel. 441/542-7104, 8am-8pm daily when a ship is in port, 8am-4pm daily otherwise)
- **St. George's** (7 Market Wharf, King's Square, tel. 441/297-0556, 10am-4pm Mon.-Sat., depending on cruise ship schedules)

Two additional visitors centers are open in Dockyard's cruise ship terminals, King's Wharf and Heritage Wharf, but are only open when a ship is in port.

MAPS

The pocket-size *Handy Reference Map,* an easy-to-read, east-to-west depiction of sights and attractions produced by the BTA, can be picked up at the VICs or at information booths at cruise terminals, the Clocktower Mall in Dockyard, and other points, along with bus and ferry schedules and brochures on restaurants, shopping, water sports, nature reserves, and the Railway Trail. Bus and ferry schedules, tokens, and passes can be purchased at the ferry terminal or the Hubert W. "Sparky" Lightbourne Central Bus Terminal, both in Hamilton.

MONEY

Bermuda's currency, formerly based on the British sterling system of pounds, shillings, and pence, went decimal in 1970, adopting colorful dollars and cents issued by the Bermuda Monetary Authority (BMA). Today, Bermuda's money is pegged to the U.S. dollar and interchangeable with it anywhere on the island.

In 2009, Bermuda released a new set of banknotes, even more striking in their design and color scheme than the originals.

Incorporating cultural icons and island landmarks, including flora and fauna, plus numerous innovative security features, the currency includes banknotes in denominations of $2 (turquoise, bluebird), $5 (violet-red, blue marlin), $10 (indigo, angelfish), $20 (green, whistling tree frog), $50 (yellow-orange, longtail), and $100 (red-orange, cardinal).

Coins are similarly artistic, especially the penny, manufactured in bronze with the image of a wild hog on the back—a tribute to the distinctive and now very rare Hogge money forged for use by settlers in the colony's early years, when tobacco-bartering was also common. Other coin denominations, in nickel, include: 5 cents (angelfish), 10 cents (lily), 25 cents (longtail), and $1 (gold, Bermuda fitted dinghy). The $1 coin was introduced in 1988 when a $1 note was discontinued and a $2 introduced. Since her coronation in 1952, all notes and coins have featured Queen Elizabeth II, though in the latest note series, her image is simply a small profile on the front bottom-left corner. Because Bermuda notes and coins are restricted to use on the island, U.S. currency is used by all island-based international companies and their non-Bermudian employees, who are paid in U.S. dollars and hold local U.S.-dollar accounts at Bermudian banks.

Changing Money

Travelers are advised to bring credit cards plus a minimum amount of cash for their Bermuda holiday. Since Bermudian currency cannot be exchanged at foreign banks, ask stores for U.S. change where possible before leaving the island (many merchants are happy to comply); HSBC's Harbourview Centre (37 Front St.) and Church Street branch (64 Church St.), both in Hamilton, have handy U.S. cash ATMs, as do the Butterfield locations (65 Front St. and 11 Bermudiana Rd.). There is also a U.S. dollar ATM at the airport. Bermuda's three licensed retail banks are HSBC (37 Front St., tel. 441/295-4000, www.hsbc.bm), Butterfield Bank (65 Front St., tel. 441/295-1111, www.bm.butterfieldgroup.com), or Clarien Bank

Collectible Currency

Bermuda launched a set of striking new banknotes in 2009 to coincide with the island's 400th anniversary of settlement. It marks the first redesign since Bermuda went decimal and introduced the Bermuda dollar (on par with its U.S. counterpart) in 1970.

The colorful notes are distinctive and popular among collectors—most notably, perhaps, for their shape: They are vertically oriented. They also feature bold designs that incorporate the island's iconic flora and fauna—tree frogs, cardinals, longtails, angelfish, and bluebirds—along with enhanced anticounterfeiting elements such as new watermarks, iridescent bands, see-through features, and serial numbers that increase in size.

The notes, released by the Bermuda Monetary Authority (BMA), are available in collector sets, along with special coin releases of the past, from the BMA offices (43 Victoria St., tel. 441/295-5278, www.bma.bm, 9am-4pm Mon.-Fri.).

(19 Reid St., tel. 441/296-6969, www.clarienbank.com). Monday and Friday are busiest, especially during lunch hours when Bermuda residents do most of their banking; the advent of online banking in recent years, however, has cut down on bank lines.

ATM machines, open 24 hours, are located at each bank's Hamilton headquarters and throughout the island at bank branches, gas stations, and supermarkets. Butterfield Bank introduced the first multicurrency ATM in 2014 in the airport's refurbished International Lounge; it dispenses Canadian dollars, British pounds, and euros.

The island's ATMs issue a maximum of BM$2,500 per day (or much less, depending on your home bank's policy, which can be as low as US$250 per day) and charge a 1.5 percent transaction fee of the dollar amount withdrawn, with a minimum fee of $2.50. Bermudians can buy foreign currency, including U.S. and Canadian dollars, British pounds, euros, and special-order currencies, from all the banks. Bank hours vary, but most are open 9am-4:30pm; Somerset, St. George's, and airport branches have restricted hours.

Credit Cards

Major credit cards (Visa, MasterCard, American Express) are accepted at most hotels, restaurants, liveries, and retailers and can be used for cash advances at all bank branches. ATMs open 24 hours around the island also distribute cash advances for Visa, MasterCard, American Express, Cirrus, and Plus cards (know your PIN number). The American Express representative is Bermuda Financial Network (British-American Bldg., 4th Fl., 133 Front St., Hamilton, tel. 441/292-1799), which offers free phone calls and emergency AmEx card-replacement services. AmEx cardholders can also make payments on their cards at this office. It also allows money to be received or sent in minutes via Western Union money-transfer services.

Lost or stolen major credit cards can be reported to these contact numbers (800 numbers are not toll-free from Bermuda):

- American Express: tel. 800/528-4800
- MasterCard: tel. 800/307-7309
- Visa: tel. 800/847-2911
- Visa Gold/Business: tel. 800/847-2911

Costs

Despite the lack of sales tax, Bermuda rates as one of the priciest destinations in the world, and many visitors are surprised by the high cost of island living, particularly restaurant tabs (which add an automatic 17 percent gratuity) and grocery bills. But budget-conscious travelers can save money in a number of ways during a Bermuda vacation.

Booking an apartment or studio via websites such as Airbnb or VRBO can save the great expense of a resort vacation and allow you to live like a local. Shopping—wisely—at grocery stores instead of breaking your budget at pricey restaurants every day can also rein in costs. Shop like Bermudians do: Farmers' roadside stands or fishers' catch of the day deliver the freshest local ingredients in season at very fair prices.

Traveling by bus and ferry is cheaper than renting a moped or taking taxis. Buying passes for public transport saves money too: A three-day pass allows you to hop on and off buses and ferries all day long. A book of 13 tokens saves money on each ride if you plan to stay a while.

As far as sights and activities go, much of what Bermuda has to offer is free: Explore the chain of forts, trek the Railway Trail and national parks, swim at umpteen beaches, wander the backstreets of Hamilton, St. George's, and Somerset—you will not only save money, but you'll leave Bermuda with a truer picture of island life than anyone sequestered in an all-inclusive cruise or fancy resort.

Tipping

Bermudians in the service industries depend on tips. Taxi drivers expect a 15 to 20 percent tip on rates, more if heavy luggage or official touring is involved. In nearly all restaurants, a 17 percent gratuity is automatically added to your bill, so there is no need to leave a tip at these establishments unless you feel the service or food is exceptional enough to deserve more; in such circumstances, islanders may leave an extra $10 or $20. Smaller, homespun eateries tend not to build a tip into the tab; check the menu or bill slip to confirm. In hotels, bellhops and door porters should receive $5 or more. Room service warrants a $5-10 tip. Depending on your length of stay and service, housekeepers typically get $3-5 per day. Bermudians tip gas-station attendants $2 or more for a fill-up (all of Bermuda's stations are full-serve).

COMMUNICATIONS AND MEDIA

Bermudians, isolated 650 miles from the nearest landfall (Cape Hatteras, North Carolina), take their communications very seriously. Thanks to a well-developed infrastructure,

Wired Island

With five undersea fiber-optic cables, telecommunications infrastructure, and nearly 100-percent Internet penetration, Bermuda is ranked as a top digital jurisdiction by the Economist Intelligence Unit, the research and analysis division of *The Economist,* and other media. Island residents and businesses enjoy fiber and high-speed wireless connectivity, and visitors can also benefit from this tech-obsessed environment. The current Premier, David Burt, is an IT entrepreneur with a master's in information systems development, and he was also one of the programmers behind the popular local Hitch app (www.hitch.bm)—Bermuda's answer to Uber.

A novel app launched by Bermudian entrepreneurs in 2017 offers a curated choice of "insider" experiences for island visitors. Winnow (www.winnow.life) delivers a handpicked selection of outdoor, culinary, fitness, cultural, and family adventures to book, with the aim of helping travelers feel more like locals.

Most Bermudian shops, restaurants, and attractions have a social-media presence; if you can't find a website, look for a Facebook page or Instagram post. Just follow #Bermuda to tap into daily happenings, news, and a slice of social life featuring Bermudians both here and abroad.

albeit threatened by seasonal hurricanes, the island provides modern telephone, Internet, wireless, and wireless-roaming services. The mail service is mostly efficient, there's no shortage of couriers, and the island is bombarded with up-to-the-minute print, digital, and broadcast media.

Mail and Courier Services

Airmail travels to and from the island daily. Mail received by 9:30am at the General Post Office (56 Church St., Hamilton, tel. 441/297-7893, gpo@gov.bm, 8am-5pm Mon.-Fri., 8am-noon Sat.) is sent out the same day but may take several days to reach its destination. Mail sent internationally via the sub-post offices in the parishes must first go to the General Post Office, sometimes taking a day or two to exit the island. Stamps for a postcard to the United States and Canada cost 70 cents; to Europe, 80 cents; to Africa, Asia, and Australasia, 90 cents. Letters weighing 10 grams are 5 cents more, plus up to 50 cents on top for each additional 10 grams. A few Parish post offices are open 8am-5pm Monday-Friday. Surface mail is airlifted to and from Bermuda frequently. International Data Express (tel. 441/297-7802), a service offered through the General Post Office, is a 48-hour mail service delivering to most international destinations; it requires mail be posted by 10:30am for same-day dispatch.

Local company Mailboxes Unlimited, at three locations, offers mail and courier services, including boxing and wrapping, as well as full-scale moving services for larger items. The main office (48 Par-la-Ville Rd., Hamilton, tel. 441/292-6563) sells boxes, envelopes, bubble wrap, labels, tape, and pens. There is also a Mailboxes Unlimited outlet in Hamilton (12 Church St., tel. 441/296-5656).

All major international courier services have offices in Bermuda, in some cases several outlets. They include FedEx (3 Mill Creek Rd., Pembroke, tel. 441/295-3854); DHL Express (17 Cox's Hill Rd., Pembroke, tel. 441/294-4848); International Bonded Couriers (IBC, 10 Park Rd., Hamilton, tel. 441/295-2467, www.ibc.bm); UPS (10 Park Rd., Hamilton, tel. 441/295-2467); and Best Shipping (6 Addendum Lane S., Pembroke, tel. 441/292-8080, www.best.bm).

Telecommunications

Bermuda's phone, fax, and wireless data services, like its Internet capabilities, are modern and efficient, though more costly than in North America or Europe. Travelers to Bermuda usually bring their own cell phones or wireless handhelds. Most North American models operate normally here. However, calling via a phone linked to an overseas network can be expensive. To avoid large roaming charges, an alternative (for GSM phones only) is to purchase prepaid SIM cards. **Digicel** (11 Church St., tel. 441/500-5000, http://www.digicelgroup.com/bm) sells $20 cards and will remove and later put back your own SIM card, providing the phone is unlocked or attached to AT&T or T-Mobile networks. **One Communications** (18 Church St. and 30 Victoria St., Hamilton; 36 Water St., St. George's; Heron Bay Plaza, 227 Middle Rd., Southampton; tel. 441/700-7000, http://one-comm.bm) offers the same service. Mobile phones can be rented from **Bermuda Cell Rental** (tel. 441/232-2355, www.bermuda-cellrental.com).

Public phones are located around the island, though often are in a shabby state or out of order—a problem most Bermudians, with their surgically attached mobiles, don't seem to notice or care about these days. For international calls, **TeleBermuda International** (Victoria Place, 31 Victoria St., Hamilton, tel. 441/296-9000, info@telebermuda.com, 9am-4:30pm Mon.-Fri.), has a retail center in Hamilton, where prepaid phone cards can be purchased.

Bermuda's international access code is 1 followed by 441 (area code) and the phone number. To dial the United States or Canada from Bermuda, simply dial 1 plus the area code and number. For operator-assisted calls, dial 00. For U.S. or Canada directory assistance, dial 1 plus the area code plus 555-1212. To make UK calls, dial 011 followed by 44, plus a city area code and a phone number. Caribbean nations take 1 or 011 as international access codes, depending on their nationality, with European islands requiring 011.

Internet Access

Bermuda Internet was first offered here in the early 1990s, and infrastructural improvements have helped keep the island in step with global trends. Speeds have doubled since the installation of fiber-optic cables after the America's Cup, which also triggered innovations such as free Wi-Fi over water (the Great Sound). Most hotels and guesthouses offer free Wi-Fi to visitors. Larger properties cater to business travelers with high-speed connections in rooms, lobby areas, and dedicated business centers. Free wireless Internet is offered at L. F. Wade International Airport.

Computer and communication supplies are extremely expensive to purchase in Bermuda, so try to come equipped, or be prepared to pay two to three times the price you would at home. Bermuda's Internet domain is .bm, though some Bermuda-based websites have .com URLs.

Media
TOURISM PUBLICATIONS
Destination Bermuda (tel. 44-19/3581-6142, www.destination-magazines.com/bermuda) is an annual magazine published in the United Kingdom and distributed free of charge to Bermuda-bound airline passengers at check-in at London's Gatwick, New York, Toronto, and other North American gateways. Photos and features highlight cultural attractions, activities, history, shopping, and business services.

Experience Bermuda (www.experience-bermuda.com), backed by the Bermuda Hotel Association, has glossy hard backed copies in hotel rooms island-wide. Included are photo features and write-ups on things to see and do, wining and dining, and weddings and honeymoons.

Bermuda.com Guide (www.bermuda.com) is a free booklet packed with ads and information on seasonal events, tours, cultural sights, restaurants, and shopping highlights. Find it at major hotels, bookstores, airport and cruise ship terminals, and Visitor Information Centres.

NEWS
Bermuda has one daily newspaper, *The Royal Gazette* (tel. 441/295-5881, www.royalgazette.com), available in hard copy ($1.50) and free online editions. Owned by Bermuda Press

Holdings, it dates back to 1828. It is a morning must-read for locals, and the online edition appeals to younger generations and overseas Bermudians and Bermudaphiles.

As an online news site, Bernews (http://bernews.com) ably competes with the *Gazette,* and often beats its team of journalists to the story. It's also more digitally savvy, with strong use of podcasts, social media, and digital advertising.

MAGAZINES

For such a small market, Bermuda has a plethora of magazines fighting for a diminishing pot of advertising dollars. Most have digital editions as well as printed copies. *RG* magazine, published six times a year and distributed free inside *The Royal Gazette,* offers newsy features and profiles of local personalities. *The Bermudian* (www.thebermudian.com), launched in 1930 in the vein of *The New Yorker,* downsized after its 75th anniversary in 2005 from a monthly to a quarterly, but its digital presence is well thought out and nicely designed. Produced by the Bermudian Publishing Company, *The Bermudian* features Bermuda history, architecture, and traditions, and a well-perused party section. The magazine's popular "Best of Bermuda Awards" issue each summer provides a well-vetted insider's list of the island's favorite shops, attractions, and services—a useful resource for visitors.

Other publications include Bermuda Media's annual *New Resident,* a resource for newcomers to the island. Business travelers should look at *Bermuda Finance, Bermuda:Re + ILS* (www.bermudareinsurancemagazine.com), and Bermuda Captive magazines, supported by many of the island's global companies; and *Bottom Line,* a free quarterly assessment by *The Royal Gazette* on domestic and international company news, including corporate profiles.

TELEVISION

North American—mostly U.S.—television fare is on the menu; major U.S. networks are affiliated with Bermuda stations, which air their programming daily, and the island's cable service offers hundreds of mainly American channels. Broadcast stations represent the U.S. television networks and also offer some local programming. Established in 1947, Bermuda Broadcasting Company (Fort Hill, Devonshire, tel. 441/295-2828) today has two commercial TV stations: ZFB-TV channel 7 (cable channel 2) is the affiliate of ABC, while ZBM-TV channel 9 (cable channel 3) airs CBS network programming. Both stations also air locally produced daily evening news, talk shows, and sports programs.

Several channels offer Bermuda-produced programming, though often of poor quality. The Bermuda Channel (channel 77) carries visitor-oriented features on sightseeing, sports, transportation, shopping, and restaurants. The Bermuda government channel CITV, or Community Information Television (channel 2), presents 24-hour coverage of government events, cultural programming, interviews, and local human interest features. Look TV (channel 1) offers local segments on island personalities, traditions, and major cultural and sporting events. Fresh TV (channel 3) broadcasts music videos, local events, and interviews with Bermudian personalities. The Bermuda Weather Channel (channel 4) airs weather warnings, storm advisories, and hurricane tracking.

RADIO

The island's radio stations offer eclectic home-grown announcers, DJs, reporters, and programming. For locals and visitors, daytime talk shows—featuring call-in segments and vociferous debates about all things Bermuda—are a highly entertaining slice of island life. ZBM-2 1340 AM, with host David Lopes, broadcasts lively local chitchat. ZFB 1230 AM, offering an easy-listening mix and local programming.

FM channels include Ocean ZBM 89.1 FM, with piped-in syndicated programming from the United States, including mellow chart favorites from the 1970s onward, plus afternoon call-in shows to local hosts. ZFB Power 95 FM carries a mix of reggae, rap, and R&B, while Irie 98.3 is 100-percent reggae. Vibe 103.3 has Top 40 hits.

Hott 107.5 FM, targeting the island's younger population, offers the most slickly produced programming, thanks to its Chicago connections—one of its founders was the former program director of WGCI. Sister station Magic 102.7 FM carries adult contemporary soul, R&B, and light rock hits from the 1970s-1990s.

ELECTRICITY

Power losses, both brief and of the lengthier variety, are unfortunately an integral part of island life. Bermuda relies on one power plant, BELCo, on Hamilton's outskirts in Pembroke, to serve the island's electricity needs. When something goes awry or a bad storm hits, Bermudians are made acutely aware of their tenuous connection to modern comforts.

Heavy winter storms and summer hurricanes usually take Bermudian homes and businesses off the grid at least temporarily. Few Bermuda homes are without flashlights, matches, lighters, candles, or batteries—the essential tools for any semblance of life after dark during power outages. Major hotels, both hospitals, and many businesses and private residences also own gas- and propane-fueled generators, which can be switched on to run basic electrical needs such as showers, water pumps, stoves, and refrigerators.

Power surges are common, so make sure to unplug laptops, phones, and other sensitive equipment after an outage; when the power returns, it sometimes shuts on and off a couple of times during testing before being fully restored. Bring a surge protector with you, or purchase one at Red Laser (8 Bakery Lane, Pembroke, tel. 441/296-6400, www.redlaser. bm). Call 955 to report outages via a recorded phone-in system that matches the caller's telephone number with the affected neighborhood address.

Like North America, Bermuda operates on 110 volts AC, 60 cycles, with U.S. flat-blade (two-pin) plug outlets, so any U.S.-manufactured appliance, such as blow-dryers and curling irons, will not require voltage converters or adapters. European visitors, however, can either bring adapters with them or purchase them at stores such as Unlimited Supplies (7 Elliott St., Hamilton, tel. 441/295-9229) or P-Tech (5 Reid St., Hamilton, tel. 441/295-5496).

PHOTOGRAPHY AND DIGITAL SERVICES

Just as it is to artists, Bermuda is a never-disappointing muse to photographers. Lensfolk rhapsodize about the unique softness of the island's light, the diffusion of water and air, the turquoise hues of its ocean, the cornucopia of pastel shades at every turn.

Digital photo printing is expensive in Bermuda (85 cents each for 4-by-6 prints, $1 for 5-by-7), so you might prefer to wait to do it at home, but there are several efficient, good-quality outlets that offer a speedy turnaround. P-Tech Photo (5 Reid St., Hamilton, tel. 441/279-5419 or 441/295-5496, www. ptech.bm, 9am-5pm Mon.-Sat.) has a full-service digital mini lab so customers can order lab-quality prints and create greeting cards. Photo files can be uploaded online and prints collected from the store. For fine-art digital printing, photo enlarging, and pre-press services, Loris Toppan at Colourlab (Somers Bldg., 2nd Fl., 15 Front St., Hamilton, tel. 441/799-6180) is a maestro.

Beware the effect of heat on cameras—do not store equipment inside parked cars or in the oven-like canisters on the back of rental mopeds. Bring a polarizing UV lens filter to take the shine off ocean shots, in particular, and be careful of sand and salt exposure at the beach or on the water (keep cameras covered when not in use). Avoid shooting in the harshness of midday if possible; Bermuda's intense sunlight 11am-2pm fills photos with deep contrasts, burnout, and shadows; dawn or early evening will provide the most alluring light conditions, not to mention soft pink sunrises and sunsets.

Wedding photo specialists include Sacha Blackburne (tel. 441/234-5089, www.sachablackburne.com); Alex Masters (tel. 441/705-2868, www.alexandermasters.com); Amanda Temple (tel. 441/236-2339, www.amandatemple.com); Meredith Andrews (tel. 441/505-3686, http://meredithandrewsphotography.com); Becky Spencer Photography (tel. 441/238-5236, www.beckyspencer.com); John Manderson (www.luminousimaging.com); Gavin Howarth (tel. 441/532-3234, www.gavinhowarth.com); Mark Tatem and Ally Lusher of Two and Quarter Photography (tel. 441/541-0214, www.twoandquarter.bm); Moongate Productions (tel. 441/300-5005, www.moongateproductions.com); and Ernie McCreight (tel. 441/295-4755, www.ernestmccreight.com).

LookBermuda's digital photographic services (tel. 441/295-3555, www.lookbermuda.com) include shooting special events and panoramas. For more contacts and portfolios, check www.bermudaphotographers.com.

Resources

Suggested Reading and Films

ISLAND LIFE AND TRAVEL

Barritt, Fred, and Peter Smith. *Bermewjan Vurds: A Dictionary of Conversational Bermudian.* 7th ed. Bermuda: Lizard Press, 2005. Hilarious collection of amazing but true local idiom and slang, updated periodically.

Berg, Daniel, and Denise Berg. *Bermuda Shipwrecks: A Vacationing Diver's Guide to Bermuda's Shipwrecks.* East Rockaway, NY: Aqua Explorers, 1991. An A-to-Z rundown of legendary wrecks discovered off Bermuda, with a brief history, plus photos of wreck sites, artifacts, and the divers who found them.

Caswell, Tracey. *Tea with Tracey: The Woman's Survival Guide to Bermuda.* Bermuda: Print Link, 1994. A cockroaches-and-all view of Bermuda by a resident expat whose introduction to island life is a highly entertaining read for anyone interested in what it's really like to live in a so-called paradise.

Emery, Llewellyn. *Nothin' But a Pond Dog.* Bermuda: Bermudian Publishing, 1996, reprinted 1999. Businessman, cedar craftsman, and author Emery paints both a humorous and poignant portrait of back o' town life as a child in the 1950s.

O'Connell, Seán. *Shark Bait.* Bermuda: Warrenden Press, 2017. Long-distance swimmer O'Connell's recounts his 1976 battle against tides, sharks, and fatigue to complete the first nonstop swim around Bermuda.

Richardson, Ralph. *The Bermuda Boater.* 2nd ed. Bermuda: Pyro Press, 2004. Written by a seasoned Bermudian navigator and boating enthusiast, this edition is an extremely useful resource for yachties and commercial or recreational boaters in Bermuda, complete with navigation and safety basics, local chart references, and island knowledge on weather, tides, emergency resources, and other tips.

Smith, Molly. *Discovering Bermuda with Paintbrush and Bike.* Bermuda: Bermudian Publishing, 2005. An island tour through the eyes of Bermudian watercolorist Smith, whose sketches, paintings, and observations along the way—including recipes, herbal remedies, and poems—paint a rich portrait of a whimsical island.

Temple, Amanda. *Tapestry of Tales.* Bermuda, 2017. A stunning collection of photographic portraits of Bermudian people at home, woven together by their stories.

Watlington, Frank. *Bermuda Kites: How to Make and Fly Them.* Bermuda, 1960. Reprint. A primer on tried-and-true methods to create the colorful tissue-paper concoctions that grace island skies over the Easter weekend. Easy-to-follow diagrams describe basic designs, papering, and looping tricks that have become a beloved Bermudian tradition.

HISTORY AND FOLKLORE

Bermuda's Architectural Heritage Series. Devonshire, St. George's, Sandys, Hamilton Parish, Smith's, Paget, Hamilton City, Pembroke. Bermuda: Bermuda National Trust, 1995-2017. In-depth parish histories researched and written by local historians, full of photos and illustrations.

Bernhard, Virginia. *Slaves and Slaveholders in Bermuda, 1616-1782.* Columbia: University of Missouri Press, 1999. Historical analysis of the complex relationship between slavery and racism in the second-oldest colony of the New World.

Cox, John. *Bermuda's Favourite Haunts.* Bermuda: John Cox, 1991. Spooky chronicle of haunted houses around the island and the ghosts that inhabit them.

Deichmann, Catherine Lynch. *Rogues & Runners: Bermuda and the American Civil War.* Bermuda: Bermuda National Trust, 2003. Companion booklet to the fascinating exhibit in the Bermuda National Trust Museum at the old Globe Hotel building in St. George's.

Evans, Jonathan Land. *Bermuda Maps.* Bermuda: National Museum of Bermuda Press, 2017. A comprehensive, beautifully illustrated survey of hundreds of Bermuda maps, with analysis of their content, presentation, and context. The maps range from crude manuscripts drawn by early settlers and seafarers to modern-day versions.

Grearson, Don. *USS Bermuda: The Rise and Fall of an American Base.* Bermuda: Great Dog Publishing, 2009. An inside look at the controversial 1995 closure of the U.S. military bases in Bermuda and the local and international politicking that followed.

Harris, Edward Cecil. *Bermuda Forts: 1612-1957.* Bermuda: Bermuda Maritime Museum Press, 1997. Harris, who is an archaeologist, historian, and the director of the National Museum of Bermuda, provides a comprehensive overview of the island's chain of fortifications, detailing their history and archaeology. It is especially topical now that the local government plans to restore many of these decaying landmarks as cultural attractions.

Jones, Rosemary. *Bermuda: Five Centuries.* Bermuda: Panatel VDS, 2004. Full-color, reader-friendly history of the island from its discovery in 1505 to the 21st century. A companion to a DVD series by the same name, the book contains time lines, contemporary accounts, and more than 360 historic images from private and public collections.

Jones, Rosemary, and Dr. Edward Harris. *Royal Bermuda.* Bermuda: National Museum Press, 2014. A pictorial history, showcasing the island's four centuries of connections to the British Crown, including Queen Elizabeth II's seven visits since 1953.

McDowall, Duncan. *Another World: Bermuda and the Rise of Modern Tourism.* London: Macmillan Education, 1999. Canadian history professor and longtime Bermudaphile McDowall describes the economic makeover that tourism gave Bermuda in this highly readable, anecdotal work.

Slayton, Marina I., ed. *Four Centuries of Friendship.* Bermuda: Bermuda Maritime Museum Press, 2009. A colorful historical overview of diplomacy and relations between the United States and Bermuda from the 1600s to today.

Smith, Jonathan D. *Island Flames: Murder, Execution and Racial Enmity: The Real Story of Bermuda's 1977 Riots.* Bermuda: Ten Ten Publications, 2015. A comprehensive account of Bermuda's darkest period, when the hanging of two murderers sparked the worst violence the island has ever seen. By a former Bermuda police commissioner.

Watts, Gordon Payne Jr. *Shipwrecked: Bermuda's Maritime Heritage.* Bermuda: National Museum of Bermuda Press, 2014. Five hundred years of history and more than 300 wrecks—the legacy of Bermuda, the shipwreck capital of the mid-Atlantic. Detailed analysis of a multitude of wrecks from the 1500s Age of Discovery to the modern day, by a foremost underwater archaeologist.

Woodward, Hobson. *A Brave Vessel: The True Tale of the Castaways who Rescued Jamestown and Inspired Shakespeare's The Tempest.* New York: Viking, 2009. A detailed and compelling narrative of the 1609 *Sea Venture* shipwreck on Bermuda, its survivors' subsequent rescue of starving colonists at Jamestown, and the tale's creative impact on history's most famous playwright. By an associate editor of the Adams Papers at the Massachusetts Historical Society.

Zuill, W. S. *The Story of Bermuda and Her People.* 3rd. ed. London: Macmillan Caribbean, 1999. Concise paperback history of the island, written by a former editor of *The Royal Gazette.*

NATURE AND THE ENVIRONMENT

Bermuda Rose Society. *Roses in Bermuda.* Bermuda: Bermudian Publishing, 1997. Packed with color photos to make identification easy, this edition highlights the wealth of roses and where to find them throughout the island, from ramblers and hybrid teas to the so-called mystery varieties. One section even details where to find Bermuda roses in the United States.

Dobson, Andrew. *A Birdwatching Guide to Bermuda.* Shrewsbury, UK: Arlequin Press, 2002. A detailed birding guide written by the president of the island's Audubon Society.

Frith, Kathleen, Jonathan Frith, James Constable, Jennifer Constable, and James Cooper. *Sporty Little Field Guide to Bermuda.* Bermuda: 2 Halves, 1997. A comprehensive paperback guide to the island's main plant and animal life, with artful illustrations accompanied by brief, informative text.

Lucas, Ron. *Bermuda Reef Portraits.* Bermuda: Bermuda Zoological Society, 2008. A full-color photographic guide to the island's marinelife, useful for divers and snorkelers.

Phillips-Watlington, Christine. *Bermuda's Botanical Wonderland: A Field Guide.* London: MacMillan Education, 1996. Whimsically illustrated edition with renditions of typical island habitats and the abundant flora within them.

Sterrer, Wolfgang. *Bermuda's Marine Life.* Bermuda: Bermuda Zoological Society, 1992. A comprehensive and highly readable look at all forms of island marinelife by a former curator of the Bermuda Zoological Society's Natural History Museum in Flatts.

Stevenson, Andrew. *Whale Song: Journeys into the Secret Lives of the North Atlantic Humpbacks.* Lanham, MD: Lyons Press, 2011. Stevenson's beautiful photographs of humpbacks off Bermuda are the result of a four-year project to learn more about these migrating mammals.

Thomas, Martin L. H. *The Natural History of Bermuda.* Bermuda: Bermuda Zoological Society, 2004. Comprehensive full-color coffee-table book with photos and detailed text on marine and terrestrial wildlife and the island's delicate ecosystem. Available at the Bermuda Aquarium, Museum & Zoo shop, and bookstores in Hamilton and St. George's.

Thomas, Martin L. H. *A Naturalist's Field Guide to Bermuda.* Bermuda: Bermuda Zoological Society, 2009. A condensed version of the author's larger work, in the form of a portable, full-color, pocket-size field guide.

Wingate, Janet. *Nonsuch Summer.* Janet Wingate, 2005. An evocative memoir written by the daughter of Bermudian naturalist David Wingate about her idyllic childhood summers spent on Nonsuch Island in Castle Harbour. Winner of a Bermuda Literary Award in the Young Adult category.

COLLECTORS

Williams, Malcolm, and Peter T. Sousa, eds. *Coins of Bermuda.* Bermuda: Bermuda Monetary Authority, 1997. A history of island coinage, from the first Hogge money and sterling coins to the decimal system.

ART AND ARCHITECTURE

Calnan, Patricia. *The Masterworks Bermudiana Collection.* Bermuda: Bermudian Publishing, 1994. Lavish edition showcasing the repatriated island artworks of Winslow Homer, Georgia O'Keeffe, and other luminaries, as collected by Bermuda's Masterworks Foundation.

Foster, Graham, and Rosemary Jones. *Hall of History: Bermuda's Story in Art.* Bermuda: National Museum of Bermuda Press, 2011. A visual feast, this oversize coffee-table edition showcases artist Foster's epic mural at the Commissioner's House, Dockyard. Annotations detail the history captured in each image. Included are sections on Foster's often humorous details, and essays chronicling how he completed the 1,000-square-foot masterpiece.

Harris, Edward, ed. *Dr. Savage's Bermuda.* Bermuda: National Museum of Bermuda Press, 2015. Recovering the forgotten landscape of Bermuda in the 1830s through a remarkable collection of paintings by the prolific Royal Artillery surgeon Johnson Savage.

Masterworks at 25. The Masterworks Foundation, 2012. Large-format edition tracing the art charity's mission to repatriate Bermuda art and its success in bringing home works by Homer, O'Keeffe, Gleizes and other world-renowned artists who had been inspired by the island.

Shorto, Sylvia, and Ian MacDonald-Smith. *Bermuda Gardens & Houses.* New York: Rizzoli International, 1996. Informative coffee-table volume written by Bermudian art historian Shorto and photographed by much-published island lensman MacDonald-Smith.

FOOD

Bottone, Edward. *Spirit of Bermuda: Cooking with Gosling's Black Seal Rum.* Bermuda: Bermudian Publishing, 1998. Vibrantly illustrated cookbook by Philadelphia chef and former resident Bottone, with all the island's favorite recipes (codfish cakes, cassava pie), as well as colorful descriptions of holiday traditions and culinary folklore.

Island Thyme: Tastes and Traditions of Bermuda. Bermuda: Junior Service League, 2004. Collection of recipes, menus, and table settings from island residents and restaurants in a full-color volume produced to raise money for one of Bermuda's core social agencies.

Ming, Fred. *Bermuda Favourites.* Bermuda: Fred Ming, 2004. A compendium of recipes from one of the island's best-known chefs and cooking teachers, including red snapper fillets, red bean soup, and nasturtium salad.

Wadson, Judith. *Bermuda: Traditions and Tastes.* Bermuda: Judith Wadson, 1998. A history of Bermudian holidays, including Cup Match and Good Friday, and the typical dishes that accompany the celebrations.

PHOTOGRAPHY

Airey, Theresa, and Edward Marshall. *Bermuda: The Quiet Years, 1883-1953.* Bermuda: Theresa Airey and Edward Marshall, 2004. A fascinating collection of 147 restored nitrate negatives portraying the island before the advent of automobiles. Photographs capture street scenes, city restaurants, lily festivals, the railway, and pristine landscapes many Bermudians would barely recognize anymore.

MacDonald-Smith, Ian. *A Scape to Bermuda.* 3rd ed. Bermuda: Ian MacDonald-Smith, 2004. All-season Bermuda, with studies of clouds, rocks, flower-strewn lanes, architecture, rainbows, and Christmas lights.

Skinner, Roland. *Picturesque Bermuda I and II.* Bermuda: Roland Skinner, 1996 and 1999. Landscapes, seascapes, and aerial shots of Bermuda by prolific lensman Skinner, a former Bermuda News Bureau staffer who now owns one of the largest Bermuda stock photo libraries and sells large-scale prints of his work.

Spurling, Ann. *Nine Parishes.* Bermuda: Ann Spurling, 2003. Pricey ($80) but satisfying photographic tour of the island by the island's premier homes-and-gardens photographer. Entertainingly written and laden with informative captions, its lush spreads feature Bermudian homes, people, cultural traditions, and pastimes. One of the best Bermuda pictorials available.

BUSINESS

Duffy, Catherine R. *Held Captive: A History of International Insurance in Bermuda.* Toronto: Oakwell Boulton, 2004. Definitive 516-page tome outlining the creation of "Bermuda Inc." in detailed CEO interviews, photos, glossaries, and corporate profiles.

Stewart, Robert. *A Guide to the Economy of Bermuda.* Toronto: Oakwell Boulton, 2003. An analysis of why Bermuda has been one of the most successful economies in the world for the past half century, written by an economics teacher and former Shell CEO who now is the director of several international Bermuda companies and investment funds.

CHILDREN

For such a small island, Bermuda boasts a surprising number of well-produced children's books, which local and visiting kids enjoy for their stories about island animals, icons, and traditions, including tree frogs, cedar trees, and sailboats. They make great souvenirs for kids back home.

Booth, Mark. Illustrated by Patricia DeCosta. *Bermuda's Sidney the Sailboat.* Bermuda: Bermudian Publishing, 1994. Compelling Cinderella tale of a neglected sailboat and its adventures. Perfect for ages four and up.

Cooper, Dana. *My Bermuda ABC.* New York: Worzalla Publishing, 1991. Bermudian commercial artist Cooper's whimsical counting and alphabet guide, inhabited by tropical touchstones like loquats, limestone, and lizards.

Donkin, Andrew. *Bermuda Triangle.* New York: Dorling Kindersley, 2000. Eerily illustrated and vividly told, this DK Readers Program book, with large text for easy reading, is a kid-pleasing synopsis of the legendary phenomenon.

Jacobs, Francine. *Bermuda Petrel: The Bird that Would Not Die.* New York: William Morrow, 1981. The story of the endemic Bermuda petrel, or cahow.

Jones, Rosemary. *Bermuda: Five Centuries for Young People.* Bermuda: Panatel VDS, 2009. This spin-off of Bermuda's narrative history is intended for a primary to middle school readership. Redesigned with new images and color-coding for easy navigation, the book has end-of-chapter questions and activities for school and home-school use.

Karwoski, Gail Langer. *Miracle: The True Story of the Wreck of the Sea Venture.* Plain City, OH: Darby Creek, 2004. Very professionally produced edition by Georgia-based writer Karwoski that's sure to captivate young imaginations with the story of Bermuda's first colonists. Kid-friendly design includes scores of illustrations, photos, and graphics, along with digestible yet historically detailed text and provoking sidebars on early navigation, island traditions, birds, and animals.

Mulderig, A. Elizabeth. *Tiny the Treefrog Tours Bermuda.* Bermuda: Bermudian Publishing, 1992. A charmingly illustrated rhyme about a quixotic tree frog and his Bermuda sightseeing exploits.

Stevenson, Kevin. Illustrated by Helen Daniel. *The Story of the Bermuda Cedar Tree.* Bermuda: Bermudian Publishing, 1997. Artfully illustrated with gouache plates, the book tells the story of Bermuda's iconic tree and its multiple uses throughout the centuries.

BERMUDA ON FILM

The Bermuda Depths, Rankin-Bass, 1978. A made-for-TV motion-picture adventure written by Arthur Rankin Jr., a Bermuda resident and Canadian cartoon producer of *Rudolph the Red-Nosed Reindeer* and *Frosty the Snowman.* The film stars Burl Ives, Leigh McCloskey, Carl Weathers, and Connie Sellecca in a ghost yarn about scientists terrorized by a giant turtle as they investigate the Bermuda Triangle. McCloskey and Sellecca's kid versions are played by Bermudian children.

Bermuda: Five Centuries, Panatel VDS, 1999. Six-part documentary series using contemporary interviews and historic and modern footage to trace the island's history via major social themes over 500 years. With companion book.

The Deep, Columbia Pictures, 1977. Peter Benchley's underwater thriller, directed by Peter Yates and starring Nick Nolte, Jacqueline Bisset, and Lou Gossett Jr., was inspired by Benchley's visits to the island and was filmed in Bermuda. A romantic interlude turns to adventure when a couple discovers gold coins and mysterious glass ampoules on a sunken World War II wreck. The film features many familiar sights—including lots of Bermudian extras. Based on Benchley's 1976 book of the same title, one of its hallmark elements was the theme song, sung by Donna Summer.

The Lion and the Mouse, Lucinda Spurling, Afflare Films, 2009. Narrated by former Bermuda resident Michael Douglas, the documentary explores the four centuries of strong connections between Bermuda and America, from early colonial days to modern times.

Mr. Happy Man, Matt Morris, 2010. Award-winning 10-minute documentary by U.S. director Morris about Bermuda's Johnny Barnes and his longtime morning ritual of waving joyfully to local commuters as they drive to work, Barnes's bid to make the world a happier place.

Neptune's Daughter, Warner Studios, 1949. This Oscar-winning musical-comedy-romance directed by Edward Buzzell and starring aquatic goddess Esther Williams, Red Skelton, and Ricardo Montalban was filmed at a pool on Agar's Island, in Bermuda's Great Sound. The production was fraught with problems, but the film ended up as the 10th highest-grossing movie of that year, propelled by the popular song, "Baby, It's Cold Outside."

Rare Bird, Lucinda Spurling, Afflare Films, 2006. Spurling's documentary details the fascinating story of the endangered Bermuda petrel, or cahow, from believed extinction to rediscovery in the 1950s, and its gradual comeback today.

Where the Whales Sing, Andrew Stevenson, 2010. An award-winning documentary featuring Stevenson's young daughter Elsa, in which she and her father try to discover the secrets of migrating humpback whales on their journeys past Bermuda to Canada and the Caribbean. The film traces Stevenson's four years of research on humpbacks (www. whalesbermuda.com).

Internet Resources

GENERAL INFORMATION

Bermuda.com
www.bermuda.com
Boasting the most hits of any Bermuda site, this comprehensive portal is owned and run by a local printer, the Bermuda Press. Thorough but advertising-driven listings for accommodations, dining, and activities understandably read like a tourism brochure.

Bermuda Tourism Authority
www.gotobermuda.com
The contemporary, easy-to-navigate Bermuda Tourism Authority website offers facts, figures, and curated resources for travelers, including events, sights, Department of Immigration and Customs rules, licensed accommodations, wedding how-to info, activities, and a reservations system.

Bermuda Online
www.bermuda-online.org
Comprising a portal linking to 128 websites, plus a digital library compiled by local resident and author Keith Forbes, the regularly updated website is now owned and supported by *The Royal Gazette*. Despite its dated design, it remains a useful repository of information—from census figures to resources for new residents.

Central Intelligence Agency (CIA) World Factbook
www.cia.gov/cia/library/publications/the-world-factbook/geos/bd.html
The Central Intelligence Agency's online fact book is crammed with constantly updated information on Bermuda, including land-use, population, literacy, and electricity-consumption statistics.

Nothing to Do in Bermuda?
www.nothingtodoinbermuda.com
Contradicting its ironic title, this site by resident Claire Hattie, which she now manages for the Bermuda Press, rebuts island naysayers by showcasing the full slate of weekly events, activities, nightlife, sports, and artistic pursuits Bermuda offers to keep boredom—or "rock fever"—at bay. Included are links to expat groups, plus loads of fun stuff to keep kids amused too.

U.S. Department of State
www.travel.state.gov
The U.S. Department of State's website posts a Consular Information Sheet on Bermuda, which gives an accurate overview of crime, communications, traffic safety, and customs issues, as well as links relevant to U.S. travelers.

GOVERNMENT

U.S. Consulate Bermuda
http://bm.usconsulate.gov
The U.S. Consulate Bermuda's website offers information on services for American citizens on the island, including assistance in the event of emergencies. It also has information about the current consul general, as well as details on U.S.-Bermuda history, visas, educational initiatives, and special events.

Corporation of Hamilton
www.cityhall.bm

The Corporation's website carries news and traffic advisories for the City of Hamilton, along with details of upcoming events, services, cruise ship schedules, and links to local resources from attractions to ferry fares and the yellow pages.

L. F. Wade International Airport
www.bermudaairport.com

L. F. Wade International Airport's website gives flight, check-in, Customs, Immigration, retail, and restaurant details, plus airport telephone numbers and web links for airlines that serve Bermuda.

Official Bermuda Government Website
www.gov.bm

The official Bermuda government website is a portal to all ministries, departments, and related bodies, including the National Anti-Money Laundering Committee (NAMLC).

ISLAND LIFE AND EVENTS
Bermemes
www.bermemes.com

Bermuda's most popular masters of social media, the Bermemes crew dish continual LOLs on the vagaries of local life via Facebook and Twitter daily. This site captures the ones gone viral, plus blogs on favorite Bermudian food, dry humor, and offbeat comments on upcoming weather, events, traditions, or funny local names, and links to the wittiest of grassroots websites (#badparking Bermuda), including video and animation. A revealing insight into the real Bermudian character.

Bermynet.com
www.bermynet.com

Covering the home-from-college scene, this site features photos from Hamilton happy hours, as well as the summer club scene, beach parties, DJs, and live web radio.

Box Office Tickets
www.premierticketsglobal.com
(www.ptix.bm)

Buy tickets online to all Bermuda's major entertainment events or movies via these sites, all of which are well used by island residents.

E-Moo
www.e-moo.bm

A morning must-see for thousands of residents, this classifieds website carries information on public events, yard sales, and stuff for sale galore, from jewelry and pianos to boats and furniture.

ACCOMMODATIONS
Airbnb
www.airbnb.com and www.vrbo.com

A global website listing accommodations in hundreds of countries, including Bermuda, Airbnb allows residents to post home and apartment rentals, allowing for a more cost-effective way to stay on the island and experience a taste of what it's really like to live here.

Bermuda Accommodations
www.bermudarentals.com

Toronto-based Bermudian Fiona Campbell is a broker for a list of island-wide vacation properties of various sizes and rates, including historic homes and long-term rentals. A map shows where they are on the island, and numbered links connect with the property's information page. Most are studios or apartments attached to local homes.

Bermuda Vacation Rentals
www.bermudagetaway.com

This website provides a listing of information, photos, and contacts for a select group of highly rated Bermuda vacation rentals, located on an island map, including beachside cottages and historic buildings. The site allows prospective renters to check availability by date and to send reservation inquiries to the property owners.

VRBO
www.vrbo.com
Offering vacation rentals from owners, VRBO is a more cost-effective way to stay on the island and allows visitors to experience a taste of what it's really like to live here.

WEDDINGS
Getting Married in Bermuda
www.bermudianweddings.com
As a favorite wedding destination, Bermuda makes getting married here a breeze. *The Bermudian* magazine's dedicated wedding website rounds up all the resources prospective brides and grooms will need, along with photos of island nuptials and blogs by experts. Individual wedding planners also have their own sites, and each can arrange every detail—from paperwork and photographers to flowers, cakes, and surfside ceremonies.

Bermuda Bride
www.bermudabride.com
Winner of the 2016 Best of Bermuda Award for Wedding Planner, Nikki Begg has orchestrated many of the island's most picture-perfect nuptials for the past 17 years—more than 1,200 weddings, according to her count. This site contains a full list of services, plus testimonials and photos of the most spectacular.

Das Fete
www.dasfete.com/what-we-do
The website for this of-the-moment event and style production house is as creative as its projects. Business and husband-wife duo Selange Gitschner and Matthew Strong offer full concierge services for weddings and other special events.

MEDIA
The Bermudian
www.thebermudian.com
Launched in 1930, *The Bermudian* magazine is a veritable institution on the island, but one that has evolved with the times. Today's editions are sleek and contemporary in look and lifestyle content, as is its website. It carries features about island life and residents, history, homes, even recipes. One great resource, with its own tab on the website, is the company's popular Best of Bermuda Awards, which laud the standouts in categories like shopping, restaurants, events, people, and places. Previous award-winners are archived here too.

Bernews
www.bernews.com
Often scooping the local newspaper (*The Royal Gazette*) with its speedy round-the-clock postings, Bernews has gained an impressive number of devotees, becoming *the* place locals go for fast-breaking island stories, news updates, even environmental and history features.

The Royal Gazette
www.theroyalgazette.com
The online edition of Bermuda's daily paper carries current-day headlines, features, sports, columns, commentary, classifieds, TV listings, and online reader polls, but the site is often slower to post daily breaking news than Bernews, and its daily edition isn't posted until midmorning.

BUSINESS INFORMATION
Bermuda Business Development Agency
www.bda.bm
The BDA promotes the island as a premier offshore business center, supports locally based international companies, and helps companies that want to move operations to the island or launch start-ups in Bermuda. The agency connects prospective business leaders with industry professionals and regulatory officials, conducts roadshows and other business development efforts overseas, and advocates for the island's reputation as a top-tier finance hub.

Bermuda Chamber of Commerce
www.bermudachamber.bm
The Bermuda Chamber of Commerce's

website represents its members, from e-business to construction companies. Included is information on how to acquire permits to sell and showcase products on the island, as well as details on cruise ship schedules and weekly Harbour Nights summer street festivals in Hamilton, Dockyard, and St. George's.

Bermuda Monetary Authority
www.bma.bm

The official website of the Bermuda Monetary Authority (BMA), the island's main regulatory body, which supervises the financial services industry, approves incorporations, oversees licenses to financial institutions, and issues banknotes and coinage. The site offers text of public legislation, and a "warning" list of bogus companies not licensed to do business on the island.

Bermuda Stock Exchange
www.bsx.com

The website of the Bermuda Stock Exchange, which, established in 1971, bills itself as the largest offshore electronic securities market. The site features market highlights, news, a daily trade report for the domestic market, plus links to trading members.

REAL ESTATE
Coldwell Banker Bermuda Realty
www.bermudarealty.com

Bermuda's largest full-service real-estate company, catering to commercial and residential sales and rentals, relocation, property management, leasing, and vacation properties.

Propertyskipper.com
www.propertyskipper.com

Don't want to leave Bermuda? This site helps house hunters find their dream home, acting as a centralized clearinghouse for the island's rental and for-sale markets, including commercial and land listings. A quick-search mechanism lets you narrow your search by parish and also carries property-related

news and a clickable listing of local real estate brokers.

Rego Sotheby's International Realty
www.regosothebysrealty.com

Founded in 1949, this is one of the island's oldest full-service real estate firms, with a focus on luxury, commercial, and hotel-tourism properties.

TELEPHONE DIRECTORIES
Bermuda Yellow Pages
www.bermudayp.com

Using the Yabsta platform, the searchable Bermuda Yellow Pages website lists thousands of island businesses, community agencies, and services, also provides free classifieds, event listings, weather updates, an airline arrivals schedule, blogs, and a visitor section with links to bus and ferry schedules, restaurant menus, wedding planner resources, and a video tour of the island.

WEATHER
Bermuda Weather Service
www.weather.bm

The official site of the Bermuda Weather Service offers current conditions, weeklong forecasts, marine conditions, climate data—and live satellite and three-hour loop radar imagery showing the approach and size of rain bands, hurricanes, and other area disturbances.

LIVE WEBCAMS
Bermuda Cahow Cam Project
www.nonsuchisland.com

The government's Department of Conservation Services is one of the parties behind this webcam that gives a live look inside a cahow burrow on protected Nonsuch Island. The once nearly extinct seabirds have made a comeback through a carefully monitored conservation program that has received worldwide kudos.

Bermuda Weather Service
www.weather.bm/webcam.asp

With images updating every two minutes, this webcam located at the weather radar site at Cooper's Island, St. George's, gives you a real-time look at how the forecast is shaping up, with views of cloud formations, passing squalls, and the East End horizon.

Port Bermuda Webcam
www.portbermudawebcam.com

A 24-7 live-streaming, HD-quality video broadcast from the lofty veranda of historic Commissioner's House at the westernmost point of the Royal Naval Dockyard. With a view over the ramparts, you can see the cruise ships make port, as well as boat traffic around Heritage and King's Wharves and in the Great Sound beyond.

328

Index

A

Aberfeldy Nurseries: 98
accommodations: 293-295
Admiralty Cove Adventure Park: 70
Admiralty House Park: 64, 66, 71
African Diaspora Trail: 204
air travel: 272-274
Albuoy's Point: 34
Alexandra Battery: 20, 214, 225
animals: 243-250
aquarium: 184-185
Arboretum: 26, 84-85, 88
Argo Group Gold Cup: 44
Ascot's: 20, 74, 76
Astwood Cove: 21, 115-116
ATMs: 310
attitudes: 296
AXIS Adrenaline Projects: 24, 190

B

Baby Beach: 25, 128, 132
Bailey's Bay: 189
Barber's Alley: 206
Barr's Bay Park: 34, 204
beaches: general discussion 21, 25, 285-286; Devonshire and Paget 87-88, 98, 100; Hamilton City and Pembroke Parish 66, 67, 69; Sandy's 148-149, 157-158, 162, 163-164; Smith's and Hamilton Parishes 178, 186, 189-190; St. George's 217, 223, 226; Warwick and Southampton 115-117, 127-129
Beachfest: 133
beer/brewery: 180
Belmont Hills Golf Club: 25, 117
Beluga Seafood Bar: 19, 41, 54
Bermuda Agricultural Exhibition: 90, 102-103
Bermuda Aquarium, Museum & Zoo (BAMZ): 24, 26, 184-185, 191
Bermuda Arts Centre: 20, 50, 154
Bermuda Athletic Association: 70
Bermuda Botanical Gardens: 20, 94-95
Bermuda cedar: 240-241
Bermuda Day Parade: 44
Bermuda Docs: 71
Bermuda Festival of the Performing Arts: 43
Bermuda Fitted Dinghy Races: 159
Bermuda Goodwill Golf Tournament: 134, 220
Bermuda Heroes Weekend: 46
Bermuda Historical Society Museum: 34-35
Bermuda Institute of Ocean Sciences (BIOS): 26, 215
Bermuda International Film Festival: 44
Bermuda International Invitational Race Week: 44
Bermuda Kitefest: 25, 133
Bermuda, map of: 2-3
Bermuda Marathon Weekend: 43-44, 90
Bermuda Musical & Dramatic Society Pantomime: 46
Bermuda National Gallery: 36
Bermuda National Sports Centre: 88
Bermuda National Trust Museum: 206
Bermuda100: 22
Bermuda Perfumery: 23, 50, 209, 210
Bermuda Regional Bridge Tournament: 133
Bermuda Sand Castle Competition: 133
Bermuda shorts: 48
Bermuda Sloop Foundation: 150
Bermuda Society of Arts: 36, 50
Bermuda Squash Racquets Association: 89
Bermuda Tourism Authority: 22, 275, 278, 288, 309
Bermuda Transport Museum: 148
Bermuda Triangle: 232
Bermuda Triple Crown Billfish Championship: 44
Bermuda Turtle Project: 188
Bermuda Underwater Exploration Institute: 131
Bermuda Underwater Exploration Institute (BUEI): 26, 69
Bermuda Waterski & Wakeboard Centre: 24, 165
Bermuda Zoological Society: 24, 131, 190
Bermúdez, Juan de: 251
Bermudian Heritage Museum: 204, 206
bicycling: general discussion 128, 282-283; Devonshire and Paget 108; Hamilton City and Pembroke Parish 78; Sandy's 149, 157, 163; Smith's and Hamilton Parishes 189, 191, 195; St. George's 227; Warwick and Southampton 117, 122, 139
Birdcage: 35
birds/bird-watching: general discussion 244, 246; Devonshire and Paget 85, 86, 97, 99; Hamilton City and Pembroke Parish 68; Sandy's 161, 164; Smith's and Hamilton Parishes 175, 186; St. George's 216, 223; Warwick and Southampton 115, 117, 126, 127
Birdsey Studio: 98-99
Black Bay: 22, 164
Black Watch Well: 67
Blue Hole Park: 185-186
Boatloft: 147
botanical gardens/arboretums: 84-85, 94-95

bowling: 118-119, 227
Breezes: 22, 159
Burnt Point Fort: 215, 225
business hours: 304-305
bus travel: 279-280
Butterfly Garden at Brighton Nurseries: 86

C

Cabinet Building: 40
cahow birds: 216
Camden House: 95-96
camping: 294
Canada Day Beach Party: 133
Carter House: 223-224
Casemate Prison: 148
caves/caverns: 175, 177, 186, 187-190
cell phones: 312-313
Cenotaph: 41
Chapel of Ease: 224
Chaplin Bay: 20, 21, 116-117
Chewstick: 38
children, activities for: general discussion 23-25; Hamilton City and Pembroke Parish 71; Sandy's 151-152; St. George's 219; Warwick and Southampton 119, 132
children, traveling with: 283, 306
Christmas Boat Parade: 25, 46
Christmas Walkabout: 209
Church Bay: 21, 128
churches/temples: Devonshire and Paget 85-86, 99; Hamilton City and Pembroke Parish 37, 38-39, 67-68; Sandy's 163; Smith's and Hamilton Parishes 174-175, 186-187; St. George's 205-206, 224; Warwick and Southampton 114, 125-126
City Hall and Arts Centre: 35-36, 43
Clarence Cove: 21, 25, 66
Clearwater Beach: 21, 226
Clearwater Playground: 226
climate: 231, 233-236
Cobb's Hill Methodist Church: 114, 204
Coconut Rockets/Bermuda Flyboard: 24, 150
Commissioner's House: 147, 152, 204
communications and media: 311-315
Coney Island: 189
Constellation: 22, 149
consulates: 285
Cooperage: 147
Cooper's Island Nature Reserve: 23, 223
costs: 311
Cottage Café & Bistro: 19, 55
courier services: 312
Crawl: 189
credit cards: 311
cricket: general discussion 166, 290-291; Devonshire and Paget 89; Sandy's 165; St. George's 219, 226-227; Warwick and Southampton 131
crime: 303-304
Cristóbal Colón: 22, 190
Crow Lane: 96-97
cruise travel: 274-275
Crystal Cave and Fantasy Cave: 19, 187-189
Cup Match: 165, 166, 219
currency: 309-311
customs regulations: 284-285

D

Daniel's Head Beach Park: 164
Darrell's Wharf: 114
Davidrose Jewelry: 23, 209
Daylesford Theatre: 43
Death Valley Playground: 132
Deep Bay: 66, 69
Deliverance: 203-204
demographics: 268-269
Devil's Isle Kitchen & Bar: 19, 56
Devonshire Bay Battery: 87
Devonshire Bay Park: 87-88
Devonshire Marsh: 86
Devonshire Parish: 82-92; map 83
Devonshire Recreation Club: 89
digital services: 315-316
Dining Room, The: 20, 27, 125, 136
disabilities, access for travelers with: 305-306
Dock, The: 19, 133, 136
Dockyard Playground: 152
Dockyard Watersports Centre: 149
Dolphin Quest: 148, 151, 152
Ducking Stool Park: 67
ducking stool reenactments: 209

E

economy: 260-267
ecosystems: 237-239
Elbow Beach: 19, 21, 25, 100
electric cars: 281-282
electricity: 315
Emancipation Day: 165
embassies: 285
emergencies: 298-299
environmental issues: 236-237, 245
Esten House: 202
etiquette: 296
Evans Pond Nature Reserve: 127
expenses: 311
extreme water sports: 24

F

family vacations: 23-25
Fanny Fox's Cottage: 202

fauna: 243-250
Ferry Island Fort: 215
Ferry Point National Park: 215-216
ferry travel: 280-281
Festa do Espiritu Santo: 176
festivals and events: 296-297
Firefly Nature Reserve: 86
Fish & Tings: 20, 39, 54
fish/fishing: general discussion 288-289;
    Hamilton City and Pembroke Parish 44, 70;
    Sandy's 158; Smith's and Hamilton Parishes
    177, 182
Flatts Village: 182; map 184
flora: 239-243
food/restaurants: 291-293
Fort Cunningham: 225
Fort Hamilton: 20, 68-69, 71, 225
Fort Prospect: 225
forts and guns: 225
Fort Scaur: 27, 162, 225
Fort St. Catherine: 20, 214-215, 219, 225
Fort Victoria: 225
Freer Cox Nature Reserve: 86

G
Garden Club of Bermuda: 102
Gates Fort: 20, 214, 225
gay and lesbian travelers: 307-309
geography: 231
Gibbet Island Beach: 178
Gibbs Hill: 27, 123, 125, 132
Glass Beach: 163
Gloria's Kitchen: 22, 167
golf: general discussion 288; Devonshire and
    Paget 88-89; St. George's 218-219; Warwick
    and Southampton 117-118, 129-130
gombeys: 45
government: 257-260
Government House: 67
gratuities: 311
Great Head Park: 224, 226
Great Sound: 27, 112

H
Hamilton, City of: 19, 32-63; map 33
Hamilton Parish: 182-195; map 183
Hamilton Princess & Beach Club: 20, 71, 76
Harbour Nights: 20, 25, 44, 45
Harbour Road: 112
Harrington Sound: 177-178
health and safety: 297-304
Heritage Rose Garden: 97
Heritage Wharf: 146
Heydon Chapel: 163
Heydon Trust Estate: 163

High Cave Magazine: 147
history: 250-257
H. M. Floating Dock: 66
Hog Bay Park: 26, 163
holidays, public: 297
Holy Trinity Cathedral: 19, 37
Holy Trinity Church: 186-187
horseback riding: general discussion 128, 289;
    Devonshire and Paget 89; Hamilton City and
    Pembroke Parish 52; Sandy's 149; Smith's
    and Hamilton Parishes 178; St. George's 219;
    Warwick and Southampton 118, 129
Horseshoe Bay: 20, 21, 127-128
Humpback Whale Research Project: 131
hurricanes: 234, 235

IJ
insurance: 298
Internet access: 312, 313
Island Tour Centre: 24, 52, 131, 149
itineraries: 19-27
Jack Lightbourn Shell Collection: 69
Jamaican Grill: 20, 39, 56
Jeremy Johnson's Village Carpentry: 50, 72
Jobson's Cove: 20, 25, 116
jogging: see running/jogging
Johnny Barnes statue: 97
John Smith's Bay: 21, 178
Jon Faulkner Gallery: 154
Juice 'n' Beans: 20, 60

KL
Kaleidoscope Art Foundation: 86
kayaking/canoeing: Devonshire and Paget 101;
    Hamilton City and Pembroke Parish 52, 70;
    Sandy's 158, 164, 165; Smith's and Hamilton
    Parishes 177, 182, 189, 191; St. George's 207-
    208, 218
Khyber Pass: 115
Kindley Community Tennis Courts: 227
King's Castle: 225
King's Square: 203
King's Wharf: 146
Labor Day March and Celebration: 44
Lagoon Park: 161
language: 270
Lennon, John: 98
lesbian and gay travelers: 307-309
L'Herminie: 22, 149
lighthouses: St. George's 224; Warwick and
    Southampton 123, 125, 132
Lili Bermuda: 20, 49, 50
Long Bay: 21, 226
Lords Oval: 226

M

magazines: 314
Magistrates Court: 37
mail: 312
Mangrove Bay: 27, 157
maps and information: 309
Marcus': 19, 73, 77
Marion Bermuda Race: 103
Martello Tower: 20, 215, 225
Masterworks Museum of Bermuda Art: 20, 50, 96
measurements: 305
medical services: 298
mobile phones: 312-313
money: 309-311
mopeds: 281, 282
Mullet Bay Playground: 219
Museum Playground: 147, 152

N

National Equestrian Centre: 89
National Museum of Bermuda: 20, 147-148, 151
nature reserves: 286-287
Newport Bermuda Race: 34, 44
news sources: 313-314
Non-Mariners Race: 159
Nonsuch Island: 216
North Hamilton: 38-39
North Rock: 24, 190
North Rock Brewing Co.: 180

OP

Old Devonshire Church: 85-86
Old Rectory: 207
Old Towne Market: 209
Oleander Cycles: 25, 108, 139
onions: 75
Open Houses and Gardens: 102
Ordnance Island: 203
packing tips: 304
Paget Marsh: 25, 99-100
Paget Parish: 92-108; map 93
Palm Grove Gardens: 86
Parapet, The: 163
parks and gardens: general discussion 286-287;
    Devonshire and Paget 84-85, 87-88, 96-97;
    Hamilton City and Pembroke Parish 34, 35, 37-
    38, 64, 66-67, 68; Sandy's 161-162; Smith's and
    Hamilton Parishes 177, 185-186; St. George's
    207; Warwick and Southampton 126-128
Parson's Road Playground: 71
passports: 18, 283
Pembroke Marsh Park: 68
Pembroke Parish: 64-78; map 65
Pembroke Youth Centre: 38
Penhurst Agricultural Park: 177

Peppercorn Ceremony: 208
Perot Post Office: 35
photography: 315-316
pink sand: 117
plane travel: 272-274
planning tips: 16-18
plants: 239-243
politics: 257-260
Pomander Road: 98
Portuguese Consulate: 176
Portuguese Cultural Association: 176
postal services: 312
Prospect: 87
Prospero's Cave Spa: 23, 191
publications: 313-314

QR

Queen Elizabeth Park: 35
Queen's Birthday Parade: 44
Queen's Exhibition Hall: 147
racism: 269-270
radio: 314-315
rail tours: 283
Railway Trail: general discussion 25, 27, 128;
    Devonshire 88; Hamilton Parish 191; Paget 101;
    Sandy's 165; Smith's 178-179; Southampton
    129; St. George's 218; Warwick 117
real estate: 262
Red Hole: 98
religion: 270
Remembrance Day Parade and Ceremony: 46
resources: 317-327
Robinson's Bay: 87
romantic retreats: 20, 22-23
Round the Sound Swim: 179, 191
Royal Bermuda Yacht Club: 34
Royal Hamilton Alexander Dinghy Club: 98
Royal Naval Cemetery: 161
Royal Naval Dockyard: 20, 23, 145-157, 225; map
    146
rugby: 90, 291
running/jogging: general discussion 290;
    Devonshire and Paget 82, 85, 88, 90, 100,
    101; Hamilton City and Pembroke Parish
    43-44, 70; Sandy's 163; Smith's and Hamilton
    Parishes 191; St. George's 219; Warwick and
    Southampton 114, 117, 118, 127, 128, 129,
    130-131

S

sailing: general discussion 289; Hamilton City
    and Pembroke Parish 52-53; Sandy's 158; St.
    George's 218
Salt Kettle: 100
Sandy's Parish: 140-168; map 143

Santa Claus Parade (Hamilton): 46
Santa Claus Parade (St. George's): 209
Sargasso Sea: 126
Science at Sea: 69
scooters: 281, 282
scuba diving/snorkeling: general discussion 21, 22; Devonshire and Paget 87, 88, 100-101; Hamilton City and Pembroke Parish 52-53, 67, 69, 70, 71; Sandy's 148-150, 158, 162, 163, 164-165; Smith's and Hamilton Parishes 177, 186, 189, 190-191; St. George's 207, 218; Warwick and Southampton 117, 128, 129
Seabreeze Lounge: 19, 102, 104
sea turtles: 188
Sea Venture: 22, 149
senior travelers: 307
Sessions House: 39-40
Seymour's Pond: 126
Shark Hole: 189-190
Shelly Bay Beach and Nature Reserve: 189
Sherwin Nature Reserve: 114-115
1609 Bar & Restaurant: 19, 73, 77
skirling ceremonies: 71
Smith's Fort: 225
Smith's Garden: 207
Smith's Parish: 172-181; map 173
smoking: 304
Snorkel Park Beach: 148, 152
snowballs: 120
soccer: Devonshire and Paget 89; Hamilton City and Pembroke Parish 70; Warwick and Southampton 131
social tensions: 269-270
Soldier Bay: 21, 226
Somers Day: 165
Somerset Bridge: 27, 162
Somerset Cricket Club: 165
Somerset Long Bay: 21, 161-162, 164
Somerset Village: 22, 27, 157-161; map 158
Somers Garden: 207
Southampton Fort: 225
Southampton Parish: 123-139; map 124
South Shore Road: 112, 118, 130
Southside: 222-228
souvenirs: 50
Spanish Point Park: 66-67, 69, 71
spas: Devonshire and Paget 89, 101-102; Hamilton City and Pembroke Parish 53-54, 70-71; Sandy's 158; Smith's and Hamilton Parishes 179, 191; St. George's 208; Warwick and Southampton 131-132
spectator sports: general discussion 290-291; Devonshire and Paget 89, 90; Hamilton City and Pembroke Parish 70; Sandy's 165, 166; St. George's 219, 226-227; Warwick and Southampton 131

Spirit of Bermuda: 150
Spittal Pond Nature Reserve: 26, 175-177
squash: 89
St. Anne's Church: 125-126
State House: 204-205
St. Catherine's Beach: 21, 217
St. David's Battery: 224, 225, 226
St. David's County Cricket Club: 226
St. David's Island: 222-228
St. David's Lighthouse: 224
St. George, old town of: 201-213; map 202
St. George's Cricket Club: 219
St. George's Historical Society & Museum, Printery, and Garden: 207
St. George's New Year's Eve celebration: 209
St. George's Parish: 20, 23, 196-228; map 199
Stiles House: 202
St. John's Church: 67-68
St. Mark's Church: 174-175
Stockdale: 202
Stonehole Bay: 20, 116-117
St. Patrick's Church: 174
St. Paul's Anglican Church: 99
St. Peter's Church: 204, 205-206
Strykz Bowling Lounge: 227
St. Theresa's Cathedral: 38-39

T

taxes: 284
taxi travel: 278-279
TEDxBermuda: 133
telephones: 312-313
television: 314
tennis: general discussion 289-290; Devonshire and Paget 98, 100, 101; Hamilton City and Pembroke Parish 70; St. George's 227; Warwick and Southampton 129, 131
time: 305
tipping: 311
tobacco: 304
Tobacco Bay: 21, 217
Tom Moore's Jungle (Walsingham Nature Reserve): 185-186
tourist information: 309
tour operators: 287
Town Cut: 214
train tours: 283
transportation: 272-283
triathlons: 290
Tucker House Museum: 206-207
Tucker Shipwreck Gallery: 69
Tucker's Town: 216-217
Turtle Bay: 21, 226
Turtle Beach: 226
Twizy: 22, 78

UV

Unfinished Church: 207
vaccinations: 18
Vasco da Gama Club: 176
Verdmont Cottage: 204
Verdmont Museum: 172, 174
Vesey Nature Reserve: 127
Victoria Park: 37-38
Victualling Yard: 147
Village Café: 22, 160
visas: 18, 283
volunteering: 309

WXYZ

Walsingham Nature Reserve: 185-186
Warwick Academy: 114
Warwick Camp: 115
Warwick Lanes: 118
Warwick Long Bay: 19, 21, 116
Warwick Parish: 112-123; map 113
Warwick Playground: 119
Watch Hill Park: 177
water sports: general discussion 24; Devonshire and Paget 87, 88, 100-101; Hamilton City and Pembroke Parish 52-53, 66, 69, 70, 71; Sandy's 148, 149-151, 158, 162, 163, 164-165; Smith's and Hamilton Parishes 177-178, 186, 189, 190-191; St. George's 207-208, 217-218; Warwick and Southampton 127-128, 129, *see also specific activity*
Waterville: 97-98
weather: 231, 233-236
weddings: 308
Well Bay: 226
Wesley Park: 35
West Whale Bay: 21, 128-129
West Whale Bay Park: 126-127
Whale Bay Fort and Battery: 225
Whalebone Bay: 217
whales/whale-watching: 131, 149, 248
wildlife/wildlife-watching: general discussion 243-250; St. George's 223; Warwick and Southampton 126, 127, *see also* birds/bird-watching; whales/whale-watching
William Joell Tennis Stadium: 70
WindReach Recreational Village: 119
women travelers: 306-307
Woody's Drive-In Two Bar & Restaurant: 22, 167
World Heritage Centre: 24, 203
World Rugby Classic: 90
yacht travel: 275-278
Zoom Around the Sound: 191
zoos and animal parks: Smith's and Hamilton Parishes 184-185; Warwick and Southampton 119

INDEX

List of Maps

Front color map
Bermuda: 2-3

Discover Bermuda
chapter divisions map: 17

City of Hamilton and Pembroke Parish
City of Hamilton: 33
Pembroke Parish: 65

Devonshire and Paget Parishes
Devonshire Parish: 83
Paget Parish: 93

Warwick and Southampton Parishes
Warwick Parish : 113
Southampton Parish: 124

Sandys Parish
Sandys Parish: 143
Royal Naval Dockyard: 146
Somerset Village: 158

Smith's and Hamilton Parishes
Smith's Parish: 173
Hamilton Parish: 183
Flatts Village: 184

St. George's Parish
St. George's Parish: 199
The Old Town of St. George: 202

Acknowledgments

Updating a guidebook of this scope takes time—and a heckuva lot of intel.

Thank you to everyone who contributed ideas, calls, texts, emails, messages, posts, likes, tags, tips, feedback, thoughts, insider info, and, especially, constructive criticism. Writers depend on every bit of source material that responds to what we report and feeds fresh content for new editions.

I'm grateful to my incredibly well-informed work colleagues, including Yvonne DeCosta, Sophie Burt, Sean Moran, Lynesha Lightbourne, Jereme Ramsay, Kevin Richards, Nicole Conrad-Morrison, Heather Bean, Justin Simons, John Narraway, Tuere Smith, and Marsha Foley, not to mention our dynamic interns Leah Amaral and Jason Gonsalves—Bermudian ambassadors all, who definitely have the inside track when it comes to the first, latest, and very best of genuine "Bermy" experiences.

For all things foodie, I defer to my indefatigable chef-CEO Ross Webber (#CutRoadCooking), an East Ender who reliably delivers the goods on every level of eatery with enviable epicurean instincts.

Kudos are also due to communications colleagues Glenn Jones and Jill Dill, whose dedication to telling the world the real story about how we live #OutHere has helped change the way the world perceives and experiences Bermuda.

Big ups to the wonderfully insightful Year 9 English classes of Emma White and Rachael Ward at Bermuda's Saltus Grammar School, who invited me to speak about the ins and outs of travel writing, then fed me loads of curated Gen Z top picks. Rock-climbing, cliff-jumping, glowworms, and county cricket were middle-school highlights.

No project like this can be done in isolation. Very proud of my Moon support team who are responsible for the final product: Kristi Mitsuda, Rue Flaherty, Kat Bennett, Holly Birchfield, and Nikki Ioakimedes have been the ultimate professionals every step of the way.

To my husband Paul and now college-bound Gabriel, who have made this dozen-year Moon journey with me—our joint adventures have always inspired these pages.

Finally, to all Bermuda visitors who bought Moon guides over the years and took the time to send back thoughtful commentary before, during, or after magical sojourns to my homeland, I thank you—for picking Moon, and Bermuda.

MOON BERMUDA
Avalon Travel
Hachette Book Group
1700 Fourth Street
Berkeley, CA 94710, USA
www.moon.com

Editor: Kristi Mitsuda
Series Manager: Kathryn Ettinger
Copy Editor: Christopher Church
Graphics and Production Coordinator: Rue Flaherty
Cover Design: Faceout Studios, Charles Brock
Interior Design: Domini Dragoone
Moon Logo: Tim McGrath
Map Editor: Kat Bennett
Cartographers: Brian Shotwell, Stephanie Poulain,
    Kat Bennett, Austin Ehrhardt
Indexer: Greg Jewett

ISBN-13: 9781631219887
Printing History
1st Edition — 2006
5th Edition — June 2018
5 4 3 2 1

Front cover photo: Warwick Long Bay
© John Manderson, Luminous Imaging, Bermuda
Back cover photo: a beach resort at St. George's
© David Biagi | Dreamstime.com
All interior photos © Rosemary Jones except
pages 1, 16, 109, 111 © Paul Shapiro; page 6 (top
right) © Earl Jones; page 8 © Andrew Stevenson;
page 247 © Gabriel Jones

Printed in Canada by Friesens